Emerging Trends in Image Processing, Computer Vision, and Pattern Recognition

Emerging Trends in Image Processing, Computer Vision, and Pattern Recognition

Edited by

Leonidas Deligiannidis

Hamid R. Arabnia

AMSTERDAM • BOSTON • HEIDELBERG • LONDON
NEW YORK • OXFORD • PARIS • SAN DIEGO
SAN FRANCISCO • SINGAPORE • SYDNEY • TOKYO

Morgan Kaufmann is an imprint of Elsevier

Executive Editor: Steve Elliot
Editorial Project Manager: Kaitlin Herbert
Project Manager: Anusha Sambamoorthy
Designer: Ines Maria Cruz

Morgan Kaufmann is an imprint of Elsevier
225 Wyman Street, Waltham, MA 02451, USA

Library of Congress Cataloging-in-Publication Data
A catalogue record for this book is available from the Library of Congress

British Library Cataloguing-in-Publication Data
A catalogue record for this book is available from the British Library

For information on all Morgan Kaufmann publications
visit our website at http://store.elsevier.com/

This book has been manufactured using Print On Demand technology. Each copy is produced
to order and is limited to black ink. The online version of this book will show color figures
where appropriate.

ISBN: 978-0-12-802045-6

Working together
to grow libraries in
developing countries

www.elsevier.com • www.bookaid.org

Contents

PART 1 IMAGE AND SIGNAL PROCESSING

PART 2 COMPUTER VISION AND RECOGNITION SYSTEMS

PART 3 REGISTRATION, MATCHING, AND PATTERN RECOGNITION

Contributors

A. Abdel-Dayem
Department of Mathematics and Computer Science, Laurentian University, Sudbury, Ontario, Canada

Ryo Aita
Graduate school of Engineering, Utsunomiya University, 7-1-2, Yoto, Utsunomiya, Tochigi, Japan

Samet Akpınar
Department of Computer Engineering, Middle East Technical University, Ankara, Turkey

Ferda Nur Alpaslan
Department of Computer Engineering, Middle East Technical University, Ankara, Turkey

Kyota Aoki
Graduate school of Engineering, Utsunomiya University, 7-1-2, Yoto, Utsunomiya, Tochigi, Japan

Hamid R. Arabnia
University of Georgia, Computer Science, Athens, GA, USA

S. Arboleda-Duque
Department of Electric, Electronic and Computer Engineering, Universidad Nacional de Colombia; Department of Telecommunications Engineering, Universidad Católica de Manizales, Manizales, Caldas, Colombia

R. Ardekani
Molecular and Computational Biology, Department of Biological Sciences, USC, Los Angeles, CA, USA

Ramazan S. Aygün
DataMedia Research Lab, Computer Science Department, University of Alabama Huntsville, Huntsville, AL, USA

Pham The Bao
Faculty of Mathematics and Computer Science, Ho Chi Minh University of Science, Ho Chi Minh City, Viet Nam

Robert Beck
Department of Computing Sciences, Villanova University, Villanova, PA, USA

Christopher Blay
YouTube Corporation, San Bruno, CA, USA

H. Chen
Department of Preventive Medicine, Keck School of Medicine, USC, Los Angeles, CA, USA

Haijung Choi
SANE Co., Ltd, Seoul, Korea

Clarimar José Coelho
Computer Science and Computer Engineering Department (CMP), Pontifical
Catholic University of Goiás (PUC-GO), Goiânia, Brazil

Eduardo Tavares Costa
Department of Biomedical Engineering, DEB/FEEC/UNICAMP, Campinas,
Brazil

Anderson da Silva Soares
Computer Science Institute (INF), Federal University of Goiás (UFG), Goiânia,
Brazil

Sepehr Damavandinejadmonfared
Department of Computing, Advanced Cyber Security Research Centre,
Macquarie University, Sydney, New South Wales, Australia

Maria Stela Veludo de Paiva
Engineering School of São Carlos (EESC), Electrical Engineering Department,
University of São Paulo (USP), São Paulo, Brazil

Leonidas Deligiannidis
Wentworth Institute of Technology, Department of Computer Science, Boston,
MA, USA

İmren Dinç
DataMedia Research Lab, Computer Science Department, University of Alabama
Huntsville, Huntsville, AL, USA

Semih Dinç
DataMedia Research Lab, Computer Science Department, University of Alabama
Huntsville, Huntsville, AL, USA

Gregory Doerfler
Department of Computing Sciences, Villanova University, Villanova,
PA, USA

Min Dong
School of Information Science and Engineering, Lanzhou University, Lanzhou,
China

Arezoo Ektesabi
Swinburne University of Technology, Melbourne, Victoria, Australia

Hany A. Elsalamony
Mathematics Department, Faculty of Science, Helwan University,
Cairo, Egypt

B. Foley
Molecular and Computational Biology, Department of Biological Sciences, USC,
Los Angeles, CA, USA

Faouzi Ghorbel
GRIFT Research Group, CRISTAL Laboratory, Ecole Nationale des Sciences de l'Informatique (ENSI), Campus Universitaire de la Manouba, Manouba, Tunisia

J.B. Gómez-Mendoza
Department of Electric, Electronic and Computer Engineering, Universidad Nacional de Colombia, Manizales, Caldas, Colombia

Marco Aurélio Granero
Department of Biomedical Engineering, DEB/FEEC/UNICAMP, Campinas; Federal Institute of Education, Science and Technology São Paulo—IFSP, Sao Paulo, Brazil

Marco Antônio Gutierrez
Division of Informatics/Heart Institute, HCFMUSP, Sao Paulo, Brazil

M. Hariyama
Graduate School of Information Sciences, Tohoku University, Sendai, Miyagi, Japan

A. Hematian
Department of Computer and Information Sciences, Towson University, Towson, MD, USA

Chuen-Min Huang
Department of Information Management, National Yunlin University of Science & Technology, Yunlin, Taiwan, ROC

Nguyen Tuan Hung
Faculty of Mathematics and Computer Science, Ho Chi Minh University of Science, Ho Chi Minh City, Viet Nam

M. Ilie
"Dunarea de Jos" University of Galati, Faculty of Automatic Control, Computers, Electrical and Electronics Engineering, Galati, Romania

Rowa'a Jamal
Electrical Engineering Department, University of Jordan, Amman, Jordan

J. Johnson
Department of Mathematics and Computer Science, Laurentian University, Sudbury, Ontario, Canada

Eui Sun Kang
Soongsil University, Seoul, Korea

Ajay Kapoor
Swinburne University of Technology, Melbourne, Victoria, Australia

A. Karimian
Department of Biomedical Engineering, Faculty of Engineering, University of Isfahan, Isfahan, Iran

Loay Khalaf
Electrical Engineering Department, University of Jordan, Amman, Jordan

Jin Young Kim
School of Electrical and Computer Engineering, Chonnam National University, Gwangju, South Korea

Manbae Kim
Department of Computer and Communications Engineering, Kangwon National University, Chunchon, Gangwon, Republic of Korea

Bernd Klässner
Technische Universität München, München, Germany

Vladimir Kulyukin
Department of Computer Science, Utah State University, Logan, UT, USA

Gustavo Teodoro Laureano
Computer Science Institute (INF), Federal University of Goiás (UFG), Goiânia, Brazil

Xiangyu Lu
School of Information Science and Engineering, Lanzhou University, Lanzhou, China

Yide Ma
School of information Science Engineering, Lanzhou University, Lanzhou, China

Saeed Mahmoudpour
Department of Computer and Communications Engineering, Kangwon National University, Chunchon, Gangwon, Republic of Korea

Karmel Manaa
Electrical Engineering Department, University of Jordan, Amman, Jordan

P. Marjoram
Department of Preventive Medicine, Keck School of Medicine, USC, Los Angeles, CA, USA

Mohamed Amine Mezghich
GRIFT Research Group, CRISTAL Laboratory, Ecole Nationale des Sciences de l'Informatique (ENSI), Campus Universitaire de la Manouba, Manouba, Tunisia

Slim M'Hiri
GRIFT Research Group, CRISTAL Laboratory, Ecole Nationale des Sciences de l'Informatique (ENSI), Campus Universitaire de la Manouba, Manouba, Tunisia

José Manuel Miranda
Facultad de Ingeniería, Universidad Autónoma del Estado de México, Toluca, Estado de México, Mexico

Hector A. Montes-Venegas
Facultad de Ingeniería, Universidad Autónoma del Estado de México, Toluca, Estado de México, Mexico

Oswaldo Morales
Superior School of Mechanical and Electrical Engineers, National Polytechnic Institute of Mexico, IPN Avenue, Lindavista, Mexico City, Mexico

Jaime Moreno
Superior School of Mechanical and Electrical Engineers, National Polytechnic Institute of Mexico, IPN Avenue, Lindavista, Mexico City, Mexico; Signal, Image and Communications Department, University of Poitiers, Poitiers, France

Dae Hyuck Park
SANE Co., Ltd, Seoul, Korea

M. Pashna
Malaysia-Japan International Institute of Technology (MJIIT), Universiti Teknologi Malaysia, Jalan semarak 54100 Kuala Lumpur, Malaysia

Alfredo Petrosino
University "Parthenope", Naples, Italy

Marc L. Pusey
iXpressGenes Inc., Huntsville, AL, USA

Maram Rabee'a
Electrical Engineering Department, University of Jordan, Amman, Jordan

Marcelo Romero
Facultad de Ingeniería, Universidad Autónoma del Estado de México, Toluca, Estado de México, Mexico

M. Saadatseresht
Department of Geomatics Engineering, College of Engineering, University of Tehran, Tehran, Iran

Maweheb Saidani
GRIFT Research Group, CRISTAL Laboratory, Ecole Nationale des Sciences de l'Informatique (ENSI), Campus Universitaire de la Manouba, Manouba, Tunisia

Giuseppe Salvi
University "Parthenope", Naples, Italy

Jeong Goo Seo
SANE Co., Ltd, Seoul, Korea

Tamara Seybold
Arnold & Richter Cine Technik, München, Germany

M. Shimoda
Second Department of Surgery, Dokkyo Medical University, Tochigi, Japan

Madhav Sigdel
DataMedia Research Lab, Computer Science Department, University of Alabama Huntsville, Huntsville, AL, USA

Madhu S. Sigdel
DataMedia Research Lab, Computer Science Department, University of Alabama Huntsville, Huntsville, AL, USA

Dominik Spinczyk
Faculty of Biomedical Engineering, Silesian University of Technology, Zabrze, Poland

Walter Stechele
Technische Universität München, München, Germany

Iulia Stirb
Computer and Software Engineering Department, "Politehnica" University of Timisoara, Timisoara, Romania

Hongjun Su
Department of Computer Science and Information Technology, Armstrong State University, Savannah, GA, USA

R. Talebi
Department of Mathematics and Computer Science, Laurentian University, Sudbury, Ontario, Canada

J.D. Tamayo-Quintero
Department of Electric, Electronic and Computer Engineering, Universidad Nacional de Colombia, Manizales, Caldas, Colombia

Ricardo Tejeida
Superior School of Mechanical and Electrical Engineers, National Polytechnic Institute of Mexico, IPN Avenue, Lindavista, Mexico City, Mexico

Md. Zia Uddin
Department of Computer Education, Sungkyunkwan University, Seoul, Republic of Korea

Vijay Varadharajan
Department of Computing, Advanced Cyber Security Research Centre, Macquarie University, Sydney, New South Wales, Australia

Keju Wang
School of Information Science and Engineering, Lanzhou University, Lanzhou, China

Chuangbai Xiao
College of Computer Science and Technology, Beijing University of Technology, Beijing, China

S. Yazdani
Malaysia-Japan International Institute of Technology (MJIIT), Universiti Teknologi
Malaysia, Jalan semarak 54100 Kuala Lumpur, Malaysia

R. Yusof
Malaysia-Japan International Institute of Technology (MJIIT), Universiti Teknologi
Malaysia, Jalan semarak 54100 Kuala Lumpur, Malaysia

Hong Zhang
Department of Computer Science and Information Technology, Armstrong State
University, Savannah, GA, USA

Hongyu Zhao
College of Computer Science and Technology, Beijing University of Technology,
Beijing, China

Huaxia Zhao
College of Computer Science and Technology, Beijing University of Technology,
Beijing, China

Acknowledgments

We are very grateful to the many colleagues who offered their services in preparing and publishing this book. In particular, we would like to thank the members of the Program Committee of IPCV'14 and IPCV'13 annual International Conferences; their names appear at: http://www.worldacademyofscience.org/worldcomp14/ws/conferences/ipcv14/committee and http://www.worldacademyofscience.org/worldcomp13/ws/conferences/ipcv13/committee. We would also like to thank the members of the Steering Committee of WORLDCOMP 2014; their names appear at http://www.worldacademyofscience.org/worldcomp14/ws and the referees who were designated by them. We would like to extend our appreciation to Steve Elliot (Elsevier Executive Editor) and Kaitlin Herbert (Elsevier Editorial Project Manager) for the outstanding professional service that they provided to us.

Preface

It gives me a great pleasure to introduce this collection of papers to the readers of the book series "Emerging Trends in Computer Science and Applied Computing" (Morgan Kaufmann/Elsevier). This book is entitled *Emerging Trends in Image Processing, Computer Vision, and Pattern Recognition*. I am indebted to Professor Leonidas Deligiannidis of Wentworth Institute of Technology (Boston, MA) for acting as the senior editor of this book. His tireless energy, leadership and strategic ability made the implementation of this project a wonderful experience.

From the computer science perspective, the core of imaging science includes the following three intertwined computer science fields, namely: image processing, computer vision, and pattern recognition. This book covers the emerging trends in these three important areas. There is significant renewed interest in each of these three fields because of the Big Data initiative with applications as diverse as computational biology, biometrics, biomedical imaging, robotics, security, knowledge engineering, and others. Although, the topic of Big Data Analytics is not explicitly addressed in this book, many algorithms and methodologies that appear in this book can be applied (some with straightforward extensions) to Big Data.

This book is composed of selected papers that were accepted for the 2013 and 2014 international conference on image processing, computer vision, and pattern recognition (IPCV'13 and IPCV'14), July, Las Vegas, USA. Selected authors were given the opportunity to submit the extended versions of their conference papers for publication consideration in this book. The IPCV annual conferences are held as part of the World Congress in computer science, computer engineering, and applied computing, WORLDCOMP. An important mission of WORLDCOMP includes "Providing a unique platform for a diverse community of constituents composed of scholars, researchers, developers, educators, and practitioners. The Congress makes concerted effort to reach out to participants affiliated with diverse entities (such as universities, institutions, corporations, government agencies, and research centers/labs) from all over the world. The congress also attempts to connect participants from institutions that have *teaching* as their main mission with those who are affiliated with institutions that have *research* as their main mission. The congress uses a quota system to achieve its institution and geography diversity objectives." Since this book is composed of the extended versions of the accepted papers of IPCV annual conferences, it is no surprise that the book has chapters from highly qualified and diverse group of authors.

I am very grateful to the many colleagues who offered their services in organizing the IPCV conferences. Their help was instrumental in the formation of this book. The members of the editorial committee included:

- Dr. Selim Aissi, Vice President, Global Information Security, Visa Inc., USA (formerly: Chief Strategist—Security, Intel Corporation, USA)
- Dr. Eng. Hamid Ali Abed Al-Asadi, Head of Computer Science Department, Faculty of Education for Pure Science, Basra University, Basra, Iraq

- Prof. Rafeeq AbdulRahman Al-Hashemi, Dean of Information Technology, Al-Hussein Bin Talal University, Jordan
- Prof. Ezendu Ariwa, Faculty of Computer Science and Technology, University of Bedfordshire, UK; Chair, IEEE Consumer Electronics & Broadcast Technology Chapter, UKRI; and Chair, IEEE Technology Management Council Chapter, UKRI, UK
- Prof. Michael Panayiotis Bekakos, Professor of Computer Systems; Director, Laboratory of Digital Systems, Department of Electrical and Computer Engineering, Democritus University of Thrace, Greece; Head, Parallel Algorithms and architectures Research Group (PAaRG); and Editor-in-Chief, The Journal of Neural, Parallel & Scientific Computations, USA
- Dr. Sidahmed Benabderrahmane, INRIA (French National Computer Science Institute), France
- Prof. Juan Jose Martinez Castillo, Director of The Acantelys Research Group and Coordinator of the Computer Engineering Department, Universidad Gran Mariscal de Ayacucho, Venezuela
- Dr. Daniel Bo-Wei Chen, Department of Electrical Engineering, Princeton University, New Jersey, USA
- Dr. Lamia Atma Djoudi, Synchrone Technologies, France
- Prof. Mary Mehrnoosh Eshaghian-Wilner, Professor of Engineering Practice, University of Southern California, California, USA and Adjunct Professor, Electrical Engineering, University of California Los Angeles, Los Angeles (UCLA), California, USA
- Prof. Oleg Finko, Krasnodar Higher Military Command Engineering School Rocket Forces, Russia and Institute of Information Technology and security, Kuban State Technological University, Russia
- Prof. Mohammad Shahadat Hossain, Department of Computer Science and Engineering, University of Chittagong, Chittagong, Bangladesh; Visiting Professor, Trisakti University, Indonesia; and Visiting Academic Staff, The University of Manchester, UK
- Prof. George Jandieri, Georgian Technical University, Tbilisi, Georgia; Chief Scientist, The Institute of Cybernetics, Georgian Academy of Science, Georgia; and Editorial Board Member: International Journal of Microwaves and Optical Technology, The Open Atmospheric Science Journal, American Journal of Remote Sensing
- Prof. Young-Sik Jeong, Department of Multimedia Engineering, Dongguk University, Seoul, South Korea and Editor-in-Chief, Journal of Information Processing Systems (JIPS)
- Dr. Sunil Kothari, HP Labs, Palo Alto, California, USA
- Prof. Joan Lu, University of Huddersfield, Huddersfield, West Yorkshire, UK
- Dr. Andrew Marsh, CEO, HoIP Telecom Ltd (Healthcare over Internet Protocol), UK and Secretary General of World Academy of BioMedical Sciences and Technologies (WABT) a UNESCO NGO, The United Nations

- Prof. James J. (Jong Hyuk) Park, Department of Computer Science and Engineering (DCSE), SeoulTech, Korea; President, FTRA, Editor-in-Chief, HCIS Springer, JoC, IJITCC; and Head of DCSE, SeoulTech, Korea
- Dr. Muhammad Imran Razzak, Department of Health Informatics, College of Public Health & Health Informatics, King Saud bin Abdulaziz University for Health Sciences, Riyadh, Kingdom of Saudi Arabia
- Prof. Gerald Schaefer, Loughborough University, Loughborough, UK
- Prof. Fernando G. Tinetti, School of Computer Science, Universidad Nacional de La Plata, La Plata, Argentina and Co-editor, Journal of Computer Science and Technology (JCS&T)
- Prof. Vladimir Volkov, The Bonch-Bruevich State University of Telecommunications, Saint-Petersburg, Russia
- Prof. Patrick S. P. Wang, Fellow: IAPR, ISIBM, WASE; Professor of Computer and Information Science, Northeastern University, Boston, Massachusetts, USA and Zijiang Visiting Chair, ECNU, Shanghai, NTUST, Taipei; iCORE Visiting Professor, University of Calgary, Canada; and Otto-von-Guericke Distinguished Guest Professor, University Magdeburg, Germany
- Prof. Shiuh-Jeng Wang, Department of Information Management, Central Police University, Taiwan; Program Chair, Security & Forensics, Taiwan, R.O.C.; and Director, Information Crypto and Construction Lab (ICCL) & ICCL-FROG
- Dr. Wei Wei, School of Computer Science and Engineering, Xi'an University of Technology, Xi'an, P. R. China and Member of China Computer Federation (CCF), P. R. China
- Prof. Mary Q. Yang (ABDA and BIOCOMP), Director, Mid-South Bioinformatics Center and Joint Bioinformatics Ph.D. Program, Medical Sciences and George W. Donaghey College of Engineering and Information Technology, University of Arkansas, USA
- Prof. Jane You, Department of Computing, The Hong Kong Polytechnic University, Hong Kong

I express my gratitude to Steve Elliot (Elsevier Executive Editor) and Kaitlin Herbert (Elsevier Editorial Project Manager). I hope that you enjoy reading this book.

Introduction

It gives me immense pleasure to present this edited book to the imaging science research community. As the title of this book (*Emerging Trends in Image Processing, Computer Vision, and Pattern Recognition*) suggests, this book addresses problems in the three intertwined areas: image processing, computer vision, and pattern recognition.

The collection of chapters compiled in the section entitled "Image and Signal Processing" presents solutions to imaging problems that use methods based on: noise reduction and removal (denoising), color filters, signal processing classifications, various forms of wavelet transformations, image quantization, processing of ultrasound and RF signals, image quality assessment, video processing, OCR, sampling methods, image coding, thresholding methods, image and mass segmentation, and a number of novel applications.

The collection of chapters compiled in the section entitled "Computer Vision and Recognition Systems" presents solutions to problems that use methods based on: machine learning, tracking, localization of areas of interests, artificial neural networks, fuzzy logic, image retrieval, action recognition, image annotation, 3D simulation, Bayesian classifiers, biometrics, various forms of principal component analysis, depth image processing, Hough transform, 3D imaging, and a number of novel applications.

Lastly, the collection of chapters compiled in the section entitled "Registration, Matching, and Pattern Recognition" presents solutions to problems that use methods based on: template and correlation approaches, geometry-based registration, surface registration, Fourier transforms, active contours, camera calibration, distortion correction, field-of-view models, image kernels, distribution functions, projections, pattern unwrapping, detection and matching approaches, and a number of novel applications.

The chapters that appear in the three sections outlined above are extended versions of selected papers that were accepted for presentation at the 2013 and 2014 international conference on image processing, computer vision, and pattern recognition (IPCV'13 and IPCV'14), July, Las Vegas, USA. I was fortunate to be a coeditor of the proceedings of the above annual conferences where the preliminary versions of these chapters first appeared. I am grateful to all authors who submitted papers for consideration. I thank all referees and members of the editorial board of IPCV and WORLDCOMP. Without their help this book project would not have been initiated nor finalized.

I hope that you learn from and enjoy reading the chapters of this book as much as I did.

Image and signal processing

PART

1

Image and signal
processing

Denoising camera data: Shape-adaptive noise reduction for color filter array image data

1

Tamara Seybold[1], Bernd Klässner[2], Walter Stechele[2]

[1]Arnold & Richter Cine Technik, München, Germany
[2]Technische Universität München, München, Germany

1 INTRODUCTION

While denoising is an extensively studied task in signal processing research, most denoising methods are designed and evaluated using readily processed image data, e.g., the well-known Kodak data set [1]. The noise model is usually additive white Gaussian noise (AWGN). This kind of test data does not correspond nowadays to real-world image or video data taken with a digital camera.

To understand the difference, let us review the color image capturing via a digital camera, which is the usual way of image capturing nowadays. One pixel captures the light intensity, thus the sensor data corresponds linearly to the lightness at the pixel position. To capture color data, a color filter array (CFA) is used, which covers the pixels with a filter layer. Thus the output of the sensor is a value that represents the light intensity for one color band at one pixel position. This sensor data cannot be displayed before the following steps are applied: the white balance, the demosaicking, which leads to a full color image and the color transformations, which adapt the linear data to displayable monitor data adapted to the monitor gamma and color space. These steps lead to a noise characteristic that is fundamentally different from the usually assumed AWGN: through demosaicking it is spatially and chromatically correlated and through the nonlinear color transformations the noise distribution is unknown.

As this noise characteristic cannot be easily incorporated into the denoising methods, we propose to apply the denoising to the raw CFA data—the mosaicked data linear to the light intensity with uncorrupted noise characteristics. In the raw data we observe noise with a known distribution and a signal-dependent variance, which can be precisely estimated based on measurements [2]. However, despite

3

the richness of denoising methods, denoising color image raw data has been less studied until now. Hirakawa extended a wavelet-based method to CFA data [3]. Zhang proposed a principle component analysis (PCA) based solution [4]. The state-of-the-art method in image denoising, BM3D [5], was combined with a noise estimation algorithm and used for image denoising and declipping [6]. The latter gives very good results, which, however, come with a high computational cost. Nonlocal methods inherently have high memory cost, as the whole image must be present in the internal memory. With high resolution image sensors this can be a limiting aspect.

In this paper, we therefore propose a local method for raw data image and video denoising, which builds on a shape-adaptive discrete cosine transform (SA-DCT) [7]. The method relies on a homogeneous neighborhood for each pixel, and a thresholding operation, which eliminates the noisy DCT coefficients. The neighborhood estimation prevents from oversmoothing, which is the prevailing denoising drawback. Foi et al. adapted the method to signal-dependent noise [8], thus it can be easily used for the noise in raw data. However, the method is still not adapted to linear and CFA data. We, therefore, propose to adapt and extend the method. We calculate the neighborhood estimation on luminance data and we propose a luminance transformation that can be directly applied to the CFA data. Additionally, we show how to adapt the shape-adaptive DCT (SA-DCT) to Bayer data, as this is the most usual CFA, and describe how the real noise characteristics from a digital camera can be obtained and included in the method. We compare our solution both to Zhang [4, 6] and evaluated the visual quality of image and video data. Finally, we discuss the computational cost. While our first results are discussed in Ref. [9], we add new results using real camera data from the ARRI image set [10] in this chapter and show how the method can be improved for video sequences.

2 CAMERA NOISE

To apply denoising on raw data, we first need a realistic model for the camera noise. Therefore, we measure the real camera noise in the raw domain based on a series of exposures and calculate the noise variance using the photon transfer method [11]. While this measurement can be performed with any camera, we use the ARRI Alexa camera, as it delivers uncompressed raw data in 16 bit precision. Since the data is uncompressed, we can expect unaltered measurement results and additionally the individual camera processing steps are known for this camera [10]. Our method can equivalently be used for other cameras.

The Alexa camera has been developed for motion picture recordings in digital cinema applications. It has a CMOS sensor with a resolution of 2880×1620. In front of the sensor, the camera has a filter pack composed of an infrared cut-off filter, an ultraviolet cut-off filter and an optical low-pass filter to reduce aliasing. The CFA, which is located between the filter pack and the sensor, is a Bayer mask.

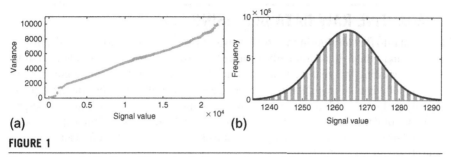

FIGURE 1

Variance and distribution of the noise in the raw domain (signal values in 16 bit precision).

The photon transfer method [11] uses two subsequent frames recorded at constant and homogenous lighting conditions. The noise variance is calculated as the mean of the difference between these two frames, the corresponding signal value is calculated as the mean over all the signal values in these frames. The graph in Figure 1 (a) shows the variance plotted over the respective mean signal value. The variance of the sensor noise can be approximated by a linear model, which matches the results reported in Ref. [12], where other cameras have been studied. We observe, however, one difference in the signal region around value 0.1×10^4. The step in the variance curve is due to a special characteristic of the Alexa sensor, the dual-gain read-out technology. The sensor read-out of the Alexa provides two different paths with different amplification (dual-gain read-out). The low amplified path provides the data for the signal range starting from 0.1×10^4. The high amplified path saturates in the high signal values, but for the low signal values it provides a significantly higher signal-to-noise ratio. The read-out noise (offset of the variance curve) is reduced, thus the dual-gain technology enhances the low light performance of the camera. The two read-out paths are combined in the region around the signal value 0.1×10^4, which explains the step in the variance curve.

The distribution is very similar to a Gaussian distribution. In Figure 1 (b) the distribution at signal level 1265 is shown with the Gaussian approximation. The difference between the approximation and the measured histogram is small, thus we can well approximate the sensor noise n in the raw domain using a Gaussian distribution with signal-dependent variance.

$$n \sim \mathcal{N}(0, \sigma(x)) \quad \text{with} \quad \sigma^2(x) = m(x)x + t(x) \tag{1}$$

The variance $\sigma^2(x)$ is approximated as a piecewise linear function depending on the signal x, with the slope $m(x)$ and the intercept $t(x)$ based on the measurement data in Figure 1 (a). Because of the dual-gain read-out the values for $m(x)$ and $t(x)$ are piecewise constant.

Based on the model for the camera noise in the raw data, we describe in the next section the shape-adaptive DCT denoising method and how to integrate the noise model in the SA-DCT.

3 ADAPTIVE RAW DATA DENOISING

Our goal is to find an algorithm, which provides a high visual quality of the denoising results, and which is additionally efficient in terms of hardware implementation costs. Regarding the visual quality, a common problem of denoising algorithms is blurring of edges or fine details in the image (oversmoothing). The shape-adaptive denoising algorithm [7] prevents from oversmoothing by using a homogenous neighborhood for denoising. As proposed by Foi we use the local polynomial approximation and intersection of confidence interval technique (LPA-ICI) to find an adequate neighborhood for each pixel.

The method has been adapted for signal-dependent noise in Ref. [8]. However, it still cannot directly be used on Bayer data, because the neighboring pixels do not have the same color due to the Bayer mask.

To find a way of estimating the neighborhood based on the Bayer data, we apply a luminance transformation. In color image denoising, a color space transformation from RGB to a luminance-chrominance color space (e.g. YCbCr) is usual. As the structural information in natural images is mostly contained in the luminance data, it is effective to perform the neighborhood estimation on the luminance channel only and use this neighborhood for denoising all three channels. In our case, we apply a similar strategy; we obtain an estimation of the luminance channel based on the Bayer data. We discuss this luminance transformation in the next section.

3.1 LUMINANCE TRANSFORMATION OF BAYER DATA

To find a luminance estimation based on the Bayer data we tested different techniques: filtering with a fixed filter kernel, partial debayering, and a new method we call "virtual luminance." Partial debayering means, we take the debayered green channel as luminance estimation directly, as the green channel is most dominant for the luminance. We used the camera debayering method (ADA), which can be applied by downloading the free "ARRIRAW Converter (ARC)" tool [14]. Another low-cost luminance estimation applies filters directly to the Bayer data. We used two different filters: a Gaussian filter kernel and a filter similar to the luminance filter by Jeon and Dubois [13]. We additionally calculated a luminance directly on the Bayer data by using the neighboring color values, which we call "virtual," because the result gives us luminance values which are located between the pixels.

The results on our test image "city" in Table 1 show that the difference in terms of peak signal-to-noise ratio (PSNR) of the denoising result is marginal. The best value

Table 1 Results of the Luminance Estimation

	Gaussian	h_L **[13]**	**Virtual**	**ADA**	**LSLCD [13]**
PSNR	36.84	36.74	36.76	36.85	36.66

PSNR of the denoising result using the respective luminance estimation method.

is reached by the camera debayering and Gaussian filtering. We use the Gaussian filtering for our method, as it shows one of the best results and additionally is a very simple and cost-efficient method.

3.2 LPA-ICI FOR NEIGHBORHOOD ESTIMATION

Once we obtained a continuous luminance estimation we can apply the LPA-ICI method [7] to find the dimension of the local homogenous neighborhood. The LPA-ICI method chooses a polynomial model (LPA) of a certain scale. Based on the ICI rule, the scale of the model is chosen and this scale defines the extent of a shape around each pixel, in which no singularities or discontinuities are present.

The LPA-ICI method is applied in eight directions. In each direction θ_k a set of directional kernels g_{h,θ_k} with the varying scale h is used to find an interval D.

$$D_{\hat{y}h_i,\theta_k} = \left[\hat{y}h_i,\theta_k - \Gamma\sigma_{\hat{y}h_i,\theta_k}, \hat{y}h_i,\theta_k + \Gamma\sigma_{\hat{y}h_i,\theta_k}\right] \tag{2}$$

$\Gamma > 0$ is a tuning parameter, which adjusts the size of the interval. The standard deviation of the estimate $\sigma_{\hat{y}h_i,\theta_k}$ is calculated by multiplying the standard deviation σ of the input with the norm $\| g_{h,\theta_k} \|_2$ of the used kernel:

$$\sigma_{\hat{y}h_i,\theta_k} = \sigma \| g_{h,\theta_k} \|_2 \tag{3}$$

The standard deviation of the input, σ, is calculated using Equation (1) with the signal value x estimated by using the noisy observation, thus the raw data pixel value. This is a very simple estimate, but we found that the improvement using a better approximation is marginal.

The largest possible scale h_i is chosen using the ICI rule.

$$\mathcal{I}_{j,\theta_k} = \bigcap_{i=1}^{j} D_{\hat{y}h_i,\theta_k} \tag{4}$$

This scale defines the shape dimension in the direction θ_k. The ICI rule is applied in all eight directions and thereby a neighborhood $\tilde{U}_x^+$ for the pixel position x is found. This neighborhood can now be used for denoising.

3.3 SHAPE-ADAPTIVE DCT AND DENOISING VIA HARD THRESHOLDING

The shape of the neighborhood is found for each pixel. Now the SA-DCT must be applied on the Bayer data to perform the denoising. Therefore the Bayer data is separated into the four sub-channels, R, G_1, G_2, and B, which each contain fourth of the total number of pixels.

For each sub-channel the SA-DCT is implemented as proposed by Foi [7]. A local estimate $\hat{y}_{\tilde{U}_x^+}$ is obtained by thresholding in the SA-DCT domain with the threshold parameter t_x set to

$$t_x = k_{\text{thr}}\sigma\sqrt{2ln|\tilde{U}_x^+| + 1} \tag{5}$$

The constant k_{thr} regulates the denoising strength. The global estimate is given by a weighted average of the local estimates.

$$\hat{y} = \frac{\sum_{x \in X} w_x \hat{y}_{\tilde{U}_x^+}}{\sum_{x \in X} w_x \chi_{\tilde{U}_x^+}} \qquad (6)$$

The weights w_x are calculated based on the size of the neighborhood $\tilde{U}_x^+$ and the noise variance σ^2. A smaller neighborhood gets higher weights, thus fine details are preserved. N_x^{har} is the number of non-zero coefficients after thresholding, thus sparse solutions are preferred over non-sparse solutions.

$$w_x = \frac{\sigma^{-2}}{(1 + N_x^{har}) | \tilde{U}_x^+ |} \qquad (7)$$

We showed how to apply neighborhood estimation on Bayer data and discussed how this neighborhood can be used for denoising with SA-DCT hard thresholding. In the following we evaluate our method and compare it to other state-of-the-art methods.

4 EXPERIMENTS: IMAGE QUALITY VS SYSTEM PERFORMANCE

We compare our method to the state-of-the-art denoising method, BM3D [5], which was specifically adapted for raw data [6], and the PCA-based method from Ref. [4].

While we also tested our method on real camera data, we compare our method quantitatively using simulated camera video sequences, as this provides us a realistic reference. This test method was described in Ref. [2] and we use it for our data similarly: we rendered the high-resolution image data and applied the camera simulation including the optical low-pass of the camera optics. We obtain a simulated reference image and including the camera noise added to the sensor data, we obtain realistic noisy images. These images are then denoised and compared to the reference. We tested the method using two different debayering methods: the ARRI debayering method, which is implemented in the camera processing tool freely available in the internet [14], and a method called "demosaicing with directional filtering and a posteriori decision" (DDFAPD) [15].

We perform a test with different noise levels. In a digital camera the noise is signal-dependent corresponding to the characteristic described in Section 2. To obtain different noise levels, we change the simulated brightness of the image and subsequently process the images with a higher ASA level to obtain comparable results. This leads to a higher noise level, as the ASA operates as a gain: The higher the ASA value, the higher the amplification and thus the lower the signal-to-noise-ratio. Three different noise levels were simulated: ASA 800, which means a low noise level, ASA1600, and ASA 3200, which corresponds to a quite high noise level.

4.1 VISUAL QUALITY OF DENOISING RESULTS

We first compare the method quantitatively, thus we calculate quality metrics enabling us to do so. We calculate the PSNR, as it is a very usual metric, and we use three additional objective quality metrics that according to Ref. [2] correlate better with the human perception of visual quality: a PSNR adapted to the human visual system (PSNR-HVS) [16], the structural similarity index (SSIM) [17] and the visual information fidelity (VIF) [18]. Tables 2–4 show the results for 800 ASA, 1600 ASA and 3200 ASA respectively. While the Bayer SA-DCT reaches the highest VIF for the 800 ASA sequences, for higher ASA values, thus higher noise levels, the ClipFoi [6] method reaches the highest metric results, while SA-DCT and PCA [4] show

Table 2 Denoising Results for the Noise Level ASA 800

ASA800	Debayering	PSNR	PSNRHVS	SSIM	VIF
Proposed	ADA	40.390	36.766	0.993	0.777
Proposed	[15]	40.703	36.777	0.993	0.810
ClipFoi	ADA	38.997	34.552	0.991	0.745
ClipFoi	[15]	39.312	34.449	0.991	0.765
Zhang	ADA	40.815	37.183	0.994	0.775
Zhang	[15]	41.325	37.265	0.994	0.802

Table 3 Denoising Results for the Noise Level ASA 1600

ASA1600	Debayering	PSNR	PSNRHVS	SSIM	VIF
Proposed	ADA	38.395	34.537	0.988	0.696
Proposed	[15]	38.682	34.787	0.988	0.737
ClipFoi	ADA	40.649	37.058	0.995	0.792
ClipFoi	[15]	41.233	36.794	0.994	0.818
Zhang	ADA	38.957	34.821	0.990	0.676
Zhang	[15]	39.458	35.089	0.990	0.703

Table 4 Denoising Results for the Noise Level ASA 3200

ASA3200	Debayering	PSNR	PSNRHVS	SSIM	VIF
Proposed	ADA	35.890	31.781	0.976	0.586
Proposed	[15]	36.120	32.239	0.979	0.631
ClipFoi	ADA	39.272	35.458	0.991	0.726
ClipFoi	[15]	39.690	35.237	0.991	0.752
Zhang	ADA	36.342	31.678	0.980	0.546
Zhang	[15]	36.726	32.031	0.981	0.567

approximately the same results. We conclude that our method achieves competitive results with respect to usual quality metrics.

When comparing the results visually, however, we think our method provides slightly better results. As the visual perception is not well represented by the metrics, we can evaluate the results comparing the difference images $I_{\text{diff}} = I_{\text{ref}} - I_{\text{denoised}}$. In the review of denoising algorithms in Ref. [19] the difference images were also used to compare denoising algorithms. An ideal difference image would look like noise; if image structure comes through, image details are lost during denoising. Figure 2 (a) shows the difference of the reference image to the image denoised by Zhang [4]: The image structure is clearly visible, which indicates that the image was blurred. In Figure 2 (b) we observe finer image structures, thus finer details seem to get lost. Additionally, the difference image is colored, which means that the error is an offset and thus the color of the denoised image does not correspond to the correct color of the reference. The difference image in Figure 2 (c) shows the difference for the proposed Bayer SA-DCT. The image is most similar to noise, thus it looks more random, which means that not much image structure is lost and no color shift must be expected.

Analyzing the results visually, we found that our method performs better due to the low spatial correlation of the error: the remaining denoising error appears less disturbing as it is less correlated. We calculated the correlation coefficient between the denoising error—also called "method noise"—at one pixel position and the denoising error at the neighboring pixel positions. The spatial correlation is shown in Figure 3 (c). The data is shown for all three color channels and for a 10×10 neighborhood. Additionally the numbers are given for the green channel and a 3×3 neighborhood in Table 5.

4.2 PROCESSING REAL CAMERA DATA

Applying image processing methods from literature to real camera data can lead to artifacts, which are due to the different characteristic of the real camera data compared to the standard test data. An investigation of the differences and resulting artifacts using debayering methods is given in Ref. [10]. When we used the method denoised by Zhang [4], we observed similar artifacts like in Ref. [10] in the highlights, shown in Figure 4 (a). To solve this, we first converted the data using a logarithmic transformation into the 12-bit logarithmic format as described in Ref. [10]. Figure 4 (b) shows the result with the logarithmic transformation: the artifacts around the highlights are almost not visible anymore. However, there are strong color shifts as it can be seen in the "U" sign and in the bottom right corner in Figure 4 (b). The result of the proposed method is shown in Figure 4 (c). We additionally calculated the PSNR of the real camera sequences using a reference image calculated as the mean image over 240 frames of a static sequence. The PSNR is clearly higher, as the proposed method does not show the mentioned color artifacts and effectively removes the noise in the image.

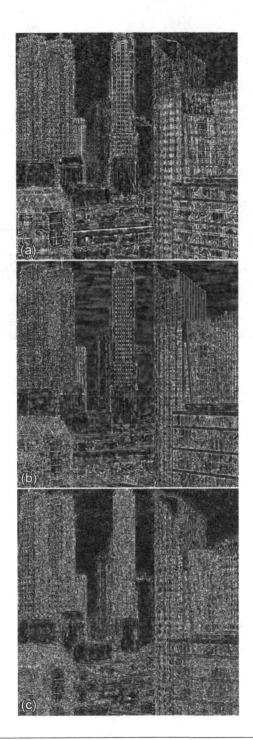

FIGURE 2

Difference to the reference for the test image "City" denoised using (a) the algorithm of Zhang [4], (b) Foi [6], and (c) the proposed version of the SA-DCT.

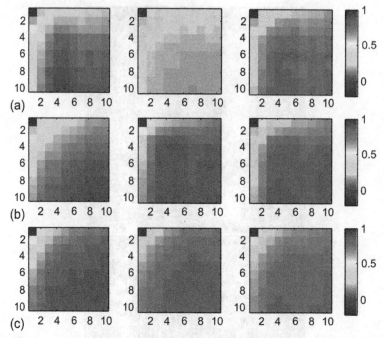

FIGURE 3

Spatial correlation of the difference images for red (left), green (middle), and blue (right) channel. Displayed is the correlation for a 10×10 neighborhood. From top to bottom: Foi [6], Zhang [4], and the proposed Bayer Data SA-DCT. Ideally only noise should be removed from the image and thus the correlation of the difference image should be low.

Table 5 Spatial Correlation of the Difference Images (Green Channel)

C_{Foi}	C_{Zhang}	$C_{\text{SA-DCT}}$
$\begin{bmatrix} 1 & 0.5672 & 0.4167 \\ 0.5893 & 0.4047 & 0.2999 \\ 0.4104 & 0.2807 & 0.2645 \end{bmatrix}$	$\begin{bmatrix} 1 & 0.4795 & 0.2767 \\ 0.5235 & 0.2826 & 0.1571 \\ 0.3119 & 0.1545 & 0.0935 \end{bmatrix}$	$\begin{bmatrix} 1 & 0.3731 & 0.2359 \\ 0.4277 & 0.2449 & 0.1846 \\ 0.2745 & 0.1923 & 0.1534 \end{bmatrix}$

The numbers correspond to the correlation of the noise at one pixel position to the noise at the neighboring pixel position. The numbers are given for a 3×3 neighborhood.

FIGURE 4

Difference to the reference for the test image "City" denoised using (a) the algorithm of Zhang [4], (b) Zhang [4] with logarithmic transformation, and (c) the proposed version of the SA-DCT.

5 VIDEO SEQUENCES

When comparing video sequences we observe that both Foi's and Zhang's method show temporal flickering. This flickering appears to be lower for the proposed Bayer SA-DCT. This is probably due to the lower spatial correlation of the remaining noise, which was shown in Figure 3 (c). Low spatial correlation means fine-grain noise, which is less visible than coarser grain noise due to the frequency-dependent color sensitivity of the human visual system. However, while the correlation is lower in the proposed SA-DCT compared to the other two methods, we still observe some temporal flickering in our results. Therefore, we extend our method using an additional temporal denoising step.

The flickering could be a consequence of the mean calculation, which dominates the result for large homogeneous areas during the denoising. Large homogeneous areas are likely to have maximum size $|\tilde{U}_x^+|$, which results in a large threshold and hence the result is mostly dominated by the mean and the DC-coefficient. As the DC-coefficient is not noise-free, temporal flickering can be observed.

To improve the visual quality in video sequences, we therefore propose to add an additional temporal denoising step. As motion estimation is difficult on Bayer data, we propose to use a very simple criterion for motion detection: when the deviation from a pixel in one frame to the same pixel in the next frame is large, we do not use it, because we assume that the pixel changed due to motion. If the pixel is similar, we use it for the temporal denoising step. A reasonable threshold depends on the noise variance.

To reduce the flickering we average over a certain number of frames N_{fr}. So the temporal smoothed output $S_{x,f}$ for every pixel x of the current frame f can be calculated from the input images $I_{x,z}$ as follows:

$$S_{x,f} = \frac{\sum_{z=f-n_1}^{f+n_2} I_{x,z}\Phi(I_{x,z}, I_{x,f})}{\sum_{z=f-n_1}^{f+n_2} \Phi(I_{x,z}, I_{x,f})} \tag{8}$$

$$\Phi(I_{x,z}, I_{x,f}) = 1 \; \forall \; I_{x,z} - I_{x,f} \leq \delta(I_{x,f}) \tag{9}$$

We use a threshold δ that depends linearly on the signal variance, which is, as described in Section 2, known from measurements.

$$\delta(I_{x,f}) = k \cdot \sigma(I_{x,f}) \tag{10}$$

Table 7 shows the results of the SA-DCT denoising with additional temporal denoising and Table 6 shows the result of the single-image SA-DCT without temporal denoising. The temporal denoising step leads to a higher PSNR and effectively reduces the flickering of the video sequence. The visual quality of the video sequence is therefore clearly higher with the temporal denoising step.

Table 6 SA-DCT Denoising Results without the Additional Temporal Denoising Step

Sequence	ASA value	PSNR	PSNRHVS	VIF	MSSIM
Color test chart	800	43.72	44.31	0.4912	0.9963
Night Odeonsplatz	800	41.18	39.33	0.7175	0.9949
Siegestor night	1600	39.89	39.22	0.6280	0.9911

The metrics are calculated and averaged over 10 frames.

Table 7 SA-DCT Denoising Results with the Additional Temporal Denoising Step

Sequence	ASA value	PSNR	PSNRHVS	VIF	MSSIM
Color test chart	800	44.63	44.88	0.5008	0.9976
Night Odeonsplatz	800	41.77	39.41	0.7308	0.9958
Siegestor night	1600	40.15	38.87	0.6492	0.9924

The metrics are calculated and averaged over 10 frames.

5.1 IMPLEMENTATION ASPECTS

Denoising algorithms like BM3D usually assume that the complete noisy image is available at each pixel position. In stream-based image processing, as it is usual in embedded systems and communication, only one pixel at a time is available. In these applications an additional buffer must be implemented to provide the neighborhood for the denoising step. For algorithms like BM3D therefore the memory cost is quite high. Our method requires only a local neighborhood for the denoising step and is therefore better suited for stream-based processing. Additionally it operates on Bayer data and the raw Bayer data has only one value per pixel whereas the processed RGB data has three values per pixel. Thus, a three times lower complexity can be expected compared to algorithms that require the fully processed image data.

While the temporal denoising step implementation requires additional frame buffers, the computational cost of the calculation is kept very low.

6 CONCLUSION

We proposed a method for real camera Bayer data denoising based on a neighborhood estimation combined with a shape-adaptive DCT. While the method has been proposed for RGB or grayscale image data, it could not be applied to Bayer data directly. To perform the SA-DCT on Bayer data we apply LPA-ICI-based neighborhood estimation to the luminance data. As the luminance data is not available in the Bayer data, we estimate the luminance efficiently using different methods. The best tradeoff between computational cost and quality was found using Gaussian filtering.

Based on the neighborhood estimation a hard thresholding is performed on the coefficients of the shape-adaptive DCT. The threshold includes the noise variance and we show how a real camera noise characteristic can be integrated. To evaluate our method we compare it with two state-of-the-art algorithms: a PCA-based CFA denoising and a BM3D-based denoising that uses noise variance estimation. While our method achieves competitive results in terms of PSNR, we show that our method can lead to better visual quality with lower computational cost. An additional temporal denoising step is proposed, which effectively reduces temporal flickering in real camera video sequences.

REFERENCES

[1] http://r0k.us/graphics/kodak/.
[2] Seybold T, Keimel C, Knopp M, Stechele W. Towards an evaluation of denoising algorithms with respect to realistic camera noise. In: Proceedings of the 2013 IEEE International Symposium on Multimedia; 2013. p. 203–10. http://dx.doi.org/10.1109/ISM.2013.39.
[3] Hirakawa K, Meng X-L, Wolfe P. A framework for wavelet-based analysis and processing of color filter array images with applications to denoising and demosaicing. In: ICASSPVol. 1; 2007. p. I-597–600. http://dx.doi.org/10.1109/ICASSP.2007.365978.
[4] Zhang L, Lukac R, Wu X, Zhang D. PCA-Based spatially adaptive denoising of CFA images for single-sensor digital cameras. IEEE Trans Image Process 2009;18 (4):797–812. http://dx.doi.org/10.1109/TIP.2008.2011384.
[5] Dabov K, Foi A, Katkovnik V, Egiazarian K. Image denoising by sparse 3-d transform-domain collaborative filtering. IEEE Trans Image Process 2007;16(8):2080–95. http://dx.doi.org/10.1109/TIP.2007.901238.
[6] Foi A. Practical denoising of clipped or overexposed noisy images. In: Proc. 16th Eur. Signal Process. Conf., EUSIPCO; 2008.
[7] Foi A, Katkovnik V, Egiazarian K. Pointwise shape-adaptive DCT for high-quality denoising and deblocking of grayscale and color images. IEEE Trans Image Process 2007;16(5):1395–411. http://dx.doi.org/10.1109/TIP.2007.891788.
[8] Foi A, Katkovnik V, Egiazarian K. Signal-dependent noise removal in pointwise shape-adaptive DCT domain with locally adaptive variance. In: EUSIPCO; 2007.
[9] Seybold T, Klässner B, Stechele W. Denoising camera data: Shape-adaptive noise reduction for color filter array image data, In: The 2014 International Conference on Image Processing, Computer Vision, and Pattern Recognition (IPCV 2014); 2014.
[10] Andriani S, Brendel H, Seybold T, Goldstone J. Beyond the Kodak image set: a new reference set of color image sequences. In: ICIP. 2013. p. 2289–93. http://dx.doi.org/10.1109/ICIP.2013.6738472.
[11] EMVA 1288. Standard for characterization of image sensors and cameras; Release 3, 2010. http://www.emva.org.
[12] Trussell HJ, Zhang R. The dominance of poisson noise in color digital cameras; 2012. p. 329–32. http://dx.doi.org/10.1109/ICIP.2012.6466862.
[13] Jeon G, Dubois E. Demosaicking of noisy bayer-sampled color images with least-squares luma-chroma demultiplexing and noise level estimation. IEEE Trans Image Process 2013;22(1):146–56. http://dx.doi.org/10.1109/TIP.2012.2214041.

[14] ARRIRAW Converter (ARC), http://www.arri.com/camera/digital_cameras/tools/arriraw_converter/.

[15] Menon D, Andriani S, Calvagno G. Demosaicing with directional filtering and a posteriori decision. IEEE Trans Image Process 2007;16(1):132–41. http://dx.doi.org/10.1109/TIP.2006.884928.

[16] Egiazarian K, Astola J, Ponomarenko N, Lukin V, Battisti F, Carli M. New full-reference quality metrics based on HVS. In: VPQM; 2006.

[17] Wang Z, Bovik AC, Sheikh HR, Simoncelli EP. Image quality assessment: from error visibility to structural similarity. IEEE Trans Image Process 2004;13(4):600–12. http://dx.doi.org/10.1109/TIP.2003.819861.

[18] Sheikh H, Bovik A. Image information and visual quality. IEEE Trans Image Process 2006;15(2):430–44. http://dx.doi.org/10.1109/TIP.2005.859378.

[19] Buades A, Coll B, Morel J. A review of image denoising algorithms, with a new one. Multiscale Model Simulat 2005;4(2):490–530.

An approach to classifying four-part music in multidimensional space

2

Gregory Doerfler, Robert Beck

Department of Computing Sciences, Villanova University, Villanova, PA, USA

1 INTRODUCTION

The four-part classifier (FPC) system began as an experiment in randomly generating four-part music that would abide by traditional four-part writing rules. The essential rules were quickly coded along with the beginnings of a program for producing valid chord sequences. But as the program evolved, it was moved in a new direction—one that could reuse the rules already written. The idea of creating a classification system which could be trained with music by known composers and tested with other music by the same composers became the driving force behind the development of this tool.

1.1 RELATED WORK

While computer classification of music is nothing new, research is lacking in the domain of classifying *four-part* music. As for four-part-specific music systems, the 1986 CHORAL system created by Ebcioglu [1] comes closest to FPC's precursor program geared toward composition. Ebcioglu's system harmonizes four-part chorales in the style of J.S. Bach via first-order predicate calculus. Newer research by Nichols et al. [2] most closely matches the mature version of FPC but is not four-part specific. Like FPC, their system operates in high-dimensional space (FPC was developed in 19-space and later expanded to 22-space) but parameterizes the musical chord *sequences* of *popular* music. FPC does not consider the order of chords in its analysis but focuses instead on chord structure and the movements between parts.

1.2 EXPLANATION OF MUSICAL TERMS

In order for FPC to be understood in the steps that follow, a basic level of musical knowledge is required.

There are 12 pitches in a chromatic scale from which are derived 12 major keys. The names of each key range from A to G and include some intermediate steps

FIGURE 1

Diatonic scale in C.

between letters such as Bb or F#. Most importantly, the key serves as a musical "anchor" for the ear. All pitches can be understood in relation to the syllable *do* (pronounced "doh"), and all chords in relation to the I chord (the tonic). Both *do* and the I chord are defined by the key.

Although each key contains 12 pitches (or steps), only 7 of them make up the diatonic scale (Figure 1)—the scale used most often in western music (*do, re, mi, fa, sol, la, ti, do*). From bottom to top, the distances between the notes of the diatonic scale follow the pattern "whole step, whole step, half step, whole step, whole step, whole step, half step." Whether traversing the diatonic scale requires multiple sharps or flats is determined by the key signature at the beginning of the piece.

From these seven diatonic notes, seven diatonic chords are possible. In four-part music, each chord is made up of four voices: soprano, alto, tenor, and bass. The arrangement of these voices produces chords in specific positions and inversions. For the sake of simplicity, the exact procedure for determining chord names and numbers has been omitted.

Notes differ not only by pitch but by duration. The shortest duration FPC handles is the eighth note followed by the quarter note, the dotted quarter note, the half note, the dotted half note, and lastly the whole note. The time signature dictates the number of beats in a measure and what type of note constitutes one beat. For example, in 3/4 time, there are three beats in a measure and a quarter note gets one beat. FPC only considers music in 3/4 or 4/4 time, so a quarter note always gets one beat.

Finally, harmonic rhythm describes the shortest regular chord duration between chord changes. For example, in 4/4 a quarter-note-level harmonic rhythm means that chords change at most every beat. Harmonic rhythm is one of the most important components of traditional four-part analysis, its reliability crucial to correctly identifying chords and chord changes. For this project, only music with quarter-note-level harmonic rhythms was chosen, removing the need to detect harmonic rhythms programmatically.

2 COLLECTING THE PIECES—TRAINING AND TEST PIECES

A collection of four-part MusicXML files was created for use as training and test data by the FPC system. Four-part pieces were collected from Web sites in two different formats: PDF and MusicXML—with the PDFs later converted to MusicXML. A few hymns were entered by hand in Finale 2011, a music notation program capable of exporting to MusicXML.

2.1 DOWNLOADING AND CONVERTING FILES

The two main Web sites used were Hymnary.org and JSBChorales.net. Hymnary is a searchable database of hymns, many of which are offered for download in PDF and MusicXML formats. For the purposes of this project, Hymnary's PDF files were found to be preferable to its MusicXML files, which were compressed, heavily formatted, and difficult to touch up. A few of the PDFs on Hymnary were simply scans and not native PDFs (ones containing font and character data), so they were entered by hand into Finale 2011 and exported to MusicXML. The other site, JSBChorales. org, offers a collection of Bach chorales entirely in MusicXML format. These MusicXML files were found to be suitable.

XML and PDF files were downloaded from these sites and renamed using the format "title—classifier.pdf" or "title—classifier.xml" where "title" is the hymntune or other unique, harmonization-specific name of the composition and "classifier" is the composer. This naming convention was maintained throughout the project. Individually, the PDF files from Hymnary were converted to MusicXML using a software program called PDFtoMusic Pro. PDFtoMusic Pro is not a text-recognition program, so it can only extract data from PDFs created by music notation software, which all of them were. The free trial version of PDFtoMusic Pro converts only the first page of PDF files, which fortunately created no issue since all but a few of the downloaded hymns were single-page documents. The XML files PDFtoMusic Pro produced carried the xml file extension and were compressed.

2.2 FORMATTING THE MusicXML

Before the XML files could be used, it was necessary to adjust their formatting and, in the case of the XML variety, remove their compression. This was done with Finale. Once open in Finale, lyrics, chord charts, and any extraneous or visually interfering markings were removed manually. If the piece was written in open staff, as was the case with every Bach chorale, a piano reduction (two staves) was created in its place. Measures with pick-up notes were deleted and if beats had been borrowed from the last measure, they were added back. For these reinstated beats, the last chord of the piece was extended.

Any time two layers exist in the same staff of the same measure, FPC expects them to start and finish out the measure together. However, publishers and editors do not like splitting note stems multiple times in a single measure if only one beat requires a split and so tend to add or drop layers mid-measure strictly for appearance (Figure 2). Anywhere these kinds of sudden splits occurred, measures were adjusted by hand (Figure 3).

If two parts in the same staff double a note in unison but the staff did not use two layers to do it (Figure 4), the parts were rewritten for that measure (Figure 5). Any rests present were replaced with the corresponding note(s) of the previous chord.

FIGURE 2

Improper layering.

FIGURE 3

Proper layering.

    Lastly, all measures were copied and pasted into a new Finale document to remove any hidden formatting. The files were then exported with the same naming convention as before and saved in a specific training piece or test piece directory for use by FPC (Figure 6).

FIGURE 4

Missing layer for presumably doubled note.

FIGURE 5

Proper layering for doubled note.

The next few sections describe how FPC works in general. Section 6 returns to the specific way FPC was used in this experiment.

3 PARSING MusicXML—TRAINING AND TEST PIECES

By clicking the "Load Training XML" or "Load Test XML" button, the user kicks-off step 1 of the data-loading process: Parsing the XML (Figure 7).

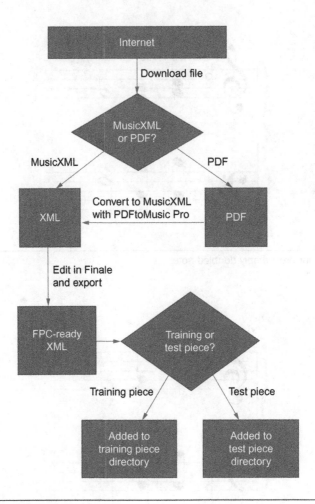

Flow chart for collecting pieces.

3.1 READING IN KEY AND DIVISIONS

First, FPC parses the key from each file, then the divisions. The number of divisions is an integer value defining quarter note duration for the document. All other note types (half, eighth, etc.) are deduced from this integer and recognized throughout the document. If a quarter note is found to be two, a half note is four.

3.2 READING IN NOTES

MusicXML organizes notes by layers within staves within measures. In other words, layer 1 of staff 1 of measure 1 comes before layer 2 of staff 1 of measure 1, which precedes layer 1 of staff 2 of measure 1, and so on. Last is layer 2 of staff 2 of the final measure. If a staff contains only one layer in a particular measure, the lower note of the

FIGURE 7

FPC upon launch.

two-note cluster (alto for staff 1, bass for staff 2) is read before the upper note (soprano or tenor, respectively). Since a measure might contain a staff with one layer and another with two, FPC was carefully designed to handle all possible combinations.

A note's pitch consists of a step and an octave (e.g., Bb and 3). A hash map is used to relate pitches to integers (e.g., "Bb3" → 18), and these integers are used to represent each voice of a four-part Chord object.

3.3 HANDLING NOTE VALUES

In 3/4 and 4/4 time, a quarter-note-level harmonic rhythm means that chords change at most each beat. Therefore, the chord produced by the arrangement of soprano, alto, tenor, and bass voices at the start of each beat carries through to the end of the beat. This also means that shorter notes moving between beats cannot command chords of their own. Quarter notes, which span a whole beat, are then the ideal notes to capture as long as they fall on the beat, which they always did. Likewise, eighth notes that fall on the beat are taken to be structurally important to the chord, so their durations are doubled to a full beat and their pitches captured, whereas those that fall between beats are assumed to be passing tones, upper and lower neighbors, and other non-chord tones, so they are ignored. For simplicity's sake, anything longer than a quarter note is considered a repeat quarter note and sees its pitch captured more than once. For instance, a half note is treated as two separate quarter notes and a whole note as four separate quarter notes. A dotted quarter note is assumed to always fall on the

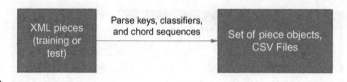

FIGURE 8

Flow chart for creating Piece objects.

beat, so it is captured as two quarter notes; the following eighth note is ignored. While it is possible for something other than an eighth note to follow a dotted quarter, it is highly unlikely in 3/4 or 4/4, and it did not happen in any of the music used.

3.4 RESULTS

Finally, for each XML file, FPC creates a Piece object comprising at the moment a key, classifier, and sequence of Chords. For each piece, it also produces a CSV file with the same information. The CSV files serve purely as logs (Figure 8).

4 COLLECTING PIECE STATISTICS

After the XML has been parsed, FPC moves immediately to the next step: Collecting Piece Statistics.

4.1 METRICS

Statistics are collected for each piece via 19 Boolean tests on each chord or chord change. These Boolean tests produce the following metrics (Diagram 111):

```
                              Bach.txt - Notepad                    –  □  ×
File  Edit  Format  View  Help
Classifier: Bach
ThirdAppearsOnlyOnceInSATRuleAvg: 93.16435185185185 (std: 2.352603590852641)
ThirdNotDoubledInUnisonRuleAvg: 98.24768518518519 (std: 1.731314361116895)
FifthDoubledInSecondInversionAvg: 60.0 (std: 37.416573867739416)
CrossOverRuleAvg: 97.77777777777779 (std: 4.4444444444444455)
SATOctaveRuleAvg: 96.22685185185185 (std: 3.546731430610151)
SevenChordDiminishedFifthRuleAvg: 74.0 (std: 24.979991993593593)
ParallelFifthsRuleAvg: 99.19710959454034 (std: 0.9862815023092376)
ParallelOctavesRuleAvg: 98.53479853479853 (std: 1.9243846940020113)
DirectFifthsInOuterVoicesRuleAvg: 99.68253968253968 (std: 0.6349206349206383)
DirectOctavesInOuterVoicesRuleAvg: 99.48717948717949 (std: 1.0256410256410278)
JumpRuleAvg: 99.17488031540411 (std: 1.0166735427357976)
StepwiseMovementsRuleAvg: 97.30637621444525 (std: 1.7111423230998217)
StepwiseSopranoMovementsAvg: 76.70824927276513 (std: 7.399696537216317)
RootPositionAvg: 65.91666666666666 (std: 3.1337360742833376)
FirstInversionAvg: 21.041666666666664 (std: 6.843494653115128)
SecondInversionAvg: 2.7037037037037037 (std: 2.3703703703703702)
ThirdInversionAvg: 2.25 (std: 2.438123139721299)
SuspensionAvg: 0.6948188080263552 (std: 0.8562296665230974)
SecondaryChords: 7.965277777777777 (std: 6.675616099555304)
NumberofPieces: 5
```

DIAGRAM 111

ThirdAppearsOnlyOnceInSAT	The percent of chords whose third appears only once in the upper three voices. In classical writing, it is preferable that the third appear just once in the upper three voices.
ThirdNotDoubledInUnison	The percent of chords whose third is not doubled in unison. Doubling the third in unison is usually avoided unless necessary.
FifthDoubledInSecondInversion	The percent of second-inversion chords whose fifth is doubled. Classically, it is preferable that the fifth be doubled in second inversion.
CrossOver	The percent of chords not containing overlapping parts. It is preferable that voices do not cross over. Doubling in unison is fine.
SETOctave	The percent of chords whose soprano and alto pitches as well as alto and tenor pitches differ by not more than an octave. This is a fairly strict rule in classical, four-part writing. The distance between the bass and tenor does not matter and may be great.
SevenChordContainsDiminishedFifth	The percent of vii° chords with a fifth. While the fifths of other chords are often omitted, the diminished fifth of a vii° chord adds an important quality and its presence is a strict requirement in classical writing.
NoParallelFifths	The percent of chord changes free of parallel fifths. This is a strict rule of classical writing.
NoParallelOctaves	The percent of chord changes free of parallel octaves. This is also a strict rule.
NoDirectFifthsInOuterVoices	The percent of chord changes free of direct fifths in the outer voices. This is a fairly important rule in classical writing.
NoDirectOctavesInOuterVoices	The percent of chord changes free of direct octaves in the outer voices. This also is a fairly important rule.
LeapingParts	The percent of chord changes involving a part jumping by a major seventh, a minor seventh, or the tri-tone. Jumping the tri-tone in a nonmelodic voice part is never acceptable in classical writing, but from time to time, leaps by major and minor sevenths and even tri-tones are permissible if in the soprano.
StepwiseMovements	The percent of chord changes in which at least one voice moves by no more than a major second. While this is not a formal rule of classical writing *per se*, good writing generally has very few chord changes in which all four parts leap.
StepwiseSopranoMovements	The percent of chord changes in which the soprano moves by not more than a major second.
RootPosition	The percent of chords in root position (root in bass).
FirstInversion	The percent of chords in first inversion (third in bass).

Continued

SecondInversion	The percent of chords in second inversion (fifth in bass).
ThirdInversion	The percent of chords in third inversion (seventh in bass).
Suspensions	The percent of chord changes involving a suspended note that resolves to a chord tone.
SecondaryDominants	The percent of chords borrowed from other keys that act as launch pads to chords that *do* belong in the key (diatonic chords). FPC handles all "V-of" chords (i.e., V/ii, Viii, V/IV, V/V, V/vi) and all "V^7-of" chords except V7/IV. "V^7-of" chords are simply recorded as "V-of" chords since they perform the same function.

After all 19 metrics are computed per piece, a TXT file is produced for backup (Figures 9 and 10).

5 COLLECTING CLASSIFIER STATISTICS—TRAINING PIECES ONLY

The previous two steps—Parsing the XML and Collecting Piece Statistics—apply to the loading of both training and test data. Step 3, however, applies to training data only. If the user has clicked "Load Training XML," FPC now begins the final step before it is ready to start classifying test pieces: Collecting Classifier Statistics.

In the sections that follow, "classifier" with a lowercase "c" refers to the Piece object's string field while "Classifier" with a capital "C" refers to the Classifier object.

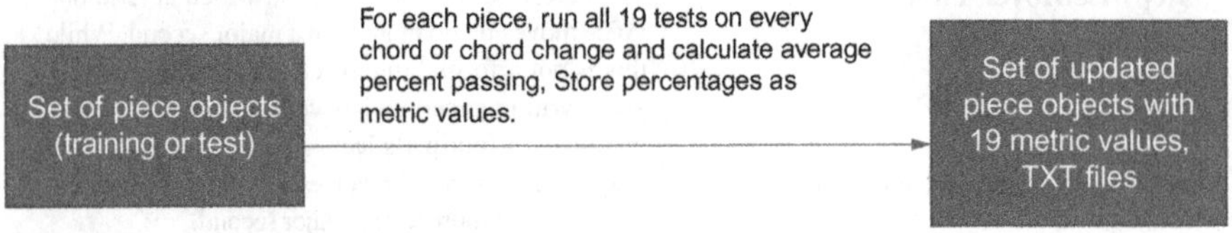

FIGURE 9

Flow chart for collecting Piece statistics.

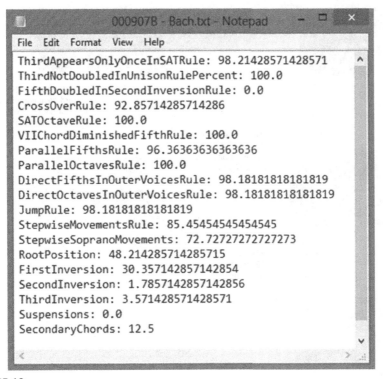

```
000907B - Bach.txt - Notepad

File  Edit  Format  View  Help

ThirdAppearsOnlyOnceInSATRule: 98.21428571428571
ThirdNotDoubledInUnisonRulePercent: 100.0
FifthDoubledInSecondInversionRule: 0.0
CrossOverRule: 92.85714285714286
SATOctaveRule: 100.0
VIIChordDiminishedFifthRule: 100.0
ParallelFifthsRule: 96.36363636363636
ParallelOctavesRule: 100.0
DirectFifthsInOuterVoicesRule: 98.18181818181819
DirectOctavesInOuterVoicesRule: 98.18181818181819
JumpRule: 98.18181818181819
StepwiseMovementsRule: 85.45454545454545
StepwiseSopranoMovements: 72.72727272727273
RootPosition: 48.214285714285715
FirstInversion: 30.357142857142854
SecondInversion: 1.7857142857142856
ThirdInversion: 3.571428571428571
Suspensions: 0.0
SecondaryChords: 12.5
```

FIGURE 10

Sample TXT file for a Bach chorale containing 19 metric values (percentages).

5.1 APPROACH

For each training piece belonging to the same classifier, a Classifier object is created. The mean and standard deviation are computed for each metric from all the pieces of the classifier and then stored in the Classifier object. For any piece, metrics outside three standard deviations of the mean are thrown out, and the means and standard deviations are recalculated. Again, the whole piece is not thrown out, just the piece's individual metric(s). FPC updates each Classifier object with the new mean(s) and standard deviation(s) and then produces TXT files with the same information. Figure 11 provides an example to illustrate the process.

6 CLASSIFYING TEST PIECES

Three techniques were used to classify test pieces from metric data: Unweighted Points, Weighted Points, and Euclidean Distance.

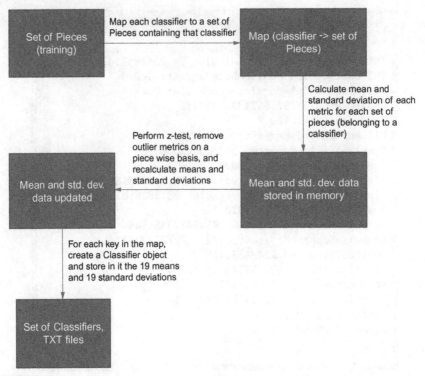

FIGURE 11

Flow chart for collecting Classifier statistics. Example: Pieces 1–10 belong to Classifier A, Pieces 11–20 to Classifier B, and Pieces 21–30 to Classifier C. The mean for metric X from Pieces 1–10 is calculated to be 15 (as in 15%) and the standard deviation is 5 (as in 5% points). If Piece 10's metric X is 31, which is greater than $15 + 3 \times 5$ (z-test upper-bound), it is an outlier. Piece 10's metric X is therefore discarded and the mean and standard deviation for metric X are recomputed using Pieces 1–9. Classifier A then receives the new mean and standard deviation for metric X, and a TXT file is written. These steps are repeated for Classifiers B and C.

6.1 CLASSIFICATION TECHNIQUES

Unweighted Points is the simplest technique. It treats each metric equally, assigning a single point to a Classifier each time one of its metrics best matches the test piece. The classifier with the most points at the end is declared the winner and is chosen as the classification for the test piece.

Weighted Points was an original approach. It works similar to Unweighted Points except metrics can be worth different amounts of points. First, it calculates metric differences from the Classifiers: For each metric, it finds the Classifier with the highest value and the one with the lowest value. It subtracts the lowest value from the

$$d(p, q) = \sqrt{(p_1 - q_1)^2 + (p_2 - q_2)^2 + \cdots + (p_n - q_n)^2}$$

FIGURE 12

Euclidean distance formula.

highest value, and the difference becomes the number of "points" that metric is worth. Then, like Unweighted Points, it looks to see which Classifier is closest to the test piece for each particular metric, only instead of assigning a single point, it assigns however many points the metric is worth.

Euclidean Distance is a standard technique for calculating distances in high-dimensional space. Here, it focuses on one Classifier at a time, taking the square root of the sums of each metric difference (between test piece and classifier) squared. This is illustrated in Figure 12, where p is the classifier, q is the test piece, and there are n metrics.

Euclidean distance is calculated for each classifier, and the classifier with the smallest distance from the test piece is chosen as the classification.

6.2 USER INTERFACE

A row of four buttons allows the user to load training XML, load test XML, classify test pieces, and clear results. Above these buttons sit textboxes displaying the paths to files FPC will read or write on the user's machine during use. At the very top of the UI is a checkbox allowing FPC to select the training and test pieces from the collection *randomly*. Randomizing training and test pieces requires XML to be loaded each time a trial is run (since Classifiers will likely contain different data). Therefore, checking this box disables the "Load Training XML" and "Load Test XML" buttons, moving their combined functionality into the "Classify Test Pieces" button. Below the row of buttons is an information area, which displays the results of each step including test piece classification. To the right of the information area can be found a panel of checkboxes giving the user control over the metrics. Metrics can be turned on or off to help the combinations producing the most accurate results be discovered. At the very bottom of FPC sits a status bar that reflects program state.

6.3 CLASSIFICATION STEPS

When the user clicks "Classify Test Pieces," test piece data from the TXT files created in step 2 (collecting piece statistics) are read and loaded into memory. It is true that if the user has performed steps in the normal order and loaded training XML before test XML, the test piece data would still be in memory, and reading from file would not be necessary. However, due to the sharing of Piece objects between training pieces and test pieces, if steps were done out of order, the Piece objects, if still in memory, might contain training data instead of test data. And because each TXT file is small, reading in the data proves a reliable way to ensure good system state if, for example, the user were to load training and test data, exit the program, and launch FPC again hoping to start classifying test pieces immediately without reloading. Here, reading from files is the simplest solution.

Next, if the Classifiers are not already in memory, the data are read in from the Classifier TXT files produced in step 3 (collecting classifier statistics). For each test piece, its metric values are compared with those of each Classifier. Each classification technique then scores the metrics and handles the results in its own, unique way.

6.4 TESTING THE CLASSIFICATION TECHNIQUES

Four-part music was selected comprising three composers: J.S. Bach, John Bacchus Dykes, and Henry Thomas Smart. Dykes and Smart were nineteenth century English hymnists, while Bach was an early eighteenth century German composer. Dykes and Smart were chosen for their similarities with one another, while Bach was chosen for his differences from them.

Using all 19 metrics, 20 trials were run per composer combination: (1) Bach versus Dykes, (2) Bach versus Smart, (3) Dykes versus Smart, and (4) Bach versus Dykes versus Smart. The averages were then computed for each classification technique. Later, 20 more trials were run for Bach versus Dykes using a subset of metrics thought most important.

Forty-five pieces in all were used—15 per composer—and randomization was employed on each trial so that training pieces and test pieces could be different each time.

6.5 CLASSIFYING FROM AMONG TWO COMPOSERS

For all three evaluation techniques, the averages of each trial, when classifying among two composers, came out well above 50%—the value expected from a two-composer coin toss. In fact, no individual trial fell below 50%.

Bach Versus Dykes—All Metrics

Technique	Correctness (%)
Unweighted Points	82.5
Weighted Points	86.8
Euclidean Distance	71.5

Bach Versus Smart—All Metrics

Technique	Correctness (%)
Unweighted Points	92.1
Weighted Points	89.3
Euclidean Distance	69.3

Dykes Versus Smart—All Metrics

Technique	Correctness (%)
Unweighted Points	74
Weighted Points	82.9
Euclidean Distance	69.3

The best technique overall was Weighted Points, demonstrating the strongest performance in two out of the three classifications.

6.6 CLASSIFYING FROM AMONG THREE COMPOSERS

For all three evaluation techniques, the averages of each trial, when classifying among three composers, came out well above 33.3%—the value expected from random, three-way guessing. In fact, no individual trial dipped below 33.3%. The technique that worked best was Unweighted Points followed by Weighted Points at a close second.

Back Versus Dykes Versus Smart—All Metrics

Technique	Correctness (%)
Unweighted Points	71
Weighted Points	68.1
Euclidean Distance	57.1

6.7 SELECTING THE BEST METRICS

If all 45 pieces were to be used to train the system, the resulting classifier data would represent what data from a randomized trial would look like on average. In this case, one can see that Bach's chord inversion statistics are far different from those of Dykes and Smart. Bach also relies more heavily on secondary chords:

Classifier Data from 45 Test Pieces

Five Metrics	Bach	Dykes	Smart
Root Position (%)	65.7	62	61.1
First Inversion (%)	22.1	20	22.02
Second Inversion (%)	2	10.72	10
Third Inversion (%)	1.1	0.6	1.9
Secondary Chords (%)	11.5	4.4	3.9

To test if FPC could even more accurately distinguish between Bach and either of the others, 20 additional trials were run for Bach and Dykes using only root position, first inversion, second inversion, third inversion, and secondary chords metrics.

Bach Versus Dykes—Five Metrics

Technique	Correctness (%)
Unweighted Points	80.7
Weighted Points	88.6
Euclidean Distance	89.3

Although Unweighted Points was 1.8% points less accurate, Weighted Points improved by 1.8% points, and Euclidean Distance was a surprising 17.8% points more accurate. Whereas Euclidean Distance performed the worst last time, this time it actually performed the best. Using only these five metrics likely removed considerable amounts of "noisy" data, which suggests Euclidean Distance performs best with low noise.

7 ADDITIONAL COMPOSER AND METRICS

Later, a fourth composer, Lowell Mason, was added as were three more metrics with similarities to the five metrics that had performed the best so far. The new metrics were introduced to see if they could rival those five metrics or supplement them.

7.1 LOWELL MASON

Before introducing the three new metrics, it was intriguing to see if the five metrics from before continued to dominate the other 14 metrics when Mason was added. Covering all 7 of the newly possible composer combinations (BM, DM, SM, BDM, BSM, DSM, and BDSM), 140 additional trials were run (20 per combination) for the original 19 metrics and again for the 5-metric subset.

Bach Versus Mason

Technique	19 Metrics (%)	5 Metrics (%)	Δ
Unweighted Points	82.3	83.3	+1
Weighted Points	79	90.4	+11.4
Euclidean Distance	69.2	88.7	+19.5

Dykes Versus Mason

Technique	19 Metrics (%)	5 Metrics (%)	Δ
Unweighted Points	67.6	72.3	+4.7
Weighted Points	76.4	68.1	−8.3
Euclidean Distance	70.6	65.7	−4.9

Smart Versus Mason

Technique	19 Metrics (%)	5 Metrics (%)	Δ
Unweighted Points	71.8	75.3	+3.5
Weighted Points	82.3	77.3	−5
Euclidean Distance	68.5	75.1	+6.6

Bach Versus Dykes Versus Mason

Technique	19 Metrics (%)	5 Metrics (%)	Δ
Unweighted Points	69	67.1	−1.9
Weighted Points	61.8	73.2	+11.4
Euclidean Distance	50.5	70.4	+19.9

Bach Versus Smart Versus Mason

Technique	19 Metrics (%)	5 Metrics (%)	Δ
Unweighted Points	71.9	67.5	−4.4
Weighted Points	70.4	71.9	+1.5
Euclidean Distance	53.5	66.3	+12.8

Dykes Versus Smart Versus Mason

Technique	19 Metrics (%)	5 Metrics (%)	Δ
Unweighted Points	55.9	58	+2.1
Weighted Points	57.6	57.9	+0.3
Euclidean Distance	53.6	57.6	+4

Bach Versus Dykes Versus Smart Versus Mason

Technique	19 Metrics (%)	5 Metrics (%)	Δ
Unweighted Points	54.5	55.1	+0.6
Weighted Points	52.6	57.6	+5
Euclidean Distance	46.3	58.4	+12.1

As seen above, the results with Mason were in keeping with the correctness levels of previous classifications, and as a whole, the five-metric subset continued to perform better than the entire set of metrics. Not surprisingly, the percent of correct answers (for all techniques and both metric sets) was overall at its lowest in the last set of trials, when all four composers were classified together. However, the percentages were well above 25% and statistically appropriate for the change from three to four composers based on past three-way classifications. They were actually much better than expected.

A look through the classifier data produced during these seven classifications revealed that Mason had a very high ThirdAppearsOnlyOnceInSAT percentage compared to the other composers, yet a relatively low standard deviation. This raised the question of whether the ThirdAppearsOnlyOnceInSAT metric was worth adding to the special set of five metrics, so the last classification was rerun to include it. Consequently, results saw a significant 3–4% point improvement, suggesting this to be another helpful metric worth isolating in the future.

7.2 ADDITIONAL METRICS

Because the five metrics that were isolated proved so useful, three new metrics were developed to analyze similar musical features. The metrics are as follows:

OpenPosition	The percent of chords considered "open" by music theory standards. In an open chord, at least one chord tone is skipped over between soprano and alto, and alto and tenor.
ClosedPosition	The percent of chords considered "closed" by music theory standards. Generally, the soprano, alto, and tenor are packed together as tightly as possible in a closed chord.
SameChordNumberDifferentInversion	The percent of chord changes in which the chord number remains the same but the inversion changes.

Like in previous classifications, the new metrics were used to classify music by all four composers in groups of two, three, and four composers at a time. The new metrics were tested on their own, in combination with the five-metric subset, and in combination with the original 19 metrics.

Interestingly, in most cases FPC was less accurate than previously in its classifications. Accuracy actually suffered the most when these three metrics were used in conjunction with the five metrics that had previously performed best. Although these new metrics were aimed at imitating the properties of the ones that had been so successful, they failed to add any value.

8 CONCLUSIONS

It has been shown how FPC uses metrics based on chord structure and chord movement as input for three classification techniques. Furthermore, it has been demonstrated that conducting multiple randomized trials with test pieces of known classification allows the accuracy of FPC's guesswork to be easily measured.

Analyzed results from multiple trials indicate FPC is most reliable when only a handful of the most effective metrics are used. Root position, first inversion, second inversion, third inversion, and secondary chords metrics have proven, at least here, to be the most important factors in distinguishing between composers. A logical direction for future work would be to test FPC's performance classifying four-part music by time period instead of composer.

REFERENCES

[1] Ebcioglu K. An expert system for chorale harmonization. In: AAAI-86 Proceedings; 1986. p. 784–8. http://www.aaaipress.org/Papers/AAAI/1986/AAAI86-130.pdf.

[2] Nichols E, Morris D, Basu S. Data-driven exploration of musical chord sequences, In: Proceedings of the 14th international conference on Intelligent user interfaces (IUI'09). ACM, New York, NY, USA; 2009. p. 227–36. http://dx.doi.org/10.1145/1502650.1502683.

[3] Doerfler G, Beck R. An approach to classifying four-part music. In: Proceedings of the 2013 International Conference on Image Processing, Computer Vision, and, Pattern Recognition (IPCV); 2013. p. 787–94.

FURTHER READING

Anders T, Miranda ER. Constraint programming systems for modeling music theories and composition, ACM Computing Surveys 2011;43(4). http://dx.doi.org/10.1145/1978802.1978809. Article 30 (October 2011), 38 pages. http://doi.acm.org/10.1145/1978802.1978809

De Prisco R, Zaccagnino G, Zaccagnino R. EvoBassComposer: a multi-objective genetic algorithm for 4-voice compositions. In: Proceedings of the 12th Annual Conference on Genetic and Evolutionary Computation (GECCO '10). ACM, New York, NY, USA; 2010. p. 817–8. http://dx.doi.org/10.1145/1830483.1830627.

Edwards M. Algorithmic composition: computational thinking in music. Comm ACM 2011;54(7):58–67. http://dx.doi.org/10.1145/1965724.1965742.

Measuring rainbow trout by using simple statistics

3

Marcelo Romero, José Manuel Miranda, Hector A. Montes-Venegas

Facultad de Ingeniería, Universidad Autónoma del Estado de México, Toluca,
Estado de México, Mexico

1 INTRODUCTION

Generally, small farms use a manual measuring and counting process when cultivating rainbow trout [1–4]. There are many reasons to perform such classification, but the most important are to feed the trout according to its size and to avoid cannibalism into the tanks [4]. Problems when doing a manual classification are, indistinctively, the stress and physical damage causes to the specimen when manipulated by the farmer. Moreover, we believe that this classification approach is not accurate, where the trout is taken from the water using a net and visually the farmer decide whether or not the trout should be changed to another tank.

Mexico, as well as many other countries in the world, has large hydric areas, which are ideal for aquaculture [5,6]. Taking advantage of both, its altitude and natural water resources, the State of Mexico (Mexico) has particular interest in increasing the trout's production as a sustainability and economic strategy for local small farmers [7]. Hence, this is a good opportunity to integrate technology to optimize the trout's production in this region.

That is the reason which motives our research interest in the field, where we have accomplished some results, including a research project [3] and a couple of bachelor in science dissertations [1,2]. In this paper we robustly evaluate our experimental procedure to measure rainbow trout [8] in a small farm located in the Valley of Toluca, Mexico [9], where we have observed a manual classification process as illustrated in Figure 1.

Therefore, robust experimental results are presented in this publication by using our statistical system [8] and a state-of-the-art rainbow trout image database specially collected for this article. These data corpus were collected by capturing 20 images for each of 30 specimens per size (fry, fingerling, and table-fish), counting 1800 rainbow trout images.

Some related work is observed in the literature. Hsieh et al. [10] proposed a technique to measure dead tuna fish using a colour pattern. In this work, the fish length is

FIGURE 1

Manual measuring-classification process generally done in small farms in central Mexico. Note that this small farms use lined earth tanks.

estimated by proportional relationship between the fish body pixel length and an image reference scale. Ibrahim and Wang [11] measure four dead fish classes by constructing a central line along the fish body from horizontal and vertical views of the fish's body. Finally, a commercial counting and measuring system is observed in Vaki System [12]; however, there is no further information about its classification procedure.

The rest of this article is as follows. First, Section 2 describes our novel prototype designed for this research. Then, Section 3 introduces our statistical measuring approach. After that, Section 4 details our experimental framework. Next, Section 5 shows our performance evaluation. Finally, Section 6 concludes this article and draws some venues for our future work.

2 EXPERIMENTAL PROTOTYPE

In this section, we describe our experimental prototype, which has been designed as part of this research.

This novel prototype is essential to collect useful trout's 2D images; therefore, we have meticulously designed it. Figure 2 shows our experimental prototype, which has evolved from a traditional squared glass fish-cube (prototype version 1). We observed relevant issues from our first prototype and that knowledge was experimentally analyzed to obtain our second model. Note that our two prototypes have been experimentally evaluated in a trout farm; so, we have gathered special knowledge about handling the rainbow trout.

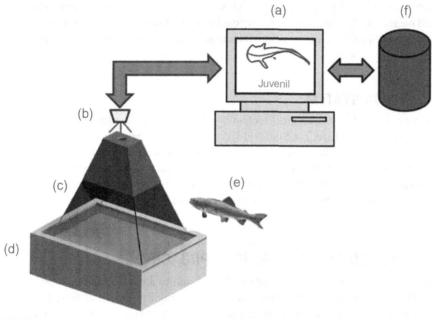

FIGURE 2

Our experimental scenario for measuring rainbow trout. (a) Statistical approach within a personal computer, (b) vision system, (c) canalization system, (d) illumination system, (e) specimen to be measured, and (f) database.

Then, as observed in Figure 2, our experimental prototype consists of three main components: canalization, illumination, and vision which are aim to collect RGB trout images using a standard personal computer.

2.1 CANALIZATION SYSTEM

We have design a novel canalization system based on opaque-glass within our prototype. This canalization system poses two main properties. The first property is regarded to its trapezoidal shape, which has been decided according to the digital camera's vision field principle. As long as such trapezoidal shape avoids reflection to be captured when taking a digital image. As its second property, we can mention that this is a two-canal tray, which prevents occlusion by taking only one fish per canal and it allows capturing two rainbow trout images per shot.

2.2 ILLUMINATION SYSTEM

To assist our vision system, we have integrated an illumination system, which distributes light in a uniform way at the bottom of the canalisation system. To do this, a light source is located to an appropriate high to distribute light uniformly over an acrylic diffuser. The light-source's high was defined by using a bisection approach and measuring the light intensity projected into the diffuser with photo resistors. We integrated this diffuse illumination to increase contrast into the image and highlighting the trout's body.

2.3 VISION SYSTEM

In order to explore economical technology for our classification system, we have used a standard 2D LifeCam Studio [13] camera in this experimentation. This camera is able to capture RGB-images with a maximum resolution of 1920×1080 pixels. In this prototype, this RGB camera is located at the top of the canalization system to capture downward-view images of the trout. Its high is proportional to the canalization base length to avoid extra data to be captured.

3 STATISTICAL MEASURING APPROACH

In this section, we present our statistical approach to measure rainbow trout.

Considering the rainbow trout natural swimming movement against the water flow and observing the trout from a downward point of view, we hypothesized that a *third- order curve* could approximate the trout's body within the water.

Different procedures can be followed to obtain a third-order curve equation. However, we prefer a simple but effective solution that could be executed online after a trout's image is captured.

Then, given n sample points (x,y) which depict the trout body, we apply minimum squares to compute a polynomial third-order equation [14]:

$$y^3 = a_0 + a_1 x + a_2 x^2 + a_3 x^3 \tag{1}$$

where a_0, a_1, a_2, a_3 are constants that gain their values by solving the $[4 \times 4]$ equation system (2):

$$
\begin{aligned}
\sum_{i=1}^{n} y_i &= n a_0 + a_1 \sum_{i=1}^{n} x_i + a_2 \sum_{i=1}^{n} x_i^2 + a_3 \sum_{i=1}^{n} x_i^3 \\
\sum_{i=1}^{n} x_i y_i &= a_0 \sum_{i=1}^{n} x_i + a_1 \sum_{i=1}^{n} x_i^2 + a_2 \sum_{i=1}^{n} x_i^3 + a_3 \sum_{i=1}^{n} x_i^4 \\
\sum_{i=1}^{n} x_i^2 y_i &= a_0 \sum_{i=1}^{n} x_i^2 + a_1 \sum_{i=1}^{n} x_i^3 + a_2 \sum_{i=1}^{n} x_i^4 + a_3 \sum_{i=1}^{n} x_i^5 \\
\sum_{i=1}^{n} x_i^3 y_i &= a_0 \sum_{i=1}^{n} x_i^3 + a_1 \sum_{i=1}^{n} x_i^4 + a_2 \sum_{i=1}^{n} x_i^5 + a_3 \sum_{i=1}^{n} x_i^6
\end{aligned} \tag{2}
$$

The equation system (2) can be easily solved using the matrix notation, $AX = B$, or more specifically: $X = BA^{-1}$.

After this computation, we obtained the best regression curve that adjusts the trout's body captured into an RGB image.

Then, we observe that this regression curve is related to the trout's length, which could be estimated by computing the Euclidean distance among the points within the regression curve.

Finally, given a probe-length (l_i) a classification can be done by comparing against training lengths. For this research, such comparison is performed by computing the Mahalanobis distance [15] from training fry, fingerling, and table-trout lengths:

$$d_i = \frac{l_i - \bar{x}}{s_{\bar{x}}} \qquad (3)$$

Hence, a probe-trout t_i is classified through its estimated length l_i by comparing its Mahalanobis distance d_i against a predefined threshold, which in fact is the number of standard deviations that is expected to be l_i to the training mean length $(\bar{x})$.

4 EXPERIMENTAL FRAMEWORK

This section presents the experimental framework to illustrate how rainbow trout is measured using our statistical approach.

As show in Figure 3, after an RGB image is taken by our prototype, we are following a five-stage image processing to get the trout's contour. As explained in Section 3, we are measuring the trout's length using this contour.

To classify the trout's image within an image, we are performing four main steps. Firstly, an RGB image of the trout is taken using our prototype (Section 2). Secondly,

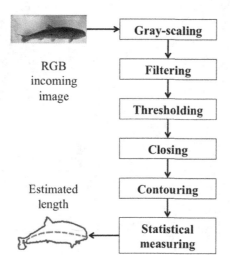

FIGURE 3

Processing an incoming RGB image to estimate the trout's length using our statistical approach.

this RGB image is processed to obtain the trout's contour. Thirdly, the trout's length is estimated by applying our statistical method (Section 3) to the trout's contour. Finally, using that estimated length, the trout is classified using a binary classification approach.

In Section 4.1, we provide more detail about our image processing step.

4.1 TESTING PROCEDURE

As illustrated in Figure 2, we have implemented a novel functional prototype which allows us to gather RGB images. After that, as shown in Figure 3, RGB images are processed using standard algorithms in the literature [16,17] until we obtain the trout's contour. Next, we apply our statistical approach to that contour, so we can estimate the trout's length. Finally, a binary classification approach is taken to classify the trout within the income image. We now detail our experimental procedure:

1. As mentioned before, we have collected a trout-image database using our prototype (illustrated in Figure 4) in a farm. This database was created

FIGURE 4

Functional prototype used within our measuring system. This prototype includes an illumination source, a pyramidal canalization compartment and a 2D camera.

Table 1 Experimental Data Images

Trout Size	Specimens	Images Per Specimen	Total Images
Fry	30	20	600
Fingerling	30	20	600
Table-fish	30	20	600
Grand total	90		1800

Table 2 Training and Testing Sets

Trout Size	Training	Testing
Fry	150	300
Fingerling	150	300
Table-fish	150	300
Total	450	900

using 30 fry, 30 fingerling, and 30 table-fish specimens, capturing 20 images per specimen. This state-of-the-art rainbow trout image database (see Table 1) was recently collected for this publication. However, for this experiment we are using only 450 images per size.

2. From our database, separate training and testing sets are defined (see Table 2). Thus, 450 images for training and 900 images for testing are used. Specifically, we have three training data sets, containing 150 images per size, namely, fry, fingerling, and table-fish trout. In every case, we selected the first five-captured images for each of the 30 specimens per size to be part of the training set. Then, we use the next 10-captured images for each of the 30 specimens for testing. By doing this, we have three testing sets (one per trout-size) containing 300 images of fry, fingerling, and table-fish, respectively.

3. From these 450 training images, training data are gathered, which in fact consist of training lengths, the arithmetic mean, and the standard deviation for each size.

4. For each testing trout image, estimated lengths are gathered as illustrated in Figures 3 and 5. To do this, we gather an RGB image using our prototype. Then, we execute a five-stage image processing: gray-scaling, filtering, thresholding, closing, and contouring. Next, we estimate the trout's length by applying our statistical approach to the contour obtained above. Finally, using this estimated length we classify the trout as fry, fingerling, or table-fish.

5. To speed up our image-processing step, our vision system gathers $[640 \times 360]$ pixels RGB-images.

6. Captured RGB values are converted into a grayscale by forming weighted sums of the R, G, and B components [16]:

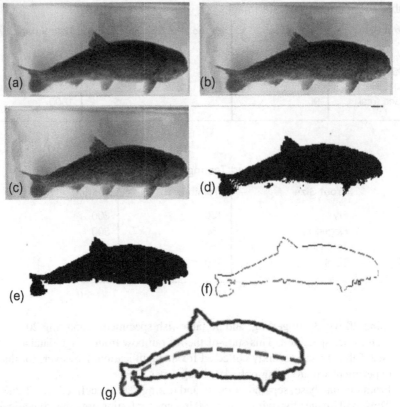

FIGURE 5

Image processing performed to measure a rainbow trout using our statistical approach.
(a) RGB incoming image sensed by the vision system; (b) gray-scaling; (c) filtering;
(d) thresholding; (e) closing; (f) contouring; and (g) trout's length estimated by a third
order regression curve (plotted as dash line).

$$0.2989 * R + 0.5870 * G + 0.1140 * B \tag{4}$$

7. Noise reduction is performed in every grayscale image by using a $[3 \times 3]$
Gaussian low-pass filter and $\sigma = 0.6$

$$G(x, y) = \frac{1}{2\pi\sigma^2} e^{-(x^2+y^2)/2\sigma^2} \tag{5}$$

8. A binary image is obtained by using a 0.245 threshold, which was calculated
experimentally from training rainbow trout images.

9. The trout's body is emphasized by using a closing operation, first erosion, and then dilation with a $[5 \times 8]$ mask. This operation is the key to eliminate small clusters of pixels around the trout's body cluster.

10. The trout's contour is obtained by removing interior pixels. In this case, a pixel is set to 0 if all its four-connected neighbours are 1, thus leaving only the boundary pixels on as shown in Equation (6):

$$\text{If } \begin{matrix} & 1 & \\ 1 & x & 1 \\ & 1 & \end{matrix} \text{ Then } \begin{matrix} & 1 & \\ 1 & 0 & 1 \\ & 1 & \end{matrix} \qquad (6)$$

11. Using the trout's contour, we apply our statistical measuring approach detailed in Section 3.

12. By definition, the trout's size is estimated by computing the Mahalanobis distance from this estimated length to training data (Equation 3).

13. For classification in this experiment, imagine that the complete testing-trout set (900 in total) is passed through a grid one by one in three steps. First, the grid is sized to filter only fry-trout. Then, every trout able to pass this grid is labelled as a fry-trout. Second, for the rest of the testing set, the grid is now sized to filter fingerling-trout. Every trout that is able to pass this grid is labelled as fingerling-trout. Third, for the rest of the testing set, the grid is now sized to filter table-fish trout.

    Remember that we are computing the Mahalanobis distance and this allows us to easily implement the approach above using fry, fingerling, and table-fish training data, respectively. Referring as training data the arithmetic mean and the standard deviation from each size.

    Another advantage in using Mahalanobis distance is that we can make our classification process as rigid as we decide, by defining a threshold in number of standard deviations.

    Then, in this article we are reporting classification figures from one to three standard deviations.

14. We are considering this experiment as a binary classification problem, as illustrated in Table 3. By doing this, we are collecting true positive (TP), false positive (FP), false negative (FN), and true negative (TN) frequencies [18].

15. Using values in Table 3, performance figures are generated by computing accuracy, repeatability, specificity, recall, and precision metrics when

Table 3 Binary Classification

	Actual Positive	**Actual Negative**
Predicted positive	TP	FP
Predicted negative	FN	TN

classifying as fry, fingerling, and table-fish trout. In every case, we are evaluating using as threshold from one to three standard deviations.

Accuracy, a degree of veracity, is a measurement of how well the binary classification test correctly identifies a rainbow trout's size.

$$Accuracy = \frac{TP+TN}{TP+TN+FP+FN} \tag{7}$$

Repeatability, a degree of reproducibility, is an indicator about how robustly a rainbow trout size can be identified:

$$Repeatability = \frac{TP}{TP+FP} \tag{8}$$

Specificity, a degree of speciality, rates how negative rainbow trout's size is correctly identified:

$$Specificity = \frac{TN}{TN+FP} \tag{9}$$

Recall measures the fraction of positive examples that are correctly labelled:

$$Recall = \frac{TP}{TP+FN} \tag{10}$$

Precision measures that fraction of examples classified as positive that are truly positive:

$$Precision = \frac{TP}{TP+FP} \tag{11}$$

5 PERFORMANCE EVALUATION

We now present performance figures when using our statistical model to measure rainbow trout in a farm.

As observed in Figure 5, our statistical approach's performance to measure a rainbow trout depends on our image processing stage. However, according to our experimental results, we believe that we have addressed main issues about capturing and processing an RGB image within our system.

As we have mentioned before, we consider this as a binary classification problem as indicated in step 13 in our experimental procedure (Section 4.1). Thus, the complete testing lengths (computed from 900 images) are compared against fry training data, using Mahalanobis distance. Then, if a testing length falls into a predefined threshold (one to three standard deviations), the respective testing trout is marked as fry-trout. Next, all remaining testing lengths are compared against fingerling training data using Mahalanobis distance as well. Again, if the testing length falls into a predefined threshold (one to three standard deviations), we label the respective testing trout as fingerling-trout. Then, every remaining testing length is compared against table-fish training data using Mahalanobis distance. Similarly, if the testing length falls into a predefined threshold (one to three standard deviations), the testing trout is labelled as table-fish-trout.

Then, as prescribed in Table 3 we count TP, FP, TN, and FN frequencies, which are summarized from Tables 4 to 6. Hence, by using these values we are able to compute accuracy, repeatability, and specificity metrics, which are presented from Tables 7 to 9 and illustrated in Figure 6.

Finally, we are computing recall and precision metrics. Tables 10 and 11 summarize these results and Figure 7 shows recall and precision results at three standard deviations.

Observing our experimental results when classifying our testing set, we score the best precision at three standard deviations: 95.93%, 93.21%, and 96.25% for fry, fingerling, and table-fish trout, respectively.

Table 4 Frequency when Classifying a Probe Set as Fry Trout at Three Standard Deviations

	1Sx	2Sx	3Sx
TP	201	259	276
FP	71	147	234
TN	529	453	366
FN	99	41	24

Table 5 Frequency when Classifying as Fingerling Trout at Three Standard Deviations

	1Sx	2Sx	3Sx
TP	149	108	39
FP	40	27	36
TN	357	309	279
FN	82	50	36

Table 6 Frequency when Classifying as Table-Fish Trout at Three Standard Deviations

	1Sx	2Sx	3Sx
TP	165	261	257
FP	7	19	10
TN	141	58	48
FN	126	21	0

Table 7 Accuracy when Classifying a Probe Set at Three Standard Deviations

Testing as	1Sx (%)	2Sx (%)	3Sx (%)
Fry	81.11	80.57	69.70
Fingerling	79.11	84.41	88.86
Table-fish	71.33	81.54	96.83

Table 8 Repeatability when Classifying a Probe Set at Three Standard Deviations

Testing as	1Sx (%)	2Sx (%)	3Sx (%)
Fry	73.90	78.84	95.93
Fingerling	63.79	80.00	93.21
Table-fish	54.12	52.00	96.25

Table 9 Specificity when Classifying a Probe Set at Three Standard Deviations

Testing as	1Sx (%)	2Sx (%)	3Sx (%)
Fry	88.17	89.92	95.27
Fingerling	75.50	91.96	75.32
Table-fish	61.00	88.57	82.76

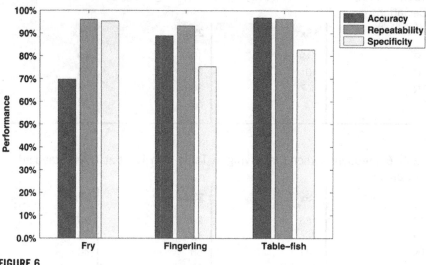

FIGURE 6

Accuracy, repeatability, and specificity performance when classifying fry, fingerling, and table-fish trout at three standard deviations using our statistical measuring system.

Table 10 Recall when Classifying Testing Sets at Three Standard Deviations

Testing as	1Sx (%)	2Sx (%)	3Sx (%)
Fry	67.00	64.50	56.70
Fingerling	86.33	68.35	92.55
Table-fish	92.00	52.00	100.00

Table 11 Precision when Classifying Testing Sets at Three Standard Deviations

Testing as	1Sx (%)	2Sx (%)	3Sx (%)
Fry	73.90	78.84	95.93
Fingerling	63.79	80.00	93.21
Table-fish	54.12	52.00	96.25

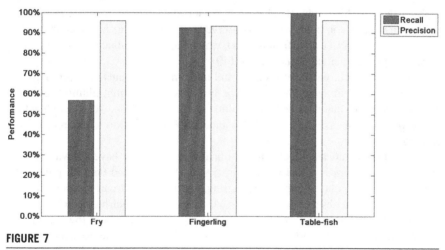

FIGURE 7

Recall-precision metrics when classifying fry, fingerling, and table-fish trout at three standard deviations using our statistical measuring system.

Furthermore, when classifying those testing lengths, we score a 100% recall and 96.25% precision when classifying table-fish trout at three standard deviations.

These experimental results are not only motivated, but also valuable evidences that indicate effectiveness in our classification system.

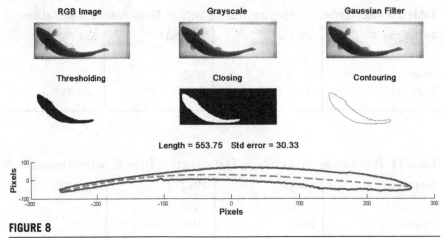

RGB Image   Grayscale   Gaussian Filter

Thresholding   Closing   Contouring

Length = 553.75   Std error = 30.33

FIGURE 8

Processing a table-fish trout image for classification using our statistical measuring system.

6 CONCLUSIONS

In this article, we have robustly evaluated our statistical system to measure rainbow trout in farm using computer vision as observed in Figure 8. This novel technique [8] is a simple but effective statistical method, which has been evaluated in a small farm in central Mexico named *Rincon del Sol* [9].

For this research, we have designed and implemented a functional prototype to collect RGB trout images. This prototype includes canalization, illumination, and vision components that have been meticulously assembled. Also, we believe that this prototype could be easily integrated into a mechanical system to interconnect lined earth tanks in farms.

Our experimental results encourage our research as they have shown that our classification system is effective, where 95.93%, 93.21%, and 96.25% precisions are observed when classifying fry, fingerling, and table-fish trout, respectively.

It is important to observe that, although our statistical approach has been inspired to measure rainbow trout, this approach can be applied to other fishes grown in farms.

As part of our future work, we are integrating water flow and stereovision into our prototype to investigate two main issues: the light reflection into the water and the presence of turbulence. Our final aim is to implement an economical classification system for small farms.

ACKNOWLEDGMENTS

Authors thank to the Research Department of the Autonomous University of the State of Mexico (UAEMex) for its financial support through the research project SIyEA/ 32742012 M. Their gratitude also goes to the Mexican Council for Science and Technology (CONACyT) for the scholarship granted to Jose Manuel Miranda (634478).

REFERENCES

[1] Mejia S. Conteo y clasificación de la trucha arcoíris utilizando visión artificial: revisión literaria y análisis [BSc. Final dissertation]. Mexico: Engineering Department, Autonomous University of the State of Mexico; 2013.

[2] Miranda J. Prototipo de un sistema clasificador de la trucha arcoíris utilizando un modelo estadístico de su longitud obtenido de imágenes 2D [BSc thesis]. Mexico: Engineering Department, Autonomous University of the State of Mexico; 2014.

[3] Romero M, Vilchis A, Portillo O. Intelligent system to count, measure and classify fishes using computer vision. Research project SIyEA 32742012 M. Mexico: Autonomous University of the State of Mexico; 2012.

[4] Woynarovich A, Hoitsy G, Moth-Poulsen T. Small-scale rainbow trout farming. FAO Fisheries and aquaculture technical paper, Food and Agriculture Organization of the United Nations; 2011.

[5] CONAGUA, Comisión Nacional del Agua. Concesión de Aprovechamiento de Aguas Superficiales. Water National Council; 2006. [Online] Available from: http://www.con agua.gob.mx/Contenido.aspx?n1=5&n2=101&n3=302&n4=302. [Accessed: 13 September 2014].

[6] DOF, Diario Oficial de la Federación. Ley de aguas nacionales. DCVII(14): 27–95. Federal Oficial News. [Online] Available from: http://dof.gob.mx/nota_detalle.php?codigo=670229&fecha=12/05/2004. [Accessed: 13 September 2014]; 2004.

[7] Gallego I, Carrillo R, García D, Sasso I, Guerrero J, Burrola C, et al. Programa maestro, sistema producto trucha del Estado de México. Government Plan for Rainbow Trout Production. Mexico, Autonomous University of the State of Mexico; 2007.

[8] Romero M, Miranda JM, Montes HA, Acosta JC. A statistical measuring system for rainbow trout, In: Proceedings on the international conference on image processing, computer vision and pattern recognition. Las Vegas NE, United States of America; 2014.

[9] Rincon del Sol. Small Trout Farm. La Marqueza, State of Mexico, Mexico; 2014. [Visited: 20 August 2014].

[10] Hsieh C, Chang H, Chen F, Liou J, Chang S, Lin T. A simple and effective digital imaging approach for tuna fish length measurement compatible with fishing operations. Comput Electron Agric 2011;75:44–51.

[11] Ibrahim M, Wang J. Mechatronics applications to fish sorting part 1: fish size identification. industrial electronics (ISIE 2009). In: IEEE international symposium; 2009.

[12] Vaki System. Bioscanner Fish Counter. [Online] Available from: http://www.vaki.is/Products/BioscannerFishCounter/. [Accessed: 10 May 2014]; 2013.

[13] LifeCam Studio. LifeCam Studio. [Online] Available from: http://www.microsoft.com/hardware/en-us/p/lifecam-studio. [Accessed: 13 September 2014]; 2014.

[14] Murray S, Schiller J, Srinivasan R. Probability and Statistics. 4th ed. USA: Mc Graw-Hill; 2012.

[15] Duda R, Hart P, Stork D. Pattern classification. 2nd ed. USA: Wiley Interscience; 2001.

[16] Gonzales R, Woods R. Digital image processing. 3rd ed. USA: Prentice Hall; 2008.

[17] Gonzales R, Woods R, Eddins S. Digital image processing using Matlab. 2nd ed. USA: Prentice-Hall; 2009.

[18] Davis J, Goadrich M. The relationship between precision-recall and ROC curves. In: Proceedings of the 23rd International Conference on Machine Learning; 2006.

Fringe noise removal of retinal fundus images using trimming regions

Arezoo Ektesabi, Ajay Kapoor

Swinburne University of Technology, Melbourne, Victoria, Australia

1 INTRODUCTION

For centuries with the rapidly growing population, the need for improvements in medical and health care systems has been felt. As one of the main sensory organs, eye has always played an important role in any individuals' life. Therefore, ophthalmological research has been of interest and closely monitored areas, especially since the 1999, with the introduction of the vision 2020 campaign [1]. The campaign has aimed to improve the prognosis, diagnosis, treatment, and posttreatment procedures.

The ophthalmological practices have always been greatly influenced as the result of the improvements in health system and biomedical approaches, leading to better understanding of the underlying causes of different diseases. The design and use of the image-capturing and -processing algorithms have also aided in early disease detection and progression, assisting the treatment and monitoring the posttreatment results. Overall in the past two decades, the procedures have become faster, more reliable, repeatable, and accurate.

The statistics provided by World Health Organization (WHO) in 2010 suggests that there are about 285 million people in the world who are currently visually impaired, consisting of 39 million who are blind and 246 million people who have low vision, including both moderate and severe visual impairment cases. It has also been indicated that the leading causes of blindness have been diseases such as cataract, glaucoma, and age-related macular degeneration [1–4].

The above findings suggest that there is still need for further improvement. The study also indicates that the majority of the observed complications occur in developing regions of the world, while 80% of these visual impairments could have been avoided if detected early [1,5]. Despite recent advancements in technology and improvements in biomedical research and ophthalmological findings, there is still the need for fast, affordable, and reliable diagnosis and treatment procedures in developing regions.

Current interest in telemedicine and the need for developing new techniques and methodologies for retinal image processing as well as a better, highly accurate, reliable, accessible, repeatable, and inexpensive system for disease diagnosis has been the key motivation of this study.

1.1 IMAGE PROCESSING

For decades image processing has been used in industrial application. However, in the past few years there has been a sudden trend and increase in use due to recognition of image-processing capabilities biomedical applications.

Usually, image processing consists of a few main steps including, detection of the object with a camera and then processing the obtained images using segmentation, normalization, feature extraction, and matching. The outcome of this can then be interpreted or displayed [6,7].

For this study, the above steps have been slightly modified and the associated flow chart is illustrated in Figure 1.

The initial step in any image-processing procedure is image acquisition. This is a very crucial step as the obtained images directly affect the precision and accuracy of the final outcome. A few points are usually considered while collecting images; some of which are the general understanding problem, the required image and possible storage capability and capacity, capturing time, resolution, lighting, camera, available resources, and available options.

The next stage would be the image preprocessing step, where the usual colored image is manipulated and prepared for the next stages. Since in majority of cases, the overall reduction in processing time is of great interest, this stage mainly concentrates on manipulation of images so that the overall complexity of the process is reduced. However, the implemented processes have to ensure that the essential information needed for the following stages are not destroyed or affected as the result. To achieve this, the RGB images are usually decomposed to the primary colors and gray scaled. With the reduction in amount of data processed, the overall processing time is also reduced. Similarly, other processes may also be implemented at this stage including the implementation of different filters and adjustment of image contrast.

Once the images have been prepared, the feature localization step would be conducted in order to localize the key features of interest. Accurate detection of the optic disk has been the key feature of interest in this study. The noiseless solution for early prognosis of diseases such as Glaucoma is presented further in this chapter.

This is then followed by feature extraction stage, where the information is extracted from the regions of interest. At this stage, the overall objective of the study is fulfilled.

FIGURE 1

Flow chart of the image-processing steps.

Lastly, the detailed information obtained in the feature extraction step is studied in depth and interpreted accordingly. The overall outcome and the key findings can also be displayed.

1.2 RETINAL IMAGE PROCESSING

In this study, image-processing implementation on retinal images is considered. Majority of the studies performed previously only consider or concentrate on the localizing, extracting stages, and detecting features such as retinal blood vessels [8–12] or optic disk [13–17]. The studies tend to ignore the preliminary stages of image processing, which could affect the overall accuracy and precision of the process.

Moreover, in automated systems, the input data may vary depending on the capturing instrumentation, their effect, response of the individual patients, image resolution, size and contrast which in turn could alter the final results if the setting is chosen properly for localizing and extracting stage.

In order to enhance the processing results and have a complete automated process, it is essential to prepare the input images to the best possible format in the preprocessing stage. There might also be times where a secondary image preprocessing stage is needed. This stage could be implemented if the preliminary results do not produce the desired outcome.

These points highlight the fact that preprocessing stage is the basis and a crucial step in image processing. As a result, for achieving the best possible outcomes a thorough and exact procedure should be suggested and conducted at this stage.

1.2.1 Ophthalmological Data

In order to start the image processing in ophthalmology, retinal images are needed. These images are captured using specialized instruments. However, for the purpose of this research the open-source databases have been used. There are several different open-source databases available online, including the digital retinal images for vessel extraction (DRIVE) [18], structured analysis of the retina (STARE) [19,20], retinal vessel image set for estimation of width [21], retinopathy online challenge [22], collection of multispectral images of the fundus [23], and MESSIDOR database [24].

For the purpose of this study, the DRIVE and STARE database has been chosen for further analysis. The collection of DRIVE database was initiated by Staal et al. It contains 20 colored retinal images, captured by Canon CR5 nonmydriatic 3CCD camera with a 45° field of view. The images are digitized to 768×584 pixels, 8 bits per color channel [18]. STARE database consists of about 400 retinal images and was initiated in 1975 by Michael Goldbaum. The images are 8 bits per color plane at 605×700 pixels and were captured by TopCon TRV-50 fundus camera with 35° field of view [19,20].

2 METHODOLOGY

An important yet overlooked stage in majority of the literature on image processing is the image preprocessing step. Depending on the requirements of the study, and the main objectives of the project, certain necessary steps and procedures should be performed in the image preprocessing step so that the image is well prepared to fit the objective of further stages.

One of the procedures that should be implemented at this stage is the noise minimization. A common problem in such cases is the noise which appears as illuminated bright spots on the edges of the retinal images [25]. The bright fringes may have been formed due to the refraction of the light within the eye, ambient light which might have affected the image if eye is not placed properly in front of the device and also the eye response itself. An example of such retinal responses can be viewed in Figure 2.

The removal of fringe noise plays an important role in the accuracy of detection in particular when the optic disk is the area of interest. This is due to the fact that the bright illuminated fringe may inaccurately be located instead of the optic disk which is commonly known to be as the brightest region in the retinal image.

There have been several approaches in order to enhance the detection precision in such instances. Majority of the previous literature suggest the use of filters or adjust the contrast of the image. Although the outcomes have been promising, many of the other crucial information may have also been lost as the result.

In this study, the trimming regions have been used as the common approach. The trimming region may be used to remove the unwanted noise and enhance the overall accuracy of detection. In order to remove all the noise, it should be noted that the radius of the proposed region should be smaller than those of the actual region of interest so that all the fringe noises are removed.

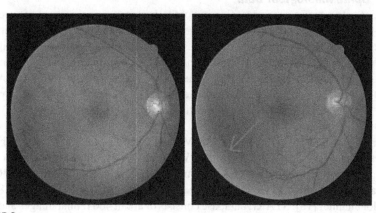

FIGURE 2

Comparison of two retinal images, no fringe noise is present in left-hand image while in the right-hand image the bright spot is completely visible.

This approach was initially suggested by Zhang et al. [25]. They introduced a trimming boundary represented by the following equations:

$$X^2 + Y^2 + AX + BY + C = 0 \tag{1}$$

$$C_x = -\frac{A}{2}$$

$$C_y = -\frac{B}{2}$$

$$r = \sqrt{\frac{A^2 + B^2}{4} - C}$$

However, the accuracy of detection of the proposed method was not 100% and there has been a need for manual observation and modification. In order to improve the success rate and create a complete automated process, the use of circular trimming circle centred (a,b) [26] has previously been suggested and implemented by the authors. The proposal is represented by the following equation:

$$(x - a)^2 + (y - b)^2 = r^2 \tag{2}$$

Equating Equation (2) with Equation (1), we can conclude that:

$$a = -\frac{A}{2} = C_x$$

$$b = -\frac{B}{2} = C_y$$

$$r = \sqrt{\frac{A^2 + B^2}{4} - C}$$

The above procedure improved the precision of detection greatly and if the chosen radius was accurately selected, the crucial information would have still been intact. Despite the great success rate of this method, it can only be implemented on retinal images where the region of interest is approximately circular. Observing multiple retinal fundus images suggest that different instrumentations and settings may also result in an oval-shaped retinal images. Examples of which are shown in Figure 3.

In these cases implementing the circular trimming region may result in an inaccurate detection of the feature of interest as well as great loss of crucial information, as illustrated in Figure 4.

To overcome this problem and preserve as much information as possible, authors propose another trimming region. The suggested elliptical trimming region is characterized by the following equations:

$$\left(\frac{x - h}{a}\right)^2 + \left(\frac{y - k}{b}\right)^2 = r^2 \tag{3}$$

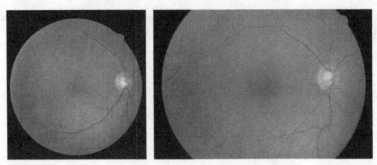

FIGURE 3

Circular- [18] and oval-shaped retinal fundus images [19,20].

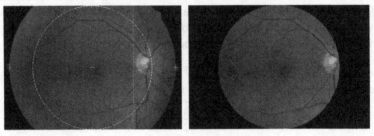

FIGURE 4

Implementation of circular trimming region to the oval-shaped retinal image.

$$h = -\frac{A}{2} = C_x$$

$$k = -\frac{B}{2} = C_y$$

$$x - \text{Radius} = a$$

$$y - \text{Radius} = b$$

Based on the retinal images and their characteristics, either the circular or elliptical trimming region may be used and implemented.

2.1 IMPLEMENTATION

The implementation of the proposed methodology is similar to what has been previously suggested by the authors [26] with minor modifications. The needed information for both the circular and elliptical trimming region is the estimated location for the center and the radius in both horizontal and vertical directions.

Initial step would be creating a mask to define the region of interest [27]. Once the region of interest is defined, the radius can then be estimated. To estimate the radius, it is important to locate the first and last nonzero pixel (white pixel) across the columns of the image. The middle value between these two estimated points can then be used as a preliminary location for the center.

This is then followed by finding the first and last nonzero pixel across the rows using the estimated center location. Recalculating the middle value of these newly found points can lead to readjustment of the center location as well as the location of the first and last nonzero pixels across the columns of the image.

In order to find the radius, the distance between the radius and the corner pixel values is calculated. For the circular trimming region, both the vertical and horizontal calculated radius would approximately be the same and so either can be used to define the trimming region. However, in the case of an elliptical trimming region, the radius in horizontal (short axis) and vertical axis (long axis) is different and so both have to be calculated and taken under consideration for defining the elliptical region of interest.

The outcome of the above procedure for both elliptical and circular trimming region can be viewed in Figure 5.

It should also be noted that for all the fringe noises to be removed, the implemented radius has to be smaller than the estimated radius. The variation in size maybe selected based on an observation for a single image in the database; this value may then be used for the remaining images.

From Figure 6, it can be seen that in case of circular trimming region, the chosen radius has to be slightly smaller than those of the actual estimated radius. However, in case of the elliptical trimming region, the modified radius, shown in dotted line, can simply be chosen using the estimated radius short and long axes.

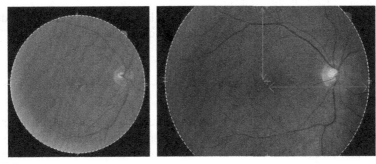

FIGURE 5

Suggested trimming regions: circular trimming region (left) and elliptical trimming region. The centers are marked as "+" and the estimated trimming region is drawn by discontinued lines. The radii are also shown as arrows.

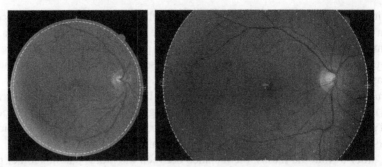

FIGURE 6

Modified radius, circular trimming region (left), and elliptical trimming region (right).

3 RESULTS AND DISCUSSION

Implementing the above procedures and observing the obtained results suggest that depending on the input image, the chosen methodology may vary. If the region of interest in the retinal image is circular in shape, the circular trimming region may be used. However, if it is more oval shaped, the elliptical trimming region may be used instead.

Automatic detection of the center and radius ensures that the best trimming region is chosen, with a simple comparison between the measured radius in horizontal and vertical direction.

The proposed methodology has been implemented on the images from the databases [17–19] and results obtained are shown in Figure 7.

From the sample outcomes depicted in Figure 7, it can be suggested that for the oval-shaped image the elliptical trimming region would provide better results in comparison to the original data and the circular trimming region. Although the circular trimming circle may also be used in this case, there seems to be loss of critical information which is highly undesirable.

On the other hand for circular image, the circular trimming region with modified radius would results in an ideal solution and feature of interest detection.

4 CONCLUSION

In conclusion, it can be said that the fringe noise present at the edges of retinal images as the result of instrumentation error or patient's response can be removed successfully using the proposed methodology. The use of automatic adaptive circular or elliptical trimming region ensures that all the illuminated bright regions are removed and features of interests such as optic disk which previously would have been inaccurately localized are now detected with a very high precision using this robust localization procedure. The highly accurate detection can then be used by ophthalmologists in

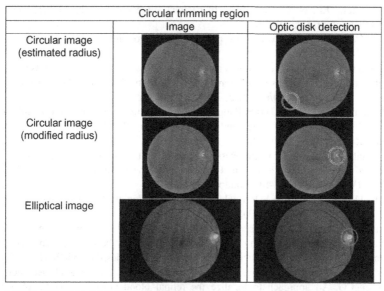

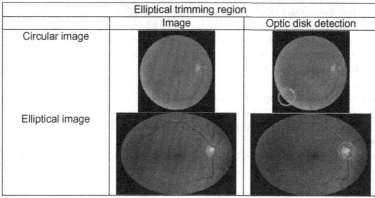

FIGURE 7

Optic disk detection under different circumstances for circular- and oval-shaped images, using the proposed circular and elliptical trimming region.

characterizing and early prognosis of diseases. For example in this case, extracting the variations in size of the optic disk would help in diagnosing diseases such as Glaucoma.

REFERENCES

[1] World Health Organisation. Global data on visual impairments 2010. viewed March 2014, http://www.who.int/blindness/GLOBALDATAFINALforweb.pdf?ua=1> 2010.
[2] Khanna R, Pujari S, Sangwan V. Cataract surgery in developing countries. Curr Opin Ophthalmol 2011;22:10–4.

[3] Lamoureux EL, et al. The impact of cataract surgery on quality of life. Curr Opin Ophthalmol 2011;22:19–27.

[4] Tan CSH. Cost effectiveness of phacoemulsification in developing countries. Eye 2010;24:1827–8.

[5] World Health Organisation. Global pattern of blindness changes with success in tackling infectious disease and as population ages, viewed June 2011, http://www.who.int/medi acentre/news/notes/2004/np27/en/; 2004.

[6] Mehrabian H, Hashemi-Tari P. Pupil boundary detection for iris recognition using graph cuts, In: Proceedings of image and vision computing, New Zealand, 2007, Hamilton, New Zealand; 2007. p. 77–82.

[7] Ektesabi A, Kapoor A. Complication prevention of posterior capsular rupture using image processing techniques. In: Proceedings of the world congress on engineering 2012 (WCE 2012), July 4-6, London, U.K., vol. I.

[8] Jamal I, Akram M, Tariq A. Retinal image preprocessing: background and noise segmentation. Telkomnika 2012;10(3):537–44.

[9] Xu X, Abramoff MD, Bertelsen G, Reinhardt JM. Retinal vessel width measurement at branching points using an improved electric field theory-based graph approach, Med Imag 2012;7(11), http://www.ncbi.nlm.nih.gov/pmc/articles/PMC3507841/.

[10] Fraz MM, Barman SA, Remagnino P, Hoppe A, Basit A, Uyyanonvara B, Rudnicka AR, Owen CG. An approach to localize the retinal blood vessels using bit planes and centerline detection, Comput Methods Prog Biomed 2012;108(2):600–16, http://www. cmpbjournal.com/article/S0169-2607(11)00227-6/pdf.

[11] Yamamoto Y, Yamamoto Y, Marugame A, Ogura M, Saito A, Ohta K, Fukumoto M, Murata T. Age-related decrease of retinal vasculature are identified with a novel computer-aided analysis system. Tohoku J Exp Med 2012;228:229–37.

[12] Cheng SC, Huang YM. A novel approach to diagnose diabetes based on the fractal characteristics of retinal images. IEEE Trans Inf Technol Biomed 2003;7:163–70.

[13] Youssif A, Ghalwash A, Ghoneim A. Optic disc detection from normalized digital fundus images by means of a vessels direction matched filter. IEEE Trans Med Imaging 2008;27:1118.

[14] Rangayyan R, Zhu X, Ayres F, Ells A. Detection of the optic nerve head in fundus images of the retina with Gabor filters and phase portrait analysis. J Digit Imaging 2010;23:438–53.

[15] Zhu X, Rangayyan R, Ells A. Detection of the optic nerve head in fundus images of the retina using the hough transform for circles. J Digit Imaging 2010;23:332–41.

[16] Sekhar S, Al-Nuaimy W, Nandi A. Automatic localization of optic disc and fovea in retinal fundus, In: 16th European signal processing conference; 2008.

[17] Welfer D, Scharcanski J, Kitamura C, Dal Pizzol M, Ludwig L, Marinho D. Segmentation of the optic disk in color eye fundus images using an adaptive morphological approach. Comput Biol Med 2010;40:124–37.

[18] Staal JJ, Abramoff MD, Niemeijer M, Viergever MA, van Ginneken B. Ridge based vessel segmentation in color images of the retina. IEEE Trans Med Imaging 2004;23:501–9.

[19] Hoover A, Kouznetsova V, Goldbaum M. Locating blood vessels in retinal images by piece-wise threhsold probing of a matched filter response. IEEE Trans Med Imaging 2000;19(3):203–10.

[20] Hoover A, Goldbaum M. Locating the optic nerve in a retinal image using the fuzzy convergence of the blood vessels. IEEE Trans Med Imaging 2003;22(8):951–8.

[21] University of Lincoln. Review: retinal vessel image set for estimation of widths, viewed Feb 2014, http://reviewdb.lincoln.ac.uk/> 2010.

[22] The University of Iowa and the ROC organizers (Michael D. Abramoff, Bram van Ginneken and Meindert Niemeijer). Retinopathy Online Challenge, viewed Feb. 2014, http://webeye.ophth.uiowa.edu/ROC/var.1/www/; 2007.

[23] School of Computer Science, The University of Birmingham. Collection of multispectral images of the fundus, viewed Feb. 2014, http://www.cs.bham.ac.uk/research/projects/fundus-multispectral/> 2014.

[24] TECHNO-VISION Project. Methods to evaluate segmentation and indexing techniques in the field of retinal ophthalmology, viewed Feb. 2014, http://messidor.crihan.fr/index-en.php; 2014.

[25] Zhang Z, Yin FS, Liu J, Wong WK, Tan NM, Lee BH, Cheng J, Wong TY. ORIGA-light: an online retinal fundus image database for glaucoma analysis and research, In: 32nd annual international conference of the IEEE EMBS, Argentina; 2010. p. 3065–8.

[26] Ektesabi A, Kapoor A. Removal of circular edge noise of retinal fundus images, In: International conference on image processing, computer vision and pattern recognition (IPCV'14), Las Vegas; 2014.

[27] Ektesabi A, Kapoor A. Exact pupil and iris boundary detection. In: International conference on control, instrumentation, and automation (ICCIA), Shiraz, vol. 2; p. 1217–21.

pSQ: Image quantizer based on contrast band-pass filtering

5

Jaime Moreno[1,2], Oswaldo Morales[1], Ricardo Tejeida[1]

[1]*Superior School of Mechanical and Electrical Engineers, National Polytechnic Institute of Mexico, IPN Avenue, Lindavista, Mexico City, Mexico*
[2]*Signal, Image and Communications Department, University of Poitiers, Poitiers, France*

1 INTRODUCTION

Digital image compression has been a research topic for many years and a number of image compression standards have been created for different applications [1, 2]. The JPEG2000 is intended to provide rate-distortion and subjective image quality performance superior to existing standards, as well as to supply functionality [3]. However, JPEG2000 does not provide the most relevant characteristics of the human visual system, since for removing information in order to compress the image mainly information theory criteria are applied. This information removal introduces artifacts to the image that are visible at high compression rates, because of many pixels with high perceptual significance have been discarded. Hence, an advanced model is necessary that removes information according to perceptual criteria, preserving the pixels with high perceptual relevance regardless of the numerical information. The Chromatic Induction Wavelet Model presents some perceptual concepts that can be suitable for it. Both contrast band-pass filtering (CBPF) and JPEG2000 use wavelet transform. CBPF uses it in order to generate an approximation to how every pixel is perceived from a certain distance taking into account the value of its neighboring pixels. By contrast, JPEG2000 applies a perceptual criterion for all coefficients in a certain spatial frequency independently of the values of its surrounding ones. In other words, JPEG2000 performs a global transformation of wavelet coefficients, while CBPF performs a local one. CBPF attenuates the details that the human visual system is not able to perceive, enhances those that are perceptually relevant, and produces an approximation of the image that the brain visual cortex perceives. At long distances, the lack of information does not produce the well-known compression artifacts; rather it is presented as a softened version, where the details with high perceptual value remain (e.g., some edges).

67

2 RELATED WORK: JPEG 2000 GLOBAL VISUAL FREQUENCY WEIGHTING

In JPEG2000, only one set of weights is chosen and applied to wavelet coefficients according to a particular viewing condition (100, 200, or 400 dpi's) with fixed visual weighting [3, Annex J.8]. This viewing condition may be truncated depending on the stages of embedding, in other words at low bit rates, the quality of the compressed image is poor and the detailed features of the image are not available since at a relatively large distance the low frequencies are perceptually more important. Table 1 specifies a set of weights which was designed for the luminance component based on the contrast sensitivity function (CSF) value at the mid-frequency of each spatial frequency. The viewing distance is supposed to be 4000 pixels, corresponding to 10 in. for 400 dpi print or display. The weight for LL is not included in the table, because it is always 1. Levels 1, 2, ..., 5 denote the spatial frequency levels in low- to high-frequency order with three spatial orientations, *horizontal, vertical*, and *diagonal*.

3 PERCEPTUAL QUANTIZATION
3.1 CONTRAST BAND-PASS FILTERING

The CBPF [4] is a low-level perceptual model of the HVS. It estimates the image perceived by an observer at a distance d just by modeling the perceptual chromatic induction processes of the HVS. That is, given an image I and an observation distance d, CBPF obtains an estimation of the perceptual image I_ρ that the observer perceives when observing I at distance d. CBPF is based on just three important stimulus properties: spatial frequency, spatial orientation, and surround contrast. This three properties allow to unify the chromatic assimilation and contrast phenomena, as well as some other perceptual processes such as saliency perceptual processes.

The perceptual image I_ρ is recovered by weighting these $\omega_{s,o}$ wavelet coefficients using the *extended contrast sensitivity function* (e-CSF). The e-CSF is an extension of the psychophysical CSF [5] considering spatial surround information (denoted

Table 1 Recommended JPEG 2000 Frequency (*s*) Weighting for 400 dpi (*s* = 1 is the Lowest Frequency Wavelet Plane)

s	Horizontal	Vertical	Diagonal
1	1	1	1
2	1	1	0.731668
3	0.564344	0.564344	0.285968
4	0.179609	0.179609	0.043903
5	0.014774	0.014774	0.000573

by r), visual frequency (denoted by v, which is related to spatial frequency by observation distance), and observation distance (d). Perceptual image I_ρ can be obtained by

$$I_\rho = \sum_{s=1}^{n} \sum_{o=v,h,dgl} \alpha(v,r)\omega_{s,o} + c_n \tag{1}$$

where $\alpha(v,r)$ is the e-CSF weighting function that tries to reproduce some perceptual properties of the HVS. The term $\alpha(v,r)\omega_{s,o}$ is considered the *perceptual wavelet coefficients* of image I when observed at distance d.

3.2 FORWARD INVERSE QUANTIZATION

Quantization is the only cause that introduces distortion into a compression process. Since each transform sample at the perceptual image I_ρ (1) is mapped independently to a corresponding step size either Δ_s or Δ_n; thus, I_ρ is associated with a specific interval on the real line. Then, the perceptually quantized coefficients Q, from a known viewing distance d, are calculated as follows:

$$Q = \sum_{s=1}^{n} \sum_{o=v,h,dgl} \text{sign}(\omega_{s,o}) \left\lfloor \frac{|\alpha(v,r)\omega_{s,o}|}{\Delta_s} \right\rfloor + \left\lfloor \frac{c_n}{\Delta_n} \right\rfloor \tag{2}$$

Unlike the classical techniques of visual frequency weighting (VFW) on JPEG2000, which apply one CSF weight per sub-band [1, Annex J.8], perceptual quantization using CBPF(pSQ) applies one CSF weight per coefficient over all wavelet planes $\omega_{s,o}$. In this section, we only explain forward perceptual quantization using CBPF (F-pSQ). Thus, Equation (2) introduces perceptual criteria of the perceptual images (1) to each quantized coefficient of the dead-zone scalar quantizer [1, Annex J.8]. A normalized quantization step size $\Delta = 1/128$ is used, namely, the range between the minimal and maximal values at I_ρ is divided into 128 intervals. Finally, the perceptually quantized coefficients are entropy coded, before forming the output code stream or bitstream.

The perceptual quantizer F-pSQ in JPEG2000 is tested on all the color images of the *Miscellaneous volume* of the University of Southern California Image Data Base [6]. The data sets are eight 256×256 pixel images and eight 512×512 pixel images, but only visual results of the well-known images *Lena*, *F-16*, and *Baboon* are depicted, which are 24-bit color images and 512×512 of resolution. The CBPF model is performed for a 19 in. monitor with 1280 pixels of horizontal resolution at 50 cm of viewing distance. The software used to obtain a JPEG2000 compression for the experiment is *JJ2000* [7].

Figure 1(a) shows the assessment results of the average performance of color image compression for each bit-plane using a dead-zone uniform scalar quantizer (SQ, function with heavy dots), and it also depicts the results obtained when applying F-pSQ (function with heavy stars).

Using CBPF as a method of forward quantization, achieves better compression ratios than SQ with the same threshold, obtaining better results at the highest

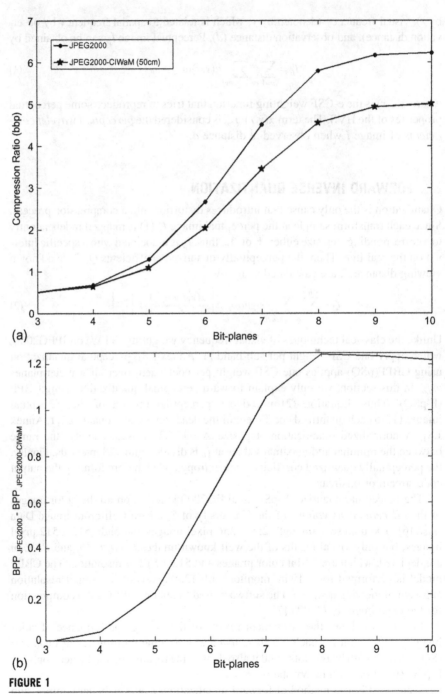

FIGURE 1

(a) JPEG2000 Compression ratio (bpp) as a function of Bit-plane. Function with heavy dots shows JPEG2000 only quantized by the dead-zone uniform scalar manner. While function with heavy stars shows JPEG2000 perceptually prequantized by F-pSQ. (b) The bit-rate decrease by each Bit-plane after applying F-pSQ on the JPEG2000 compression.

bit-planes, since CBPF reduces unperceivable features. Figure 1(b) shows the contribution of F-pSQ in the JPEG2000 compression ratio, for example, at the eighth bit-plane, CBPF reduces 1.2423 bits per pixel than the bit rate obtained by SQ, namely, in a 512×512 pixel color image, CBPF estimates that 39.75 kB of information is perceptually irrelevant at 50 cm.

Both Figures 2 and 3 depict examples of recovered images compressed at 0.9 and 0.4 bits per pixel, respectively, by means of JPEG2000 (a) without and (b) with F-pSQ. Also these figures show that the perceptual quality of images forward quantized by pSQ is better than the objective one.

FIGURE 2

Examples of recovered images of Lenna compressed at 0.9 bpp. (a) JPEG2000 PSNR $= 31.19$ dB and (b) JPEG2000-F-pSQ PSNR $= 27.57$ dB.

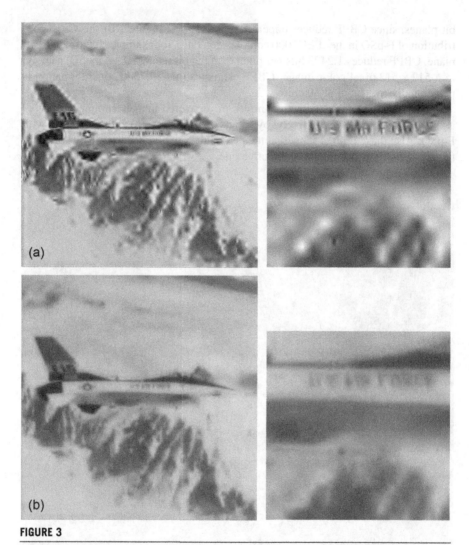

FIGURE 3

Examples of recovered images of F-16 compressed at 0.4 bpp. (a) JPEG2000
PSNR = 25.12 dB. (b) JPEG2000-F-pSQ PSNR = 24.57 dB.

Figure 4 shows examples of recovered images of *Baboon* compressed at 0.59, and
0.45 bits per pixel by means of JPEG2000 (a) without and (b) with F-pSQ. In Figure 4
(a) PSNR = 26.18 dB and in Figure 4(b) PSNR = 26.15 dB but a perceptual metrics
like WSNR [8], for example, assesses that it is equal to 34.08 dB. Therefore, the
recovered image forward quantized by pSQ is perceptually better than the one only
quantized by an SQ. Since the latter produces more compression artifacts, the pSQ
result at 0.45 bpp (Figure 4(b)) contains less artifacts than SQ at 0.59 bpp. For

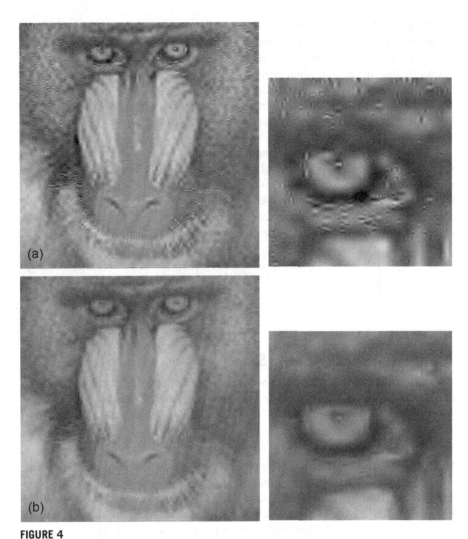

FIGURE 4

Examples of recovered images of Baboon. (a) JPEG2000 compressed at 0.59 bpp.
(b) JPEG2000-F-pSQ compressed at 0.45 bpp.

example, the *Baboon*'s eye is softer and better defined using F-pSQ and it additionally saves 4.48 kB of information.

3.3 PERCEPTUAL INVERSE QUANTIZATION

The proposed perceptual quantization is a generalized method, which can be applied
to wavelet transform-based image compression algorithms such as EZW, SPIHT,
SPECK, JPEG2000, or H*i*-SET.

The main challenge underlies in to recover not only a good approximation of coefficients Q but also the visual weight $\alpha(v,r)$ (Equation 2) that weighted them. A recovered approximation $\hat{Q}$ with a certain distortion Λ is decoded from the bitstream by the entropy decoding process. The VFWs were not encoded during the entropy encoding process, since it would increase the amount of stored data. A possible solution is to embed these weights $\alpha(v,r)$ into $\hat{Q}$. Thus, our goal is to recover the $\alpha(v,r)$ weights only using the information from the bitstream, namely, from the forward quantized coefficients $\hat{Q}$.

The reduction of the dynamic range is uniformly made by the perceptual quantizer; thus, the statistical properties of I are maintained in $\hat{Q}$. Therefore, our hypothesis is that an approximation $\hat{\alpha}(v,r)$ of $\alpha(v,r)$ can be recovered applying CBPF to $\hat{Q}$, with the same viewing conditions used in I. That is, $\hat{\alpha}(v,r)$ is the recovered e-CSF. Thus, the perceptual inverse quantizer or the recovered $\hat{\alpha}(v,r)$ introduces perceptual criteria to inverse scalar quantizer and is given by

$$\hat{I} = \begin{cases} \displaystyle\sum_{s=1}^{n} \sum_{o=v,h,dgl} \text{sign}(\hat{\omega}_{s,o}) \left\lfloor \frac{\Delta_s(|\hat{\omega}_{s,o}| + \delta)}{\hat{\alpha}(v,r)} \right\rfloor + (|\hat{c}_n| + \delta)\Delta_n, & \hat{\omega}_{s,o} > 0 \\ 0, & \hat{\omega}_{s,o} = 0 \end{cases} \quad (3)$$

4 EXPERIMENTAL RESULTS

For the sake of showing that the encoded VFWs are approximately equal to the decoded ones, that is, $\alpha(v,r) \approx \hat{\alpha}(v,r)$, we perform two experiments.

4.1 BASED ON HISTOGRAM

Histogram of $\alpha(v,r)$ and $\hat{\alpha}(v,r)$. The process of this short experiment is shown in Figure 5. Figure 5(a) depicts the process for obtaining losslessy both encoded and decoded visual weights for the 512×512 *Lena* image, Channel Y at 10 m. While Figure 5(b) and (c) shows the frequency histograms of $\alpha(v,r)$ and $\hat{\alpha}(v,r)$, respectively. In both graphs, the horizontal axis represents the sort of VFW variations, whereas the vertical axis represents the number of repetitions in that particular VFW. The distribution in both histograms is similar and they have the same shape.

4.2 CORRELATION ANALYSIS

Correlation analysis between $\alpha(v,r)$ and $\hat{\alpha}(v,r)$. We employ the process shown in Figure 5(a) for all the images of the CMU, CSIQ, and IVC image databases. In order to obtain $\hat{\alpha}(v,r)$, we measure the lineal correlation between the original $\alpha(v,r)$ applied during the F-pSQ process and the recovered $\hat{\alpha}(v,r)$. Table 2 shows that there is a high similarity between the applied VFW and the recovered one, since their correlation is 0.9849, for gray-scale images, and 0.9840, for color images.

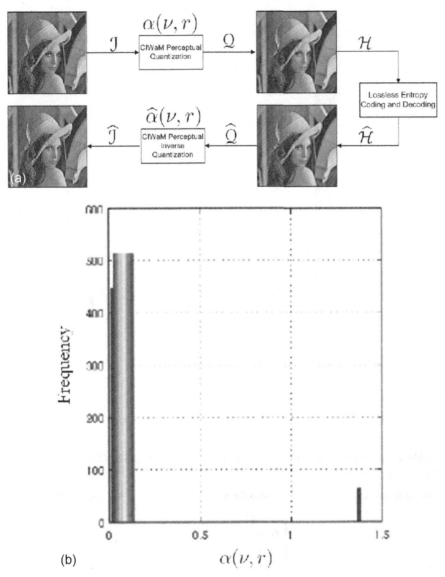

FIGURE 5

(a) Graphical representation of a whole process of compression and decompression.
histograms of (b) $\alpha(v, r)$ and

(Continued)

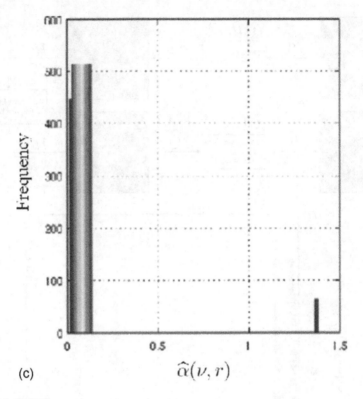

(c) $\widehat{\alpha}(\nu, r)$

FIGURE 5, CONT'D

(c) $\hat{\alpha}(v, r)$ visual frequency weights for the 512×512 image *Lenna*, channel Y at 10 m.

Table 2 Correlation Between $\alpha(v, r)$ and $\hat{\alpha}(v, r)$ Across CMU, CSIQ, and IVCIMAGE Databases

Image Database	8 bpp Gray-Scale	24 bpp Color
CMU	0.9840	0.9857
CSIQ	0.9857	0.9851
IVC	0.9840	0.9840
Overall	0.9849	0.9844

Figure 6 depicts the PSNR difference (dB) of each color image of the CMU database, that is, the gain in dB of image quality after applying $\hat{\alpha}(v, r)$ at $d = 2000$ cm to the $\hat{Q}$ images. On average, this gain is about 15 dB. Visual examples of these results are shown in Figure 7, where the right images are the original images, central images are perceptual quantized images after applying $\alpha(v,r)$, and left images are recovered images after applying $\hat{\alpha}(v,r)$.

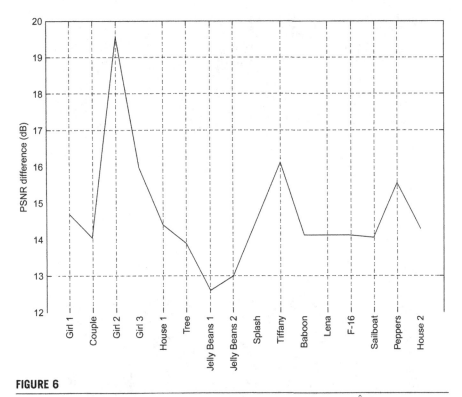

FIGURE 6

PSNR difference between Q image after applying $\alpha(v, r)$ and recovered $\hat{I}$ after applying $\hat{\alpha}(v, r)$ for every color image of the CMU database.

After applying $\hat{\alpha}(v, r)$, a visual inspection of these 16 recovered images shows a perceptually lossless quality. We perform the same experiment for gray-scale and color images with $d = 20, 40, 60, 80, 100, 200, 400, 800, 1000,$ and 2000 cm, in addition to test their objective and subjective image quality by means of the PSNR and MSSIM metrics, respectively.

In Figures 8 and 9, green functions denoted as F-pSQ are the quality metrics of perceptual quantized images after applying $\alpha(v, r)$, while blue functions denoted as I-pSQ are the quality metrics of recovered images after applying $\hat{\alpha}(v, r)$ in CMU image data base. Thus, for either gray-scale or color images, both PSNR and MSSIM estimations of the quantized image $\hat{Q}$ decrease regarding d, the longer the d the greater the image quality decline. When the image decoder recovers Q and it is perceptually inverse quantized, the quality barely varies and is close to perceptually lossless, no matter the distance

Results obtained both in the categorical subjective image quality image database [9] (Figures 10 and 11) and image and video-communication image database [10] (Figures 12 and 13) show that for either gray-scale or color images, both PSNR

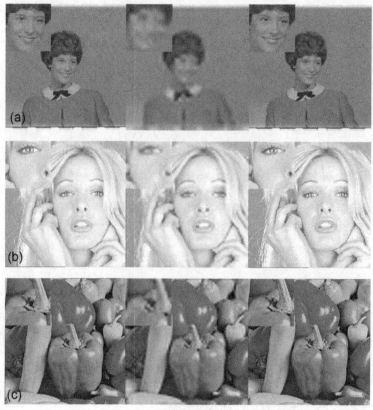

FIGURE 7

Visual examples of perceptual quantization. Left images are the original images, central images are forward perceptual quantized images (F-pSQ) after applying $\hat{\alpha}(v, r)$ at $d=2000$ cm, and right images are recovered I-pSQ images after applying $\hat{\alpha}(v, r)$. (a) Girl 2. (b) Tiffany. (c) Peppers.

and MSSIM estimations of the quantized image Q decrease regarding d, the longer the d the greater the image quality decline. When the image decoder recovers $\hat{Q}$ and it is perceptually inverse quantized, the quality barely varies and is close to perceptually lossless, no matter the distance.

5 CONCLUSIONS

In this work, we defined both forward (F-pSQ) and inverse (I-pSQ) perceptual quantizer using CBPF. We incorporated it to Hi-SET, testing a perceptual image compression system Hi-SET+pSQ. In order to measure the effectiveness of the perceptual quantization, a performance analysis is done using 13 assessments such as PSNR or

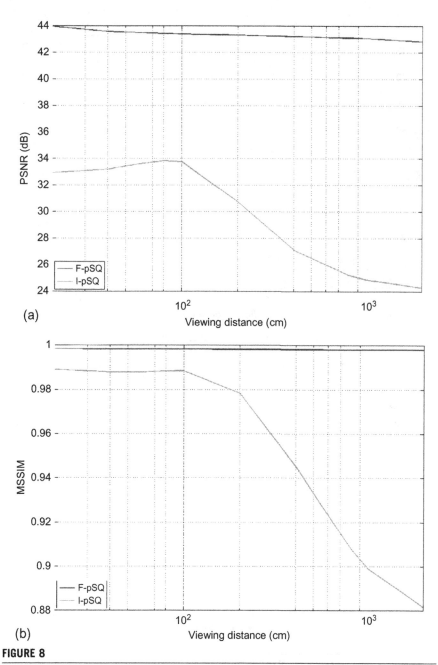

FIGURE 8

PSNR and MSSIM assessments of compression of gray-scale images (Y Channel) of the CMU image database. Green functions denoted as F-pSQ are the quality metrics of forward perceptual quantized images after applying $\alpha(v, r)$, while blue functions denoted as I-pSQ are the quality metrics of recovered images after applying $\hat{\alpha}(v, r)$. (a) PSNR. (b) MSSIM.

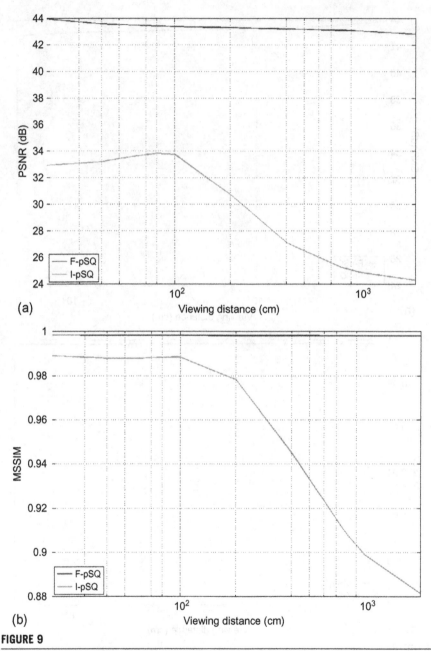

FIGURE 9

PSNR and MSSIM assessments of compression of Color Images of the CMU image database. Green functions denoted as F-pSQ are the quality metrics of forward perceptual quantized images after applying $\alpha(v, r)$, while blue functions denoted as I-pSQ are the quality metrics of recovered images after applying $\hat{\alpha}(v, r)$. (a) PSNR. (b) MSSIM

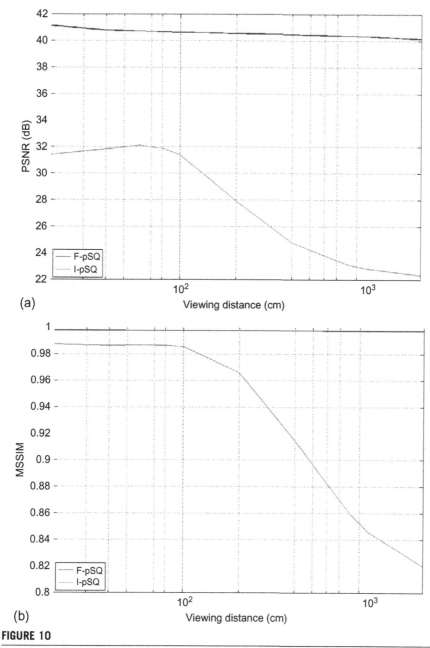

(a)

(b)

FIGURE 10

Compression of gray-scale images (Y Channel) of the CSIQ image database. (a) PSNR. (b) MSSIM.

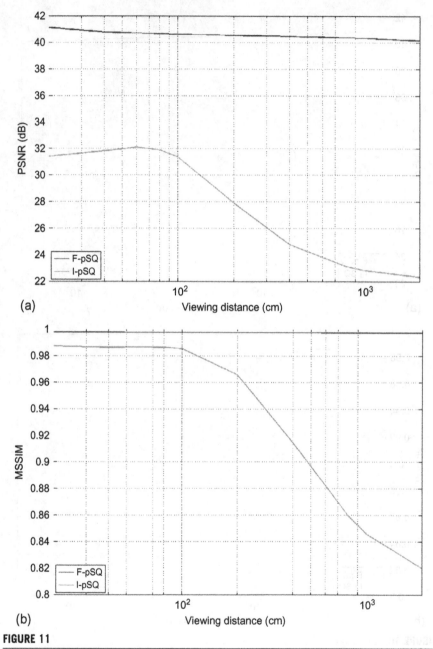

(a)

(b)

FIGURE 11

Perceptual quantization of color images of the CSIQ image database. (a) PSNR. (b) MSSIM.

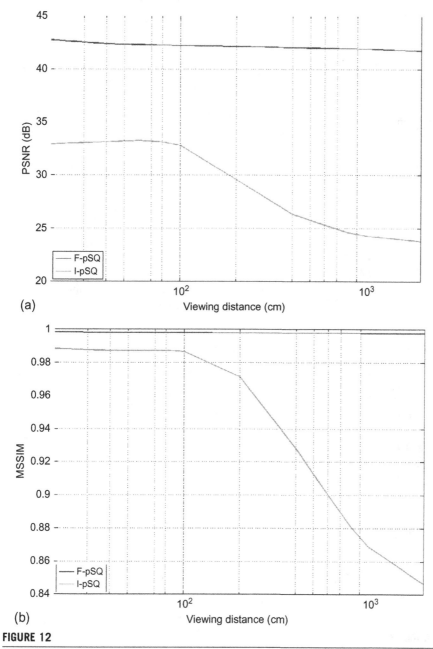

FIGURE 12

Perceptual quantization of gray-scale images (Y Channel) of the IVC image database.
(a) PSNR. (b) MSSIM.

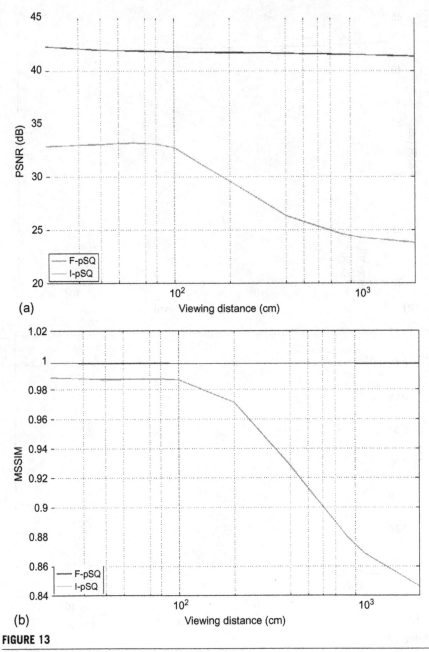

FIGURE 13

Perceptual quantization of color images of the IVC image database. (a) PSNR. (b) MSSIM.

MSSIM, for instance, which measured the image quality between reconstructed and original images. The experimental results show that the solely usage of the forward perceptual quantization improves the JPEG2000 compression and image perceptual quality.

ACKNOWLEDGMENT

This work is supported by National Polytechnic Institute of Mexico by means of Project No. 20140096, the Academic Secretary and the Committee of Operation and Promotion of Academic Activities (COFAA), National Council of Science and Technology of Mexico by means of Project No. 204151/2013, and LABEX Σ-LIM France, Coimbra Group Scholarship Programme granted by University of Poitiers and Region of Poitou-Charentes, France.

REFERENCES

[1] Moreno J, Morales O, Tejeida R. pSQ: image quantizer based on contrast band-pass filtering, In: International conference on image processing, computer vision, and pattern recognition of the world congress in computer science, computer engineering, and applied, computing; 2014. p. 256–61.

[2] Moreno J, Otazu X. Image coder based on Hilbert scanning of embedded quadTrees: an introduction of Hi-SET coder, In: IEEE international conference on multimedia and expo; 2011.

[3] Boliek M, Christopoulos C, Majani E. Information technology: JPEG2000 image coding system, JPEG 2000 Part I final committee draft version 1.0 ed., ISO/IEC JTC1/SC29 WG1, JPEG 2000; April 2000.

[4] Otazu X, Parraga C, Vanrell M. Towarda unified chromatic induction model". J Vis 2010;10(12):6.

[5] Mullen K. The contrast sensitivity of human color vision to red-green and blue-yellow chromatic gratings. J Physiol 1985;359:381–400.

[6] S. I.P. I. of the University of Southern California. (1997) The USC-SIPI image database. Signal and Image Processing Institute of the University of Southern California. [Online]. Available: http://sipi.usc.edu/database/.

[7] C. Research, École Polytechnique Fédérale de Lausanne, and Ericsson. JJ2000 implementation in Java. Cannon Research, École Polytechnique Fédérale de Lausanne and Ericsson. [Online]. Available: http://jj2000.epfl.ch/; 2001.

[8] Mitsa T, Varkur K. Evaluation of contrast sensitivity functions for formulation of quality measures incorporated in halftoning algorithms. In: IEEE international conference on acoustics, speech and signal processing, vol. 5; 1993. p. 301–4.

[9] Larson EC, Chandler DM. Most apparent distortion: a dual strategy for full-reference image quality assessment. Proc SPIE 2009;742:1–17.

[10] le Callet P, Autrusseau, F. Subjective quality assessment IRCCyN/IVC database, http://www.irccyn.ec-nantes.fr/ivcdb/; 2005.

Rebuilding IVUS images from raw data of the RF signal exported by IVUS equipment

6

Marco Aurélio Granero[1,2], Marco Antônio Gutierrez[3], Eduardo Tavares Costa[1]

[1]Department of Biomedical Engineering, DEB/FEEC/UNICAMP, Campinas, Brazil
[2]Federal Institute of Education, Science and Technology São Paulo—IFSP, Sao Paulo, Brazil
[3]Division of Informatics/Heart Institute, HCFMUSP, Sao Paulo, Brazil

1 INTRODUCTION

Among the different modalities of medical images, ultrasound is arguably the most difficult in which to perform segmentation. This is evident from a study of the first papers on segmentation, in which it was only possible to apply a threshold to the image in order to separate the background from foreground due to the poor quality of the acquired data [1].

At the same time, subsequent technological development has greatly increased the quality of ultrasound images, especially in terms of signal-to-noise ratio and contrast-to-noise ratio (CNR), resulting in improvements to image quality. Several studies have been highlighted that aim to develop algorithms for the design of edges on objects contained in ultrasound images [1].

Ultrasonic tissue characterization (UTC) has become a well-established research field since its first publication [2]. Thijssen [3] defines UTC as the assessment by ultrasound of quantitative information about the characteristics of biological tissue and their pathology. This quantitative information is extracted from echographic data from radiofrequency (RF) data.

UTC applications abound in the literature and include classification of breast tissue [4,5], liver [5], heart [6,7], eyes [8], skin [9], kidney [10], and prostate [11].

Szabo [12] defines two general goals for UTC which can be applied to the above areas:

(i) reveal the properties of tissues by analyzing the RF signal backscattered by ultrasound transducer and

(ii) use information about the properties of the tissue to distinguish between the state of tissue (healthy or diseased) or to detect changes in these properties when subjected to stimuli or long periods of time in response to natural processes or medication.

Reaching these goals can be challenging since the interaction between biological tissue and sound waves is extremely difficult to model and the process evolved in image segmentation is strongly influenced by the quality of data and by the different parameters used during the acquisition process of an image.

Parameters like contrast, brightness, and gain are adjusted by physicians to improve the visualization of regions during the examination. These changes determine the digital imaging and communications (DICOM) images that are recorded and the result cannot be changed after the image has been acquired. This greatly complicates the comparison between patients and the use of images in studies of groups of patients.

Thus, to avoid these complications and make image reconstructed independent of the parameters set by the physician, a reconstruction method from Intravascular ultrasound (IVUS) images is proposed. This method is based on the RF signal stored by the equipment during medical imaging examinations of IVUS.

The process of rebuilding starts with applying a band-pass filter to the RF signal to eliminate signals that do not come from the transducer. In the next step, a time gain compensation (TGC) function is applied to compensate for attenuation loss. After this, the envelope of the signal is computed and the result is log-compressed and normalized in a grayscale image.

After the process of rebuilding, the grayscale image, in polar coordinators, is submitted to a digital development process (DDP) responsible for enhancing the contrast and edge emphasis. So, the image is interpolated to cartesian coordinators. The cartesian image is further processed with an intensity transformation function to improve the contrast of the final cartesian grayscale IVUS image.

The above processes are described in more detail in Section 2 and the results obtained are shown in Section 3. In Section 4 a comparison is made between reconstructed images and DICOM images from an examination. Section 4 also presents the conclusions and possibilities for future work. This article is an extended version of the paper presented in the 2014 International Conference on Image Processing, Computer Vision, and Pattern Recognition [13].

2 METHOD FOR IVUS IMAGE RECONSTRUCTION

An IVUS examination is carried out by inserting a catheter into coronary arteries via femoral or brachial vessels. At the tip of this catheter there is an ultrasound emitter and a piezoelectric transducer that collect the echoes reflected by internal structures of the vessel as RF signal.

A schematic representation of the execution of an IVUS examination is shown in Figure 1(a), where the IVUS equipment collects data from patient and stores it in the workstation. Figure 1(b) shows an IVUS rotational catheter.

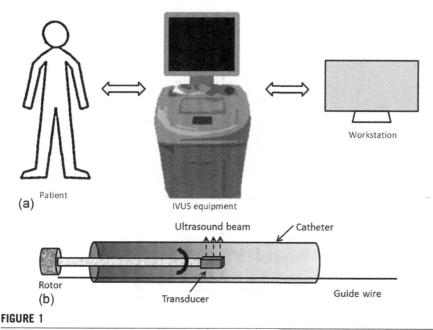

FIGURE 1

(a) IVUS *in vivo* analysis typical scenario and (b) rotational IVUS catheter.

During an IVUS exam, the acquired images are stored in DICOM format and exported to the databank of the clinical centre to be used for clinical diagnosis.

To improve the quality of the images, in terms of CNR, physicians frequently need to adjust parameters like contrast and brightness to improve the visualization of the region of interest (ROI).

In addition to the images in DICOM format, the equipment allows the RF signal to be recorded, which are used in the manufacture of images in a proprietary format.

The proposal of this article is to process the RF signal data according to the steps shown in Figure 2 and detailed below, to rebuild the IVUS images with an independent and fixed set of parameters.

2.1 RF DATASET

The data were taken from examinations in the Department of Hemodynamic in the Heart Institute of the Medical School of the University of São Paulo (Heart Institute, HCFMUSP), Brazil, using iLab IVUS equipment (Boston Scientific, Fremont, USA), equipped with a 40-MHz catheter Atlantis SR 40 Pro and anonymized to avoid the identification of the patient and used only for research purposes.

The RF File Reader (designed by Boston Scientific) is an xml file that contains information about the examination. This file allows us to identify the number of rows, columns, and frames from each exam. Beyond this, the reader contains the distance from each pixel in the image, in millimeters.

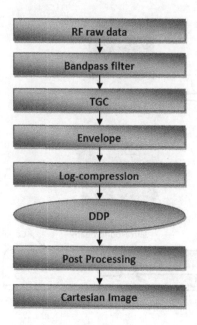

FIGURE 2

Block diagram of reconstruction process.

Once image attributes have been found using the RF File Reader, it is possible to extract the data. These data were placed in a tri-dimensional matrix. The rows of this matrix represent the lines in A-mode, each line with radial information about the vessel, the columns represent the distance to the tip of catheter and the slices, third dimension, represent each time frames of the exam. The study of IVUS used in this work results in a 3D matrix, where the dimensions represents the size of each image and the third dimension being the number of frames.

After this, each frame was submitted to the reconstruction shown in Figure 2.

2.2 BAND-PASS FILTER

A Butterworth band-pass filter was applied to dataset in order to eliminate frequencies that do not come from the transducer. The manufacture of transducer describes the central frequency emitted by transducer at the tip of catheter as 40 MHz and frequency sample rate as 200 MHz.

Each line in A-mode was filtered by a Butterworth finite impulse response (FIR) filter. The frequency range was adjusted between 20 and 60 MHz as can be viewed in Figure 3(a).

2.3 TIME GAIN COMPENSATION

The ultrasound is a mechanical wave and due to this nature, the intensity of the ultrasound beam is attenuated as it penetrates the tissue.

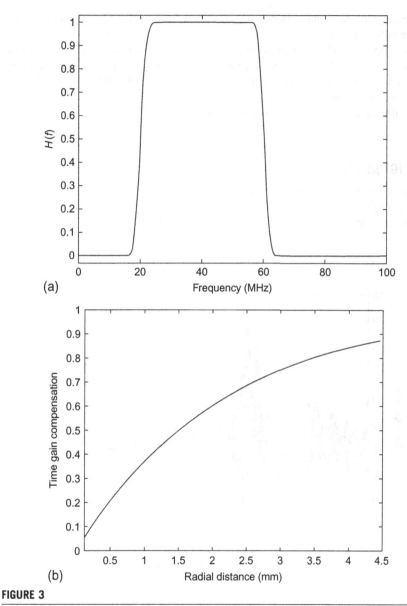

(a)

(b)

FIGURE 3

(a) Frequency response of the Butterworth FIR filter and (b) profile of TGC function.

To compensate for this loss in signal intensity, TGC is applied to each line in A-mode, which is defined as

$$T(r) = 1 - e^{-\beta r} \tag{1}$$

where β is the coefficient of attenuation and r is the radial distance from tip of catheter.

The range of the radial distance was extracted from the RF File Reader of exam ranging until 4.48 cm.

In Ciompi [14], RF signal of *in vivo* and *ex vivo* was used to develop a multiclass classifier to the problem of characterization of the atherosclerotic plaque. They define a value for the coefficient of attenuation as $\beta = 0.4605\,\mathrm{dB/cm}$, which was adopted in this work.

The profile of TGC function is shown in Figure 3(b).

2.4 SIGNAL ENVELOPE

To show the changes stemming from the texture and not from the wave profile, the envelope of the signal is obtained simply applying the Hilbert transform to each line in A-mode from the RF signal, Figure 4(a).

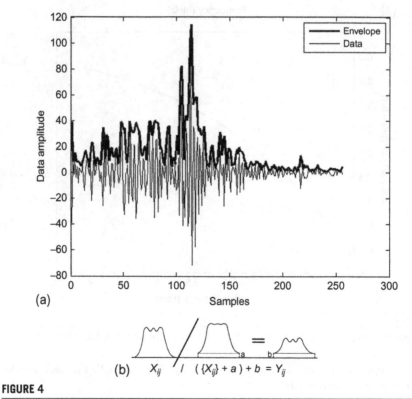

FIGURE 4

(a) RF envelope is shown as a black line over the wave profile of RF signal gray line (data) and (b) DDP transformation.

2.5 LOG-COMPRESSION

The next stage in the procedure described in Figure 2, is to normalize the RF signal providing values between 0 and 1 in order to permit work with a homogeneous range for all IVUS images. After this, the RF signal undergoes a transformation whose purpose is to map a narrow range of grayscale values in an input image to a wide range of output levels [15]. This transformation is defined as

$$I_{log} = \frac{1}{t} log \left[1 + (e^t - 1) I_{nor} \right] \quad (2)$$

where I_{nor} represents the RF signal normalized and t is a constant empirically obtained to improve the log-compression.

2.6 DIGITAL DEVELOPMENT PROCESS

The DDP consist of a nonlinear intensity transformation, used frequently in photography, to emphasize dark regions in images with a large dynamic range, without saturation or overexposure of brighter areas.

This way, in order to emphasize the edges borders and improve contrast gain, a DDP was applied to the image [15].

Each pixel value of an image was modified by the following equation to produce an image with better CNR:

$$Y_{ij} = k \left(\frac{X_{ij}}{\{X_{ij}\} + a} \right) + b \quad (3)$$

where X_{ij} is obtained by applying a Gaussian low-pass filter, with order 3 and $\sigma = 0.5$, to the original image. The parameters a and b control the radial contrast gain and were empirically determined to improve the CRN, Figure 4(b).

The parameter k is a simple gain and the term $\left(\frac{X_{ij}}{\{X_{ij}\} + a} \right)$ control the edge emphasis.

2.7 POSTPROCESSING

This step in the rebuilding process aims to expand the gray level dynamic band, in term of saturation of the image. It was obtained applying a gamma correction intensity transformation to the image [15].

After this, the image was converted and interpolated to cartesian form, resulting in an image with 512×512 pixels and 256 gray levels.

Finally, a two-dimensional (2D) Gabor filter was applied to the image to enhancing the changes streaming from texture and to evidence the edges.

A 2D Gabor filter is a complex field sinusoidal, modulated by a 2D gaussian function in the spatial domain [16].

3 EXPERIMENTAL RESULTS

The results of the rebuilding process of the IVUS images are shown in Figure 5, which the major structures visible in an IVUS examination are identified.

Figure 5(a) shows the segmentation of lumen and the media-adventitia borders and Figure 5(b) shows the stent and an artifact generated by the wire guide. Figure 5(c) shows a region with calcification and the acoustic shadow behind it, with an arrow pointing to an artifact generated by the wire guide.

Figure 5(e) and (h) shows a bifurcation region, with calcification. A stent is visible in Figure 5(d) and (i), and it is possible to identify the malposition of the stent in Figure 5(i).

Figure 5(f) shows the shadow of the pericardium and Figure 5(g) the acoustic shadow of a big calcification and the lumen and media-adventitia borders.

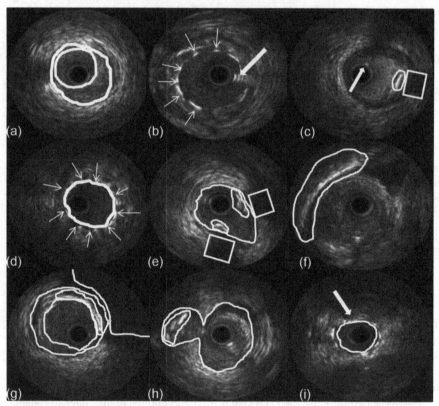

FIGURE 5

Nine images from the reconstruction process showing different regions (a) lumen-adventitia borders, (b) stent, (c) calcification, (d) stent, (e) bifurcation region, (f) pericardium shadow, (g) calcification, (h) bifurcation, and (i) malposition stent.

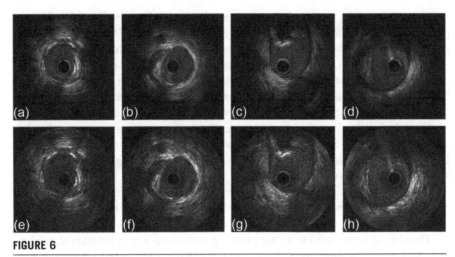

FIGURE 6

(a)–(d) DICOM images and (e)–(h) rebuilt images.

Figure 6 shows both the rebuild image and the DICOM images, Figure 6(a)–(d) as possible to see DICOM images and in Figures 6(e)–(h) the images rebuilding by the method propose in this article.

As can be seen, the rebuilt images show the same structures as DICOM images, and in all cases the contrast of the rebuild images is better than the DICOM images. What is perhaps most noticeable is the difference in visibility in the outer region of the lumen. The reconstructed image shows fine detail where the DICOM shows only a black region.

4 DISCUSSION, CONCLUSION, AND FUTURE WORK

IVUS is an examination that can provide a good quality image of the cross-section of blood vessel allowing the assessment of inner structures.

In an IVUS medical examination, sets of hundreds or even thousands of images are acquired and used as the basis for a medical diagnosis.

These images are subject to a variability of interpretation inter and intra operator because a set of parameter are adjusted to improve the visualization of an ROI. Once the images are acquired, these parameters cannot be changed, restricting the comparison between different examinations or patients.

To avoid this limitation, this work describes a methodology for reconstructing IVUS images from RF raw data, which are independent of the parameters adjusted by the physician during the exam and which can be processed to improve the CNR of the image.

The RF signal is processed according to the theoretic model proposed in Section 2 and illustrated in Figure 2. The parameters used in the model were adjusted to maximize CNR enabling identification of the main structures of the vessel.

The results of the proposed model were presented in Figures 5 and 6 and compared with the DICOM images generated by the equipment. The proposed model produces images with superior CNR which can be used for clinical purposes.

In the figures, it is possible to see the main structures of the vessel and this result can be used to perform segmentation to help the physician in diagnosis process. Beyond this, it is possible to identify bifurcations and calcifications regions to be submitted a percutaneous coronary intervention.

Considering the data used in this work, the propose method was proved to be robust with regard to fidelity in the reconstruction of structures in comparison with DICOM image and, in all cases the CNR in reconstructed images was higher than DICOM images (Figure 6).

The study of RF signal plays a fundamental role in the rebuilding process and can be used to development of automatic segmentation algorithm of the structures of the vessel and to development of automatic classifiers by tissue characterization.

Thereby, as future works, we are planning to develop a segmentation algorithm and automatic classifiers to perform a tissue classification based on texture and spectral analysis of the RF signal.

ACKNOWLEDGMENTS

The authors want to thank the Department of Hemodynamic of Heart Institute to provide the RF dada set. Beyond this, this work would not be possible without the help of Mariana, Paulo, and John, great friends of my life, and the financial support of the Brazilian National Institute of Science and Technology in Medicine Assisted by Scientific Computing (INCT—MAAC) and National Council for Scientific and Technological Development (CNPq).

REFERENCES

[1] Noble JA. Ultrasound image segmentation and tissue characterization. Proc Inst Mech Eng H: J Eng Med 2010;224:307. http://dx.doi.org/10.1243/09544119JEIM604.

[2] Mountford RA, Wells PNT. Ultrasonic liver scanning: the A-scan in the normal and cirrhosis. Phys Med Biol 1972;17:261–9.

[3] Thijssen JM. Ultrasonic speckle formation, analysis and processing applied to tissue characterization. Pattern Recogn Lett 2003;24:659–75.

[4] Tsui P-H, Yeh C-K, Chang C-C, Liao Y-Y. Classification of breast masses by ultrasonic Nakagami imaging: a feasibility study. Phys Med Biol 2008;53:6027–44.

[5] Molthen RC, Shankar PM, Reid JM, Forsberg F, Halpern EJ, Piccoli CW, et al. Comparisons of the Rayleigh and K distribution models using in vivo breast and liver tissue. Ultrasound Med Biol 1998;24:93–100.

[6] Clifford L, Fitzgerald P, James D. Non-Rayleigh first-order statistics of ultrasonic backscatter from normal myocardium. Ultrasound Med Biol 1993;19:487–95.

[7] Nillesen MM, Lopata RGP, Gerrits IH, Kapusta L, Thijssen JM, de Korte CL. Modeling envelope statistics of blood and myocardium for segmentation of echocardiographic images. Ultrasound Med Biol 2008;34(4):674–80.

[8] Lizzi FL, Greenbaum M, Feleppa EJ, Elbaum M, Coleman DJ. Theoretical framework for spectrum analysis in ultrasonic tissue characterization. J Acoustic Soc Am 1983;73:1366–73.

[9] Raju BI, Swindells KJ, Gonzalez S, Srinivasan MA. Quantitative ultrasonic methods for characterization of skin lesions in vivo. Ultrasound Med Biol 2003;29(6):825–38.

[10] Engelhorn ALDV, Engelhorn CA, Salles-Cunha SX, Ehlert R, Akiyoshi FK, Assad KW. Ultrasound tissue characterization of the normal kidney. Ultrasound Quart 2012;28(4).

[11] Moradi M. A new paradigm for ultrasound-based tissue typing in prostate cancer [Tese de doutorado]. School of Computing, Queen's University; 2008.

[12] Szabo TL. Diagnostic ultrasound imaging inside out. Hartford, Connecticut: Elsevier; 2004.

[13] Granero MA, Gutierrez MA, Costa ET. Rebuilding IVUS images from raw data of the RF signal exported by IVUS equipment, In: The 2014 international conference on image processing, computer vision, and pattern recognition, 2014, Las Vegas, IPCV '14; 2014. p. 57–62.

[14] Ciompi F. Ecoc-based plaque classification using in-vivo and ex-vivo intravascular ultrasound data [Master thesis]. Computer Vision Center, Universitat Autonoma de Barcelona; 2008.

[15] Gonzalez RC, Woods RE, Eddins SL. Digital image processing using Matlab. Prentice Hall; 2004.

[16] Pratt WK. Digital image processing: PIKS Scientific inside. 4th ed John Wiley & Sons; 2007.

XSET: Image coder based on contrast band-pass filtering

7

Jaime Moreno[1,2], Oswaldo Morales[1], Ricardo Tejeida[1]

[1]*Superior School of Mechanical and Electrical Engineers, National Polytechnic Institute of Mexico, IPN Avenue, Lindavista, Mexico City, Mexico*

[2]*Signal, Image and Communications Department, University of Poitiers, Poitiers, France*

1 INTRODUCTION

Digital image compression has been a research topic for many years and a number of image compression standards have been created for different applications. The JPEG2000 is intended to provide rate-distortion and subjective image quality performance superior to existing standards, as well as to supply functionality [1]. However, JPEG2000 does not provide the most relevant characteristics of the human visual system, since for removing information in order to compress the image mainly information theory criteria are applied. This information removal introduces artifacts to the image that are visible at high compression rates, because of many pixels with high perceptual significance have been discarded. Hence, it is necessary an advanced model that removes information according to perceptual criteria, preserving the pixels with high perceptual relevance regardless of the numerical information. The Chromatic Induction Wavelet Model presents some perceptual concepts that can be suitable for it. Both CBPF and JPEG2000 use wavelet transform. CBPF uses it in order to generate an approximation to how every pixel is perceived from a certain distance taking into account the value of its neighboring pixels. By contrast, JPEG2000 applies the perceptual criteria for all coefficients in a certain spatial frequency independently of the values of its surrounding ones. In other words, JPEG2000 performs a global transformation of wavelet coefficients, while CBPF performs a local one. CBPF attenuates the details that the human visual system is not able to perceive, enhances those that are perceptually relevant and produces an approximation of the image that the brain visual cortex perceives. At long distances, the lack of information does not produce the well-known compression artifacts, rather it is presented as a softened version, where the details with high perceptual value remain (e.g., some edges).

The block diagram of the X-SET engine for encoding and decoding is shown in Figure 1. The source data are an RGB image, which comprises three components, then a color transformation is first applied over all three components. After the color

FIGURE 1

General block diagram for βSET encoding and decoding.

transformation, each component is decomposed with a discrete wavelet transform into a set of planes of different spatial frequencies by means of a forward wavelet transformation (9/7 analysis Filter). Then, these coefficients are forward perceptually quantized using CBPF, for reducing the precision of data in order to make them more perceptually compressible. Perceptual quantization is the only responsible that introduces imperceptible lossless distortion into the image data. Then, Hi-SET algorithm is employed for entropy encoding among quantized coefficients forming the output bit stream. The decoding process is the inverse of the encoding one. The bit stream is first entropy decoded by means of Hi-SET, perceptually dequantized, inverse discrete wavelet transformed and finally inverse color transformed, getting as a result the reconstructed image data.

2 RELATED WORK: JPEG2000 GLOBAL VISUAL FREQUENCY WEIGHTING

In JPEG2000, only one set of weights is chosen and applied to wavelet coefficients according to a particular viewing condition (100, 200, or 400 dpi's) with fixed visual weighting [1, Annex J.8]. This viewing condition may be truncated depending on the stages of embedding, in other words at low bit rates, the quality of the compressed image is poor and the detailed features of the image are not available since at a relatively large distance the low frequencies are perceptually more important. Table 1 specifies a set of weights which was designed for the luminance component based on the CSF value at the mid-frequency of each spatial frequency. The viewing distance is supposed to be 4000 pixels, corresponding to 10 in. for 400 dpi print or display. The weight for *LL* is not included in the table, because it is always 1. Levels 1,2,...,5 denote the spatial frequency levels in low-to-high-frequency order with three spatial orientations, *horizontal*, *vertical*, and *diagonal*.

Table 1 Recommended JPEG2000 Frequency (s) Weighting for 400 dpi'S (s=1 is the Lowest Frequency Wavelet Plane)

s	Horizontal	Vertical	Diagonal
1	1	1	1
2	1	1	0.731 668
3	0.564 344	0.564 344	0.285 968
4	0.179 609	0.179 609	0.043 903
5	0.014 774	0.014 774	0.000 573

3 IMAGE ENTROPY ENCODING: XSET ALGORITHM
3.1 PERCEPTUAL QUANTIZATION

(1) *Contrast band-pass filtering*: The contrast band-pass filtering (CBPF) [2] is a low-level perceptual model of the HVS. It estimates the image perceived by an observer at a distance d just by modeling the perceptual chromatic induction processes of the HVS. That is, given an image I and an observation distance d, CBPF obtains an estimation of the perceptual image I_ρ that the observer perceives when observing I at distance d. CBPF is based on just three important stimulus properties: spatial frequency, spatial orientation, and surround contrast. These three properties allow unifying the chromatic assimilation and contrast phenomena, as well as some other perceptual processes such as saliency perceptual processes.

The perceptual image I_ρ is recovered by weighting these $\omega_{s,o}$ wavelet coefficients using the *extended contrast sensitivity function* (e-CSF). The e-CSF is an extension of the psychophysical CSF [3] considering spatial surround information (denoted by r), visual frequency (denoted by v, which is related to spatial frequency by observation distance), and observation distance (d). Perceptual image I_ρ can be obtained by

$$I_\rho = \sum_{s=1}^{n} \sum_{o=v,h,dgl} \alpha(v,r)\omega_{s,o} + c_n \tag{1}$$

where $\alpha(v,r)$ is the e-CSF weighting function that tries to reproduce some perceptual properties of the HVS. The term $\alpha(v,r)\omega_{s,o}$ is considered the *perceptual wavelet coefficients* of image I when observed at distance d.

(2) *Forward quantization (F-pSQ)*: Quantization is the only cause that introduces distortion into a compression process. Since each transform sample at the perceptual image I_ρ (1) is mapped independently to a corresponding step size either Δ_s or Δ_n, thus I_ρ is associated with a specific interval on the real line. Then, the perceptually quantized coefficients Q, from a known viewing distance d, are calculated as follows:

$$Q = \sum_{s=1}^{n} \sum_{o=v,h,dgl} \text{sign}(\omega_{s,o}) \left\lfloor \frac{|\alpha(v,r)\omega_{s,o}|}{\Delta_s} \right\rfloor + \left\lfloor \frac{c_n}{\Delta_n} \right\rfloor \tag{2}$$

Unlike the classical techniques of visual frequency weighting (VFW) on JPEG2000, which apply one CSF weight per subband [1, Annex J.8], perceptual quantization using CBPF (pSQ) applies one CSF weight per coefficient over all wavelet planes $\omega_{s,o}$. In this section, we only explain forward perceptual quantization using CBPF (F-pSQ). Thus, Equation (2) introduces perceptual criteria of the perceptual images (1) to each quantized coefficient of the dead-zone scalar quantizer [1, Annex J.8]. A normalized quantization step size $\Delta = 1/128$ is used, namely, the range between the minimal and maximal values at I_ρ is divided into 128 intervals. Finally, the perceptually quantized coefficients are entropy coded, before forming the output code stream or bitstream.

(3) *Inverse quantization (I-pSQ)*: The proposed perceptual quantization is a generalized method, which can be applied to wavelet-transform-based image compression algorithms such as EZW, SPIHT, SPECK, or JPEG2000. In this work, we introduce both forward (F-pSQ) and inverse perceptual quantization (I-pSQ) into the Hi-SET coder [4–6]. An advantage of introducing pSQ is to maintain the embedded features not only of Hi-SET algorithm but also of any wavelet-based image coder. Thus, we call CBPF quantization + Hi-SET=CHi-SET or XSET.

Both JPEG2000 and XSET choose their VFWs according to a final viewing condition. When JPEG2000 modifies the quantization step size with a certain visual weight, it needs to explicitly specify the quantizer, which is not very suitable for embedded coding. By contrast, XSET needs neither to store the visual weights nor to necessarily specify a quantizer in order to keep its embedded coding properties.

The main challenge underlies in to recover not only a good approximation of coefficients Q but also the visual weight $\alpha(v,r)$ (Equation 2) that weighted them. A recovered approximation $\hat{Q}$ with a certain distortion Λ is decoded from the bitstream by the entropy decoding process. The VFWs were not encoded during the entropy encoding process, since it would increase the amount of stored data. A possible solution is to embed these weights $\alpha(v,r)$ into $\hat{Q}$. Thus, our goal is to recover the $\alpha(v,r)$ weights only using the information from the bitstream, namely, from the Forward quantized coefficients $\hat{Q}$. Thus, our goal is to recover the $\alpha(v,r)$ weights only using the information from bitstream, namely, from the forward quantized coefficients.

The reduction of the dynamic range is uniformly made by the perceptual quantizer, thus the statistical properties of I are maintained in $\hat{Q}$.

Therefore, our hypothesis is that an approximation $\hat{\alpha}(v,r)$ of $\alpha(v,r)$ can be recovered applying CBPF to $\hat{Q}$, with the same viewing conditions used in I. That is, $\hat{\alpha}(v,r)$ is the recovered e-CSF. Thus, the perceptual inverse quantizer or the recovered $\hat{\alpha}(v,r)$ introduces perceptual criteria to inverse scalar quantizer and is given by

$$\hat{I}=\begin{cases} \displaystyle\sum_{s=1}^{n}\sum_{o=v,h,dgl} \text{sign}(\hat{\omega}_{s,o})\left\lfloor \frac{\Delta_s(|\hat{\omega}_{s,o}|+\delta)}{\hat{\alpha}(v,r)}\right\rfloor + (|\hat{c}_n|+\delta)\Delta_n, & \hat{\omega}_{s,o}>0 \\ 0, & \hat{\omega}_{s,o}=0 \end{cases} \qquad (3)$$

3.2 STARTUP CONSIDERATIONS

(1) *Hilbert space-filling Curve*: The Hilbert curve is an iterated function, which can be represented by a parallel rewriting system, more precisely an L-system. In general, the L-system structure is a tuple of four elements:
(a) *Alphabet*: the variables or symbols to be replaced.
(b) *Constants*: set of symbols that remain fixed.

(c) *Axiom* or *initiator*: the initial state of the system.

(d) *Production rules*: how variables are replaced.

In order to describe the Hilbert curve alphabet let us denote the upper left, lower left, lower right, and upper right quadrants as W, X, Y, and Z, respectively, and the variables as U *(up, W-X-Y-Z), L (left, W-Z-Y-X), R (right, Z-W-X-Y)*, and D *(down, X-W-Z-Y)*. Where - indicates a movement from a certain quadrant to another. Each variable represents not only a trajectory followed through the quadrants, but also a set of 4^m transformed pixels in m level. The structure of the proposed Hilbert Curve representation does not need fixed symbols, since it is just a linear indexing of pixels. It is appropriate to say that the original work made by David Hilbert [7], proposes an axiom with a D trajectory (Figure 2(a)), while it is proposed to start with an U trajectory (Figure 2(b)). This proposal is based on the most of the image energy is concentrated where the higher subbands with lower frequencies are, namely, at the upper-left quadrant. The first three levels are portrayed in left-to-right order by Figure 2(a) and (b).

The production rule set of the Hilbert curves is defined as follows: U is changed by the string $LUUR$, L by $ULLD$, R by $DRRU$ and D by $RDDL$. In this

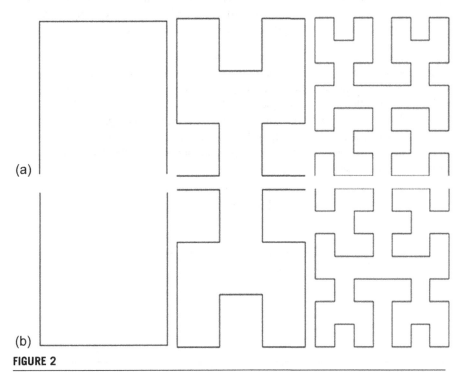

(a)

(b)

FIGURE 2

First three levels of a Hilbert Curve. (a) Axiom = D proposed by David Hilbert [7].
(b) Axiom = U employed in this chapter.

way, high-order curves are recursively generated replacing each former level curve with the four later level curves.

The Hilbert Curve process remains in an area as long as possible before moving to the neighboring region. Hence, the correlation between pixels is maximized, which is an important image compression issue. Since the higher the correlation at the preprocessing, the more efficient the data compression.

(2) *Linear Indexing*: A linear indexing is developed in order to store the coefficient matrix into a vector. Let us define the wavelet transform coefficient matrix as H and the interleaved resultant vector as $\hat{H}$, being $2^{\gamma} \times 2^{\gamma}$ be the size of H and 4^{γ} the size of H, where γ, is the Hilbert curve level. Algorithm 1 generates a Hilbert mapping matrix θ with level γ, expressing each curve as four consecutive indexes.

The level γ of θ is acquired concatenating four different θ transformations in the previous level, $\gamma - 1$. Algorithm 1 generates the Hilbert mapping matrix θ, where $\tilde{\beta}$ refers a 180° rotation of β and β^{T} is the linear algebraic transpose of β. Thus, each wavelet coefficient at $H_{(i,j)}$ is stored and ordered at $\vec{H}_{\theta(i,j)}$, being $\theta(i,j)$ the location index into $\vec{H}$.

(3) *SignificanceTest*: Asignificance test is defined as the trial of whether a coefficient subset achieves the predetermined significance level or threshold in order to be a significant or insignificant. It defines how these subsets are formed and what are the coefficients considered significant.

With the aim of recovering the original image at different qualities and compression ratios, it is not needed to sort and store all the coefficients $\vec{H}$ but just a subset of them: the subset of significant coefficients. Those coefficients H_i such that $2^{thr} \leq \left|\vec{H}_i\right|$ are called *significant* otherwise they are called *insignificant*. The smaller the *thr*, the better the final image quality and the lower the compression ratio.

Let us define a bit-plane as the subset of coefficients S_0 such that $2^{thr} \leq |S_0| \leq 2^{thr+1}$. The significance of a given subset S_0 among a particular bit-plane is store at $\hat{H}_{sig}$ and can be defined as:

$$\hat{H}_{sig} = \begin{cases} 1, & 2^{thr} \leq |S_0| \leq 2^{thr+1} \\ 0, & \text{otherwise} \end{cases} \tag{4}$$

Input: γ
Output: θ
1 if $\gamma = 1$ then
2 $\quad \theta = \begin{bmatrix} 1 & 4 \\ 2 & 3 \end{bmatrix}$
3 else
4 $\quad \beta = \textbf{Algorithm 1} \ (\gamma - 1)$
5 $\quad \theta = \begin{bmatrix} \beta^{T} & (\tilde{\beta})^{T} + (3 \times 4^{\gamma-1}) \\ \beta + 4^{\gamma-1} & \beta + (2 \times 4^{\gamma-1}) \end{bmatrix}$

ALGORITHM 1

Function to generate Hilbert mapping matrix θ of size $2^{\gamma} \times 2^{\gamma}$.

Data: $\mathcal{S}_o$, *thr*
Result: $\mathcal{S}_1$, $\mathcal{S}_2$, $\mathcal{S}_3$, $\mathcal{S}_4$ and $\widehat{\mathcal{H}_{sig}}$
1 $\gamma = \log_4(length\ of\ \mathcal{S}_o)$
2 The cell 1 of the subsets $\mathcal{S}_1$, $\mathcal{S}_2$, $\mathcal{S}_3$ and $\mathcal{S}_4$ is declared with $4^{\gamma-1}$ elements, while the cell 2 with just one element.
3 $i = 1$
4 $\widehat{\mathcal{H}_{sig}}$ is emptied.
5 **for** $j=1$ **to** 4^{γ} **do**
6   Store $\mathcal{S}_o\left[from\ j\ to\ \left(i \times 4^{\gamma-1}\right)\right]$ into $\mathcal{S}_i(1)$.
7   **if** $2^{thr} \leq \max|\mathcal{S}_i(1)| < 2^{thr+1}$ **then**
8          $\mathcal{S}_i(2) = 1$
9   Add **1** at the end of the $\widehat{\mathcal{H}_{sig}}$.
10   **else**
11         $\mathcal{S}_i(2) = 0$
12   Add **0** at the end of the $\widehat{\mathcal{H}_{sig}}$.
13   i and j are incremented by 1 and $4^{\gamma-1}$, respectively.

ALGORITHM 2

Subset significance test.

Algorithm 2 shows how a given subset S_0 is divided into four equal parts (line 6) and how the significance test (lines 7-12) is performed, resulting in four subsets (S_1, S_2, S_3, and S_4) with their respective significance stored at the end of $\hat{H}_{sig}$. Subsets S_1, S_2, S_3, and S_4 are four 2×1 cell arrays. The fist cell of each array contains one of the four subsets extracted from $S_0(S_i(1))$ and the second one stores its respective significance test result ($S_i(2)$).

3.3 CODING ALGORITHM

Similar to SPIHT and SPECK [8,9], Hi-SET considers three coding passes: initialization, sorting, and refinement, which are described in the following subsections. SPIHT uses three ordered lists, namely, the *list of insignificant pixels* (LIP), the *list of significant sets* (LIS), and the *list of significant pixels* (LSP). The latter list represents just the individual coefficients, which are considered the most important ones. SPECK employs two of these lists, the LIS and the LSP. Whereas Hi-SET makes use of only one ordered list, the LSP.

Using a single LSP place extra load on the memory requirements for the coder, since the total number of significant pixels remains the same even if the coding process is working in insignificant branches. That is why Hi-SET employs spare lists, storing significant pixels in several sub-lists. These smaller lists have the same length than significant coefficients founded in the processed branch. With the purpose of expediting the coding process it is used not only spare lists, but also spare cell arrays, both are denoted by an prime, LSP', H', or S_1', for instance.

(1) *Initialization Pass*: The first step is to define threshold thr as

$$\text{thr} = \left\lfloor \log_2\left(\max\left\{\vec{H}\right\}\right)\right\rfloor, \tag{5}$$

that is, thr is the maximum integer power of two not exceeding the maximum value found at $\vec{H}$.

Data: S_1, S_2, S_3, S_4, *thr* and γ
Result: *LSP* and $\hat{\mathcal{H}}$
1 *LSP* and $\hat{\mathcal{H}}$ are emptied.
2 **if** $\gamma = 0$ **then**
3   **for** $i = 4$ to 1 **do**
4   **if** $S_i(2)$ *is significant* **then**
5   Add $S_i(1)$ at the beginning of the *LSP*.
6   **if** $S_i(1)$ *is positive* **then**
7   Add **0** at the beginning of the $\hat{\mathcal{H}}$.
8   **else**
9   Add **1** at the beginning of the $\hat{\mathcal{H}}$.

10 **else**
11   **for** $i=1$ to 4 **do**
12   **if** $S_i(2)$ *is significant* **then**
13   Call **Algorithm 2** with $S_i(1)$ and *thr* as input data and Store the results into S'_1, S'_2, S'_3, S'_4 and $\hat{\mathcal{H}}'$.
14   Add $\hat{\mathcal{H}}'$ at the end of the $\hat{\mathcal{H}}$.
15   Call **Algorithm 3** with S'_1, S'_2, S'_3, S'_4, *thr* and $\gamma - 1$ as input data and Store the results into $\hat{\mathcal{H}}'$ and *LSP'*.
16   Add $\hat{\mathcal{H}}'$ at the end of the $\hat{\mathcal{H}}$.
17   Add *LSP'* at the end of the *LSP*.

ALGORITHM 3

Sorting pass.

The second step is to apply Algorithm 2 with thr and $\vec{H}$ as input data, which divides $\vec{H}$ into four subsets of $4^{\gamma-1}$ coefficients and adds their significance bits at the end of $\hat{H}$.

(2) *Sorting Pass*: Algorithm 3 shows a simplified version of the classification or sorting step of the H*i*-SET Coder. The H*i*-SET sorting pass exploits the recursion of fractals. If a quadtree branch is *significant* it moves forward until finding an individual pixel, otherwise the algorithm stops and codes the entire branch as *insignificant*.

Algorithm 3 is divided into two parts: Sign Coding (lines 2-9) and Branch Significance Coding (lines 11-16). The algorithm performs *the Sign Coding* by decomposing a given quadtree branch up to level, $\gamma=0$, i.e., the branch is represented by only 4 coefficients with at least one of them being *significant*. The initial value of γ is $\log_4\left(\text{length of } \vec{H}\right) - 4$. Only the sign of the significant coefficients is coded, 0 for positives and 1 for negatives. Also, each significant coefficient is added into a spare LSP or LSP'.

The Branch Significance Coding calls Algorithm 2 in order to quarter a branch in addition to call recursively an entire sorting pass at level, $\gamma - 1$ up to reach the elemental level when, $\gamma=0$. The Significance Test results of a current branch (obtained by the Algorithm 2) and the ones of next branches (acquired by Algorithm 3, denoted as $\hat{H}$) are added at the end of $\hat{H}$. Also, all the significant coefficients found in previous branches (all the lists LSP') are added at the end of the LSP. This process is repeated for all four subsets of $\vec{H}$.

(3) *Refinement Pass*: At the end of $\hat{H}$, the (thr -1)-th most significant bit of each ordered entry of the LSP, including those entries added in the last sorting pass, are added. Then, thr is decremented and another sorting pass is performed. the sorting and refinement steps are repeated up to thr $=1$.

The decoder employs the same mechanism as the encoder, since it knows the fractal applied to the original image. When the bitstream $\hat{H}$ is received, by itself describes the significance of every variable of the fractal. Then with these bits, the decoder is able to reconstruct both partially and completely, the same fractal structure of the original image, refining the pixels progressively as the algorithm proceeds.

4 EXPERIMENTS AND RESULTS

For the sake of comparing the performance between the JPEG2000 [10] and XSET coders, both algorithms are tested according to the process depicted in Figure 3. First an XSET compression with certain viewing conditions is performed, which gives a compressed image with a particular bit-rate (bpp). Then, a JPEG2000 compression is performed with the same bit-rate. Once both algorithms recover their distorted images, they are compared with some numerical image quality estimators such as: MSSIM [11], PSNR [12], SSIM [13], VIF [14], UQI [15], and WSNR [16].

This experiment is performed across the CMU [17] and IVC [18] Image Databases. Image quality estimations are assessed by the six metrics mentioned before.

Figures 4 and 5 show the perceptual quality, estimated by Figure 4(a) MSSIM, Figure 4(c) SSIM, Figure 5(a) UQI, Figure 5(b)VIF and Figure 5(c) WSNR, in addition to the objective quality Figure 4(b) PSNR, of the recovered color images both

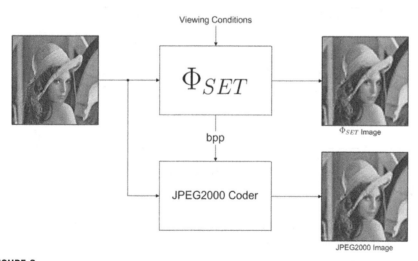

FIGURE 3

Process for comparing JPEG2000 and XSET. Given some viewing conditions a XSET compression is performed obtaining a particular bit-rate. Thus, a JPEG2000 compression is performed with such a bit-rate.

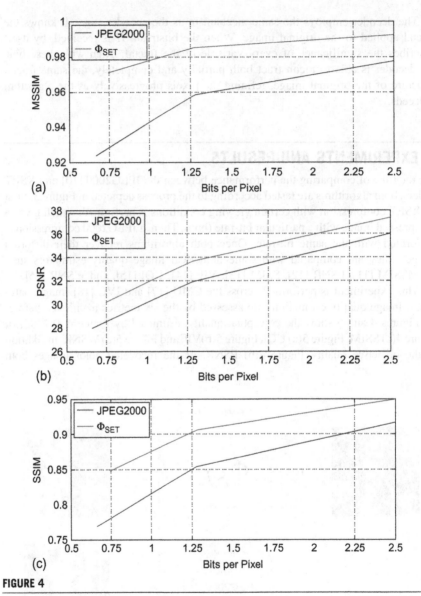

FIGURE 4

Comparison between XSET (green functions; light gray in print versions) and JPEG2000 (blue functions; dark gray in print versions) image coders. Compression rate versus image quality assessed by (a) MSSIM, (b) PSNR and (c) in the CMU image database.

for JPEG2000 (Blue function; dark gray in print versions) and XSET (Green function; light gray in print versions) as a function of their compression rate. For this experiment, we employ the CMU Image Database and the *Kakadu* implementation for JPEG2000 compression [19]. On the average, a color image compressed at 1.0 bpp (1:24 ratio,

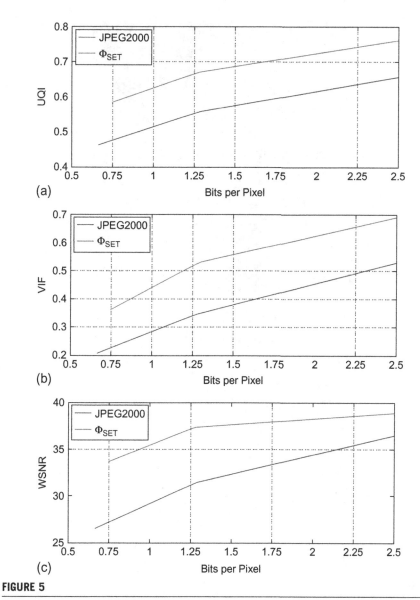

FIGURE 5

Comparison between XSET (green functions; light gray in print versions) and JPEG2000 (blue functions; dark gray in print versions) image coders. Compression rate versus image quality assessed by (a) UQI, (b) VIF, and (c) WSNR in the CMU image database.

stored in 32 kB) by JPEG2000 coder has MSSIM$=0.9424$, SSIM$=0.8149$, UQI$=0.5141$, VIF$=0.2823$ and WSNR$=29.2$ of perceptual image quality, and PSNR$=30.11$ of objective image quality, while by XSET has MSSIM$=0.9780$, SSIM$=0.8758$, UQI$=0.6249$, VIF$=0.4387$, WSNR$=35.41$ and PSNR$=31.84$. In Figure 6, we can see these differences when images (a-b) *Lenna*, (c-d) *Girl2*, and

FIGURE 6

Example of recovered color images *Lenna*, *Girl2*, and *Tiffany* of the CMU image database compressed at (a and d) 0.92 bpp, (b and e) 0.54 bpp, and (c and f) 0.93 bpp, respectively. JPEG2000 Images are compressed using Table 1 and $s=3$. (a) JPEG2000, MSSIM$=0.9595$; (b) JPEG2000, MSSIM$=0.9742$;

FIGURE 6, CONT'D

(c) JPEG2000, MSSIM = 0.9274; (d) XSET, MSSIM = 0.9829;

(Continued)

FIGURE 6, CONT'D

(e) XSET, MSSIM=0.9948; and (f) XSET, MSSIM=0.9798.

(e-f) *Tiffany* are compressed at 0.92, 0.54, and 0.93 bpp, respectively, by JPEG2000 and XSET. For example, for these three images, the average difference of MSSIM is 0.0321 in favor of XSET. Therefore, for this image database, XSET has clearly improvement of visual quality than JPEG2000.

5 CONCLUSIONS

The main goal of this chapter is to introduce perceptual criteria on the image compression process. These perceptual criteria are used to identify and to remove non-perceptual information of an image. These aspects are used to propose a perceptual image compression system. Additionally, the coder based on Hilbert scanning (Hi-SET) is also presented.

The Hi-SET coder, presented in Section 3, is based on Hilbert scanning of embedded quadTrees. It has low computational complexity and some important properties of modern image coders such as embedding and progressive transmission. This is achieved by using the principle of partial sorting by magnitude when a sequence of thresholds decreases. The desired compression rate can be controlled just by chunking the stream at the desired file length. When compared to other algorithms that use Hilbert scanning for pixel ordering, Hi-SET improves image quality by around 6.20 dB. Hi-SET achieves higher compression rates than JPEG2000 coder not only for high and medium resolution images but also for low resolution ones where it is difficult to find redundancies among spatial frequencies. Table 2 summarizes the average improvements when compressing the TID2008 Image Database [20].

The Hi-SET coder improves the image quality of the JPEG2000 coder around $PSNR = 1.16$ dB for gray-scale images and 1.43 dB for color ones. Furthermore, it saves around 0.245 bpp for high-resolution gray-scale images. Thus, the results across the CMU image database resulted Hi-SET improved the results of JPEG2000 not only objectively but also by metrics like MSSIM, VIF, or WPSNR, which are perceptual indicators.

This is why in Section 3.1 Forward (F-pSQ) and Inverse (I-pSQ) perceptual quantizer using CBPF are defined. When F-pSQ and I-pSQ are incorporated to Hi-SET, a perceptual image compression system XSET is proposed. In order to measure the effectiveness of the perceptual quantization, a performance analysis is done using the most important image quality assessments such as PSNR, MSSIM, VIF, or WSNR. In addition, when both forward and inverse perceptual quantization are applied into Hi-SET, namely, using XSET, it significatively improves the results regarding the JPEG2000 compression.

Table 2 Average PSNR(DB) Improvement of Hi-SET in Front of JPEG2000 for TID2008 Image Database

Components	Y		YC_bC_r	
Resolution	Low	Medium	Low	Medium
Compression ratio (bpp)	0.55	0.17	0.93	0.33
Image quality (dB)	1.84	0.43	1.79	1.06

ACKNOWLEDGMENT

This work is supported by National Polytechnic Institute of Mexico by means of Project No. 20140096, the Academic Secretary and the Committee of Operation and Promotion of Academic Activities (COFAA), National Council of Science and Technology of Mexico by means of Project No. 204151/2013, and LABEX Σ-LIM France, Coimbra Group Scholarship Programme granted by University of Poitiers and Region of Poitou-Charentes, France.

REFERENCES

[1] Boliek M, Christopoulos C, Majani E. Information Technology: JPEG2000 Image Coding System, JPEG 2000 Part I final committee draft version 1.0 ed., ISO/IEC JTC1/SC29 WG1, JPEG 2000; April 2000.

[2] Otazu X, Párraga C, Vanrell M. Toward a unified chromatic induction model. J Vis 2010;10(12), No. 6, 1–24.

[3] Mullen K. The contrast sensitivity of human color vision to red-green and blue-yellow chromatic gratings. J Physiol 1985;359:381–400.

[4] Moreno J, Otazu X. Image coder based on Hilbert Scanning of Embedded quadTrees, In: IEEE Data compression conference; 2011.

[5] Moreno J, Otazu X. Image coder based on Hilbert Scanning of Embedded QuadTrees. Data Compression Conference (DCC) 2011:470,470, 29–31 Mar.

[6] Moreno J, Otazu X. Image coder based on Hilbert Scaning of Embedded quadTrees: an introduction of Hi-SET coder, In: IEEE international conference on multimedia and expo, July 2011; 2011.

[7] Hilbert D. Über die stetige Abbildung einer Linie auf ein Flächenstück. Math Ann 1891;38(3):459–60.

[8] Pearlman WA, Said A. Image wavelet coding systems: part II of set partition coding and image wavelet coding systems. Found Trends Sig Process 2008;2(3):181–246.

[9] Pearlman WA, Said A. Set partition coding: part I of set partition coding and image wavelet coding systems. Found Trends Sig Process 2008;2(2):95–180.

[10] Taubman DS, Marcellin MW. JPEG2000: image compression fundamentals, standards and practice. Boston, Dordrecht, London: Kluwer Academic Publishers; 2002. ISBN: 079237519X.

[11] Wang Z, Simoncelli E, Bovik A. Multiscale structural similarity for image quality assessment. In: Conference record of the thirty-seventh asilomar conference on signals, systems and computers, 2; 2003. p. 1398–402.

[12] Huynh-Thu Q, Ghanbari M. Scope of validity of PSNR in image/video quality assessment. Electron Lett 2008;44(13):800–1.

[13] Sheikh H, Bovik A. Image information and visual quality. IEEE Trans Image Process 2006;15(2):430–44.

[14] Wang Z, Bovik A, Sheikh H, Simoncelli E. Image quality assessment: from error visibility to structural similarity. IEEE Trans Image Process 2004;13(4):600–12.

[15] Wang Z, Bovik A. A universal image quality index. IEEE Sig Process Lett 2002; 9:81–4.

[16] Mitsa T, Varkur K. Evaluation of contrast sensitivity functions for formulation of quality measures incorporated in halftoning algorithms. In: IEEE international conference on acoustics, speech and signal processing, vol. 5. p. 301–4.

[17] S.I.P.I. of the University of Southern California. The USC-SIPI image database. Signal and Image Processing Institute of the University of Southern California. [Online]. Available: http://sipi.usc.edu/database/; 1997.

[18] le Callet P, Autrusseau F. Subjective quality assessment IRCCyN/IVC database. http://www.irccyn.ec-nantes.fr/ivcdb/; 2005.

[19] Taubman D. Kakadu software. [Online]. Available: http://www.kakadusoftware.com/; July 2010.

[20] Ponomarenko N, Lukin V, Zelensky A, Egiazarian K, Carli M, Battisti F. TID2008 -a database for evaluation of fullreference visual quality assessment metrics. Adv Modern Radioelect 2009;10:30–45.

Security surveillance applications utilizing parallel video-processing techniques in the spatial domain

8

Leonidas Deligiannidis[1], Hamid R. Arabnia[2]

[1]Wentworth Institute of Technology, Department of Computer Science, Boston, MA, USA
[2]University of Georgia, Computer Science, Athens, GA, USA

1 INTRODUCTION

One of the most important goals of security surveillance is to collect and disseminate real-time information and provide situational awareness to operators and security analysts [1]. Only then educated decisions and future reasoning can be made and prevent undesirable incidents [2]. The need for surveillance spans in many domains, including commercial buildings, law enforcement, the military, banks, parking lots, city settings as well as hallways and entrances to buildings, etc. Most of today's surveillance is used primarily as a forensic tool, to investigate what has already happened, and not to prevent an incident. Detection of objects, people, peoples' faces [3], cars, and their pattern of movement is necessary to enhance automated decision making and alarming. This is a difficult problem to solve [4]. One of the most common approaches to solving this problem is background subtraction [4–6] where each pixel is compared to its intensity value and if the change is above a threshold, it is marked as motion detected. In Ref. [2] the authors developed an object detection system that is based on pixel and region analysis and gives better results in sudden pixel intensity variations. Many times motion detection alone may not be enough. The identity of the object or person that triggers the motion detector may need to be identified. Other times the trajectory of the moving entity may need to be tracked [7–9].

2 GRAPHICAL PROCESSING UNIT AND COMPUTE UNIFIED DEVICE ARCHITECTURE

Originally, graphics processors were used primarily to render images. In recent years, however, these graphical processing units (GPUs) are also used to solve problems involving massive data-parallel processing. Thus, GPUs have been transformed to general purpose graphical processing units (GPGPUs) and can be viewed as external devices that can perform parallel computations for problems that don't only involve graphics.

Lately, GPUs have experienced a tremendous growth, mainly driven by the gaming industry. GPUs are now considered to be programmable architectures and devices consisting of several many-core processors capable of running hundreds of thousands of threads concurrently.

NVIDIA Corporation provides a new API that utilizes C/C++ to program their graphics cards. This API is called CUDA (Compute Unified Device Architecture) [10] and enables us to utilize relatively easily data-parallel algorithms [11–13]. CUDA has been used in simulations [14–16], genetic algorithms [17], DNA sequence alignment [18], encryption systems [19,20], image processing [21–29], digital forensics [30], and other fields.

CUDA is available for most operating systems, and it is freely available; CUDA is restricted to NVidia graphics cards, however, CUDA is a highly parallel computing platform and programming model and provides access to an elaborate GPU memory architecture and parallel thread execution management. Each thread has a unique identifier. Each thread can then perform the same operation on different sets of data.

A CUDA program consists of two main components. The program that runs on the host computer and functions (called kernels) that run on the GPU. Each kernel is executed as a batch of threads organized as a grid of thread blocks. The size of the grid and blocks is user configurable to fit the problem's requirements. These blocks can be configured as 1D, 2D, or 3D matrices. This architecture is built around a scalable array of multithreaded streaming multiprocessors. CUDA uses a single instruction multiple thread architecture that enables us to write thread-level parallel code.

CUDA also features several high-bandwidth memory spaces to meet the performance requirements of a program. For example, Global memory is memory accessed by the host computer and by the GPU. Other memory types are only accessible by the kernels and reside within the chip and provide a much lower latency: a read-only constant memory, shared memory (which is private for each block of threads only), a texture cache and, finally, a two-level cache that is used to speed up accesses to the global memory. Coordination between threads within a kernel is achieved through synchronization barriers. However, as thread blocks run independently from all others, their scope is limited to the threads within the thread block. CPU-based techniques can be used to synchronize multiple kernels.

Generally, in a CUDA program, data are copied from the host memory to the GPU memory across the PCI bus. Once in the GPU memory, data are processed by kernels (functions that run in the GPU), and upon completion of a task the data need to be copied back to the host memory. Newer GPUs support host page-locked memory where host memory can be accessed directly by kernels, but that reduces the available memory to the rest of the applications running on the host computer. On the other hand, this eliminates the time needed to copy back and forth data from host to GPU memory and vice versa. Additionally, for image generation and manipulation application, we can use the interoperability functionality of OpenGL with CUDA to improve further the performance of an application. This is because we can render an image directly on the graphics card and avoid copying the image data from the host to GPU, and back, for each frame.

3 PARALLEL ALGORITHMS FOR IMAGE PROCESSING

Spatial domain filtering (or image processing and manipulation in the spatial domain) can be implemented using CUDA where each pixel can be processed independently and in parallel. The spatial domain is a plane where a digital image is defined by the spatial coordinates of its pixels. Another domain considered in image processing is the frequency domain where a digital image is defined by its decomposition into spatial frequencies participating in its formation. Many image-processing operations, particularly spatial domain filtering, are reduced to local neighborhood processing [31].

Let S_{xy} be the set of coordinates of a neighborhood (normally a 3×3 or 5×5 matrix) that is centered on an arbitrary pixel (x,y) of an image f.

Processing a local neighborhood generates a pixel (x,y) in the output image g. The intensity of the generated pixel value is determined by a specific operation involving the pixel in the input image at the same coordinates [32]. The spatial domain processing can be described by the following expression:

$$g(x, y) = T(f(x, y))$$

where $f(x, y)$ is the intensity value of the pixel (x,y) of the input image, $g(x, y)$ is the intensity value of the pixel (x,y) of the output image, and T is an operator defined on a local neighborhood of the pixel with coordinates (x,y), shown in Figure 1.

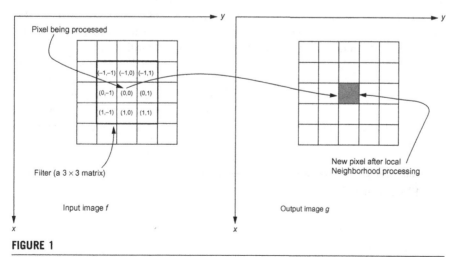

FIGURE 1

Local neighborhood processing with a 3×3 filter of an input pixel (x,y). New pixel value is stored in the output image at the same coordinates.

Because an operation of local neighborhood in the spatial domain is based on processing the local and limited area (typically a 3×3 or 5×5 matrix; also called filter kernel) around every pixel of the input image, these operations can be implemented separately and independently for each pixel, which provides the opportunity for these operations to be performed in parallel. The linear spatial filtering of an image of size $N \times M$ with a filter of size $m \times n$ is defined by the expression:

$$g(x, y) = \sum_{s=-a}^{a} \sum_{t=-b}^{b} w(s, t) f(x+s, y+t)$$

where $f(x, y)$ is the input image, $w(s, t)$ are the coefficients of the filter, and $a = \frac{n-1}{2}$, and $b = \frac{m-1}{2}$.

The pseudo-code of the algorithm is shown below. An image f of size $N \times M$ is being processed where a filter w of size $n \times m$ is applied, and the result is placed in the output image g (see Pseudo-code 1).

PSEUDO-CODE 1

```
for x=1 to N do
 for y=1 to M do
  Out=0;
  for s=-a to a do
   for t=-b to b do
    // calculate the weighted sum
    Out=Out+f(x+s, y+t) * w(s,t)
  g(x,y)=Out
```

Normally, the filter size is small in size, ranging from 3×3 to 5×5 matrices. The image size is, however, could be in thousands of pixels especially when we are working with high-definition images and video. In the above algorithm, we see four nested loops. However, only the outer two loops need to be iterated many times; since the inner two loops iterate nine times total for a 3×3 filter. Thus, to speed up performance we need to parallelize the outer two loops first, before even considering to parallelize the two inner loops. We can visualize the entire image as a long one-dimensional array of pixels; that's how it is stored in memory anyway. Now we can rewrite the above algorithm as such (see Pseudo-code 2).

PSEUDO-CODE 2

```
foreach pixel p in f do
 x=p.getXcoordinates()
 y=p.getYcoordinates()
 Out=0
 for s=-a to a do
  for t=-b to b do
```

```
// calculate the weighted sum
Out=Out+f(x+s, y+t) * w(s,t)
g(x,y)=Out
```

The above algorithm collapses the two outer loops. Now, using Cuda's built-in thread and block identifiers, we can launch $N \times M$ threads where each thread will be processing a single pixel and thus eliminating the expensive two outer loops. Note that the two inner loops are not computationally expensive and can be left alone. So the revised parallel algorithm will look like Pseudo-code 3:

PSEUDO-CODE 3

```
x=getPixel(threadID).getXcoordinates()
y=getPixel(threadID).getYcoordinates()
Out=0
for s=-a to a do
 for t=-b to b do
  // calculate the weighted sum
  Out=Out+f(x+s, y+t) * w(s,t)
g(x,y)=Out
```

The same CUDA function can be called for different filtering effects by passing a reference to a filter. Since the filters do not change, they can be placed in Constant memory for decreased access time. The Cuda kernel is shown below in Code 1. The filter is placed in Constant memory for increased performance. *ptr is a pointer to the input image, and *result is a pointer to the output image. Since this kernel is invoked on RGB images, the filter is applied on all three colors and the result is constrained to values from 0 to 255 using our T() function.

4 APPLICATIONS FOR SURVEILLANCE USING PARALLEL VIDEO PROCESSING

Based on the topics described earlier, we can implement several algorithms for practical surveillance applications. These algorithms that we will describe can run serially, but for improved performance we can run them in parallel. To implement and execute these algorithms we used a Lenovo W530 running Windows 8 Pro 64-bit, equipped with an i7@2.6GHz CPU, and 8GB of memory. The GPU is an NVIDIA Quadro K1000M with 192 CUDA cores.

CODE 1

```
__global__ void Parallel_kernel(uchar4 *ptr, uchar4 *result,
      const int filterWidth, const int filterHeight) {
 // map from threadIdx/BlockIdx to pixel position
```

```
int x = threadIdx.x + blockIdx.x * blockDim.x;
int y = threadIdx.y + blockIdx.y * blockDim.y;
int offset = x + y * blockDim.x * gridDim.x;
if( offset >= N*M ) return; // in case we launched more threads than we
need.
int w = N;
int h = M;
float red = 0.0f, green = 0.0f, blue = 0.0f;
//multiply every value of the filter with corresponding image pixel.
//Note: filter dimensions are relatively very small compared to the
dimensions of an image.
for(int filterY = 0; filterY < filterHeight; filterY++) {
  for(int filterX = 0; filterX < filterWidth; filterX++) {
    int imageX = ((offset%w) - filterWidth / 2 + filterX + w) % w;
    int imageY = ((offset/w) - filterHeight / 2 + filterY + h) % h;
    red += ptr[imageX + imageY*w].x * filterConst[filterX
+filterY*filterWidth];
    green += ptr[imageX + imageY*w].y * filterConst[filterX
+filterY*filterWidth];
    blue += ptr[imageX + imageY*w].z * filterConst[filterX+
filterY*filterWidth];
  }
}
//truncate values smaller than zero and larger than 255, and store the
result.
result[offset].x = T(int(red));
result[offset].y = T(int(green));
result[offset].z = T(int(blue));
}
```

For a camera, we used an Axis P13 series network camera attached to a Power Over Ethernet 100 Gbit switch. We wrote software that communicates with the camera using the HTTP protocol, to instruct the camera when to begin and end the video feed as well as changing the resolution of the feed. The camera transmits the video in Motion JPG format. Each frame is delimited with special tags and the header for each image frame contains the length of the data frame. We used the std_image (http://nothings.org/stb_image.c) package to decode each JPG image before passing the image frame to our processing algorithms.

4.1 MOTION DETECTOR

The first algorithm detects motion in the field of view of the camera. To implement this algorithm, we need to keep track of the previous frame to see if the current and the previous frames differ and by how much. We first calculate the square difference of the previous and the current frame; this operation is done for every pixel.

If this difference is above a set threshold, we fire a "Motion Detected" event, which can activate a sound alarm, etc., to get the attention of the operator. We can adjust the threshold value to make the detector more or less sensitive to pixel value changes. We can also display the pixels that triggered the alarm visually. The parallel algorithm is shown in Pseudo-code 4:

PSEUDO-CODE 4

```
//one thread for each pixel
foreach pixel p do
  color_diff=prev_color(p) - curr_color(p)
  // square of different
  color_diff *=color_diff
  // update previous color
  prev_color(p)=curr_color(p)
  // empirically chosen value.
  // can be adjusted to make detector more
  // or less sensitive to changes.
  threshold=5000
  if( color_diff>threshold ) then
    fire "Motion Detected" event
    current_color(p)=RED
  else
    leave pixel unchanged
    OR make pixel gray
    OR anything you want
```

4.2 OVER A LINE MOTION DETECTOR

Even though the Motion Detector algorithm presented earlier is a simple and useful algorithm, many times we are interested only in a section of the live video feed. This algorithm is applicable when, for example, there is a busy road on the left and a restricted area on the right of the field of view of the camera. A single line can divide the live video feed into two areas. Since a line is defined but only two points, an operator only needs to define these two points. Alarm events get generated only if there is motion above the user-defined line. To implement this algorithm, we will use the dot product of two vectors. There are two ways of calculating the dot product of two vectors:

$$a \cdot b = \|a\| \|b\| \cos \theta$$

$$a \cdot b = a1b1 + a2b2 + \cdots + anbn$$

We will use the second formula to calculate the dot product. To determine if a pixel C with coordinates (Cx, Cy) is above the user-specified line, which is defined by points A and B with coordinates (Ax, Ay) and (Bx, By) respectively, we need to do the following, as illustrated in Figure 2.

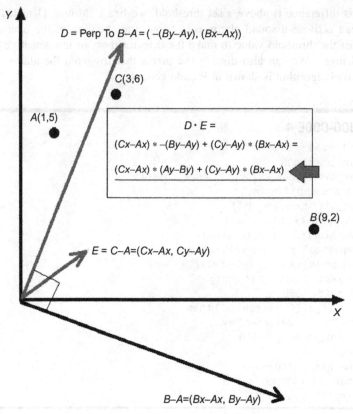

FIGURE 2

Using dot product to determining if a point is over or below a user-specified line.

First we need to find the vector that is perpendicular to the line that is defined by points A and B; we will call it vector D. We then need to find the vector E that is equal to the difference of vectors C and A. If the dot product of D and E is greater than 0, point C is above the line defined by points A and B. If it is equal to 0, point C is right on the line, otherwise point C is below the line. The parallel algorithm in pseudo-code is shown in Pseudo-code 5.

4.3 LINE CROSSING DETECTOR

Line Crossing Detector is a similar algorithm to Over a Line Detector.

PSEUDO-CODE 5

```
//one thread for each pixel
foreach pixel p do
 color_diff = prev_color(p) - curr_color(p)
```

```
// square of different
color_diff *= color_diff
// update previous color
prev_color(p) = curr_color(p)
// empirically chosen value.
// can be adjusted to make detector more
// or less sensitive to changes.
threshold = 5000
Cx = p.getXcoordinates()
Cy = p.getYcoordinates()
// calculate dot product, see Figure 2
r = (Cx-Ax)*(Ay-By) + (Cy-Ay)*(Bx-Ax)
if( r > 0 ) then // OVER THE LINE
  if ( color_diff > threshold ) then
    fire "Motion Detected" event
    current_color(p) = RED
  else
   over the line but below threshold.
   could make pixel transparent
  else // BELOW THE LINE
   do nothing, we are not
   interested in this area
```

PSEUDO-CODE 6

```
//one thread for each pixel
foreach pixel p do
 color_diff = prev_color(p) - curr_color(p)
 // square of different
 color_diff *= color_diff
 // update previous color
 prev_color(p) = curr_color(p)
 // empirically chosen value.
 // can be adjusted to make detector more
 // or less sensitive to changes.
 threshold = 5000
 Cx = p.getXcoordinates()
 Cy = p.getYcoordinates()
 // calculate dot product, see Figure 2
 r = (Cx-Ax)*(Ay-By) + (Cy-Ay)*(Bx-Ax)
 if( r >= -200 && r <= 200 ) then
  if ( color_diff > threshold ) then
    fire "On Line Motion Detected" event
    current_color(p) = RED
  else
   pixel on line, but no motion detected.
```

```
could make pixel green to show line
else // OVER or BELOW THE LINE
do nothing, we are not
interested in these areas
```

It is similar in that this algorithm is also using a line defined by two points and the dot product. However, if the dot product computed in Over a Line Motion Detector is equal to zero, then the pixel in question is located on the line.

This algorithm detects motion on the line. Because the line could be very skinny, depending on its slope, only a few pixels could end up exactly on the line. For this reason, we can make the line thicker by adjusting the limits of the dot product. Instead of checking if the dot product is equal to exactly zero, we can check if the dot product is between the positive and negative n, where n is a user-specified value. The algorithm in Pseudo-code 6 illustrates the Line Crossing Detector.

One problem with this algorithm is that the thickness of the line depends on the distance between the points A and B that specify the line. To fix this, we need to calculate the distance (length) between the two points as shown below:

```
// find length of line
distX=Ax-Bx;
distY=Ay-By;
LEN = sqrt(distX*distX+distY*distY);
if(LEN equals 0) then
  LEN=0.001;
```

and then we need to replace in Pseudo-code 6

```
if ( r >= -200 && r <= 200 ) then
```

with

```
X=4.0
if (r/LEN >= -X && r/LEN <= X) then
```

Now the width of the line does not depend on the distance of the A and B points. The value of X specifies the thickness of the line, and it does not depend on the length of the vector $\overrightarrow{AB}$. This is very useful when the user wants to dynamically adjust the position and orientation of the line by manipulating the points A and B.

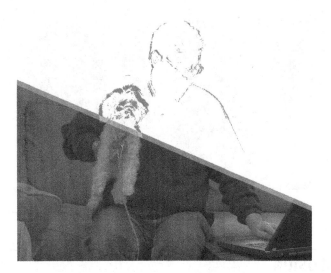

FIGURE 3

Snapshot showing motion detected above a user-specified line and on the line.

Figure 3 is a snapshot of our application showing motion detection above a user-specified line and also motion on the line, in real time on a video feed with resolution 1920×1080.

4.4 AREA MOTION DETECTOR

We can modify the Over a Line Motion Detector algorithm and instead of specifying one line, we can specify multiple lines. We can specify several detached areas or one area defined by a polygon. This algorithm can be used easily to define an area of interest or exclude the defined area; this can be done by simply reversing the order of the points that define the area. We will need to compute N number of dot products where N is the number of lines.

4.5 FIRE DETECTION

As a next step, we wanted to detect not only motion but also some type of an emergency event such as fire. If we classify the pixels that contain fire, then we can highlight these pixels (change their color, enhance their brightness, etc.) and also notify an operator. This is a difficult problem to solve as it is not very trivial to classify and recognize pixels that contain fire, flame, or smoke. We used Refs. [33,34] to figure out how to detect fire in a video stream. Then we implemented the algorithm in Ref. [33] which produced relatively accurate results as shown in Figure 4. The angle of the camera seemed to influence the fire detection, but if the fire was close to the camera, this algorithm seemed to produce accurate results. We should note here that we did not incorporate the "Compute Area" part of the algorithm presented in [33] and that could be the reason of not having our implementation producing very accurate results.

FIGURE 4

Fire detection in a video stream.

5 CONCLUSION

In this article, we presented several algorithms that are easily implemented even by undergraduate students. These algorithms have many applications in Security and more specifically in security surveillance. Using CUDA, these algorithms can be executed in parallel for increased performance. This can be done because using CUDA we can launch one thread per pixel. So, a high-resolution image or video feed can be processed in almost the same amount of time as a low resolution image or video stream. When our students implemented these algorithms as programming assignments we found that the biggest delay in the application was the network feeding the camera video stream to the application. In this paper we present the extended results of our paper initially published in Ref. [35].

ACKNOWLEDGMENTS

We would like to thank NVIDIA Corporation for providing equipment and financial support through their CUDA Teaching Center initiative. We would also like to thank Axis Communications for donating more than 20 network-enabled surveillance cameras. Their support is greatly appreciated.

REFERENCES

[1] Olsina L, Dieser A, Covella G. Metrics and indicators as key organizational assets for ICT security assessment. In: Akhgar B, Arabnia HR, editors. Emerging trends in computer science & applied computing. Emerging trends in ICT security Elsevier Inc.; 2013, ISBN: 978-0-12-411474-6.

[2] Collins RT, Lipton AJ, Fujiyoshi H, Kanade T. Algorithms for cooperative multisensor surveillance. Invited paper, Proc IEEE 2001;89(10):1456–77.

[3] Introna LD, Wood D. Picturing algorithmic surveillance: the politics of facial recognition systems. In: Norris C, McCahill M, Wood D, editors. Surveillance & Society CCTV Special, vol. 2; 2004. p. 177–98, 2/3.

[4] Toyama K, Krumm J, Brumitt B, Meyers B. Wallflower: principles and practice of background maintenance. In: Proceedings of the international conference computer vision, Corfu, Greece; 1999. p. 255–61.

[5] Haritaoglu I, Harwood D, Davis LS. W4: Real-time surveillance of people and their activities. IEEE Trans Pattern Anal Mach Intell 2000;22:809–30.

[6] Stauffer C, Grimson WEL. Learning patterns of activity using real-time tracking. IEEE Trans Pattern Anal Mach Intell 2000;22:747–57.

[7] Jiang X, Motai Y, Zhu X. Predictive fuzzy logic controller for trajectory tracking of a mobile robot. In: Proceedings of IEEE mid-summer workshop on soft computing in industrial applications; 2005.

[8] Klancar G, Skrjanc I. Predictive trajectory tracking control for mobile robots, In: Proceedings of power electronics and motion control conference; 2006. p. 373–8.

[9] Ma J. Using event reasoning for trajectory tracking. In: Akhgar B, Arabnia HR, editors. Emerging trends in computer science & applied computing. Emerging trends in ICT security Elsevier Inc.; 2013, ISBN: 978-0-12-411474-6.

[10] Nvidia Corporation's CUDA download page. https://developer.nvidia.com/cuda-down loads. Retrieved Nov. 26 2013.

[11] Husselmann AV, Hawick, KA. Spatial agent-based modeling and simulations—a review. Technical Report CSTN-153, Computer Science, Massey University, Albany, Auckland, New Zealand, October 2011. In Proc. IIMS Postgraduate Student Conference, October 2011.

[12] Husselmann AV, Hawick KA. Simulating species interactions and complex emergence in multiple flocks of birds with gpus". In: Gonzalez T, editor. Proceedings IASTED international conference on parallel and distributed computing and systems (PDCS 2011), Dallas, USA, 14-16 Dec 2011. IASTED; 2011. p. 100–7.

[13] Husselmann AV, Hawick KA. Parallel parametric optimization with firefly algorithms on graphical processing units. In: Proceedings of the international conference on genetic and evolutionary methods (GEM'12), number CSTN-141, Las Vegas, USA; 2012. p. 77–83.

[14] Sang J, Lee C-R, Rego V, King C-T. A fast implementation of parallel discrete-event simulation. In: Proceedings of the international conference on parallel and distributed processing techniques and applications (PDPTA); 2013.

[15] Rego VJ, Sunderam VS. Experiments in concurrent stochastic simulation: the eclipse paradigm. J Parallel Distrib Comput 1992;14(1):66–84.

[16] Johnson MGB, Playne DP, Hawick KA. Data-parallelism and GPUs for lattice gas fluid simulations. In: Proc. of the Int. Conf. on Parallel and Distributed Processing Techniques and Applications (PDPTA); 2010.

[17] Tadaiesky VWA, de Santana ÁL, Dias LdJC, Oliveira IdId, Jacob Jr AFL, Lobato FMF. Runtime performance evaluation of GPU and CPU using a genetic algorithm based on neighborhood model. In: Proceedings of the international conference on parallel and distributed processing techniques and applications (PDPTA); 2013.

[18] He J, Zhu M, Wainer M. Parallel sequence alignments using graphics processing unit. In: Proceedings of the international conference on bioinformatics and computational biology (BIOCOMP); 2009.

[19] Wang Z, Graham J, Ajam N, Jiang H. Design and optimization of hybrid MD5-blowfish encryption on GPUs. In: Proceedings of the international conference on parallel and distributed processing techniques and applications (PDPTA); 2011.

[20] Bobrov M, Melton R, Radziszowski S, Lukowiak M. Effects of GPU and CPU loads on performance of CUDA applications. In: Proceedings of international conference on parallel and distributed processing techniques and applications, PDPTA'11, July 2011, Las Vegas, NV, vol. II; 2011. p. 575–81.

[21] Colantoni P, Boukala N, Da Rugna J. Fast and accurate color image processing using 3d graphics cards. In: 8th International Fall Workshop: Vision Modeling and Visualization; 2003.

[22] Ahmadvand M, Ezhdehakosh A. GPU-based implementation of JPEG2000 encoder. In: Proceedings of the international conference on parallel and distributed processing techniques and applications (PDPTA); 2012.

[23] Sánchez MG, Vidal V, Bataller J, Verdú G. Performance analysis on several GPU architectures of an algorithm for noise removal. In: Proceedings of the international conference on parallel and distributed processing techniques and applications (PDPTA); 2012.

[24] Sánchez MG, Vidal V, Bataller J, Arnal J. A fuzzy metric in GPUs: fast and efficient method for the impulsive image noise removal. In: Proceedings of the international symposium on computer and information sciences (ISCIS); 2011.

[25] Stone SS, Haldar JP, Tsao SC, Hwu WW, Liang Z-P, Sutton BP. Accelerating advanced MRI reconstructions on GPUs. In: Proceedings of the 5th international conference on computing, frontiers; 2008.

[26] Xu W, Mueller D. Learning effective parameter settings for iterative ct reconstruction algorithms. In: Fully 3D image reconstruction in radiology and nuclear medicine conference; 2009.

[27] Li L, Li X, Tan G, Chen M, Zhang P. Experience of parallelizing cryo-EM 3D reconstruction on a CPU-GPU heterogeneous system. In: Proceeding HPDC 11 proceedings of the 20th international symposium on high performance distributed computing; 2011.

[28] Anderson RF, Kirtzic JS, Daescu O. Applying parallel design techniques to template matching with GPUs, vol. 6449. New York: Springer-Verlag New York Inc.; 2011.

[29] Sánchez MG, Vidal V, Bataller J, Arnal J. Implementing a GPU fuzzy filter for impulsive image noise correction. In: Proceedings of the international conference computational and mathematical methods in science and engineering (CMMSE); 2010.

[30] Chen C-h, Wu F. An efficient acceleration of digital forensics search using GPGPU, In: Proceedings of the 2013 international conference on security and management (SAM); 2012.

[31] Gonzalez RC, Woods RE. Digital image processing. 3rd ed. Prentice Hall; Upper Saddle River, NJ. 2008, ISBN: 9780131687288.

[32] Shiffman D. Learning processing: a beginner's guide to programming images, animation, and interaction. In: Morgan Kaufmann series in computer graphics. USA: Morgan Kaufmann, Elsevier; 2008, ISBN: 9780123736024.

[33] Patel P, Tiwari S. Flame detection using image processing techniques. Int J Comput Appl 2012;58(18):13–6.

[34] Çelik T, Özkaramanlı H, Demirel H. Fire and smoke detection without sensors: image processing based approach. In: 15th European signal processing conference (EUSIPCO 2007), Poznan, Poland; 2007.

[35] Deligiannidis L, Arabnia HR. Parallel video processing techniques for surveillance applications. In: Proceedings of the 2014 international conference on computational science and computational intelligence (CSCI'14), Las Vegas, NV, USA; 2014. p. 183–9.

Highlight image filter significantly improves optical character recognition on text images ☆

9

Iulia Stirb

Computer and Software Engineering Department, "Politehnica"
University of Timisoara, Timisoara, Romania

1 INTRODUCTION

Many often, the choice of the image filter is done nonautomatically, by humans, as a result of observing the characteristics of the image (color of the text and background, shape or thickness of characters in the image, noise around characters). Researches reveal that specific filters are used for certain images. For instance, if the original image is blurred and the expected result is an image with higher clarity than Sharpen filter can be used and on the other hand, if less level of details is desired in the resulting image, then Blur filter would be the right choice.

The process of selecting the scale of a filter in order to perform edge detection over the image can be automated [1]. Overall, researches have been carried out regarding the automated selection of the parameters of many filters [2, p. 86]. In other words, once the proper filter to apply to the image has been choose by humans, the filter's parameter is selected by a computer depending on the desired output image.

However, an automated analysis of the image properties in order to select the proper filters to be applied to it would be a complicated, expensive, and time-consuming process since the analysis depends on many factors (e.g., noise, clarity, or contrast of the input image).

The image filter which I named it "Highlight" is designed to be a universal filter for improving optical character recognition (OCR) rate of success on a large variety of text images and because of its large applicability it avoids the automated selection of the proper filter to be applied to a specific image.

In the Section 1, the article contains the description of the new image filter, namely, Smart Contrast, and afterwards, one major section in which the new image filter, entitled Highlight, is detailed and snippets of code from its implementation are

---

☆IPCV paper: Highlight Image Filter Significantly Improves OCR on Text Images

provided. Both sections include an overview on some already existing filters such as the nonoptimized and optimized version (using "color matrix" technique) of Contrast image filter. In the following section, the optimization technique (i.e., "byte buffer" technique) of Smart Contrast and Highlight image filters is presented, but nevertheless, "byte buffer" techniques can be applied to any image filter. Conclusions section presents the major benefit Highlight image filter brings in improving the success rate of OCR in comparison to other filters and describes the visual effect of Highlight filter on images.

1.1 PROPERTIES OF HIGHLIGHT IMAGE FILTER

Highlight image filter detects the edges of the features in the image, i.e., edges of the characters in a text image, highlights and sharpens the text, and increases the contrast in a selective manner (in a way similar to Smart Contrast image filter), that is predominantly in the areas of sudden change in color intensity like it is in the case of the edges of the characters [3, pp. 391-397].

What Highlight filter brings new regarding the way contrast is normally done is that it performs a selection between two types of transformations and chooses the proper one to be applied. Instead of simply applying the same transformation to all components of each pixel like Contrast filter would do, the selection is done for each component (e.g., Red) of each pixel separately. This improvement made by Highlight image filter (and Smart Contrast as well) regarding the way contrast is increased produces even more contrast between the text in an image and the background in cases when this is needed such as when the color of the text is close to the color of the background making the text more visible than it would be by simply applying Contrast filter.

2 DESCRIPTION OF SMART CONTRAST IMAGE FILTER

Smart Contrast filter compares the value of each component (e.g., Red) of each pixel with 127 (255/2, note that the range in which the components Red, Green, and Blue vary is 0-255 when it comes to RGB images as in this case) and if the value is less than 127, it performs a certain transformation to that specific component, if greater it performs a different transformation. As a case study, if an image that contains some text is considered and the color of the text would be $(R_t,G_t,B_t) = (126,126,125)$ and the color of the background would be $(R_b,G_b,B_b) = (130,137,136)$, then the colors would be pretty similar, so the text would be hard to recognize even for the human eye. In this case, which may often occurs, Smart Contrast filter decreases more the color of the text and increases more the color of the background than Contrast filter would do, making the text more visible and more easily to be detected by OCR. Thus, Smart Contrast keeps the good work Contrast filter does and, in addition, produces good results for edge cases.

2.1 CONTRAST IMAGE FILTER

Contrast filter is based on the transformation in Equations (1a)–(1c) where contrast is the contrast scale (the degree to which the contrast is increased) and red, green, and blue are the values of the components of a pixel:

$$((red/255.0 - 0.5) \times contrast + 0.5) \times 255.0 \tag{1a}$$

$$((green/255.0 - 0.5) \times contrast + 0.5) \times 255.0 \tag{1b}$$

$$((blue/255.0 - 0.5) \times contrast + 0.5) \times 255.0 \tag{1c}$$

The graphic representation for transformation in Equations (1a)–(1c) is represented in Figure 1 (blue plot). In the same figure, the identity function it is also drawn (green plot) to spot how pixel component values increase or decrease according to the transformation. If the value of the pixel component is less than zero, it is set to zero and if it is greater than 255, it is set to 255.

So far, the same transformation is being applied to all components of each pixel. Thus, this is how Contrast filter performs; however, the property is also specific to many other filters (e.g., Invert, Color).

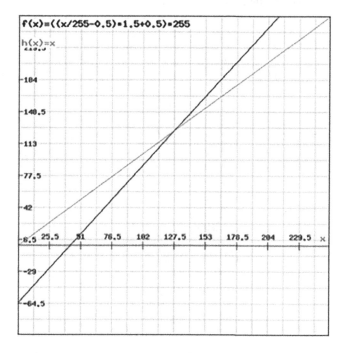

FIGURE 1

Contrast filter transformation (function f).

2.1.1 Description of the optimized implementation of contrast image filter using "color matrix" technique

Figure 2 presents an example of how "color matrix" optimization technique performs on one pixel having the, e.g., Red component equal to 51 and scaled down to 0.2 (=51/255). The input vector represents the original pixel with its components Red, Green, Blue, and Alpha in this order [4,5]. The values of the components vary in a range from 0 (=0/255) to 1 (=255/255). The last element of the input vector is used for additional computations, if needed. After the calculation of the output array, the values are scaled again to the fit into the interval [0;255].

The matrix content is specific to each filter separately and exemplified in Figure 3 for Contrast image filter. *diff* is obtained as in Equation (2) by refactoring Equations (1a)–(1c), and *scale* is the desired degree of Contrast (usually varies from 1 to 6). The fact that diff is computed only once for all pixels in the image before the filter is actually applied to the image saves a great amount of execution time spent per pixel, compared to the standard version of contrast that uses the transformation in Equations (1a)–(1c). To be more specific, this optimization technique implies successive divisions (for scaling all pixels values to the range [0;1]) and multiplications (for scaling all pixels values back to range [0;255]) which can be performed in parallel on several floating-point units provided by the underlying hardware architecture, which considerably decreases the execution time (Contrast image filter was speedup 8 times on HD images):

$$
\begin{bmatrix} 0.2 & 0.7 & 0.5 & 1.0 & 1.0 \end{bmatrix} \times
\begin{pmatrix}
2 & 0 & 0 & 0 & 0 \\
0 & 1 & 0 & 0 & 0 \\
0 & 0 & 1 & 0 & 0 \\
0 & 0 & 0 & 1 & 0 \\
0.5 & 0.1 & 0.2 & 0 & 1
\end{pmatrix}
= \begin{bmatrix} 0.9 & 0.8 & 0.7 & 1.0 & 1.0 \end{bmatrix}
$$

FIGURE 2

ColorMatrix example of multiplication for one pixel.

scale	0	0	0	0
0	scale	0	0	0
0	0	scale	0	0
0	0	0	scale	0
diff	diff	diff	diff	1

FIGURE 3

Color matrix for Contrast image filter.

$$\text{diff} = -0.5 \times (\text{scale} - 1.0) - 0.5/255.0 \tag{2}$$

The main advantages of using "color matrix" optimization technique are the significant increase in execution time (8 times for Contrast filter) and the fact that the contrast of each component, e.g., Red can be increased in a different manner than another, e.g., Green.

The drawback of "color matrix" optimization techniques is that the one and the same set of transformations must be applied to all pixels in the image.

This optimization technique should be used when the image filter performs many computations per pixel such as Contrast.

2.2 NEW IMAGE FILTER: SMART CONTRAST

Smart Contrast performs two similar transformations depending on the value of the pixel component. For less than 127 (255/2) values, the formula is illustrated by

$$((\text{value}/255.0 - 0.6) \times \text{contrast} + 0.6) \times 255.0 \tag{3}$$

Equation (4) shows the formula for values of the pixel components greater than 127.

$$((\text{value}/255.0 - 0.4) \times \text{contrast} + 0.4) \times 255.0 \tag{4}$$

Value 127 is the threshold for Smart Contrast filter and the value of the threshold is chosen to be the median value in the range from 0 to 255 (i.e., 0 is lowest value and 255 the highest value of color intensity).

As a remark, the same pixel could be the result of applying two types of transformations to its components (e.g., Red, Green, or Blue). For instance, we could focus on an arbitrary pixel that has the coordinates (x,y) relative to the upper-left corner of the image. By assuming that Equation (3) is applied to the Red component of that pixel and Equation (4) is applied to the Blue component of the same pixel, we are facing a possible situation that could arise in the algorithm. Despite this fact exemplified before, not more than one transformation will be applied to a single component of a pixel (e.g., Red component could not possibly be the result of applying Equations (3) and (4), it will have to be either (3) or (4), but not both).

Furthermore, two different pixels could be the result of applying different transformations to the same component of the two pixels, e.g., the filtered Red component of the first pixel that has the coordinates (x_1,y_1) could be the result of applying Equation (3) and the filtered Red component of the second pixel that has the coordinates (x_2,y_2) could be the result of applying Equation (4). The graphic representation of the two transformations is shown in Figure 4(a), together with the identity function that helps in spotting the way pixel components are increased or decreased. Figure 4(b) highlights the difference between Contrast and Smart Contrast algorithms. If the value of the pixel component is less than threshold 127, the blue plot describes the transformation that is applied to that certain component, else the transformation shown in the red plot is the one applied to the component.

Since the one and the same transformation is not applied to all pixels in the image, the "color matrix" optimization techniques cannot be used when it comes to Smart

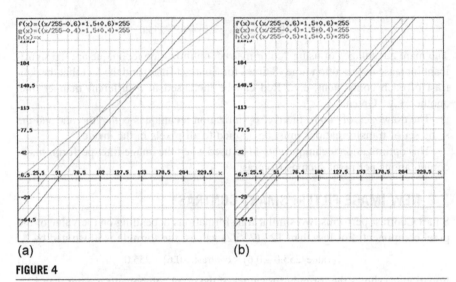

(a)   (b)

FIGURE 4

(a) Smart Contrast transformation (functions f and g) and the identity function h. (b) Smart Contrast (functions f and g) and contrast transformation (function h).

Contrast image filter. Another optimization technique is applied to this filter, as well as to the further image filter, namely, Highlight, and will be detailed at the end of the description of both image filters.

Best OCR rate of success for the filtered images using Smart Contrast filter is produced when contrast scale is set to 1.5.

2.3 VISUAL RESULT OF APPLYING SMART CONTRAST ON IMAGES

Smart Contrast filter produces the results shown in Figure 5. The results produced by Contrast filter are also shown in Figure 5 in order to spot the improvements made by Smart Contrast. The effect of applying Smart Contrast filter would be that, in most of the cases, contrast is increased in areas where edges of the objects (e.g., characters) appear in the image. Exceptions occur when the color of the characters is close to the

FIGURE 5

The visual effect of Smart Contrast image filter.

color of the background, but both are close to either the lowest color intensity or the highest color intensity. This drawback is solved in Highlight filter.

3 DESCRIPTION OF HIGHLIGHT IMAGE FILTER

This filter decreases more the values of pixel components (i.e., Red, Green, and Blue) that are less than 127 (using Equation 3) and increases more the values greater than 127 (using Equation 4) than Contrast filter would do. OCR benefits from Highlight filter's improved way of contrasting the image (which is similar to how Smart Contrast filter performs in the way that it chooses between the same transformations as Smart Contrast) and from the other two properties that are sharpening and highlighting the edges of the features in the image (e.g., the characters).

Highlight filter emphasized the areas of rapid intensity change (i.e., edges) like LoG (Laplacian of Gaussian) filter would do. Once the edges are detected, they are being sharpened, which would produce a visual effect that is similar to what Sharpen filter would do to an image. Still, the implementation of Highlight image filter has no similarities with Sharpen and LoG filters' implementation.

In addition, Highlight filter creates shadows behind characters (the color of the shadows contrasts with the color of the characters) and those shadows create a uniformly colored area that covers the noise around characters and this way it leaves no isolated noise pixel around the text that could damage the correctness of the OCR process. In a specific stage of it, the OCR engine transforms the colored filtered text image into a black and white one in which the contours of the characters are unbroken because of the uniformly colored shadows, turned to whether black or white, that fill the characters (i.e., shadows will be white if the characters are turned to white, and respectively, black if the characters are turned to black).

Precisely, all these combined properties of Highlight image filter, namely, selective contrast, sharpening and highlighting the characters, and creating contrasting shadows behind text, contribute to a high success rate of OCR on text images.

3.1 DESCRIPTION OF THE IMAGE FILTERS' VISUAL EFFECTS THAT ARE INCLUDED IN HIGHLIGHT'S VISUAL EFFECT

Smart Contrast produces an effect similar to what Contrast does, that is increasing the contrast of the image. In addition, Smart Contrast decreases more the values of pixel components that are less than 127 and increases more the values greater than 127 than Contrast would do. Highlight filter contrasts the image in a way similar to Smart Contrast.

Sharpen filter accentuates edges, but it does as well as with the noise [6], which is undesired and could make the OCR produce worse results than with the unfiltered image. Highlight filter takes the concept of spotting the edges from Sharpen filter, but does not accentuate the noise as well.

LoG combines the effects of Laplacian filter and Gaussian filter (which blurs the images in order to reduce the sensitivity to noise). While Laplacian detects the regions of rapid intensity change therefore being used in edge detection, LoG sharpens edges between two regions of uniform color but different intensities [7].

3.2 NEW IMAGE FILTER: HIGHLIGHT

Highlight filter gathers together visual effects similar to the ones produced by Smart Contrast, Sharpen, and LoG filters. The implementation is carried out in an original manner using no template convolution (masks) like the last two mentioned filters do.

Highlight filter performs a different contrast increase for each component of each pixel in the image. A component—let's take as an example the Red component—of the current pixel is increased or decreased depending on the value of the Red component of the current pixel and the two other filled with Red color pixels as in Figure 6 that shows a small 3×3 area within an image. The pixels that are not filled with Red color in Figure 6 do not contribute to the new value of the Red component of the current pixel.

Pixels that contribute to the new value of the current pixel in Figure 6 are placed in a diagonal manner. Because of this, both vertical and horizontal edges of the characters are detected.

For each component of each pixel, a contrast scale is computed separately. The way contrast scale of each component of the current pixel (x,y) is computed is emphasized in Equations (5a)–(5c), where r, g, and b indicate the Red, Green, and Blue components, respectively, and x_1y_1, x_2y_2 indicate the pixels with coordinates $(x-1,y-1)$ and $(x-2,y-2)$. For instance, $r\_x_2y_2$ is the value of the Red component of the pixel with coordinates $(x-2,y-2)$.

$$(100 + |r\_x_1y_1 - r\_xy| + |r\_x_2y_2 - r\_x_1y_1|)/100 \tag{5a}$$

$$(100 + |g\_x_1y_1 - g\_xy| + |g\_x_2y_2 - g\_x_1y_1|)/100 \tag{5b}$$

$$(100 + |b\_x_1y_1 - b\_xy| + |b\_x_2y_2 - b\_x_1y_1|)/100 \tag{5c}$$

Equations (5a)–(5c) produce values in the range from 1.0 to 6.1 and are not applied to the left and top edges of the image. Once the contrast scale for each component of each individual pixel in the image has been recorded, the algorithm is ready to be applied.

current pixel

FIGURE 6

Pixels (placed on the main diagonal) that count in computing the value of the contrast scale of each individual component (i.e., Red, Green, and Blue) of the current pixel.

The starting point of Highlight filter algorithm is based on the fact that human eye is sensitive to a difference of at least 30 between the values of at least one of the same component of two adjacent pixel when it comes to perceive and recognize characters. To be more specific, if we would have to write some characters on a background which is uniformly colored with the intensity $(R_b,G_b,B_b)=(0,0,0)$, the color of the text would have to be $(R_t,G_t,B_t)=(0+40,31+0,0)$ or $(R_t,G_t,B_t)=(0,0+31,0)$ or any other combination that would meet the above request, in order for the human eye to recognize what is written. Figure 7 proves what is being said before.

A reasonable assumption that is made from the start is that characters that would not be perceived by the human eye are not expected to be recognized by a machine using OCR, but every character perceive by the human eye must also be recognized by a machine (assuming there is no noise), or at least expect to be recognized. Thus, for the text that could not be perceived by the human eye, the performances of OCR are not improved by filtering first the text image using Highlight filter.

The core of the algorithm is described in the following. Since an example makes the general case more explicit, let's bring into discussion the Blue component of the pixel having the coordinates (x,y) relative to the upper-left corner of the image.

If the absolute difference between the value of the Blue component of the pixel with coordinates $(x-1,y-1)$ and the value of the Blue component of the pixel having the coordinates (x,y) is greater than 15 and the absolute difference between the value of the Blue component of the pixel with coordinates $(x-2,y-2)$ and the value of the Blue component of the pixel with coordinates $(x-1,y-1)$ is also greater than 15 than a certain transformation will be applied to the Blue component of the pixel having the coordinates $(x-2,y-2)$ (assuming x and y are greater than 2).

The requests described before is shown in Equations (6a)–(6c) and will be as well tested separately for the other two components, i.e., Red and Green of each pixel in the image, except for the pixels in the right and bottom edges of the image (those will not be filtered). This remark is valid for Equations (6a)–(6c), but as well for all the following formulas:

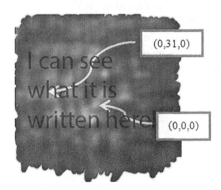

FIGURE 7

The condition to be met for the characters to be recognized by the human eye.

$$|r\_x_1y_1 - r\_xy| > 15, \quad |r\_x_2y_2 - r\_x_1y_1| > 15 \qquad (6a)$$

$$|g\_x_1y_1 - g\_xy| > 15, \quad |g\_x_2y_2 - g\_x_1y_1| > 15 \qquad (6b)$$

$$|b\_x_1y_1 - b\_xy| > 15, \quad |b\_x_2y_2 - b\_x_1y_1| > 15 \qquad (6c)$$

Why 15(30/2)? Let's assume that the text in an image has some noise around it and the transition between the color of the text and the color of the background is done through an intermediary pixel which could be called "noise pixel" which has a different color. This situation appears frequently in the real scenarios. Then, the minimum difference of 30 between the values of the color component of the background and the color component of the text is spread among three adjacent pixels (background pixel, noise pixel, and text pixel placed as the colored ones in Figure 6) with three different colors instead of just two adjacent pixels, i.e., text pixel and background pixel as in Figure 7. For instance, if the intensity of the color of the background would be $(R_b,G_b,B_b) = (0,0,0)$, the intermediate color (noise color) would have to be at least $(R_n,G_n,B_n) = (0,0,16)$ and the text color would have to be at least $(R_t,G_t,B_t) = (0,0,32)$, for the condition in Equation (6c) to be fulfilled.

Because of the diagonal manner in which the pixels which contribute to the new value of the current pixels are placed, meaning that the direction of the gradient is a diagonal direction, all the noise around curve edges that follow this direction is eliminated. Noise around vertical and horizontal edges, which form an angle of $-45°$ and $45°$ with the diagonal direction, is as well almost eliminated. Anyway, the noise affects more the curve edges than the horizontal and vertical edges.

Figure 8 shows the visual representation of all possible cases that fulfill the condition in Equation (6c), which refers to the Blue component that will be taken as an example further on. The visual representation for the Red and Green component can be obtained in the same way.

Before getting to the point where a specific transformation is applied, another condition, in addition to the one described in Equation (6c), must be first met. The new condition is described in Equation (7c).

If the conditions in Equation (7c) are fulfilled, then there is a diagonal "blue" gradient. If Equations (6c) and (7c) are met, then whether transformation (3) or (4) is applied to the Blue component of the current pixel so, therefore, the contrast for the component is increased depending on the result of the comparison with 127 (255/2):

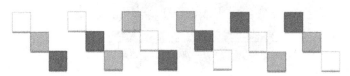

FIGURE 8

Possible cases for the condition in Equation (6c) to be fulfilled.

$$|r\_x_2y_2 - r\_xy| > 30 \qquad (7a)$$

$$|g\_x_2y_2 - g\_xy| > 30 \qquad (7b)$$

$$|b\_x_2y_2 - b\_xy| > 30 \qquad (7c)$$

Figure 9 spots the two of the six possible cases shown in Figure 8, showing the visual representation of the situations when condition in Equation (7c) is met.

If the condition in Equation (7c) is not fulfilled, then the intensity of the Blue component will be increased or decreased depending on whether the condition in Equation (8c) described below is met or not. To be more specific, if the condition in Equation (8c) is fulfilled, the intensity of the Blue component is decreased using a transformation in Equation (3) and in the opposite case, it is increased using transformation in Equation (4). Both transformations are applied, this time, regardless of the value of the Blue component:

$$|r\_x_2y_2 - r\_x_1y_1| > 0 \qquad (8a)$$

$$|g\_x_2y_2 - g\_x_1y_1| > 0 \qquad (8b)$$

$$|b\_x_2y_2 - b\_x_1y_1| > 0 \qquad (8c)$$

Transformations in Equations (3) and (4) are applied to the value of each component, i.e., *value* variable and the result depends on the contrast scale, i.e., *contrast* variable.

Figure 10 spots the two of the four left possible cases shown in Figure 8 (the first two of them were already discussed and matched with the condition in Equation (7c).

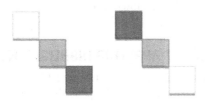

FIGURE 9

Possible cases for the condition in Equation (7c) to be fulfilled.

FIGURE 10

Possible cases for the condition in Equation (8c) to be fulfilled.

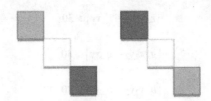

FIGURE 11

Possible cases while condition in Equation (8c) is not fulfilled.

More exactly, Figure 10 shows the visual representation of the cases which fulfill the condition in Equation (8c).

In case the condition in Equation (8c) is not fulfilled, the two left cases that were not discussed before, out of six spotted in Figure 8, are shown in Figure 11.

It was not said before what happens if the condition (6c) is not met and this will be the appropriate time to be speaking about this. Well, if the condition is not fulfilled, another condition is being tested as shown in Equation (9c).

$$|r\_x_2y_2 - r\_x_1y_1| > 15 \tag{9a}$$

$$|g\_x_2y_2 - g\_x_1y_1| > 15 \tag{9b}$$

$$|b\_x_2y_2 - b\_x_1y_1| > 15 \tag{9c}$$

If neither (9c) is fulfilled, no transformation will be applied to the Blue component of the pixel with coordinates $(x-2, y-2)$. If Equation (9c) is met, the condition in Equation (8c) will be tested again. The visual representation of the cases that meet the condition in Equation (9c) is shown in Figure 12.

3.3 VISUAL RESULTS OF APPLYING HIGHLIGHT FILTER ON IMAGES

Highlight image filter produces the results in Figure 13. It can be seen how this filter detects the edges of the characters and sharpens them (the best example would be "ALL CHANNELS" image) and how it creates contrasting shadows behind the characters (the black shadows can be best seen on white colored "Golf: Women's British Open" text in the image).

This pixel does not count

FIGURE 12

Possible cases for the condition in Equation (9c) to be fulfilled.

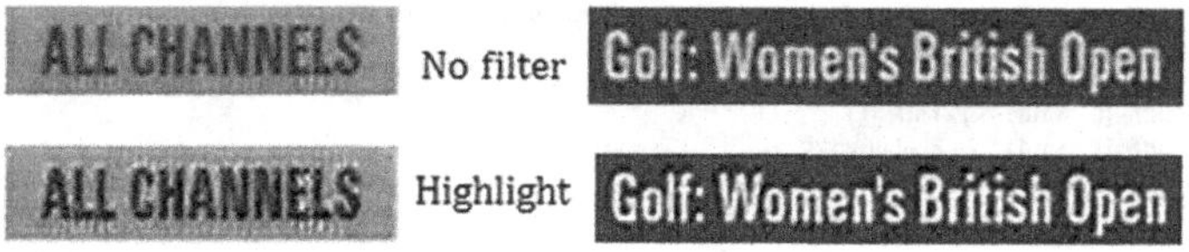

FIGURE 13

The visual effect of Highlight image filter.

Because of the shadows behind the sharpened edges of the characters and because of the increased contrast of the edges, the characters appear to be highlighted in the filtered image (a slightly 3D effect), which is the main visual effect of Highlight image filter.

3.4 HIGHLIGHT IMAGE FILTER PROGRAM CODE AND VISUAL REPRESENTATION

Part of the C# code that corresponds to Highlight image filter is being listed in Code 1. The *buffer* array stores the image representation, more exactly the Blue, Green, Red, and Alpha components in this order for the first pixel, then the components for the second pixel in the same order and so on for the rest of the pixels in the image.

The visual representation of the algorithm is shown in Figure 14. The six cases next to the first `if` are the visual representation of the condition. In other words, if the condition in Equation (6c) is met, we will found ourselves in one of the six possible cases. So far for the rest of Figure 14, the possible cases that meet the conditions are shown next to the `if`-s and `else`-s, as it is also in the case of the second `if`, for which its condition is represented visually by two out of six possible cases.

4 DESCRIPTION OF THE OPTIMIZED IMPLEMENTATION OF SMART CONTRAST AND HIGHLIGHT USING "BYTE BUFFER" TECHNIQUES

The byte buffer stores byte representation of the image, namely, Blue, Green, Red, and Alpha components in this order for each pixel as in Figure 15. An additional buffer is required for filters such as Sharpen or Blur to avoid altering the original pixels, since the new value of the current pixel depends on its neighboring pixels for these filters.

First step in the optimization algorithm is to obtain an object of type `BitmapData` (more details about this predefined class and the next ones can be found from Refs. [4,5] Web site) using `LockBits` method of `Bitmap` C# class. In next step, `Scan0` property is accessed on the obtained object in order to get the address of the first pixel in the image. Once we have this address, all the image data from it are copied to the byte buffer using the overloaded `Copy` method of `Marshal` C# class. The third step is

```
public void EdgeIntensityChange(byte[] buffer, double[] contrastBuffer, int Stride, int k)
{
    int diff01 = buffer[k - Stride * 2 - 8] - buffer[k - Stride - 4];
    int diff12 = buffer[k - Stride - 4] - buffer[k];
    int diff02 = buffer[k - Stride * 2 - 8] - buffer[k];
    // if there is a diagonal gradient
    if (Math.Abs(diff01) > 15 && Math.Abs(diff12) > 15)
    {
        if (Math.Abs(diff02) > 30) // if there is a gradient
        {
            // increase or decrease the component depending on its value, if less than 127 decrease the component value, else increase it
            buffer[k - Stride * 2 - 8] = contrastPixelComponent1(0, buffer[k – Stride * 2 - 8], contrastBuffer[k]);
        }
        else
        {
            // if the intensity of the component of the pixel with coordinates (x-2,y-2) is greater than the one of the component of the pixel with
            // coordinates (x-1,y-1)
            if (diff01 > 0)
            {
                // turn component whiter regardless of its value
                buffer[k - Stride * 2 - 8] = contrastPixelComponent1(2,
                buffer[k – Stride * 2 - 8], contrastBuffer[k]);
            }
            else
            {
                // turn component darken regardless of its value
                buffer[k - Stride * 2 - 8] = contrastPixelComponent1(1,
                buffer[k – Stride * 2 - 8], contrastBuffer[k]);
            }
        }
    }
    else if (Math.Abs(diff01) > 15)
    {
        if (diff01 > 0)
        {
            buffer[k - Stride * 2 - 8] = contrastPixelComponent1(2,
            buffer[k - Stride * 2 - 8], contrastBuffer[k]);
        }
        else
        {
            buffer[k - Stride * 2 - 8] = contrastPixelComponent1(1,
            buffer[k – Stride * 2 - 8], contrastBuffer[k]);
        }
    }
}
```

CODE 1

Part of Highlight image filter's algorithm.

different from a filter to another and represents the calculations done on the byte buffer in order to filter the image. Finally, the byte buffer will contain the byte representation of the filtered image. By using the buffer, we avoid calling SetPixel method on a Bitmap object each time the pixels needs to be set to the filtered value, which would be time consuming since the Bitmap object is accessed as many times as the number of pixels in the image. The next step is to copy the filtered buffer back to the address of the first pixel of the image using the overloaded Copy method. The last step is to unlock the Bitmap object, using UnlockBits method.

This optimization can be applied to any filter since it focuses on reducing the execution time related to image processing, not to the filter's action. The average speedup using this optimization technique is 22 times considering filters such as Smart Contrast, Highlight, Sharpen, Blur, Invert and Color.

if

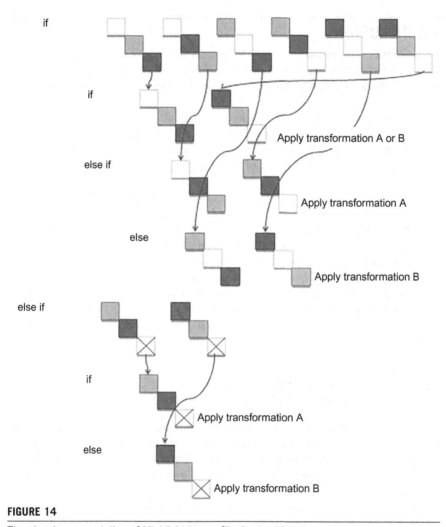

Apply transformation A or B

Apply transformation A

Apply transformation B

else if

if

Apply transformation A

else

Apply transformation B

FIGURE 14

The visual representation of Highlight image filter's algorithm.

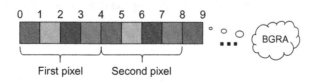

First pixel   Second pixel

FIGURE 15

Image representation storage in the byte buffer that keeps each pixel's four components.

5 CONCLUSIONS

Smart Contrast is proved to be very useful especially in edge cases, which occur actually very often, such as when the color of the characters in a text image is close to the color of the background, but nevertheless would do a great work whenever a contrast increase is desired.

I recommend the usage of Highlight filter rather than other filters in situations when the image contains areas of narrow text (but sure one can also successfully use it when the text in the image is wide). After applying this filter in the situation mentioned above, the success rate of OCR on the filtered image is considerably increased.

Probably, the most important thing to mention regarding Highlight image filter is that it eliminates the noise in the image, more exactly, it focuses on eliminating the noise located all around the edges of characters in the text image by covering the isolated noise pixels with a uniform contrasting colored area around the contour of the characters that forms the shadow of the text. Beside the actions (sharpen, contrast, highlight) of this filter, the diagonal gradient direction also contributes to removing the noise from the filtered image. The image could be also a bit blurred (not too much) and still, the OCR is improved.

In few words, Highlight filter determines outstanding OCR results on text images in which,

- Text is narrow.
- Noise is present (could be around characters).
- Any other situation (e.g., lack of contrast, too much blurring).

The effect of Highlight image filter is detecting the edges and once detected it sharpens them. As well, this filter increases the contrast in a selective manner, more exactly especially in the areas of the text image where this is the most needed (i.e., edges of the characters), saving the time that would be spent with contrasting the rest of the image. Overall, it highlights the edges.

The visual effect on characters that are present in the image would be sharpening them and increasing their contrast, creating shadows (behind them) that contrast with their color and obviously highlighting them by creating a slightly 3D effect.

As a result, Highlight filter consists of an appropriate combination of the following visual effects, which contribute together to increased performances to 98% of OCR (by first applying the filter before passing the text image to the OCR engine):

- Sharpen.
- Selective contrast.
- Highlight.

Many techniques, such as adaptive restoring of text image, have been tried [8, pp. 778-781]. Image filtering has also made an improvement in important areas, such as medicine, as described by Barber and Daft [9], but lately, improving OCR performance using filtering has become and will be a great challenge. When developing Smart Contrast, which is a nonlinear image filter, I had as a starting point the Contrast filter. Beside Smart Contrast's incontestable performances in improving OCR, this filter was actually just the triggering point for my following creation, namely, Highlight image filter, as well nonlinear, which overcomes the challenge of performing OCR with a very high success rate on text images.

NOMENCLATURE

LoG Laplacian of Gaussian
OCR optical character recognition
HD high dimension

REFERENCES

[1] Lindeberg T. Edge detection and ridge detection with automatic scale selection, Diva Academic ArchiveInt J Comput Vis 1998;30:117–54. http://www.csc.kth.se/cvap/abstracts/cvap191.html, [Accessed: 1st March 2014].

[2] Rajwade A, Rangarajan A, Benerjee A. Automated filter parameter selection using measures of noiseness. Comput Robot Vis 2010;86–93, IEEE Xplore Digital Library. Available from: http://ieeexplore.ieee.org. [Accessed: 3rd March 2014].

[3] Stirb I. Highlight image filter significantly improves optical character recognition on text images. In: Arabnia HR, editor. Proceedings of the 2014 international conference on image processing, computer vision and pattern recognition. United States of America: CSREA Press; 2014.

[4] Microsoft. ColorMatrix Class. [Online] Available from: http://msdn.microsoft.com/en-us/library/system.drawing.imaging.colormatrix(v=vs.110).aspx [Accessed: 30th July 2013]; 2014.

[5] Microsoft. Bitmap Class. [Online] Available from: http://msdn.microsoft.com/en-us/library/system.drawing.bitmap(v=vs.110).aspx [Accessed: 29th July 2014]; 2014.

[6] The GIMP Help Team. Enhanced Filters. Sharpen. [Online] Available from: http://docs.gimp.org/en/plug-in-sharpen.html. [Accessed: 1st August 2013]; 2012.

[7] Fisher R, Perkins S, Walker A, Wolfart E. Laplacian/Laplacian of Gaussian. [Online] Available from: http://homepages.inf.ed.ac.uk/rbf/HIPR2/log.htm [Accessed: 15th August 2013]; 2003.

[8] Stubberud P, Kanai J, Kalluri V. Adaptive image restoration of text images that contain touching or broken characters. In: Proceedings of the third international conference on document analysis and recognition, vol. 2; 1995, p. 778–81, IEEE Xplore Digital Library. Available from: http://ieeexplore.ieee.org [Accessed: 3rd September 2013].

[9] Barber JC, Daft C. Adaptive filtering for reduction of speckle in ultrasonic pulse-echo images. Ultrasonic 1986;24:41–4.

A study on the relationship between depth map quality and stereoscopic image quality using upsampled depth maps [*]

10

Saeed Mahmoudpour, Manbae Kim

Department of Computer and Communications Engineering, Kangwon National University, Chunchon, Gangwon, Republic of Korea

1 INTRODUCTION

The attractive 3D video applications such as 3D television (3DTV) and free-view point-video (FVV) have led to numerous researches in 3D video display technologies. Using depth information of the scene, user can experience 3D perception on 3DTV and FVV enables users to choose the desired scene view point interactively. Despite of rapid advances in 3D technology, the quality evaluation of 3D contents without a full subjective test is still difficult and human viewers are needed to judge the quality of images or videos that is a costly and time consuming task. Objective quality assessment tools like peak signal-to-noise ratio (PSNR) and structural similarity index measure (SSIM) can evaluate the 2D image quality much faster without human interference and can be implemented in a machine. Therefore, a reliable objective quality assessment tool for 3D applications is desirable. However, besides visual quality that represents the image quality regardless of depth information, several other aspects like depth quality, naturalness, visual fatigue, and discomfort should be taken into account for 3D quality evaluation [1]. As these 3D aspects are still under investigation [2,3] and in the absence of a reliable 3D quality metric, different studies attempted to evaluate the 3D quality by considering depth map properties [4,5].

Bosc et al. [6] examined the reliability of 2D image metrics in 3D evaluation considering the artifacts of stereoscopic images generated from seven different depth

---

[*]IPCV paper title: Optimum Image Quality Assessment for 3D Perception of Stereoscopic Image Generated from Upsampled Depth Map

image-based rendering (DIBR) algorithms. Considering the results, they proposed objective measurements based on analysis of shift of the contours and mean SSIM score. To investigate the correlation between depth map quality as a grayscale image and 3D video quality, different probable artifacts are applied to depth maps in Ref. [7]. In other similar research [8], the performance of three quality metrics including PSNR, SSIM, and video quality metric on coded stereoscopic images is compared with subjective test.

In this research, subjective quality assessment is utilized to measure the effect of artifacts generated from different depth map upsampling approaches on the final reconstructed stereoscopic image. Image upsampling is the method of increasing spatial resolution of images and depth map upsampling is of great importance in 3D applications. The high-speed time-of-flight cameras extract reliable depth maps. However, the spatial resolution of depth maps is relatively low in comparison with original images. Therefore, diverse depth map upsampling approaches are provided to obtain high-resolution depth maps. Also, it is important to evaluate the upsampling quality in order to realize upsampling performance on 3D content quality.

In this article, test depth maps are upsampled using seven well-known upsampling algorithms as each method can yield different artifacts. Then, the quality of each upsampled depth map is evaluated using different objective image quality assessment (IQA) tools. Also, the subjective quality assessment is used to evaluate the effect of depth map upsampling artifacts on the reconstructed stereoscopic image quality. Investigating the similarity between 2D quality evaluation and 3D perception, we will search for the most accurate IQA tool(s) for 3D quality evaluation. Using the proper automatic objective IQA tool will help to predict the quality of 3D image without using the expensive subjective test and even free of watching the stereoscopic image.

Since it is difficult to investigate all methods, seven approaches are selected to be utilized in this work. The *bilinear upsampling* uses average weighted of four neighboring pixels for interpolation to achieve upsampled depth map. A similar method called *bicubic upsampling* (BCU) is based on 16 neighboring pixels. The *bilateral upsampling* (BU) [9] is a prevalent approach that combines a spatial filter and a range filter to preserve the edge regions in upsampling process. Another upsampling method based on the BU is *joint bilateral upsampling* (JBU) [10] which utilizes both a color data and its low-resolution depth map. The *variance-based upsampling* (VBU) [11] avoids the usage of the constant variance by computing a variance for each pixel block. The disadvantage of the JBU is that it is sensitive to homogeneous regions and the weighting function can be assigned a wrong variance in nonedge regions. To solve this problem, an *adaptive bilateral upsampling* method (ABU) [12] has been proposed, where a large weight is assigned to color image at edge pixels and a large weight is assigned to depth data at nonedge pixels. To overcome the limitation in reducing blur at low-gradient edge regions in prior methods, a *distance transform-based bilateral upsampling* (DTBU) [13] has been proposed.

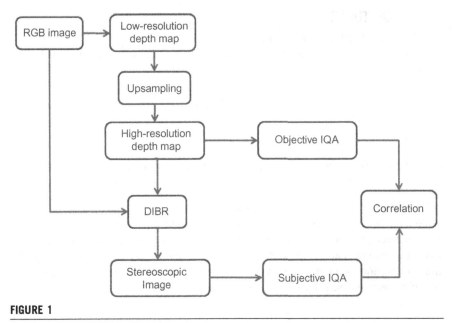

FIGURE 1

The flow diagram of experiment.

The Pearson, Spearman, and Kendall correlations are three proper approaches for similarity measurement between each objective assessment result and the subjective IQA. Comparing the objective and subjective scores, it will be inferred that which objective IQA tools show the most correspondence with human judgment and have superiority for 3D quality assessment. DIBR or 2D + Depth is used to generate a stereoscopic image. Figure 1 shows the overall framework that examines the relation between upsampling methods and 3D perception.

This article is organized as follows. In Section 2, different IQA tools considered in this work are described. Section 3 presents the subjective quality assessment methodology and the experimental results are provided in Section 4. Finally, we summarize our work in Section 5.

2 OBJECTIVE QUALITY ASSESSMENT TOOLS

Full-reference image quality assessment (FR IQA) compares test and reference images, therefore, both ground-truth and upsampled depth map are needed. The no-reference/blind image quality assessment (NR IQA) refers to quality assessment of images by an algorithm where only the distorted image is accessible and no information about the reference image is available. In this article, several FR IQA and NR IQA tools are used to evaluate the performance of different upsampling methods. The quality metrics are introduced in the following section:

2.1 FR IQA TOOLS

2.1.1 Peak signal-to-noise ratio

PSNR is one of the most prevalent tools for image quality evaluation defined by the following equation:

$$PSNR = 10 \cdot \log \left[\frac{\sum (D^h - D^u)^2}{255^2} \right] \tag{1}$$

where D^h and D^u are ground-truth and upsampled depth maps, respectively.

2.1.2 Structural similarity index measure

A sophisticated tool for image quality evaluation is SSIM [14] that measures the similarity between two images and considered to be correlated with the quality perception of the human visual system (HVS). SSIM principle is based on the modeling any image distortion as a combination of luminance distortion, contrast distortion, and loss of correlation. SSIM value for two images f and g is expressed by

$$SSIM = l(f, g)c(f, g)s(f, g) \tag{2}$$

$$l(f, g) = \frac{2\mu_f \mu_g + C_1}{\mu_f^2 + \mu_g^2 + C_1}, \quad c(f, g) = \frac{2\sigma_f \sigma_g + C_2}{\sigma_f^2 + \sigma_g^2 + C_2}, \quad s(f, g) = \frac{\sigma_{fg} + C_3}{\sigma_f + \sigma_g + C_3}$$

where $l(f,g)$, $c(f,g)$, and $s(f,g)$ are luminance, contrast, and structure comparison functions, respectively. σ_f and σ_g denote standard deviations, μ_f and μ_g are mean values and σ_{fg} is covariance. C_1, C_2, and C_3 are positive constants added to avoid a null denominator. The SSIM is a value between 0 and 1 that higher value shows more similarity.

2.1.3 Visual information fidelity

Visual information fidelity (VIF) [15] is a full-reference image quality metric that uses information theoretic criterion for image fidelity measurement. In an information-theoretic framework, the information that could ideally be extracted by the brain from the reference image and the loss of this information to the distortion are quantified in VIF method using natural scene statistics (NSS), HVS, and an image distortion (channel) model. The VIF is derived from a quantification of two mutual information quantities: the mutual information between the input and the output of the HVS channel when no distortion channel is present (called the *reference image information*) and the mutual information between the input of the distortion channel and the output of the HVS channel for the test image. Similar to SSIM, the assessment result is represented using a value between 0 and 1.

2.2 NR IQA TOOLS

2.2.1 Sharpness degree

Sharpness degree [16] is used to represent the extent of sharpness of the image and is defined by the following equation:

$$\text{Sharpnees degree} = \frac{1}{MN}\sum_{i=0}^{M-1}\sum_{j=0}^{N-1}G^{2}(x,y) \tag{3}$$

where

$$G(x,y) = \sqrt{(D(x,y)-D(x-1,y))^{2}+(D(x,y)-D(x,y-1))^{2}}$$

2.2.2 Blur metric

Another tool for measuring blur attempts to obtain the spread of the edges. First, an edge detector (e.g., a Sobel edge detector) is applied to a grayscale image. We scan each row of the image for pixels corresponding to an edge location. The start and end positions of the edge are defined as the locations of the local extrema closest to the edge. The spread of the edge is then given by the distance between the end and start positions and is identified as the local blur measure for this edge location. The global blur measure for the whole image is obtained by averaging the local depth values over all edges found [17]:

$$\text{Blur Metric} = \frac{\text{Sum of all edge widths}}{\text{Number of edges}} \tag{4}$$

2.2.3 Blind image quality index

Blind image quality index (BIQI) [18] identifies the likeliest distortion in the image and then quantifies this distortion using an NSS-based approach. Given a distorted image, the algorithm first estimates the presence of a set of distortions in the image that consists of JPEG, JPEG2000, white noise, Gaussian Blur, and Fast fading. The amount or probability of each distortion in the image is denoted as p_i $\{i=1,2,\ldots,5\}$. The method performs quality assessment in two stages. This first stage is a classification and the second stage attempts to evaluate the quality of the image along each of these distortions. The quality of the image is then expressed as a probability-weighted summation:

$$\text{BIQI} = \sum_{i=1}^{5}p_i \cdot q_i \tag{5}$$

where q_i $\{i=1,2,\ldots,5\}$ represents the quality scores from each of the five quality assessment algorithms (corresponding to the five distortions).

2.2.4 Natural image quality evaluator

Natural image quality evaluator (NIQE) [19] is a completely blind image quality analyzer that only uses measurable deviations from statistical regularities observed in natural images, without training on human-rated distorted images. Unlike current general purpose NR IQA algorithms which require knowledge about anticipated distortions in the form of training examples and corresponding human opinion scores, NIQE uses a quality aware collection of statistical features based on the simple and successful space domain, the NSS model. These features are derived from a corpus of natural, undistorted images.

The quality scores for both BIQI and NIQE are expressed by a value between 0 and 100 (0 represents the best and 100 the worst quality).

3 3D SUBJECTIVE QUALITY ASSESSMENT

During the subjective quality evaluation, the quality of each reconstructed stereoscopic image is rated by observers according to double stimulus continuous quality scale subjective test, as described in the International telecommunication union's recommendation on subjective quality assessment [20]. Fifteen nonexpert observers are participated in this experiment. In the first stage, original stereoscopic images were displayed to each participant for 10 s and another stereoscopic image made by an upsampled depth map for the same period of time. For each image data, similar viewing was carried out in order to examine the 3D perception. Depth perception is subjectively judged based on scales of 1 (bad), 2 (poor), 3 (fair), 4 (good), and 5 (excellent) in terms of 3D perception.

To detect outliers, a rejection analysis was performed on subjective results. An observer rating is considered as outlier if the correlation between Mean Opinion Score (MOS) and subject's rating results for all images is less than 0.7. According to correlations, there were no outliers among subjects.

4 EXPERIMENTAL RESULTS

The quality performance of the 7 upsampling methods is evaluated using 10 test depth maps from Middlebury stereo dataset [21]. The test RGB images and related depth maps are shown in Figure 2. In order to obtain low-resolution depth maps, the original data are downsampled to lower resolution first and then the high-resolution depth maps are constructed using seven upsampling methods (Figure 3).

Table 1 represents the average subjective quality score of each upsampling method and Table 2 shows the mean scores of different objective quality metrics on upsampled depth maps. The results are derived from averaging the quality scores of the collection of 10 images. As upsampling artifacts are important in edge locations, edge PSNR (E-PSNR) and nonedge PSNR (NE-PSNR) are also computed.

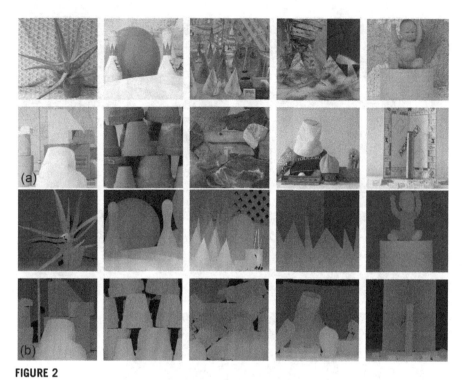

FIGURE 2

(a) Test RGB and (b) depth maps provided by Middlebury.

Table 1 Average Subjective Measurement Data of Upsampled Depth Maps

	BLU	BCU	BU	JBU	VBU	ABU	DTBU
MOS	3.76	3.64	3.89	3.84	4.03	3.46	3.99

Table 2 Average Objective Measurement Data of Upsampled Depth Maps (PSNR unit: dB)

Depth Map	BLU	BCU	BU	JBU	VBU	ABU	DTBU
PSNR	35.85	35.71	35.64	34.15	35.64	33.16	34.86
E-PSNR	23.68	23.55	23.66	22.82	23.38	20.97	22.93
NE-PSNR	38.07	37.94	37.78	37.50	37.93	35.43	36.92
Sharpness	39.5	42.2	49.51	49.09	31.92	88.31	68.14
Blur	8.48	11.38	10.29	10.87	10.51	9.00	9.89
SSIM	0.976	0.955	0.975	0.956	0.971	0.962	0.972
VIF	0.518	0.539	0.424	0.422	0.478	0.398	0.438
BIQI	57.8	66.34	63.11	32.81	41.94	29.15	72
NIQE	15.95	13.11	13.94	11.82	12.47	13.41	13.82

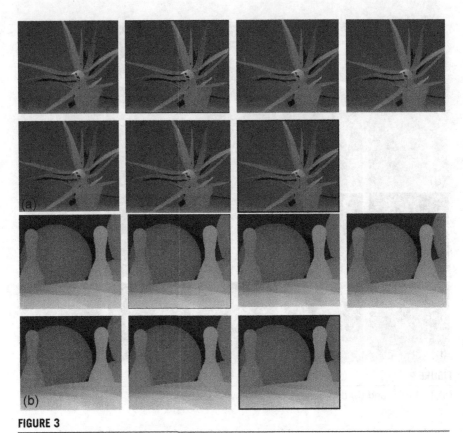

FIGURE 3

Upsampled depth maps of *aloe* (a) and *bowling* (b) obtained by BLU, BCU, BU, DTBU, JBF, ABU, and VBU in the scan order.

The 3D perception grades of upsampling methods in Table 1 are based on 3D visual discomfort.

Quality scores of upsampled depth maps obtained from each IQA metric are considered as a group of seven samples. All values are normalized by scaling between 0 and 1 and the similarity of samples distribution in each IQA group is compared with subjective evaluation samples group using Pearson, Spearman, and Kendall correlation coefficients. Table 3 shows the correlation results.

Before evaluating the strength of correlation using different correlation coefficients, it is worth mentioning that Pearson's correlation coefficient takes into account both the number and degree of concordances and discordances, whereas Kendall's tau correlation coefficient shows only the number of concordances and discordances. Spearman's correlation is in between of the Pearson's and Kendall's, reflecting the degree of concordances and discordances on the rank scale. The disadvantage of Pearson is the sensitivity to outliers (an observation that is numerically distant from the rest of the data). In this case, Spearman and Kendall are less sensitive to outliers and preferable.

Table 3 Pearson, Spearman, and Kendall Correlation Coefficients Between Subjective and Objective Measurements

	PSNR	E-PSNR	NE-PSNR	Sharpness	Blur Metric	SSIM	VIF	BIQI	NIQE
Pearson	0.528	0.608	0.554	−0.522	0.273	0.505	0.019	−0.34	0.132
Spearman	0.035	0.142	0.035	−0.321	0.142	0.357	0.107	−0.321	0.107
Kendall	0.047	0.142	0.047	−0.142	0.047	0.142	0.142	−0.238	0.142

According to Table 3, edge PSNR shows higher value of correlation compare to common PSNR and nonedge PSNR. Also, Pearson coefficient is much higher than Spearman result which indicates the distribution is nonlinear. In this case, Spearman and Kendall results are more reliable.

Sharpness degree and blur metric show negative and positive correlation values, respectively. These two results confirm the fact that image with high spatial frequency (sharper) reveals much noticeable visual discomfort than that with low frequency [22].

SSIM uses luminance, contrast, and structure features to measure quality. Similar to PSNR, Pearson coefficient is higher than two other correlation coefficients in this metric. SSIM has the highest Spearman value among other metrics. Thus, it is the most similar metric to visual fatigue in the case of samples order.

VIF results are based on NSS, HVS, and an image distortion (channel) model in wavelet domain and shows a positive but low correlation to visual fatigue.

BIQI and NIQE are two NR IQA metrics that are expected to show lower correlation in comparison to FR IQA metrics. JPEG, JPEG2000, white noise, Gaussian Blur, and Fast fading are five distortions that are considered in BIQI method for quality measurements. Similar to negative results of sharpness degree, BIQI is not correlated with subjective results.

NIQE metric delivers a positive correlation using Pearson coefficient. Also, Spearman and Kendall correlation results are comparative to some results derived from FR IQA methods. NIQE results are close to VIF, therefore, it can be inferred that NIQE is an acceptable quality assessment tool when there is no access to reference image. Figure 4 shows correlation values for different quality metrics in column diagram mode.

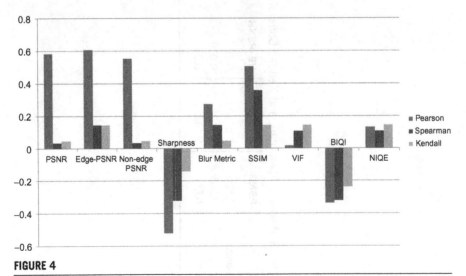

FIGURE 4

Column diagram of correlation between image quality metrics and subjective evaluation in descending order using Pearson, Spearman, and Kendall.

5 CONCLUSION

In this article, the performance of 2D objective quality tools for 3D quality evaluation is studied. Seven upsampling algorithms that yield different artifacts are implemented to construct high-resolution depth maps. Comparing the quality evaluation results of upsampled depth maps with subjective ratings of reconstructed stereoscopic images, we successfully achieved a reasonable relation between objective IQA results and subjective assessment. As a result, PSNR and SSIM show the highest Pearson correlation coefficients. Sharpness degree has a negative correlation which indicates that the sharp edge is a reason for visual discomfort. Also, VIF is not an appropriate tool due to small correlation coefficient.

REFERENCES

[1] Urvoy M, Barkowsky M, Le Callet P. How visual fatigue and discomfort impact 3D-TV quality of experience: a comprehensive review of technological, psychophysical, and psychological factors. Ann Telecommun 2013;68(11–12):641–55.

[2] Banks MS, Akeley K, Hoffman DM, Girshick AR. Consequences of incorrect focus cues in stereo displays. J Soc Inf Disp 2008;24(7):7.

[3] Tam WJ. Human stereoscopic vision: research applications for 3D-TV. SID International Symposium Digest of Technical Papers 2007;1(38):1216–9.

[4] Mahmoudpour S, Kim M. Optimum image quality assessment for 3D perception of stereoscopic image generated from upsampled depth map. In: Proceedings of the international conference on image processing and computer vision; 2014.

[5] Yasakethu S, Hewage C, Fernando W, Worrall S, Kondoz A. Quality analysis for 3D video using 2D video quality models. IEEE Trans Consumer Electron 2008;54(4):1969–76.

[6] Bosc E, Pepion R, Le Callet P, Koppel M, Ndjiki-Nya P, Pressigout M, et al. Towards a new quality metric for 3D synthesized view assessment. IEEE Trans Selected Topics Signal Process 2011;5(7):1332–43.

[7] Banitalebi-Dehkordi A, Pourazad MT, Nasiopoulos P. A study on the relationship between depth map quality and the overall 3D video quality of experience. In: Proceedings of the IEEE international conference on 3DTV: the true vision-capture, transmission and display of 3D video; 2013. p. 1–4.

[8] Hewage C, Worrall S, Dogan S, Kondoz A. Prediction of stereoscopic video quality using objective quality models of 2-D video. IET Electron Lett 2008;44(16):963–5.

[9] Tomasi C, Manduchi R. Bilateral filtering for gray and color image, In: Proceedings of the IEEE international conference on computer vision; 1998. p. 836–46.

[10] Kopf J, Cohen MF, Lischinski D, Uyttendaele M. Joint bilateral upsampling. ACM Trans Graphics 2007;26(3):1–6.

[11] Jang S, Lee D, Kim S, Choi H, Kim M. Depth map upsampling with improved sharpness. Broadcast Eng 2012;17(6):933–44.

[12] Pham C, Ha S, Jeon J. A local variance-based bilateral filtering for artifact-free detail and edge-preserving smoothing. In: Proceedings of the international conference on advances in image and video technology, South Korea; 2011. p. 60–70.

[13] Yeo D, Haq E, Kim J, Baig M, Shin H. Adaptive bilateral filtering for noise removal in depth upsampling. In: Proceedings. Conference on SoC design incheon, South Korea; 2010. p. 36–9.

[14] Wang Z, Bovik AC, Sheikh HR, Simoncelli EP. Image quality assessment: from error visibility to structural similarity. IEEE Trans Image Process 2004;13(4):600–12.

[15] Sheikh H, Bovik A. Image information and image quality. IEEE Trans Image Process 2006;12(2):430–44.

[16] Tsai C, Liu H, Tasi M. Design of a scan converter using the cubic convolution interpolation with canny edge detection. In: Proceedings of the international conference on electric information and control engineering; 2011. p. 5813–6.

[17] Marziliano P, Dufaux F, Winkler S, Ebrahimi T. Perceptual blur and ringing metrics: application to JPEG2000, In: Proceedings of the International Workshop on Multimedia, Signal Processing; 2008. p. 403–8.

[18] Moorthy AK, Bovik A. A two-step framework for constructing blind image quality assessment. IEEE Trans Signal Process Lett 2010;17(5):513–6.

[19] Mittal A, Soundararajan R, Bovik AC. Making a 'completely blind' image quality analyzer. IEEE Trans Signal Process Lett 2013;20(3):209–12.

[20] Methodology for the subjective assessment of the quality of television pictures, International Telecommunications Union/ITU Radio Communication Sector, ITU-R BT.500–11; January 2002.

[21] Scharstein D, Szeliski R. A taxonomy and evaluation of dense two-frame stereo correspondence algorithms. Comput Vis 2002;47(1–3):7–42.

[22] Kim D, Sohn K. Visual fatigue prediction for stereoscopic image. IEEE Trans Circuits Syst video Technol 2011;21(3):231–6.

ρGBbBShift: Method for introducing perceptual criteria to region of interest coding

11

Jaime Moreno[1,2], **Oswaldo Morales**[1], **Ricardo Tejeida**[1]

[1]*Superior School of Mechanical and Electrical Engineers, National Polytechnic Institute of Mexico, IPN Avenue, Lindavista, Mexico City, Mexico*
[2]*Signal, Image and Communications Department, University of Poitiers, Poitiers, France*

1 INTRODUCTION

Region of interest (ROI) image coding is a feature that modern image coders have, which allows to encode n specific region with better quality than the rest of the image or background (BG). ROI coding is one of the requirements in the JPEG2000 image coding standard [2,3], which defines two ROI methods [4,5]:

(1) Based on general scaling [4]
(2) Maximum shift (MaxShift) [5]

The general ROI scaling-based method scales coefficients in such a way that the bits associated with the ROI are shifted to higher bitplanes than the bitplanes associated with the BG, as shown in Figure 1(b). It implies that during an embedded coding process, any BG bitplane of the image is located after the most significant ROI bitplanes into the bitstream. But, in some cases, depending on the scaling value, φ, some bits of ROI are simultaneously encoded with BG. Therefore, this method allows to decode and refine the ROI before the rest of the image. No matter φ, it is possible to reconstruct with the entire bitstream a highest fidelity version of the whole image. Nevertheless, if the bitstream is terminated abruptly, the ROI will have a higher fidelity than BG.

The scaling-based method is implemented in five steps:

(1) A wavelet transform of the original images is performed.
(2) An ROI mask is defined, indicating the set of coefficients that are necessary for reaching a lossless ROI reconstruction, Figure 2.

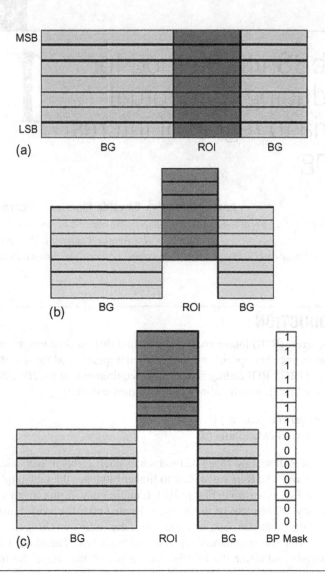

FIGURE 1

JPEG2000ROI Coding. (a) NoROI coding, (b) scaling-based ROI coding method ($\varphi = 3$), and (c) MaxShift method, $\varphi = 7$. Background is denoted as BG, region of interest as ROI, and bitplane mask as BPmask. MSB is the most significant bitplane and LSB is the least significant bitplane.

(3) Wavelet coefficients are quantized and stored in a sign magnitude representation, using the most significant part of the precision. It will allow to downscale BG coefficients.

(4) A specified scaling value, $\tilde{\varphi}$, downscales the coefficients inside the BG.

(5) The most significant bitplanes are progressively entropy encoded.

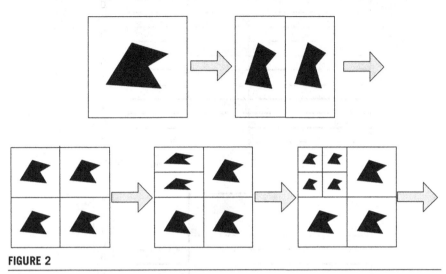

FIGURE 2

ROI mask generation, wavelet domain.

The input of ROI scaling-based method is the scaling value φ, while MaxShift method calculates it. Hence, the encoder defines from quantized coefficients this scaling value such that,

$$\varphi = \lceil \log_2(\max\{M_{BG}\} + 1) \rceil \tag{1}$$

where $\max\{MBG\}$ is the maximum coefficient in the BG. Thus, when ROI is scaled up φ bitplanes, the minimum coefficient belonging to ROI will be place one bitplane up of BG (Figure 1(c)). Namely, 2^{φ} is the smallest integer that is greater than any coefficient in the BG. MaxShift method is shown in Figure 1(c). Bitplane mask (BPmask) will be explained in Section 2.1.

At the decoder side, the ROI and BG coefficients are simply identified by checking the coefficient magnitudes. All coefficients that are higher or equal than the φth bitplane belong to the ROI, otherwise, they are a part of BG. Hence, it is not important to transmit the shape information of the ROI or ROIs to the decoder. The ROI coefficients are scaled down φ bitplanes before inverse wavelet transformation is applied.

2 RELATED WORK

2.1 BbB SHIFT

Wang and Bovik proposed the bitplane-by-bitplane shift (BbBShift) method in Ref. [6]. BbBShift shifts bitplanes on a bitplane-by-bitplane strategy. Figure 3(a) shows an illustration of the BbBShift method. BbBShift uses two parameters,

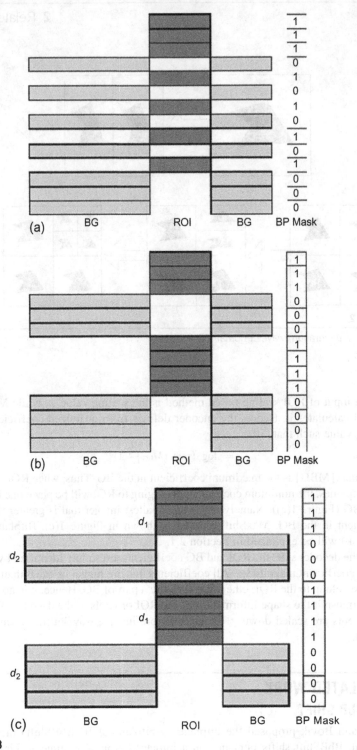

FIGURE 3

ROI coding methods. (a) BbBShift, $\varphi 1 = 3$ and $\varphi 2 = 4$, (b) GBbBShift and (c) pGBbBShift. Background is denoted as BG (for pGBbBShift method is perceptually quantized by pSQ at d_2), region of interest as ROI (for pGBbBShift method is perceptually quantized at d_1 by pSQ) and bitplane mask as BPmask.

$\varphi 1$ and $\varphi 2$, whose sum is equal to the number of bitplanes for representing any coefficient inside the image, indexing the top bitplane as bitplane 1. Summarizing, the BbBShift method encodes the first $\varphi 1$ bitplanes with ROI coefficients, then, BG and ROI bitplanes are alternately shifted, refining gradually both ROI and BG of the image (Figure 3(a)). The encoding process of the BbBShift method is defined as

(1) For a given bitplane bpl with at least one ROI coefficient:
- If $bpl \leq \varphi 1$, bpl is not shifted.
- If $\varphi 1 < bpl \leq \varphi 1 + \varphi 2$, bpl is shifted down to $\varphi 1 + 2\,(bpl - \varphi 1)$
(2) For a given bitplane bpl with at least one BG coefficient:
- If $bpl \leq \varphi 2$, bpl is shifted down to $\varphi 1 + 2bpl - 1$
- If $bpl > \varphi 2$, bpl is shifted down to $\varphi 1 + \varphi 2 + bpl$

2.2 GBbBShift

In practice, the quality refinement pattern of the ROI and BG used by BbBShift method is similar to the general scaling-based method. Thus, when the image is encoded and this process is truncated in a specific point, the quality of the ROI is high while there is no information of BG.

Hence, Wang and Bovik [7] modified BbBShift method and proposed the generalized bitplane-by-bitplane shift (GBbBShift) method, which introduces the option to improve visual quality either of ROI or BG or both. Figure 3(b) shows that with GBbBShift method it is possible to decode some bitplanes of BG after the decoding of same ROI bitplanes. It allows to improve the overall quality of the recovered image. This is possible gathering BG bitplanes. Thus, when the encoding process achieves the lowest bitplanes of ROI, the quality of BG could be good enough in order to portray an approximation of BG.

Therefore, the main feature of GBbBShift is to give the opportunity to arbitrary chose the order of bitplane decoding, grouping them in ROI bitplanes and BG bitplanes. This is possible using a binary bitplane mask or BPmask, which contains one bit per each bitplane, that is, twice the amount of bitplanes of the original image. An ROI bitplane is represented by 1, while a BG bitplane by 0. For example, the BPmask for MaxShift method in Figure 1(c) is 11111110000000, while for BbBShift in Figure 3(a) and GBbBShift in Figure 3(b) are 11101010101000 and 11100011110000, respectively.

At the encoder side, the BPmask has the order of shifting both the ROI and BG bitplanes. Furthermore, BPmask is encoded in the bitstream, while the scaling values φ or $\varphi 1$ and $\varphi 2$ from the MaxShift and BbBShift methods, respectively, have to be transmitted.

3 PERCEPTUAL GBbBShift

3.1 QUANTIZATION

In order to generate an approximation to how every pixel is perceived from a certain distance taking into account the value of its neighboring pixels the Chromatic Induction Wavelet Model (CBPF) is used. CBPF attenuates the details that the human visual system (HVS) is not able to perceive, enhances those that are perceptually relevant and produces an approximation of the image that the brain visual cortex perceives. CBPF takes an input image I and decomposes it into a set of wavelet planes $\omega_{s,o}$ of different spatial scales s (i.e., spatial frequency ν) and spatial orientations o. It is described as:

$$I = \sum_{s=1}^{n} \sum_{o=v,h,dgl} \omega_{s,o} + c_n \tag{2}$$

where n is the number of wavelet planes, c_n is the residual plane, and o is the spatial orientation either *vertical*, *horizontal*, or *diagonal*. The perceptual image I_ρ is recovered by weighting these $\omega_{s,o}$ wavelet coefficients using the *extended Contrast Sensitivity Function* (e-CSF), which considers spatial surround information (denoted by r), visual frequency (v related to spatial frequency by observation distance), and observation distance (d). Perceptual image I_ρ can be obtained by

$$I_\rho = \sum_{s=1}^{n} \sum_{o=v,h,dgl} \alpha(v,r)\omega_{s,o} + c_n \tag{3}$$

where $\alpha(v,r)$ is the e-CSF weighting function that tries to reproduce some perceptual properties of the HVS. The term $\alpha(v,r)\,\omega_{s,o} \equiv \omega_{s,o};\rho,d$ can be considered the *perceptual wavelet coefficients* of image I when observed at distance d. For details on the CBPF and the $\alpha(v,r)$ function, see Ref. [8].

We employ the perceptual quantizer (ρSQ) either forward (F-ρSQ) and inverse (I-ρSQ), defined by Moreno et al. [1]. Each transform sample at the perceptual image I_ρ (from Equation 3) is mapped independently to a corresponding step size either Δs or Δn, thus I_ρ is associated with a specific interval on the real line. Then, the perceptually quantized coefficients Q(F-ρSQ), from a known viewing distance d, are calculated as follows:

$$Q = \sum_{s=1}^{n} \sum_{o=v,h,dgl} \text{sign}(\omega_{s,o}) \left\lfloor \frac{|\alpha(v,r)\omega_{s,o}|}{\Delta_s} \right\rfloor + \left\lfloor \frac{c_n}{\Delta_n} \right\rfloor \tag{4}$$

The perceptual inverse quantizer (I-ρSQ) or the recovered $\hat{\alpha}(v,r)$ introduces perceptual criteria to the classical Inverse Scalar Quantizer and is given by

$$\hat{I} = \begin{cases} \sum_{s=1}^{n} \sum_{o=v,h,dgl} \text{sign}(\hat{\omega}_{s,o}) \left\lfloor \frac{\Delta_s(|\hat{\omega}_{s,o}|+\delta)}{\hat{\alpha}(v,r)} \right\rfloor + (|\hat{c}_n|+\delta)\Delta_n, & \hat{\omega}_{s,o} > 0 \\ 0, & \hat{\omega}_{s,o} = 0 \end{cases} \tag{5}$$

3.2 ρGBbBShift *ALGORITHM*

In order to have several kinds of options for bitplane scaling techniques, a perceptual generalized bitplane-by-bitplane shift (ρGBbBShift) method is proposed. The ρGBbBShift method introduces to the GBbBShift method perceptual criteria when bitplanes of ROI and BG areas are shifted. This additional feature is intended for balancing perceptual importance of some coefficients regardless of their numerical importance and for not observing visual difference at ROI regarding MaxShift method, improving perceptual quality of the entire image.

Thus, ρGBbBShift uses a binary bitplane mask or BPmask in the same way that GBbBShift (Figure 3(c)). At the encoder, shifting scheme is as follows:

(1) Calculate φ using Equation (1).
(2) Verify that the length of BPmask is equal to 2φ.
(3) • For all ROI Coefficients, forward perceptual quantize them using Equation (4) (F-ρSQ) with viewing distance d_1.
  • For all BG coefficients, forward perceptual quantize them using Equation (4) (F-ρSQ) with viewing distance d_2, being $d_2 \gg d_1$.
(4) Let τ and η be equal to 0.
(5) For every element i of BPmask, starting with the least significant bit:
  • If BPmask$(i)=1$, Shift up all ROI perceptual quantized coefficients of the $(\varphi-\eta)$th bitplane by τ bitplanes and increment η.
  • Else: Shift up all BG perceptual quantized coefficients of the $(\varphi-\tau)$th bitplane-by-η-bitplanes and increment τ.

At the decoder, shifting scheme is as follows:

(1) Let $\varphi=$ length of $BP_{mask}/2$ be calculated.
(2) Let τ and η be equal to 0.
(3) For every element i of BPmask, starting with the least significant bit:
  • If BPmask$(i)=1$, Shift down all perceptual quantized coefficients by τ bitplanes, which pertain to the $(2\varphi-(\tau+\eta))$th bitplane of the recovered image and increment η.
  • Else: Shift down all perceptual quantized coefficients by η bitplanes, which pertain to the $(2\varphi-(\tau+\eta))$th bitplane of the recovered image and increment τ.
(4) Let us denote as $c_{i,j}$ a given non-zero wavelet coefficient of the recovered image with 2φ bitplanes and $c_{i,j}$ as a shifted down c obtained in the previous step, with φ bitplanes:
  • If $(c_{i,j}\&$ BPmask$)>0$, inverse perceptual quantize $\bar{c}_{i,j}$ using Equation (5) (I-ρSQ) with d_1 as viewing distance.
  • If $(c_{i,j}\&$ BPmask$)=0$, inverse perceptual quantize $\bar{c}_{i,j}$ using Equation (5) (I-ρSQ) with d_2 as viewing distance.

4 EXPERIMENTAL RESULTS

The ρGBbBShift method, as the other methods presented here, can be applied to many image compression algorithms such as JPEG2000 or Hi-SET [9]. We test our method applying it to Hi-SET and the results are contrasted with MaxShift method in JPEG2000 and Hi-SET. The setup parameters are φ =8 for MaxShift and BPmask = 1111000110110000, d_1 = 5H and d_2 = 50H, where H is picture height (512 pixels) in a 19-in. LCD monitor, for ρGBbBShift. Also, we use the *JJ2000* implementation when an image is compressed by JPEG2000 standard [10].

4.1 APPLICATION IN WELL-KNOWN TEST IMAGES

Figure 4 shows a comparison among methods MaxShift and GBbBShift applied to JPEG2000, in addition to, ρGBbBShift applied to Hi-SET. The 24-bpp image *Barbara* is compressed at 0.5 bpp. It can be observed that without visual difference at ROI, the ρGBbBShift method provide better image quality at the BG than the general based methods defined in JPEG2000Part II [2].

In order to better qualify the performance of MaxShift, GBbBShift, and ρGBbBShift methods, first, we compared these methods applied to the Hi-SET coder

FIGURE 4

512 × 640 pixel Image Barbara with 24 bpp. ROI is a patch of the image located at [341 280 442 442], whose size is 1/16 of the image. Decoded images at 0.5 bpp using MaxShift method in JPEG2000 coder ((a) φ=8), GBbBShift method in JPEG2000 coder ((b) BPmask = 1111000110110000), and ρGBbBShift method in Hi-SET coder ((c) BPmask = 1111000110110000). (a) MaxShift in JPEG2000 coder, 0.5 bpp.

FIGURE 4, CONT'D

(b) GBbBShift in JPEG2000 coder, 0.5 bpp. (c) ρGBbBShift in Hi-SET coder, 0.5 bpp.

and then, we compare MaxShift and ρGBbBShift methods applied to the JPEG2000 standard and Hi-SET, respectively. We compress two different grayscale and color images of *1600*, from CSIQ image database [11], and *Lenna* [12] at different bit-rates. ROI area is a patch at the center of these images, whose size is 1/16 of the image. We employ the perceptual quality assessment proposed by Moreno et al. [13] called P2SNR, which weights the mainstream PSNR by means of a chromatic induction model, so we renamed this image quality assessment as CwPSNR.

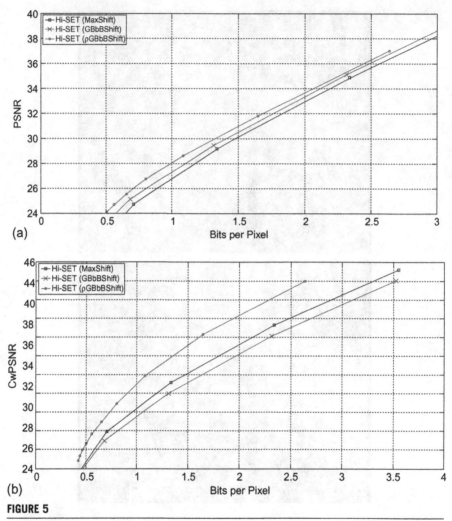

FIGURE 5

Comparison among MaxShift (Blue Function), GBbBShift (Green Function) and ρGBbBShift (Red Function) methods applied to H*i*-SET coder. 512 × 512 pixel Image *1600* with (a-b) 8 and (c-d) 24 bpp are employed for this experiment. ROI is a patch at the center of the image, whose size is 1/16 of the image. The overall image quality of decoded images at different bits per pixel is contrasted both (a and c) objectively and (b and d) subjectively. (a) PSNR grayscale. (b) CwPSNR grayscale.

Figure 5 shows the comparison among MaxShift (Blue Function), GBbBShift (Green Function), and ρGBbBShift (Red Function) methods applied to H*i*-SET coder. 512 × 512 pixel Image *1600* both for grayscale and color are employed for this experiment. These figures also show that the ρGBbBShift method gets the better

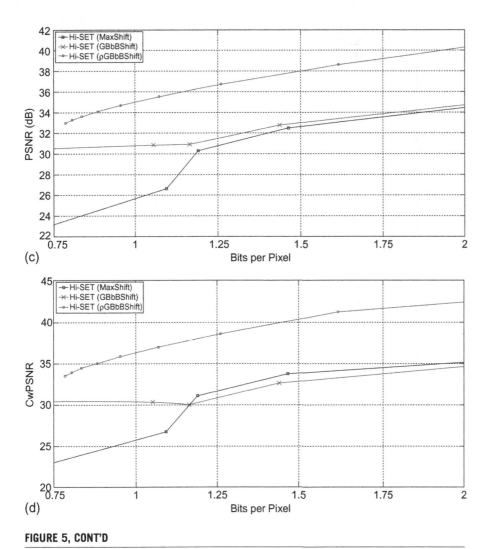

FIGURE 5, CONT'D

(c) PSNR color. (d) CwPSNR color.

results both in PSNR (objective image quality) and CwPSNR (subjective image quality) in contrast to MaxShift and GBbBShift methods.

When MaxShift method applied to JPEG2000 coder and ρGBbBShift applied to Hi-SET coder are compared, in the whole image quality assessment of image *1600*, JPEG2000 obtains better objective quality both for grayscale and color images (Figure 6(a) and (c), respectively). But when the subjective quality is estimated ρGBbBShift coded images are perceptually better.

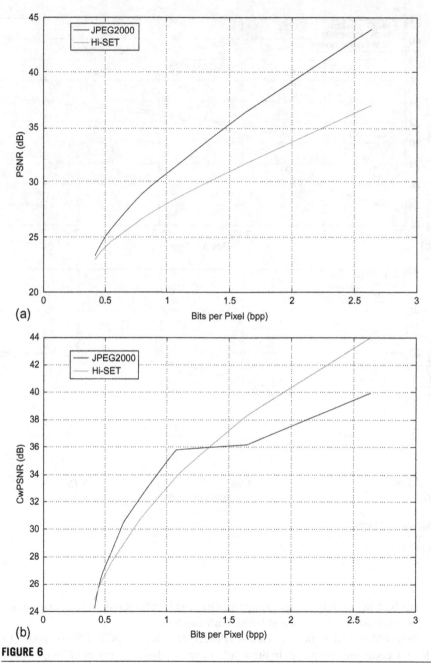

(a)

(b)

FIGURE 6

Comparison between MaxShift method applied to JPEG2000 coder and rGBbBShift applied to Hi-SET coder. 512 x 512 pixel Image 1600 with (a-b) 8 and (c-d) 24 bits per pixel are employed for this experiment. ROI is a patch at the center of the image, whose size is 1/16 of the image. The overall image quality of decoded images at different bits per pixel are contrasted both (a and c) objectively and (b and d) subjectively.

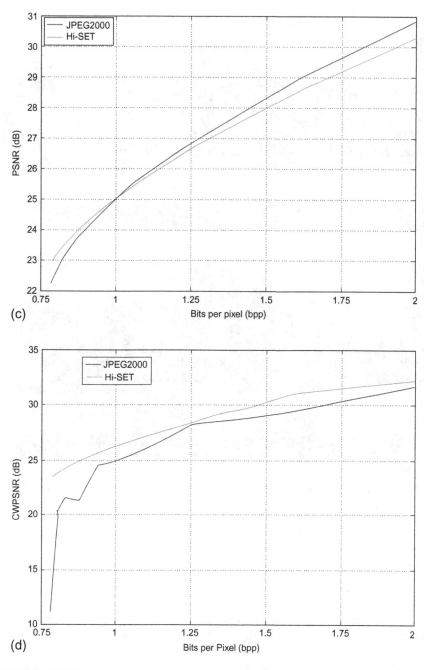

(c)

(d)

FIGURE 6, CONT'D

FIGURE 7

512 × 512 pixel Image *1600* from CSIQ image data base with 8 bpp. ROI is a patch at the center of the image, whose size is 1/16 of the image. Decoded images at 0.42 bpp using $\varphi = 8$ for MaxShift method (a) in JPEG2000 coder and (b) in H*i*-SET coder, and BPmask = 1111000110110000 for (c) GBbBShift and (d) ρGBbBShift methods in H*i*-SET coder.

A visual example is depicted by Figure 7, where it can be shown that there is no perceptual difference between ROI areas besides the perceptual image quality at BG is better when ρGBbBShift is applied to the H*i*-SET coder (Figure 7(d)). Furthermore, Figure 7(b) and (c) shows the examples when MaxShift and GBbBShift methods, respectively, are applied to the H*i*-SET coder.

Similarly, when an ROI area is defined in Image Lenna, Figure 8(a) and (b) shows the comparison among MaxShift (Blue Function), GBbBShift (Green Function), and

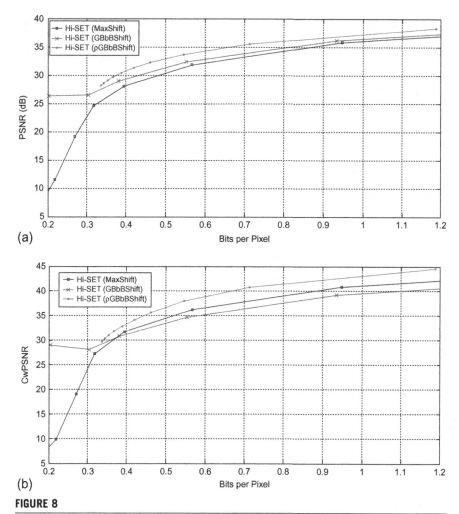

FIGURE 8

(a and b) Comparison among MaxShift (Blue Function), GBbBShift (Green Function) and ρGBbBShift (Red Function) methods applied to H*i*-SET coder. (c and d) Comparison between MaxShift method applied to JPEG2000 coder and ρGBbBShift applied to H*i*-SET coder. 512 × 512 pixel Image *Lenna* with 8 bpp is employed for this experiment. ROI is a patch at the center of the image, whose size is 1/16 of the image. The overall image quality of decoded images at different bits per pixels are contrasted both (a and c) objectively and (b and d) subjectively.

GBbBShift (Red Function) methods applied to H*i*-SET coder. 512 × 512 pixel Image Lenna for grayscale is employ for this experiment. These figures also show that the ρGBbBShift method gets the better results both in PSNR (objective image quality, Figure 8(a)) and CwPSNR (subjective image quality, Figure 8(b)) in contrast to

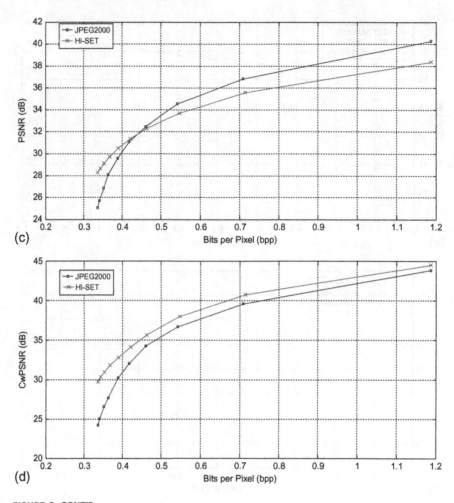

FIGURE 8, CONT'D

MaxShift and GBbBShift methods. In addition, when MaxShift method applied to JPEG2000 coder and ρGBbBShift applied to Hi-SET coder are compared, ρGBbBShift obtains less objective quality (Figure 8(c)), but better subjective quality for grayscale images (Figure 8(d)).

Figure 9 shows a visual example, when image *Lenna* is compressed at 0.34 bpp by JPEG2000 and Hi-SET. Thus, it can be observed that ρGBbBShift provides an important perceptual difference regarding the MaxShift method (Figure 9(d)). Furthermore, Figure 9(b) and (c) shows the examples when MaxShift and GBbBShift methods, respectively, are applied to the Hi-SET coder.

FIGURE 9

512512 pixel Image Lenna from CMU image database with 8 bpp. ROI is a patch at the center of the image, whose size is 1/16 of the image. Decoded images at 0.34 bpp using $\varphi = 8$ for MaxShift method (a) in JPEG2000 coder and (b) in Hi-SET coder, and BPmask = 1111000110110000 for (c) GBbBShift and (d) ρGBbBShift methods in Hi-SET coder.(a) MaxShift method in JPEG2000 coder, 0.34 bpp. (b) MaxShift method in Hi-SET coder, 0.34 bpp.

(Continued)

FIGURE 9, CONT'D

(c) GBbBShift method in H*i*-SET coder, 0.34 bpp. (d) ρGBbBShift method in H*i*-SET coder, 0.34 bpp.

4.2 APPLICATION IN OTHER IMAGE COMPRESSION FIELDS

The usage of ROI coded images depends on an specific application, but in some fields such as manipulation and transmission of images is important to enhance the image quality of some areas and to reduce it in others [14,15]. In telemedicine or in remote sensing (RS) it is desirable to maintain the best quality of the ROI area, preserving relevant information of BG, namely, the most perceptual frequencies.

Thus, in medical applications an image is by itself an $ROI\phi$ area of the human body, a mammography is an area of chest, for instance. That is why, it is important to know where is this $ROI\phi$ located, in order to ease the interpretation of a given ROI coded image. In addition, according Federal laws in some countries, ROI areas must be lossless areas [16]. ρGBbBShift is able to accomplish these two features.

Figure 10 shows an example of medical application. A rectangular ROI of the Image *mdb202* from PEIPA image database [17], coordinates [120 440 376 696],

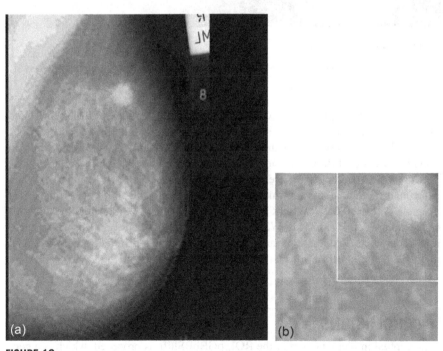

FIGURE 10

Example of a medical application. 1024 x 1024 pixel Image mdb202 from PEIPA image database. ROI is a patch with coordinates [120 440 376 696], whose size is 1/16 of the image. Decoded images at 0.12 bpp using MaxShift method ((a-b) $\varphi = 8$) in JPEG2000 coder and ρGBbBShift method ((c-d) BPmask = 1111000110110000) in H*i*-SET coder. (a) MaxShift method in JPEG2000 coder, 0.12 bpp. (b) Patch of (a) portrayed both ROI and BG areas.

(Continued)

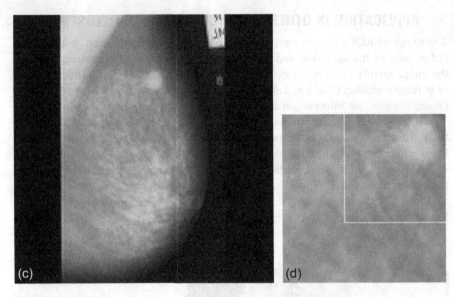

FIGURE 10, CONT'D

(c) ρGBbBShift method in H*i*-SET coder, 0.12 bpp. (d) Patch of (c) portrayed both ROI and BG areas.

is coded at 0.12 bpp by JPEG2000 and H*i*-SET, employing MaxShift and ρGBbBShift methods, respectively. The overall image quality measured by PSNR in Figure 10(a) (MaxShift method applied to JPEG2000) is 37.21 dB, while in Figure 10(c) (ρGBbBShift method applied to H*i*-SET) is 36.76 dB. Again, PSNR does not reflect perceptual differences between images (Figure 10(b) and (d)). When perceptual metrics assess the image quality of the ρGBbBShift coded image, for example, VIFP = 0.6359, WSNR = 34.24 and C*w*PSNR = 40.88, while for MaxShift coded image VIFP = 0.3561, WSNR = 31.34, and C*w*PSNR = 37.18. Thus, these metrics predicts that there is an important perceptual difference between ROI methods, being ρGBbBShift method better than MaxShift method.

5 CONCLUSIONS

A perceptual implementation of the ROI, ρGBbBShift, is proposed, which is a generalized method that can be applied to any wavelet-based compressor. We introduced ρGBbBShift method to the H*i*-SET coder and it visually improves the results obtained by previous methods like MaxShift and GBbBShift. Our experiments show that ρGBbBShift into H*i*-SET provides an important perceptual difference regarding the MaxShift method into JPEG2000, when it is applied to conventional images like *Lenna* or *Barbara*.

ACKNOWLEDGMENT

This work is supported by National Polytechnic Institute of Mexico by means of Project No. 20140096, the Academic Secretary and the Committee of Operation and Promotion of Academic Activities (COFAA), National Council of Science and Technology of Mexico by means of Project No. 204151/2013, and LABEX Σ-LIM France, Coimbra Group Scholarship Programme granted by University of Poitiers and Region of Poitou-Charentes, France.

REFERENCES

[1] Moreno J, Fernandez C, Saucedo S. pGBbBShift: method for introducing perceptual criteria to region of interest coding, In: International conference on image processing, computer vision, and pattern recognition of the world congress in computer science, computer engineering, and applied computing; 2013. p. 111–7.

[2] Boliek M, Majani E, Houchin JS, Kasner J, Carlander M, Information technology: JPEG2000 image coding system (extensions), JPEG 2000 part II final committee draft ed., ISO/IEC JTC 1/SC 29/WG 1; December 2000.

[3] Boliek M, Christopoulos C, Majani E, Information technology: JPEG2000 image coding system, JPEG 2000 Part I final committee draft version 1.0 ed., ISO/IEC JTC1/SC29 WG1, JPEG 2000; April 2000.

[4] Taubman DS, Marcellin MW. JPEG2000: image compression fundamentals, standards and practice. Boston, Dordrecht, London: Kluwer Academic Publishers; 2002. ISBN: 079237519X.

[5] Atsumi E, Farvardin N. Lossy/lossless region-of-interest image coding based on set partitioning in hierarchical trees. In: International conference on image processing, vol. 1; p. 87–91.

[6] Wang Z, Bovik AC. Bitplane-by-bitplane shift(Bb BShift)—a suggestion for JPEG2000 region of interest image coding. IEEE Signal Process Lett 2002;9(5):160–2.

[7] Wang Z, Banerjee S, Evans BL, Bovik AC. Generalized bitplane-by-bitplane shift method for JPEG2000 ROI coding" In: IEEE international conference on image processing, vol. 3; p. 81–4.

[8] Otazu X, Párraga C, Vanrell M. Toward a unified chromatic induction model. J Vis 2010;10(12):6.

[9] Moreno J, Otazu X. Image coder based on Hilbert scanning of embedded quad trees: an introduction of Hi-SET coder, In: IEEE international conference on multimedia and expo; 2011.

[10] C. Research, École Polytechnique Fédérale de Lausanne, and Ericsson. JJ2000 implementation in Java. Cannon Research, École Polytechnique Fédérale de Lausanne and Ericsson. [Online]. Available: http://jj2000.epfl.ch/; 2001.

[11] Larson EC, Chandler DM. Most apparent distortion: a dual strategy for full-reference image quality assessment" Proc SPIE 2009;742:1–17.

[12] S. I.P. I. of the University of Southern California. The USC-SIPI image database. Signal and Image Processing Institute of the University of Southern California. [Online]. Available: http://sipi.usc.edu/database/; 1997.

[13] Moreno J. P2SNR: perceptual full-reference image quality assessment for JPEG2000, In: International conference on image processing, computer vision, and pattern recognition of the world congress in computer science, computer engineering, and applied, computing; 2012. p. 835–41.

[14] Bartrina-Rapesta J, Auli-Llinas F, Serra-Sagrista J, Zabala-Torres A, Pons-Fernandez X, Maso-Pau J. Region of interest coding applied to map overlapping in geographic information systems, In: IEEE international geoscience and remote sensing symposium; 2007. p. 5001–4.

[15] Gonzalez-Conejero J, Serra-Sagrista J, Rubies-Feijoo C, Donoso-Bach L. Encoding of images containing no-data regions within JPEG2000 framework, In: 15th IEEE international conference on image processing; 2008. p. 1057–60.

[16] Wilson B. Ethics and Basic Law for Medical Imaging Professionals. Philadelphia: F.A. Davis Co; 1997.

[17] PEIPA. Pilot European image processing archive, available at http://peipa.essex.ac.uk/ [Online]; 2004.

DT-Binarize: A decision tree based binarization for protein crystal images

12

İmren Dinç[1], Semih Dinç[1], Madhav Sigdel[1], Madhu S. Sigdel[1], Ramazan S. Aygün[1], Marc L. Pusey[2]

[1]DataMedia Research Lab, Computer Science Department, University of Alabama Huntsville, Huntsville, AL, USA
[2]iXpressGenes Inc., Huntsville, AL, USA

1 INTRODUCTION

Protein crystallography is one of the major research areas in the drug discovery industry since it gives information about the 3D structure of the protein and its functionality [1]. Growing a protein crystal structure is a complex process that comprises of several sensitive stages. Every stage requires high attention since some parameters, such as pH, temperature, type, and portion of the salt and the precipitant need to be set carefully. (Note that it is possible to generate millions of different solutions using different chemicals for protein crystallization process.) Therefore, growing a crystal usually requires many trials, and most of the trials do not yield a desired protein crystal [2]. In non-automated systems, hundreds of images of proteins need to be checked manually by the experts in order to detect the crystal formation, which is a time consuming process [1]. For this reason, detecting and analyzing of protein crystals using an automated system is significantly important for the experts to save time and effort. There are several examples of automated systems in use, and most of them use typically regional, geometrical or texture features of the protein images to detect and classify crystals. In order to extract the features correctly, accurate image segmentation is required for these systems.

Image binarization (thresholding) is one of the widely used preprocessing tasks in most of the systems. Thresholding is an operation that converts grayscale image into a black and white image using a threshold value τ. This τ value can be selected using different techniques. Therefore, image thresholding can be mainly grouped into two based on the selection of τ value: global and local thresholding. If an image is binarized using a single τ value, it is called "global thresholding." If τ value varies depending on pixel position due to some local features of the image, then it is called "local thresholding" [3]. In the literature, there are many studies that focus on different aspects of the problems. The studies focus on their own problem domain to find the best approach for binarization [4], and there is not an optimal solution that works for all cases.

All thresholding techniques have been developed based on some assumptions, and all of the methods have some strengths and weaknesses. Therefore, all methods may fail under some circumstances. For example, Otsu's thresholding method, which is one of the popular thresholding methods in the literature, is affected by the size of the objects in the image. If the object size is too large or too small, this method will probably fail in segmentation operation. This may lead extraction of incorrect features for the system [5]. As another example, most of document binarization methods assume that document has whitish background color. This means that if the document has dark background, those methods will generate improper binary images. Thus, there is no single thresholding method that can generate proper binary images for all images in the datasets such as medical images, biological images, and especially protein crystallization images.

Crystal images are anticipated to have characteristic features such as high intense regions, clear edges, and proper geometric shapes. These features are mostly used in classification process, but in some cases, they may not be observed clearly due to focusing or reflection problems in the image. Capturing clear images is an important step to extract reliable features as well as to binarize images correctly. Most of protein images have non-uniform illumination, low contrast, and noise since proteins are grown in a liquid solution. This makes thresholding process more complex task. In this study, we investigated several thresholding methods for protein crystal imagery. In most cases, while one method generates proper binary images for some of the protein images, another method generates better results for the others. Obviously, a single type of thresholding technique is not enough to generate a useful binary image to use in classification of the protein images. Thus, it is very important to select the correct binarization method for these types of images in the classification process. Improper binary image may lose some important information or it may keep some unnecessary information such as tiny noisy pixels. Furthermore, incorrect thresholding method may lose a blurred crystal in the image or it may crop a regular object around its borders leading incorrect classification.

In our previous work [6], we used three thresholding techniques (Otsu's Threshold (Otsu), 90th Percentile Green Intensity Threshold (g90), and Max Green Intensity Threshold (g100)) together not to lose any informative feature for classification of protein crystallization images. However, this also leads incorporation of unnecessary features that may yield incorrect classification results. To avoid this problem, in this study, we propose an alternative approach, *DT-Binarize*, recently introduced in [7]. It selects the best thresholding technique for a particular image using decision tree.

In DT-Binarize, we train a decision tree using some basic features of the protein images on our pre-labeled samples. Each label indicates a different thresholding technique that properly fits for that particular image. In the test stage, the best thresholding method is selected for a given test image using the same features. Our technique tries to select the most useful and reliable binarization methods for the protein crystallization images. In this way, the complexity of our system may be reduced since we are dealing with less number of features (i.e., features from a single thresholded image are used rather than from multiple thresholded images).

This research uses protein crystallization images dataset provided by iXpress-Genes, Inc. As our earlier work, we classify the protein images into three main groups (non-crystals, likely-leads, and crystals). Each category has its own specific characteristics that need to be considered independently. In this paper, we focus on "crystals" only and propose a solution to select the best thresholding technique for each image.

The rest of the chapter is structured as follows. The image binarization techniques are described in Section 2. Our approach to select the best binarization technique is explained in Section 3. Experimental results are provided in Section 4. Finally, our chapter is concluded in Section 5.

2 BACKGROUND
2.1 IMAGE BINARIZATION METHODS

Image binarization is a technique for separating foreground and background regions in an image. For the protein images consisting of crystals, the crystal regions are expected to be represented as the foreground in the binary images. Some of the sample protein images are provided in Figure 1 (a-c). While a thresholding technique may perform well for an image, it may not perform as good as other thresholding techniques for another image. Thus, we consider three image thresholding techniques described below: Otsu's threshold (Otsu), 90th percentile green intensity threshold (g90), and max green intensity threshold (g100).

2.1.1 Otsu threshold
For Otsu's thresholding [8], firstly a gray level image is generated from an input color image. Then, for each possible intensity threshold, the variance of spread of pixels in the foreground and background region is calculated. The intensity (τ_0) for which the sum of foreground and background spreads is minimal is selected as the threshold. Pixels with gray level intensity higher than (τ_0) form the foreground region while the remaining pixels form the background. Figure 1 (d-f) shows some sample binary images of Otsu's method.

2.1.2 90th Percentile green intensity threshold (g90)
When green light is used as the excitation source for fluorescence based acquisition, the intensity of the green pixel component is observed to be higher than the red and blue components in the crystal regions [6]. 90th percentile green intensity threshold

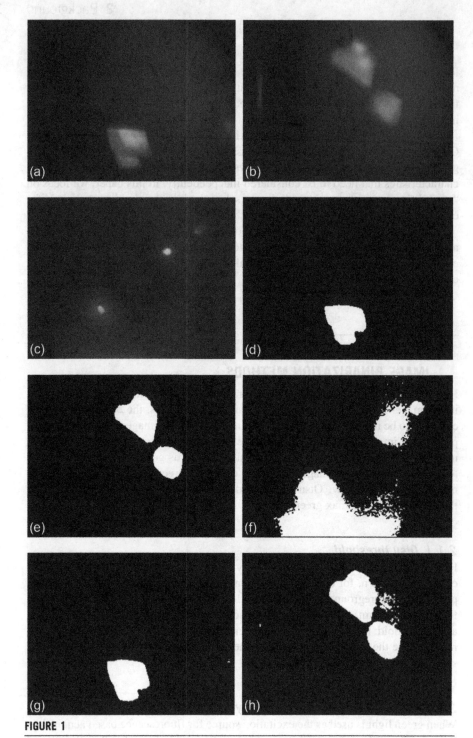

FIGURE 1

Sample images for all thresholding techniques: (a-c) original images,(d-c) Otsu results, (g-i) g90 results, and (j-l) g100 results. Note that (e), (g), and (l) are outputs of the best thresholding method for each case.

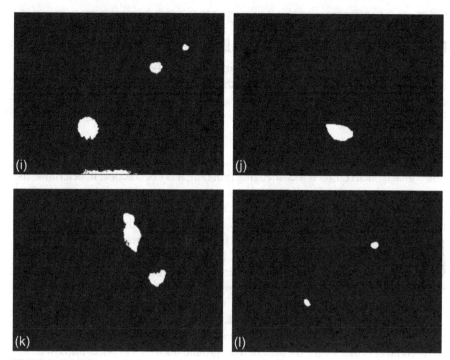

FIGURE 1, CONT'D

utilizes this feature for image binarization. First, the threshold intensity (τ_{g90}) is computed as the 90th percentile intensity of the green component in all pixels. This means that the number of pixels in the image with the green component intensity below this intensity constitutes around 90% of the pixels. Also, a minimum gray level intensity condition ($t_{min} = 40$) is applied. All pixels with gray level intensity greater than t_{min} and having green pixel component greater than (τ_{g90}) constitute the foreground region while the rest constitute the background region [3]. Some sample binary images of g90 are shown in Figure 1 (g-i).

2.1.3 Maximum green intensity threshold (g100)

This technique is similar to the 90th percentile green intensity threshold described earlier. In this method, the maximum intensity of green component (τ_{g100}) is used as the threshold intensity for green component. All pixels with gray level intensity greater than t_{min} and having green pixel component equal to (τ_{g100}) constitute the foreground region. The foreground (object) region in the binary image from this method is usually smaller than the foreground region from the other two techniques [3]. Figure 1 (j-l) shows some sample binary images of g100.

3 DT-BINARIZE: SELECTION OF BEST BINARIZATION METHOD USING DECISION TREE

In this section, first we describe DT-Binarize that can be used in any image binarization problem. Then, we briefly define the methods used at intermediate stages of our algorithm. Finally, we provide application of this method to the protein image binarization problem.

3.1 OVERVIEW

Since image binarization is a challenging problem, it is not practical to determine the optimal threshold value for all cases. There are some weaknesses and strengths of the all image binarization methods [9]. Based on this fact, in this research, we target an algorithm that selects the best binarization method rather than a single threshold value. Our goal is to exploit the powerful features of different binarization methods and use them whenever they perform well. For this reason, we propose using a supervised classification method (decision trees) to determine the best binarization method for any image dataset based on some basic features such as standard deviation, mean, max intensity, etc.

We first build a training set that is labeled with the best thresholding technique by the experts. In other words, the best thresholding technique for each image is used as the class label in that stage. We benefit from ground truth data to select the best binarization method as a class label. According to our algorithm we first generate a training dataset, in which training samples are labeled with the binarization methods that provides best binary image. Then in the training stage, we build the decision tree based on the basic features of the images in the training dataset. Once we have the decision tree, we are able to determine the best binarization method for any test image by using the same statistical features. Figure 2 shows the mechanism of the DT-Binarize algorithm. Following steps provide a brief summary of our algorithm:

1. resizing and noise reduction of the images,
2. labeling training images with best binarization methods,
3. extracting statistical features of the images,
4. building the decision tree based on the statistical features,
5. predicting the best binarization method for a test image using the decision tree,
6. applying chosen binarization method to a given test image.

3.2 STAGES OF THE ALGORITHM

3.2.1 Median filter

Median filter is one of the well-known order-statistic filters due to its good performance for some specific noise types such as "Gaussian," "random," and "salt and pepper" noises [3]. According to the median filter, the center pixel of a $M \times M$ neighborhood is replaced by the median value of the corresponding window. Note that noise pixels are considered to be very different from the median. Using this idea

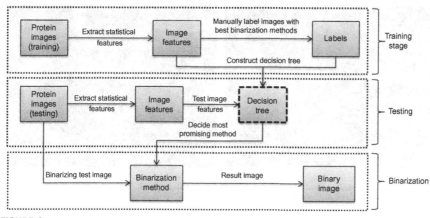

FIGURE 2

Overview of the DT-Binarize.

median filter can remove this type of noise problems [3]. We use this filter to remove the noise pixels on the protein crystal images before binarization operation.

3.2.2 Contrast stretching

Contrast stretching is a normalization method that enhances the informative features of the image by expanding the histogram of the intensities. It maps the pixel values into a new range in a linear fashion [3]. We can apply contrast stretching to the images by using Equation (1),

$$I_{out} = (I_{in} - P_{in}) \left(\frac{P'_{max} - P'_{min}}{P_{ax} - P_{min}} \right) + P'_{min} \tag{1}$$

where I_{in} and I_{out} are the input and output images, P_{min} and P_{max} are the minimum and the maximum intensity value of the input images, and P'_{min} and P'_{max} are the minimum and the maximum intensity values of the output image, respectively. We include contrast stretching in our research, because our dataset contains some low contrast images that may cause incorrect thresholding for our dataset. Figure 3 shows a problematic image and contrast stretching result. Note that informative features of the result image are magnified without loosing the structure of the crystal, and contrast stretching is not applied all the images in the dataset.

3.2.3 Decision tree

Decision tree [10] is a rule-based classifier that employs a tree structure for data classification. It is a supervised classification technique that comprises of training and testing stages. In the training stage the tree is generated based on the entropy of the data features. In the testing stage, each test sample is classified using the tree built in the training stage. Decision tree is a classifier that requires relatively less time to create training model. In addition, testing is quite fast after building the tree.

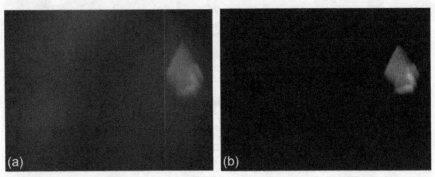

FIGURE 3

Contrast stretching example: (a) original image and (b) image after applying contrast stretching.

3.3 APPLICATION OF DT-BINARIZE ON PROTEIN CRYSTAL IMAGES

Protein image binarization problem is a convenient application area of DT-Binarize, since there is no single thresholding method that can generate proper binary images for all datasets. In our problem, we labeled the protein crystallization images with one of the three different thresholding methods: Otsu's threshold 90th Percentile Green Intensity threshold, and Max Green Intensity threshold. We use the training images to build the decision tree based on only standard deviation of the pixel intensities. 75% of the data is selected as the training set, and the remaining is used for the testing. Figure 4 shows the decision tree of the training stage. In Figure 4, "g90" is selected as the best binarization method if standard deviation of the test sample is less than 12.86. However, if the standard deviation is between 12.86 and 24.99, the best

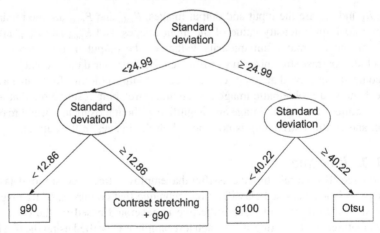

FIGURE 4

Decision tree for selecting the best threshold method.

binarization method is selected as "Contrast Stretching + g90." Similarly, other binarization methods may be selected depending on the standard deviation of the test image.

We have employed this tree to our test dataset. For a test sample, we take the standard deviation and find the corresponding class label of the tree. The method represented with that label is selected to binarize the test image. The following section provides some numerical and visual results of DT-Binarize with several examples.

4 EXPERIMENTS AND RESULTS

This section provides objective evaluation of each binarization technique using the ground truth (reference) image dataset that is manually generated by our research group. The correctness of a binary image is calculated using several well-known performance measures. DT-Binarize technique is also compared with the given methods.

4.1 DATASET

The protein crystal images may be grouped into five main categories: "posettes and spherulites" "needles," "2D plates," "small 3D crystals," and "large 3D crystals." Distinctive features of these categories may be identified as high intense regions, straight edges, and proper geometric shapes. Our dataset consists of totally 114 protein crystal images that consist of three subcategories of crystals: "2D plates (40%)," "small 3D crystals (10%)," and "large 3D crystals (50%)." The size of each image is 320×240, and all images have been captured by a special imaging system under green light. In the following sections, we are going to explain protein crystal subcategories briefly.

4.1.1 2D Plates

2D Plates have quadrangular shapes. In some specific cases, we may not be able to observe all the edges of a quadrangular shape because of focusing issues. 2D Plates may have small or large sizes, and they may be located as a stack of regions. The mean intensities of 2D Plates are lower than the mean intensities of 3D crystals. This means intensity change between the foreground and the background may not be as significant as for 3D crystals. Figure 5 (a-c) shows a group of sample images for this category.

4.1.2 Small 3D crystals

The areas of small 3D crystals are smaller than those of large 3D crystals. They have higher intensities than 2D plates. This causes a significant intensity change between 3D objects and background in images. Generally, it is hard to detect all the edges of this category due to small size. Figure 5 (d-f) shows some sample images of this category.

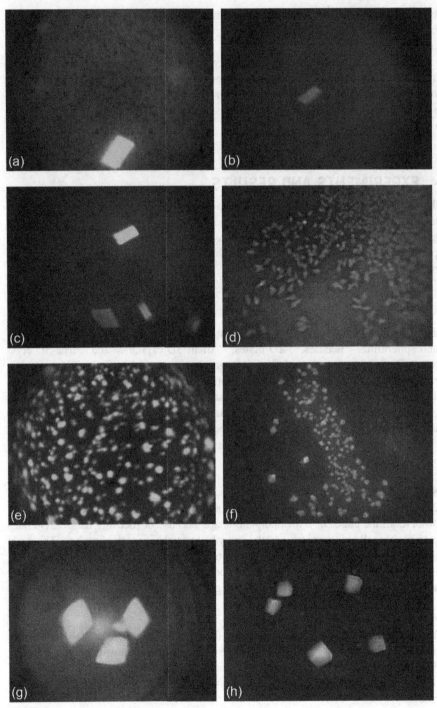

FIGURE 5

Protein crystallization image samples: (a-c) 2D plates, (d-f) small 3D crystals, and (g-i) large 3D crystals.

FIGURE 5, CONT'D

4.1.3 Large 3D crystals

This category generally has regions with high intensity, and these regions generally have proper geometric shapes. The 3D structure of large 3D crystals can be observed in images. In some particular cases, it is difficult to detect all the edges of 3D objects because of focusing and light reflection problems. The instances of this category have larger sizes than small 3D crystals. Some sample images of this category are shown in Figure 5 (g-i).

4.2 CORRECTNESS MEASUREMENT

Most image binarization studies need to deal with a common difficulty regarding the correctness of their proposed system. Because a simple visual comparison of the binary images would not provide an objective and dependable results, numerical results are expected as well as the visual results. For this reason, we decided to generate a reference (ground-truth) binary image of each protein image manually in our dataset. We extracted the protein instances in a image using an image editing software [11] that has the capability of auto selection of the objects in an image. This software also provides fine level adjustments on the object areas. Finally, all reference images were checked by the domain experts to minimize the human error.

The success of a binarization method can be measured in terms of the "similarity" of its output binary image to the corresponding reference binary image. If the similarity is high then it can be considered as a successful method. In order to measure similarity between two binary images, in this study, we used a simple technique called "weighted sum." In this technique we basically sum (overlap) two binary images, after we multiply the reference image by 2,

$$I_S = 2 \times I_R + I_O \tag{2}$$

where I_S, I_R, and I_O are the sum image, reference binary image, and the output binary image, respectively. Suppose that the values of the pixels of protein instances are

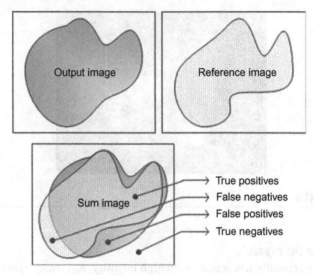

FIGURE 6

Example sum image.

represented by "1" and the background area is represented by "0" in the images. After the "weighted sum" operation, the sum image will include "0s," "1s," "2s," and "3s." Every number has a special meaning to measure the similarity. If the pixel value p_{ij} of the sum image is "3," it is a *hit*, which is also called as a True Positive (TP). If the pixel value is "2," it is a *miss*, which is called as a False Negative (FN). Similarly, if the pixel value is "1," it is a *false alarm*, which is called as a False Positive (FP). Finally if the pixel value is "0," it is a *correct reject*, which is called as a True Negative (TN). We can use these 4 values (TP, TN, FN, and TN) to measure the correctness of the output binary image. Figure 6 shows an example sum image that includes four regions.

In the literature there are several measures that may provide correctness information from different perspectives. It is important to use a proper accuracy measure that is more relevant to the characteristics of our study. For example, the classical accuracy measure may not be a proper technique for our study. Because in a typical protein binary image, there are usually few number of foreground pixels compared to the background pixels. This means that the TN pixels can easily suppress the accuracy even if there are no TP pixels. To avoid bias towards a specific measurement method, we use and compare 4 well-known measures: Accuracy, F-Score (F-measure), Matthews correlation coefficient (MCC), and Jaccard (Jacc) similarity. These can provide more reliable measures for a variety of confusion matrices [12]. Following equations show the formula of each measurement:

$$M_{\text{acc}} = \frac{\text{TP} + \text{TN}}{\text{TP} + \text{TN} + \text{FP} + \text{FN}} \tag{3}$$

$$M_{\mathrm{F1}} = \frac{2 \times \mathrm{TP}}{(2 \times \mathrm{TP}) + \mathrm{FP} + \mathrm{FN}} \qquad (4)$$

$$M_{\mathrm{MCC}} = \frac{(\mathrm{TP} \times \mathrm{TN}) - (\mathrm{FP} \times \mathrm{FN})}{\sqrt{(\mathrm{TP} + \mathrm{FP})(\mathrm{TP} + \mathrm{FN})(\mathrm{TN} + \mathrm{FP})(\mathrm{TN} + \mathrm{FN})}} \qquad (5)$$

$$M_{\mathrm{Jacc}} = \frac{\mathrm{TP}}{\mathrm{TP} + \mathrm{FP} + \mathrm{FN}} \qquad (6)$$

4.3 RESULTS

In the experimentation stage we generate four binary images using the three binarization techniques (g90, g100, and Otsu) and DT-Binarize (see Figure 8). Correctness of each binary image is measured based on reference binary images (ground truth). Four different correctness measures are employed at this stage in order to evaluate the results objectively. This process is done for all test images in the dataset. Table 1 shows the average results of each measure. DT-Binarize achieves 98.44% accuracy on our protein dataset, but accuracy is not a reliable measure for our dataset since true negative pixels are much more than true positive pixels in the image. Therefore, F-measure, MCC, and Jaccard similarity measures are more reliable to evaluate DT-Binarize. According to Table 1, our method could reach 81.06%, 82.36%, and 71.03% for F-measure, MCC, and Jaccard respectively. DT-Binarize outperforms all other methods by 10% on the average.

Figure 7 shows a visual representation of the results is given in Table 1.

In almost all cases, DT-Binarize was able to generate the best binary image in the testing stage. Figure 8 shows a sample test case in which our technique can successfully generate the best result.

However, there are also few cases that our technique could not provide proper binary image of the protein crystal. Figure 9 shows a sample image for that case.

Please note that success of DT-Binarize depends on the thresholding methods that are chosen for the problem domain. If none of the thresholding techniques provide a correct result, our method will not provide a good result either. It means that there is a performance limit that DT-Binarize can achieve. We call this limit as the

Table 1 Comparison of the Techniques by Different Measures

	G100	G90	Otsu	DT-Binarize
Acc	0.9787	0.9569	0.8911	0.9844
F1	0.6935	0.6230	0.6212	0.8106
MCC	0.7184	0.6632	0.6516	0.8236
Jaccard	0.5907	0.4960	0.5396	0.7103

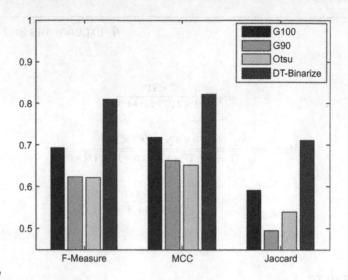

FIGURE 7

Comparison of the results.

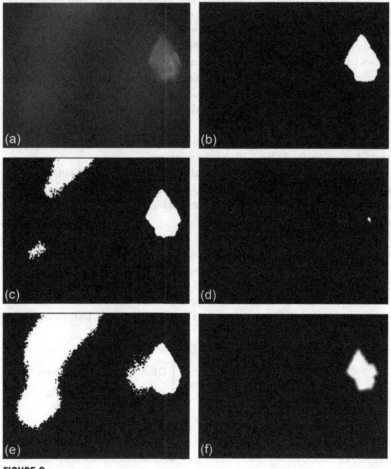

FIGURE 8

A sample test case: (a) original image, (b) ground truth image, (c) g90 threshold, (d) g100 threshold, (e) Otsu threshold, and (f) DT-Binarize.

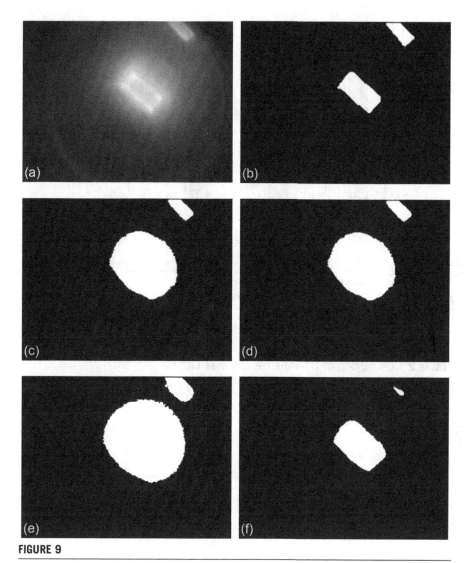

FIGURE 9

Example of a bad binarization result: (a) original image, (b) ground truth image, (c) g90 threshold, (d) g100 threshold,(e) Otsu threshold, and (f) DT-Binarize.

"Max Limit." If we select the best thresholding method for every image out of the provided techniques, we can reach the "Max Limit." In this case, DT-Binarize is considered to perform well when it chooses the same thresholding techniques that are chosen manually. Figure 10 shows the comparison of the correctness of our technique with respect to the best labeling. The closeness to the max limit indicates the success of DT-Binarize in this problem. Numerical results are presented in Table 2. The max

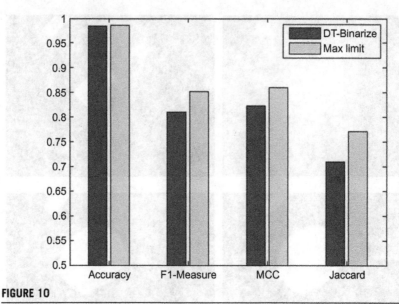

FIGURE 10

Comparison with theoretical max limit.

Table 2 Comparison of DT-Binarize and max Limit

	Max Limit	DT-Binarize
Acc	0.987	0.9844
F1	0.852	0.8106
MCC	0.86	0.8236
Jacc	0.771	0.7103

limit of F-measure is 85.2%, and DT-Binarize could achieve 81.06%. It means that DT-Binarize can reach 95% of the max limit for protein image dataset.

5 CONCLUSION

This paper presents a new technique for image binarization problem using a group of different thresholding methods. DT-Binarize is a supervised method with training and testing stages. In the training stage, a decision tree is built using the standard deviation of the protein images. Leaf nodes of the tree represent different thresholding techniques that provide the best binarization method for a specific group of images. In the testing stage, using the decision tree, we select the best thresholding technique for the test sample and then generate the binary image using that technique.

We evaluate the performance of our approach with four different accuracy measures. For all cases, DT-Binarize outperformed other single thresholding methods. Experimental results show that our technique improves the binarization accuracy by 10% on the average and provides high accuracy by reaching 95% of the expert choices.

ACKNOWLEDGMENT

This research was supported by National Institutes of Health (GM090453) grant.

REFERENCES

[1] Zhu X, Sun S, Bern M. Classification of protein crystallization imagery. Engineering in Medicine and Biology Society; 2004, IEMBS '04. 26th Annual International Conference of the IEEE, vol. 1; 2004. p. 1628–31.

[2] Rupp B, Wang J. Predictive models for protein crystallization, Methods 2004;34 (3):390–407. Available: http://www.sciencedirect.com/science/article/pii/S1046202304001203.

[3] Gonzalez R, Woods R. Digital image processing. Pearson/Prentice Hall; 2008. Available: http://books.google.com/books?id=8uGOnjRGEzoC.

[4] Sezgin M, Sankur B. Survey over image thresholding techniques and quantitative performance evaluation. J Electron Imaging 2004;13(1):146–68. Available: http://dx.doi.org/10.1117/1.1631315.

[5] Ray N, Saha B. Edge sensitive variational image thresholding. IEEE International Conference on Image Processing, ICIP 2007, vol. 6; 2007, p. VI37–VI40.

[6] Sigdel M, Pusey ML, Aygun RS. Real-time protein crystallization image acquisition and classification system. Crystal Growth Design 2013;13(7):2728–36. Available: http://pubs.acs.org/doi/abs/10.1021/cg3016029.

[7] Dinç I, Dinç S, Sigdel M, Sigdel MS, Pusey ML, Aygün RS. Dt-binarize: A hybrid binarization method using decision tree for protein crystallization images. Proceedings of the 2014 International Conference on Image Processing, Computer Vision & Pattern Recognition, ser. IPCV'14; 2014, p. 304–11.

[8] Otsu N. A threshold selection method from gray-level histograms. Automatica 1975;11 (285–296):23–7.

[9] Roy S, Saha S, Dey A, Shaikh S, Chaki N. Performance evaluation of multiple image binarization algorithms using multiple metrics on standard image databases 2014; 249:349–60. Available: http://dx.doi.org/10.1007/978–3–319–03095–1_38.

[10] Tan PN, Steinbach M, Kumar V. Introduction to data mining. 1st ed. Boston, MA, USA: Addison-Wesley Longman Publishing Co., Inc.; 2005.

[11] Corporation C. Corel draw; 2014. Available: http://www.corel.com/corel/category.jsp?rootCat=cat20146&cat=cat3430091.

[12] Sigdel M, Aygün RS. Pacc – a discriminative and accuracy correlated measure for assessment of classification results. Proceedings of the 9th International Conference on Machine Learning and Data Mining in Pattern Recognition, ser. MLDM'13. Springer-Verlag: Berlin, Heidelberg; 2013. p. 281–95. Available, http://dx.doi.org/10.1007/978–3–642–39712–7_22.

Automatic mass segmentation method in mammograms based on improved VFC snake model

13

Xiangyu Lu, Min Dong, Yide Ma, Keju Wang
School of Information Science and Engineering, Lanzhou University, Lanzhou, China

1 INTRODUCTION

Breast cancer is one of the common malignant tumors and remains the leading cause of cancer death among females, accounting for 23% of the total cancer cases and 14% of the cancer deaths in the world [1]. Mammography is a preferred method for early detection and also the most efficient and reliable tool for early prevention and diagnosis of breast cancer [2]. Mammograms are always with low contrast and the lesions are blurry and irregular, the shape and size of each mass or calcification are changeful, which cause the high misdiagnosis rate of breast cancer. For the past few years, computer-aid diagnosis has become the international research hot spot worldwide [3], which offers the doctors a reliable "second suggestion."

Breast mass is an important symptom and its accurate segmentation is crucial to the treatment of breast cancer. Different algorithms for early lesion area detection in mammograms have been widely studied [4–7]. Kumar and Sureshbabu [4] detected mass in mammogram automatically using wavelet transform modulus maximum (WTMM), which located the region of interest (ROI) by multithreshold and then extracted the contour of ROI by WTMM method. Song et al. [5] proposed a hybrid segmentation method, which defined a local cost function for dynamic programming based on the rough region of mass obtained by template-matching technique, and the performance was evaluated by measuring the similarity. A new mass segmentation and automatic estimation method were presented based on robust multiscale feature-fusion and maximum *a posteriori* [6]. Before delineating the final mass, the dynamic contrast improvement, template matching, and posterior probabilities were used to obtain the mass candidate points. This method can segment the ill-defined or spiculated lesions.

Novel image detection methods are appearing along with the development of technology. In recent years, the active contour model (Snake) [8] is widely used in image processing, computer vision, etc. [9,10], and among which VFC (vector field convolution) Snake [11] model performs more excellent characteristics in segmentation of boundaries such as low dependence to initial contour, capability of convergence and superior noise robustness. While it doesn't work well when we apply the typical VFC Snake method to extract the mass in mammograms, because of that the mass boundaries are always with low contrast and appearing blurry in the whole image.

Considering the disadvantage mentioned above, we proposed an integrated approach for mass autosegmentation in breast based on the improved VFC Snake model. The present method can detect the regions of masses in mammograms automatically and achieve promising results. This chapter is organized as follows. In Section 2, we present the methodology for mass localization and segmentation. Section 3 illustrates some experiments to verify the proposed method. Besides, the comparisons with typical VFC Snake model and the discussion also can be found in Section 3. Section 4 gives the conclusions of this chapter.

2 METHODOLOGY

The proposed methodology of breast mass segmentation can be schematically described in Figure 1. The method consists of four main processing steps: (1) obtaining the mammogram images; (2) mammogram preprocessing, to remove the label and enhance the image; (3) mass localization: for determining the regions of interest and mass location parameters; and (4) mass accurate segmentation.

2.1 MAMMOGRAM DATABASE

The mammograms used in this work are taken from digital database for screening mammography (DDSM) [12] and mammography image analysis society (MIAS) [13]. These two databases are widely used in studies on mammogram analysis, because they are freely available and consist of plenty cases. For DDSM database, there are as many as 2620 cases and each image contains about 3000×5000 pixels with 16-bit or 12-bit gray level, we map the intensity value into the range [0–255] by using brightness adjustment method. The full raw mammograms provided in this database are with a format of LJPEG which is hard to read under Windows, thus we first convert it to the usable PNG format by a DDSM-software proposed by Chris [14]. The suspicious regions of each abnormality were provided with chain code data by experts. The MIAS database contains 322 mammograms and each image is 1024×1024 pixels with 8-bit gray level, the abnormality is given by a circle. These two databases also offered some other corresponding information such as type, severity, character, and so on.

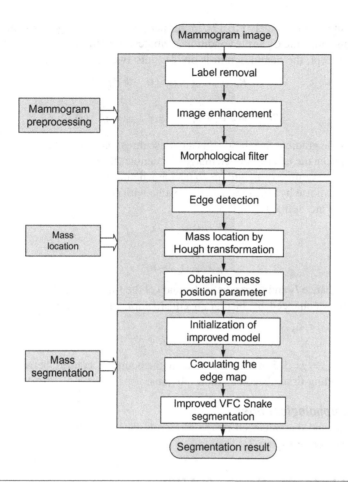

FIGURE 1

Flow chart of mass segmentation methodology.

2.2 MAMMOGRAM PREPROCESSING

2.2.1 Label removal

The mammogram image usually includes of breast region, pectoral muscle, background and label. In order to reduce the processing time and further study, the label should be removed. Here, we use the standard local threshold method which has been proved to be a convenient method to remove the label.

2.2.2 Image enhancement

To extract the mass region accurately and eliminate noise, the rough set (RS) theory [15] is applied. Traditional gray level transformation is not working well since the gray values between mass region, pectoral muscle, and gland are similar. RS theory that is used in reasoning from imprecise data is applied in information processing and artificial intelligence widely [16,17]. In this part, we choose image gradient attribute C_1 and noise attribute C_2 as the condition attributes. According to the indiscernibility relation concept, the mammogram is divided into two sub-images:

$$R_{C_1}(i,j) = \{(i,j) | : f(i,j) > P\} \tag{1}$$

$$R_{C_2}(s) = \underset{m}{U}\,\underset{n}{U}\,\{s_{mn} | : \text{int}|\bar{s}_{mn} - \bar{s}_{m\pm1,n\pm1}| > Q\} \tag{2}$$

where P is the gradient threshold, Q is the noise threshold, $f(i,j)$ is the gradient value calculated from the label-removed image, "s" denotes the sub-block. Considering s_{mn} as each pixel examine its neighbors to decide whether it is noise or not. If it is, then eliminate the noise by replacing the pixel value with Q. The sub-images that need to be enhanced are defined as follows:

$$I_1 = R_{C_1}(i,j) - R_{C_2}(s) \tag{3}$$

$$I_2 = \bar{R}_{C_1}(i,j) - R_{C_2}(s) \tag{4}$$

Next, we enhance I_1 and I_2, respectively, and get the final image by merging the sub-images: I_2 is enhanced by histogram equalization method and I_1 is transformed below:

$$g(i,j) = \rho \cdot I_1(i,j)^\gamma \tag{5}$$

Here, we set $\rho = \gamma = 1.5$. After enhancement, the boundary contrast between the mass and surrounding tissue becomes more obvious.

2.2.3 Morphological filter

Then we amend the enhanced image using morphological filter. The preprocessed image is shown in Figure 2.

2.3 ROI EXTRACTION AND LOCATION

2.3.1 Edge extraction

The preprocessed image is composed of pectoral muscle and mass region. Before removing the pectoral muscle, the edge detection operator is used to extract the edge first.

2.3.2 Hough transform detection

From Figure 3, the edge of pectoral muscle appears as a triangle while mass edge usually appears as an ellipse or circle; thus, we can obtain the approximate edge of mass by performing the linear Hough transform (LHT) [18] and circular Hough transform (CHT) on the extracted edge image, which, respectively, are defined as formulas (6) and (7). Here, Ω_{pectoral} is the pectoral muscle detected by LHT on edge image, Ω_{mass} is the initially segmented mass obtained by CHT on the region $\Omega_{\text{edge-pectoral}}$, where Ω_{pectoral} is removed. (a_i, b_i) is the center position of the circle and R is the radius. The location results are shown in Figure 3:

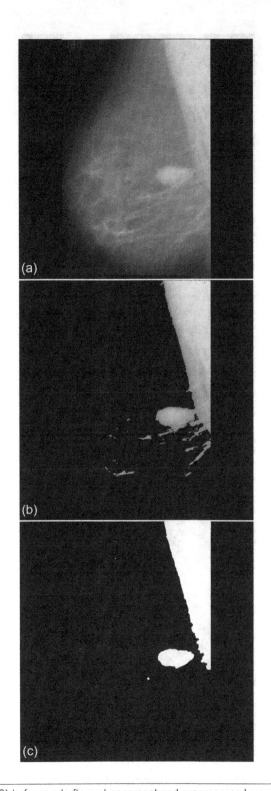

FIGURE 2

Image(from MIAS) before and after enhancement and preprocessed results.

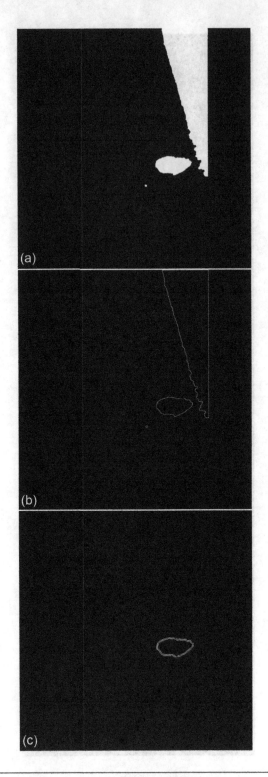

FIGURE 3

Edge extraction and mass location results (1024 × 1024 pixels).

$$\Omega_{\text{edge}} \to \Omega_{\text{pectoral}} : (\rho, \theta) = \text{LHT}(x_i, y_j) \tag{6}$$

$$\Omega_{(\text{edge-pectoral})} \to \Omega_{\text{mass}} : ((a_i, b_i), R) = CHT((x_i, y_i), r_{\min}, r_{\max}) \tag{7}$$

2.3.3 Mass location parameter

For a further work, we obtain the mass position coordinate by defining a circle, whose center corresponds to the center of extracted mass egde, and the radius of which is a middle value of the distance from boundary pixel to the center position, indicating as: (cx, cy) and r. For Figure 3, the parameter is: (682, 586), $r = 46$. The parametric circle could be used as the initial contour of deformable model followed by.

2.4 MASS SEGMENTATION

The results of mass location are rough and exist certain gap with the actual boundary, we utilize the Snake model to perform an accurate segmentation further.

2.4.1 Typical VFC Snake model

The Snake model defined a parametric curve guided by external forces and internal forces that pull it toward the edge of ROI until the energy function achieves the minimum. The curve $v(s)$ and the minimizing energy function $E(v)$ forms are

$$v(s) = [x(s) . y(s)]^{\text{T}}, \quad s \in [0, 1] \tag{8}$$

$$E(v) = \int_0^1 (E_{\text{int}}(v(s)) + E_{\text{ext}}(v(s))) ds \tag{9}$$

$$E_{\text{int}}(v(s)) = \frac{1}{2} [\alpha |v'(s)|^2 + \beta |v''(s)|^2] \tag{10}$$

where E_{int} is the internal energy decided by the curve, α and β control the continuity and smoothness, respectively. E_{ext} is the external energy decided by the image information. The VFC Snake is an active contour model whose external force is VFC field. First defined a vector field kennel:

$$\mathbf{k}(\mathbf{x}, \mathbf{y}) = [\mathbf{u_k}(\mathbf{x}, \mathbf{y}), \mathbf{v_k}(\mathbf{x}, \mathbf{y})] = m(x, y)\mathbf{n}(\mathbf{x}, \mathbf{y}) \tag{11}$$

where $m(x, y)$ is the vector magnitude and $n(x, y)$ is the unit vector pointing to the kennel origin (0, 0):

$$m(x, y) = (r + \varepsilon)^{-\gamma} \tag{12}$$

$$\mathbf{n}(\mathbf{x}, \mathbf{y}) = [-\mathbf{x}/\mathbf{r}, -\mathbf{y}/\mathbf{r}] \tag{13}$$

Here, $r = (x^2 + y^2)^{1/2}$. The external force is calculated by convoluting the vector field kennel $k(x, y)$ and the edge map $f(x, y)$, defined as

$$f_{\text{vfc}} = f(x, y) \times \mathbf{k}(\mathbf{x}, \mathbf{y}) = [f(x, y) \times \mathbf{u_k}(\mathbf{x}, \mathbf{y}), f(x, y) \times \mathbf{v_k}(\mathbf{x}, \mathbf{y})] \tag{14}$$

2.4.2 Improved VFC Snake model

First, we use the typical VFC Snake model to detect the lesion area; however, there are obvious distortions in the segmented results. By analyzing the force field of the model, we observe that the distribution of which is disordered (Figure 4(b) and (c)), and this causes the misleading of the active contour to the interference tissues rather than the real mass boundaries. Thus, the main idea of our proposed segmentation algorithm is to improve the force field by defining a new and clear edge map $f(x, y)$. First, the gradient value of each pixel is improved using RS theory method by setting a gradient threshold to judge whether the pixel belongs to a potential boundary or not. If it is, then these pixels should be enhanced. Next, the edge map $f(x, y)$ is calculated by performing the Canny operator [19], which is considered to have more excellent features like stability and accuracy compared to the gradient operator. As shown in Figure 4(d) and (e), it is obvious that the improved force field distribution turns to be more regular, which appears much evenly near the boundaries and the areas mixed in normal glands.

Besides, the performance of typical VFC Snake model depends on the position of initial contour around the mass, which usually is a circle formed by the coordinate position and radius. Here, we set the initial contour by using the parametric circle obtained in the mass location part.

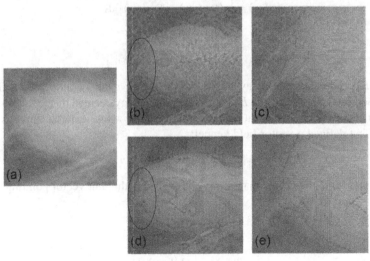

FIGURE 4

Force field of typical and improved VFC Snake and the enlarged images.

3 EXPERIMENT RESULTS AND DISCUSSION

Our proposed method was totally tested on 400 mammograms with abnormal breast regions from DDSM and MIAS database and the experimental results are shown in Figures 5 and 6, respectively. We can observe that our approach can achieve much

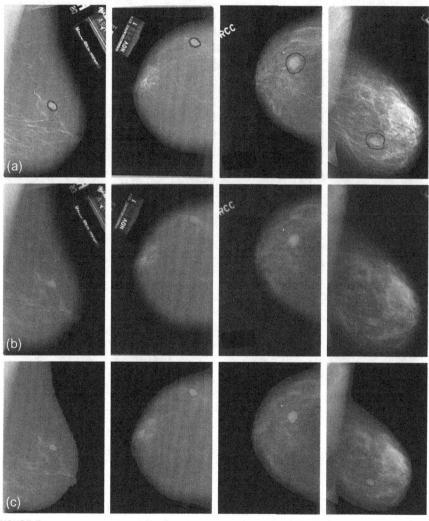

FIGURE 5

Experimental results of mammograms from DDSM database: (a)–(d) The "thumbnails". (a-1)–(d-1) Full raw images. (a-2)–(d-2) Results by our proposed method. (a-3)–(d-3) Results by typical VFC Snake model. (a-4)–(d-4) Results by manually.

Continued

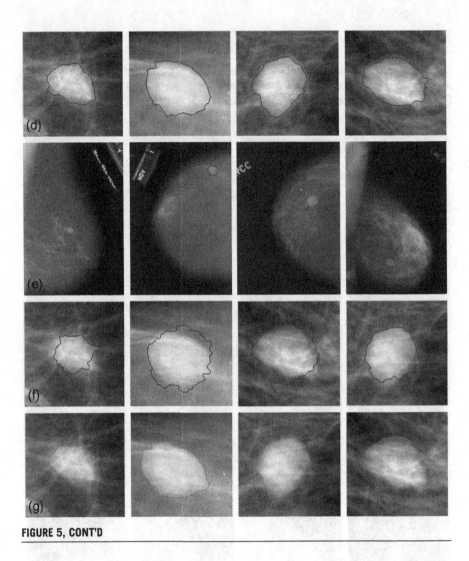

FIGURE 5, CONT'D

better results in comparison with the typical VFC Snake method. During this test, we set the parameter of VFC Snake model as: $\alpha = 0.5$, $\beta = 0.2$, and the iteration is about 30. To fully explain the superiority of our proposed method in visual, the illustrated mammograms consist of craniocaudal and mediolateral oblique view, whose severity includes benign and malignant, and each case contains only one abnormality.

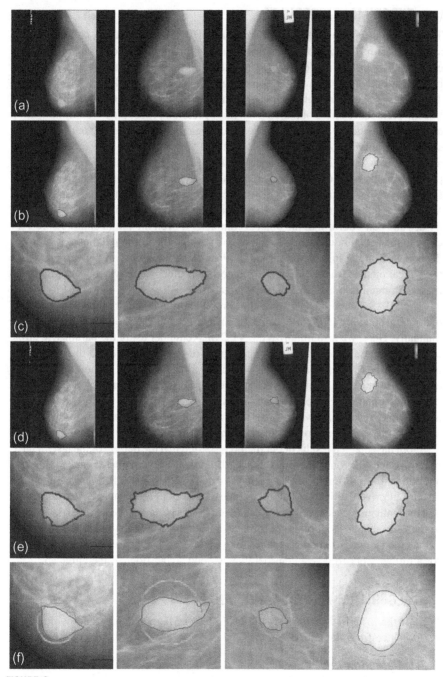

FIGURE 6

Experimental results of mammograms from MIAS database: (a)–(d) Original images.
(a-1)–(d-1) Results by the proposed method. (a-2)–(d-2) Results by typical VFC Snake model.
(a-3)–(d-3) The ground truth.

3.1 EXPERIMENTS RESULTS

The suspicious regions of full raw images from DDSM were given by chain code data as ground truth. This database also provided thumbnail images for visual browsing of each case as shown in Figure 5(a)–(d). The severity of these selected images is benign and the approximate abnormal regions have been marked in this database. To contrast, we illustrate the manual-segmented results in (a-4)-(d-4). Here, we utilize the parametric circle obtained from mass location procedure as the initialization of VFC Snake model and segment the lesion area. Results gained by our method are shown in Figure 5(a-2)–(d-2), labels in these mammograms have been removed already. From the enlarged images, we can clearly see that the contours converge precisely to the real boundaries in all cases and are much similar to the manual ones. For comparison, Figure 5(a-3)–(d-3) states the same cases detected by the typical VFC Snake model, unfortunately, these results are seriously influenced by the blurry tissues and can't deform to the objects completely, even the initial contours are very close to the actual boundaries. Thus, we can say that the improved model is in lower dependence on the initial contour and with stronger capability of convergence than the typical method, that is, our approach performs much better when we segment the masses in mammograms from DDSM database.

The MIAS database has offered the central coordinate and radius of each abnormal region showing in Figure 6(a-3)–(d-3), as well was the ground truth segmented manually. Here, we also initialize the VFC Snake model using the parametric circle obtained by mass location. From Figure 6(a-2)–(d-2), we observe that the results segmented by the typical method exist serious distortions and the contours can hardly converge to the real boundaries. Compared with the typical model, our proposed method can completely remove the labels or interference and achieve more robust and accurate results. As we can see, the curves are much more close to the ground truth and precisely tend to the object even in blurry regions.

From the enlarged results of our method, we find that the margin of the last image is rough and the other ones are smooth, that is because the severity between the last lesion and the rest are different, the last lesion is malignant while others are benign. Our results objectively reflect the pathology characteristics of actual masses to some extent that the malignant masses are always with burrs. This performance is somewhat benefit to the early diagnosis of breast cancer. Therefore, for a CAD system, we are able to extract the features of our detected results and determine the severity of abnormalities for a further work to give a considerable "second suggestion" to the clinician.

3.2 ALGORITHM PERFORMANCE ANALYSIS

We test the proposed method on the DDSM and MIAS database and evaluate the performance from three aspects.

3.2.1 Detection rate

First, we compute the detection rate, our evaluation principle is that the autosegmented region by the proposed method is completely within the criterion region by the experts. In the case of DDSM database, the criterion region is the outline formed by chain code data, and for MIAS database, the criterion region is the circle formed by the center coordinates and the radius. The detection rates of masses for each database are shown in Table 1. As we can see, 362 images are successfully extracted in total and the average detection rate is 90.5%, and even reaches up to 91.47% for the DDSM images. While it is lower for the MIAS images, the lesions in dense breast images of MIAS are always embedded in the gland and we can hardly obtain the mass position by location or edge map by edge detection operator for the deformable model.

3.2.2 Segmentation accuracy

To further explain the accuracy of our algorithm, we introduce another area-based evaluation method then. The area overlap ratio criteria are the most common evaluation criteria in medical images, which are the ratio of overlapped area between the segmented region of VFC Snake method and the criterion region of ground truth segmented manually. The performance of the proposed method and the typical VFC Snake method is tested on the successfully detected mammograms of MIAS by the following equation:

$$o = \frac{S_{L \cap T}}{S_{L \cup T}} \tag{15}$$

where L is the area segmented by VFC Snake model, T is the area of ground truth. $S_{L \cap T}$ and $S_{L \cup T}$ are the intersection area and union set area of the two regions, respectively. The average area overlap ratio and the variance of the segmentation results are shown in Table 2. We can see that the average area overlap ratio of improved method

Table 1 Mass Detection Rate by the Proposed Method

Database	Tested Images	Detected Images	Nondetected Images	Detection Rate (%)
DDSM	340	311	29	91.47
MIAS	60	51	9	85.0
Total	400	362	38	90.5

Table 2 Area Overlap Ratio of Different Methods

Method	Mean (%)	Variance (%)
Typical method	76.0151	11.5249
Improved method	90.4073	2.1556

is much higher than the typical method, and the variance is much lower, that is to say, our auto-segmented results are generally much more close to the ground truth. It is proved that our approach indeed performs much more excellent results compared with the typical method.

3.2.3 Segmentation similarity

Finally, we introduce a new measure method of medical image segmentation which is based on boundary distance-based similarity [20]. The above-mentioned area-based criteria have reflected the difference between the region of arithmetic-segmented result and manual-segmented result, while it could neither reflect the difference nearby the contour nor estimate whether the arithmetic-segmented curve is bigger or smaller than the ground truth.

The new evaluation index is described as expression (16), where m_{outside} and σ_{outside} are the mean and standard deviation of the bigger portion, which consist of points from segmented contour outside the ground truth (segmented manually), and m_{inside} and σ_{inside} are the mean and standard deviation values of the smaller portion, which are inside. R_{equ} is the radius of a circle equivalent to the segmented region. Here, the value of σ reflects the level of similarity, the smaller the σ value is, the higher similarity level has been reflected.

$$\left(\frac{m_{\text{outside}}}{R_{\text{equ}}} \pm \frac{\sigma_{\text{outside}}}{R_{\text{equ}}}\right) - \left(\frac{m_{\text{inside}}}{R_{\text{equ}}} \pm \frac{\sigma_{\text{inside}}}{R_{\text{equ}}}\right) \tag{16}$$

For the arithmetic-segmented contour $A = \{a_1, a_2, \ldots, a_k\}$ and the manual-segmented curve B, if there are m points outside B and n points inside B, then,

$$m_{\text{outside}} = \frac{1}{m} \sum_{i=1}^{m} \min\left(d(a_i, B)\right) \tag{17}$$

$$\sigma_{\text{outside}} = \sqrt{\frac{\sum_{i=1}^{m} \left[\min\left(d(a_i, B)\right) - m_{\text{outside}}\right]^2}{m-1}} \tag{18}$$

$$m_{\text{inside}} = \frac{1}{n} \sum_{j=1}^{n} \min\left(d(a_j, B)\right) \tag{19}$$

$$\sigma_{\text{inside}} = \sqrt{\frac{\sum_{j=1}^{n} \left[\min\left(d(a_j, B)\right) - m_{\text{inside}}\right]^2}{n-1}} \tag{20}$$

Here, d stands for the Euclidean distance. In this part, we access the similarity of eight mammograms which illustrated in Figures 5 and 6.

From Table 3, compare the corresponding values of m and σ of each image, we can find that most of the m_{outside}, m_{inside} and almost all σ_{outside}, σ_{inside} values obtained by modified method are much smaller than the typical results. The m value shows how much the curves deviated, and the smaller m indicates that the curve is much

Table 3 The Similarity of Different Methods

| Image | Evaluation $(m_{outside}/R_{equ} \pm \sigma_{outside}/R_{equ}) - (m_{inside}/R_{equ} \pm \sigma_{inside}/R_{equ})$ | |
	Typical Method	Improved Method
Figure 5(a)	$(0.0813 \pm 0.0055) - (0.1709 \pm 0.0040)$	$(0.0589 \pm 0.0035) - (0.0637 \pm 0.0016)$
Figure 5(b)	$(0.1727 \pm 0.0099) - (0.0628 \pm 0.0147)$	$(0.0298 \pm 0.0018) - (0.0425 \pm 0.0080)$
Figure 5(c)	$(0.1021 \pm 0.0124) - (0.0589 \pm 0.0033)$	$(0.0477 \pm 0.0039) - (0.0456 \pm 0.0014)$
Figure 5(d)	$(0.2076 \pm 0.0092) - (0.1180 \pm 0.0087)$	$(0.0758 \pm 0.0003) - (0.0592 \pm 0.0028)$
Figure 6(a)	$(0.0505 \pm 0.0020) - (0.1508 \pm 0.0089)$	$(0.0465 \pm 0.0022) - (0.1691 \pm 0.0036)$
Figure 6(b)	$(0.1289 \pm 0.0058) - (0.1008 \pm 0.0074)$	$(0.1171 \pm 0.0054) - (0.0659 \pm 0.0041)$
Figure 6(c)	$(0.5395 \pm 0.0201) - (0.2628 \pm 0.0204)$	$(0.1627 \pm 0.0153) - (0.3878 \pm 0.0185)$
Figure 6(d)	$(0.1328 \pm 0.0025) - (0.1239 \pm 0.0044)$	$(0.0510 \pm 0.0027) - (0.1265 \pm 0.0029)$

close to the real ones. The σ can exactly reflects the level of similarity of two curves, the smaller σ is, the much similar to the manual-segmented results. Thus, we can come to the conclusion that the contours obtained by modified method are more similar to the manual-segmented results compared with the typical method.

4 CONCLUSIONS

In this work, we present an effective integrated approach based on the improved VFC Snake model for mass automatic segmentation in mammogram which with low contrast and blurry boundaries. First of all, the local threshold method, RS theory, and morphological filter are applied to preprocess the mammograms to remove the labels and enhance the whole image. Then we use the LHT and CHT algorithms to locate the massive lesions and the position of which parametrically indicated as an approximate circle. The mass segmentation stage uses the parametric circle to initialize the deformable method which is defined by improving the force field of typical VFC Snake model and extract the mass boundary accurately. The proposed approach is tested on DDSM and MIAS database, respectively, and the results show that our algorithm achieves a higher detection rate and superior segmentation accuracy compared with the typical VFC Snake model. What's more, the segmented contours are much similar to the actual boundary of objects. In conclusion, the improved approach can not only locate and segment the mass automatically, but also in lower dependence on the initial active contour and with stronger capability of convergence. Besides, this algorithm is robust to the interference of blurry areas and tissue and able to converge precisely to the object. In addition, the results conform to the pathology characteristics of actual masses to some extent and benefit to early detection of breast cancer. That is to say, the proposed approach can provide some important basis to improve the CAD system.

This is an extension of the paper published on the IPCV'14 [21]. Here, we further evaluate the performance of our proposed algorithm using a novel distance-based boundary similarity measure based on the manual-segmented result mainly. In future work, we would like to classify the breast masses to benign and malignant based on the auto-segmented results of this chapter.

ACKNOWLEDGMENTS

Authors would like to thank the retrieval of DDSM and MIAS database from the Internet for the experiments of this chapter. This work is jointly supported by the National Natural Science Foundation of China (Grant No. 61175012), Science Foundation of Gansu Province of China (Grant Nos. 1208RJZA265 and 145RJZA181), Specialized Research Fund for the Doctoral Program of Higher Education of China (Grant No. 20110211110026), and the Fundamental Research Funds for the Central Universities of China (Grant No. lzujbky-2013-k06).

REFERENCES

[1] Jemal A, Bray F, Center MM, Ferlay J, Ward E, Forman D. Global cancer statistics. CA Cancer J Clin 2011;61(2): 69–90.

[2] Xu G, Li K, Feng G. Comparison of three imaging methods in the early diagnosis of breast cancer. J Capital Med Univ 2009;30(3):293–7.

[3] Ouyang C, Ding H, Wang G. Segmentation of masses in mammograms. Beijing Biomed Eng 2007;26(3):237–41.

[4] Kumar P, Sureshbabu R. Segmentation of region of interest and mass auto detection in mammograms based on wavelet transform modulus maximum. Digit Image Process 2011;3(7):415–21.

[5] Song E, Xu S, Xu X, Zeng J, Lan Y, Zhang S, Hung CC. Hybrid segmentation of mass in mammograms using template matching and dynamic programming. Acad Radiol 2010;17(11):1414–24.

[6] Abbas Q, Celebi M, Garcia I. Breast mass segmentation using region-based and edge-based methods in a 4-stage multiscale system. Biomed Sig Process Control 2013;8(2):204–14.

[7] Wang Y, Tao D, Gao X, Li X, Wang B. Mammographic mass segmentation: embedding multiple features in vector-valued level set in ambiguous regions. Pattern Recogn 2011;44(9): 1903–15.

[8] Kass M, Witkin A, Terzopoulo D. Snakes: active contour models. Int J Comput Vis 1988;1(4): 321–31.

[9] Mouelhi A, Sayadi M, Fnaiech F. A supervised segmentation scheme based on multilayer neural network and color active contour model for breast cancer nuclei detection. In: 2013 International conference on electrical engineering and software applications (ICEESA); 2013. p. 1–6.

[10] Guo M, Wang Z, Ma Y, Xie W. Review of parametric active contour models in image processing. J Conv Inf Technol 2013;8(11):248–58.

[11] Li B, Scott T. Active contour external force using vector field convolution for image segmentation. IEEE Trans Image Process 2007;16(8):2096–106.

[12] Heath M, Bowyer K, Kopans D, Moore R, Kegelmeyer W. The digital database for screening mammography. The Fifth International Workshop on Digital Mammography. 2001.

[13] Suckling J, Parker J, Dance DR, Astley S, Hutt I, Boggis C. The mammographic image analysis society digital mammogram database; 1994.

[14] Chris R. Software. [Online]. Available: http://microserf.org.uk/academic/Software.html.

[15] Pawlak Z. Rough set approach to knowledge-based decision support. Eur J Oper Res 1997;99(1):48–57.

[16] Hassanien A, Abraham A, Peters J, Schaefer G, Herry C. Rough sets and near sets in medical imaging: a review. IEEE Trans Inf Technol Biomed 2009;13(6):955–68.

[17] Liu Y, Ma Y, Xia C, Li S. Rough sets theory and its applications in image processing. Appl Res Comput [Jisuanji Yingyong Yanjiu] 2007;24(4):176–8.

[18] Hough PV. Method and means for recognizing complex patterns. U.S. Patent 3069654; 1962.

[19] Canny J. A computational approach to edge detection. IEEE Trans Pattern Anal Mach Intell 1986;8(6):679–98.

[20] Ha Z, Li C, Wang J, Zhou K, Yang Z. A new evaluation method for medical image segmentation. Beijing Biomed Eng 2008;27(4):385–8.

[21] Lu X, Ma Y, Xie W, Li T. Automatic mass segmentation method in mammograms based on improved VFC Snake model. The 2014 International conference on image processing, computer vision, and pattern recognition; 2014.

Correction of intensity nonuniformity in breast MR images

14

S. Yazdani[1], R. Yusof[1], A. Karimian[2], M. Pashna[1], A. Hematian[3]

[1]*Malaysia-Japan International Institute of Technology (MJIIT), Universiti Teknologi Malaysia, Jalan semarak 54100 Kuala Lumpur, Malaysia*

[2]*Department of Biomedical Engineering, Faculty of Engineering, University of Isfahan, Isfahan, Iran*

[3]*Department of Computer and Information Sciences, Towson University, Towson, MD, USA*

1 INTRODUCTION

Breast cancer is the second factor for death among women around the world [1]. Mammography is considered as one of the primary studies on tumor diagnosis and breast disease. It is not recommended to have frequent MRIs for high-risk women because of radiation. Scientists are looking for the best way for quantifying breast densities of MR images in healthy women to assessment of healthy breast composition. They are trying to find the link between breast cancer and breast composition. In addition, these assessments can help future researches to estimate potential risk of breast cancer. Our goal is normalizing MR images for quantifying density of the breast accurately, because this factor is an important marker in diagnosis of breast cancer. However, MR images has some limitations, such as, they sometimes are in low contrast, the dependence of MR image quality upon the condition the image is acquired, ideal image situation is never realized practically, bias field, etc.

One of the main problems of MR images is bias field [2]. Bias field has been a challenging problem in MR image segmentation. It is a smooth and low-frequency signal that corrupts MRI images specially those produced via old MRI machines. Bias field is attributed to eddy current, poor radio frequency (RF) coil uniformity, and patient anatomy [3]. Bias field eliminate high-frequency contents of MRI image like contours and edges, blur the images, change the intensity of image pixels, as a result, same tissues have different gray level distribution in the image. In order to decrease the aforementioned restriction, research teams throughout the world have conducted some studies on bias field correction in mammographic images [4,5].

According to their studies there are two main methods for bias field correction: prospective and retrospective methods. The prospective methods try to solve this problem in the process of acquisition by using special hardware. These approaches can only delete inhomogeneities due to hardware imperfections.

Retrospective approaches have been more developed; they are classified into two groups: first group uses the segmentation-based methods for computing the bias field and the second one works directly on data.

Although the segmentation-based approaches, such as expectation maximization (EM) algorithm [6], FCM-based methods [7,8], maximum likelihood [9,10], and MAP-based approaches [11,12], have obtained suitable result, they have some disadvantages such as: they work solely on intensity of image and they are able only to estimate and correct low amplitude intensity inhomogeneities [13].

These methods work directly on MRI image data such as SPM99 [14]. These methods has a problem of entropy minimization. Another method in this category is N3 (nonparametric intensity nonuniformity normalization) [3], which we used it in this chapter for bias field correction. N3 method was determined to be the best method on the recent studies [3].

After digitalizing the images, N3 method was used for bias field estimation and correction. The input of proposed method includes different percentages of intensity inhomogeneities, while the output consists of bias field corrected images with very high quality, which indicate breast regions more precisely.

2 PREPROCESSING STEPS

The main purpose of the preprocessing stage is to enhance the image quality for further processing steps by reducing or correcting the unrelated artifacts in the mammogram images. Mammograms image analysis is problematic due to existence of different artifacts that make the processing step complicated. Therefore, preprocessing stage is essential to improve the image quality. It will prepare the mammogram image for the next processing stages.

2.1 NOISE REDUCTION

Magnetic resonance images are corrupted by Rician distribution that arises from complex Gaussian noise in the original frequency domain measurements.

The Rician probability density function for the corrupted MR image intensity x is demonstrated as follows:

$$p(x) = \frac{x}{\sigma^2}\exp\left(-\frac{x^2+A^2}{2\sigma^2}\right)I_0\left(\frac{xA}{\sigma^2}\right) \tag{1}$$

where σ is the standard deviation of the noise, A is the underlying true intensity, and I_0 is the modified Bessel function of the first kind with order zero [15]. Median filter is one of the most popular nonlinear spatial filters for noise reduction that is more efficient than convolution when the purpose is to preserve borders and decrease noise simultaneously. This method is simple, computationally efficient, and also has a well denoizing power.

The median filter replaces the value of a given pixel with the median pixel value within a region of interest. A median filter with properly selected window size can smooth the noise in the original image. It may also virtually eliminate the main tissues information from the MR image. Therefore, there will be a trade-off between noise reduction and the preservation of information from image. Clearly, by increasing the size of the median window, both noise signals and signals from main tissues are being suppressed. For the 7×7 case, it removed more of the useful information than the 5×5 case. Therefore, the 5×5 median is the best for noise removal and preservation of brain tissue information [16].

The operation of median filtering technique is presented as:

$$f(x, y) = \text{median}_{(s, t) \in Sxy}\{g(s, t)\} \tag{2}$$

Let Sxy and median be the set of coordinates in a subimage window which is centered at (x,y) and the median value of the window, respectively.

2.2 BIAS FIELD REDUCTION

It is also called intensity inhomogeneity or intensity nonuniformity, which is one of the main problematic and challenging issues in MRI. It is a low-frequency undesirable signal that blurs MR images and thus decreases the high-frequency contents of MRI such as contours and edges.

Bias field is not always visible to the human eye and has a negative effect on segmentation results. For analysis techniques such as image segmentation, the presence of intensity nonuniformity may reduce its reliability and accuracy dramatically, as per the hypothesis that intensity is uniform in each tissue class being no longer verified.

Thus, the correction of intensity nonuniformity can improve the application of many quantitative analyses.

Bias field is the smooth intensity variation in MR images caused by different factors such as:

- Nonuniform reception sensitivity
- Inhomogeneous RF
- Nonuniform reception sensitivity

Other less important parameters causing the bias field include:

- Eddy currents
- Mistuning of the RF coil
- Geometric distortion
- Patient movement

These parameters cause intensity variation over the image and the totality of the imaged object [17]. Different methods exist to compensate for the inhomogeneity problem [18–22]. The aim of this study is to show how to restore the corrupted image for MR images that corrupted by bias field. We used two-step normalization method.

2.3 LOCALLY NORMALIZATION STEP

One of the problems, which happen in quantitative analysis of MRI, is that the results are not comparable between consecutive scans, different anatomical regions and within the same scan.

In order to segment MRI images in an effective approach, undesirable signals must be suppressed before segmentation process. Thus, one of the major challenges is eliminating the bias field. A normalization filter is required to remove low-frequency magnetic field variations within the MR images in order to regulate image brightness and contrast while preserving details.

In our normalization method, a sliding window is applied to slide vertically on each MRI image to compensate the current image bias field effects through histogram analysis.

In order to calculate the normalization factor, all the pixels within the region of the sliding window are gathered as the input data. Then the standard deviation of all gathered pixel values is calculated (SD1) beside the standard deviation of the mid-line of the sliding window (SD2). All the pixel data in the mid-line need to be shifted to the desired offset where the SD2 meets the SD1 value. At this point, the difference in the SD1 and SD2 is added to the pixel values of the mid-line to compensate the bias field effect. When the minimum and maximum pixel values of the mid-line are obtained, the mid-line pixel data are then stretched to its maximum data resolution (8-bit, 0–255) where the minimum value is zero and the maximum value is 255 (see Equation 3):

$$N_p = \frac{(P - P_m) \times R_M}{P_M - P_m} \tag{3}$$

where N_p is the normalized pixel value, p is the pixel value, P_m is the minimum pixel value in the image, P_M is the maximum pixel value in the image, and R_M is the maximum value of pixel bit depth.

In this step, a locally normalization via a resizable sliding window is performed to compensate intensity nonuniformity in MR images.

2.4 HYBRID METHOD FOR BIAS FIELD CORRECTION

Nonparametric intensity nonuniformity normalization (N3) was proposed by Sled et al. [3] for solving the problem of artifacts in MRI images. It is an iterative method, which estimates multiplicative bias field and true tissue intensity distribution. This method is an intensity model-based or histogram-based approach. Unlike some other methods such as EM, N3 does not rely on tissue classification.

One of the main advantages of nonparametric methods is that they do not make any assumptions about the patient anatomy. In addition, it is fully automatic, accurate, and robust method. In this step, a combination of N3 algorithm and singularity function analysis (SFA) model is used in breast MR images.

2.4.1 Bias field model

The following equation is the basis of the N3 method [23]. Bias field is often modeled as a multiplicative field:

$$v(\mathbf{x}) = u(\mathbf{x})f(\mathbf{x}) + n(\mathbf{x}) \tag{4}$$

In which, f is an unknown bias field or intensity inhomogeneity, v is the observed image, x designates the spatial position or voxel, u is the true image, and n is the noise which assumed to be independent of u.

The main stage for correcting bias field is estimating its distribution (f). The mixture of multiplicative and additive model makes this stage difficult.

The challenging problem of bias field correction consists of recovering $u(x)$ from information about the multiplicative factor $f(x)$ and the additive term $n(x)$. Due to the simultaneous presence of $n(x)$ and $f(x)$, it is difficult to solve the problem. Thus, a common solution is to neglect the $n(x)$ that is an additive noise. For the two-dimensional discrete image case and using a log transform, the bias field is made additive.

Consider a case without noise in which u and f are independently distributed random variables. Instead of v, u, f, we deal with $\log v, \log u, \log f$, then the formation model becomes additive:

$$\log v(i,j) = \log u(i,j) + \log f(i,j) \tag{5}$$

Let $V(u,v)$, $U(u,v)$, and $F(u,v)$ present the probability densities of $v(i,j)$, $u(i,j)$, and $f(i,j)$, respectively. Equation (5) can be expressed as

$$V(u,v) = U(u,v) + F(u,v) \tag{6}$$

Making the approximation that $\ln u$ and $\ln f$ are uncorrelated random variables, Equation (6) is found by convolution as follows:

$$V(\hat{v}) = F(\hat{v}) + U(\hat{v}) \tag{7}$$

The multiplication corrupts the field and a division can undo the corruption. In the frequency domain, multiplications and divisions convert to convolutions and deconvolutions as follows:

$$V(\hat{v}) = F(\hat{v}) \times U(\hat{u}) = F(\hat{v} - \hat{u})U(\hat{u})d(\hat{u}) \tag{8}$$

In which V, U, and F are probability densities. After this stage, the uniformity distribution (F) is modeled and viewed as blurring intensity distribution U that is the main stage for correcting bias field.

2.4.2 Correction step

An straightforward technique for image bias field correction would be that if the spatial frequencies of $u(i,j)$ (the true image) and $f(i,j)$ bias field are disjointed, the bias field can be removed by filtering out the spatial frequencies illustrating the bias field. In some cases, useful knowledge in MRI related to higher spatial frequencies than the intensity nonuniformity. Thus, by removing low spatial frequencies, intensity nonuniformity can be suppressed. The problem is that in most cases, spatial frequency information of the bias field and true image are not perfectly separated, and they have some overlapped components. For example, in MRI scans, when low spatial frequencies are removed, the spatial image will be considerably changed, implying the existence of useful knowledge at low spatial frequency bands. In such situations, using low pass filtering eliminates not only bias field but also useful knowledge in the true image, therefore decreasing the quality of the bias field corrected breast image. Another group of bias field correction methods relies on the assumption that anatomical knowledge in MRI occurs in the higher spatial frequency bands than intensity nonuniformity. These methods remove the bias field by filtering out highest spatial frequency bands demonstrating anatomical knowledge. One of the disadvantages of these methods is that the results depend on anatomy.

In this chapter, we used SFA idea [17], which assumes that anatomical information of MRI occurs in the high spatial frequencies in the image. In this method, after low pass filtering, since useful low spatial frequencies are removed during the filtering process, the filtered version of the ideal signal does not look like the original unbiased signal. SFA models recover the removed low-frequency information via reconstructing spatial information from the rest of high spatial frequencies.

In general, we applied a model that uses the assumption that bias field does not corrupt high spatial frequency bands in the image. Consequently, we first removed all low spatial frequencies without recognizing important information. Second, we recreated the spatial image from the remained higher spatial frequencies. The low spatial frequencies, which are related to intensity nonuniformity, are thus removed in the recreated image, leading to an intensity nonuniformity corrected breast image.

2.4.3 Field estimation

Using the distribution of U, we can estimate bias field estimation as follows. For a measurement $\hat{v}$ at some location x, $\hat{u}$ can be estimated using the distributions F and U ($\hat{u} = [\log(u)]$).

The estimated value of $\hat{u}$ given a measurement v_j is defined as follows:

$$E(\hat{u}) \frac{\displaystyle\int_{-\infty}^{\infty} \hat{u} F(\hat{v} - \hat{u}) U(\hat{u}) d(\hat{u})}{\displaystyle\int_{-\infty}^{\infty} F(\hat{u}) U(\hat{u}) d(\hat{u})} \tag{9}$$

By using the estimation of $\hat{u}$, the estimation of f can be found as follows:

$$\hat{f}_e(\hat{v}) = \hat{v} - E\lceil \hat{u} | \hat{v} \rceil \tag{10}$$

where $\hat{f}_e$ is the estimation of f_e, based on the single measurement of $\hat{v}$ at location x.

The difference between v and computed expectation of real signal, given the measured signal. Finally, the distribution U is estimated applying a deconvolution filter as follows:

$$\widetilde{G} = \frac{\widetilde{F}^*}{|\widetilde{F}|^2 + Z^2} \tag{11}$$

In which * defines complex conjugate, $\widetilde{F}$ is the Fourier transform of F, Z is a constant term for limiting the magnitude of G.

This estimation is then used to estimate a corresponding field.

In addition to processing stages were described above, there are some steps for practical impletion of applied algorithm.

- Estimating V distribution by using an equal-size bins histogram and Parzen window [24].

$$V(\hat{v}_j) = \frac{1}{N}\sum_{i=1}^{N}\frac{1}{h}\varphi\left[\frac{\hat{v}_j - v(\mathbf{x}_i)}{h}\right]$$
(12)

$$\varphi(s) = \begin{cases} 1 - |s|, & |s| < 1 \\ 0, & \text{elsewhere} \end{cases}$$
(13)

In which h is the distance between $\mathrm{O}v_j$, x_i is the location, N is the set of measurements $v(x_i)$, $\hat{v}_j$ is the centers of the bins

- Smoothing the bias field by using the B-spline technique [25]. For doing this stage, the MRI data should resample into subsamples (coarser resolution). This step is carried out because smoothing the bias field at full resolution is computationally difficult.

The smoothing stage is a challenging stage and the manner of smoothing, effects on bias field correction performance. The proposed approach for smoothing is approximating data by using linear combination of smooth basis functions. B-spline is a suitable basis, which is compactly supported spline. In comparison with conventional filtering approaches the proposed technique is superior regarding to missing data. Filtering methods are not suitable for this step because of boundary effects, which degraded overall performance substantially. The boundary of the chest wall of fatty tissues may be smoothed out to be close to outside background [13].

- Resampling to original resolution and using it for correcting original volume.
- Terminating the iterations using the variation coefficient, as follows:

$$e = \frac{6\{rn\}}{\mu\{rn\}}, \quad n = 1\ldots N$$
(14)

where rn is the ratio between subsequent field estimates at the location, 6 is the standard deviation, and μ is the mean.

When e falls below determined threshold, the iteration is stopped. In this chapter, breast MR images including variety percentages of bias field were used.

By using mentioned method, the bias field is removed and the specialist can assess and quantify the density of the breast accurately, and also the bias field corrected images are ready for another processing such as segmentation.

More importantly, segmentation and bias field estimation are mutually influenced by each other and the performance of MRI segmentation can be degraded significantly by the presence of bias field. If the bias field is corrected, the segmentation would be more powerful and it helps to specialist to have an accurate assessment.

3 EXPERIMENTAL RESULTS

This chapter demonstrated recent progress on MR image bias field correction. As mentioned above there are different methods, which are popular to bias field correction such as low pass filtering and statistical methods. Low pass filtering techniques are fast, easy to code, in addition, they can also be adaptive to image data. One of the main disadvantages of low pass filtering method is assuming the bias field as low-frequency signal. This methods also assume that the other image component have higher frequency, which is usually wrong for some cases. In addition, they tend to corrupt low-frequency components in tissue.

Statistical techniques are easy to integrate with other knowledge such as registration, segmentation, or some image feature but one of the disadvantages of these methods is that they often have relied on Gaussian distribution for modeling the intensity distribution of tissues, but experimental results show that intensity distribution of tissue do not indicate a Gaussian mixture exactly. This method fails to present some tissues [26].

Overall, the N3 method is superior to the other methods in robustness and high performance point of view [27].

In this part, we show the efficacy of proposed algorithm for clinical breast MRIs. All of the images were acquired by 1.5 T clinical MR scanner in "Isfahan radiology Medical Center." Figure 1(a) demonstrates a breast MR image corrupted by bias field and bias field corrected image using mentioned algorithm.

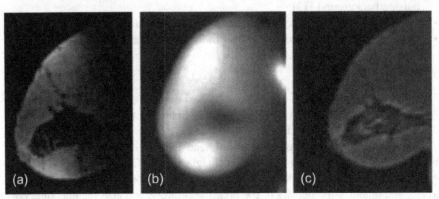

FIGURE 1

From left to right: (a) Original MR image with severe bias field, (b) Estimated bias field and (c) Corrected image.

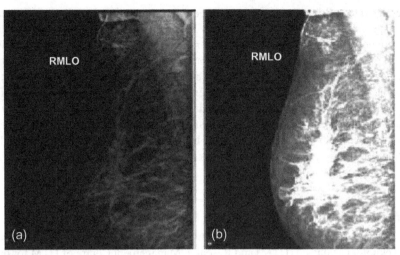

FIGURE 2

From left to right: (a) Original MR image, (b) corrected image.

Mentioned algorithm estimated bias field, corrected it, and improved the image contrast and quality dramatically. Figure 2 indicates other examples of breast MRI.

We can see that the bias field in our clinical database is 30–40% and the algorithm has removed the bias field successfully.

In Figures 1 and 2, MRI digitalized images have different percentages of bias field. These images are blurred because of bias field existence and breast compositions are not clearly shown. In the images, which are normalized through mentioned algorithm, these regions are presented clearly in Figures 1(c) and 2(b). In these images, the dynamic range is increased and the fatty tissues became brighter than before and they can be separated from fibroglandular tissues.

4 CONCLUSION

The bias field is the challenging problem of MR images. It changes the intensity values of pixels in MRI image and corrupts these images. The correction of this problem is necessary for subsequent computerized quantitative analysis. The high importance of bias field correction, motivated us to use a fast, reliable, and robust algorithm to solve this problem. It is expected that a fully automated algorithm for bias field correction in breast MRI may have great potential in clinical MRI applications.

In this chapter, an effective, robust, and accurate method is used for bias field correction in breast MR images. We proposed a new combination of locally normalization, N3, and SFA methods. The proposed technique takes advantage of N3 and SFA methods and not only preserves simplicity, but also has the potential to be generalized to multivariate versions adapted for segmentation applying multimodality images (e.g., T1, T2, and PD images). N3 method is an iterative algorithm and does not need any model assumption. This method does not rely on any prior knowledge of pathological data as a result can be applied at early stage and it is a substantial advantage in automated data analysis. Breast MRI image as an input enters into the proposed package and after different processing steps, the output is an image which indicates breast compositions and density measurement of the breast. The efficacy of the algorithm is presented on clinical breast MRIs and the results show the potential of method to extract useful information for breast disease detection. Extension of this method for tumor and disease detection is the next challenging task for the future.

ACKNOWLEDGMENTS

The authors would like to thank Ministry of Education of Malaysia (MoE), University Teknologi Malaysia (UTM) and Research Management Centre of UTM for providing financial support under the GUP Research Grant No. 04H40, titled "Dimension reduction and Data Clustering for High Dimensional and Large Datasets."

REFERENCES

[1] Avril N, Schelling M, Dose J, Weber WA, Schwaiger M. Utility of PET in breast cancer. Clin Positron Imaging 1999;2:261–71.

[2] Roy S, Carass A, Bazin PL, Prince JL. Intensity inhomogeneity correction of magnetic resonance images using patches. In: SPIE 7962, Medical imaging: 2011. p. 9621F.

[3] Sled JG, Zijdenbos AP, Evans AC. A nonparametric method for automatic correction of intensity nonuniformity in MRI data. IEEE Trans Med Imaging 1998;17:87–97.

[4] Kim K, Habas P, Rajagopalan V, Scott J, Rousseau F, Glenn O, et al. Bias field inconsistency correction of motion-scattered multislice MRI for improved 3D image reconstruction. IEEE Trans Med Imaging 2011;30.

[5] Wels M, Zheng Y, Huber M, Hornegger J, Comaniciu D. A discriminative model-constrained EM approach to 3D MRI brain tissue classification and intensity nonuniformity correction. Phys Med Biol 2011;56:3269.

[6] Dempster AP, Laird NM, Rubin DB. Maximum likelihood from incomplete data via the EM algorithm. J R Stat Soc Series B Stat Methodol 1977;1–38.

[7] Pham DL, Prince JL. An adaptive fuzzy C-means algorithm for image segmentation in the presence of intensity inhomogeneities. Pattern Recognit Lett 1999;20:57–68.

[8] Clarke L, Velthuizen R, Camacho M, Heine J, Vaidyanathan M, Hall L, et al. MRI segmentation: methods and applications. Magn Reson Imaging 1995;13:343–68.

[9] Van Leemput K, Maes F, Vandermeulen D, Suetens P. Automated model-based bias field correction of MR images of the brain. IEEE Trans Med Imaging 1999;18:885–96.

[10] Gispert JD, Reig S, Pascau J, Vaquero JJ, García-Barreno P, Desco M. Method for bias field correction of brain T1-weighted magnetic resonance images minimizing segmentation error. Hum Brain Mapp 2004;22:133–44.

[11] Wells III W, Grimson W, Kikinis R, Jolesz F. Adaptive segmentation of MRI data. IEEE Trans Med Imaging 1996;15:429–42.

[12] Guillemaud R, Brady M. Estimating the bias field of MR images. IEEE Trans Med Imaging 1997;16:238–51.

[13] Manjón JV, Lull JJ, Carbonell-Caballero J, García-Martí G, Martí-Bonmatí L, Robles M. A nonparametric MRI inhomogeneity correction method. Med Image Anal 2007;11:336–45.

[14] Ashburner J, Friston KJ. Voxel-based morphometry—the methods. Neuroimage 2000;11:805–21.

[15] Nobi M, Yousuf M. A new method to remove noise in magnetic resonance and ultrasound images. J Sci Res 2011;3.

[16] Singh WJ, Nagarajan B. Automatic diagnosis of mammographic abnormalities based on hybrid features with learning classifier. Comput Methods Biomech Biomed Eng 2013;16:758–67.

[17] Luo J, Zhu Y, Clarysse P, Magnin I. Correction of bias field in MR images using singularity function analysis. IEEE Trans Med Imaging 2005;24:1067–85.

[18] Ivanovska T, Laqua R, Wang L, Völzke H, Hegenscheid K. Fast implementations of the levelset segmentation method with bias field correction in MR images: full domain and mask-based versions. Pattern recognition and image analysis, vol. 7887. Berlin, Heidelberg: Springer; 2013. p. 674–81.

[19] Adhikari SK, Sing J, Basu D, Nasipuri M, Saha P. Segmentation of MRI brain images by incorporating intensity inhomogeneity and spatial information using probabilistic fuzzy c-means clustering algorithm. In: International Conference on Communications, Devices and Intelligent Systems (CODIS), 2012; 2012. p. 129–32.

[20] Fletcher E, Carmichael O, DeCarli C. MRI non-uniformity correction through interleaved bias estimation and B-spline deformation with a template. In: 2012 Annual International Conference of the IEEE Engineering in Medicine and Biology Society (EMBC); 2012. p. 106–9.

[21] Verma N, Cowperthwaite MC, Markey MK. Variational level set approach for automatic correction of multiplicative and additive intensity inhomogeneities in brain MR Images, In: 2012 Annual International Conference of the IEEE Engineering in Medicine and Biology Society (EMBC); 2012. p. 98–101.

[22] Uwano I, Kudo K, Yamashita F, Goodwin J, Higuchi S, Ito K, et al. Intensity inhomogeneity correction for magnetic resonance imaging of human brain at 7T. Med Phys 2014;41:022302.

[23] Lin M, Chan S, Chen JH, Chang D, Nie K, Chen ST, et al. A new bias field correction method combining N3 and FCM for improved segmentation of breast density on MRI. Med Phys 2011;38:5.

[24] Gao G. A parzen-window-kernel-based CFAR algorithm for ship detection in SAR images. IEEE Geosci Remote Sens Lett 2011;8:556–60.

[25] Csébfalvi B. An evaluation of prefiltered B-spline reconstruction for quasi-interpolation on the body-centered cubic lattice. IEEE Trans Vis Comput Graph 2010;16:499–512.

[26] Lee JD, Su HR, Cheng PE, Liou M, Aston J, Tsai AC, et al. MR image segmentation using a power transformation approach. IEEE Trans Med Imaging 2009;28:894–905.

[27] Hou Z. A review on MR image intensity inhomogeneity correction. Int J Biomed Imaging 2006;2006:1–11.

Traffic control by digital imaging cameras☆ 15

Rowa'a Jamal, Karmel Manaa, Maram Rabee'a, Loay Khalaf

Electrical Engineering Department, University of Jordan, Amman, Jordan

1 INTRODUCTION

Road crashes are considered as one of the major causes of death and injury. Over the years, there has been a noticeable steady increase in traffic violations and problems. This led the search for ways to control traffic with the intentions of reducing collisions by enforcing traffic laws, including traffic light violation, red-light violation, and speed violation. Over the last couple of decades, researchers have deliberately worked on improving the control at traffic intersections and traffic lights to reduce traffic jams and accidents [1]. The bottleneck in traffic problems is related to the limited resources in the current infrastructure, such as road crossing or merging. The traffic problems get worse with time, since the number of vehicles is increasing significantly.

The use of automated traffic control technologies is now wide spread throughout the world. Worldwide, despite of variation in the nature of these applications, they have provided positive road safety benefits. The first red-light camera was introduced in 1965 in the Netherlands. This camera was based on using tubes stretched across the road to detect the violation and subsequently trigger the camera [2]. New York's red-light camera program went into effect in 1993 [3].

The first digital camera system was introduced in Canberra in December 2000, and digital cameras have increasingly replaced the old film cameras in other locations since then [4]. From the late 1990s, digital cameras began to be introduced, those cameras can be installed with a network connection to transfer real-time live images to a central processing unit, for that they have advantages over film cameras in speed monitoring. However, film-based systems may provide superior image quality in the variety of lighting conditions encountered on roads. New film-based systems are still being used, but digital ones are providing greater proficiency, lower maintenance and are now more popular.

☆IPCV paper: Traffic Control by Digital Imaging Cameras.

2 PAPER OVERVIEW

This paper discusses the production of a traffic control camera used to obtain red-light violation, license plate recognition, and speed detection of the vehicles. The proposed camera is designed to be used at the bottleneck of traffic; intersections with traffic lights. Since there are several technologies used to obtain the same aim of this study, other characteristics were taken into consideration to make it more attractive.

The major step in using such cameras is monitoring the traffic at the red light by capturing a video. Then the video is processed by using image-processing techniques. The image-processing code was developed using Matlab 7.7, whereby the program reads video file, converts it to frames, and then by character segmentation, it can recognize the type of the violation and license plate number. The main tasks of this camera include detection of the red-light violation. Simply, the camera will check the color of the light, if it was red, it will compare between a saved picture for the street in such red-light case (the street in front of the traffic light must be empty) and the captured one. If there is any violation, the camera will capture a photo for the car and perform plate recognition.

On the other hand, for the speed violation, the camera will measure the distance between two points passed by the car and the time elapsed through this distance. Then, it will calculate the speed of the car by dividing the distance over the time. Also, if there is any violation in the speed, it will capture and perform plate recognition for the car. The system continuously monitors the traffic signal and the camera is triggered by any vehicle entering the intersection. Automatic number plate recognition can be used for purposes unrelated to enforcement of traffic laws. In principle, any agency or person with access to data either from traffic cameras or cameras installed for other purposes can track the movement of vehicles for any purpose.

3 IMPLEMENTATION

The main effort of this research is the use of image processing of captured images of a digital camera. The images used in this project and the video were taken by an inexpensive Canon 500 D, digital camera of 15 megapixel and 3.00 × zoom (as shown in Figure 1). It records videos with very high accuracy, full HD with 30 frames/s. Throughout this section, the design essentials, basics, and procedure will be discussed separately.

The desired system should be able to meet the requirements and goals stated below:

- Ability to detect the speed of the vehicle that crosses the traffic light with accuracy of 15%.
- Ability to recognize the vehicle registration plate with accuracy of 75%.
- Ability to identify cars crossing the red light.

FIGURE 1

Canon 500 D digital camera.

4 TRAFFIC DETECTORS

This section describes current technology associated with traffic control.

4.1 INDUCTION LOOPS

Inductive-loop detector technology has been in use for the detection of vehicles since the early 1960s. It consists of a loop of wire and an electronic detection unit. Simply, the operation is based on the principle of metal detection, relying on the fact that a moving metal will induce an electrical current in a nearby conducting wire. With a vehicle detector, the loop is buried in the roadway and the object to be detected is a vehicle (as shown in Figure 2).

Vehicle-detection loops are used to detect vehicles passing a certain area; for our approach, a traffic light. An insulated, electrically conducting loop is installed in the pavement. The electronic unit transmits energy into the wire loops at frequencies between 10 and 200 kHz, depending on the model. The inductive-loop system behaves as a tuned electrical circuit in which the loop wire is considered as the inductive elements. When a vehicle passes over the loop or is stopped over the loop, the vehicle induces eddy currents in the wire loops, which decrease their inductance. The decreased inductance actuates the electronics unit output relay or solid-state optically isolated output, which sends a pulse to the traffic signal controller signifying the passage or presence of a vehicle.

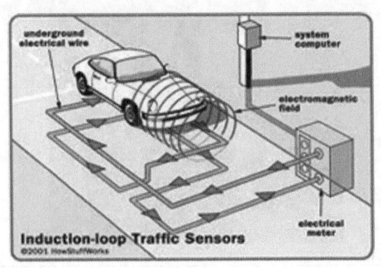

FIGURE 2

Induction loop.

4.2 MICROWAVE RADAR

Radar is an object-detection system which uses radio waves to determine the range, direction, or speed of objects. It can be used to detect motor vehicles. The radar antenna transmits pulses of radio waves which bounce off any object in their path. The object returns a small part of the wave's energy to the receiver antenna which is usually located at the same site as the transmitter.

The basic use of the traffic radars is the measurement of the speed of the vehicle. Traffic radar calculates speed from the reflections it receives. It uses a phenomenon of physics known as the Doppler principle. The classic example is heard along roads. As the car approaches, you hear the high pitch sound of the car horn. The instant the car passes and begins to move away, you hear a lower pitch sound. The car itself is making the same sound for both coming and going, but for a stationary listener, the speed of the car adds to the pitch of its sound as it approaches, and subtracts as it departs. This change from true pitch is called the Doppler shift, and the magnitude of the change depends upon the speed of the car. The Radar compares the shifted frequency of the reflection to the original frequency of the beam it sent out and from the difference it calculates speed. Figure 3 shows how microwave radar detects the speed of the vehicle.

4.3 INFRARED SENSORS

Active and passive infrared sensors are manufactured for traffic flow monitoring applications. Active infrared sensors illuminate detection zones with low-power infrared energy transmitted by laser diodes operating in the near infrared region of the electromagnetic spectrum. A portion of the transmitted energy is reflected

FIGURE 3

Microwave radar.

or scattered by vehicles back toward the sensor. The diodes operated in the near infrared spectrum at 880 nm. The signal modulation prevented interference from other
sources of infrared energy, including sunlight. Two transmitter-receiver systems
measured the vehicle speed and one measured the vehicle height. When trucks sus-
ceptible to rollover or jackknifing were encountered, flashers were activated to warn
drivers to reduce speed [5].

Passive sensors do not transmit energy; they detect energy from two sources:

1. Energy emitted from vehicles, road surfaces, and other objects in their field-of-view.
2. Energy emitted by the atmosphere and reflected by vehicles, road surfaces, or
   other objects into the sensor aperture

The energy captured by infrared sensors is focused by an optical system onto an
infrared-sensitive material mounted at the focal plane of the optics. This material
converts the reflected and emitted energy into electrical signals. Real-time signal
processing is used to analyze the signals for the presence of a vehicle. The sensors
are mounted overhead to view approaching or departing traffic. They can also be
mounted in a side-looking configuration. Infrared sensors are utilized for signal control; volume, speed, and class measurement; detection of pedestrians in crosswalks;
and transmission of traffic information to motorists.

4.4 VIDEO DETECTION

Video detection is based on real-time image processing providing efficient wide-area
detection well suited for registration of incidents on roads and in tunnels. Connected
to Traffic Controllers, the application can also be used for vehicle detection at

signalized intersections where it is difficult or expensive to install inductive loops. Video-detection systems are also considered nonintrusive.

Video detection combines real-time image processing and computerized pattern recognition in a flexible platform; it uses a vision processor to analyze real-time changes in the image. In this system, cameras called image sensors capture images and provide a video signal to the vision processor. The video signal is analyzed and the results are recorded. Video image detection is one of the leading alternatives to the commonly used loop detectors. It is progressively being used to detect traffic intersections and interchanges. This is because video detection is often cheaper to install and maintain than inductive loop detectors at multilane intersections. In addition to speed, volume, queues, and headways, it provides traffic engineers with many other traffic characteristics, such as level of service, space mean speed, acceleration, and density. Video detection is also more readily adaptable to changing conditions at intersections (e.g., lane reassignment and temporary lane closure for work zone activities). This is one of the biggest advantages of video image detection. It provides traffic managers with the means to reduce congestion and improve roadway planning. Additionally, it is used to automatically detect incidents in tunnels and on freeways, thus providing information to improve emergency response times of local authorities [6].

Through the discussion about the image-processing cameras, it is noticeable that they have these advantages:

- Monitors multiple lanes and multiple detection zones/lane.
- Easy to add and modify detection zones.
- Rich array of data available.
- Provides wide-area detection when information gathered at one camera location can be linked to another.
- Generally cost effective when many detection zones within the camera field-of-view or specialized data are required.

5 IMAGE PROCESSING

Image processing is defined as a process involving the change in the natural appearance of an image. It consists of an input and an output. The input is an image, whereas the output is a set of characteristics related to the image, also the output may be an image.

The main aim of image processing lies in converting the image for better human interpretation and machine perception. The operation of image processing may contain several actions including making the images to appear sharper, removing motion blur from images, removing noise from images, obtaining the edges of an image and removing details from an image [7].

5.1 BASIC TYPES OF IMAGES

There are a total of four basic types of images, namely, binary, grayscale, true color or red-green-blue (RGB), and indexed. The descriptions of all these images are provided in the following sections.

5.1.1 Binary image

A binary image is a digital image that has only two possible values for each pixel. The pixel is made up of either in black or white color. Binary images are also called bi-level or two levels. This means that each pixel can be stored as a single bit in either binary "0" or "1." Figure 4 shows a binary image.

5.1.2 Grayscale image

A grayscale digital image is an image in which the value of each pixel is not the same. The only colors are shades of gray. Each image pixel is made up of shades of gray from 0 (black) to 255 (white). Each pixel can be represented by 1 byte or 8 bits. The reason for having such an image was because less information is needed to be provided for each pixel (Figure 5).

5.1.3 True color or RGB image

Each pixel will have a particular color that is being described by the amount of red, green, and blue in it. If each of the components has a range of 0-255, this will give a total of 2^{24} different possible colors in an image. Each pixel will require 24 bits and they are called 24-bit color images (Figure 6).

FIGURE 4

Binary image.

FIGURE 5

Grayscale image.

FIGURE 6

RGB image.

5.1.4 Indexed images

Each pixel has a value that does not give its color but an index to the color in the map which has a list of all the colors used in that image.

6 PROJECT DESIGN

The procedure followed to obtain the interruption whether for the red violation or the speed violation is shown in Figure 6.

Image Acquisition: The proposed design was performed through recording a video by using a digital camera with a focus of 14 mm then converting this video to a series of images in order to obtain the principle of image processing through MATLAB 7.7.0 version. Whereas all the images obtain will be JPEG format.

Preprocessing
- *Cropping*: The basic type of preprocessing refers to image cropping. Cropping refers to the removal of the outer parts of an image to improve framing, accentuate subject matter or change aspect ratio. In other words, it refers to removing unwanted areas from a digital image capture. This is needed in the project in the part of the vehicle registration plate.

  Image cropping can be performed either by manually or by defining the selected spatial coordinates [*a b c d*]. *a* is the pixels from left, *b* is the pixels from bottom, *c* is the width of the selected area, and finally *d* is the height of the selected area.
- *Bwarea Function*: This function from the MATLAB basically removes from a binary image all the connected components (objects) which are lower than the defined pixel. After which it will reproduce another binary image with the entire pixel that are higher or equal to the defined pixel.

Segmentation: Segmentation is the process of assigning a label to every pixel. In other words, the segmentation is partitioning a digital image into multiple segments "pixels." The goal of segmentation is to simplify the representation of an image into something that is more meaningful and easier to analyze. Whereas the result of image segmentation is a set of segments that cover the entire image, or a set of contours extracted from the image. The simplest method of image segmentation is called the threshold method. This method is based on threshold value to turn a grayscale image into a binary image. During this process, every pixel in an image is called as object pixel if the value is greater than the threshold value and it is named as background pixel if the value is lower than the threshold value. An object pixel is being given a "1" value while the background pixel is given the "0" value. After which a binary image is being created with all the object and background pixels.

Representation and Description
- *Edge Detection*: Edge detection is the process for detecting meaningful discontinuities in intensity values; to find places where in an image where the intensity changes rapidly. Using: Sobel, Prewitt, Roberts or Canny method. What has been used in this project is Sobel edge detection.
- *Strel Function*: It is a function used to create a structuring element. It has many syntaxes; one from them is "strel('rectangle', MN)" which was used in this project to create the plate rectangular shape and MN represents a two-element vector of nonnegative integers (Figure 7).

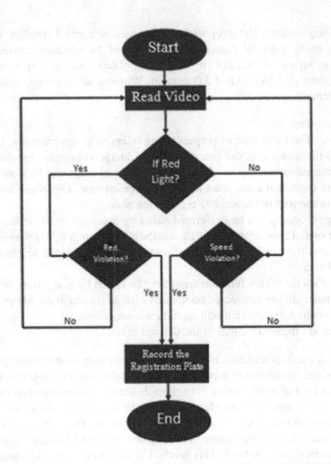

FIGURE 7

System flow chart.

6.1 RED-LIGHT VIOLATION

This part has been made by taking the absolute difference between the current inputs with a reference one. So it could be known if the car had passed the red line.

By applying the following steps:

- Define the red-light position in the traffic light.
- Define the reference frame to compare with (when the street is empty).
- Define the frame where the violation occurred.
- Take the absolute difference between the two frames.

For that it could be known if the car had passed the red line showed in Figure 8.

FIGURE 8

Reference of red light violation.

6.2 SPEED VIOLATION

This part is to determine if the car has crossed a certain speed limit which was chosen to be 600 pixel/s for normal traffic conditions. Two reference points have been defined $c1 = [162\ 260]$, $c2 = [445\ 504]$, $r1 = [691\ 700]$, and $r2 = [567\ 577]$ (as shown in Figure 9). This operation reads the video frames and first if there was a crossing found in them, it takes the difference which is the pixel difference between the points. The absolute difference is taken between the reference defined by ($c1$ and $r1$) and the read frame. The difference is defined as start frame, and it takes another absolute difference between ($c2$, $r2$) and the read frame, where the difference is defined as the final frame.

The difference is made by:

$$\text{Framdiff} = \text{finalfram} - \text{startfram} \tag{1}$$

The time can be known from the following equation where 30 is the frame rate:

$$\text{Time} = \frac{\text{framdiff}}{30} \tag{2}$$

Then the speed is calculated by the following equation, where 310 is the difference in pixels:

$$\text{Speed} = \frac{310}{\text{time}} \tag{3}$$

FIGURE 9

Speed violation.

6.3 PLATE NUMBERS RECOGNITION

This is done by first determining the plate position, then taking the numbers from the plate and from a look-up table to compare. The numbers are detected by taking the ones that have the maximum correlations. The look-up table is a template that contains the numbers from 0 to 9.

The action of recognition includes many functions to obtain the exact result. The image will be transformed to grayscale. Then the extended-maxima transform is computed. Edge detection and Strel functions are also used. Finally, plate shaping and filter processing are used to obtain the final result.

Plate position determination is made by the following steps:

- Transform the image to grayscale.
- Compute the extended-maxima transform.
- Apply edge-detection-type Sobel.
- Determine the line by Strel function.
- Dilate the image.
- Verify the rectangular plate shape.

Plate number recognition (PNR) consists of three parts:

- PNR: in this M-file, the image is being read and then opens a text document where the result is being displayed at. In this M-file, the plate numbers are being divided each separately in order to the compare. As shown in Figure 10.

FIGURE 10

Templates for the plate numbers.

- Creatt: in this M-file, the templates have been made.
- Recognize_numb: in this M-file, it computes the correlation between template and input image and takes the maximum correlation. Its output is a string containing the letter.

The correlation is made by this part of the code:

$$\text{for } n = 1 : \text{all}_{\text{numb}} \tag{4}$$

where all_{numb} is from the PNR M-file which is the size templates

$$\text{corr} = \text{corr2}(\text{templates}\{1, n\}, \text{cropped}) \tag{5}$$

This comutes the correlation between the templates and the input image

$$\text{corr}_{\text{values}} = [\text{corr}_{\text{value}} \, \text{corr}] \tag{6}$$

After applying this part of the project the result of the plate number will appear in a text document.

The templates that were used in finding the maximum correlation are provided in the subsequent sections.

7 PERFORMANCE ANALYSIS

The project was tested using a video for speed and red violations. For the plate position determination and number recognition, a few images were tested.

7.1 SPEED VIOLATION

A video was tested for any speed violation; in the tested video, the car speed was 615 pixel/s which violate the limit, while the other cars in the street had a speed in the range of (500-580)pixel/s.

There is a ratio for transformation from pixel to meter each 1 pixel equals 0.000264583 m, but this is not quit accurate since the zoom ratio affect number and size of the pixel.

7.2 RED VIOLATION

For the same video, the car has violated the red light, and the project code was able to detect it.

7.3 PLATE POSITION DETERMINATION

This part from the project has worked efficiently with some errors.

The proposed design was tested at 25 plates; the accuracy percentage was determined by the following:

$$\text{Accuracy percentage} = \text{number of matching numbers/total number} \qquad (7)$$

Note: Any addition number appears in the result count as an error, Table 1 shows the results and the percentage of error.

Table 1 Results Summary

Plate Number	Result	Error Percentage	Accuracy Percentage
22-4444	22-4444	0	100
2-70000	2 70000	0	100
4-44444	4-44444	0	100
14-17772	-1477772	25	75
34-444	34444	0	83.33
15-55000	1555000	12.5	87.5
10-5000	10-5000	0	100
10 952	7952	40	60
21-2	2162	25	75
60-13583	80013583	25	75
71-6516	75685-8	71.43	28.57
18-80964	809614	37.5	62.5
15-74995	157754742895	50	50
22-95951	22185851	37.5	62.5
7-6628	748828	50	50
7-3052	743052	16.67	83.33
71-9810	71488-10	37.5	62.5
187687	167667	33.33	66.67
20-67120	2087120	25	75
20-74717	23	87.5	12.5
55555	55555	0	100
11-8880	498880	42.86	57.14
11-430	1-433	33.33	66.67
11-1111	4941411	57.14	42.86
10-962	10-862	16.67	83.33
			Total accuracy = 70.38

Figure 11 represents the PNR result:

Figure 12 represents the correlation between the input numbers and the templates, in the illustrated plate. Figure 12 shows the correlation for the first element number (2) and the templates. Figure 12 shows that its maximum correlation was with templates of number (2).

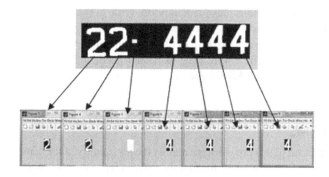

FIGURE 11

PNR.

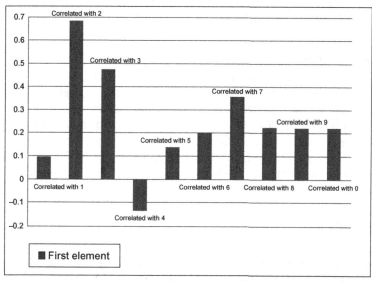

FIGURE 12

Correlation of number (2).

8 GENERAL CONCLUSION

Based on the results and the observation of the performance of the project code, the following conclusions can be drawn:

- MATLAB was a very helpful programe to use; it has all the required toolboxes and demos.
- The results of image processing were very good for the purpose of this project, the operations used to edit the images have done the task successfully.
- The camera specifications played an important role in the accuracy of the code, as it is better, the accuracy will be better.
- This project can make a good drop in the cost comparing to the other systems are being used in the traffic controlling, as it only needs a computer, high-quality camera, and the MATLAB license.

8.1 PROBLEMS

The problems faced in this project were mainly the low quality of the camera used since the video contains a moving car, for that the camera lens and zoom must be at a high quality, and it also needs a high processor computer for the MATLAB to work properly.

In the red violation, our tested zone was an intersection of three lanes so the moving cars left no space for us to put our testing points, which implies that we need a higher position of camera to see the empty space needed for testing points.

In the plate recognition what we faced that some of the plates have some nails on them or some stains which make it harder to extract the numbers correctly.

8.2 FUTURE WORK

This code was implemented using image processing in MATLAB, It can be implemented by using SCILAB which have the required toolboxes, and it is free to use which can also be used in LINUX and for which reduce the cost even more sine it is an open source, but SCILAB is harder to deal with rather than MATLAB.

The same approach that was used in this project can be used to detect the traffic congestion in a street and therefore control the traffic light signaling depending on the numbers of cars in the street, which can reduce the congestion on the streets.

REFERENCES

[1] Jamal R, Manna K, Rabee M, Khalaf L. Traffic control by digital imaging cameras. In: IPCV'14, The 2014 World congress in computer science, computer engineering, and applied computing (WORLDCOMP'14), Las Vegas, USA; 2014.
[2] Retting R, Ferguson S, Hakkert A. Effects of red light cameras on violations and crashes—a review of the international literature. Traffic Inj Prev 2003;4(1):17–23.

[3] Dailey DJ, Li L. 'Video image processing to create a speed sensor. Research Report, University of Washington; April 2000.

[4] Peter Clack. World-first digital camera to nab red light runners; November 26, 2000.

[5] Ralph Gillman. Office of highway policy information.

[6] http://www.mountain-plains.org/pubs/html/mpc-04-166/pg1.php; May, 2012.

[7] Matlab tutorial fundamental programming. http://in.mathworks.com/help/pdf_doc/matlab/matlab_prog.pdf retrieved; Nov. 18, 2014.

Night color image enhancement via statistical law and retinex

16

Huaxia Zhao, Chuangbai Xiao, Hongyu Zhao

College of Computer Science and Technology, Beijing University of Technology, Beijing, China

1 INTRODUCTION

The night color image enhancement is of great importance in both the computational photography and computer vision. First, it can effectively increase the visibility and surrealism of the scene. Second, artificial illumination light distributes unevenly at night leading to weakening the quality of monitoring photos and increasing the difficulty of surveillance. Thus, the night color image enhancement can promote the video surveillance. Last, the input images of most computer vision algorithms (e.g., the photometric analysis algorithm) are daytime images. Thus, the night color image enhancement can increase the scope of such algorithms by enhancing nighttime images.

However, the night color image enhancement is a challenging task. Currently, the main techniques for the night image enhancement are the image fusion and image enhancement. Image fusion techniques include two categories: one is the fusion of the nighttime image and visible image [1,2] and another is the fusion of the night-time image and infrared image [3,4]. These methods require multiple different spectral images collected in the same scene and have high computational complexity. The main techniques for the image enhancement include contrast stretching, slicing, histogram equalization, and some algorithms based on the retinex [5–11], etc. Of all these algorithms, the algorithm based on the retinex has acceptable results, but it will produce the "halo effect" and high time complexity.

In this article, we propose a novel algorithm for enhancing the night color image based on the statistical law and the retinex. We assume that there is a transformation on the brightness components of the pixel values between the nighttime image and illumination image. Therefore, through this transformation, we can accurately and quickly get the illumination image. Then, we can get the resulting image successfully based on the retinex. The resulting image retains image details and exhibits higher brightness, so that the overall image looks more harmonious and natural. Our algorithm is simpler and faster compared to the other algorithms.

The rest of this article is organized as follows. In Section 2, overview of retinex theory is given. In Section **3**, the proposed algorithm is described in detail, which contains two parts: analysis of the transformation law and enhancing the nighttime image. Finally, the experimental results are presented to demonstrate the efficiency of the proposed algorithm in Section 4. The conclusion is in Section 5.

2 OVERVIEW OF RETINEX THEORY
2.1 THE BASIC IDEA OF RETINEX THEORY

The Retinex theory deals with the removal of unfavorable illumination effects from a given image. A commonly assumed model suggests that any given image S is the pixel-wise multiplication of two images, the reflection image R, and the illumination image L. This model is given in the following equation:

$$S = R \cdot L \tag{1}$$

Therefore, if we can get the illumination image, we can quickly get the reflection image. In the actual calculation, a look-up-table log operation transfers this multiplication into an addition, resulting with $s = \log(S) = \log(L) + \log(R) = 1 + r$.

2.2 THE "HALO EFFECT"

The Retinex algorithm often results in the "halo effect." It is mainly based on the position of surrounding pixels to give different weights to estimate the current pixel illumination in the calculation of the illumination, while ignoring the pixel itself. This often leads to mutual influence between different pixels in the intense chiaroscuro edge region: the estimated illumination of high pixels is lower affected by adjacent low pixels, the estimated illumination of low pixels is higher affected by adjacent high pixels. The distortion of the estimated illumination leads to the "halo effect."

3 ANALYZING THE TRANSFORMATION LAW AND ENHANCING THE NIGHTTIME IMAGE

We first transform the original RGB space to HSV space, because processing the color image directly in RGB space will lead to color distortion. The HSV space is closer to human visual perception in color perception. Our transformation law is only used in brightness component of HSV space.

Currently, most algorithms often use the filtering method to estimate the illumination image, and achieve good results. In this article, we use the processing results of some algorithms (the algorithm of Michael Elad [12] and MSRCR [13,14]) as illumination images. Through these two algorithms, we get three images. One is the nighttime image and the other two are the corresponding illumination images. Their brightness components of HSV space are denoted as L, M, and N. For analyzing the transformation law, we get pixels which value is i $(0-255)$ from L. Then, we have a set of coordinates through known pixels. In the same coordinates, we get two sets of pixel values from M and N. The average (j, k) of these two sets are the corresponding value to i. Figure 1 displays the correspondence between i and j, k. In order to facilitate observation, we add a linear which is $y=x$.

By observing Figure 1, we find the curve of MSRCR on the figure can be represented by a circular arc. But it is too close to the linear which is $y=x$ resulting in that the enhanced image is too bright and loses details seriously. The curve of Michael Elad is roughly like a circular arc except a small part. It is the reason that the resulting images processed by the algorithm of Michael Elad have a stronger noise. Overall, we can use a circular arc to represent the relationship between the input image and illumination image. Obviously, the fitting circular arc should pass the point

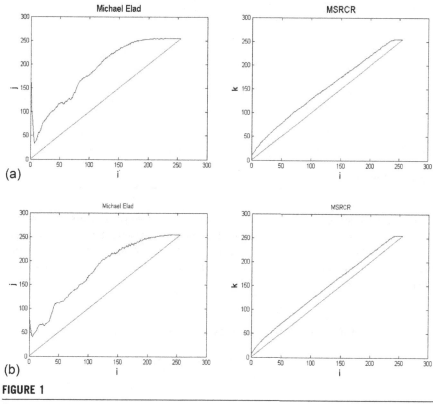

FIGURE 1

The corresponding graphs of pixel values of source images and illumination images obtained by the algorithm of Michael Elad and MSRCR algorithm. Panels (a–d) are the processing results of four different pictures.

(Continued)

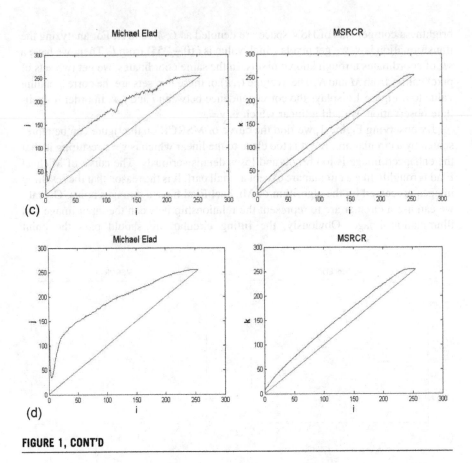

FIGURE 1, CONT'D

(255,255). In order to facilitate the calculation, we use two parameters to represent the circular arc. One parameter is x-coordinate (x_0) of the circular center. Another is the intersection $(0, \lambda)$ of arc and y positive axle. According to the nature of the circle, the y-coordinate (y_0) of the circular center can be expressed as the following equation:

$$y_0 = \frac{255^2 - \lambda^2/2 - 255 \times x_0}{255 - \lambda} \tag{2}$$

The radius (r) of the circular arc can be expressed as follows:

$$r = \sqrt{(x_0 - 255)^2 + (y_0 - 255)^2} \tag{3}$$

The circular arc can be expressed as follows:

$$y = \sqrt{r^2 - (x - x_0)^2} + y_0 \tag{4}$$

Using Equation (4), we can get the illumination image directly and quickly. The circular arc is shown in Figure 2.

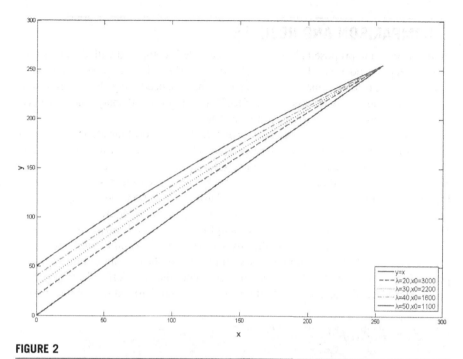

FIGURE 2

Fitting circular arc.

According to Equation (4), we can know that the circular arc takes two parameters called x_0 and λ. The smaller x_0 is, the more obvious the brightness enhancement is. The greater λ is, the more obvious the brightness enhancement is. It can be seen that the darker the input image is, the smaller x_0 is and the greater λ is, and vice versa. Therefore, we assign the average pixel value of the source image to λ. x_0 is represented by the following formula:

$$x_0 = \max\left(127, \text{round}\left(6000 \times \exp^{-\lambda/30}\right)\right) \tag{5}$$

Where round () is the rounding function which is used to improve the algorithm speed. The minimum size of x_0 is limited to 127 to prevent image distortion. Therefore, we have got a no-argument function to show the relationship between the original image and the corresponding illumination image.

The algorithm is given below:

(1) Transform the original RGB data to the HSV data.
(2) Get the illumination image using Equations (4) and (5).
(3) Enhance the nighttime image through the retinex theory and the obtained illumination image.
(4) Transform the HSV data to the RGB data and show the enhanced image.

4 COMPARISON AND RESULTS

In this section, the proposed algorithm of this article is compared with the algorithm of Michael Elad and MSRCR algorithm. Figures 3-8 show the experimental results of five scenes. (a) is the original image. (b) shows the enhanced image by the algorithm of Michael Elad. (c) is obtained by MSRCR algorithm. (d) displays the enhanced image by the proposed algorithm in this article.

It can be clearly seen from the figures that the three algorithms all have a certain enhancement effect on the nighttime images. The processing results of MSRCR algorithm are too bright leading to atomization phenomenon and loss of details, as shown in Figures 4(c), 5(c), 6(c), and 8(c). The processing results of Michael Elad's algorithm tend to produce excessive sharpening phenomenon in highlighting edges and the "halo artifacts" phenomenon which is shown in Figures 6(b), 7(b), and 8(b). Moreover, it often leads to noisy amplification in dark areas, as shown in Figure 3(b), which is mainly due to the unsmooth curve (shown in Figure 1) between source images and illumination images. Compared with the two algorithms, the proposed algorithm can better recover details, eliminates the "halo effect" and suppress noise. Moreover, the results of our algorithm look more harmonious and natural.

FIGURE 3

Scene 1. (a) original image; (b) enhanced image by Michael Elad; (c) enhanced image by MSRCR; (d) enhanced image by the proposed algorithm.

FIGURE 4

Scene 2. (a) original image; (b) enhanced image by Michael Elad; (c) enhanced image by MSRCR; (d) enhanced image by the proposed algorithm.

FIGURE 5

Scene 3. (a) original image; (b) enhanced image by Michael Elad; (c) enhanced image by MSRCR; (d) enhanced image by the proposed algorithm.

FIGURE 6

Scene 4. (a) original image; (b) enhanced image by Michael Elad; (c) enhanced image by MSRCR; (d) enhanced image by the proposed algorithm.

FIGURE 7

Scene 5. (a) original image; (b) enhanced image by Michael Elad; (c) enhanced image by MSRCR; (d) enhanced image by the proposed algorithm.

FIGURE 8

Scene 6. (a) original image; (b) enhanced image by Michael Elad; (c) enhanced image by MSRCR; (d) enhanced image by the proposed algorithm.

For a more definite description of the experimental results, this article also uses objective evaluation criteria to test the effectiveness of our algorithm. We examine our algorithm in mean value, standard deviation and time-consuming (Computer configuration: CPU: Pentium(R) 3.00 GHz; Memory: 3.00 GB; Programming Language: Matlab). The image mean reflects the brightness level of the image; the standard deviation reflects the image contrast; the time-consuming reflects the time complexity of the algorithm. The results are shown in Tables 1–4.

As can be seen in Tables 1–6, in terms of the mean, MSRCR algorithm has the most significant effect of improving mean, but the enhanced images are too bright overall to protect details. Compared with the algorithm of Michael Elad, the proposed algorithm has a better enhancing effect of the mean which displays the brightness of the whole picture is consistent with human visual perception. In terms of

Table 1 Criteria of Assessment of Figure 3

	Mean	**Standard Deviation**	**Time Consuming (s)**
Source image	32.290669	37.976650	
Michael Elad	74.522833	34.043863	125.203029
MSRCR	122.023486	33.550094	8.073667
proposed algorithm	92.0300	38.6720	1.246996

Table 2 Criteria of Assessment of Figure 4

	Mean	Standard Deviation	Time Consuming (s)
Source image	19.074728	28.879643	
Michael Elad	54.979484	32.582415	174.404951
MSRCR	105.600284	41.911008	14.030690
proposed algorithm	87.0683	46.6404	1.724475

Table 3 Criteria of Assessment of Figure 5

	Mean	Standard Deviation	Time Consuming (s)
Source image	42.871070	57.089267	
Michael Elad	74.523826	51.653054	177.822975
MSRCR	125.407817	52.732457	11.619577
proposed algorithm	81.8586	61.3861	1.39663

Table 4 Criteria of Assessment of Figure 6

	Mean	Standard Deviation	Time Consuming (s)
Source image	43.9788	37.4953	
Michael Elad	85.4186	28.9512	177.513603
MSRCR	145.5552	27.6842	13.096727
proposed algorithm	94.7658	32.4271	1.450654

Table 5 Criteria of Assessment of Figure 7

	Mean	Standard Deviation	Time Consuming (s)
Source image	37.186166	32.700994	
Michael Elad	87.693053	47.901984	306.097388
MSRCR	141.732310	45.151938	27.631109
proposed algorithm	101.8945	55.9020	2.418071

Table 6 Criteria of Assessment of Figure 8

	Mean	Standard Deviation	Time Consuming (s)
Source image	19.9751	37.1902	
Michael Elad	61.4820	36.6652	163.483256
MSRCR	98.9313	36.8997	14.983709
proposed algorithm	84.8932	43.4253	1.330059

standard deviation, the proposed algorithm is better than the other two algorithms. The proposed algorithm has remarkable enhancement of the image contrast and significant effect of image detail recovery. In terms of time consuming, the proposed algorithm has lower time complexity than the other two algorithms. Moreover, our algorithm does not need manual control parameters increasing the adaptability of our algorithm.

5 APPLICATION

Besides above applications, there are other applications. Because this algorithm uses the properties of the image itself. We process overexposed images by means of this algorithm and get good results. Our algorithm avails several applications due to its fundamentality and the special properties in processing natural images.

Overexposed images often have high brightness, low contrast, and invisible details. This algorithm can effectively restore the contrast and brightness to a suitable standard for human senses by means of the transformation between the original image and illumination image. The processing results of overexposed images are listed (seen in Figures 9–10). Panel (a) is the original image and (b) displays the enhanced image by the proposed algorithm in this article. It can be clearly seen from the figures that this algorithm has a good restoration of overexposed images, making the images more in line with human senses. This approach enhances significant edges, making structures visually pleasing.

6 THE CONCLUSION

In this article we present an effective algorithm for enhancing the nighttime image. In our algorithm, we propose a statistical law to present the relation of the original image and illumination image. Using this statistical law and retinex theory, we

FIGURE 9

Scene 6.

FIGURE 10

Scene 7.

can accurately and quickly get the resulting image. The algorithm is validated through subjective and objective evaluation, which shows it can eliminate the "halo effect," enhance the image contrast, recover image details and have low time complexity. In summary, our algorithm is effective to complete the challenging task of enhancing the nighttime image [15].

REFERENCES

[1] Raskar R, Ilie A, Jingyi Y. Image fusion for context enhancement and video surrealism. In: Proceedings NPAR 2004—3rd international symposium on non-photorealistic animation and rendering, 2004. Annecy, France: Association for Computing Machinery; 2004. p. 85–93.

[2] Yamasaki A, Takauji H, Kaneko S, et al. Denighting: enhancement of nighttime images for a surveillance camera. In: 2008 19th international conference on pattern recognition, ICPR 2008, 2008. Tampa, FL, United States: Institute of Electrical and Electronics Engineers Inc; 2008.

[3] Xiaopeng Z, Sim T, Xiaoping M. Enhancing photographs with near infrared images. In: 26th IEEE conference on computer vision and pattern recognition, CVPR, 2008. Anchorage, AK, United States: Institute of Electrical and Electronics Engineering Computer Society; 2008.

[4] Shaojie Z, Xiaopeng Z, Xiaoping M, et al. Enhancing low light images using near infrared flash images. In: 2010 17th IEEE international conference on image processing, ICIP 2010, 2010. Hong Kong: IEEE Computer Society; 2010. p. 2537–40.

[5] Brainard D, Wandell B. Analysis of the retinex theory of color vision. J Opt Soc Am 1986;3:1651–61.

[6] McCann J. Lessons learned from Mondrians applied to real images and color gamuts. In: Final program and proceedings of the 7th IS and T/SID color imaging conference: color science, systems and applications, 1999. Scottsdale, AZ, United States: Society for Imaging Science and Technology; 1999. p. 1–8.

[7] Funt B, Ciurea F, McCann J. Retinex in Matlab. In: Final program and proceedings of the 8th IS and T/SID color imaging conference: color science, systems and applications,

2000. Scottsdale, AZ, United States: Society for Imaging Science and Technology; 2000. p. 112–21.

[8] Jobson D, Rahman Z, Woodell GA. Properties and performance of a center/surround retinex. IEEE Trans Image Process 1997;6(3):451–62.

[9] Rahman Z, Jobson DJ, Woodell GA. Multi-scale retinex for color image enhancement. In: Proceedings of the 1996 IEEE international conference on image processing, ICIP'96. 1996. Lausanne, Switz: IEEE; 1996. p. 1003–6.

[10] Tomasi C, Manduchi R. Bilateral filtering for gray and color images. In: Proceedings of the 1998 IEEE 6th international conference on computer vision, 1998. Bombay, India: IEEE; 1998. p. 839–46.

[11] Meylan L, Susstrunk S. High dynamic range image rendering with a retinex-based adaptive filter. IEEE Trans Image Process 2006;15(9):2820–30.

[12] Elad M. Retinex by two bilateral filters. In: Proceedings of the scale-space conference, vol. 9(7); 2005. p. 217–29.

[13] Jobson DJ, Rahman Z, Woodell GA. Multiscale retinex for bridging the gap between color images and the human observation of scenes. IEEE Trans Image Process 1997;6(7):965–76.

[14] Rahman Z, Jobson DJ, Woodell GA. Retinex processing for automatic image enhancement. J Electron Imag 2004;13(1):100–10.

[15] Huaxia Z, Chuangbai X, Hongyu Z. Night color image enhancement via statistical law and retinex. In: Proceedings of the 2014 world congress in computer science, computer engineering, and applied computing, IPCV 2014, 2014. Las vegas, Nevada, USA: WORLDCOMP'14 Steering Committee; 2014.

PART 2

Computer vision and recognition systems

PART

2

Computer vision
and recognition
systems

Trajectory evaluation and behavioral scoring using JAABA in a noisy system

17

H. Chen[1], P. Marjoram[1], B. Foley[2], R. Ardekani[2]

[1]*Department of Preventive Medicine, Keck School of Medicine, USC, Los Angeles, CA, USA*
[2]*Molecular and Computational Biology, Department of Biological Sciences, USC,*
Los Angeles, CA, USA

1 INTRODUCTION

Behavioral studies commonly rely upon extensive time-series observation of animals, and characterization of their movement, activities and social interactions. Historically this involved scientists (or their students) recording observations by hand—a laborious and error-prone process. More recently, automation has promised to dramatically increase the quantity and detail of data collected, and a variety of methods have recently become popular in the important area of automated tracking, for example, the CTRAX ethomics software [1], and the proprietary EthoVision [2].

Most available solutions demand restricted experimental conditions that may not be desirable for the question of interest, or feasible in the field, (or even the lab). For example, in *Drosophila melanogaster* experiments, it is common to restrict the possibility of flight, and use a backlit glass substrate for contrast [1]. A majority of *D. melanogaster* social interactions occur on food, and glass is not representative of their normal habitat. Additionally, many tracking algorithms perform poorly when the number of objects being tracked is not fixed. In such contexts, it is difficult to determine whether a large "blob" of pixels in fact represents a single object or two overlapping objects. Such close contact happens commonly during aggression, courtship and mating events.

We are particularly interested in describing spontaneous group assembly, and describing the resultant behavior in those groups. That is, we need to analyze setups with variable numbers of flies that frequently come into close contact. As a test-case, we consider data from a set of experiments in which we recorded fly behavior in an environment consisting of four food patches, modeled on a published experiment conducted with still cameras [3]. Each patch was recorded independently, and flies could freely move among patches, or be off patch (and thus not recorded). To model group assembly, we need to accurately count individuals on patches, and measure joining and leaving. We are currently able to detect objects (blobs or putative flies) in video frames against a static background. This method is designed to be relatively robust to nonoptimal experimental conditions.

Behavioral annotation requires that we move from static blobs, to individual-fly identification and tracking. Here, we build upon our work presented in [4], and describe a three-stage process from video processing to behavioral annotation. First, we present an algorithm that enables us to assemble trajectories even through multi-fly blobs. Second, we then utilize these trajectories in freely available machine-learning behavioral annotation software. The Janelia Automatic Animal Behavior Annotator (JAABA) is a commonly used animal-behavior annotation software [5]. We use JAABA to manually flag errors in our tracking algorithm for "single fly" versus "multifly" blobs. This enables subsequent trajectory correction and behavioral annotation. Finally, from the subset of trajectories consisting of high-likelihood single-fly blobs, we train a sex classifier to distinguish males from females. We also train a chasing classifier, which together with sex annotation allows us to score important social behaviors, namely courtship and aggression.

2 METHODS

Videos are recorded using four high-resolution Grasshopper digital video cameras (Point Grey Research Inc., Richmond, Canada) simultaneously filming individual patches at 30 Hz, RGB, and 800×600 resolution. Videos are processed as single frames, by identifying blobs against an averaged background [6]. Blobs may contain from one to many individual flies, or be spurious artifacts. Features of the blobs are extracted using the cvBlobslib package [7]. The borders of the patch are defined manually, using the ImageJ software ellipse tool [8], and are calculated as length of the radius from centroid of the patch. All flies outside this radius are considered "off patch." Lighting was ambient room lighting. Videos were recorded for 1 h intervals, and a subset were scored for joining and leaving by hand, to evaluate accuracy.

To facilitate tracking and individual-fly (sex and genotype) identification, we painted a small color-coded dot on each fly (either blue or yellow). For color detection problems there are drawbacks to the RGB color space. First, there is a high correlation between red, green, and blue channels; moreover, they are not robust to lighting conditions. In many situations, one needs to be able to separate the color components from intensity [9–11]. There are many linear and nonlinear color spaces that achieve better color constancy, effective bandwidth reduction, and robust color image processing [12]. In particular, HSV has been shown to have better performance than RGB space for color recognition [9]. For color recognition on silhouettes, RGB values of each pixel were converted to HSV using the equations of [12]. We selected thresholds in 3D HSV space, which were most effective for distinguishing blob colors. Each pixel within the fly silhouette was assigned to a color based on h, s, and v, and values, and pixels which were not within these thresholds were disregarded. The paint color was inferred by the majority of pixels.

Blobs are identified for each frame, or time T. The number of blobs, and blob statistics for each T, were output. Blob statistics include the blob X and Y centroids (B_X and B_Y); fitted-ellipse major and minor axes (B_A, B_B); and blob area (in pixels, B_P). Blobs with centroids outside the perimeter of the patch are excluded. Every blob is assigned a unique identifier within a frame (B_i). Each blob is subsequently assigned an inferred fly number (B_n, below).

Flies are taken to be nonfissible blob units. We infer the number and identity of flies within blobs by tracking fusion and fission events. We construct tracks by making three simplifying assumptions (based on observation). First, that flies do not often move a greater distance than their body length between frames. Second, that the noise in blob area estimation is not large between consecutive frames (i.e., less than half the actual fly area). Third, (on the scale of 30 frames a second) that flies do not join and leave patches often, that is, we conservatively assume fly number does not change, unless there is no other explanation for the data. TABU is implemented in R [13].

Trajectories are constructed by initializing the first frame assuming each blob is a single fly. Subsequently, we implement the following algorithm at each frame:

1. *Identify Neighborhoods*: For each pair of frames T_t and T_{t+1}, we construct a graph by drawing edges between blobs that (a) are in different frames and (b) overlap. We define overlapping as having centroids within the distance of the major axis B_A of the blob ellipse. We define two degrees of overlapping: mutual and unidirectional. A mutual overlap occurs when the B_A of both blobs is longer than the distance between their centroids. If only one B_A is this long, the overlap is unidirectional. A "neighborhood" is defined as group of blobs linked by mutual edges.

2. *Check "Joins" and "Leaves"*: We test for probable joining and leaving events by examining blobs that are not in a neighborhood with other blobs, using the more-relaxed unidirectional overlap. Flies in blobs in T_t with no unidirectional matches in T_{t+1} are assumed to have left, and flies in blobs in T_{t+1} with no unidirectional matches in T_t are assumed to have joined. Otherwise, the unmatched blobs are assigned to their nearest unidirectional match.

3. *Assign flies to blobs*: In the simplest case, a neighborhood is comprised of a single blob in T_t and T_{t+1}. If so, all flies in the blob at T_t are assigned to the blob at T_{t+1}. In more complex cases, we assign flies between blobs to minimize the difference between summed fly-area and their respective B_P. Every fly inherits the blob-specific statistics of its assigned blob. During fission events if there are fewer flies than blobs we update fly numbers. Thus, we arrive at our count of flies. Each blob is also assigned a count of the number of flies it contains, B_N.

4. *Update statistics*: Each fly is assigned a number of fly-specific statistics. These include a unique index for each fly (F_j); fly area in pixels (F_P); and fly area from the fitted ellipse ($F_e = B_A B_B \pi$). Statistics are running averages, updated only when a fly is inferred to be in a single-fly blob. An error parameter is also updated (F_S) to alert us when there is a mismatch between observed blob

properties and the inferred fly state, for instance, if the ratio between F_P and F_e is much smaller than 0.9, there is a high likelihood the blob contains multiple flies.

5. *Resolve probable errors*: For cases where error deviance F_S has grown too large, we attempt to reduce mismatch between imputed fly and blob matches by imputing leaving events, or evaluating group assignment.

We have found that this method gives us correct fly counts in blobs >85% of the time, but is subject to several systematic biases (see Section 3). For example, it deals poorly with occlusion due to mounting which may last for seconds, and mating, which lasts for up to 20 min. It also may incorrectly infer several small flies instead of a single large fly. We therefore attempt a subsequent analysis aimed at correcting these remaining biases using machine learning (ML).

2.1 ML IN JAABA AND TRAJECTORY SCORING

Once TABU has been applied, the trajectories become compatible with JAABA, allowing us to conveniently score behavior using its video annotation capabilities. We then fit various ML algorithms. The first, GentleBoost, is natively implemented within JAABA. The others (GradientBoost, logistic regression, and Support Vector Machine [SVM] with linear and Gaussian kernels [gSVM and lSVM]) we implemented ourselves using the Python Scikit-learn [14] package. For boosting, we use decision stumps as the weak rules, and to ensure fair comparison default parameter values were used for all other methods.

Training of ML Algorithms: We used JAABA to calculate a number of internal single-frame fly statistics, as well as multiframe window features. Window features are normalized to have mean 0 and variance 1. It is these features that were used for the ML classifiers. Users define behaviors, and score positive and negative cases for trajectories in the JAABA Graphical User Interface (GUI), by observation in the video window. Since the ML algorithms are binary classifiers, we scored instances of behavior as a binary outcome: Multifly = 1 for blobs labeled as having more than one fly, Multifly = 0 otherwise; Sex = 0 for female (or 1 for male); and Chase = 1 (or 0 for other behaviors).

We then fit ML classifiers using threefold cross-validation analysis in which the training data uses the manual annotations that we input using JAABA. After fitting, the performance of each model was evaluated using accuracy, specificity, sensitivity, precision, and area under the curve. Here, accuracy is defined as the proportion of times that the fly state is correctly called, for a total number of validation calls. All other performance measures follow the usual statistical definitions. Sex and Multifly classifiers were trained on 4000 frames from a single training video, and evaluated on 400 randomly picked frames. The Chase classifier was trained on 2000 frames, and evaluated on 500. At the same time, using the Multifly classifier, we evaluated the performance of the TABU input trajectories by scoring whether our B_N statistic accurately described blob fly count.

Sex classification was performed after trajectory scoring, and incorporated both an ML classifier (as above) and color information. Because the color scoring was more accurate than the Sex classifier, integration was performed by applying the Sex classifier to frames where the color of the painted marker is uncertain.

In order to understand the biological significance of the Chase classifier, we need to understand the sex of the individuals involved in the behavior. Courtship and aggression are known to be important components of fly social behavior [3]. These are usually male initiated, often characterised by chasing, and are directed at females and males respectively. Females rarely if ever chase other flies. Taking Chase together with Sex and Multifly, we created two composite behaviors: Aggression and Courtship. In the case where Multifly $=0$, Sex $=1$, and Chase $=1$, Aggression was defined as a male chasing another male, and Courtship was defined as a male chasing a female. To compare our test videos, we created a composite behavior profile for each. That profile comprised of the percentage of frames that (a) contained Multifly blobs; (b) contained at least one female; (c) contained Aggression; and (d) contained Courtship.

3 RESULTS

We begin by evaluating the performance of the basic blob-recognition algorithm from Ardekani et al. [6], and the change in accuracy after processing the data with TABU, for the basic task of recognizing fly number and for joining and leaving events. The empirical "real" results are obtained from manual annotation. Results are shown in Table 1. Let e be the estimated number of flies in a frame for a given method, n be the actual (manually annotated) number, and τ be the total number of frames. We estimate overall counting error, E, as $E = \frac{1}{\tau}\sum_{\tau}\frac{|e-n|}{n+1}$ (where the denominator is $n+1$ to avoid division by zero). This represents an approximate per-fly probability of being miscounted. Directionality, D, is calculated similarly, $D = \frac{1}{\tau}\sum_{\tau}\frac{e-n}{n+1}$, and demonstrates the chances of being consistently over- or under-counted. Joining or leaving events, "Jump," are reported as the per-frame probability

Table 1 Performance of the Blob Algorithm Output (Blob), and TABU Trajectory Output

Rep	Blob E	TABU E	Blob D	TABU D	Real Jump	Blob Jump	TABU Jump
1	0.177	0.106	−0.145	0.074	0.013	0.085	0.031
2	0.138	0.197	−0.101	0.192	0.009	0.116	0.017
3	0.156	0.106	0.077	0.036	0.011	0.023	0.014
4	0.11	0.09	0.025	0.048	0.003	0.023	0.015
5	0.123	0.124	−0.074	0.098	0.012	0.127	0.042
Mean	0.141	0.125	−0.044	0.090	0.010	0.075	0.024

Counting error (E), and directionality (D) bias in counting is shown. Empirical (Real) and estimated fly patch-joining or leaving rates (Jump) are also shown for raw blob data and processed trajectories.

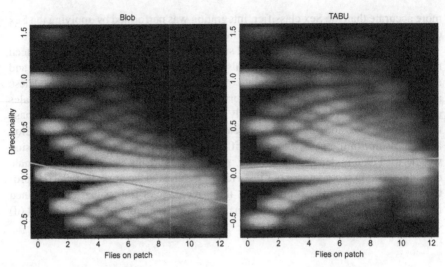

FIGURE 1

Heat map of the distribution of per-fly over- and under-counts (D) as function of the number of flies on a patch for each frame across five test videos.

of either a change in blob number, or a trajectory starting or ending. Results are shown for five separate videos (Rep).

By using TABU to create our trajectories, we have obtained more accurate data than was provided by the raw blob counts (Table 1). We have also greatly reduced the correlation between bias and fly number in our estimates (Figure 1). While the raw output overestimates the number of flies on a patch at low fly numbers, it tends to underestimate fly numbers when there are more flies on a patch (Blob bias: est $= -0.034$, df $= 442,173$, $t = -309.1$, $P < 0.001$). However, TABU does show evidence of a consistent bias towards over-counting, which becomes slightly stronger at high numbers of flies (Tabu bias: est $= 0.0075375$, df $= 495,300$, $t = 71.67$, $P < 0.001$). Application of the Tabu algorithm reduces the number of spurious patch joining and leaving events to about 30% over the raw blob data (Table 1). However, even for the TABU output, the number of inferred joining and leaving events is still more than $2 \times$ the actual data, offering potential for improvement through subsequent application of ML.

We now investigate whether application of ML methods to our TABU trajectories can identify miscalled blob counts B_N. Threefold cross-validation model-fit results are shown in Table 2. Here algorithms were trained using a period of 10 K frames. We see that all models have an accuracy above 0.98. The two SVM models rank highly on almost all metrics, while logistic regression ranks poorly on most metrics. While JAABA is not top ranked on any metric, we note that it performs very well overall.

The critical practical question is whether models trained on one part of a video will be equally effective when applied to later periods of the same video, or to

Table 2 Performance Measures of ML Algorithms for Multifly Calling on Threefold Cross Validation

Algorithms	Accuracy	Sensitivity	Specificity	Precision	AUC
JAABA	0.994(2)	0.994(3)	0.994(2)	0.994(2)	–
GradientBoost	0.988(5)	0.989(5)	0.987(3)	0.987(5)	0.994(4)
Logistic	0.989(4)	0.993(4)	0.984(5)	0.985(3)	0.997(3)
lSVM	0.991(3)	0.996(1)	0.985(4)	0.986(4)	0.998(2)
gSVM	0.995(1)	0.996(2)	0.995(1)	0.995(1)	0.998(1)

The accuracy, sensitivity, specificity, and area under the curve scores are shown for each. Ranks among ML methods for each performance score are given in brackets.

completely new video. Fly behavior is known to change over time, and varies among different genotypes and in different social contexts. We tested the performance of all algorithms on four videos that were not used in the training of the algorithm. This included different genotypes and sex ratios, as well as slightly different lighting and focus, than the algorithms were trained on. Results are shown in Table 3. The performance of all ML methods dropped slightly under these new conditions. All the ML methods improved upon the trajectory input data from TABU. The performance ranking of the ML algorithms remained broadly the same in this new data. The gSVM did very well, and logistic regression did relatively poorly. Again JAABA (GentleBoost) did very well overall.

Sex Annotation: We found that the various ML algorithms had accuracies in Sex calling ranging between 0.73 and 0.89 (Table 4). Logistic regression, GradientBoost and JAABA all had similar accuracies, above 0.88. The video blob-processing annotation based on the colored marker, however, was the most accurate of all the Sex classifiers (with an accuracy of 0.93). Integrating this classifier together with the JAABA scores improved the performance statistics for Sex calling to 0.95 and above.

On the nontraining data, the performance of the Sex classifier for JAABA was very similar to that on the trained video (with an accuracy above 0.90), suggesting

Table 3 Evaluation of the ML Algorithm Performance for Multifly Calling on Nontraining Videos

Algorithms	Accuracy	Sensitivity	Specificity
TABU	0.823–0.994	0.747–0.994	0.884–0.995
JAABA	0.986–0.995	0.982–0.994	0.989–0.996
GradientBoost	0.981–0.990	0.979–0.993	0.977–0.987
Logistic	0.983–0.993	0.979–0.992	0.977–0.990
lSVM	0.983–0.992	0.978–0.998	0.976–0.987
gSVM	0.984–0.993	0.975–0.992	0.984–0.993

The minimum to maximum range of accuracy, sensitivity, and specificity scores are shown for each, in comparison with the input trajectory data (TABU).

Table 4 Performance Measures of the Sex Classifier on Threefold Cross Validation

Algorithms	Accuracy	Sensitivity	Specificity	Precision	AUC
blobColor	0.939	0.904	0.975	0.997	–
JAABA	0.883	0.913	0.852	0.860	–
GradientBoost	0.882	0.893	0.871	0.874	0.953
Logistic	0.893	0.867	0.919	0.915	0.952
lSVM	0.816	0.906	0.727	0.769	0.949
gSVM	0.731	0.827	0.635	0.695	0.884
blobColor + JAABA	0.967	0.947	0.987	0.986	–

The accuracy, sensitivity, specificity, precision, and area under the curve scores are shown for each.

Table 5 Evaluation of the Sex Classifier Performance on Nontraining Videos

Algorithms	Accuracy	Sensitivity	Specificity
JAABA	0.919	0.941	0.877
GradientBoost	0.925	0.942	0.895
Logistic	0.872	0.940	0.779
lSVM	0.957	0.932	0.981
gSVM	0.854	0.848	0.859

The mean accuracy, sensitivity, and specificity scores across the videos are shown.

Table 6 Evaluation of the Chase Classifier Performance on Threefold Cross Validation

Algorithms	Accuracy	Sensitivity	Specificity	Precision	AUC
JAABA	0.887	0.920	0.867	0.809	–
GradientBoost	0.884	0.919	0.827	0.896	0.917
Logistic	0.859	0.913	0.770	0.866	0.888
lSVM	0.844	0.813	0.895	0.927	0.861
gSVM	0.781	0.696	0.919	0.933	0.885

The accuracy, sensitivity, specificity, precision, and area under the curve scores are shown for each.

that this classification is very robust (Table 5). Indeed, all ML methods however (particularly lSVM) performed somewhat better when applied to the nontraining data, perhaps suggesting that the training dataset was a particularly difficult dataset for which to call sex.

Behavior Annotation: The ultimate goal of trajectory analysis, and the implementation of JAABA on tracking data, is to evaluate behaviors in a diversity of experimental manipulations. In scoring Chasing, JAABA, GradientBoost, and logistic regression all performed well, with accuracy above 0.85 (Table 6). Even on the

Table 7 Evaluation of the Chase Classifier Performance on Nontraining Videos

Algorithms	Accuracy	Sensitivity	Specificity
JAABA	0.826	0.949	0.764
GradientBoost	0.801	0.989	0.750
Logistic	0.871	0.987	0.766
lSVM	0.880	0.915	0.839
gSVM	0.762	0.932	0.668

The accuracy, sensitivity, and specificity scores are shown for each.

Table 8 Behavioral Profiles of the Five Fly Videos (v1–v5), with the Number of Females:Males in the Experiment (but not Necessarily in Frame) Shown in Brackets

Behaviors	v1(15:5)	v2(15:5)	v3(10:10)	v4(10:10)	v5(5:15)
Multifly %	32.61	28.09	15.43	22.46	17.23
Sex=0%	51.34	63.54	22.75	44.72	24.28
Aggression %	0.29	0.987	1.40	1.73	1.45
Courtship %	0.66	0.915	0.82	1.65	0.73

The percentage of frames containing at least one of these behaviors is shown. Behavioral annotations were obtained using JAABA.

nontraining dataset, all the methods besides the Gaussian SVM had accuracy greater than 0.8, but logistic regression and the linear SVM performed best (Table 7).

Intriguingly, we found gross differences in fly behavior between the videos, which generally reflected the sex ratio composition of their respective experiments. It is precisely differences such as these that we hope we will be able to detect using methods such those we have developed here, so this is an encouraging result. A higher proportion of females results in a greater likelihood of observing females on patch, as well as an increased prevalence of Multifly blobs (Table 8). There was a trend towards more frequent aggression with an increase in male numbers, while courtship was observed more frequently at intermediate sex ratios. These results are entirely consistent with what we understand about fly behavior, which again provides encouragement regarding the usefulness of automated annotation of fly behavior such as that we present here.

4 DISCUSSION

In this paper we have developed a method for generating, and error correcting, tracking data from video recordings of *Drosophila* made in nonideal conditions. Nonoptimal conditions cause problems at the initial image processing stage, due to poor performance of background subtraction routines, occlusion caused by proximity between animals, and uncertainty in the number of objects that need to be tracked (*c.f.* [1]). This leads to subsequent poor performance of tracking data. However, imperfect conditions will apply for a majority of behavioral observation systems in nature. Even in many lab situations, experimenters often have to work with such conditions to collect relevant data. Our methods offer the potential for investigators to more successfully work with such data.

Our simple TABU tracking algorithm, by making a few realistic assumptions about the persistence of flies across frames and within blobs, greatly reduces the uncertainty of the initial image processing data from the algorithm of Ardekani et al. [6]. It allows us to count flies on patches with more certainty, and reduces the apparent degree of fly movement on and off of patches. Error rates are still non-zero, but it is clear that subsequent application of any of the ML methods we tested here has the potential to increase correct allocation of flies among blobs from around 90% to over 98%.

Among the algorithms we evaluated, there is no clear winner among the ML methods in terms of performance. However, for ease of implementation, and robustly high performance, the GentleBoost algorithm natively implemented in JAABA represents a reasonable choice for future work. It performed well for the Multifly classifier, and consistently well for Sex and Chase. We emphasize that use of JAABA (and all the behavioral annotation algorithms we tested) requires fly tracking data as input, thereby necessitating pre-processing using an algorithm such as TABU before use. Such a pre-processing algorithm needs to be able to construct tracks successfully in nonideal conditions, and when the number of objects being tracked is unknown, a problem that is known to be extremely challenging [1].

In the test videos, we were able to integrate multiple classifiers, such as painted marker color and Sex to improve our ability to score accurately. We were also able to integrate Sex and Chase in order to obtain richer biological data than was available from individual classifiers. We recapitulated the experimental sex ratio conditions (i.e., higher rates of observation of female prevalence correspond with higher female sex ratios) in the untrained videos. Importantly, we detected interesting patterns in behavioral differences among the trials related to sex ratio—there were trends in the frequency of male-male Aggression, but not, interestingly, Courtship. It might be that as males spend more time fighting, they have less time or opportunity to court. The ability to detect such meaningful behavioral trends, in naturalistic setups, will be of great interest to ethologists.

In sum, our methods produce improved performance both in terms of accurate identification of the number of flies in a blob (and, therefore, the number of flies in a frame at any given moment), and in terms of generation of tracks for individual flies. Both of these types of information are crucial for analysis of fly (and other animal) group behavior. Flies are social animals that actively aggregate and interact in groups. The sizes of these groups is therefore a key diagnostic of the behavior of those flies, and varies with factors such as genotype, sex ratio, etc. Therefore, the methods we present here provide the opportunity for researchers to use automated methods to generate large quantities of such data in an experimental context. A more difficult remaining challenge is to automatically recognize interactions between flies, such as courtship and acts of aggression. Methods (including JAABA) are being developed to attack this problem. Creating, and error correcting, fly trajectories is a necessary first step in taking advantage of this work.

ACKNOWLEDGMENTS

The authors gratefully acknowledge funding from NSF and NIMH through awards DMS 1101060 and MH100879. The material contained in this chapter reflects the views of the authors, and not necessarily those of NSF or NMH.

REFERENCES

[1] Branson K, Robie AA, Bender J, Perona P, Dickinson MH. High-throughput ethomics in large groups of *Drosophila*. Nat Methods 2009;6:451–7.

[2] Noldus L, Spink A, Tegelenbosch R. EthoVision: a versatile video tracking system for automation of behavioral experiments. Behav Res Methods Instrum Comput 2001;33:398–414.

[3] Saltz J, Foley BR. Natural genetic variation in social niche construction: social effects of aggression drive disruptive sexual selection in *Drosophila melanogaster*. Am Nat 2011;177:645–54.

[4] Chen H, Foley B, Marjoram P. Trajectory scoring using JAABA in a noisy system, In: Worldcomp iPCV; 2014.

[5] Kabra M, Robie A, Rivera-Alba M, Branson S, Branson K. JAABA: interactive machine learning for automatic annotation of animal behavior. Nat Methods 2013;10:64–U87.

[6] Ardekani R, Biyani A, Dalton JE, Saltz JB, Arbeitman MN, Tower J, et al. Three-dimensional tracking and behaviour monitoring of multiple fruit flies. J R Soc Interface 2013;10(78):20120547.

[7] Bradski, G., 2000. The openCV library. Dr. Dobb's Journal of Software Tools.

[8] Abramoff M, Magalhaes P, Ram S. Image Processing with ImageJ. Biophoton Int 2004;11:36–42.

[9] Park S, Kim K. Color recognition with compact color features. Int J Commun Syst 2012;25(6):749–62.

[10] Saber E, Tekalp A, Eschbach R, Knox K. Automatic image annotation using adaptive color classification. Graph Model Image Process 1996;58:115–26.

[11] Sural S, Qian G, Pramanik S. Segmentation and histogram generation using the hSV color space for image retrieval, In: International conference on image processing (iCIP); 2002.

[12] Wyszechi G, Stiles W. Color science: concepts and methods. 2nd ed. New York, USA: Wiley; 1982.

[13] R Development Core Team. R: a language and environment for statistical computing. Vienna, Austria: R Foundation for Statistical Computing; 2006.

[14] Pedregosa F, Varoquaux G, Gramfort A, Michel V, Thirion B, Grisel O, et al. Scikit-learn: machine learning in Python. J Mach Learn Res 2011;12:2825–30.

An algorithm for mobile vision-based localization of skewed nutrition labels that maximizes specificity

18

Vladimir Kulyukin[1], Christopher Blay[2]

[1]*Department of Computer Science, Utah State University, Logan, UT, USA*
[2]*YouTube Corporation, San Bruno, CA, USA*

1 INTRODUCTION

Many nutritionists and dieticians consider proactive nutrition management to be a key factor in reducing and controlling cancer, diabetes, and other illnesses related to or caused by mismanaged or inadequate diets. According to the U.S. Department of Agriculture, U.S. residents have increased their caloric intake by 523 calories per day since 1970. Mismanaged diets are estimated to account for 30-35% of cancer cases [1]. A leading cause of mortality in men is prostate cancer. A leading cause of mortality in women is breast cancer. Approximately 47,000,000 U.S. residents have metabolic syndrome and diabetes. Diabetes in children appears to be closely related to increasing obesity levels. The current prevalence of diabetes in the world is estimated to be at 2.8% [2]. It is expected that by 2030 the diabetes prevalence number will reach 4.4%. Some long-term complications of diabetes are blindness, kidney failure, and amputations. Nutrition labels (NLs) remain the main source of nutritional information on product packages [3,4]. Therefore, enabling customers to use computer vision on their smartphones will likely result in a greater consumer awareness of the caloric and nutritional content of purchased grocery products.

In our previous research, we developed a vision-based localization algorithm for horizontally or vertically aligned NLs on smartphones [5]. The new algorithm, presented in this chapter, improves our previous algorithm in that it handles not only aligned NLs but also those that are skewed up to 35-40° from the vertical axis of the captured frame. Figure 1 shows an example of such a skewed NL with the vertical axis of the captured frame denoted by a white line. Another improvement designed and implemented in the new algorithm is the rapid detection of the presence of an NL in each frame, which improves the run time, because the new algorithm fails fast and proceeds to the next frame from the video stream.

FIGURE 1

Skewed NL with vertical axis shown.

The new algorithm targets medium- to high-end mobile devices with single or quad-core ARM systems. Since cameras on these devices capture several frames per second, the algorithm is designed to minimize false positives rather than maximize true ones, because, at such frequent frame capture rates, it is far more important to minimize the processing time per frame.

Our chapter is organized as follows. In Section 2, we present our previous work on accessible shopping and nutrition management to give the reader a broader context of the research and development presented in this chapter. In Section 3, we outline the details of our algorithm. In Section 4, we present the experiments with our algorithm and discuss our results. In Section 5, we present our conclusions and outline several directions for future work.

2 PREVIOUS WORK

In 2006, our laboratory began to work on ShopTalk, a wearable system for independent blind supermarket shopping [6]. In 2008-2009, ShopTalk was ported to the Nokia E70 smartphone connected to a Bluetooth barcode pencil scanner [7].

In 2010, we began our work on computer vision techniques for eyes-free barcode scanning [8]. In 2013, we published several algorithms for localizing skewed barcodes as well as horizontally or vertically aligned NLs [5,9]. The algorithm presented in this chapter improves the previous NL localization algorithm by relaxing the NL alignment constraint for up to 35-40° in either direction from the vertical orientation axis of the captured frame.

Modern nutrition management system designers and developers assume that users understand how to collect nutritional data and can be triggered into data collection with digital prompts (e.g., email or SMS). Such systems often under-perform, because many users find it difficult to integrate nutrition data collection into their daily activities due to lack of time, motivation, or training. Eventually, they turn off or ignore digital stimuli [10].

To overcome these challenges, in 2012 we began to develop a Persuasive NUTrition Management System (PNUTS) [5]. PNUTS seeks to shift current research and clinical practices in nutrition management toward persuasion, automated nutritional information extraction and processing, and context-sensitive nutrition decision support. PNUTS is based on a nutrition management approach inspired by the Fogg Behavior Model [10], which states that motivation alone is insufficient to stimulate target behaviors. Even a motivated user must have both the ability to execute a behavior and a trigger to engage in that behavior at an appropriate place or time.

Another frequent assumption, which is not always accurate, is that consumers and patients are either more skilled than they actually are or that they can be quickly trained to obtain the required skills. Since training is difficult and time consuming, a more promising path is to make target behaviors easier and more intuitive to execute for the average smartphone user. Vision-based extraction of nutritional information from NLs on product packages is a fundamental step in making proactive nutrition management easier and more intuitive, because it improves the user's ability to engage into the target behavior of collecting and processing nutritional data.

3 SKEWED NL LOCALIZATION
3.1 DETECTION OF EDGES, LINES, AND CORNERS

Our NL detection algorithm uses three image processing methods: edge detection, line detection, and corner detection. Edge detection transforms images into bitmaps where every pixel is classified as belonging or not belonging to an edge. The algorithm uses the Canny edge detector (CED) [11]. After the edges are detected (see Figure 2), the image is processed with the hough transform (HT) [12] to detect lines (see Figure 3). The HT algorithm finds paths in images that follow generalized polynomials in the polar coordinate space.

Corner detection is done primarily for text spotting because text segments tend to contain many distinct corners. Thus, image segments with higher concentrations of corners are likely to contain text. Corners are detected with the dilate-erode

FIGURE 2

Original NL (left); NL with detected edges (right).

FIGURE 3

NL with edges (right); NL with detected lines (right).

method [13] (see Figure 4). Two stages of the dilate-erode method with different 5×5 kernels are applied. Two stages of dilate-erode with different kernels are applied. The first stage uses a 5×5 cross dilate kernel for horizontal and vertical expansions. It then uses a 5×5 diamond erode kernel for diagonal shrinking. The resulting image is compared with the original and those pixels which are in the corner of an aligned rectangle are found.

The second stage uses a 5×5 X-shape dilate kernel to expand in the two diagonal directions. A 5×5 square kernel is used next to erode the image and to shrink it horizontally and vertically. The resulting image is compared with the original and those pixels which are in a $45°$ corner are identified. The resulting corners from both steps are combined into a final set of detected corners.

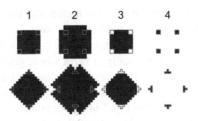

FIGURE 4

Corner detection steps.

In Figure 4, the top sequence of images corresponds to stage one when the cross and diamond kernels are used to detect aligned corners. The bottom sequence of images corresponds to stage two when the X-shape and square kernels are used to detect 45° corners. Step one shows the original input of each stage, step two is the image after dilation, step three is the image after erosion, and step four is the difference between the original and eroded versions. The resulting corners are outlined in red (dark gray in print versions) in each step to provide a basis of how the dilate-erode operations modify the input.

Figure 5 demonstrates the dilate-erode algorithm used on an image segment that contains text. The dilate steps are substantially whiter than their inputs, because the appropriate kernel is used to expand white pixels. Then the erode steps partially reverse this whitening effect by expanding darker pixels. The result is the pixels with

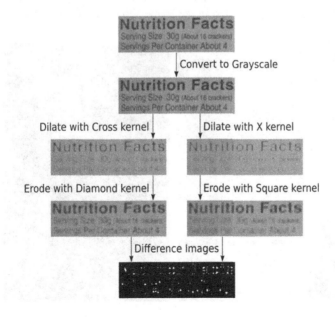

FIGURE 5

Corner detection for text spotting.

the largest differences between the original image and the result image. Figure 5 shows corners detected on an image segment with text.

Our previous NL localization algorithm [5] was based on the assumption that the NL exists in the image and is horizontally or vertically aligned with the smartphone's camera. Unfortunately, these conditions sometimes do not hold in the real world due to shaking hands or failing eyesight. The exact problem that the new algorithm addresses is twofold. Does a given input image contain a skewed NL? And, if so, within which aligned rectangular area can the NL be localized? In this investigation, a skewed NL is one which has been rotated away from the vertical alignment axis by up to 35-40° in either direction, i.e., left or right. An additional objective is to decrease processing time for each frame to about 1 s.

3.2 CORNER DETECTION AND ANALYSIS

Before the proper NL localization begins, a rotation correction step is performed to align inputs which may be only nearly aligned. This correction is performed by taking advantage of high numbers of horizontal lines found within NLs. All detected lines that are horizontal within 35-40° in either direction (i.e., up or down) are used to compute an average horizontal rotation. This rotation is used to perform the appropriate correcting rotation. Corner detection is executed after the rotation. The dilate-erode corner detector is applied to retrieve a two-dimensional bitmap where true white pixels correspond to detected corners and all other false pixels are black. Figure 5 shows main steps of the dilate-erode corner detection algorithm. Figure 6 (right) shows the corners detected in the frame shown in Figure 6 (left).

FIGURE 6

Visualization of the corner detection output.

The dilate-erode corner detector is used specifically because of its high sensitivity to contrasted text, which is why we assume that the region is bounded by these edges contains a large amount of text. Areas of the input image which are not in focus do not produce a large amount of corner detection results and tend not to lie within the needed projection boundaries.

Two projections are computed after the corners are detected. The projections are sums of the true pixels for each row and column. The image row projection has an entry for each row in the image while the image column projection has an entry for each column in the image. The purpose of these projections is to determine boundaries for the top, bottom, left, and right boundaries of the region in which most corners lie. Each value of the projection is averaged together and a projection threshold is set to twice the average. Once a projection threshold is selected, the first and last indexes of each projection greater than the threshold are selected as the boundaries of that projection.

3.3 SELECTION OF BOUNDARY LINES

After the four corner projections have been computed, the next step is to select the Hough lines that are closest to the boundaries selected on the basis of the four corner projections. In two images of Figure 6, the four light blue (white in print) lines are the lines drawn on the basis of the four corner projection counts. The dark blue (dark gray in print) lines show the lines detected by the HT. In Figure 7 (left), the bottom light blue (white in print) line is initially chosen conservatively where the row corner projections drop below a threshold. If there is evidence that there are some corners

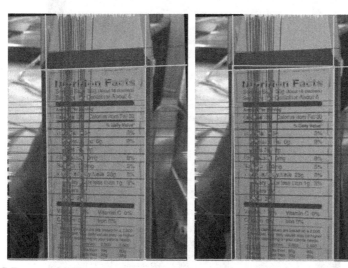

FIGURE 7

Initial boundaries (left); final boundaries (right).

present after the initially selected bottom lines, the bottom line is moved as far below as possible, as shown in Figure 7 (right).

When the bounded area is not perfectly rectangular, which makes integration with later analysis where a rectangular area is expected to be less straightforward. To overcome this problem, a rectangle is placed around the selected Hough boundary lines. After the four intersection coordinates are computed (see Section 3.3 for details), their components are compared and combined to find a smallest rectangle that fits around the bounded area, as shown in Figure 7. This rectangle is the final result of the NL localization algorithm. As was stated before, the four corners found by the algorithm can be passed to other algorithms such as row dividing, word splitting, and Optical Character Recognition (OCR). Row dividing, world splitting, and OCR are beyond the scope of this chapter. Figure 8 shows a skewed NL localize by our algorithm.

3.4 FINDING INTERSECTIONS IN CARTESIAN SPACE

Each Hough line returned by the HT is described as (ρ, θ), where ρ is the length of the normal from the line to the origin of the polar coordinate system and θ is the angle specifying the rotation of the line about the origin. Given $l_1 = (\rho_1, \theta_1)$ and $l_2 = (\rho_2, \theta_2)$ in the polar coordinate system, we need to find the intersection of these lines in the Cartesian system in order to find the four intersection coordinates shown in Figure 7. If $\theta_1 = \theta_2$ and $\rho_1 = \rho_2$, then l_1 and l_2 are the same line and there are infinitely many

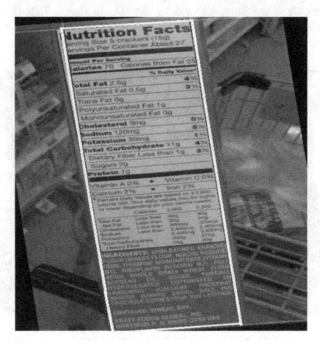

FIGURE 8

Localized skewed NL.

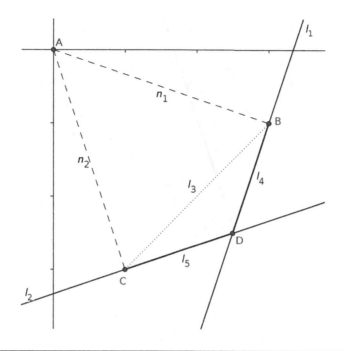

FIGURE 9

Case 1: Intersection D is between two normals.

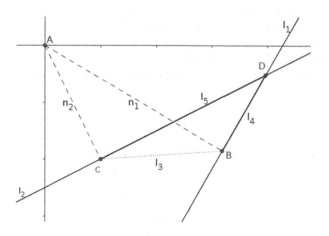

FIGURE 10

Case 2: Intersection D is above two normals.

intersections. If $\theta_1 = \theta_2$ and $\rho_1 \neq \rho_2$, then l_1 and l_2 are parallel lines and have no intersections. If l_1 and l_2 do not coincide and are not parallel, there are three cases to consider, shown in Figures 8, 9, and 10. In each case, there are two normals AB and AC, denoted as n_1 and n_2, respectively (see Figure 8) to l_1 and l_2. The normal n_1 goes from the origin A to point B on l_1 whereas the normal n_2 goes from the origin A to point C

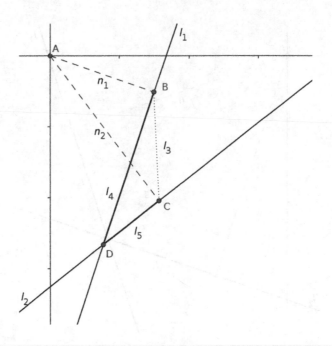

FIGURE 11

Case 3: Intersection D is below two normals.

on l_2. The segment BC, denoted as l_3, completes the triangle T_1 consisting of points A, B and C. Another triangle T_2 consists of points B, C, and D, where point D is the sought intersection of l_1 and l_2. Consider the line segments BD and CD denoted as l_4 and l_5, respectively (see Figures 9, 10, or 11). Once l_4 is found, point D is found by adding vectors n_1 and l_4. Technical details of this computation are given in [14].

4 EXPERIMENTS
4.1 COMPLETE AND PARTIAL TRUE POSITIVES

We assembled 378 images captured from a Google Nexus 7 Android 4.3 smartphone during a typical shopping session at a local supermarket. Of these images, 266 contained an NL and 112 did not. Our skewed NL localization algorithm was implemented and tested on the same platform with these images.

We manually categorized the results into five categories: complete true positives, partial true positives, true negatives, false positives, and false negatives. A complete true positive is an image where a complete NL was localized. A partial true positive is an image where only a part of the NL was localized by the algorithm. Figure 12 shows examples of complete and partial true positives.

Figure 13 shows another example of complete and partial true positives. The image on the left was classified as a complete true positive, because the part of

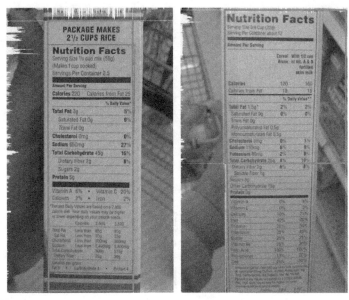

FIGURE 12

Complete (left) vs. partial (right) true positives.

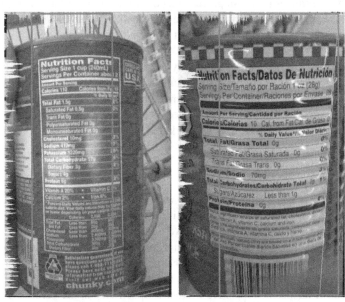

FIGURE 13

Complete (left) vs. partial (right) true positives.

FIGURE 14

Complete (left) vs. partial (right) true positives.

the NL that was not detected is insignificant and will likely be fixed through simple padding in subsequent processing. The image on the right, on the other hand, was classified as a partial true positive. While the localized area does contain most of the NL, some essential text in the left part of the NL is excluded, which will likely cause failure in subsequent processing.

In Figure 14, the left image technically does not include the entire NL, because the list of ingredients is only partially included. However, we classified it as a complete true positive since it includes the entire table on nutrition facts. The right image of Figure 14, on the other hand, is classified as a partial true positive, because some parts of the nutrition facts table is not included in the detected area.

4.2 RESULTS

Of the 266 images that contained NLs, 83 were classified as complete true positives and 27 were classified as partial true positives, which gives a total true positive rate of 42% and a false negative rate of 58%. All test images with no NLs were classified as true negatives. The remainder of our analysis was done via precision, recall, and specificity, and accuracy. Precision is the percentage of complete true positive matches out of all true positive matches. Recall is the percentage of true positive matches out of all possible positive matches. Specificity is the percentage of true negative matches out of all possible negative matches. Accuracy is the percentage of true matches out of all possible matches.

Table 1 NL Localization Results

PR	TR	CR	PR	SP	ACC
0.7632	0.422	0.3580	0.1475	1.0	0.5916

Table 1 gives the NL localization results where PR stands for "precision," TR for "total recall," CR for "complete recall," PR for "partial recall," SP for "specificity," and ACC for "accuracy." While total and complete recall numbers are somewhat low, this is a necessary trade-off of maximizing specificity. Recall from Section 1 that we have designed our algorithm to maximize specificity. In other words, the algorithm is less unlikely to detect NLs in images where no NLs are present than in images where they are present. As we argued above, lower recall and precision may not matter much because of the fast rate at which input images are processed on target devices, but there is definitely room for improvement.

4.3 LIMITATIONS

The majority of false negative matches were caused by blurry images. Blurry images are the result of poor camera focus and instability. Both the CED and dilate-erode corner detector require rapid and contrasting changes to identify key points and lines of interest. These points and lines are meant to correspond directly with text and NL borders. These useful data cannot be retrieved from blurry images, which results in run-time detection failures. The only recourse to deal with blurry inputs is improved camera focus and stability, both of which are outside the scope of this algorithm, because it is a hardware problem. It is likely to work better in later models of smartphones. The current implementation on the Android platform attempts to force focus at the image center but this ability to request camera focus is not present in older Android versions. Over time, as device cameras improve and more devices run newer versions of Android, this limitation will have less impact on recall but it will never be fixed entirely.

Bottles, bags, cans, and jars have a large showing in the false negative category due to Hough line detection difficulties on curved lines (see Figure 15). One possibility to get around this limitation is a more rigorous line detection step in which a segmented HT is performed and regions which contain connecting detected lines are grouped together. These grouped regions could be used to warp a curved image into a rectangular area for further analysis.

Smaller grocery packages (see Figure 16) tend to have irregular NLs that place a large amount of information into tiny spaces. NLs with irregular layouts present an extremely difficult problem for analysis. Our algorithm better handles more traditional NL layouts with generally empty surrounding areas. As a better analysis of corner projections and Hough lines is integrated into our algorithm, it will become possible to classify inputs as definitely traditional or more irregular. If this classification can work reliably, the method could switch to a much slower and generalized

FIGURE 15

NL with curved lines.

localization to produce better results in this situation while still quickly returning results for more common layouts.

5 CONCLUSIONS

We have made several interesting observations during our experiments. The row and column projects have two distinct patterns. The row projection tends to create evenly spaced short spikes for text in each line of text within the NL while the column projection tends to contain one very large spike where the NL begins at the left due to the sudden influx of detected text. We have not performed any in-depth analysis of these patterns. However, the projection data were collected for each processed image. We plan to do further investigations of these patterns, which will likely allow for run-time detection and corresponding correction of inputs of various rotations.

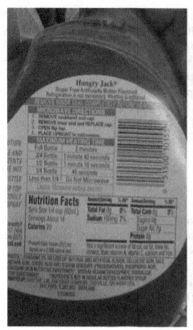

FIGURE 16

Irregular NL layouts.

For example, the column projections could be used for greater accuracy in determining the left and right bounds of the NL while row projections could be used by later analysis steps such as row division. Certain projection profiles could eventually be used to select customized localization approaches at run time.

During our experiments with and iterative development of this algorithm, we took note of several possible improvements that could positively affect the algorithm's performance. First, since input images are generally not square, the HT returns more results for lines in the longer dimension, because they are more likely to pass the threshold. Consequently, specifying different thresholds for the two dimensions and combining them for various rotations may produce more consistent results.

Second, since only those Hough lines that are nearly vertical or horizontal are of use to this method, improvements can be made by only allocating bins for those Θ and ρ combinations that are considered important. Fewer bins means less memory to track all of them and fewer tests to determine which bins need to be incremented for a given input.

Third, both row and column corner projections tend to produce distinct patterns which could be used to determine better boundaries. After collecting a large amount of typical projections, further analysis can be performed to find generalizations resulting in a faster method to improve boundary selection.

Fourth, in principle, a much more intensive HT method can be developed that would divide the image into a grid of smaller segments and perform a separate HT within each segment. One advantage of this approach is to look for the skewed, curved, or even zigzagging lines between segments that could actually be connected into a longer line. While the performance penalty of this method could be quite high, it could allow for the detection and dewarping of oddly shaped NLs. Finally, a more careful analysis of the found Hough lines during the early rotation correction could allow us to detect and localize NLs of all possible rotations, not just skewed ones.

The U.S. Food and Drug Administration recently proposed some changes to the design of NLs on product packages [15]. The new design is expected to change how serving sizes are calculated and displayed. Percent daily values are expected to shift to the left side of the NL, which allegedly will make them easier to read. The new design will also require information about added sugars as well as the counts for Vitamin D and potassium. We would like to emphasize that this redesign, which is expected to take at least 2 years, will not impact the proposed algorithm, because the main tabular components of the new NL design will remain the same. The nutritional information in the new NLs will still be presented textually in rows and columns. Therefore, the corner and line detection and their projections will work as they work on the current NL design [16].

REFERENCES

[1] Anding R. Nutrition made clear. Chantilly, VA: The Great Courses; 2009.
[2] Rubin AL. Diabetes for dummies. 3rd ed. Hoboken, NJ: Wiley, Publishing, Inc; 2008.
[3] Nutrition Labeling and Education Action of 1990. http://en.wikipedia.org/wiki/Nutrition_Labeling_and_Education_Act_of_1990.
[4] Food Labelling to Advance Better Education for Life. Available at www.flabel.org/en.
[5] Kulyukin V, Kutiyanawala A, Zaman T, Clyde S. Vision-based localization and text chunking of nutrition fact tables on android smartphones. In: Proceedings of the International Conference on Image Processing, Computer Vision, and Pattern Recognition (IPCV 2013). Las Vegas, NV: CSREA Press; 2013. p. 314–20, ISBN 1-60132-252-6.
[6] Nicholson J, Kulyukin V. ShopTalk: independent blind shopping = verbal route directions + barcode scans. In: Proceedings of the 30th Annual Conference of the Rehabilitation Engineering and Assistive Technology Society of North America (RESNA 2007), June 2007, Phoenix, Arizona; 2007. Avail. on CD-ROM.
[7] Kulyukin V, Kutiyanawala A. Accessible shopping systems for blind and visually impaired individuals: design requirements and the state of the art. Open Rehabil J 2010;2:158–68. http://dx.doi.org/10.2174/1874943701003010158, ISSN 1874–9437.
[8] Kulyukin V, Kutiyanawala A, Zaman T. Eyes-free barcode detection on smartphones with Niblack's binarization and support vector machines. In: Proceedings of the 16th International Conference on Image Processing, Computer Vision, and Pattern Recognition (IPCV 2012), Vol. 1. Las Vegas, NV: CSREA Press; 2012. p. 284–90, July 16–19. ISBN 1-60132-223-2, 1-60132-224-0.
[9] Kulyukin V, Zaman T. Vision-based localization of skewed UPC barcodes on smartphones. In: Proceedings of the International Conference on Image Processing, Computer

Vision, & Pattern Recognition (IPCV 2013). Las Vegas, NV: CSREA Press; 2013. p. 344–50. ISBN: 1-60132-252-6, 314–320.

[10] Fog BJ. A behavior model for persuasive design. In: Proceedings of the 4th International Conference on Persuasive Technology, Article 40. New York, USA: ACM; 2009.

[11] Canny JF. A computational approach to edge detection. IEEE Trans Pattern Anal Mach Intell 1986;8:679–98.

[12] Duda RO, Hart PE. In: Use of the hough transformation to detect lines and curves in pictures. Comm. ACM, vol. 15; 1972, p. 11–15. January.

[13] Laganiere R. OpenCV 2 computer vision application programming cookbook. UK: Packt Publishing Ltd; 2011.

[14] Blay C. On mobile detection and localization of skewed nutrition fact tables. Department of Computer Science, Utah State University; 2013, M.S. Thesis. http://digitalcommons.usu.edu/etd/2015/.

[15] Tavernise S. New F.D.A. nutrition labels would make 'serving sizes' reflect actual servings. New York Times, February 27, 2014.

[16] Kulyukin V, Blay C. An algorithm for mobile vision-based localization of skewed nutrition labels that maximizes specificity. In: Proceedings of the International Conference on Image Processing, Computer Vision, & Pattern Recognition (IPCV 2014). Las Vegas, NV: CSREA Press; 2014 p. 3–9, ISBN: 1-60132-280-1.

A rough fuzzy neural network approach for robust face detection and tracking

19

Alfredo Petrosino, Giuseppe Salvi
University "Parthenope", Naples, Italy

1 INTRODUCTION

Visual location and tracking of objects of interest, particularly, human faces in video sequences, are a critical task and an active field in computer vision applications that involves interaction with the human face by using surveillance, human-computer interface, biometrics, etc. As the face is a deformable target and its appearance easily changes because of the face-camera pose, sudden changes in illumination and complex background, tracking it is very difficult. Common methods of face detection include skin color [1,2], boosting [3,4], neural networks (NNs) [5], support vector machines (SVMs) [6,7], and template matching [8]. The results of the skin-color-based method are strongly influenced by sudden changes in lighting and the method often fails to detect people with different skin colors. In many cases, the results of the boosting, SVMs, and in particular, the NN methods suffer from the disadvantage of being strongly linked to the set of images selected for learning. For this type of approach, as face characteristics are implicitly derived from a window, a large number of face and nonface training examples are required to train a well-performed detector. To describe the face by template matching several standard patterns of a face are stored. The face detection is then computed through the correlations between an input image and the stored standard patterns. This approach, if one the one hand is simple to implement, on the other hand, has proven to be inadequate for face detection because of its extreme sensitivity to changes in both pose and orientation. Face detection may be performed on gray-scale or color images. To detect faces of different sizes and varying orientations in gray-scale images, the input image has to be rotated several times and it has to be converted to a pyramid of images [3–7] by subsampling it by a factor. Therefore, the computational complexity will increase with a complicated and time-consuming classifier. Detection using color information may be independent of face size and rotation within the color image. This approach avoids the image-scaling problem and appears to be a more promising method for a real-time face-tracking application. For this reason, in this study, we have performed face detection by using color images. The main purpose of face detection is to localize and extract with certainty a subset of pixels which satisfy some specific criteria like chromatic or textural homogeneity, the face region, from the background also to hard variations of scene conditions, such as the presence of a complex background and uncontrolled illumination. Rough set theory offers an interesting and a new mathematical approach the manage uncertainty that has been used to various soft computing techniques as: importance of features, detection of data dependencies, feature space dimensionality reduction, patterns in sample data, and classification of objects. For this reason, rough sets have been successfully employed for various image processing tasks including image classification and segmentation [9–12]. Multiscale representation is a very useful tool for handling image structures at different scales in a consistent manner. It was introduced in image analysis and computer vision by Marr and others who appreciated that multiscale analysis offers many benefits [13–18]. In this study, we have particularly proposed to make scale space according to the notion of rough fuzzy sets, realizing a system capable of efficiently clustering data coming from image analysis tasks. The hybrid notion of rough fuzzy sets comes from the combination of two models of uncertainty like coarseness by handling rough sets [19] and vagueness by handling fuzzy sets [20]. In particular the rough sets defines the contour or uniform regions in the image that appear like fuzzy sets and their comparison or combination generates more or less uniform partitions of the image. Rough fuzzy sets, and in particular C-sets first introduced by Caianiello [21], are able to capture these aspects together, extracting different kinds of knowledge in data. Based on these considerations, we report a new face-detection algorithm based on rough fuzzy sets and online learning by NN [11], able to detect skin regions in the input image at hand and thus independently from what previously seen. The extracted features at different scales by rough fuzzy sets are clustered from an unsupervised NN by minimizing the fuzziness of the output layer. The new method, named multiscale rough neural network (MS-RNN), was designed to detect frontal faces in color images and to be not sensitive to variations of scene conditions, such as the presence of a complex background and uncontrolled illumination. The proposed face-detection method has been applied to real-time face tracking using Kalman filtering algorithm [22], this filter is used to predict the next face-detection window and smooth the tracking trajectory. The article is structured as follows. In Section 2, we explain the basic theories behind the proposed method, i.e., rough sets, fuzzy sets, and their synergy. Section 3 describes the face-detection method and illustrates how these theories are applied to the process of digital images relative to the proposed method, which is specifically described in Sections 4 and 5. Section 6 introduces the proposed face-tracking method. Section 7 reports the results obtained using the proposed method, through an extensive set of experiments on CMU-PIE [23], color FERET [24,25], IMM [26], and CalTech [27] face databases; in addition, the effectiveness of the proposed model is shown when applied to the face-tracking problem on a database of YouTube video and the standard

IIT-NRC [28] facial video database, comparing them with the recent results on the same topic. Lastly, some concluding remarks are presented in Section 8.

2 THEORETICAL BACKGROUND

Let $X = \{x_1, \ldots, x_n\}$ be a set and $\mathcal{R}$ an equivalence relation on X, i.e., $\mathcal{R}$ is reflexive, symmetric, and transitive. As usual, $X/\mathcal{R}$ denotes the quotient set of equivalence classes, which form a partition in X, i.e., $x\mathcal{R}y$ means the x and y cannot be took apart. The notion of rough set [19] borns to answer the question of how a subset T of X can be represented by means of $X/\mathcal{R}$. It consists of two sets:

$$RS^-(T) = \{[x]_\mathcal{R} | [x]_\mathcal{R} \cap T \neq \varnothing\}$$

$$RS_-(T) = \{[x]_\mathcal{R} | [x]_\mathcal{R} \subseteq T\}$$

where $[x]_\mathcal{R}$ denotes the class of elements $x, y \in X$ such that $x\mathcal{R}y$ and $RS^-(T)$ and $RS_-(T)$ are, respectively, the *upper* and *lower approximation* of T by $\mathcal{R}$, i.e.,

$$RS_-(T) \subseteq T \subseteq RS^-(T).$$

These definitions are easily extended to fuzzy sets for dealing with uncertainty. The definition of rough fuzzy sets we propose to adopt here takes inspiration, as firstly made in Ref. [29], from the notion of composite sets [21,11]. Let $F = \{(x_i, \mu_{x_i}), i = 1, \ldots, n\}$ a fuzzy set on T defined by adding to each element of T the degree of its membership to the set through a mapping $\mu_F : T \rightarrow [0,1]$. The operations on fuzzy sets are extensions of those used for conventional sets (intersection, union, comparison, etc.). The basic operations are the intersection and union as defined as follows:

$$\mu_{A \cap B} = \max\{\mu_A(x), \mu_B(x)\}, \quad x \in T$$

$$\mu_{A \cup B} = \min\{\mu_A(x), \mu_B(x)\}, \quad x \in T$$

The previous are only a restricted set of operations applicable among fuzzy sets, but they are the most significant for our aim. A *composite set* or *C*-set is a triple $C = (\Gamma, m, M)$ (where $\Gamma = \{T_1, \ldots, T_p\}$ is a partition of T in p disjoint subsets $T_1, \ldots, T_p$, while m and M are mappings of kind $T \rightarrow [0,1]$ such that $\forall x \in T, m(x) = \sum m_i \mu_{T_i}(x)$ and $M(x) = \sum M_i \mu_{T_i}(x)$ where

$$m_i = \inf\{f(x) | x \in T_i\}, \quad M_i = \sup\{f(x) | x \in T_i\} \tag{1}$$

for each choice of function $f : T \rightarrow [0,1]$. Γ and f uniquely define a composite set. Based on these assumptions, we may formulate the following definition of rough fuzzy set:

1. If f is the membership function μ_F and the partition Γ is made with respect to a relation $\mathcal{R}$, i.e., $\Gamma = T/\mathcal{R}$, a fuzzy set F gets two approximations $RS^-(F)$ and

$RS_-(F)$, which are again fuzzy sets with membership functions defined as Equation (1), i.e., $m_i = \mu_{RS_-(F)}$ and $M_i = \mu_{RS^-(F)}$. The couple of sets $(RS^-(F), RS_-(F))$ is a *rough fuzzy set*.

2. Let $C = (\Gamma, m, M)$ and $C' = (\Gamma', m', M')$ two rough fuzzy sets related, respectively, to partitions $\Gamma = (T_1, \ldots, T_s)$ and $\Gamma' = (T'_1, \ldots, T'_s)$ with $m(m')$ and $M(M')$ indicating the measures expressed in Equation (1). The *product* between two C-sets C and C', denoted by $\otimes$, is defined as a new rough fuzzy set $C'' = C \otimes C' = (\Gamma'', m'', M'')$ where Γ'' is a new partition whose elements are $T''_{i,j} = T_i \cap T'_j$ and m'' and M'' are obtained by:

$$m''_{i,j} = \sup\{m_i, m'_j\}, \quad M''_{i,j} = \inf\{M_i, M'_j\}$$

As shown in Ref. [29], this computation scheme generalizes the concept of fuzzy set to rough fuzzy set. It has been also demonstrated in Ref. [30,31] that recursive application of the previous operation provides a refinement of the original sets, realizing a powerful tool for measurement and a basic signal-processing technique.

3 FACE-DETECTION METHOD

The RGB color space is considered native to computer graphics (the encoding of files, CRT monitors, CCD cameras and scanners, and the rasterization of graphics cards usually use this model), and is therefore the most widespread. It is an additive model, in which the colors are produced by adding, the primary colors red, green, and blue, with white having all the colors present and black representing the absence of any color. RGB is a good space for computer graphics but not so for image processing and analysis. RGB's major defects are the high correlation between the three channels (varying the intensities, all three components change) and the fact that it is not perceptually uniform. However, this color space can be used to generate other alternative color formats, including YC_bC_r, HSI, and CIE*Lab*. CIE*Lab* is the most complete color space specified by the International Commission on Illumination (CIE). This color space is based on the opponent-colors theory of color vision, which says that a single values can be used to describe the red/green and the yellow/blue attributes as two colors cannot be both green and red at the same time, nor blue and yellow at the same time. When a color is expressed in CIE*Lab*, L defines lightness ($L=0$ denotes black and $L=100$ indicates diffuse white), the chromaticity coordinates (a, b), which can take both positive and negative values, denote, respectively, the red $(+a)$/green $(-a)$ value and the yellow $(+b)$/blue $(-b)$ value. The CIE*Lab* color space covers the entire spectrum visible to the human eye and represents it in a uniform way. It thus enables description of the set of visible colors independent of any graphics technology. This color space has two advantages:

1. It was designed to be perceptually uniform, i.e., perceptually similar images have the same chromaticity components.
2. The chromaticity coordinates (a, b) are distinct and independent of the lightness L.

The smooth shape and curve of a face, in some cases, may be varied considerably the intensity of the light reflected from it. The chromaticity components, instead, remain relatively unchanged and it can be used to detect skin regions. For this reason, to separate the skin from the non-skin regions, we analyze only the chromaticity distribution of an image, in particular, those relating to the chromaticity component a regardless of the lightness component. After detection of the skin regions, the luminance component of the colors is used to capture the details of the face (eyes, nose, lips, eyebrows, beard, etc.). The overall algorithm for face detection is given as a flow chart in Figure 1, where the input to the algorithm is an RGB image.

The luminance component L and the chrominance components a are used to create the skin map at each pixel (x, y) as follows:

$$SM(x, y) = SM_L(x, y) \cap SM_a(x, y)$$

where $SM_L(x, y)$ and $SM_a(x, y)$ are obtained as the output of a specialized NN incurred from the integration of the rough-fuzzy-set-based scale space transform and neural clustering, and separately applied to the L component image, and a component image, as depicted in Figure 1. Finally, the skin map SM is fed as input to an algorithm for the detection of elliptical objects, as an extension of the technique reported in Ref. [32].

In Figure 2, we have presented the results obtained by applying this method to some images of CalTech database. It can be observed from the figures that the a component identifies the skin region, while the L component is used mainly to obtain the details of the face (eyes, nose, lips, eyebrows, beard, etc.).

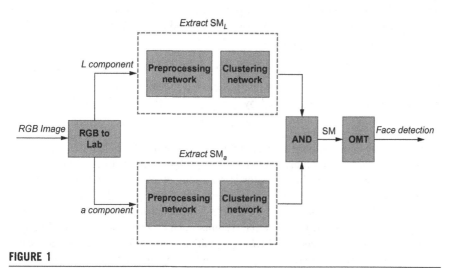

FIGURE 1

Overall face-detection method.

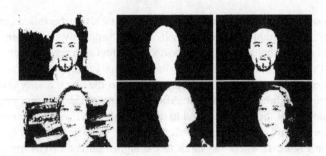

FIGURE 2

L component, *a* component, and skin map (SM).

3.1 THE PROPOSED MULTISCALE METHOD

Let us consider an image as a set X of picture elements, i.e., a Cartesian product $[0,\ldots,N-1] \times [0,\ldots,M-1]$. $X/\mathcal{R}$ is a discretization grid in classes of pixels, such that $[x]_{\mathcal{R}}$ denotes the class of pixels containing x and μ is the luminance function of each pixel. Given a subset T of the image not necessarily included or equal to any $[x]_{\mathcal{R}}$, various approximations ($RS^-(T)$ and $RS_-(T)$) of this subset can be obtained. As instance, this subset defines the contour or uniform regions in the image. On the contrary, regions appear rather like fuzzy sets of gray levels and their comparison or combination generates more or less uniform partitions of the image. Rough fuzzy sets, and in particular C-sets, seem to capture these aspects together, trying to extract different kinds of knowledge in data. In particular, let us consider four different partitions $Y^i, i = 1,2,3,4$, of the set-image X, such that each element of Y^i is a sub-image of dimension $w \times w$ and Y^2, Y^3, Y^4 are taken as shifted versions of Y^1 in the directions of $0\,°$, $-45\,°$, and $-90\,°$ of $w-1$ pixels. In such a case, each pixel of the image can be seen as the intersection of four corresponding elements of the partitions Y^1, Y^2, Y^3, Y^4 as shown in Figure 3.

$$Y^i, \quad i = 1,2,3,4$$

Since for each partition, it is possible to define a C-set, each pixel can be seen as belonging to the partition obtained by the product of the original four C-set:

$$C = C^1 \otimes C^2 \otimes C^3 \otimes C^4$$

where C^i is the composite set corresponding to partition Y^i. We shall define as *scale* the size w of each partition element. The product operator is neither idempotent nor increasing. The fact that this operator is not idempotent allows it to be iteratively applied to the input signal in order to construct the scales pace. The multiscale construction follows that of a fuzzy NN [33,34]. Specifically, it consists of two pyramidal-layered networks with fixed weights, each looking upon an $2^n \times 2^n$ image. By fixing the initial dimension of *CRC* (*C*andidate *R*egion to be *C*ategorized), each pyramidal network is constituted by $n-R$ multiresolution levels. Each processing element (i,j) at the rth level of the first pyramid (respectively, second pyramid)

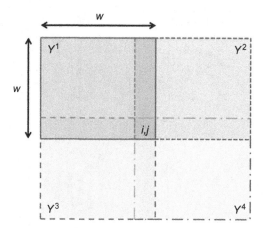

FIGURE 3

Each image pixel can be seen as the intersection of four elements of the partitions.

computes the minimum value (respectively maximum value) over a $2w \times 2w$ area at the $(r-1)$th level. The pyramidal structures are computed in a top-down manner, firstly analyzing regions as large as possible and then proceeding by splitting regions turned out to be not of interest. The mechanism of splitting operates as follows. If we suppose to be at the rth level of both pyramid-networks and analyze a region $w \times w$ which is the intersection of four $2w \times 2w$ regions, the minimum and maximum values computed inside are denoted by $m_{s,t}$ and $M_{s,t}$, $s=i,\ldots,i+w,t=j,\ldots,j+w$. The combination of the minima and maxima values is made up at the output layer, i.e.,

$$c_{i,j}^1 = \min_{s,t}[M_{s,t}], \quad c_{i,j}^2 = \max_{s,t}[m_{s,t}]$$

If $c_{i,j}^1$ and $c_{i,j}^2$ satisfy a specific constraint, the region under consideration is seen as RC (*R*egion to be *C*ategorize) and the values are retained as elementary features of such a region. Otherwise, the region is divided in four sub-regions each of dimension equal to $w/2$. The preprocessing subnetwork is applied again to the newly defined regions. The fuzzy intersections computed by the preprocessing subnetwork are fed to a clustering subnetwork which is described in the following.

3.2 CLUSTERING SUBNETWORK

Each node in the clustering sub network receives, as shown in Figure 4, two input values from each corresponding neuron at the previous layer. In particular, at each iteration, a learning step is applied to the clustering subnetwork according to the minimization of a *Fuzzines Index* (FI), applying, and somewhere extending, the learning mechanism proposed in Ref. [35].

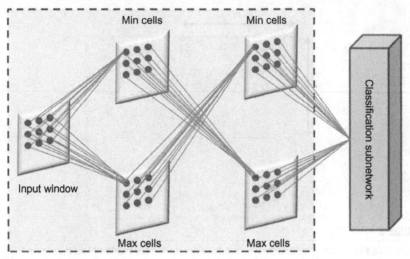

FIGURE 4

The preprocessing networks.

The output of a node j is then obtained as:

$$o_j = f(I_j), \quad I_j = g\left(\underline{O}_i, \underline{W}_{ji}\right)$$

where $\underline{O}_i = \left(o_i^{2,1}, o_i^{2,2}\right)$ and $\underline{W}_{ji} = \left(w_{j,i}^1, w_{j,i}^2\right)$, where $w_{j,i}^q$ indicates the connection weight between the jth node of the output layer and the ith node of the previous layer in the qth cell-plane, $q = 1, 2$. Each sum is intended over all nodes i in the neighborhood of the jth node at the upper hidden layer. f (the *membership function*) can be sigmoidal, hyperbolic, Gaussian, Gaborian, etc. with the accordance that if o_j takes the value 0.5, a small quantity (usually 0.001) is added; this reflects into dropping out instability conditions. g is a similarity function, e.g. correlation, Minkowsky distance, etc. To retain the value of each output node o_j in [0, 1], we apply the following mapping to each input image pixel g:

$$g' = \frac{g - g_{\min}}{g_{\max} - g_{\min}}$$

where $g_{\min}$ and $g_{\max}$ are the lowest and highest gray levels in the image.

The subnetwork has to self-organize by minimizing the fuzziness of the output layer. Since the membership function is chosen to be sigmoidal, minimizing the fuzziness is equivalent to minimizing the distances between corresponding pixel values in both cell-planes at the upper hidden layer. Since random initialization acts as noise, all the weights are initially set to unity. The adjustment of weights is done using the gradient descent search, i.e., the incremental change $\Delta w_{j,i}^l, l = 1, 2$, is taken as proportional to the sum of the negative gradient $-\eta(\partial E/\partial o_i) f'(I_i) o_j$. The adjustment rule is then the following:

$$w_{j,i}^l = w_{j,i}^l + \eta \Delta w_{j,i}^l$$

Specifically, we adopted the Linear Index of Fuzziness (LIF), whose updating rules look as follows, where E indicates the energy-fuzziness of our method and $n = M \times N$. LIF learning:

$$\Delta w_{j,i}^1 = \begin{cases} -\eta_{\text{LIF}}(1 - o_j)o_j o_i^{2,2} & \text{if } 0 \le o_j \le 0.5 \\ \eta_{\text{LIF}}(1 - o_j)o_j o_i^{2,2} & \text{if } 0.5 < o_j \le 1 \end{cases}$$

$$\Delta w_{j,i}^2 = \begin{cases} -\eta_{\text{LIF}}(1 - o_j)o_j o_i^{2,1} & \text{if } 0 \le o_j \le 0.5 \\ \eta_{\text{LIF}}(1 - o_j)o_j o_i^{2,1} & \text{if } 0.5 < o_j \le 1 \end{cases}$$

where $\eta_{\text{LIF}} = \eta \times 2/n$.

The previous rules hold also for the determination of an exact threshold value, θ, adopted for dividing the image into skin regions and nonskin regions, when convergence is reached. According to the properties of fuzziness, the initial threshold is set to be 0.5; this value allows to determine an hard decision from an unstable condition to a stable one. As said before, the updating of weights is continued until the network stabilizes. The method is said *stable* (the learning stops) when:

$$E(t+1) \le E(t) \quad \text{and} \quad |O(t+1) - O(t)| \le \gamma$$

where $E(t)$ is the method fuzziness computed at the tth iteration, γ is a prefixed very small positive quantity and $O(t) = \sum_{j:o_j \ge 0.5} o_j$. After convergence, the pixels j with $o_j > \theta$ are considered to constitute the skin map of the image; they are set to take value 255, in contrast with the remaining which will constitute the background (value 0). Figure 5 shows, with a 3D representation, the segmentation process (b) and (c) performed by the MS-RNN method on the input image depicted in (a).

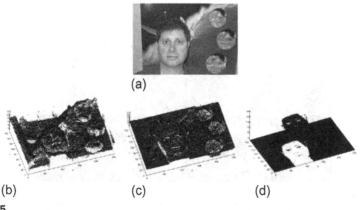

(a)

(b)   (c)   (d)

FIGURE 5

(a) Original images, (b) *L* component, (c) *a* component, and (d) skin map (SM).

4 SKIN MAP SEGMENTATION

We transformed the image model into CEI*Lab* and normalized the luminance component L and the chrominance components a in the range of $[0, 255]$. To realize multiclass image segmentation, the *CRC* must satisfy a homogeneity constraint, i.e., the difference between $c_{i,j}^1$ and $c_{i,j}^2$ must be less than or equal to a prefixed threshold. In such a case, the region is seen as uniform and becomes *RC* otherwise, the *CRC* is split into four newly defined *CRC*, letting w be $w/2$. The parameters of the preprocessing subnetwork have been set to the following values:

- $w_0 = 8$, $w_t = w_{t-1/2}$ (t denotes iteration)
- $\theta = 50$

The output of the preprocessing subnetwork normalized in the $[0, 1]$ range is fed to a clustering subnetwork. The parameters of the clustering subnetwork have been set to the following values:

- $\eta = 0.2$ (learning rate)
- $\gamma = 0.001$ (convergence rate)

The reason for these choices resides in a most successful skin-detection system, both for detecting skin and suppressing noise, while requiring the minimum amount of computation or, equivalently, minimum number of iterations to converge.

4.1 SKIN MAP SEGMENTATION RESULTS

Several experiments were performed on real images to test the efficacy of the proposed method. In Figures 6 and 7, we present the results obtained by applying this method to some images.

FIGURE 6

Images of CalTech, IMM, and CMU face database and skin map obtained by the algorithm proposed.

FIGURE 7

Multiface image and the skin map obtained by the algorithm proposed.

5 FACE DETECTION

Face detection is achieved by detecting elliptical regions in the skin map by properly modifying the *Orientation Matching* (OM) technique reported in Ref. [32]. The technique detects circular objects of radius in the interval $[r_m, r_M]$, computing the OM transform of the input image and taking the peaks of the transform, which correspond to the centers of the circular patterns. To customize the technique for handling our problem of detecting elliptical pattern in the skin map, we performed a statistical analysis on 500 images taken from the databases used to test the method to find a proper ratio between major and minor semi-axis of ellipses around faces. We statistically found this ratio as 0.75. In Figures 8 and 9, we present the results achieved by applying this method to the binary skin map obtained as the output of the multiscale method.

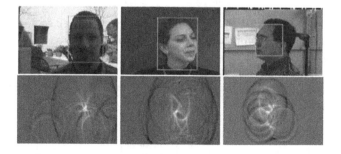

FIGURE 8

Images of CalTech, IMM, and CMU face database and the results of the OM technique.

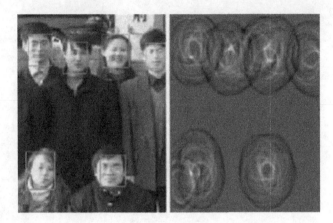

FIGURE 9

Multiface image and the result of the OM technique.

6 FACE TRACKING

The use of our MS-RNN method for face tracking relies on the fact that the skin color is invariant to face orientation and is insensitive to partial occlusion. Also, our system proved insensitive to variations of scene conditions, such as the presence of a complex background and uncontrolled illumination. Based on these considerations, we applied the MS-RNN method at any frames of video sequences and the Kalman filter algorithm [22]. Kalman filtering helps to predict the next face-detection window and smooth the tracking trajectory. Face detection is performed within a predicted window instead of an entire image region to reduce computation costs. The $x-y$ coordinates and height of the face region are initially set to the values given by the face-detection process, while the velocity values of the state vector are set to 1. The face motion model used in our tracking method can be defined by the following set of space-state equations:

$$x_{k+1} = \Phi x_k + w_k, \quad z_{k+1} = Hx_{k+1} + v_k$$

where x_k represents the state vector at the time k, characterized by five parameters consisting of the $x-y$ coordinates of the center point of the face region (c_x, c_y), the velocity in the x and y directions (v_x, v_y), and the height H_k of the face-bounded region. The width of the face-bounded region is always assumed to be 0.75 times the size of the calculated height. The transition matrix, Φ, which relates the current state to the predicted state after the time interval Δt is given as:

$$\Phi = \begin{bmatrix} 1 & 0 & \Delta t & 0 & 0 \\ 0 & 1 & 0 & \Delta t & 0 \\ 0 & 0 & 1 & 0 & 0 \\ 0 & 0 & 0 & 1 & 0 \\ 0 & 0 & 0 & 0 & 1 \end{bmatrix}$$

The vector $z_k \in \mathbb{R}^3$ represents the face position and height observed with the observation matrix:

$$H = \begin{bmatrix} 1 & 0 & \Delta t & 0 & 0 \\ 0 & 1 & 0 & \Delta t & 0 \\ 0 & 0 & 0 & 0 & 1 \end{bmatrix}$$

and w_k and v_k are the zero-mean, white, Gaussian random processes modeling the system noise. The whole filtering procedure consists of prediction and correction steps, which are carried out alternatively. The state in the next time step is predicted from the current state using:

$$x_{k+1|k} = \Phi x_{k|k}, \quad z_{k+1|k} = H x_{k+1|k}$$

Face detection is performed on the window of height $H_{k+1|k}$ and width $0.75 H_{k+1|k}$ centered at a predicted position. Detection within the window instead of the whole image helps to reduce the detection time, which is important for real-time operations. The Kalman corrector is

$$x_{k+1|k+1} = x_{k+1|k} + K_{k+1}\left(z_{k+1} - z_{k+1|k}\right)$$

where K_{k+1} is the Kalman gain, computed as

$$K_{k+1} = P_{k+1} H^T \left[H P_{k+1|k} K H^T + R_{k+1}\right]^{-1}$$

The covariance matrix P is updated as follows:

$$P_{k+1|k} = \Phi P_{k|k} \Phi^T + Q_k, \quad P_{k+1|k+1} = [I - Kk + 1 H_{k+1}] P_{k+1|k}$$

where $Q_k = E[w_k w_k^T], R_k = E[v_k v_k^T]$ and $P_{0|0} = E[x_0 x_0^T]$. The face detector and the tracker are used simultaneously. The overall algorithm for face tracking is given as a flow chart in Figure 10.

7 EXPERIMENTS

7.1 FACE-DETECTION EXPERIMENTS

7.1.1 Experiment 1

To form an experimental dataset and evaluate the effectiveness of the proposed color face-detection method in terms of face-detection performance, a total of 7266 facial images from 980 subjects were collected from three publicly available face databases, CMU-PIE [23], color FERET [24,25], and IMM [26]. A total of 2847 face images of 68 subjects were collected from CMU-PIE; for one subject, the images had different expressions and 21 lighting variations with "room lighting on" conditions. From Color FERET, a total of 4179 face images of 872 subjects were collected; for one subject, the images included five different pose variations. Specifically, the pose angles were in the range from $-45°$ to $+45°$. From IMM, a total of 240 face images of 40 subjects were collected; for 1 subject, the images include 6 different pose variations. Specifically, the pose angles were in the range from $-30°$ to $+30°$. The face images used in Experiment 1 were scaled down to their one-fourth size. Figure 11 shows some of the test images and SM results.

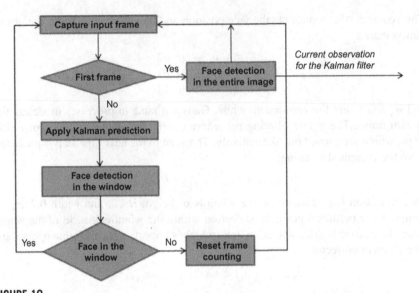

FIGURE 10

Overall face-tracking algorithm.

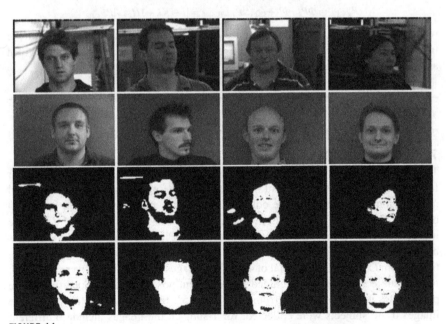

FIGURE 11

Eight of the 7266 images in Experiment 1 and skin map segmentation results.

Table 1 Experimental Results on CMU-PIE, Color FERET, and IMM Databases

Database	Detection Rate (%)	False Alarms
CMU-PIE	92.16	175
color FERET	96.53	16
IMM	98.65	0

To evaluate the performance of the face-detection algorithm, a number of detection rates and false alarms are used. The detection rate is defined as the ratio between the number of faces correctly detected and the actual number of faces, while a false alarm is a detection of the face where there is no face. Table 1 shows the results of the MS-RNN face-detection method on CMU-PIE, color FERET, and IMM databases.

Table 1 shows that the proposed algorithm for face-detection exhibits very good performance in detecting faces, which is also affected by scene condition variations, such as the presence of a complex background and uncontrolled illumination. However, the MS-RNN method is noted to be sensitive to the images where the background (neutral illumination) is turned off, mainly those obtained from CMU-PIE database.

7.1.2 Experiment 2
This experiment used the CalTech [27] face database. A total of 450 frontal images of 27 people of different races and facial expressions were included. Each image was of 896×592 pixels. The experiment employed detection and false alarms to evaluate the face-detection performance. Figure 12 shows some detection results.

Table 2 shows the comparison of the results of the MS-RNN face-detection method on CalTech databases with other fast face-detection methods reported in Refs. [6,9], which may be applied to real-time face tracking. Specifically, the first method used for comparison extends the detection in gray-images method presented in Ref. [6] to detection in color images. The second method segments skin colors, in the HSV color space, using a self-organizing Takagi-Sugeno fuzzy network with support vector learning [9]. A fuzzy system is used to eliminate the effects of

FIGURE 12

Face-detection results by the proposed method in Experiment 2.

Table 2 Experimental Results on CalTech Database

Method	Detection Rate (%)	False Alarms
Texture+SVM [6]	95.7	91
SOTFN-SV+IFAT [9]	95.7	67
Proposed method	98.43	20

illumination, to adaptively determine the fuzzy classifier segmentation threshold according to the illumination of an image. The proposed method showed the highest detection rate as well as the smallest number of false alarms, when compared with other methods.

7.2 FACE-TRACKING EXPERIMENTS

The proposed system was written in Visual C++ and implemented on a personal computer with an Intel Core i3 3.1 GHz CPU and Windows 7 operating system. The proposed detection system took 0.516 (s) for an image measuring 720×576 pixels. During the tracking process, the detection window size was 200×200 pixels, and the detection time was about 0.08 s if only the detection operation was conducted. The real-time tracking system uses a SONY CCD camera to capture images, and each image measured 720×576 pixels. At the start, a face was detected from the whole captured image, and subsequently, a face was detected within a predicted search region measuring 200×200 pixels.

7.2.1 Experiment 1

In this experiment, we tested the quality of the proposed face-tracking system on the standard IIT-NRC facial video database compared with the incremental visual tracker (IVT). This database contains short videos that show large changes in facial expression and orientation of the users taken from a web-cam placed on the computer monitor. In Figure 13, we have illustrated the tracking results of our approach and IVT on the IIT-NRC facial video database. We noted that our method, unlike the

FIGURE 13

Results of our approach and IVT tracker on the IIT-NRC facial video database.

IVT approach, is capable of tracking the target presenting a pose (190, 206), expression (89, 104), and size (89) variation, and maintaining the size of the face detected, which allows the use of the frames tracked in the recognition.

7.2.2 Experiment 2
In this experiment, we tested the quality of the proposed face-tracking system on a set of 500 video clips collected from YouTube. The frame size ranged from (320×240) to (240×180) pixels. Despite the heavy rate of noise in the video used, mostly due to the low resolution and high compression rate, our tracker successfully tracked 90% of the video clips. In Figure 14, we have presented examples of well-tracked videos. The level of performance obtained by our tracker is more than satisfactory by taking into account the low quality and high variability in the data tested.

7.2.3 Experiment 3
Figure 15 shows the tracking results for a succession of captured frames. These results show that, the proposed system can correctly track a subject under various complex motion and partial occlusion. By tracing the center point of the face detected in each frame, we obtained a motion signature as shown in Figure 16. Such motion signatures can be used to characterize human activities.

FIGURE 14

Face-tracking results on YouTube video clips.

FIGURE 15

Face tracking of a subject under various complex motion and partial occlusion.

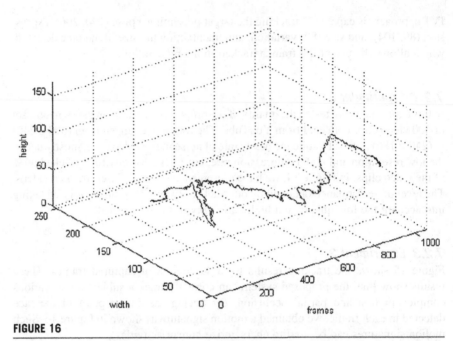

FIGURE 16

The motion signature obtained by tracing the center point of the face detected in each frame.

8 CONCLUSIONS AND FUTURE WORKS

A new method for face tracking and detection has been presented in this study, which has been designed to detect frontal faces in color images without *a priori* knowledge about the number of faces or the size of the faces in a given image. All our experiment results show that the proposed method can obtain high detection rates in the presence of both simple and complex backgrounds. SM detection may not be suitable for certain cases, such as when there are colors in the image that resemble the skin, but are not skin pixels. To overcome this problem OM transform could be employed to correctly detect the face region in the SM image. The ongoing work involves increasing the speed of our proposed method as well as adopting parallel processing provided by GPUs. In addition, the method is also being adopted as a pre-processor for a face recognition system, such that false positives may be rejected by the face validation process of the recognition system.

ACKNOWLEDGMENTS

This work was supported by MIUR—FIRB Project IntelliLogic (cod. RBIPO6MMBW) funded by Minister of Education, University and Research of Italy.

REFERENCES

[1] Sun YB, Kim JT, Lee WH. Extraction of face objects using skin color information. In: Proceedings of the IEEE international conference on communications, circuits and systems and West Sino expositions; 2002. p. 1136–40.

[2] Soriano M, Martinkauppi B, Huovinen S, Laaksonen M. Adaptive skin color modeling using the skin locus for selecting training pixels. Pattern Recogn 2003;36(3):681–90.

[3] Viola P, Jones MJ. Robust real-time face detection. Int J Comput Vis 2004;57(2):137–54.

[4] Lienhart R, Maydt J. An extended set of Haar-like features for rapid object detection. In: Proceedings of the IEEE international conference on image processing, vol. 1; p. 900–3.

[5] Rowley H, Baluja S, Kanade T. Neural network-based face detection. IEEE Trans Pattern Anal Mach Intell 1998;20(1):23–38.

[6] Sun Z, Bebis G, Miller R. Object detection using feature subset selection. Pattern Recogn 2004;37(11):2165–76.

[7] Juang CF, Chang SW. Fuzzy system-based real-time face tracking in a multi-subject environment with a pan-tilt-zoom camera. Expert Syst Appl 2010;37(6):4526–36.

[8] Kim HS, Kang WS, Shin JI, Park SH. Face detection using template matching and ellipse fitting. IEICE Trans Inf Syst 2000;11:2008–11.

[9] Hassanien AE. Fuzzy-rough hybrid scheme for breast cancer detection. Image Comput Vis J 2007;25(2):172–83.

[10] Mitra S, Banka H, Pedrycz W. Rough-fuzzy collaborative clustering systems. IEEE Trans Man Cybern B 2006;36(4):795–805.

[11] Petrosino A, Salvi G. Rough fuzzy set based scale space transforms and their use in image analysis. Int J Approx Reasoning 2006;41:212–28.

[12] Sarkar M. Rough-fuzzy functions in classification. Fuzzy Sets Syst 2002;132(3):353–69.

[13] Marr D, Ullman S, Poggio T. Bandpass channels, zero-crossing, and early visual information processing. J Opt Soc Am 1979;69:914–6.

[14] Bangham JA, Ling PD, Harvey R. Scale-space from nonlinear filters. IEEE Trans Pattern Anal Mach Intell 1996;18:520–8.

[15] Cantoni V, Cinque L, Guerra C, Levialdi S, Lombardi L. 2-D object recognition by multi-scale tree matching. Pattern Recogn 1998;31(10):1443–54.

[16] Dyer CR. Multiscale image understanding. In: Uhr L, editor. Parallel computer vision. New York: Academic Press; 1987. p. 171–213.

[17] Rosenfeld A, editor. Multiresolution image processing and analysis. Berlin: Springer; 1984.

[18] Ueda N, Suzuki S. Learning visual models from shape contours using multi-scale convex/concave structure matching. IEEE Trans Pattern Anal Mach Intell 1993;15(4):337–52.

[19] Pawlak Z. Rough sets. Int J Comput Inform Sci 1982;11(5):341–56.

[20] Zadeh LA. Fuzzy sets. Inform Control 1965;8:338–53.

[21] Caianiello ER. A calculus of hierarchical systems. In: Proceedings of the international conference on pattern recognition, Washington, DC; 1973. p. 1–5.

[22] Catlin DE. Estimation, control, and the discrete Kalman filter. New York: Springer-Verlag; 1989.

[23] Sim T, Baker S. The CMU pose illumination and expression database. IEEE Trans Pattern Anal Mach Intell 2003;25(12):1615–7.

[24] Phillips PJ, Wechsler H, Huang J, Rauss P. The FERET database and evaluation procedure for face recognition algorithms. Image Vis Comput J 1998;16(5):295–306.

[25] Phillips PJ, Moon H, Rizvi SA, Rauss PJ. The FERET evaluation methodology for face recognition algorithms. IEEE Trans Pattern Anal Mach Intell 2000;22(10):1090–104.

[26] Stegmann MB, Ersbøll BK, Larsen R. FAME–a flexible appearance modeling environment. IEEE Trans Med Imag 2003;22(10):1319–31.

[27] Markus W. Face database collection of Markus Weber. [Online] 02 February 2006. Available: http://www.vision.caltech.edu/Image_Datasets/faces/.

[28] Gorodnichy DO. Associative neural networks as means for low resolution video-based recognition. In: International joint conference on neural networks (IJCNN); 2005.

[29] Dubois D, Prade H. Rough fuzzy sets and fuzzy rough sets. In: International conference on fuzzy sets in informatics, Moscow, September 20–23; 1993.

[30] Caianiello ER, Ventre A. A model for C-calculus. Int J General Syst 1985;11:153–61.

[31] Caianiello ER, Petrosino A. Neural networks, fuzziness and image processing. In: Cantoni V, editor. Machine and human perception: analogies and divergencies. New York: Plenum Press; 1994. p. 355–70.

[32] Ceccarelli M, Petrosino A. The orientation matching approach to circular object detection. In: Proceedings of the IEEE international conference on image processing; 2001. p. 712–5.

[33] Lee S, Lee E. Fuzzy neural networks. Math Biosci 1975;23:151–77.

[34] Simpson PK. Fuzzy min-max neural networks—part I: classification. IEEE Trans Neural Netw 1992;3:776–86.

[35] Ghosh A, Pal NR, Pal SK. Self-organization for object extraction using a multilayer neural network and fuzziness measures. IEEE Trans Fuzzy Systems 1993;1:54–68.

A content-based image retrieval approach based on document queries

20

M. Ilie

"Dunarea de Jos" University of Galati, Faculty of Automatic Control, Computers, Electrical and Electronics Engineering, Galati, Romania

1 INTRODUCTION

The necessity of the content-based image retrieval (CBIR) phenomenon was imposed by the problems encountered in different areas. Initially, the image classification was done based on text labels, which was proven to be very time consuming and error prone. Starting from this problem, the image processing techniques have been improved, combined, and extended across a vast number of fields, like duplicate detection and copyright, creating image collections, medical applications, video surveillance and security, document analysis, face and print recognition, industrial, military, and so on. The term of "content" implies that the images are deconstructed into descriptors, which are analyzed and interpreted as image features, as opposed to image metadata, like annotations, geo-tags, file name, or camera properties (flash light on/off, exposure, etc.).

The traditional CBIR approaches try to solve this problem by extracting a set of characteristics from one image and comparing it with another one, representing a different image. The results obtained until now are promising but still far from covering all the requirements risen by a real world scenario. Also, the current approaches target specific problems in the image processing context. Because of that most of the CBIR implementations work in a rather similar way, on homogenous data. This causes significant performance drops whenever the test data originate from a different area than the training set.

This chapter proposes a CBIR architecture model with descriptors originating in different search areas. In order to be able to classify images originating in document scans, we have added an extra module, responsible for the document image segmentation stage. The user is offered the possibility of querying the engine with both document scans and regular images in order to retrieve the best N matches.

During the implementation stage we have faced multiple problems, as specified below:

- image preprocessing;
- extraction of characteristics from various spaces;
- implementation of a supervised machine learning module;
- document image segmentation;
- benchmarking the overall performance.

We have reached the conclusion that a CBIR engine can obtain better results in the presence of multiple sets of descriptors, from different search spaces or from the same one, even if the test images originate in very different areas.

2 RELATED WORK

The CBIR engines are trying to mimic the human behavior when executing a classification process. This task is very difficult to accomplish due to a large series of factors.

The CBIR queries may take place at different levels [1]:

- feature level (find images with $X\%$ red and $Y\%$ blue);
- semantic level (find images with churches);
- affective level (find images where a certain mood prevails). There is no complete solution for the affective queries.

All the CBIR implementations use a vector of (global or local) characteristics which originate in different search spaces—color, texture, or shape.

In the color space there are many models but recently the focus is set on various normalizations of the RGB one in the attempt of obtaining invariant elements. Two of the most interesting ones are c1c2c3 (which eliminates both shadows and highlight areas) and l1l2l3 (which eliminates only the shadows, but keeps the highlight areas) [2].

There are four large categories for determining the texture descriptors [3]:

- statistical (Tamura features, Haralick's co-occurrence matrices);
- geometrical (Voronoi tesselation features);
- spectral (wavelets [4], Gabor and ICA filters);
- model based (MRFs [5], fractals).

One of the most widely embraced approach is to use local binary patterns [6].

In what regards the local descriptors, probably the most famous algorithm (scale invariant feature transform—SIFT) was introduced by Lowe [7]. Since then, many approaches have been developed. Some of the most popular ones are based on speeded up robust feature (SURF) [8], histogram of oriented gradients (HOG) [9], gradient location and orientation histogram (GLOH) [10], or local energy-based shape histogram (LESH) [11].

3 OUR APPROACH

The proposed approach targets to classify a mixed set of images, containing real world scenes and document scans. The system mainly follows the standard CBIR architecture as it can be seen in Figure 1. It is composed of two interconnected submodules:

- the training and learning module;
- the document classification module.

A valid use case scenario contains the below stages:

- the system is trained on a set of images;
- each image is analyzed and decomposed in relevant descriptors;
- the descriptors are provided as input to a machine learning module, which is in charge of setting the class boundaries;
- each new regular image (not document) is decomposed and classified accordingly;
- each new document scan is preprocessed and segmented. The extracted images are then classified;
- the system extracts the 10 most relevant results and provides them as an answer to the user query.

The indexing process is based on supervised machine learning and is conducted on regular images. The user is allowed to enter queries based on both image types.

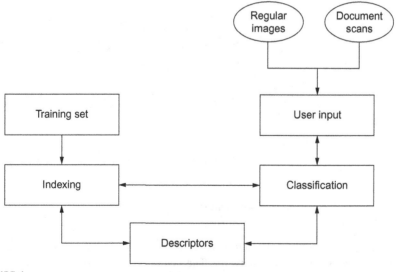

FIGURE 1

The basic system architecture.

We are using a mixed set of image characteristics:

- different color spaces;
- texture space;
- local descriptors.

We have not used any shape descriptors, as the preliminary tests showed that in this area these do not produce a noticeable improvement. The main problem was caused by the fact that the objects contained in the images may be affected by problems like occlusion or clutter.

In the color descriptors area, we have used four sets of characteristics, as it follows:

- *c1c2c3 and l1l2l3*. As explained above, these color spaces are very useful when applied on real world images. The coordinates are described by the equations below:

$$c_1 = \arctg \frac{R}{\max(G,B)} \tag{1}$$

$$c_2 = \arctg \frac{G}{\max(R,B)} \tag{2}$$

$$c_3 = \arctg \frac{B}{\max(R,G)} \tag{3}$$

$$l_1(R,G,B) = \frac{(R-G)^2}{(R-G)^2 + (R-B)^2 + (B-G)^2} \tag{4}$$

$$l_1(R,G,B) = \frac{(R-G)^2}{(R-G)^2 + (R-B)^2 + (B-G)^2} \tag{5}$$

$$l_1(R,G,B) = \frac{(R-G)^2}{(R-G)^2 + (R-B)^2 + (B-G)^2} \tag{6}$$

- the whole image in RGB coordinates;
- the RGB histogram, with 256 bins.

Each of the four sets of characteristics is used as an input for a standard feed forward/back propagation neural network. The neural networks' outputs are then collected by a simplified weighted majority voting module, as it can be observed in Figure 2.

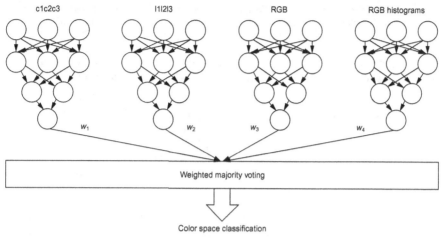

FIGURE 2

Color space classification.

The weighted module works according to the below algorithm:

- let n be the number of accepted classes and k be the number of classifiers;
- each neural network will produce on the final layer a vector $C_x = \{c_1, c_2, \ldots, c_n\}$, where $1 \leq x \leq k$;
- the weight associated to the output layer will be $W = \{w_1, w_1, \ldots, w_k\}$;
- the weighted result will be provided by the wiCi sum, as specified below, where $R \in [1, n]$, max(C) represents the maximum value obtained for a certain class, and idx represents the position of this class in the final vector

$$R = \mathrm{idx}\left(\max\left(\sum_{i=1}^{k} w_i C_i \right) \right) \qquad (7)$$

In the texture space area we have chosen an approach based on local binary pattern descriptors, mainly because of their invariant properties for color or rotation.

For the local descriptors we have chosen two sets of characteristics, based on SIFT and histogram of oriented gradients (HOG). Traditionally, the HOG descriptors are used in order to train an SVM classifier, but since we are dealing with a multiple classification problem, we have used neural networks in the learning stage for both descriptors. The two types of local descriptors produced similar results during the tests, therefore the combined classifier for SIFT and HOG uses equal weights of 50%.

The final classifier includes an additional weighted majority voting module, as shown in Figure 3.

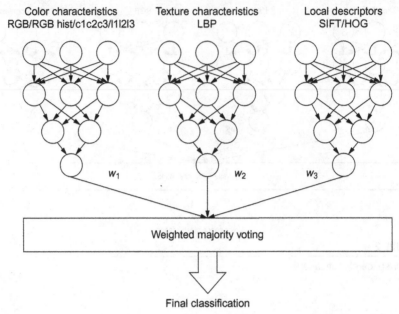

FIGURE 3

The final classification.

Since the aim is to classify document scans as well as regular images, we have also included an additional document analysis module. Its purpose is to process the scans and extract the images included in the document, in order to pass them subsequently to the module in charge of extraction of descriptors and to classify them accordingly. We are not interested in text segmentation, therefore this module will only binarize the document and go through a bottom-up [12] image segmentation stage, based on the below steps:

- text filtering, implemented as a simplified *XY* axis projection module [13];
- the document is split in tiles, which are analyzed according to their average intensity and variance. The decision criteria is that in a particular tile, an image tends to be more uniform than the text;
- the remaining tiles are clustered through a K-Means algorithm, which uses as a decision metric the Euclidean distance;
- the clusters are filtered according to their connectivity and scarcity scores in order to eliminate tiles containing text areas with different fonts, affected by noise/poor illumination or by page curvature;
- the final clusters are exposed to a reconstruction stage and merged into a single image, which is provided as an input to the modules in charge of descriptors extraction/classification (Figure 4).

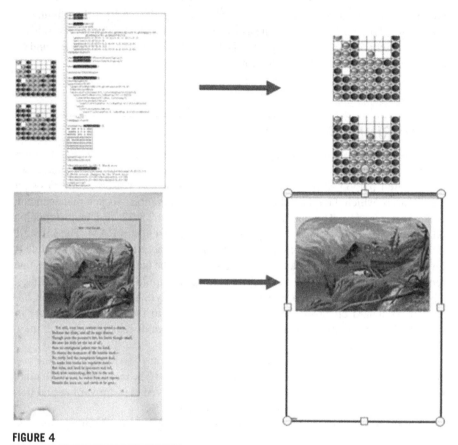

FIGURE 4

Document image segmentation results.

All the neural networks have the same structure. The transfer function is sigmoid and the images in the training set have been split in three groups:

- 60% for training;
- 20% for cross-validation;
- 20% for testing.

In order to validate the neural network progress, we have used gradient checking on the cost function specified below:

$$J(\theta) = -\frac{1}{m}\left[\sum_{i=1}^{m}\sum_{k=1}^{K}\left(y_k^{(i)}\log\left(h_\theta\left(x^{(i)}\right)\right)_k + \left(1 - y_k^{(i)}\right)\log\left(1 - h_\theta\left(x^{(i)}\right)\right)_k\right)\right]$$
$$+ \frac{\lambda}{2m}\sum_{l-1}^{L-1}\sum_{i=1}^{s_l}\sum_{j=1}^{s_l+1}\left(\theta_{ji}^{(l)}\right)^2 \tag{8}$$

with the following notations: $\{(x^{(1)}, y^{(1)}), (x^{(2)}, y^{(2)}), \ldots, (x^{(m)}, y^{(m)})\}$ is the (input, output) vector, $h_\theta(x) \in R^K$ is the hypothesis function, L is the number of layers, s_l is the number of neurons in a specific layer l, K is the number of classes, with $y \in R^K$, and Θ, the matrix which stores the weights for each layer.

4 EXPERIMENTAL SETUP

We aimed to create a scalable application, portable between different architectures and operating systems. Therefore, in what regards the programming language, we have chosen python over Matlab or Octave, for practical reasons, especially for the libraries which facilitate the user interface generation, socket management, and data processing. The operating system is a 12.04 LTS 32 bit Ubuntu, running on a machine with two cores with hyper threading and 4 GB of RAM. The software architecture is modular to facilitate any subsequent refactoring; each sub-module is implemented in a class. In order to make better use of the hardware, the modules that require resources intensively use multi-threading and multi-processing techniques. The data are stored in a MySQL database, based on MyISAM. The application follows the standard client-server architecture, in order to facilitate the exposure of functionalities to multiple users at once. So far, we have disregarded the user management problems.

We have restricted the number of recognized classes at 10 so far. The training was conducted on a CIFAR data set, provided by Ref. [14]; it includes 60,000 small (32×32 pixels) color images. The author's tests involved feed forward neural networks as well, with performances revolving around 87%.

The document scans data consisted of 1380 images, obtained from two sources:

- scans of old, degraded documents, used as a benchmark in the ICDAR 2007 conference [15];
- high quality copies, containing mostly manuals and documentation for the Ubuntu 12.04 operating system. In order to be able to use them, we have previously converted them from the pdf format to the jpeg one.

Initially we have tried replicating the CIFAR benchmark results. We have also used a neural network approach, based on RGB descriptors only; we obtained similar performances (85%). However, when we tried to classify an image originating from a different image set (document scans), the accuracy dropped significantly, by more than 10%. Therefore, we started experimenting with various combinations of RGB/c1c2c3/l1l2l3 descriptors. The results are described in Table 1 [16].

As we can observe, the presence of the c1c2c3 and l1l2l3 color spaces produces an improvement of over 10%, leading to the below conclusions:

- the experiments conducted on real world images confirm the necessity of additional color space descriptors;

Table 1 Color Space Experiments

Combined Descriptors	Results (%)
RGB+l1l2l3	82
RGB+c1c2c3	84
RGB+RGB histograms	69
RGB	71

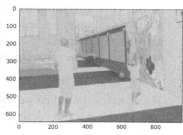

FIGURE 5

c1c2c3 normalization.

- c1c2c3 produces the most solid performance boost. After analyzing the images in the data set, we have observed the presence of many pictures with shady areas, which shows that this color space is adequate for these conditions. Figure 5 shows the effects of the c1c2c3 normalization on an image containing highlight and shadow areas;
- introducing the RGB histograms as a global descriptor actually produced a performance drop, as two different images may have very similar color histograms, yet a very different content. This was mainly caused by the surrounding conditions in which the picture of a certain object was taken. Also, the presence of the shadow areas affects the histograms and implicitly the classification result.

After experimenting with various color space weight values we have chosen the below values:

- the RGB histograms weights have been set to $w_4 = 10\%$, which improved the overall performance. We have kept this set of descriptors for situations where the color plays a more important role in the classification process. In this case, the user will be able to adjust this value accordingly;
- the rest of the weights have been set to $w[1:3] = 30\%$ (for the RGB/c1c2c3/l1l2l3 descriptors). This lead to a combined overall performance of 86%. As we

mentioned before, the UI offers the user the possibility of manually adjusting the global color relevance (associated to the RGB histograms) in the final result. As an example, the user can choose a combination like $w_1 = 20\%$, $w_2 = 20\%$, $w_3 = 20\%$, and $w_4 = 40\%$.

The next set of experiments was conducted in the texture space, with the LBP descriptor. The main problems in this area were related to choosing the cell shape and size, along with the number of pixels which compose the final descriptor. After a series of tests we concluded the below:

- choosing radial cells over square cells produces an overall performance increase of over 10%, going over 95%;
- the execution times are larger when using radial cells, especially due to the trigonometric calculus;
- over-increasing the cell size leads to performance drops, as the small textures are ignored.

The conclusion was that we will use square cells of 3×3 pixels and 8 pixels to compose the local texture descriptor.

Subsequently, we have started experimenting with the rest of the descriptors. For the HOG and SIFT algorithms we have used the authors' implementations. The tests involved the usage of singular descriptors and combining all of them together; the final weights have been set as it follows:

- $W_1 = 30\%$ for the color space;
- $W_2 = 30\%$ for the texture space;
- $W_3 = 40\%$ for the local descriptors. These have been considered more representative than the global descriptors.

The results are presented in Table 2 [16].

The results show that combining multiple types of descriptors from multiple search spaces lead to performance improvements. On the above-mentioned data set, the results are promising and show an increase of over 5%. Also, the proposed architecture is able to correctly classify images obtained from document scans as well as regular images.

Table 2 Experiments Involving All Descriptor Spaces

Descriptor Type	Results (%)
Color space	86
Texture space (LBP)	85
SIFT	82
HOG	85
All of the above	92

All the experiments conducted so far have been performed on document images which have been correctly segmented. The next set of experiments have used images affected by different types of noise, specific for the document analysis and recognition area.

As shown in Ref. [17], the document scans can be affected by different alterations:

- extra characters or images being present in the scan, due to the paper transparency;
- page curvature introduces distortions;
- incorrect exposure to light;
- machine malfunctioning;
- additional ink spots, water stains, anchoring devices, other marks, etc.

Each of the above factors may affect the segmentation process and the overall classification results. Therefore we have used the CVSEG algorithm presented in Ref. [17] applied on a mixed set of documents.

There are two areas which may be affected by the problems described above—the binarization stage or the segmentation stage. In what follows, we will describe how the binarization results affect the segmentation stage and the overall performance.

The CVSEG binarization tests have used four types of binarization algorithms. The experiments showed that the best options are NLBIN (a nonlinear binarization algorithm, recommended by the authors of the Ocropus library [18]) and Sauvola's algorithm [19]. Both algorithms have similar results and are usually affected as described below:

- the binarized image includes large black areas, especially in old scan documents;
- rotated images introduce skew angle estimation errors; these are usually introduced by the human operator or by the anchoring devices;
- threshold-related problems (usually these are caused by the low contrast or by the quality of the paper), which cause some details to be eroded and others to be enhanced.

The classification algorithm was then tested only against documents which contained the problems described above (the segmentation process was 100% accurate). The overall classification results have been affected as it is presented in Table 3.

The most impacting effect is caused by the old document area in the context of the binarization stage. When the large black areas are introduced, they usually cover the

Table 3 Binarization Experiments

Binarization Problem	Overall Results (%)
Large black areas	75.5
Skew angle estimation	90.8
Threshold problems	89.1

FIGURE 6

Binarization problems.

images as well, not only the text. This causes all the next processing stages (segmentation and classification) to fail. Figure 6 is affected by this problem—the drawing in the upper area has been completely covered and the only visible area is the one containing text.

The next performance drop is caused by the threshold problems, which may erode some details until they completely vanish. Specifically, in the over-dilated images the small details are usually merged into black tiles and in the over-eroded images the details composed of thin line disappear completely. Under these circumstances, the classification algorithm is not be able to extract the same amount of descriptors therefore the accuracy dropped by 3%.

There is also a small performance drop when processing rotated images but usually this problem is solved by the rotation invariance characteristic in the descriptors.

In what regards the segmentation experiments, we have used the CVSEG algorithm [17]. We have also found some problems in what regards processing the images at this stage. Usually they are caused by:

- incorrect binarization results—this may lead to segmentation results which include too much or too little from the original image;
- usage of different font types—some of the larger fonts may get included in the result;
- page layout, borders, page rotation, objects which did not belong in the original document, etc.

Table 4 Segmentation Experiments

Segmentation Problem	Overall Results (%)
Binarization	74.2
Font type	91.0
Page layout	91.1

Table 5 Overall Classification Performance Fluctuations

Images	Average Results (%)	Performance Drop (%)
Binarization problems	85.13	6.87
Segmentation problems	85.43	6.57
Mixed images	89.58	2.42

The results are described in Table 4.

Again, the binarization results have an important impact on the overall performance. As mentioned before, the segmentation module cannot extract the correct image from a document which has not been correctly binarized, because in many cases the original drawings/images have been masked by the large black areas. Subsequently, the classification module cannot extract the appropriate descriptors and fails to correctly classify the image.

There are some small performance drops in the remaining two areas as well but usually, even the segmentation results contain erroneous areas (page borders or extra text) they have little or no impact at all in the classification stage. Most of the problems in this area have been caused by the incomplete images originating in the segmentation results.

The last experiments have been conducted on mixed images, with problems in both the binarization and segmentation stages, or no problems at all, originating from the ICDAR dataset and from the Ubuntu documentation. The combined results are described in Table 5.

As expected, the overall performance dropped especially because of the results obtained in the binarization stage, which impact the remaining stages as well. The difference however is not very large, mostly because the classification module can still identify over-dilated images or incomplete images.

5　FUTURE RESEARCH

In the future we would like to continue the research conducted so far. There are many areas which can be improved and also, upon refactoring they can provide new functionalities:

- we intend to add a module in charge of collecting a user score for the result vector, which can be used later for altering automatically the default weights in the majority voting module. This way, the CBIR engine will be able to provide more representative results for the user.
- we have started to develop a user interface which will allow the user to configure the classification module according to his/her needs—this involves selecting the desired binarization/segmentation algorithms and tuning the majority voting modules. The user score module and this module can be combined with a user management module so that the system can recall the user's preferences;
- we also intend to insert a module that can analyze a certain image and compute how many shadow areas it contains. This module would help in deciding which color space is more adequate for each particular situation;
- the number of characteristics is very large; only the SIFT descriptors may go over 100,000 for 640×480 images. In order to be able to compute the results much faster, we are considering the possibility of adding a module in charge of reducing the dimensionality;
- in the document processing area, the system is currently cropping out the images from a scan. In order to have more accurate results, we intend to add an OCR module, which can extract the text content as well. The text can be later on reduced to keywords, which can be used in the classification and retrieval process.

ACKNOWLEDGMENTS

The authors would like to thank the Project SOP HRD/107/1.5/S/76822—TOP ACADEMIC of University "Dunarea de Jos" of Galati, Romania.

REFERENCES

[1] Sebe, N. Feature extraction & content description—DELOS—MUSCLE Summer School on Multimedia digital libraries, Machine learning and cross-modal technologies for access and retrieval. www.videolectures.net. [Online] February 25, 2007. www.videolectures.net/dmss06_sebe_fecd/.

[2] Gevers T, Smeulders AW. Colour-based object recognition. Pattern Recogn 1999;32:453–64.

[3] Vassilieva, N. RuSSIR—Russian Summer School in Information Retrieval. [Online] 2012. http://videolectures.net/russir08_vassilieva_cbir/.

[4] Cao X, Shen W, Yu LG, Wang YL, Yang JY, Zhang ZW. Illumination invariant extraction for face recognition using neighboring wavelet coefficients. Pattern Recogn 2012;45:1299–305.

[5] Bhavsar AV, Rajagopalan AN. Range map superresolution-inpainting, and reconstruction from sparse data. Comput Vis Image Underst 2012;116(4):572–91.

[6] Wikipedia. Local binary patterns. www.wikipedia.org. [Online] November 08, 2011. http://en.wikipedia.org/wiki/Local_binary_patterns.

[7] Lowe DG. Object recognition from local scale-invariant features. In: International Conference on Computer Vision. 1999. p. 1150–7.

[8] Bay H, Tuytelaars T, Van Gool L. Speeded-up robust features (SURF). Comput Vis Image Underst 2008;110:346–59, Zurich, Leuven, Belgia: s.n.

[9] Dalal N, Triggs B. Histograms of oriented gradients for human detection. Int Conf Comput Vis Pattern Recognit 2005;1:886–93.

[10] Mikolajczyk K, Schmid C. A performance evaluation of local descriptors. IEEE Trans Pattern Anal Mach Intell 2005;27:1615–30.

[11] Sarfraz S, Hellwich O. Madeira, Portugal. Head pose estimation in face recognition across pose scenarios. Proceedings of VISAPP 2008, Int. Conference on Computer Vision Theory and Applications; 2008, p. 235–242.

[12] Chen N, Blostein D. A survey of document image classification: problem statement, classifier architecture and performance evaluation. IJDAR 2007;10:1–16.

[13] Ha J, Haralick RM. Recursive X-Y cut using bounding boxes of connected components. Doc Anal Recognit 1995;2:952–5.

[14] Krizhevsky A, Sutskever I, Hinton GE. ImageNet classification with deep convolutional neural networks. In: Pereira F, Burges CJC, Bottou L, Weinberger KQ, editors. Advances in neural information processing systems 25. Curran Associates, Inc; 2012. p. 1097–1105.

[15] Antonacopoulos A, Bridson D, Papadopoulos C. ICDAR 2007 Page Segmentation Competition. ICDAR. [Online] 2007. http://www.primaresearch.org/ICDAR2007_competition/.

[16] Ilie M. A content based image retrieval approach based on document queries, IPCV'14—The 2014 International Conference on Image Processing, Computer Vision, and Pattern Recognition; 2014.

[17] Ilie M. Document image segmentation through clustering and connectivity analysis, The International Conference on Multimedia and Network Information Systems—MISSI'14; 2014.

[18] Google. Ocropus, April 21, 2013, http://code.google.com/p/ocropus/.

[19] Sauvola J, Seppanen T, Haapakoski S, Pietikainen M. Adaptive document binarization, Ulm, Germany: s.n., 1997. International Conference on Document Analysis and Recognition. p. 147–152.

Optical flow-based representation for video action detection

21

Samet Akpınar, Ferda Nur Alpaslan

Department of Computer Engineering, Middle East Technical University, Ankara, Turkey

1 INTRODUCTION

Video action recognition is a field of multimedia research enabling us to recognize the actions from a number of observations. The observations on video frames depend on the video features derived from different sources. While textual features include high-level semantic information, they cannot be automated. The recognition strongly depends on the textual sources which are commonly created manually. On the other hand, audio features are restricted to a supervisor role. As the audio does not contain strong information showing the actions conceptually, it can be used as an additional resource supporting visual and textual information. Visual video features provide the basic information for the video events or actions. Although it is difficult to obtain high levels of semantics by using visual information, a convincing way to construct an independent fully automated video annotation or action recognition model is to utilize visual information as the central resource. This way takes us to content-based video information retrieval.

Content-based video information retrieval is the automatic annotation and retrieval of conceptual video items such as objects, actions, and events using the visual content obtained from video frames. There are various methods to extract visual features and use them for different purposes. The visual feature sets they use vary from static image features (pixel values, color histograms, edge histograms, etc.) to temporal visual features (interest point flows, shape descriptors, motion descriptors, etc.). Temporal visual features combine the visual image features with the time information. Representing video information using temporal visual features generically means modeling the visual video information with temporal dimension, i.e., constructing temporal video information.

We need to represent the temporal video information formally for developing video action recognition methods. Visual features such as corners and visual interest points of video frames are the basics for constructing our model. These features are used for constructing a more complicated motion feature, namely, optical flow. In our work, we propose a new temporal video segment representation method to retrieve video actions for formalizing the video scenes as temporal information. The representation is fundamentally based on the optical flow vectors calculated for the frequently selected frames of the video scene. Weighted frame velocity concept is put forward for a whole video scene together with the set of optical flow vectors. The combined representation is used in the action-based temporal video segment classification. The result of the classification represents the recognized actions.

The main contribution of this work is the proposed temporal video segment representation method. It is aimed to be a generic model for temporal video segment classification for action recognition. The representation is based on optical flow concept. It uses the common way of partitioning optical flow vectors according to their angular features. An angular grouping of optical flow vectors is used for each selected frame of the video. We propose the novel concept of weighted frame velocity as the velocity of the cumulative angular grouping of a temporal video segment in order to represent the motion of the frames of the segments more descriptively.

The outline of this article is as follows. In Section 2, related work is proposed. Section 3 discusses the temporal segment representation. Optical flow is described in Section 4 and optical flow-based segment representation is discussed in Section 5. The inspiration of representation in cut detection is given in Section 6. In Section 7, experiments and results are presented. Finally, in Section 8, the conclusion is proposed.

2 RELATED WORK

There are different approaches followed for the representation of temporal video segments for content-based video information retrieval problems such as video action recognition, event detection, cut detection, etc. The studies in Refs. [1–4] focus on the perception of the visual world and bring us facts about how to detect the visual features and in which context more philosophically. Regarding the visual features, mentioned approaches can generally be figured out. Key-frame-, bag-of-words- (BoW), interest points-, and motion-based approaches are the groups of approaches reflecting the way of representation.

Key-frame-based representation approaches focus on detecting key frames in the video segments in order to use them in classification. This kind of representation is used in Refs. [5–8] for video scene detection and video summarization. The study of Vasileios et al. [5] contains the segmentation of videos into shots, and key-frames are extracted from these shots. In order to overcome the difficulty of having prior knowledge of the scene duration, the shots are assigned to visual similarity groups. Then, each shot is labeled according to its group and a sequence alignment algorithm is applied for recognizing the shot labels change patterns. Shot similarity is estimated using visual features and shot orders are kept while applying sequence alignment. In Ref. [6], a novel method for automatic annotation of images and videos is presented with keywords among the words representing concepts or objects needed in content-based image retrieval. Key-frame-based approach is used for videos. Images are represented as the vectors of feature vectors containing visual features such as color and edge. They are modeled by a hidden Markov model, whose states represent concepts. Model parameters are estimated from a training set. The study proposed in Ref. [7] deals with automatic annotation and retrieval for videos using key frames. They propose a new approach automatically annotating video shots with semantic concepts. Then, the retrieval carried out by textual queries. An efficient method extracting semantic candidate set of video shots is presented based on key frames. Extraction uses visual features. In Ref. [8], an innovative algorithm for key frame extraction is proposed. The method is used for video summarization. Metrics are proposed for measuring the quality.

Histogram-based BoW approaches represent the frames of the video segments over a vocabulary of visual features. References [9,10] are the examples of such approaches. Ballan et al. [9] propose a method interpreting temporal information with the BoW approach. Video events are conceptualized as vectors composed of histograms of visual features, extracted from the video frames using BoW model. The vectors, in fact, can be behaved as the sequences, like strings, in which histograms are considered as characters. Classification of these sequences having difference in length, depending on the video scene length, is carried out by using SVM classifiers with a string kernel that uses the Needlemann-Wunsch edit distance. In Ref. [10], a new motion feature is proposed, Expanded Relative Motion Histogram of Bag-of-Visual-Words (ERMH-BoW) implementing motion relativity and visual relatedness needed in event detection. Concerning the ERMH-BoW feature, relative motion histograms are formed between visual words representing the object activities and events.

Despite their performance issues in terms of time, above approaches lack the flow features and temporal semantics of motion although they are efficient in spatial level. On the other hand, motion-based approaches deal with motion features which are important in terms of their strong information content and stability over spatiotemporal visual changes. Motion features such as interest points and optical flow are used for modeling temporal video segments. References [11–14] are the studies using motion features. Ngo et al. [11] propose a new framework in order to group the similar shots into one scene. Motion characterization and background segmentation are the most important concepts in this study. Motion characterization results in the video representation formalism, while background segmentation provides the background reconstruction which is integrated to scene change detection. These two concepts and the color histogram intersection together become the fundamental approach for calculating the similarity of scenes. The study of Sand and Teller [12] presents a new approach which implements motion estimation in video scenes. The representation of video motion is carried out by using some sort of particles. Each particle is an image point with its trajectory and other features. In order to optimize the particle trajectories, appearance stability along the particle trajectories and distortion between the particles are measured. The motion representation can be used in many areas. It cannot be constructed using the standard methods such as optical flow or feature tracking. Optical flow is a spatiotemporal motion feature describing the motion of visual features. Optical flow-based representation is especially strong for video segment classification. References [13,14] present methods for representing video segments with optical flow. Lertniphonphan et al. [13] propose a representation structure based on direction histograms of optical flow. In Ref. [14], video segments are tried to be represented by using histogram of oriented optical flow (HOOF). By the help of this representation, human actions are recognized by classifying HOOF time series. For this purpose, a generalization of the Binet-Cauchy kernels to nonlinear dynamical systems is proposed.

Temporal video segment classification is an important subproblem in content-based video information retrieval addressing video action classification in our study. By definition, it is the classification of scenes in a video. The classification highly depends on the representation of temporal video information and the classification methods working on this representation.

Authors of Refs. [15–18] propose the approaches based on 3D interest points. These methods tackle the problem of video segment classification by putting new interest points or visual features forward by enriching with time dimension. Therefore, the features in the studies can be conceptualized as space-time shapes.

The methods proposed in Refs. [19,20] view the problem from the point of spatiotemporal words. The segments are seen as bag-of-features and make the classification according to the code words.

Authors of Refs. [13,14,21–23] present optical flow-based methods for video segment classification. Optical flow histograms are constructed and utilized in segment representation. By using this representation, segment classification is carried out.

3 TEMPORAL SEGMENT REPRESENTATION

Temporal video segment representation is the problem of representing video scenes as temporal video segments. While this problem generally runs through the video information including visual, audio, and textual features, our study deals with visual features only. Mentioned problem is originated from representing the temporal information. Temporal information provides a combined meaning composed of time and magnitude for a logical or physical entity. Robot sensor data, web logs, weather, video motion, and network flows are common examples of temporal information. Independent from domain, both representation and processing methods of temporal information are important in the resulting models. Regarding the processing methods, prediction, classification, and mining can be considered as first comers for the temporal information. In most cases, the representation is also a part of the processing methods due to the specific problem. While the representation and processing methods are handled together, the focus is especially on the processing methods rather than on the representation in these cases. Temporal data mining and time-series classification can be exemplified for the approaches on temporal information retrieval.

The types of the features and their quality on describing the domain knowledge also influence the temporal information processing and its application. Also, having high dimensionality makes the effective representation of temporal information with more complicated features important. Therefore, feature definitions, construction, and feature extraction methods play an important role in processing the temporal information. As the focus here is feature extraction and construction, the improvements are measured with common methods.

In content-based video information retrieval, visual video data behave like temporal information containing frame sequences over time. Each frame of the video has its visual information along with its time value. The temporal information representation highly depends on the visual content of video frames. The basic and the most primitive representation of temporal video information can be done by using the video with all pixel intensities of all frames. While this representation includes the richest visual information, processing and interpreting information is impractical. In a 600×480 frame size for a 10 s scene (30 frames/s, fps), 86.4M features exist with this approach. Therefore, there is a need for efficient representation formalisms.

Key-frame-based representation is one of the candidate approaches for representing temporal information in videos. For each scene, a key-frame is selected based on some calculations using visual features. The entire scene is represented and feature size of the representation is decreased by using this key frame. But, there is an important problem in key-frame-based approaches; i.e., lack of the important information resulting from the motion in videos.

Another approach is BoW approach for frame sequences. In this kind of representation, frames are behaved as code words obtained from grouping of the frames according to the visual features. With these code words, frame sequences are represented as sentences. This kind of representation contains temporal nature of the scenes. But, the most important disadvantage of this representation is the restricted nature of code words. Representing a visually rich frame with a label means losing an important amount of information. The representation is restricted with the variety of the code words. Therefore, limitless types of frames will be reduced to very limited number of labels.

Interest points-based representation is an alternative formalism for temporal video information. Interest points are the "important" features that may best represent the video frames invariant from the scale and noise. This representation alternative is very successful in reducing the huge frame information into small but descriptive patterns. But, it is again disadvantageous in detecting motion features despite its descriptiveness. As the motion features include flow with time, it is important to track the features along the time. Using interest points for representation lacks the motion-based information.

State-space methods are also used for representing temporal video information. The state-space methods define features which span the time. The space-time interest point concept is proposed by Laptev and Lindeberg [16]. Interest points that are spatially defined and extracted in 2D are extended with time. With this extension, interest points gain a 3D structure with time. Therefore, a space-time 3D sketch of frame patterns can be obtained and they are ready for processing. State-space approaches best fit the representation of video information temporally as they can associate the time with the visual information in a descriptive and integrated way.

In our study, a state-space-based representation approach is proposed. Optical flow is the motion feature—integrating time with visual features—utilized for constituting the state-space method.

4 OPTICAL FLOW

Theoretically, optical flow is the motion of visual features such as points, objects, and shapes through a continuous view of the environment. It represents the motion of the environment relative to an observer. James Jerome Gibson first introduced the optical flow concept in the 1940s, during World War II [24]. He was working on pilot selection, training, and testing. He intended to train the perception of pilots during the war. Perception was considered for the effect of the motion on the observer. In this context, shape of objects, movement of entities, etc. are handled for perception. During his study on aviation, he discovered optical flow patterns. He found that the environment observed by the pilot tends to move away from the landing point, while the landing point does not move according to the pilot. Therefore, he joined this concept with the pilot perception on the observed environment.

In the perception of an observer, there may be two options for approaching/departing optical flow around a point. In the first option, the observer may be moving through the target point. This makes the optical flow departing from the point. In the second option, the environment around the point may be moving through the motionless observer. This also gives the same effect, having the optical flow departing from the point. These two options are also valid for approaching optical flow. If the observer departs from the target point or the point departs from the motionless observer, the optical flow is seen as approaching through the point.

In video domain, optical flow is commonly known as the apparent motion of brightness patterns in the images. More specifically, it can be conceptualized as the motion of visual features such as corners, edges, ridges, and textures. through the consecutive frames of a video scene. Optical flow, here, is materialized by optical flow vectors. An optical flow vector is defined for a point (pixel) of a video frame. In optical flow estimation of a video frame, selection of "descriptive" points is important. This selection is done using visual features. It is clear that using an edge point or corner point is more informative than using an ordinary point semantically as the motion perception of human is based on prominent entities instead of ordinary ones. Optical flow vectors are, then, the optical flow of video frame feature instances instead of all frame points.

Two problems arise in the optical flow estimation of video frames: (1) detection and extraction of the features to be tracked, (2) calculation of the optical flow vectors of the extracted features. Optical flow estimation aims to find effective solutions to these problems. Calculation of optical flow vectors of the extracted features can be reduced to the following problem; *Given a set of points in a video frame, finding the same points in another frame.*

4.1 DERIVATION OF OPTICAL FLOW

There are various approaches concerning the estimation of optical flow. *Differential, region-based, energy-based,* and *phased-based* methods are the main groups of approaches [25]. All of these groups include many algorithms proposed so far. Each of these algorithms reflects the theoretical background of its group of approach.

Here, the meaning of optical flow estimation is discussed from a *differential* point of view. The explanation is based on the change of pixels with respect to time. The solution of the problem can be reduced to the solution of the following equation [26]:

$$I(x+\delta x, y+\delta y, t+\delta t) = I(x, y, t) \tag{1}$$

The equation is written for a point in a video frame. The point is assumed to change its pixel value over time. (x, y, t) is defined as the 3D point composed of the 2D coordinates (pixel value) of the given point at time t. I represents the intensity function giving the image intensity value of a given pixel value at a given time. The equation is based on the assumption that enormously small amount of change in the pixel position of the point in enormously small amount of time period converges to zero change in the intensity value. In other words, the intensity value of a pixel in a frame is equal to the intensity value of another pixel having the same point (the point in the former pixel) in the next frame. The point moves enormously small amount of distance (pixel change) in enormously small amount of time.

LHS of the equation is expanded by using the Taylor Series Expansion [26]:

$$I(x, y, t) + \frac{\partial I}{\partial x}\delta x + \frac{\partial I}{\partial y}\delta y + \frac{\partial I}{\partial t}\delta t + HOT \tag{2}$$

$$I(x, y, t) + \frac{\partial I}{\partial x}\delta x + \frac{\partial I}{\partial y}\delta y + \frac{\partial I}{\partial t}\delta t = I(x, y, t) \tag{3}$$

By some further derivations on Equation (3), we obtain Equations (7) (8). The variables represented by I_x, I_y, I_t are the derivatives of intensity function according to all dimensions.

$$\frac{\partial I}{\partial x}\delta x + \frac{\partial I}{\partial y}\delta y + \frac{\partial I}{\partial t}\delta t = 0 \tag{4}$$

$$\frac{\partial I}{\partial x}\frac{\delta x}{\delta t} + \frac{\partial I}{\partial y}\frac{\delta y}{\delta t} + \frac{\partial I}{\partial t}\frac{\delta t}{\delta t} = 0 \tag{5}$$

$$\frac{\partial I}{\partial x}\frac{\delta x}{\delta t} + \frac{\partial I}{\partial y}\frac{\delta y}{\delta t} + \frac{\partial I}{\partial t} = 0 \tag{6}$$

$$I_x V_x + I_y V_y = -I_t \tag{7}$$

$$\nabla I. \ \overrightarrow{V} = -I_t \tag{8}$$

Now, the problem converges to the solution of $\overrightarrow{V}$. The solution will be the estimation of optical flow. As there are two unknowns in the equation, it cannot be solved; additional constraints and approaches are needed for solution. This problem is known as *aperture problem*.

4.2 ALGORITHMS

Many algorithms according to different approaches have been proposed for optical flow estimation. According to Barron et al. [25], optical flow estimation algorithms can be grouped according to the theoretical approach while interpreting optical flow. These are *differential techniques, region-based matching, energy-based methods and phase-based techniques.*

4.2.1 Differential Techniques

Differential techniques utilize a kind of velocity estimation from spatial and temporal derivatives of image intensity [25]. They are based on the theoretical approach proposed by Horn and Schunck [26]. The proposed approach results in Equation (3). Differential techniques are used for solving the problem generally represented by this equation. Horn-Shunck method [26] is a fundamental method among the differential techniques. Global smoothness concept is also used in the approach. Lucas-Kanade method [27] is also an essential method solving the mentioned differential equation for a set of neighboring pixels together by using a weighted window. Nagel [28] and Uras et al. [29] use second-order derivatives generating the optical flow equations. Global smoothness concept is also used as well as the Horn-Shunck method. Niebles et al. [30] propose a distance-based method efficient for real-time systems. The method is analyzed according to time-space complexity and its tradeoff. Harris and Stephens Proesmans et al. [31] suggest a classical differential approach. But, it is combined with correlation-based motion descriptors.

4.2.2 Region-Based Matching

Region-based matching approaches alternate the differential techniques in case differentiation and numerical operations is not useful due to noise or small number of frames [25]. In region-based matching, the concepts such as velocity and similarity are defined between image regions. Shi and Tomasi [32] and Ali [33] propose region-based matching methods for optical flow estimation. In Ref. [32], the matching is based on Laplacian pyramid while [33] recommends a method based on sum of squared distance computation.

4.2.3 Energy-Based Methods

Energy-based methods are based on the output energy of filters tuned by the velocity [25]. Laptev and Lindeberg [34] propose an energy-based method fitting spatiotemporal energy to a plane in frequency space. Gabor filtering is used in the energy calculations.

4.2.4 Phase-Based Techniques

Different from energy-based methods velocity is defined as filter outputs having phase behavior. References [35–37] are the examples of phase-based techniques using spatiotemporal filters.

5 OPTICAL FLOW-BASED SEGMENT REPRESENTATION

In this study, an optical flow-based temporal video information representation is proposed. Optical flow vectors are needed to be calculated for the selected sequential frames. Optical flow estimation is important as the basic element of the model is optical flow vectors. As mentioned in Section 4, detection of features and estimation of optical flow according to these features are the main steps of optical flow estimation. The methods and approaches for both steps are discussed below [38].

5.1 OPTICAL FLOW ESTIMATION

In our approach, *Shi-Tomasi* algorithm proposed in Ref. [39] is used for feature detection. As it is mentioned before, Shi-Tomasi algorithm is based on Harris corner detector [40] and finds corners as interest points. Harris matrix shown in Equation (10) is obtained from the Harris corner detector:

$$S(u, v) = \sum_x \sum_y [u\ v] w(x, y) \otimes \begin{bmatrix} I_x^2 & I_x I_y \\ I_x I_y & I_y^2 \end{bmatrix} \begin{bmatrix} u \\ v \end{bmatrix} \tag{9}$$

$$M = \begin{bmatrix} I_x^2 & I_x I_y \\ I_x I_y & I_y^2 \end{bmatrix} \tag{10}$$

Shi-Tomasi algorithm uses the eigenvalues of the Harris matrix. In this context, it differs from Harris corner detector. The algorithm assumes that minimum of two eigenvalues of Harris matrix determines the cornerness (C) of the point. Therefore, the corner decision is done using the eigenvalues of the matrix. Shi-Tomasi algorithm gives more accurate results compared with Harris detector. The algorithm is also more stable for tracking.

For estimating optical flow, Lucas-Kanade algorithm is selected [27]. With videos having sufficient information and excluding noise, Lucas-Kanade algorithm is successful. The algorithm works for the corners obtained from Shi-Tomasi algorithm. Basically, the following function should be minimized for each detected corner point as seen in differential approaches:

$$\epsilon(\delta x, \delta y) = I(x, y) - I(x + \delta x, y + \delta y) \tag{11}$$

With suitable δx and δy, optical flow vectors can be obtained. But, aperture problem is not solved yet with this minimization. The solution approach for aperture problem is reflected to the function definition $\epsilon(\delta x, \delta y)$ as follows:

$$\epsilon(\delta x, \delta y) = \sum_{u_y - w_y}^{u_y + w_y} \sum_{u_x - w_x}^{u_x + w_x} [I(x, y) - I(x + \delta x, y + \delta y)] \tag{12}$$

Summation on the $x - y$ direction is a solution for the aperture problem. By using a window w centering the point (x, y), the estimation of optical flow of the point is extended with the neighboring points.

In our approach, Lucas-Kanade algorithm is applied to the corner points detected with Shi-Tomasi algorithm. Video frames are selected according to a frequency of 6 fps (30 fps videos are used) from *Hollywood Human Actions* dataset [41]. In Figure 1, two frequently sequential frames obtained from the mentioned dataset are shown.

Figure 2 shows the optical flow vectors estimated for the detected points in the former video frame in the sequence.

In our method, optical flow vectors are calculated for every detected point in all frequently selected frames. The set of optical flow vectors is the temporal information source for our representation.

The model below forms the back bone for our representation formalism. Optical flow vector set with an operator constructs the representation.

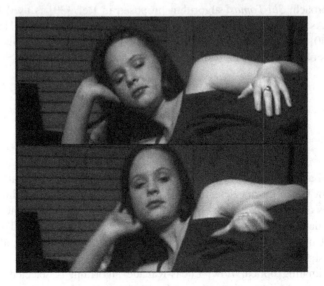

FIGURE 1

Consecutive frames for optical flow estimation.

FIGURE 2

Frame with optical flow vectors.

$$R = [S(V), \Phi] \qquad (13)$$

$S(V)$ is the set of optical flow vectors while Φ is the descriptor operator. Operator defines the relation of the elements of the optical flow vector set of the frames. This relation exposes the temporal representation of video information. The operator may change according to the complexity of the model. It may vary from just counting the vectors to complex relations between the optical flow vectors. This generic representation can easily be adapted to different problems such as segment classification or cut detection. Choice of the operator and the optical flow representation may change drastically in different problems.

5.2 PROPOSED REPRESENTATION

Usage of optical flow in video information representation is encountered in many studies including [14,17,42]. These studies are the state-of-the-art techniques motivating us for an optical flow-based representation. Optical flow histogram is the most common way of optical flow-based video representation. In [42], optical flow histograms are used for characterizing the motion of a soccer player in a soccer video. A motion descriptor based on optical flow is proposed and a similarity measure for this descriptor is described. The study of Barron et al. [17] uses optical flow by splitting it into horizontal and vertical channels. The histogram is calculated on these channels. Each channel is integrated over the angularly divided bins of optical flow vectors. In Ref. [14], HOOF is simply used according to angular segments for each frame. The feature vectors are constructed with these angular values and combined for all frames of the video segment. The essential part for contribution here is the classification method. The classification is done with a proposed novel time-series classification method including a metric for comparing optical flow histograms. The study in Ref. [21] proposes an optical flow-based representation which groups the optical flow vectors of whole video segment according to angular values. Then, average histogram is computed for each of these angular groups. The resulting histogram is the feature vector.

In our approach, histogram-based optical flow approaches are enriched with a newly defined velocity concept, *Weighted Frame Velocity*. The idea, here, is originated from the inadequacy of optical flow histograms for interpreting information. Using optical flow histogram is discarded as the most important drawback of using histograms in segment representation is that the histogram similarity does not always mean the real similarity for motion characterization. Optical flow vectors are divided into angular groups and according to these groups, optical flow vectors are summed and integrated with the new velocity concept instead of a histogram-based approach.

Estimating the optical flow vectors for each frame is the first step. Then, Equation (6) giving the generic representation is adapted to segment representation. In this aspect, Φ is the operator defining the relations between the optical flow vectors and giving their meaning for representing the video segment composed of the set of optical flow vectors $S(V)$.

In our adaptation of the above representation to segment representation, the description of Φ is important. The parameters used in the definition are shown in Table 1.

The parameters above are the basic building blocks for constructing the representation model and the descriptor operator Φ. The following definitions are done for this purpose. The definition of $S(V_f, \alpha, \beta)$ is made as follows:

$$S(V_f, \alpha, \beta) = \{V(r, \angle\varphi) \in V_f \,|\, \alpha < \varphi \le \beta\} \tag{14}$$

Let's assume that $|F| = n$, m is the number of angle intervals and l is the length of the video segment in terms of seconds. With these assumptions, the representation of a video segment using average of optical flow vectors with angular grouping can be formulized as

$$R = \left[\left\| \sum_{S(V_{vf}, \alpha_1, \alpha_2)} V(r, \angle\varphi) \right\|, \left\| \sum_{S(V_{vf}, \alpha_2, \alpha_3)} V(r, \angle\varphi) \right\|, \dots, \left\| \sum_{S(V_{vf}, \alpha_m, \alpha_{m+1})} V(r, \angle\varphi) \right\| \right] \tag{15}$$

Above vector representation is composed of m dimensions each of which is the magnitude of the sum of optical flow vectors for angle intervals. This is the common way

Table 1 Segment Representation Model Parameters

Parameter	Definition
F	Set of frames in the video segment
$S(V_f)$	Set of optical flow vectors in frame f
$S(V_f, \alpha, \beta)$	Set of optical flow vectors having angle between $\alpha - \beta$ in frame f
$A(\alpha, \beta)$	Weighted frame velocity of the whole segment direction having angle between $\alpha - \beta$
$\tau_f(\alpha, \beta)$	Threshold function for optical flow vectors having angle between $\alpha - \beta$ in frame f
$V(r, \angle\varphi)$	Optical flow vector having magnitude r and angle φ

of optical flow representation except the usage of vectors instead of histograms. This representation is descriptive as it utilizes the movement of a segment in different angel intervals by using the vector sum and magnitude calculation. But, it lacks the temporal information in terms of velocity. This means that the flow details throughout the frame sequence are discarded by only looking at the resulting direction and magnitude information. If this vector is extracted for each frame and combined for solving the problem as it is done in Ref. [14], curse of dimensionality problem arises. The dimension of the resulting vector will be *mxnxl*. For a 30-fps video of 5 s length with 30 angular intervals, for example, a vector of 4500 features is obtained for representing a segment. Using a frequency filter of 0.2 (6 frames selected from a second of the video) will decrease the dimension into 900, but the problem will not be able to be solved yet. This yields to the need for tackling the curse of dimensionality problem as it is handled in Ref. [14] with the newly proposed time-series classification method including the new distance metric for the feature vectors.

In our approach, we enrich the representation to make the temporal information more descriptive without causing the curse of dimensionality problem. For this purpose, a new component is needed for the above feature representation based on movement magnitude of the segment in different directions. Velocity is selected as the fundamental idea for the new component as the velocity of the frames strongly affects the nature of video motion such as in walk and run events. For this purpose, weighted frame velocity concept is proposed. Abstractly, the velocity component is added to the feature vector to contain distance-velocity pair.

Weighted frame velocity is a metric which measures the velocity of a segment in a given dimension. It is weighted with the vector count in its direction. Theoretically, weighted frame velocity is formulated inspiring from the general velocity calculation $V = \frac{\Delta d}{\Delta t}$:

$$A(\alpha, \beta) = \frac{\sum_{i=0}^{n-1}\left[\| \sum_{S(V_{f_i}, \alpha, \beta)} V(r, \angle\varphi) \| \cdot |S(V_{f_i}, \alpha, \beta)|\right]}{\sum_{i=0}^{n-1}|S(V_{f_i}, \alpha, \beta)|} \tag{16}$$

Equation (9) calculates the weighted distance for each angular interval of each frame. Weight concept, here, is the weight of the frame to the segment. The weighted distances are summed up and averaged according to the number of vectors in the segment. The resulting value is the weighted velocity of the frames.

When this approach is analyzed, one can notice that another problem occurs. As the velocity is weighted according to the number of vectors in the given angle interval of the frame, the noise or errors resulting from optical flow estimation and insignificant number of vectors in one dimension unfairly dominate the values of that feature. In order to avoid this problem, thresholding is used as a common way of noise reduction. Therefore, a threshold function depending on the frame and angle interval is proposed to be used in the weighted frame velocity function.

$$\tau_{f_i}(\alpha, \beta) = \begin{cases} \dfrac{S(V_{f_i}, \alpha, \beta)}{S(V_{f_i}, 0, 2\pi)}, & \dfrac{S(V_{f_i}, \alpha, \beta)}{S(V_{f_i}, 0, 2\pi)} < C \\ 1, & \text{otherwise} \end{cases} \tag{17}$$

The above function is based on the ratio of the optical flow vectors of the given angle interval for the given frame. This ratio's being smaller or bigger according to the threshold value C directly determines the result of the function. At this point, estimation of threshold becomes important. The estimation will be done during the classification phase. Thus, the weighted frame velocity function is updated accordingly.

$$A(\alpha, \beta) = \frac{\sum_{i=0}^{n-1} \left[\| \sum_{S(V_{f_i}, \alpha, \beta)} V(r, \angle\varphi) \| \cdot |S(V_{f_i}, \alpha, \beta)| \cdot \tau_{f_i}(\alpha, \beta) \right]}{\sum_{i=0}^{n-1} |S(V_{f_i}, \alpha, \beta)|} \tag{18}$$

The function affects the weighted contribution of each frame into the velocity of the segment in an angle interval according to whether its vectors' are noisy or not.

As it is mentioned before, the weighted frame velocity is, now, a new component of the feature vector representation based on the movement of the segment. Thus, the new representation is as follows:

$$R = \left[A(\alpha_1, \alpha_2), \| \sum_{S(V_{vf}, \alpha_1, \alpha_2)} V(r, \angle\varphi) \|, A(\alpha_2, \alpha_3), \| \sum_{S(V_{vf}, \alpha_2, \alpha_3)} \right.$$
$$\left. V(r, \angle\varphi) \|, \ldots, A(\alpha_m, \alpha_{m+1}), \| \sum_{S(V_{vf}, \alpha_m, \alpha_{m+1})} V(r, \angle\varphi) \| \right] \tag{19}$$

Now, the operator Φ in the generic optical-based representation model $R = [S(V), \Phi]$ is defined in this specific problem. The operator maps the optical flow vector set $S(V)$ to the feature vector R for a video scene.

$$\Phi : S(V) \rightarrow R \tag{20}$$

The function of the above mapping is shown in the obtained final representation. Mainly, it constructs the representation by applying the operator to the optical flow vectors. The operator Φ, in fact, is the symbolic representation of our method.

The practical use of the representation is classifying the segments. The representation is used for each video segment and has the size $m \times 2$. The segment classification, constant estimations, and experiments with results and comparisons will be held in Section 7.

6 CUT DETECTION INSPIRATION

Temporal video segmentation is the problem of splitting the video information temporally into coherent scenes. Temporal video segmentation is generally originated from the needs of video segment classification. As it is needed in our study, the video scenes are needed to be extracted from whole video information in many cases in order to classify them semantically as segments. On the other hand, in some cases, video segment classification and temporal video segmentation are held together. This kind of methods tackles the problem with an integrated approach by trying to carry out the scene extraction with the classification of related semantic information.

As temporal video information is composed of visually complicated and continuous sequence of video frames, analyzing the temporal boundaries of video events, actions, etc. is an important field of study. From this point of view, event boundary detection, temporal video segmentation, cut detection, etc. are similar concepts dealing with this problem.

Again, textual and audio features together with visual features are important sources of information for temporal video segmentation likewise in temporal video segment representation. Our main concern about automaticity and dependency of textual features to manual creation also continues here. Therefore, visual features' domination proceeds in this problem, too.

Regarding this domination, detecting the cuts between video scenes using visual features is an important problem. Optical flow is the key concept behaving as an operator inspiring from the representation proposed for action recognition in this study. The fundamental idea, here, is that some sort of change in optical flow character determines the cuts. In detail, the hypothesis is that the difference of intensity values between the pixels (mapped with optical flow vectors) of consecutive frames changes at the cut points. Calculated optical flow vectors in the first phase, video segment representation, can also be used here as building block features operating on pixel difference calculations to represent scene changes. This yields to a decrease in the computational complexity because of the fact that the feature base, optical flow vectors, is same and singularly calculated for both phases.

Estimated optical flow vectors for each frame in the previous part can be used. The equation $R = [S(V), \Phi]$ giving the optical flow-based generic representation, defined in Section 5, can be handled and adapted to cut detection. From this point of view, Φ is the operator defining the relations between the optical flow vectors $S(V)$ and giving their meaning for representing cuts.

In our adaptation of the above representation to temporal video segmentation—cut detection, the description of Φ is important. In order to make this description, the parameters used in the definition should be described.

7 EXPERIMENTS AND RESULTS

Temporal segment classification for action recognition uses the vector representation proposed in Section 5. Support Vector Machines (SVM) is used for nonlinear classification. Gaussian radial basis function—using standard deviation σ for two feature vectors x_i, x_j —is selected as SVM kernel.

$$K(x_i, x_j) = e^{\left(-\frac{1}{2\sigma^2}\|x_i - x_j\|^2\right)} \tag{21}$$

Hollywood Human Actions dataset [41] is used for evaluation. Hollywood dataset includes video segments composed of human actions from 32 movies. Each segment is labeled with one or more of 8 action classes: *AnswerPhone, GetOutCar, Hand-Shake, HugPerson, Kiss, SitDown, SitUp,* and *StandUp.* While, the test set is obtained from 20 movies, training set is obtained from 12 other movies different from those in the test set. The training set contains 219 video segments and the test set contains 211 samples with manually created labels.

After the optical flows are estimated, the calculations for constructing feature vectors are carried out accordingly and feature vectors are obtained for the test data. The number of angular intervals is taken as 30 as in Ref. [14]. The threshold C in the threshold function below, as discussed in this section, was determined experimentally.

$$\tau_{f_i}(\alpha, \beta) = \begin{cases} \dfrac{S(V_{f_i}, \alpha, \beta)}{S(V_{f_i}, 0, 2\pi)}, & \dfrac{S(V_{f_i}, \alpha, \beta)}{S(V_{f_i}, 0, 2\pi)} < C \\ 1, & \text{otherwise} \end{cases} \tag{22}$$

The result of the experiments for determining the best threshold value which is 0.025 is shown in Figure 3. The experiments on Hollywood dataset were carried out using this threshold value.

Comparison is made with the popular state-of-the-art Weizmann dataset. The dataset contains the actions "walk," "run," "jump," "side," "bend," "one-hand wave," "two-hands wave," "pjump," "jack," and "skip."

First, the threshold estimation is carried out for this set again. As shown in Figure 4, the threshold values $0.020 - 0.025$ gave the best results. These values were used in evaluating the results over this dataset.

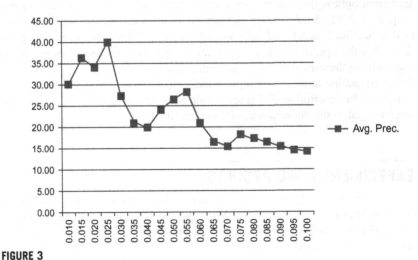

FIGURE 3

Threshold estimation in segment representation for Hollywood Human Actions.

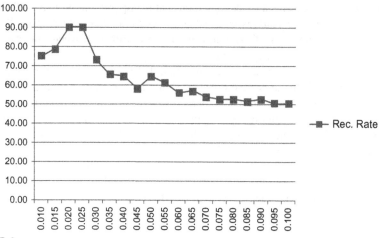

FIGURE 4

Threshold estimation in segment representation for Weizmann dataset.

Table 2 Comparison of the Results of Video Segment Classification for Weizmann Dataset

Methods	Recognition Rates (%)
Chaudry et al. [14]	94.44
Ali et al. [15]	92.60
This article	90.32
Niebles et al. [20]	90.00
Lertniphonphan [13]	79.17
Niebles and Fei-Fei [19]	72.80

   The comparison of our method in terms of recognition rates with the essential studies having different viewpoints in human action recognition and segment classification is shown in Table 2.

   The methods shown in Table 2 are some of the well-known reference studies tackling with the temporal segment classification problem. The approach in Ref. [15] uses new interest point features having time dimension. The classification is done according to these novel 3D features. Royden and Moore [13] and Gianluigi and Raimondo [14] propose optical flow-based classification, whereas Gianluigi and Raimondo [14] focuses on representing the segments frame by frame optical flows with high dimensions causing curse of dimensionality problem. Instead of dealing with the representation, the method aims to contribute by finding new metrics and time-series patterns in this high-dimensional data. Royden and Moore [13], on the other hand, propose a representation structure based on direction histograms of optical flow.

Niebles et al. [20] presents a model based on spatiotemporal words. This method sees the segments as bag-of-features and makes the classification according to the code words. A bag-of-features method is also proposed in Ref. [19] where interest points are extracted and used as bag-of-features.

When we analyze the results, we have seen that the methods proposing interest point-based new 3D features are more successful than the other models. But, the features are specific to the dataset which makes the solution dependent on dataset types. Methods focusing on mining the highly over-descriptive data in terms of time domain exhibit high success rates as they develop the model independent from the contributions in video features. But, they are disadvantageous with their high-dimensional representation regarding time complexity. Our optical flow-based method better results than the approaches using optical flow-based segment representation. It is also more successful than the BoW-based methods.

8 CONCLUSION

In this study, we tried to solve a combination of different problems on action recognition. The fundamental problem inspires us is the representation of temporal information. In many fields, representation of temporal information is essential to retrieve information from a temporal dataset. The solution to the problem varies from representing each temporal entity in a different time slice to representing a simple summary of the whole time interval. Efforts for finding a solution between these two endpoints should try to tackle the problem from different point of views. This is because, the level of representation changes with the source of the problem. For instance, to represent all the information in all time slices for symbolizing the temporal information having high-frequency over time, one should handle the curse of dimensionality problem. On the other hand, representing a single summary will cause the problem of lacking the flow of temporal information. In these cases, the focus of approaches will be finding supportive information from different sources and integration of these sources in a singular representation.

We aimed to solve the temporal information representation problem in video domain. As the video information is a perfect example of high-frequency temporal information, representation of video information is essential for the purposes based on video information retrieval. Video action recognition is selected as our specific domain. The problem domain is reduced to the temporal video segment classification. The study is shaped on visual features of the video information for the automaticity concerns. As it is mentioned below, the representation level determines the reduced problem. In this context, our aim is to represent the video scenes avoiding the lack of temporal information flow while without causing the curse of dimensionality problem. Therefore, using more descriptive and high-level visual features having the ability to host the additional temporal nature of the simpler features such as color, edge, corner, etc. becomes unavoidable. This will pass the high load of temporal information residing in high-dimensional representation to the mentioned high-level features.

The discussion summarized above took us to the complex visual features having temporal dimension. In our research, we observed that space-time related 3D features obtained from combining 2D features with temporal information [16,18] are proved to be successful. Space-time interest points and space-time shapes for actions are proposed in these studies. We also observed high-level state-of-the-art features such as optical flow describing the motion of frame features are calculated and used in temporal video information representation as in Refs. [13,14,21]. Curse of dimensionality problem occurs as all frames are represented using optical flow vectors [14]. The problem is solved by using time-series analysis and metrics.

An optical flow-based approach is proposed in this paper for representing temporal video information by inspiring from the above studies. This generic approach is applied in both temporal video segment classification and temporal video segmentation. The adaptation of the model to video segment classification is presented. The weighted frame velocity concept is proposed to strengthen the representation with the velocity of video frames. This representation formalism is tested with SVM-based classification of video segments. The results show that the proposed method produces encouraging results.

The main advantage of the method is the multipurpose temporal video representation model proposed for video action recognition domain. The new formalism described here is especially important for simplifying the computational complexity for high-dimensional information.

REFERENCES

[1] Burton A, Radford J. Thinking in perspective: critical essays in the study of thought processes. London, UK: Routledge; 1978.
[2] Warren DH, Strelow ER. In: Electronic spatial sensing for the blind: contributions from perception, rehabilitation, and computer vision. Nato Science Series. Dordrecht, Netherlands: Martinus Nijhoff Publishers; 1985.
[3] Ibson JJ. The perception of the visual world. Boston, MA, USA: Houghton Mifflin; 1950.
[4] Royden CS, Moore KD. Use of speed cues in the detection of moving objects by moving observers. Vis Res 2012;59:17–24.
[5] Vasileios TC, Aristidis CL, Nikolaos PG. Scene detection in videos using shot clustering and sequence alignment. IEEE Trans Multimed 2009;11(1):89–100.
[6] Ghoshal A, Ircing P, Khudanpur S. Hidden Markov models for automatic annotation and content based retrieval of images and video, In: Proceedings of SIGIR; 2005.
[7] Chang LW, Lie WN, Chiang R. Automatic annotation and retrieval for videos. In: Proceedings of PSIVT 2006. Lecture Notes in Computer Science, vol. 4319; 2006. p. 1030–40.
[8] Gianluigi C, Raimondo S. An innovative algorithm for key frame extraction in video summarization. J Real-Time Image Procees 2006;1(1):69–88.

[9] Ballan L, Bertini M, Del Bimbo A, Serra G. Video event classification using string kernels. Multimed Tools Appl 2009;48:69–87.

[10] Wang F, Jiang Y, Ngo C. Video event detection using motion relativity and visual relatedness. In: ACM Multimedia '08, October 26-31; 2008.

[11] Ngo C, Pong T, Zhang H. Motion-based video representation for scene change detection. Int J Comput Vis 2002;50(2):127–42.

[12] Sand P, Teller S. Particle video: long-range motion estimation using point trajectories. Int J Comput Vis 2008;80:72–91.

[13] Lertniphonphan K, Aramvith S, Chalidabhongse T. Human action recognition using direction histograms of optical flow. In: ISCIT; 2011.

[14] Chaudry R, Ravichandran A, Hager G, Vidal R. Histograms of oriented optical flow and Binet-Cauchy kernels on nonlinear dynamical systems for the recognition of human actions. In: Proceedings of CVPR'09, Miami, US; 2009.

[15] Ali S, Basharat A, Shah M. Chaotic invariants for human action recognition, In: IEEE international conference on computer vision; 2007.

[16] Laptev I, Lindeberg T. Space-time interest points, In: Proceedings of ICCV'03, Nice, France; 2003. p. 432–9.

[17] Tran D, Sorokin A. Human activity recognition with metric learning, In: European conference on computer vision; 2008.

[18] Gorelick L, Blank M, Shechtman E, Irani M, Basri R. Actions as space-time shapes. IEEE Trans Pattern Anal Mach Intellig 2007;29(12):2247–53.

[19] Niebles JC, Fei-Fei L. A hierarchical model of shape and appearance for human action classification. In: IEEE international conference on computer vision and pattern recognition, June; 2007.

[20] Niebles JC, Wang H, Fei-Fei L. Unsupervised learning of human action categories using spatial-temporal words. Int J Comput Vis 2008;79:299–318.

[21] Erciş F. Comparison of histograms of oriented optical flow based action recognition methods [MS thesis]. Turkey: Middle East Technical University; 2012.

[22] Little S, Jargalsaikhan I, Clawson K, Nieto M, Li H, Direkoglu C, et al. An information retrieval approach to identifying infrequent events in surveillance video. In: Proceedings of the 3rd ACM Conference on International Conference on Multimedia Retrieval (ICMR '13). New York, NY, USA: ACM; 2013.

[23] Wang T, Snoussi H. Histograms of optical flow orientation for abnormal events detection, In: IEEE International Workshop on Performance Evaluation of Tracking and Surveillance (PETS); 2013. p. 45–52.

[24] Gibson JJ. The perception of the visual world. Boston, MA, USA: Houghton Mifflin; 1950.

[25] Barron J, Fleet D, Beauchemin S. Performance of optical flow techniques. Int J Comput Vis 1994;12:43–7.

[26] Horn BKP, Schunck BG. Determining optical flow. Artif Intell 1981;17:185–203.

[27] Lucas B, Kanade T. An iterative image registration technique with an application to stereo vision, In: Proceedings of DARPA IU Workshop; 1981. p. 121–30.

[28] Nagel HH. On the estimation of optical flow relations between different approaches and some new results. Artif Intell 1987;33:299–324.

[29] Uras S, Girosi F, Verri A, Torre V. A computational approach to motion perception. Biol Cybern 1988;60:79–97.

[30] Camus T. Real-time quantized optical flow. J Real-Time Imaging 1997;3:71–86, Special Issue on Real-Time Motion Analysis.

[31] Proesmans M, Van Gool L, Pauwels E, Oosterlinck A. Determination of optical flow and its discontinuities using non-linear diffusion, In: 3rd European conference on computer vision, ECCV'94, vol. 2; 1994. p. 295–304.

[32] Anandan P. A computational framework and an algorithm for the measurement of visual motion. Int J Comput Vis 1989;2:283–310.

[33] Singh A. An estimation-theoretic framework for image-flow computation. In: Proceedings of ICCV, Osaka; 1990. p. 168–77.

[34] Heeger DJ. Optical flow using spatiotemporal filters. Int J Comput Vis 1988;1:279–302.

[35] Waxman AM, Wuand J, Bergholm F. Convected activation proles and receptive fields for real time measurement of short range visual motion, In: Proceedings of IEEE CVPR, Ann Arbor; 1988. p. 717–23.

[36] Fleet DJ, Jepson AD. Computation of component image velocity from local phase information. Int J Comput Vis 1990;5:77–104.

[37] Buxton B, Buxton H. Computation of optical flow from the motion of edge features in image sequences. Image Vis Comput 1984;2:59–74.

[38] Akpınar S, Alpaslan FN. Video action recognition using an optical flow based representation. In: International conference on image processing, computer vision, and pattern recognition (IPCV '14), Las Vegas, USA; 2014.

[39] Shi J, Tomasi C. Good features to track, In: IEEE conference on computer vision and pattern recognition (CVPR'94), Seattle, June; 1994.

[40] Harris C, Stephens M. A combined corner and edge detector, In: Proceedings of the 4th Alvey Vision conference; 1988. p. 147–51.

[41] Laptev I, Marszalek M, Schmid C, Rozenfeld B. Learning realistic human actions from movies, In: Proceedings of CVPR'08, Anchorage, US; 2008.

[42] Efros A, Berg A, Mori G, Malik J. Recognizing action at a distance, In: IEEE international conference on computer vision; 2003. p. 726–33.

Anecdotes extraction from webpage context as image annotation

22

Chuen-Min Huang

Department of Information Management, National Yunlin University of Science & Technology,
Yunlin, Taiwan, ROC

1 INTRODUCTION

Due to the rapid growth of digital technology, it is impractical to annotate a huge amount of images manually. Traditional research in this area focuses on content based image retrieval (CBIR), however, recent research reveals a significant gap between image annotation interpretered based on visual features and image semantics understandable by humans.

A glimpse of related studies show that the typical method of bridging the semantic gap is through the automatic image annotation (AIA) which extracts semantic features using machine learning techniques including support vector machine (SVM) [1,2], Bayesian [3] and selforganizing feature map [4,5]. In addition, various text processing techniques that support content identification based on word cooccurrence, location, and lexical-chained concepts have been elaborated in [6–8]. However, the aforementioned techniques suffer the drawbacks of heavy computation for multidocument processing, which will consume lots of memory and may incur run-time overhead. Furthermore, these feature-based or text processing techniques tend to assign the same annotation to all the images in the same cluster without considering the latent semantic anecdotes of each image. Thus, many relevant images can be missed from the retrieval list if a user does not type the exactly right keyword. To alleviate this problem, we propose a customized, relatively light computation way of anecdote identification, namely "Chinese lexical chain processing (CLCP)." The CLCP method was to extract meaningful concatenated words based on lexical chain (LC) theory from the image-resided webpage that allows sharing characters/words and facilitating their use at fine granularities without prohibitive cost. Results demonstrated that applying our method can successfully generate anecdotal descriptors as image annotations. The precision rate achieves 84.6%, and the acceptance rates from experts and users reach 84% and 76.6%, respectively. The performance testing was also very promising.

The remainder of the chapter is organized as follows. Section 2 presents the related work including AIA, keyword extraction, and LC. Then, we address the intent of our experiment in Section 3. The experimental result and evaluation method are described in Section 4. Finally, in Section 5, we draw conclusions and suggest future work.

2 LITERATURE BACKGROUND

2.1 AUTOMATIC IMAGE ANNOTATION

There have been a number of models applied for image annotation. In general, image annotation can be categorized into three types: retrieval-based, classification-based, and probabilistic-based [7]. The basic notion behind retrieval-based annotation is that semantic-relevant images are composed of similar visual features. CBIR has been proposed in 1992 [9]. Since then, more and more studies annotated the images based on this method [10].

CBIR is applied by the use of images features, including shape, color, and texture. Once images are classified into different categories, each category is annotated with a concept label such as bird, cat, mammal, and building. However, this method is limited by the training data set and the hidden semantics or abstract concepts can't be extracted because the keywords are confined to predefined terms. Consequently, the results of CBIR are usually not satisfactory.

The second type, also known as the supervised learning approach, treats annotation as classification using multiple classifiers. The images are classified based on the extracted features. This method processes each semantic concept as an independent class, and assigns each concept as one classifier. Bayesian [3] and SVM [11] are the most often used approaches.

The third type is constructed by estimating the correlations between images and concepts with a particular emphasis on the term-term relationship and intends to solve the problem of "synonym" and "homograph." Frequent used approaches include cooccurrence model [12], LSA [5], PLSA [13], and hidden Markov model (HMM) [14]. Notwithstanding the efforts made on the enhancement of annotation quality, the aforementioned approaches tend to assign the same annotation to all the images in the same cluster thereafter they suffered the lack of customized annotation for each image.

2.2 KEYWORD EXTRACTION

In the field of information retrieval, keyword extraction plays a key role in summarization, text clustering/classification, and so on. It aims at extracting keywords that represents the text theme. One of the most prominent problems in processing Chinese texts is the identification of valid words in a sentence, since there are no delimiters to separate words from characters in a sentence. Therefore, identifying words/phrases is difficult because of segmentation ambiguities and the frequent occurrences of newly formed words.

In general, Chinese texts can be parsed using dictionary lookup, statistical, or hybrid approaches [15]. The dictionary lookup approach identifies keywords of a string by mapping well-established corpus. For example, the Chinese string "蔡英文北監探扁會面一小時" (Ying-wen Tsai went to Taipei prison to visit Shui-bian Chen and talk for an hour) will be parsed as: "[蔡英文]," "[北監]," "[探]," "[扁]," "[會面]," and "[一小時]" by a well-known dictionary-based CKIP (Chinese Knowledge and Information Processing) segmentation system in Taiwan. This method is very efficient while it fails to identify newly formed or out-of-the-vocabulary words and it is also blamed for the triviality of the extracted words.

Since there is no delimiters to separate words from Chinese string except for the usage of quotation marks in special occasion, word segmentation is a challenge without the aid of dictionary. The statistical technique extracts elements by using n-gram (bi-gram, tri-gram, etc.) computation for the input string. This method relies on the frequency of each segmented token and a threshold to determine the validity of the token. The above string through n-gram segmentation will produce: "[蔡英], [英文], [文北], [北監], [監探], [探扁], [扁會], [會面], [面一], [一小], [小時]"; "[蔡英文], [英文北], ..., [一小時]" and so on. The application of this method has the benefit of corpus-free and the capability of extracting newly formed or out-of-the-vocabulary words while at the expense of huge computations and the follow-up filtering efforts.

Recently, a number of studies proposed substring [9], significant estimation [16], and relational normalization [17,18] to identify words based on statistical calculations. The hybrid method conducts dictionary mapping to process the major task of word extraction and handle the leftovers through n-gram computation, which significantly reduces the amount of terms under processing and takes care both the quality of term segmentation and the identification of unknown words. It has gained popularity and adopted by many researchers [19,20].

Since the most important task of annotation is to identify the most informative parts of a text comparatively with the rest. Consequently, a good text segmentation shall help in this identification. In the IR theory, the representation of documents is based on the vector space model [21]: A document is a vector of weighted words belonging to a vocabulary $V: d = \{w_1, \ldots, w_{|v|}\}$. Each w_v is such that $0 \leq w_v \leq 1$ and represents how much the term t_n contributes to the semantics of the document d. In the term frequency-inverse document frequency model, the weight is typically proportional to the term frequency and inversely proportional to the frequency and length of the documents containing the term. Some studies [22,23] proposed other considerations to assign different weights to words, such as word length and location.

2.3 LEXICAL CHAIN

A LC is a sequence of words, which is in lexical cohesion relations with each other, and the chained words tend to indicate portions of the context that form semantic units while it is independent of the grammatical structure of the text. LCs could serve further as a basis for a segmentation [24]. This method is usually applied in a summarization generation [25]. For instance, the string "向量空間模型" (vector space model) may be parsed as "[向量]," (vector) "[空間]," (space), and "[模型]" (model) if there is no further merging process undergoing. Thereby the most informative compound "[向量空間模型]" will be left out. Usually LCs are constructed in a bottom-up manner by taking each candidate word of a text, and finding an appropriate semantic relation offered by a thesaurus. Instead, the paper [26] proposes a top-down approach of linear text segmentation based on lexical cohesion of a text. Some scholars suggested to use machine learning approaches to create a set of rules to calculate the rate of forming a new word by characters for entity recognition including the maximum entropy model and HMM and claimed this method was able to achieve reasonable performance with minimal training data [27,28].

3 RESEARCH DESIGN
3.1 RESEARCH MODEL OVERVIEW

This study covers three tasks: Text processing, anecodote extraction, and annotation evaluation. Since image captions are written by journalists, it is assumed that a man-made caption would be faithful to an image scenario. We assigned the extracted anecdotes with the highest weight as the primary annotation and the second and the third places as secondary annotations. The framework of our research is depicted as Figure 1. We conducted CLCP and term weighting for the input data to extract anecodotes and evaluated the annotations by using the image caption mapping and human judgment, respectively. In the following section, we will introduce the way of anecodote extraction and the way of annotation evaluation.

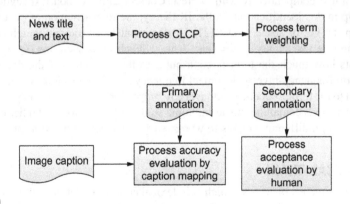

FIGURE 1

Research model.

3.2 CHINESE LEXICAL CHAIN PROCESSING

The fundamental idea of building CLCP is a bottom-up concatenating process based on the significance degree of distribution rate to extract the most meaningful LCs as anecodotes from a string. We treated a news document as a long string composed of a series of characters and punctuations.

Most of the traditional studies identify words from the whole context and store all the processed tokens for further processing as Figure 2. In this way, even a moderate-sized document may require hundreds of thousands of tokens, which will consume lots of memory and may incur unacceptable run-time overhead. Due to the number of distinct tokens processed is less than that in the document, we adopted a sharing concept to allow reuse of the identical tokens. We considered each character as a basic unit from which to build compounds as a composite, which in turn can be grouped to form larger compounds. Since the character and compound will be treated uniformly, it makes the application simple.

By doing so, we adopted the concept of flyweight and composite design patterns proposed by the GOF (Gang of Four) [29] to implement this design. Figure 3 shows the flyweight as a shared object that can be used in the whole context simultaneously. Figure 4 represents the part-whole hierarchy of texts and the way to use recursive composition. By applying flyweight design pattern, it supports the use of large numbers of fine-grained objects efficiently. By applying composite design pattern, it makes the application easier to add new components.

FIGURE 2

Traditional document processing.

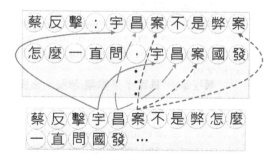

FIGURE 3

Flyweight design concept.

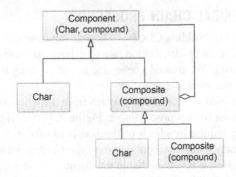

FIGURE 4

Composite text structure.

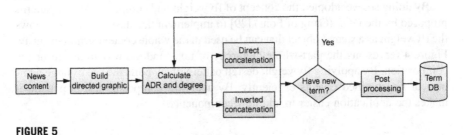

FIGURE 5

CLCP steps.

The CLCP steps are depicted as Figure 5, and Figure 6 displays a fractional code of the iterative concatenating process. The detailed description with an example is addressed next.

3.2.1 Step 1: Build a directed graph

A directed graph (or digraph) is a set of nodes connected by edges, where the edges have a direction associated with them. For example, an arc (x, y) is considered to be directed from x to y, and the arc (y, x) is the inverted link. Y is a direct successor of x, and x is a direct predecessor of y.

We use the string: "蔡反擊:宇昌案不是弊案,怎麼一直問,宇昌案國發基金為何一再放棄權利…" (Tsai fired back and stated that Yu Chang case is not a scandal, why did you keep asking for this and why the National Development Fund abandoned its rights repeatedly?) as an example to explain the construction process. After removing duplicate characters and replacing punctuations with new lines, a digraph is built as Figure 7, in which a solid line indicates the directed link and a dash line means the inverted link.

```
//Building Directed Graphic and Calculate Vertex Distribution Rates and iteration
protected void iteration(String[] sentences){
    for(String sentence : sentences){
        System.out.println(sentence);
            for(int i = 0;i<sentence.length();i++){
                boolean isContain = false;
                //System.out.println("Identify Char");
                if(!chrisstring.isNumber(sentence.substring(i,i+1))){
                Term t = new Term(sentence.substring(i,i+1));
                //System.out.println(sentence.substring(i,i+1));
                for(Term term : terms){
                    if(t.equals(term)){
                        isContain = true;
                        t = term;
                        break;
                    }
                }
            }
            try{
                String s = sentence.substring(i+1,i+2);
                if(!sentence.substring(i+1, i+2).equals(" ") ){
                    t.addNext(chrisstring.getTheNext(s,sentence, i+1));
                }
            }catch(StringIndexOutOfBoundsException s){
                //System.out.println("StringIndexOutOfBoundsException");
            }
```

FIGURE 6

A fractional code of iterative merging.

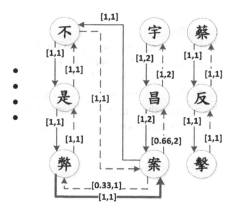

FIGURE 7

A fraction of digraph.

3.2.2 Step 2: Calculate average distribution rate and degree to concatenate vertices

This step is to calculate the average distribution rate (ADR or intensity) and the number of links (degree) of a digraph. To determine whether two vertices can be concatenated, we applied the criteria listed in (1) and (2).

$$D(i,j) \geq T \cap (\mathrm{Digraph}(\mathrm{Node}_i) > 1) \qquad (1)$$

$$D(p,q) \geq T \cap (\mathrm{Inv}D(\mathrm{Node}_p) > 1), \qquad (2)$$

where $D(i, j)$ and $D(p, q)$ represent the ADR of the arcs (i, j) and (p, q); Digraph (Node$_i$) and InvD (Node$_p$) indicate the number of direct links for vertex i and inverted links for vertex p, respectively. T is the threshold value of ADR determined by 10 runs of experiments with the value of 0.1-0.9 assigned to 500 documents and the result was verified by five subject specialists with respect to semantics of anecodotes. The result in our previous study [30] using 100 documents as a testing data set showed that 0.4 outperforms the others, while this study used five times of previous samples reveal that the accuracy rate of 0.5 reaching 82% is the best cut of intensity as Figure 8. It implies both 0.4 or 0.5 are competitive thresholds. Based on the term frequency theory, it infers that the significance of the concatenation will be proportional to its frequency. Since this study was to identify anecodotes from single documents, we set a minimum degree as 2.

Figure 9 shows a digraph with ADR and degree, the arc (宇, 昌) (Yu, Chang) with the expression [1, 2] indicating that the intensity is 1 and the degree is 2, therefore it will be concatenated as "[宇昌]" (Yu Chang) because it meets the criteria (1). In [31], we considered only on directed links but failed in detecting significant concatenations from inverted links. For example, the LC "[弊案]" (Scandal) with the value [0.33, 2] of the direct link (弊, 案) will not be concatenated if we don't consider its inverted link (案,弊) with the value [1,2] which meets the criteria (2).

3.2.3 Step 3: Run iteration

The above steps will be iterated until no concatenation can be found, and this iteration process will generate a series of short and long LCs as anecdotes. A long LC is believed to carry more anecdotes than a short LC could possibly do. For example, it is obvious that "[向量空間模型]" is a better anecdote than its substring "[向量]" or "[空間]" or "[模型]." To enhance the semantics of candidate anecdotes, we will take a further concatenation process as the last step to finalize the CLCP.

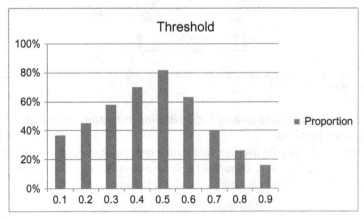

FIGURE 8

Thresholds scatter diagram of ADR.

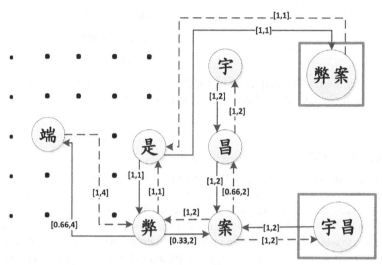

FIGURE 9

Digraph with concatenate vertices.

3.2.4 Step 4: Execute postprocessing

In the final step, significant words are determined by observing the information mutually shared by two-overlapped LCs using the following significance estimation (SE) function as (3)

$$SEi = \frac{fi}{fa + fb - fi},\tag{3}$$

where i denotes the LC_i to be estimated, that is, $i = i_i \cdot i_2, \ldots, i_n$; a and b represent the two longest compound substrings of LC_i with the length $n-1$, that is, $a = i_i \cdot i_2, \ldots, i_{n-1}$ and $b = i_2 \cdot i_3, \ldots, i_n$. The f_a, f_b and f_i are the frequencies of a, b, and i, respectively. In the above example, the term i, "[宇昌案]" (Yu Chang case), shall gain the SE value of 0.83 based on its frequency 5 and the frequency 6 of its substring a, "[宇昌]" (Yu Chang), as well as the frequency 5 of the other substring "[昌案]" (Chang case). In this case, we will retain term i "[宇昌案]" and its substring a "[宇昌]" because the frequency of "[宇昌案]" is less than "[宇昌]" indicating "[宇昌]" carries useful meanings. Likewise, we will discard the substring b "[昌案]" because both terms have the same frequency indicating the long term "[宇昌案]" can replace its substring "[昌案]." As stated above, since $f_i < f_a$, we retain both terms, and discard "[昌案]" because $f_i = f_b$.

3.2.5 Term weighting

It is suggested that the most significant content description often appears in the title and the first paragraph. In addition, word frequency and word length are also accepted as the indicators of term discrimination value in a document. Given a word LC_i, the term weighting algorithm may be defined as (4).

$$\text{Weight}_i = tf_i \times (\text{val}_1 + \text{val}_2 + \text{length}_i)$$

$$\text{val}_1 = \begin{cases} 2, \text{word}_i \in \text{title} \\ 0, \text{otherwise} \end{cases} \quad \text{val}_2 = \begin{cases} 2, \text{word}_i \in \text{FP} \\ 0, \text{otherwise} \end{cases} \tag{4}$$

where tf_i represents the frequency of LC_i; val_1 and val_2 express the added double weights on the news title and the first paragraph, respectively.

4 EVALUATION

In this experiment, we collected 18,000 images-resided web pages from Taiwan news website udn.com including the categories of politics, society, local news, world news, finance, and life as the data sets. To verify the effectiveness of our proposed CLCP method, we used the image caption as the ground truth label for the primary annotation to understand the degree to which it matches the caption. We also invited subject experts and users to assess the appropriateness of the secondary annotations. In the end, we measured the performance of the CLCP method in a real-time mode.

4.1 EVALUATION OF PRIMARY ANNOTATION

Due to the fact of discrepancy in interpreting the context semantics by humans, therefore the exact number of correct annotations of an image may not be easily identified. For example, the LC "[總統馬英九]" (President Ma Ying-jiu) is better than its substrings "[總統]" and "[馬英九]" even though these two substrings are also valid annotations. Thus, the recall measurement did not apply to this study. A precision measurement was used to understand the proportion of primary annotations actually matched the image captions as (5).

$$p = \frac{\text{number of matched PAs in captions}}{\text{total number of PAs}} \tag{5}$$

where PAs represent the primary annotations from 18,000 documents. After the CLCP processing, the total number of matched PAs in captions are 15,228. We obtained a precision rate of 84.6%.

4.2 EXPERT EVALUATION OF SECONDARY ANNOTATION

To evaluate the validity of the secondary annotations, we invited five subject experts to participate in the assessment. Thirty pieces of news were randomly selected from which we extracted 60 secondary annotations. To reduce ambiguous judgements, each annotation was evaluated based on a method of dichotomic classification to which the annotation represents the image content. Each expert could only identify either "agree" or "disagree" for each annotation. The result showed that the number of check marks of consent is 252 of 300. It implies that the agreement of the appropriateness of the secondary annotations to the images achieves 84%.

4.3 USER EVALUATION OF SECONDARY ANNOTATION

To evaluate the appropriateness of the secondary annotation, we conducted another survey to understand the differences between the image annotation and the users' expectation. Sixty graduate and undergraduate students were recruited from National Yunlin University of Science & Technology, Taiwan to participate in the assessment. One hundred pieces of news were randomly selected from which we collected 200 secondary annotations. Students were divided into four groups, and each group was given 25 images for the evaluation. To assist the assessment, we provided news title, text and caption for references. Each annotation was evaluated by three participants to understand the degree to which the annotations appropriately address the image content. The result in Table 1 shows that the number of check marks of agreement is much higher than that of disagreement. The agreement rate of user evaluation reaches 76.6%.

4.4 RESULTS OF IMAGE ANNOTATION

The following three examples display the results after conducting CLCP. For copyright consideration, we refer the indicated image to its url address for reference. Table 2 is a local news entitled "汽車救生圈 歐洲科賽奪金牌" (The automobile life-saving buoy, Europe science competition won the gold medal). The primary and secondary annotations were generated, including "[正修科大電子系博士張法憲]" (Dr. Zhang Faxian, Department of Electronic Engineering at Cheng Shiu University), "[組合式救援浮力模組]" (Combined Type of Rescue buoyancy Suite), and "[汽車的救生圈]" (The automobile life-saving buoy). Note that our method

Table 1 Results of User Agreement

Highly Agree	Agree	Average	Disagree	Highly Disagree	Total
1380	920	423	204	73	3000

Table 2 Example 1

News title	The automobile life-saving buoy, Europe science competition seizes the gold medal
Image link	https://s2.yimg.com/bt/api/res/1.2/sPmFSiNcFapEMkRGOuZVdg--/YXBwaWQ9eW5ld3M7Y2g9MjQwO2NyPTE7Y3c9Mzlw O2R4PTA7ZHk9MDtmaT11bGNyb3A7aD0xNDM7cT04NTt3PTE5MA--/http://media.zenfs.com/zh_hant_tw/News/ftv/2014526U02M1.jpg
Caption	The automobile life-saving buoy, Europe science competition won the gold medal, special award
CLCP	Dr. Zhang Faxian, Department of Electronic Engineering at Cheng Shiu University | Combined Type of Rescue buoyancy Suite | The automobile life-saving buoy

Table 3 Example 2

News title	The First Lady of Taiwan Chow Mei-Ching attends the exhibition of the Imperial Palace in Tokyo
Image link	http://wscdn.bbc.co.uk/worldservice/assets/images/2014/08/04/140804110249_cn_chow_mei_ching_tokyo_624x351_afp.jpg
Caption	Chow Mei-Ching's visit to Japan but was ultimately received a cold-should by the media
CLCP	Special Exhibition of the Treasured Masterpieces from National Palace Museum, Taipei | Taiwan | Chow Mei-Ching's visit to Japan

Table 4 Example 3

News title	France committed to deal with the flight crash in Algeria
Image link	http://wscdn.bbc.co.uk/worldservice/assets/images/2014/07/26/140726222034_francois_hollande_624x351_reuters.jpg
Caption	After meeting with the families of the victims François Hollande made a commitment
CLCP	Algeria Airlines Flight 5017 | Three days of national mourning | 118 victims

extracts "[正修科大電子系博士張法憲]," the inventor of this awarded buoy, is not mentioned in the news title and it is so specific and completely fit the picture. Table 3 is an international news entitled "台灣總統夫人周美青東京出席故宮展" (The First Lady of Taiwan Chow Mei-Ching attends the exhibition of the Imperial Palace in Tokyo). The primary and secondary annotations were generated, including "[台北國立故宮博物院神品至寶特別展]" (Special exhibition of the Treasured masterpieces from National Palace Museum, Taipei), "[台灣]" (Taiwan), and "[周美青訪日]" (Chow Mei-Ching's visit to Japan). Note that our method extracts "[台北國立故宮博物院神品至寶特別展]," the complete description of the exhibition, is the main theme of the visit. With the three annotations, it clearly describes the picture. Table 4 is an international news entitled "阿爾及利亞墜機 法國承諾處理遺體" (France committed to deal with the flight crash in Algeria). The primary and secondary annotations were generated, including "[阿爾及利亞航空公司5017航班]" (Algeria Airlines Flight 5017), "[三天的全國哀悼]" (Three days of national mourning), and "[118名罹難者]" (118 victims). Note that the three extracted annotations depict the implicit content of the press conference, which enhance understanding the picture.

4.5 PERFORMANCE TESTING

After the annotation validity and acceptance evaluation, we conducted a performance testing with respect to the time spent of processing from an event trigger to system response. Often real-time response times are understood to be in milliseconds and sometimes microseconds. Our testing data sets consist of 18,000 pieces of news; the processing time is 126 s in total with 0.007 s on average for each piece of news.

5 CONCLUSION

Unlike recent feature-based or text processing techniques tend to assign the same annotation to all the images in the same cluster without considering the latent semantic anecdotes of each image. This study proposed a corpus-free, relatively light computation of term segmentation, namely "CLCP method" to identify pertinent anecdotes for image annotation.

This chapter contributes to image annotation research in several ways. First, it demonstrates that a corpus-free, lightweight computation of a single document can effectively generate pertinent anecdotes for image annotation. This finding indicates that a greater deployment of the CLCP needs to be undertaken in order to provide customized image annotation that has been neglected by current CBIR and text-based image processing. Second, for performance consideration, this method adopted the concept of flyweight and composite design patterns that allows sharing characters/words and facilitating their use at fine granularities without prohibitive cost. This finding implies that whether the CLCP applied to a single document or multidocument processing will gain the same benefit. Third, this study demonstrates that the extracted anecdotes truly depict the implicit content of the news, which enhance understanding the picture.

Results showed that this method achieves a significant precision rate and gains high acceptance from experts and users. The performance testing was also very promising. The proposed model, along with the empirical findings, sheds new light on AIA.

ACKNOWLEDGMENTS

This study was supported by the National Science Council, Taiwan, Republic of China, under the project of special research projects of free software (NSC101-2221-E-224-056).

REFERENCES

[1] Gao S, Wang D-H, Lee C-H. Automatic image annotation through multi-topic text categorization. In: 2006 IEEE international conference on acoustics, speech and signal processing; 2006.

[2] Lei Z, Jun M. Image annotation by incorporating word correlations into multi-class SVM. Soft Comput 2011;15:917–27.

[3] Luong-Dong N, Ghim-Eng Y, Ying L, Ah-Hwee T, Liang-Tien C, Joo-Hwee L. A Bayesian approach integrating regional and global features for image semantic learning. In: IEEE international conference on multimedia and expo 2009, 28 June to 3 July 2009; 2009. p. 546–9.

[4] Chow TWS, Rahman MKM. A new image classification technique using tree-structured regional features. Advanced Neurocomput Theory Methodol 2007;70:1040–50.

[5] Huang C-M, Chang C-C, Chen C-T. Automatic image annotation by incorporating weighting strategy with CSOM classifier. In: The 2011 international conference on image processing, computer vision, & pattern recognition (IPCV'11). Monte Carlo Resort, Las Vegas, Nevada, USA; 2011.

[6] Barnard K, Duygulu P, Forsyth D, De Freitas N, Blei DM, Jordan MI. Matching words and pictures. J Mach Learn Res 2003;3:1107–35.

[7] Su JH, Chou CL, Lin CY, Tseng VS. Effective image semantic annotation by discovering visual-concept associations from image-concept distribution model. In: Proc. IEEE international conference on multimedia; 2010. p. 42–7.

[8] Zhu S, Liu Y. Semi-supervised learning model based efficient image annotation. IEEE Signal Process Lett 2009;16:989–92.

[9] Kato T. Database architecture for content-based image retrieval. In: Proc. SPIE 1662, image storage and retrieval systems; 1992. p. 112–23.

[10] Jing L, Shao-Ping M, Min Z. Automatic image annotation based-on model space. In: Proc. 2005 IEEE international conference on natural language processing and knowledge, engineering 30 Oct–1 Nov 2005; 2005. p. 455–60.

[11] Gao Y, Fan J, Xue X, Jain R. Automatic image annotation by incorporating feature hierarchy and boosting to scale up SVM classifiers. In: Proc. of the 14th annual ACM international conference on multimediaSanta Barbara, CA: ACM; 2006.

[12] Mori Y, Takahashi H, Oka R. Image-to-word transformation based on dividing and vector quantizing images with words. In: First international workshop on multimedia intelligent storage and retrieval management; 1999.

[13] Monay F, Gatica-Perez D. PLSA-based image auto-annotation: constraining the latent space. In: Proc. 12th annual ACM international conference on multimediaNew York, NY: ACM; 2004.

[14] Carneiro G, Vasconcelos N. Formulating semantic image annotation as a supervised learning problem. In: IEEE computer society conference on computer vision and pattern recognition, USA; 2005.

[15] Wang Z, Xu J, Araki K, Tochinai K. Word segmentation of Chinese text with multiple hybrid methods. In: 2009 International conference on computational intelligence and software engineering; 2009.

[16] Horng JT, Yeh CC. Applying genetic algorithms to query optimization in document retrieval. Inform Process Manag 2000;36:737–59.

[17] Fuketa M, Fujisawa N, Bando H, Morita K, Aoe JI. A retrieval method of similar strings using substrings, In: 2010 Second international conference on computer engineering and applications; 2010.

[18] Kim MS, Whang KY, Lee JG, Lee MJ. Structural optimization of a full-text n-gram index using relational normalization. VLDB J 2008;17:1485–507.

[19] Hong C-M, Chen C-M, Chiu C-Y. Automatic extraction of new words based on Google News corpora for supporting lexicon-based Chinese word segmentation systems. Expert Syst Appl 2009;36:3641–51.

[20] Tsai RT-H. Chinese text segmentation: a hybrid approach using transductive learning and statistical association measures. Expert Syst Appl 2010;37:3553–60.

[21] Salton G, Mcgill MJ. Introduction to modern information retrieval. New York: McGraw-Hill Book Company; 1983.

[22] Troy AD, Zhang G-Q. Enhancing relevance scoring with chronological term rank. In: Proc. 30th annual international ACM SIGIR conference on research and development in information retrievalAmsterdam, The Netherlands: ACM; 2007.

[23] Yan H, Ding S, Suel T. Compressing term positions in web indexes. In: Proc. 32nd international ACM SIGIR conference on research and development in information retrieval-Boston, MA: ACM; 2009. p. 147–54 1571969.

[24] Tatar D, Kapetanios E, Sacarea C, Tanase D. Text segments as constrained formal concepts. In: 12th international symposium on symbolic and numeric algorithms for scientific computing (SYNASC), 23–26 Sept. 2010; 2010. p. 223–8.

[25] Shanthi V, Lalitha S. Lexical chaining process for text generations. In: International conference on process automation, control and computing (PACC); 2011.

[26] Tatar D, Mihis AD, Czibula GS. Lexical chains segmentation in summarization. In: 10th international symposium on symbolic and numeric algorithms for scientific computing, 26–29 Sept. 2008; 2008. p. 95–101.

[27] Ageishi R, Miura T. Named entity recognition based on a hidden Markov model in part-of-speech tagging. In: First international conference on the applications of digital information and web technologies; 2008.

[28] Chiong R, Wang W. Named entity recognition using hybrid machine learning approach. In: The 5th IEEE international conference on cognitive informatics; 2006.

[29] Gamma E, Helm R, Johnson R, Vlissides J. Design patterns: elements of reusable object-oriented software. Indianapolis, IN: Pearson Education Co; 1995.

[30] Huang C-M. Applying a lightweight Chinese lexical chain processing in web image annotation. In: The 2014 international conference on image processing, computer vision, & pattern recognition (IPCV'14), Las Vegas, Nevada, USA; 2014.

[31] Huang C-M, Chang Y-J. Applying a lightweight iterative merging Chinese segmentation in web image annotation. In: Perner P, editor. 2013 International conference on machine learning and data mining, New York, USA. Berlin Heidelberg: Springer; 2013. p. 183–94.

Automatic estimation of a resected liver region using a tumor domination ratio

23

M. Hariyama[1], M. Shimoda[2]

[1]*Graduate School of Information Sciences, Tohoku University, Sendai, Miyagi, Japan*
[2]*Second Department of Surgery, Dokkyo Medical University, Tochigi, Japan*

1 INTRODUCTION

3D simulation, recently, plays an important role in surgical planning for hepatectomy since the liver has a complex structure, that is, some different vessels exist complexly as shown in Figure 1. The estimation of regions perfused by the portal vein is especially one important task in anatomical hepatectomy, since the hepatocellular carcinoma (HCC), cancerous liver tumor, tends to metastasize via the portal vein [1–3]. Figure 2 explains how HCC metastasizes through the portal vein and what a perfused region is. The tumor is fed by the nearest parts of the portal vein, and HCC metastasizes in the downstream direction through the portal vein. Therefore, the cancer-related regions can be estimated based on the perfused region.

Overestimating the perfused region tends to prevent metastasizing and reduce recurrence of HCC since a large region including the tumor is resected. However, it increases the possibility of the postoperative liver failure. Therefore, the volume of the perfused region should be minimized while including all the perfused regions of the portal vein feeding the tumor.

Some practical software programs for 3D simulation and preoperative planning have been developed like Hepavision (MeVis Medical Solutions AG, Bremen, Germany) [4], OVA (Hitachi, Tokyo, Japan) [5], and Synapse VINCENT (Fujifilm Medical, Tokyo, Japan) [6]. In preoperative planning, surgeons search for the combination of the cut-points on the portal vein in a trial-and-error way until the tumor is covered by the perfused regions of the portal-vein cut-points. However, it is difficult and time-consuming for surgeons to find optimal or near-optimal combination since the portals vein has complex structure, that is, it has many branches. As a result, surgeons tend to select simple combinations, and this leads to overestimation of the perfused region.

To solve this problem, the method to compute the optimal perfused regions has been developed, where the volume is minimized while including all the perfused region of the tumor-related portal vein [7]. In order to find the tumor-related part

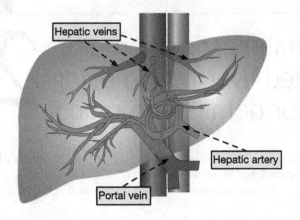

FIGURE 1

Vascular system of the liver.

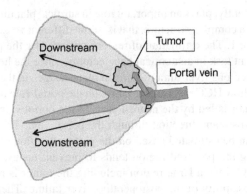

FIGURE 2

HCC (cancer) metastasizing model.

of the portal vein accurately, the tumor domination ratio (TDR) is defined which reflects how much volume of the tumor a portal-vein point feeds. The TDR allows to pick up all the tumor-related points of the portal vein, and the total of the regions perfused by them is determined to be the resected region. This chapter extends the work [7] by adding explanations, evaluations, and a method considering a more practical condition.

The rest of this chapter is organized as follows. In Section 2, the basic method to find the ideal resected region is explained where practical conditions used in the real surgeries are not considered. In Section 3, its extension is explained where practical conditions such as the branch points and the radiuses of the vessels are considered. Section 4 describes more practical estimation considering hepatic veins as well as portal veins. Section 5 is conclusion.

2 ESTIMATING AN IDEAL RESECTED REGION USING THE TDR

Perfused regions are typically estimated by using a Voronoi diagram [3]. Figure 3 shows how to compute perfused regions using Voronoi diagram. A Voronoi diagram is a way of dividing space into a number of regions as shown in Figure 3(a). A set of points (called seeds) is specified beforehand and for each seed there will be a corresponding region consisting of all points closer to that seed than to any other. The corresponding regions are called Voronoi cells. In estimating perfused regions, a seed and Voronoi cell in a Voronoi diagram correspond to a point on a portal vein and a region perfumed by the portal point, respectively, as shown in Figure 3(b). Note that, in Figure 3(b), portal-vein points (seeds) exist continuously, whereas seeds in the original Voronoi diagram are located apart from each other. As a result, the liver region is divided into small regions of the same number as the portal-vein points.

The TDR of a portal-vein point P is defined as

$$TDR = \frac{\text{Volume of the region perfused of } P \text{ in the tumor}}{\text{Volume of the tumor}} \times 100 \ [\%] \qquad (1)$$

where the denominator and enumerator are illustrated in Figure 3(c). The TDR reflects how much the portal-vein point feed the tumor and is also affected by the tumor.

Given a tumor location, let us compute an ideal resected region by using the TDR, where the ideal resected region means a minimum region including all subregions perfused by tumor-related portal points. The ideal resected region is estimated by following steps (Figure 4).

Step 1: Among the portal-vein points with TDR larger than 0 on a branch, select the point closest to the main stem as a cut-point of the branch. For example, in Figure 4(a), P_i ($i = 1, 2, \cdots, 6$) are the portal-vein points with TDR larger than 0; P_1 and P_4 are selected as cut-points on branches B_1 and B_2, respectively.

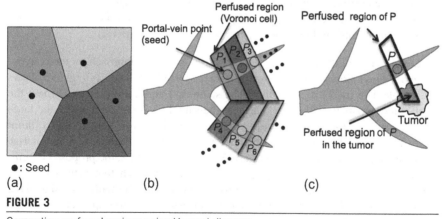

● : Seed
(a)   (b)   (c)

FIGURE 3

Computing perfused regions using Voronoi diagram.

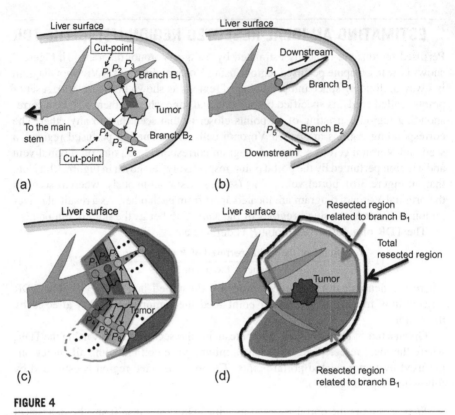

FIGURE 4

Computing ideal resected region.

Step 2: For each branch, the downstream part of the cut-point is computed by region growing (Figure 4(b)). For all the portal-vein points of these downstream parts, the perfused regions are computed as shown in Figure 4(c).

Step 3: The ideal resected region is given by a union of all the perfused regions of all the points on downstream parts as shown in Figure 4(d).

Let us compare the proposed method with the manual approach on the conventional 3D simulation software program (Synapse VINCENT ver.2). Figure 5 shows the sample date used for evaluation. The samples 1 and 2 are the cases where the small tumor exists near the liver surface; the sample 3 is the case where the large tumor exists near the main stem of the portal vein. The liver, vessels, and a tumor are extracted in advance by the other software programs. Tables 1–3 summarize the results for samples 1–3, respectively. From Tables 1 and 2, the proposed optimization method is very useful compared to the manual approach, that is, the volume of the estimated resected region by the proposed method is much smaller than that of the manual approach. This is because the degree of freedom of cut-point selection is high and the effect of optimization is large for the case where the small tumor exists near

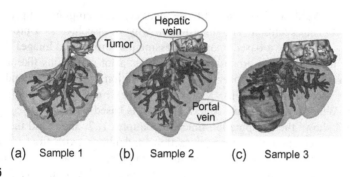

(a) Sample 1   (b) Sample 2   (c) Sample 3

FIGURE 5

Samples for evaluation.

Table 1 Comparison Results for Sample 1

Sample 1	Manual Approach by a Surgeon	Proposed
Resected volume (cc)	192	66
The number of cut-points	1	2
Results	Resected region	Resected region

Table 2 Comparison Results for Sample 2

Sample 2	Manual Approach by a Surgeon	Proposed
Resected volume(cc)	325	42
The number of cut-points	2	4
Results	Resected region	Resected region

Table 3 Comparison Results for Sample 3

Sample 3	Manual Approach by a Surgeon	Proposed
Resected volume (cc)	550	476
The number of cut-points	5	10
Results	Resected region	Resected region

the liver surface. On the other hand, from Table 3, the optimization is not very effective when the tumor exists near the main stem of the portal vein since the degree of freedom of cut-point selection is low.

Let us evaluate the computation time. The computing platform that we use is a PC with a Core-i7 CPU and a 24 GB memory. The operating system and programming language are Windows 7 and Java 1.6, respectively. The program simply designed for single-thread execution. The main reason why we use Java as a programming language is that the Java-based image-processing platform called ImageJ [8] is easy to use for medical image processing. ImageJ has a lot of plugins like a DICOM reader, basic 2D/3D image processing and visualization, and can be extended easily by adding user-defined plugins. Moreover, ImageJ runs on multiplatforms like Microsoft Windows, Linux, and MacOS since it is based on Java.

Table 4 shows the computation times for samples 1, 2, and 3 and their details. Note that vessel extraction, liver extraction, and tumor extraction are done in advance as explained above, and that their computation times are not included. The time for "computing perfused regions" is the one for *Step 1* and *Step 2*; the time for "computing resected regions" is the one for *Step 3*. The computation times vary depending on the volumes of the perfused regions and the cut region. The larger the volumes are, the longer the computation time is. The computation time for any sample is <3 min. This computation time is acceptable in real preoperative planning since the conventional preoperative planning by surgeons takes about 30–60 min for estimating a resected region. The computation time can be much speeded up by multithreading since estimating the perfused regions and cut regions has the high degree of pixel-level parallelism.

3 ESTIMATING AN OPTIMAL RESECTED REGION UNDER THE PRACTICAL CONDITIONS IN SURGERY

Although the method described in the previous section greatly reduces the volume of the estimated resected region, it is difficult for surgeons to use the results directly in the real surgery since the number of cut-points may be much larger than that of the manual approach, and since cut-points may be sometimes set on such tiny vessels that surgeons cannot identify in the real surgery. In order to solve this problem, the method described in the previous section is extended considering the practical conditions: branch points and the radius of the vessels. The optimization procedure starts with obtaining the ideal cut-points by the method described in the previous section (Figure 6(a)). These ideal cut-points are refined considering the practical conditions as shown in Figure 6(b). Each cut-point is moved toward the upstream

Table 4 Computation Time for Estimating an Ideal Resected Region

Processing	Sample 1	Sample 2	Sample 3
Computing perfused regions(s)	58	87	84
Computing resected region(s)	2	1	72
3D reconstruction(s)	18	17	11
Total(s)	78	105	167

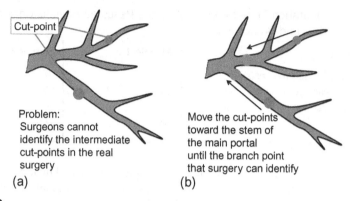

Cut-point

Problem:
Surgeons cannot
identify the intermediate
cut-points in the real
surgery

(a)

Move the cut-points
toward the stem of
the main portal
until the branch point
that surgery can identify

(b)

FIGURE 6

Refining the cut-points considering the practical conditions.

Table 5 Results of the Optimization Considering the Practical Conditions for Sample 1

Sample 1	Manual Approach by a Surgeon	Proposed (Radius: 6 mm)	Proposed (Radius: 8 mm)
Resected volume (cc)	192	112	178
The number of cut-points	1	2	1
Results	Resected region	Resected region	Resected region

Table 6 Results of the Optimization Considering the Practical Conditions for Sample 2

Sample 2	Manual Approach by a Surgeon	Proposed (Radius 6 mm)	Proposed (Radius 8 mm)
Resected volume (cc)	352	170	346
The number of cut-points	2	3	2
Results	Resected region	Resected region	Resected region

direction in such a way that the cut-point is set on a branch point and the radius of the vessel is larger than the predetermined value.

Tables 5 and 6 summarize the results of the optimization considering the practical conditions for samples 1 and 2, respectively. The radius of the vessel is set to 6 or 8 mm. These results show that the estimated resected region is minimized keeping the number of cut-points small appropriately for real surgery.

Table 7 Computation Time for Estimating the Resected Regions Considering a Vessel Radius and Branch-Point

Processing	Sample 1	Sample2
Computing perfused regions(s)	58	87
Computing resected region(s)	30	82
3D reconstruction(s)	18	16
Total(s)	106	185

Table 7 shows the computation times for samples 1 and 2 and their details. Note that the optimization considering a vessel radius and a branch point is included in "computing resected region." Although this optimization requires additional computation time, the computation time is still acceptable since it is much smaller than the time for planning by surgeons.

4 MODIFYING A RESECTED REGION CONSIDERING HEPATIC VEINS

For preoperative planning, not only portal veins but also hepatic veins should be considered due to a blood congestion problem by cutting hepatic veins. Figure 7 explains the blood congestion problem. There are three large hepatic veins in the liver: right, middle, and left hepatic veins, and their major function is to carry blood from the tissue back to the heart. Similar to the tumor metastasizing model described in Section 1, each hepatic vein is thought to absorb blood from its closest tissue as shown in Figure 7. If a hepatic vein is cut at a point as shown in Figure 7(b), blood congestion occurs in the region related to the end part from the cut-point since the end part cannot absorb the blood; this blood-congestion region is damaged, and its liver function reduces significantly. Hence, the congestion region is thought to be

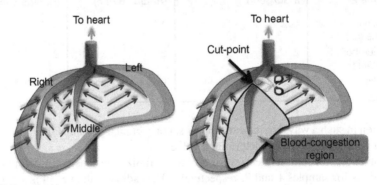

FIGURE 7

Blood congestion problem.

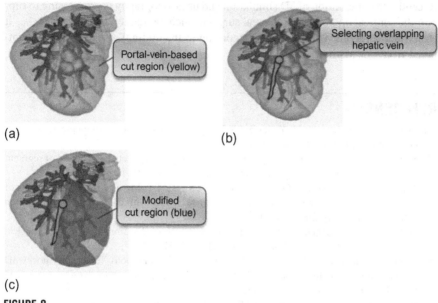

FIGURE 8

Modifying the portal-vein-based resected region considering hepatic veins.

equivalently a loss of the liver as well as a resected region. Therefore, if the total volume of the congestion region and the resected region is large for the liver function of the patient, it would cause liver failure. If the hepatic veins overlap with a portal-vein-based resected region, the resected region is limited so as not to overlap with any major hepatic vein.

In conventional software, surgeons must draw complex cutting surfaces manually considering hepatic veins, and it is very time-consuming since 3D surface is difficult to draw and not accurate.

To solve this problem, we extend the portal-vein-based estimation so as to consider hepatic veins easily as shown in Figure 8. At first, the resected region is obtained from portal-based estimation (Figure 8(a)). The yellow region denotes the portal-based cut region. Next, it is checked whether the resected region overlap with hepatic veins or not. If overlapping (Figure 8(b)), the original resected region is limited so as not to overlap with the hepatic vein (Figure 8(c)). This modified resected region is denoted by the blue region.

5 CONCLUSION

In order to minimize the resected volume while preventing metastases, the automatic method that finds the optimal combination of cut-points is proposed. The domination ratio is a key to success to find such optimal combination in a systematic way.

Recently, the integration of 3D simulation and ultrasonography is progressing to support the surgical operations in the real surgery. Such navigation technology makes it easier that surgeons resect the liver according to the optimal resected regions computed from our method.

REFERENCES

[1] Makuuchi M, Hasegawa H, Yamazaki S. Ultrasonically guided subsegmentectomy. Surg Gynecol Obstet 1985;161:346–50.

[2] Kishi Y, Hasegawa K, Kaneko J, Aoki T, Beck Y, Sugawara Y, et al. Resection of segment VIII for hepatocellular carcinoma. Br J Sur 2012;99(8):1105–12.

[3] Takamoto T, Hashimoto T, Ogata S, Inoue K, Maruyama Y, Miyazaki A, et al. Planning of anatomical liver segmentectomy and subsegmentectomy with 3-dimensional simulation software. Am J Surg 2003;206(4):530–8.

[4] Selle D, Preim B, Schenk A, Peitgen HO, et al. Analysis of vasculature for liver surgical planning. IEEE Trans Med Imaging 2002;21:1344–57.

[5] Saito S, Yamanaka J, Miura K, Nakao N, Nagao T, Sugimoto T, et al. A novel 3D hepatectomy simulation based on liver circulation: application to liver resection and transplantation. Hepatology 2005;41:1297–304.

[6] Ohshima S. Volume analyzer SYNAPSE VINCENT for liver analysis. J Hepatobiliary-Pancreat Sci 2014;21(4):235–8.

[7] Hariyama M, Okada M, Shimoda M, Kubota K. Estimation of resected liver regions using a tumor domination ratio. In: Proc. international conference on image processing, computer vision, and pattern recognition (IPCV); 2014. p. 52–6.

[8] Rasband WS. ImageJ, U. S. National Institutes of Health, Bethesda, Maryland, USA, http://imagej.nih.gov/ij/, (1997–2014).

Gesture recognition in cooking video based on image features and motion features using Bayesian network classifier

24

Nguyen Tuan Hung[1], Pham The Bao[1], Jin Young Kim[2]

[1]Faculty of Mathematics and Computer Science, Ho Chi Minh University of Science,
Ho Chi Minh City, Viet Nam
[2]School of Electrical and Computer Engineering, Chonnam National University,
Gwangju, South Korea

1 INTRODUCTION

As you know, cooking and eating are our routines which all of us must do in order to stay healthy. Although these are simple tasks that anyone would have to go through every day in life, they account for a very important position because of healthy impact. On the other hand, in a modern society, time has become more precious than ever before. Everyone does not have much time for cooking themselves and it leads to a direct impact on the health of everyone. Therefore, the question "How could we have a delicious and nutritious dish with less cooking time?" has been raised for a while.

In recent years, researchers all over the world have been building various intelligent kitchen systems, which are anticipated as the answer for the above question. They expect that these systems can help everyone cook faster and more efficiently. In these systems, there is not only a single solution but also the solutions of many different problems such as object recognition problem, human action recognition, or nutritious meals computation which are combined together. All of the above problems have been actually raised in the "Multimedia for Cooking and Eating Activities" workshop from 2009. Until now, many complex challenges still exist and there is not any complete solution. Among these problems, we evaluated that the human's cooking action recognition is the most challenge problem.

One of its challenges is action recognition problem. Its objection is how a computer program can recognize cooking actions based on training dataset.

379

Furthermore, based on sequences of cooking actions, it could predict what kind of dishes. In reality, we expect that when this program is being executed, it observes actions of user(s), recognizes these actions, and either warns user(s) if there is any wrong or suggests next cooking steps. Therefore, we realize that solving problem of cooking action recognition is the most important task to complete our intelligent kitchen system. This problem has been mentioned in a contest [1] of ICPR2012 conference as an interesting topic in video retrieval field. Through this contest and many different researches, there are numerous solutions from many researchers. Moreover, plenty of dataset are created and distributed to researchers. One of them is new "Actions for Cooking Eggs" (ACE) Dataset [2], which we used for evaluating our method in experiments, was presented in contest [1].

In this chapter, a novel method for recognizing human's actions in cooking video is proposed. Our proposed method derives from combination between image features and motion features for gesture recognition. Because of complexity of this problem, we divide it into four subproblems which include cooking action representation by image features, cooking action representation by motion features, combination of image features and motion features, and cooking action classification. From a cooking video, first, the cooking actions are represented by some image features such as pyramid histogram of oriented gradient (PHOG) [3], or scale invariant feature transform (SIFT) [4] and motion feature such as dense motion [5]. We also detect objects in each frame and compute the relative positions between them. We try to represent actions more exactly, so that classification result would be better. Hence, the feature extraction step is very important and the features must be chosen carefully. There is another subproblem which is to combine these above features. According to research from others using only one kind of feature is not good enough in accuracy and combining different features, accuracy gets higher. However, the efficient way of combination is still a complex problem since it depends on datasets and kinds of feature. In this chapter, we use both early fusion and late fusion techniques for combining features [6,7].

Last but not least, to solve cooking action classification problem, we use Bayesian network (BN) classifier. The first reason is automatic structure learning which means we do not need to concern about the network's structure. In addition, in cooking video, the sequence of actions for each kind of dishes has its characteristics. So we can learn this feature and use it in classifier to achieve better classification results. This is the second reason for us to choose BN classifier. Other advantages are easy to update parameters of nodes in the network and modify network's structure by adding or removing nodes in the network. For three main reasons, we have chosen BN as the classifier for our system.

To build a gesture recognition system, our main contributions are as follows:

- Representing cooking motion by image features including color histogram, local binary pattern (LBP), edge oriented histogram (EOH), PHOG, SIFT, and also the relative positions of objects.

- Representing cooking motion by motion features using dense trajectories motion feature.
- Combination of image features and motion features by both early fusion and late fusion techniques.
- Using BN classification for gesture recognition.

2 RELATED WORK

As soon as the flourishing period of computer visions, human's action recognition problem has appeared in many applications especially for smart devices. Generally, a typical human's action recognition system works by extracting some kind of features or/and combining them in a certain way. Most of these systems usually use both global and local image features. Until now, many researchers have been trying to answer which feature is the best for describing human's action and whether different features are supplements for each other. These following features have been deeply studied to answer the above question for recently years.

An answer came from a successful system built by a research team from Columbia University. It used SIFT [4] as an image feature, Space-time interest points (STIP) [8] as a motion feature and Mel Frequency Cepstral Coefficients [9] as a sound feature. Overall, STIP was the best motion feature for human's action description. However, to achieve better results, different kinds of them, which were supplemental features, should be combined together including image features, motion features, and even sound features. This is an important conclusion that other teams agree with.

Researchers from International Business Machines Corporation (IBM) built another human's action recognition system [10]. It used many image features including SIFT [4], GIST [11], color histogram, color moment, wavelet texture, etc. For motion features, it uses STIP [8] combining with HOG/HOF [12]. According to their experiment's result, they concluded that a combination of some features raised the accuracy of recognition. This conclusion is the same as Columbia team [13]. Besides, Nikon team's system is a simple system [14]. It used scene cut detection to extract key frames. This method depends on kind of videos, and length of videos. Although this method is not the best method, it is a good idea that we can use in our system.

In ICPR 2012 conference, there were six systems submitted to. To describe their cooking action system, researchers from Kyushu University, Japan [15] used local features including FAST detector and CHOG3D descriptor, and combined with hand motion feature which was extracted from depth images. In that research, they achieved some spectacular results. The average accuracy for action recognition in their experiment is 50.6% in case of using depth local feature and 53.0% when they used local feature. Then, when they combine these kinds of feature, the accuracy is achieved 57.1%.

The winning entry was by a team from Chukyo University, Japan. Their method uses heuristic approach using image features with some modifications. Then, in postprocessing step, they use some methods to avoid unnatural labeling results.

Their result proved that this approach is more effective than other approaches in practical use. Besides, the other recognition systems from other teams are also interesting. They use motion history image feature, spatio-temporal interest point description feature, trajectories feature, and context information. Moreover, they use one-versus-all linear Support Vector Machine (SVM) classifier as an action model. In postprocessing, they apply 1D Markov random field on the predicted class labels.

According to these methods, we could conclude that an effective action recognition method usually uses some different features and combines them to achieve the better result. Besides, the information such as context information and cooking action sequence are also important for improving the accuracy of our method.

3 OUR METHOD

3.1 OUR RECOGNITION SYSTEM OVERVIEW

Below there are two diagrams, which, respectively, shows training framework and testing framework of our recognition system. As depicted in Figure 1, the main steps in these frameworks are the same.

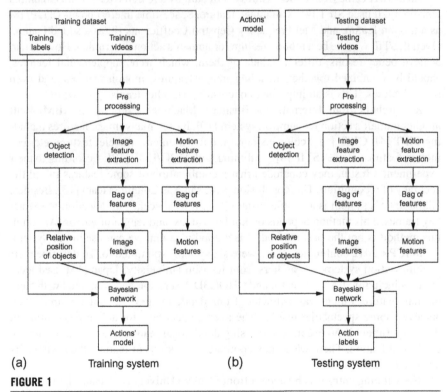

FIGURE 1

Diagrams to describe our method's systems (a) is our training system and (b) is our testing system.

First of all, the input videos are preprocessed through some minor-steps including calibrations, segmentation, objects and human detection, and hands detection. Next, some features are extracted from both depth images and color images. According to basic action recognition methods, they extract motion features in the videos and perform discriminative analysis for action recognition. For cooking action recognition problem, however, some actions cannot be described by using a motion feature alone. Hence, we propose to extract both human's motion feature and image features from cooking video.

For matching the feature vectors, there are some matching methods. However, for this problem, there is a large of feature vectors, which cannot be applied the original matching methods. Therefore, we use bag of feature (BoF) [16] to describe image features and motion features for speeding up the matching step. For each frame, we detect objects and also compute their relations. Moreover, using the training labels, we can learn some rules about the sequences of actions. Finally, we apply BN construction and parameters learning.

For the last step, we create three BNs first, and then train their parameters. The output of training system is a model which describes the cooking actions. In the testing system, we use the trained model to classify cooking actions. Besides, action labels of the previous actions are used as an additional input data for BN classifier. The action label of each frame is the output of testing system. Lastly, we evaluate our method based on the output by calculating accuracy score from precision and recall manner.[1] Their harmonic, after that, is calculated by following formula

$$F = \frac{2}{\left(\dfrac{1}{\text{Precision}} + \dfrac{1}{\text{Recall}}\right)}. \tag{1}$$

The final score is given by averaging all F-measures of all cooking motion label.

3.2 PREPROCESSING INPUT DATA

In preprocessing step, we have prepared data for available to use in the following steps. First of all, we calibrate depth images because there is a distance separates depth camera and color camera. The Kinect disparity is related to a normalized disparity

$$d = \frac{1}{8} \times (d_{\text{off}} + k_{\text{d}}) \tag{2}$$

where d is a normalized disparity, k_{d} is the Kinect disparity, and d_{off} is an offset value particular to a given Kinect device. According to a technical Kinect calibration report [17], d_{off} is typically around 1090. Moreover, in every depth image, there is a small

---

[1]http://www.murase.m.is.nagoya-u.ac.jp/KSCGR/evaluation.html.

black band on the right of the image which we expect to eliminate for mapping the depth image to color image later.

For fast segmentation, we use depth images to segment table area and floor area. We choose some first frames then find a border that separates table and floor areas. Because there is no human in these frames, it is easy for segmentation. Border detection is based on the sum of grayscale of the depth image for each row and also the ratio of disparity of two adjacent rows. In the case that this ratio is higher than a threshold, this row is the border separated table and floor areas.

For human detection, we use both depth image and segmented floor area information, which is detected in previous step. When human appears in scene, the distance from depth sensor to human body is much nearer than floor area. It means the pixels, whose grayscale are higher than average grayscale of floor area, are ones of human body.

Next step, for hand detection, we use color images and skin detection, too. First, we choose some points, which are in skin area. Based on the color of these points, we obtain the range of the color of pixels in skin area. Then, each pixel is classified by its color. Then, we eliminate areas that their size are not in range [hand_size_min, hand_size_max], which are the thresholds to determine size of hands. In case there are still more than two areas, only two largest areas are selected because the smaller areas are almost noises.

Besides, we also apply some object detection models. Objects in this case mean cooking tools such as fry pan, pan, chopstick; and ingredients such as egg, ham, and seasoning. For object detection, we use color images because they contain more information than depth images. For each object, we collect the image samples which are about 100 images. Then, image feature for each of image is calculated and a training data is made using one-versus-all SVM classification. When testing system is executed, a slide window is used to detect objects and recognize which kind of object.

3.3 IMAGE FEATURE EXTRACTION

Image feature has an important role in motion representing and they are extracted faster than other features. To solve our problems, we use image feature as one of main features for fast motion describing. In addition, there are many kinds of image feature can be used to solve our problem. We need to consider which features are the most characteristic for motion representing.

Following preprocessing step, first, image features are extracted from every frame in video. However, in practice, we only extract feature from key-frames which are chosen by one frame for each k frames in video. In our experiment, we use $k = 10$ to reduce the amount of computation because in ten continuous frames there are not many differences. In our research, LBP [18], EOH [19], PHOG [3], and SIFT [4] are used because they can characterize the content of frames including information about the context and are easy to be extracted.

To extract image feature more detail, each image feature is extracted from cells of a 4×8 grid of frame. For PHOG feature, we extract with eight gradient bins and the highest level 1=2. Moreover, for SIFT features, we apply BoF method [16] to increase the effectiveness of recognition. After key point detection step, histogram of these keypoints is calculated based on codebook which is the collection of millions of keypoints. Then, we gain many different kinds of feature vectors. Next, we apply early fusion technique in [6] to join these feature vectors together to obtain only one feature vector, which is known as the image feature vector characterized for a frame in video.

3.4 MOTION FEATURE EXTRACTION

For solving our problem, motion feature is indispensable because of their efficient in motion representation. However, this feature requires an enormous computation and is much more complex than image feature. Therefore, in our research, we use one of fastest and most density motion feature which was studied by Wang et al. [5].

Being parallel with the image features extraction, we extract motion features from videos. In our method, we use dense trajectories and motion boundary histogram (MBH) description [5] for action representation. The main reason for choosing this motion feature is every cooking actions are characterized by different simple motions, such as cutting action is related to vertical motions while mixing action is almost described by turn around motions. Moreover, there are many fine motions in cooking videos, so that we use dense trajectories feature that is the best feature for representing even the fine motions. Besides, MBH descriptor expresses only boundary of foreground motion and eliminates background and camera motion. Thus, it is completely appropriate to be applied in this step for action representation.

To compute the optical flow from above dense samples, we use FarneBack algorithm [20] because it is one of the fastest algorithm to compute a dense optical flow. Next, we track in optical flows to find out trajectories in a sequence of 15 continuous frames. To describe motion feature, each video is separated to many blocks, which are $N \times M \times L$-size blocks. It means scaling each optical flow matrix to size $N \times M$ and each block containing L optical flow. Then, each block is divided into $n_\sigma \times n_\sigma \times n_t$ cells. Lastly, we calculate MBH feature for each cell and join them together. For motion feature, we also use BoFs [16] to increase effectiveness of recognition as SIFT feature from image features.

3.5 BNS TRAINING

Because of three main reasons in the first section, we choose BNs as our classifier. In our approach, we use three separate networks that play different roles in this classification step. Since there are some categories of features from label information, image features and motion features, we use different BNs for training and classifying each of categories. By using three different BNs, the classification result would be better than using only one network. Moreover, we can train three different networks at the same time which means training time could be reduced.

In this step, we create three BNs to classify feature vectors into a certain action class. First of all, we have a BN from ground-truth label data which represents the possibility of subsequence action's label based on previous identified action labels. It is calculated by using Bayes's theorem formula

$$P_{\text{NEXT}}(A_i) = P(A_i|\text{PALs}) \tag{3}$$

where A_i is the ith action and PALs are previous action labels.

For the second BN, we have a graph in which nodes' value are extracted from high-level feature. In this BN, see Figure 2, we have human node which determines whether human exists in this frame. Similarly, hand node is node which determines whether hands are in frame or not. Besides, nodes including tool using node, container using node, and food using node are determined based on the relative position between the hands and the objects. In addition, there is a status changing node, which expresses the changing of ingredient inside cooking container. Finally, the action label nodes are based on the above-identified nodes, whose conditional probability formula is below

$$P_{\text{IMAGE}}(A_i) = P(A_i|\text{SC}, \text{TU}, \text{CU}, \text{FU}) \times P(\text{CU}|\text{Hd}) \times P(\text{FU}|\text{Hd})$$
$$\times P(\text{TU}|\text{Hd}) \times P(\text{SC}|\text{Hm}) \times P(\text{Hd}|\text{Hm}) \times P(\text{Hm}) \tag{4}$$

where SC is status changing, TU is tool using, CU is container using, FU is food using, Hd is hand, and Hm is Human.

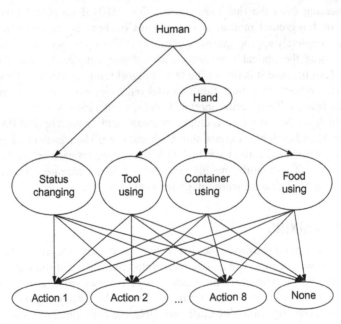

FIGURE 2

The second Bayesian network in our method.

The last BN represents the possibility of an action based on motion features of sequence of images surround the current frame.

$$P_{\text{MOTION}}(A_i) = P(A_i|\text{MF}) \tag{5}$$

where MF is motion feature.

The probability of the ith action class calculated by the first BN is called $P_{\text{NEXT}}(A_i)$, by the second BN is called $P_{\text{IMAGE}}(A_i)$, and by the last one is called $P_{\text{MOTION}}(A_i)$. We can compute the probability of an action label based on P_{NEXT} and P_{IMAGE} only by multiply probabilities, or P_{NEXT} and P_{MOTION}. After that, we combine these probability values to obtain the probability of the ith action

$$P(A_i) = w_1 \times P_{\text{NEXT}}(A_i) \times P_{\text{IMAGE}}(A_i) + w_2 \times P_{\text{NEXT}}(A_i) \times P_{\text{MOTION}}(A_i). \tag{6}$$

4 EXPERIMENTS
4.1 DATASET

In our experiments, we use ACE dataset, which contains five sets for training and two sets for testing. There are five menus of cooking eggs and eight kinds of cooking actions performed by actors in dataset. In addition, the ingredients and cooking utensils, which are used in dataset, are egg, ham, milk, oil, salt and frying pan, saucepan, bowl, knife, chopsticks, etc. The videos were captured by a Kinect sensor, which provides synchronized color and depth image sequences. Each of the videos was from 5 to 10 min long containing from 2000 to over 10,000 frames. Each frame is 480×640-size and is assigned to a certain action label indicating type of action performed by the actors in video.

In this dataset, all dishes are based on egg, sometimes ham or some seasons are added to. Each dish has its own color such as boiled egg has white or brown color from eggshell color while omelet has yellow and pink color from egg and ham. Therefore, we used image features such as color histogram, color moment feature which are extracted to classify different dish. Besides, because each cooking action requires different cooking tool, which has characterized shape, we use image features related to edge features such as cutting action requires knife while mixing action requires chopsticks.

4.2 PARAMETER SETTING

There are some parameters throughout our processes such as in preprocessing step, the parameter $d_{\text{off}} = 1090$ which depends on a certain Kinect device. Other parameters are the thresholds determining hands are hand_size_min and hand_size_max which are obtained from training data. For motion extraction, there are also some other parameter including $N \times M = 480 \times 640$, $L = 20$, $n_\sigma = 2$, and $n_t = 3$.

Lastly, we simply use $w_1 = w_2 = 1$ in Equation (6) because the problem of optimizing value for w_1 and w_2 is hard problem. However, by using $w_1 = w_2 = 1$ we also obtain a good result as we expected.

4.3 RESULTS

Our original work which was published as paper in IPCV2014 [21] has been extended by adding some more features. We evaluate the recognition precision of image features, motion features, and combination of them in ACE dataset. The evaluation results of using either image features or motion features singly are shown in the first and the second columns of Table 1. When using only image features, some actions such as boiling, breaking, and seasoning cannot be classified, which precision is 0%. While other actions include baking action and cutting action achieved has better precisions which are 36.9 and 26.1%. However, in case we apply only motion features, all actions have better precision than using only image features.

Therefore, we find out that the motion features are more efficient to represent the cooking actions than the image features, especially for the actions with large amplitude such as baking or cutting using a big cooking tool as a knife. It is successful to recognize based on the image features. However, they do not describe the other actions which have small amplitude or use tiny cooking tools. On the other hand, when we use only image features, the actions with no color changing or no use any cooking tools such as boiling, breaking, or seasoning could not be recognized by image features including color feature or edge feature. After that, we combine both of image features and motion features to obtain better results as we have expected.

The result of a combination is shown in the last column of Table 1. Compared with two first cases, the combination of the two features improves the recognition results. In this case, some actions are also well recognized, especially the actions "baking" and "turning," because they are the ones with large amplitude. However, some action recognitions are not improved while comparing with motion features because image features may not describe exactly these actions. To solve the problems, one way is to modify the high-level image feature extraction to describe more exactly such as determining exactly which cooking tools are being used. The other way is to combine these features in more efficient way such as trying to find better parameters w_1 and w_2.

Table 1 Action Recognition Precision (%)

Action	Image Features	Motion Features	Our Method
Breaking	0.0	12.7	15.0
Mixing	0.0	22.0	22.5
Baking	36.9	38.4	41.9
Turning	0.0	54.5	54.6
Cutting	26.1	17.3	17.4
Boiling	0.0	29.2	29.1
Seasoning	0.0	15.9	16.0
Peeling	0.0	27.5	27.5
Average	7.9	27.2	28.0

Table 2 Recognition Precision (%) on Testing Videos

Video No.	Image Features	Motion Features	Our Method
1	24.4	25.0	26.3
2	8.3	41.6	43.3
3	12.2	23.1	24.2
4	7.1	16.1	15.9
5	6.0	29.1	30.1
6	20.5	21.2	23.5
7	7.2	15.7	17.1
8	0.0	18.4	18.5
9	4.8	27.1	28.2
10	12.3	32.8	33.9

Moreover, the recognition results of each testing video are shown in Table 2. Each video contains a sequence of actions to cook a certain dish. In our experiment, the best precision is over 40% for all frames in a video. Although the average of precision is approximate 30%, it proves that our approach is appropriate. If we optimize the parameters and improve our implementation, the result would be definitely improved. Therefore, our works still need to be continued in near future.

As we have mentioned in the first section, this problem has been raised in the contest [1]. Until the end of contest, there are five teams who submit their works and results. We compare our method with their results as in Figures 3 and 4. Although in general our method's result is not as high as top of results, there are some advantages comparing with other methods. Some other methods cannot recognize

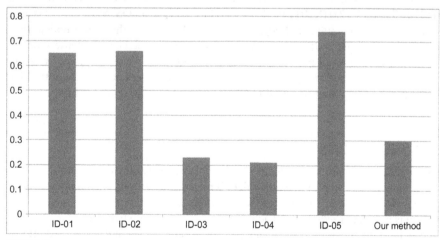

FIGURE 3

Comparing evaluation result with other researches.

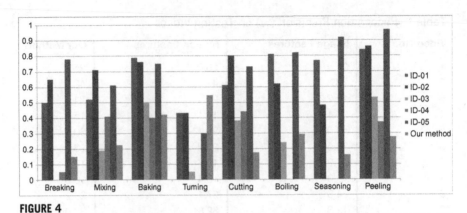

FIGURE 4

Comparing evaluation result in each gesture with other researches.

some action but our method can recognize every kind of action. Therefore, in future, we can improve to achieve higher accuracy for all actions which can be easy to obtain by applying postprocess into test framework.

In addition, our method has achieved the best result in "tuning" action recognition which is one of the hardest actions for correctly recognizing. Because our method uses the appropriate features including image features and motion features, it achieves a good result in this action. However, for some other action, its performance is not as good as other methods because the combination method needs improving to achieve better result. Hence, in next our research, we keen on studying some different way to combine the different feature vectors.

In our research, we use a PC with CPU Intel core i7-2600 3.4 GHz, 8 GB RAM, and MATLAB 7.12.0 (R2011a) 64-bit on Windows 7 64-bit OS. Most of time is used to extract motion features although we have applied one of the fastest optical flow computing algorithms. It requires much more running time because dense trajectories in each sequence of images are extracted. In addition, we only use one PC in our research. If our method is applied on a parallel system such as the clusters or the high performance computing using GPU-CPU, the result will be improved more.

5 CONCLUSIONS

In this chapter, we proposed a method using both image features and motion features for gesture recognition in cooking video. It means the motions in cooking video are represented by image feature vector and motion feature vectors. In our method, BN model is model to predict which action class a certain frame belongs to based on the action class of previous frames and cooking gesture in present frame. Additional information such as the sequence of actions is also applied into BN model to improve classification result.

According to our results, our proposed method is a good approach for solving action recognition in video. Although its performance is not good enough when comparing with the best method, we are certain this method can be improved to achieve higher performance. In addition, it is a completely flexible method as we can add easily more action or other features. Furthermore, we can also reconstruct BNs and update their parameters in nodes easily too. Thus, our method can be applied for other action recognition systems even there are many complex actions.

In the future, we are going to improve motion feature extraction, which is acceleration of feature extraction because now it account to over 80% of the running time. Another problem that we can improve in near future is using high level features. In our research, at present, there is still limitation in high-level features application because they still require more computation and time now.

ACKNOWLEDGMENTS

We would like to thank Atsushi Shimada, Kazuaki Kondo, Daisuke Deguchi, Géraldine Morin, and Helman Stern for organizing KSCGR contest and Tomo Asakusa et al. from Kyoto University, Japan for creating and distributing Actions for Cooking Egg dataset.

REFERENCES

[1] ICPR 2012 Contest, Kitchen Scene Context based Gesture Recognition http://www.murase.m.is.nagoya-u.ac.jp/KSCGR/index.html.

[2] Shimada A. Kitchen scene context based gesture recognition: a contest in ICPR2012. In: Advances in depth image analysis and applications. Berlin Heidelberg/New York: Springer; 2013.

[3] Bosch A, Zisserman A, Munoz X. Representing shape with a spatial pyramid kernel. In: Proc. of the 6th international conference on image and video retrieval (CIVR), Amsterdam; 2007.

[4] Lowe DG. Distinctive image features from scale-invariant keypoints. Int J Comput Vis 2004;60:91–110.

[5] Wang H, Klaser A, Schmid C, Liu CL. Action recognition by dense trajectories. In: IEEE conference on computer vision & pattern recognition, Colorado Springs, USA, June; 2011. p. 3169–76.

[6] Snoek C, Worring M, Geusebroek JM, Koelma DC, Seinstra FJ. The MediaMill TREC-VID 2004 semantic video search engine. In: Proc. TRECVID Workshop. Gaithersburg, MD: NIST Special Publication; 2004.

[7] Westerveld T, de Vries AP, Ballegooij A, de Jong F, Hiemstra D. A probabilistic multimedia retrieval model and its evaluation. EURASIP JASP 2003;186–97.

[8] Laptev I. On space-time interest points. Int J Comput Vis 2005;64:107–23.

[9] Mermelstein P. Distance measures for speech recognition, psychological and instrumental. In: Chen CH, editor. Pattern recognition and artificial intelligent. New York: Academic Press; 1976. p. 374–88.

[10] Matthew H, Gang H, Apostol N, John RS, Lexing X, Bert H, et al. IBM research trecvid-2010 video copy detection and multimedia event detection system. In: NIST TRECVID Workshop, Gaithersburg, MD, USA; 2010.

[11] Oliva A, Torralba A. Modeling the shape of the scene: a holistic representation of the spatial envelope. Int J Comput Vis 2001;42:145–75.

[12] Dalal N, Triggs B. Histograms of oriented gradients for human detection. In: CVPR; 2005. p. 886–93, vol. 1.

[13] Yu GJ, Xiaohong Z, Guangnan Y, Subhabrata B, Dan E, Mubarak S, et al. Columbia-UCF TRECVID2010 multimedia event detection: combining multiple modalities, contextual concepts, and temporal matching. In: NIST TRECVID Workshop, Gaithersburg, MD, USA; 2010.

[14] Matsuo T, Nakajima S. Nikon multimedia event detection system. In: NIST TRECVID Workshop, Gaithersburg, MD, USA; 2010.

[15] Ji Y, Ko Y, Shimada A, Nagahara H, Taniguchi R. Cooking gesture recognition using local feature and depth image. In: ICPR; 2012.

[16] Cruska G, Dance CR, Fan L, Willamowski J, Bray C. Visual categorization with bags of keypoints. In: Workshop on statistical learning in computer vision, ECCV; 2004. p. 886–93.

[17] Bueno JG, Slupska PJ, Burrus N, Moreno L. Textureless object recognition and arm planning for a mobile manipulator. In: 2011 Proc. ELMAR, 14–16 September; 2011, p. 59, 62.

[18] Ojala T, Pietikainen M, Harwood D. A comparative study of texture measures with classification based on feature distributions. Pattern Recognit 1996;29:51–9.

[19] Freeman WT, Michal R. Orientation histograms for hand gesture recognition. In: IEEE international workshop on automatic face and gesture recognition, Zurich, June; 1995.

[20] Farneback G. Two-frame motion estimation based on polynomial expansion. Lect Notes Comput Sci 2003;2749:363–70.

[21] Tuan Hung N, Thanh Binh N, Bao PT, Young Kim J. Gesture recognition in cooking video based on image features and motion features using Bayesian network classifier. In: The 2014 international conference on image processing, computer vision, and pattern recognition (IPCV2014); 2014.

Biometric analysis for finger vein data: Two-dimensional kernel principal component analysis

25

Sepehr Damavandinejadmonfared, Vijay Varadharajan

Department of Computing, Advanced Cyber Security Research Centre,
Macquarie University, Sydney, New South Wales, Australia

1 INTRODUCTION

Traditionally, private information is considered as passwords and personal identification numbers (PINs) among the society, which is easy to use but vulnerable to the risk of exposure and being stolen or forgotten. Biometrics [1,2], however, has been attracting researchers' and industry's attention more and more as it is believed that biometrics is a promising alternative to the traditionally used password or PIN-based authentication techniques [3]. Nowadays, there are several different biometrics systems under research such as face recognition, finger print, palm print, voice recognition, iris recognition, and so on [1,4–7]. There are two main challenges in terms of biometrics systems. The first one is that the main element by which the identity is verified or identified is accessible and forgeable, and the second one is that the rate of reliability of the mentioned systems in terms of having a satisfactory accuracy rate is not acceptable. For instance, finger and palm prints are usually frayed; iris images and voice signature are easily forged; face recognition could be considered difficult and unreliable when there are occlusions or face-lifts. Finger vein recognition [8–11], however, is more secure and convenient and has none of the mentioned drawbacks because of the following three reasons: (1) human veins are mostly invisible and located inside the body; therefore, it is difficult to be forged or stolen, (2) it is more acceptable for the user as capturing finger vein images is noninvasive and contactless, and (3) the finger vein data can only be captured from a live individual. It is thus a convincing proof that the subject whose finger vein [12] is successfully captured is alive.

Because the data in finger vein recognition are "image," there are several methods for analyzing and classifying the images in such a recognition system.

Principal component analysis (PCA) [3,13] is one of the common and powerful methods of pattern recognition and feature extraction which has been used a lot in biometrics. There have been several improvements on PCA such as kernel PCA (KPCA) [13,14], and kernel entropy PCA (KECA) [15–17] so far. See the book [18] for kernel methods in pattern analysis. One-dimensional (1D) KPCA [19] and KECA [20,21] have been proposed for finger vein recognition which led to promising results [22]. The main drawback of 1D PCA, however, is that after converting the 2D matrix to 1D, the dimension of the data is too high which results in having a very time-consuming and even inaccurate system. A highlighted improvement on 1DPCA is 2DPCA [23–26] in which the image matrix is not converted to 1D. This method has two main advantages over 1DPCA which are being much faster, and having higher accuracy. After proposing 2DPCA, kernel 2DPCA [25] was introduced in which the data are first mapped to another space using different kernel methods and then 2DPCA is implemented on the mapped data. It is believed that by transforming the data into the appropriate space first and applying 2DPCA on the mapped data, the accuracy rate will have a dramatic increase. This work is an extension of Ref. [27] presented in IPCV 2014 conference. As 2DPCA is applied on 2D image matrixes directly, there has been a great amount of research on the direction of the analysis. 2DPCA can be applied in row direction, column direction, or both. In this paper, however, different directions of the matrixes for mapping the data into kernel space are argued. We chose kernel polynomial degree one as mapping function and applied input images in row and column directions. The direction of mapping is important in our system because 2DPCA is applied on the mapped data and extracts as many eigenvectors as the dimension of the mapped data, meaning that if we have an $(N \times N)$ matrix, we will have N eigenvectors and their corresponding eigenvalues. For example, assuming our input matrixes are 60×180, applying the mapping function in row and column directions will result in 60×60 and 180×180 matrixes, respectively. Applying 2DPCA on 60×60 or 180×180 matrixes will lead to a great difference in accuracies and time duration for the system.

The remaining of this paper is organized as follows: in Section 2, image acquisition is explained. In Section 3, 2D principal component is introduced briefly. In Section 4, kernel mapping along row and column direction is explained. In Section 5, finger vein recognition algorithm is proposed. In Section 6, experimental results on the finger vein database are discussed. Finally, Section 7 concludes the paper.

2 IMAGE ACQUISITION

In this section, we briefly explain how the finger vein images were captured and what devices were used building the scanner. Based on the proven scientific fact that the light rays can be absorbed by deoxygenated hemoglobin in the vein, absorption coefficient of the vein is higher than other parts of finger. Having said that we designed a scanner consisting of four low-cost prototype devices such as infrared

FIGURE 1

A subset of samples captured from a subject.

LEDs (830 nm wavelength) and the control circuit to drive the LEDs properly, a camera to capture the images, an infrared pass filter and a computer to process the images. To make the camera sensitive to the IR light, there have been some modifications to it; the IR blocking filter was removed and replaced with an IR pass filter which blocks visible wavelengths of light and passes the IR light (Figure 1).

3 TWO-DIMENSIONAL PRINCIPAL COMPONENT ANALYSIS

The main idea of two-dimensional principal component analysis (2DPCA) is to project the image A, which is represented as a random $m \times n$ matrix, onto X that is an n-dimensional unitary column vector:

$$Y = AX \tag{1}$$

Therefore, the projected feature vector of image A is achieved from Equation (1). Finding the appropriate projection vector (X) is the goal. To evaluate the discriminatory power of X, the total scatter of projected samples can be used, which could be characterized by tracing the covariance matrix of projected features vectors. The following criterion is introduced from this point of view:

$$J(X) = \text{tr}(S_x) \tag{2}$$

where S_x represents the covariance matrix of the projected feature vector and $\text{tr}(S_x)$ is the trace of S_x. To maximize the criterion in Equation (2), the appropriate projection direction X needs to be found. S_x is introduced by

$$\begin{aligned} S_x &= E(Y - EY)(Y - EY)^T \\ &= E[(AX) - E(AX)][(AX) - E(AX)]^T \\ &= E[(A - EA)X][(A - EA)X]^T \end{aligned}$$

Therefore,

$$\text{tr}(S_x) = X^T \left[E(A - EA)^T (A - EA) \right] X \tag{3}$$

Defining the image covariance scatter matrix, we have

$$G_t = E \left[(A - EA)^T (A - EA) \right] \tag{4}$$

We now obtain the $n \times n$ matrix of G_t from all training images, where there are m training images of size $m \times n$. Thus, G_t can be evaluated by

$$G_t = 1/ < \sum_{i=1}^{M} \left(A_i - \overline{A} \right)^{\mathrm{T}} \left(A_i - \overline{A} \right) \tag{5}$$

where $\overline{A}$ is the mean matrix of input images and finally we have

$$J(X) = X^{\mathrm{T}} G_i X \tag{6}$$

First, the $n \times n$ matrix of G_t is calculated from all of the training images. Then, the unitary vectors X are obtained by getting the eigenvector matrix of G_t. This stage decides how many eigenvectors are to be used in the projection of data. To achieve this, the eigenvalues of the corresponding eigenvectors are arranged in a descending order, and a subset of the higher values is selected. Assuming d eigenvectors (with optimal projection axes $X_1, X_2, \ldots, X_d$) are selected, then how to achieve feature extraction and classification stages are explained in the next section.

4 KERNEL MAPPING ALONG ROW AND COLUMN DIRECTION

4.1 TWO-DIMENSIONAL KPCA

The main idea of using kernel function in PCA is that the data are first mapped into another space using a mapping function and then PCA is performed on the nonlinearly mapped data. 2DPCA is better than 1D PCA in terms of speed and accuracy. The idea of using kernel function in 2DPCA is to improve the accuracy of the system. With N input images, let A_i be the ith image, where $i = 1, 2, \ldots, N$, and A_i^j be the jth row of the matrix A_i, where $j = 1, 2, \ldots, n$. The nonlinear mapping is defined as follows:

$$\Phi(A_i) = \begin{bmatrix} \Phi\left(\left(A_i^1 \right)^{\mathrm{T}} \right)^{\mathrm{T}} \\ \vdots \\ \Phi\left(\left(A_i^n \right)^{\mathrm{T}} \right)^{\mathrm{T}} \end{bmatrix} \tag{7}$$

The total scatter matrix in kernel 2DPCA can be calculated as

$$G_i^{\Phi} = \sum_{i=1}^{N} \Phi(A_i) \Phi(A_i)^{\mathrm{T}} \tag{8}$$

Thus,

$$= \sum_{i=1}^{n} \begin{bmatrix} \Phi\left(\left(A_i^1 \right)^{\mathrm{T}} \right)^{\mathrm{T}} \\ \vdots \\ \Phi\left(\left(A_i^n \right)^{\mathrm{T}} \right)^{\mathrm{T}} \end{bmatrix} \left[\Phi\left(\left(A_i^1 \right)^{\mathrm{T}} \right), \ldots, \Phi\left(\left(A_i^n \right)^{\mathrm{T}} \right) \right]$$

$$G_i^{\Phi} = \sum_{N}^{i=1} \sum_{i=1}^{n} \Phi\left(\left(A_i^j\right)^{\mathrm{T}}\right) \Phi\left(\left(A_i^j\right)^{\mathrm{T}}\right)^{\mathrm{T}} \tag{9}$$

In kernel 2DPCA, after achieving $B_i = [Y_1^i, Y_1^i, \ldots, Y_d^i]$ and G_t^{Φ}, obtaining projecting axes and the projection and classification procedures are same as in 2DPCA.

4.2 KERNEL MAPPING IN ROW AND COLUMN DIRECTIONS AND 2DPCA

Equations (7)–(9) demonstrate how the kernel mapping is performed on the input data. Our argument here is that by applying this mapping in different directions (along row and column directions), we will end up having two different data having different dimensions. To further elaborate this, let us assume we have $m \times n$ input matrixes ($n > m$). By applying the kernel mapping function along the row direction (we have m rows meaning that there are m elements for the kernel matrix to be made of), the kernel matrix will be ($m \times m$). In this case, by applying kernel mapping, we reduce the number of input data and its dimension in kernel space which is ($n \times n$). However, if the kernel function is applied along column direction, the kernel matrix will be ($n \times n$). In this case, we have expanded the input data to a higher dimensional space and we have more information to analyze by 2DPCA. Figure 2 shows the detailed diagram of the kernel mapping and 2DPCA on the mapped data in two different directions. It is observed from the diagram that by applying the kernel function from row or column direction, the kernel matrix (K) is squared and with dimension of n or m.

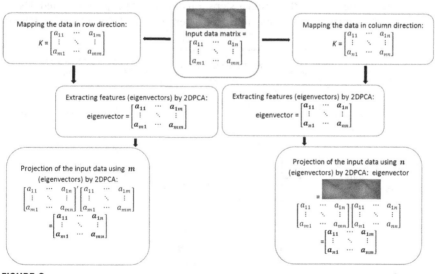

FIGURE 2

Flow diagram of kernel mapping along row and column direction and applying 2DPCA.

This argument is indispensable because the dimension of the data affects the output of the 2DPCA greatly. Having higher dimension and more information and features does not guarantee ending up more promising results and higher accuracies. Furthermore, the higher the dimension, the more time consuming the system is. On the other hand, there has to be a balance between the dimension of the data, the number of used features, and the algorithm that is used to analyze the data.

5 FINGER VEIN RECOGNITION ALGORITHM

Our proposed finger vein recognition algorithm is explained in this section. As it is shown in Figure 3, the algorithm consists of five steps; first step is to extract the region of interest (ROI). Second one is to normalize the images. Third step is to map the data into kernel space along the row and column directions which was explained in Section 4. In the fourth step, 2DPCA is applied on the data and features are extracted. Last step is to classify the data using Euclidian distance. The flow diagram of the proposed algorithm is indicated in Figure 3. All steps except for steps 3 and 4, which were explained in Section 4, are introduced in the succeeding part of this section.

5.1 ROI EXTRACTION

The unwanted black area around the images should be cropped as this area reduces the accuracy and is considered as nothing but noise. To crop images optimally, the used algorithm consists of three major steps. First of all, the edge is detected. Using the detected edges two horizontal lines are determined and the image is cropped

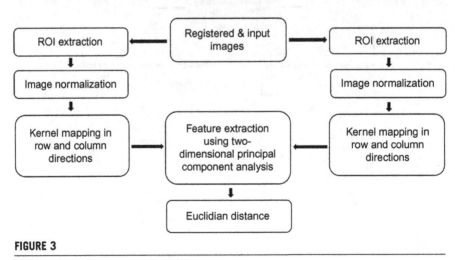

FIGURE 3

Flow diagram of the proposed algorithm.

horizontally according to the detected lines. Last but not least, the image is cropped vertically at 5% from the left border and 15% from the right border.

5.2 IMAGE NORMALIZATION

In order to achieve the highest accuracy in least time, images are normalized to smaller size after ROI extraction. It is obvious that the smaller the size, the faster the system is. However, if the size of the image is too small, it may cause too much loss of information as well. Therefore, there has to be a balance between size of the images and the accuracy of the system. Based on our experiments, when using 2DPCA to extract the features, the optimal size of finger vein images resulting in both least time consumption and highest accuracy is 20×60. Thus, all images are normalized into 20×60.

5.3 FEATURE EXTRACTION AND CLASSIFICATION METHOD

As it was mentioned before, Euclidian distance is used as a classifier in this system. Euclidian distance is a very fast method which, we believe, is appropriate for this system because after using kernel map and 2DPCA, the dimension of the data is reduced and therefore the Euclidian distance is sufficient to be used.

Given an image sample A and the optimal projection axes (selected eigenvectors, $X_1, X_2, \ldots, X_d$), the projection will be as follows:

$$Y_k = AX_k, \quad k - 1, 2, \ldots, d \qquad (10)$$

Using d axes to project the data onto, we will get d projected feature vectors $Y_1 Y_2, \ldots, Y_d$. These vectors are the principal component of the sample image A. Putting these vectors in the form of a matrix, we will get feature matrix of the image A, which is $m \times d$, $B = [Y_1, \ldots, Y_d]$.

Then, a nearest neighbor classifier is used to classify the data after transferring all images by 2DPCA and obtaining the feature matrix of them. Considering $B_i = [Y_1^i, Y_1^i, \ldots, Y_d^i]$ and $B_j = [Y_1^i, Y_1^i, \ldots, Y_d^i]$, the Euclidian distance between them is defined as follows:

$$d(B_i, B_j) = \sum_{k=1}^{d} \|Y_k^{(i)} - Y_k^{(j)}\|_2 \qquad (11)$$

6 EXPERIMENTAL RESULTS ON FINGER VEIN DATABASE

In this section, the experiments conducted on finger vein data are given and explained. Experimental results are explained in two subsections; column direction analysis in Section 6.1 and row direction analysis in Section 6.2. Our database consists of 10 samples for each of 100 individuals which results in a total number of 1000 images. In each different part of the experiments, three different types of training and testing were used. The size of image samples also varies as well as the number of testing and training. We used two different sizes ($[20 \times 60]$ and $[10 \times 20]$) in our experimental section. 2, 3, and 4 random selected images were used to train each time and, respectively, the remaining 8, 7, and 6 images to test. All implementations in each part were repeated as many times as the number of total eigenvectors.

6.1 EXPERIMENTAL SETUP-1

In this section, we explain the analysis with respect to the images with size of (20×60) for the sake of understanding. To analyze the system in column direction and get the output, we first restate that the images are in dimension of (20×60) meaning that if we map them in column direction, there will be 60 samples with the dimension of 20 to map. The output of such a mapping function will be a matrix with the dimension of (60×60). By applying 2DPCA on this matrix, there will be 60 eigenvectors extracted with the dimension of 20. In this step, there are 60 different dimensions which could be reduced using projection in 2DPCA meaning that there are 60 different projections using different number of eigenvectors. We conducted the algorithm 60 times in each of three different types (2, 3, and 4 samples to train and 8, 7, and 6 samples to test, respectively) of our implementation and calculated the accuracy rate in each point. The obtained results were then gathered and shown in Figure 4. As it was expected, by adding the number of samples for train, the accuracy goes up no matter which method to use. Another expectation was that by using more eigenvectors, the accuracy rate goes higher up to its optimized point, which here is almost near the dimension of 20. It is observed from Figure 4 that using 2, 3, and 4 images to train leads to the accuracy rate of around 90%, 95%, and 97%, respectively. Another prime issue is that the time consumed for this experiment is much more than the next as there are 60 and 20 eigenvectors in column direction mapping. It is also observed that by making the image size smaller the accuracy rate drops. It is because by making the size of images smaller, some information are lost.

6.2 EXPERIMENTAL SETUP-2

To analyze the system in row direction, the input images were used in a way that each image consists of 20 samples with the dimension of 60 to map. The output of such a mapping function will be a (20×20) matrix. By applying 2DPCA on this matrix, there will be 20 eigenvectors extracted with the dimension of 20. In this step, there are 20 different dimensions which could be reduced using projection in 2DPCA meaning that there are 20 projection manners using different number of eigenvectors. Figure 5 demonstrates the accuracy rate of the experiments along the row direction. Implementing this method using 2, 3, and 4 images to train results to the accuracy rate of around 95%, 97%, and 99%, respectively, which is clearly higher than the column direction. Mapping the input data along the row not only achieves higher

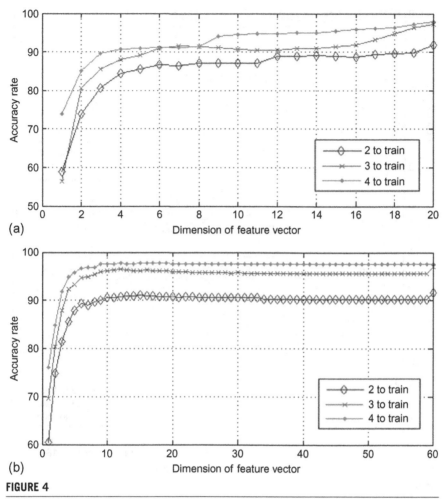

FIGURE 4

Accuracy rates obtained using K2DPCA in column direction on finger vein database:
(a) (10×20) sample size and (b) (20×60) sample size.

accuracy but also has less consumption of time as there are only 20 dimensions of
data to be reduced. Same as the previous experimental setup, the overall accuracy
rate in (10×20) is not as high as that of (20×60). However, in row direction experiments, in both cases $((10 \times 20)$ and (20×60) sample sizes), the accuracy rate goes
upper than that of column direction method with less time-consumption duration.

In this part, we give a summary of the whole experiments and their corresponding
results for the sake of a better comparison. We have chosen the highest accuracies of
each method in all implementations and their corresponding dimension of feature

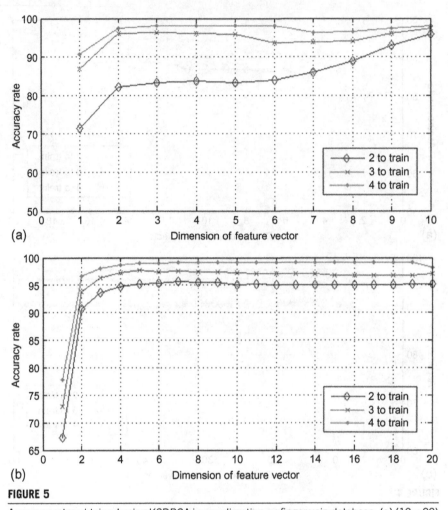

FIGURE 5

Accuracy rates obtained using K2DPCA in row direction on finger vein database: (a) (10 × 20) sample size and (b) (20 × 60) sample size.

vector. All the mentioned information are indicated in Table 1 in addition to the duration of time each algorithm consumed to analyze the data. As Table 1 shows, the maximum accuracy of the row direction analysis is higher than that of column direction in all the different experiments. Furthermore, it is observed that not only it leads to higher accuracy, but also its dimension of feature vector is much less than that of column method in all implementations implying that the row direction method can be even faster than the column direction method in real-time system as it reaches the higher accuracy using less feature vectors.

Table 1 Comparison of the Proposed Algorithm in Row and Column Direction

Method (20×60)	Images to Train	Max Accuracy (%)	Feature Vector No	Duration of Experiments (s)	Method (10×20)	Images to Train	Max Accuracy (%)	Feature Vector No	Duration of Experiments (s)
Column direction analysis	2	91.63	60	1324.8372	Column direction analysis	2	91.55	20	78.8433
	3	97	60	1676.553		3	95.14	20	103.7921
	4	97.83	15	1805.3797		4	97.83	20	120.3972
Row direction analysis	2	95.75	7	223.73	Row direction analysis	2	95.75	10	33.3856
	3	97.71	5	311.2961		3	96.14	2	39.109
	4	99.17	7	318.9148		4	98.17	3	50.4346

7 CONCLUSION

In this paper, we have proposed a new method to enhance the performance of finger vein recognition and analyzed two different aspects of applying it in order to determine the most appropriate one. Our algorithm uses kernel mapping in two different directions to transfer the input data to another space where applying 2DPCA merits the final output of the system. We also used Euclidian distance as classifier in the last step of the algorithm. Extensive experiments were conducted on our database using three different numbers of images for training. Results demonstrate that mapping the data in row direction reaches both having higher accuracy and consuming less time compared to the column direction method meaning that the proposed method has the highest accuracy when mapping the data along the row direction.

REFERENCES

[1] Jain AK, Ross A, Prabhakar S. An introduction to biometric recognition. IEEE T Circuit Syst 2004;14(1):4–20.

[2] Schouten B, Jacobs B. Biometrics and their use in e-passports. Image Vis Comput 2009;27(3):305–12.

[3] Beng TS, Rosdi BA. Finger-vein identification using pattern map and principal component analysis, In: 2011 IEEE international conference signal image processing applications, November; 2011. p. 530–4.

[4] Kumar A, Zhou Y. Human identification using finger images. IEEE T Image Process 2012;21(4):2228–44.

[5] Zhao W, et al. Face recognition: A literature survey. Acm Computing Surveys (CSUR) 2003;35(4):399–458.

[6] Chellapa SR, Wilson CL, Sirohey S. Human and machine recognition of faces: a survey. Proc IEEE 1995;83:705–40.

[7] Yang G, Xi X, Yin Y. Finger vein recognition based on a personalized best bit map. Sensors (Basel) 2012;12(2):1738–57.

[8] Song W, Kim T, Kim HC, Choi JH, Kong H-J, Lee S-R. A finger-vein verification system using mean curvature. Pattern Recogn Lett 2011;32(11):1541–7.

[9] Yang J, Shi Y, Yang J. Personal identification based on finger-vein features. Comput Hum Behav 2011;27(5):1565–70.

[10] Wu J-D, Ye S-H. Driver identification using finger-vein patterns with radon transform and neural network. Expert Syst Appl 2009;36(3):5793–9.

[11] Wu J-D, Liu C-T. Finger-vein pattern identification using principal component analysis and the neural network technique. Expert Syst Appl 2011;38(5):5423–7.

[12] Bishop CM. Pattern recognition and machine learning. Vol. 1. New York: Springer, 2006.

[13] Kim KI, Jung K, Kim HJ. Face recognition using kernel principal component analysis. Signal Process 2002;9(2):40–2.

[14] Ebied RM. Feature extraction using PCA and Kernel-PCA for face recognition. Int Conf Inform Syst 2012;8:72–7.

[15] Hu P, Yang A. Indefinite Kernel entropy component analysis. Sci Tech 2010;3:0–3.

[16] Jenssen R. Kernel entropy component analysis. IEEE Trans Pattern Anal Mach Intell May 2010;32(5):847–60.

[17] Shekar BH, Sharmila Kumari M, Mestetskiy LM, Dyshkant NF. Face recognition using kernel entropy component analysis. Neurocomputing 2011;74(6):1053–7.

[18] Shawe-Taylor J, Cristianini N. Kernel methods for pattern analysis. New York, NY: Cambridge University Press; 2004, p. 462.

[19] Damavandinejadmonfared S, Mobarakeh AK, Suandi SA, Rosdi BA. Evaluate and determine the most appropriate method to identify finger vein. Procedia Eng 2012;41:516–21.

[20] Damavandinejadmonfared S. Kernel entropy component analysis using local mean-based k-nearest centroid neighbour (LMKNCN) as a classifier for face recognition in video surveillance camera systems, In: IEEE international conference on intelligent computer communication and processing (ICCP); 2012. p. 253–6.

[21] Damavandinejadmonfared S. Finger vein recognition using linear Kernel entropy component analysis, In: IEEE international conference on intelligent computer communication and processing (ICCP); 2012. p. 249–52.

[22] Damavandinejadmonfared S, Varadharajan V. Effective Kernel mapping for one-dimensional principal component analysis in finger vein recognition, In: The 2014 international conference on image processing, computer vision, and pattern recognition; 2014.

[23] Hsieh P-C, Tung P-C. A novel hybrid approach based on sub-pattern technique and whitened PCA for face recognition. Pattern Recogn 2009;42(5):978–84.

[24] Yang L. A human face recognition method by improved modular 2DPCA, In: IT in Medicine and Education (ITME), 2011 international symposium, vol. 2; 2011. p. 7–11.

[25] Nhat VDM, Lee S. Kernel-based 2DPCA for face recognition, In: 2007 IEEE international symposium on signal processing and information technology, December; 2007. p. 35–9.

[26] Yu C, Qing H, Zhang L. K2DPCA plus 2DPCA: an efficient approach for appearance based object recognition, In: 2009 3rd international conference on bioinformatics and biomedical engineering, June; 2009. p. 1–4.

[27] Damavandinejadmonfared S, Varadharajan V. Finger vein recognition in row and column directions using two dimensional Kernel principal component analysis, In: The 2014 international conference on image processing, computer vision, and pattern recognition; 2014.

A local feature-based facial expression recognition system from depth video

26

Md. Zia Uddin

Department of Computer Education, Sungkyunkwan University, Seoul, Republic of Korea

1 INTRODUCTION

Facial expression recognition (FER) provides machines a way of sensing emotions that can be considered one of the mostly used artificial intelligence and pattern analysis applications [1–10]. In case of extracting peoples' expression images through Red Green Blue (RGB) cameras, most of the FER works used principal component analysis (PCA), which is really well known for dimension reduction and used in many earlier works. In Padgett and Cottrell [3], PCA was used to recognize facial action units (FAUs) from the facial expression images. In Donato et al. [5] as well as Ekman and Priesen [6], PCA was used for FER with the facial action coding system.

Very recently, independent component analysis (ICA) has been extensively utilized for FER based on local face image features [5,10–21]. In Bartlett et al. [14], the authors used ICA to extract local features and then classified several facial expressions. In Chao-Fa and Shin [15], ICA was used to recognize the FAUs. Besides ICA, local binary patterns (LBP) has been used lately for FER [22–24]. The main property of LBP features is their tolerance against illumination changes as well as their computational simplicity. Later on, LBP was improved by focusing on face pixel's gradient information and named as local directional pattern (LDP) to represent local face features [25]. As like as LBP, LDP features also have the tolerance against illumination changes but they represent much robust features than LBP due to considering the gradient information for each pixel as aforementioned [25].

Thus, LDP can be considered to be a robust approach and hence can be adopted for FER. To make LDP facial expression features more robust, linear discriminant analysis (LDA) can be applied as LDA is a strong method to be used to obtain good discrimination among the face images from different expressions by considering linear feature spaces. Hidden Markov model (HMM) is considered to be a robust tool to model and decode time-sequential events [21,26–28]. Hence, HMM seems an appropriate choice to train and recognize features of different facial expressions for FER.

For capturing face images, RGB cameras are used most widely but the faces captured through a RGB camera cannot provide the depth of the pixels based on the far and near parts of human face in the facial expression video where the depth information can be considered to contribute more to extract efficient features to describe the expression more strongly. Hence, depth videos should allow one to come up with more efficient person independent FER.

In this chapter, a novel FER approach is proposed using LDP, PCA, LDA, and HMM. Local LDP features are first extracted from the facial expression images and further extended by PCA and LDA. These robust features are then converted into discrete symbols using vector quantization and then the symbols are used to model discrete HMMs of different expressions. To compare the performance of the proposed approach, different comparison studies have been conducted such as PCA, PCA-LDA, ICA, and ICA-LDA as feature extractor in combination with HMM. The experimental results show that the proposed method shows superiority over the conventional approaches.

2 DEPTH IMAGE PREPROCESSING

The images of different expressions are captured by a depth camera [29] where the camera generates RGB and distance information (i.e., depth) simultaneously for the objects captured by the camera. The depth video represents the range of every pixel in the scene as a gray level intensity (i.e., the longer ranged pixels have darker and shorter ones brighter values or vice versa). Figure 1 shows the basic steps of proposed FER system.

Figure 2(a) represents a depth image from a surprise expression. It can be noticed that in the depth image, the higher pixel value represents the near (e.g., nose) and the lower (e.g., eyes) the far distance. The pseudo-color image corresponding to the depth image in Figure 2(b) also indicates the significant differences among different face portions where the color intensities. Figure 3(a)–(c) shows five generalized depth faces from a happy, surprise, and disgust expressions, respectively.

3 FEATURE EXTRACTION

The feature extraction of the proposed approach consists of three fundamental stages: (1) LDP is performed first on the depth faces of the facial expression videos, (2) PCA is applied on the LDP features for dimensionality reduction, and (3) LDA is then applied to compress the same facial expression images as close as possible and to separate the different expression class images as far as possible.

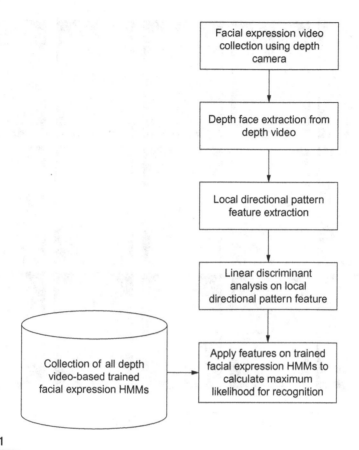

FIGURE 1

Basic steps involved in the proposed facial expression recognition system.

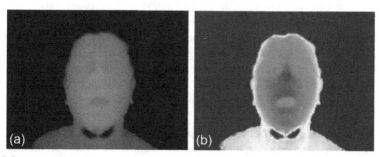

FIGURE 2

(a) A depth image and (b) corresponding pseudo color image of a surprise image.

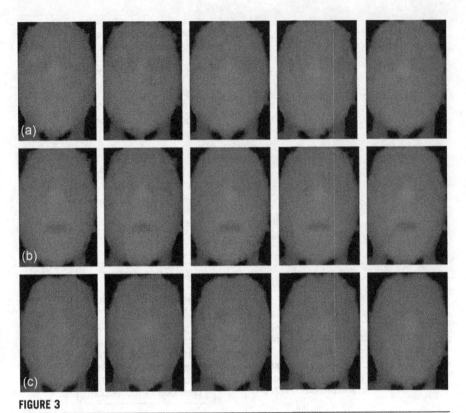

FIGURE 3

A sequential depth facial expression images of (a) happy, (b) surprise, and (c) disgust.

3.1 LDP FEATURES

The LDP assigns an 8-bit binary code to each pixel of an input depth image. This pattern is then calculated by comparing the relative edge response values of a pixel in eight different directions. Kirsch, Prewitt, and Sobel edge detector are some of the different representative edge detectors that can be used. Amongst which, the Kirsch edge detector [20] detects the edges more accurately than the others as it considers all eight neighbors. Given a central pixel in the image, the eight directional edge response values $\{m_k\}$, $k=0, 1, \ldots, 7$ are computed by Kirsch masks M_k in eight different orientations centered on its position [18]. Figure 4 shows these masks.

The presence of a corner or an edge represents high response values in some particular directions and therefore, it is interesting to know the p most prominent directions in order to generate the LDP. Here, the top-p directional bit responses b_k are set to 1. The remaining bits of 8-bit LDP pattern are set to 0. Finally, the LDP code

$$\begin{bmatrix} -3 & -3 & 5 \\ -3 & 0 & 5 \\ -3 & -3 & 5 \end{bmatrix} \qquad \begin{bmatrix} -3 & 5 & 5 \\ -3 & 0 & 5 \\ -3 & -3 & -3 \end{bmatrix} \qquad \begin{bmatrix} 5 & 5 & 5 \\ -3 & 0 & -3 \\ -3 & -3 & -3 \end{bmatrix} \qquad \begin{bmatrix} 5 & 5 & -3 \\ 5 & 0 & -3 \\ -3 & -3 & -3 \end{bmatrix}$$

East direction M_0 North east direction M_1 North direction M_2 North west direction M_3

$$\begin{bmatrix} 5 & -3 & -3 \\ 5 & 0 & -3 \\ 5 & 3 & -3 \end{bmatrix} \qquad \begin{bmatrix} -3 & -3 & -3 \\ 5 & 0 & -3 \\ 5 & 5 & -3 \end{bmatrix} \qquad \begin{bmatrix} -3 & -3 & -3 \\ -3 & 0 & -3 \\ 5 & 5 & 5 \end{bmatrix} \qquad \begin{bmatrix} -3 & -3 & -3 \\ -3 & 0 & 5 \\ -3 & 5 & 5 \end{bmatrix}$$

west direction M_4 South west direction M_5 South direction M_6 South east direction M_7

FIGURE 4

Kirsch edge masks in eight directions.

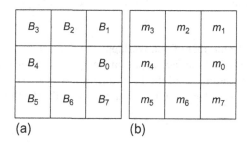

(a)   (b)

FIGURE 5

(a) Edge response to eight directions and (b) LDP binary bit positions.

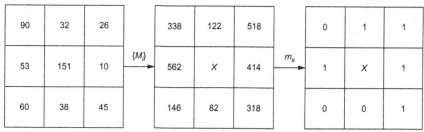

Local directional pattern binary = 10011011
Local directional pattern decimal = 155

FIGURE 6

LDP code.

is derived in Equation (1). Figure 5 shows the mask response as well as LDP bit positions and Figure 6 an exemplary LDP code considering five top positions, that is, $p = 5$.

$$\mathrm{LDP}_p = \sum_{k=0}^{7} B_k \left(m_k - m_p \right) \times 2^k, \quad B_k(a) = \begin{cases} 1 & a \geq 0 \\ 0 & a < 0 \end{cases} \tag{1}$$

where m_p is the pth most significant directional response.

Thus, an image is transformed to the LDP map using LDP code. The image textual feature is presented by the histogram of the LDP map of which the qth bin can be defined as

$$T_q = \sum_{x,y} I\{\text{LDP}(x, y) = q\}, \quad q = 0, 1, \ldots n - 1, \tag{2}$$

where n is the number of the LDP histogram bins (normally $n = 256$) for an image I. Then, the histogram of the LDP map is presented as

$$H = (T_0, T_1, \ldots, T_{n-1}). \tag{3}$$

To describe the LDP features, a depth silhouette image is divided into nonoverlapping rectangle regions and the histogram is computed for each region. Furthermore, the whole LDP feature F is expressed as a concatenated sequence of histograms

$$F = (H^1, H^2, \ldots, H^s), \tag{4}$$

where s represents the number of nonoverlapped regions in the image. After analyzing the LDP features of all the face depth images, there are some positions from all the positions corresponding to all the face images have values >0 and hence these positions can be ignored. Thus, the LDP features from the depth faces can be represented as D.

3.2 PCA ON LDP FEATURES

PCA is very popular method to be used for data dimension reduction. PCA is a subspace projection method which transforms the high-dimensional space to a reduced space maintaining the maximum variability. The principal components of the covariance data matrix Y of the LDP features D can be calculated as

$$E^T (YY^T) E = \lambda, \tag{5}$$

where λ represents the eigenvalue matrix and P the eigenvector matrix. The eigenvector associated with the top eigenvalue means the axis of maximum variance and the next one with the second largest eigenvalue indicates the axis of second largest variance and so on. Thus, m number of eigenvectors are chosen according to the highest eigenvalues for projection of LDP features. The PCA feature space projections V of LDP features can be represented as

$$F = \text{DP}_m. \tag{6}$$

3.3 LDA ON PCA FEATURES

To obtain more robust features, LDA is performed on the PCA feature vectors F. Basically, LDA is based on class specific information which maximizes the ratio of the within, Q_w and between, Q_b scatter matrix. The optimal discrimination matrix W_{LDA} is chosen from the maximization of ratio of the determinant of the between and within class scatter matrix as

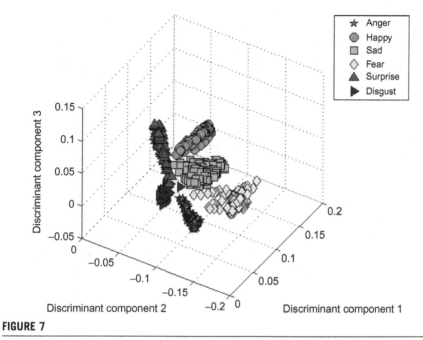

FIGURE 7

3D plot of LDP-PCA-LDA features of depth faces from six expressions.

$$W_{\mathrm{LDA}} = \arg \max_{\mathrm{LDA}} \frac{|W^\mathrm{T} Q_b W|}{|W^\mathrm{T} Q_w W|}, \tag{7}$$

where W_{LDA} is the discriminant feature space. Thus, the LDP-LDA feature vectors of facial expression images can be obtained as follows:

$$J = F W_{\mathrm{LDA}}^\mathrm{T}. \tag{8}$$

Figure 7 shows an exemplar plot of 3D LDA representation of the LDP-PCA features of all the facial expression depth images that shows a good separation among the representation of the depth faces of different classes.

3.4 HMM FOR EXPRESSION MODELING AND RECOGNITION

To decode the depth information-based time-sequential facial expression features, discrete HMMs are employed. HMMs have been applied extensively to solve a large number of complex problems in various applications such as speech recognition [30].

An HMM is a collection of states where each state is characterized by transition and symbol observation probabilities. A basic HMM can be expressed as $H = \{S, \pi, R, B\}$ where S denotes possible states, π the initial probability of the states, R the transition probability matrix between hidden states, and B observation symbols' probability from every state. If the number of activities is N then there will be a

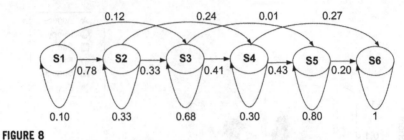

FIGURE 8

A HMM transition probabilities for sad expression after training.

dictionary $(H_1, H_2, \ldots, H_N)$ of N trained models. We used the Baum-Welch algorithm for HMM parameter estimation as applied in [21]. Figure 8 shows the structure and transition probabilities of a sad HMM after training.

To test a facial expression video for recognition, the obtained observation sequence O from the corresponding depth image sequence is used to determine the proper model by highest likelihood L computation of all N trained expression HMMs as follows:

$$L = \arg \ \max_{k=1}^{N} (P(O|H_k)). \tag{9}$$

4 EXPERIMENTS AND RESULTS

The FER database was built for six expressions: namely Surprise, Sad, Happy, Disgust, Anger, and Fear. Each expression video clip was of variable length and each expression in each video starts and ends with neutral expression. A total of 20 sequences from each expression were used to build the feature space. To train and test each facial expression model, 20 and 40 image sequences were applied, respectively.

The average recognition rate using PCA on depth faces is 62.50% as shown in Table 1. Then, we applied LDA on PCA features and obtained 65.83% average

Table 1 FER Confusion Matrix Using Depth Faces with PCA

Expression	Anger	Happy	Sad	Surprise	Fear	Disgust
Anger	**50%**	0	20	0	15	15
Happy	5	**50**	10	10	20	10
Sad	0	17.5	**70**	12.50	0	0
Surprise	0	0	0	**80**	15	5
Fear	0	5	25	10	**60**	0
Disgust	0	5	30	0	0	**65**
Average			**62.50**			

Bold values indicate correct expression recognition and others indicate incorrect recognition.

recognition rate as shown in Table 2. As PCA-based global features showed poor recognition performance, we tried ICA-based local features for FER and obtained 83.33% average recognition rate as reported in Table 3. To improve ICA features, we applied LDA on the ICA features and as shown in Table 4, the average recognition rate utilizing ICA representation on the depth facial expression images is 83.50%, which is higher than that of depth face-based FER applying PCA-based features.

Table 2 FER Confusion Matrix Using Depth Faces with PCA-LDA

Expression	Anger	Happy	Sad	Surprise	Fear	Disgust
Anger	**50%**	0	20	0	15	15
Happy	0	**55**	10	10	20	10
Sad	0	15	**72.50**	12.50	0	0
Surprise	0	0	0	**85**	10	5
Fear	0	5	25	5	**65**	0
Disgust	0	2.50	30	0	0	**67.50**
Average			**65.83**			

Bold values indicate correct expression recognition and others indicate incorrect recognition.

Table 3 FER Confusion Matrix Using Depth Faces with ICA

Expression	Anger	Happy	Sad	Surprise	Fear	Disgust
Anger	**80%**	0	10	0	0	10
Happy	0	**82.50**	10	7.25	0	0
Sad	0	0	**85**	15	0	0
Surprise	0	0	0	**85**	15	0
Fear	0	5	15	0	**85**	0
Disgust	0	0	15	2.50	0	**82.50**
Average			**83.33**			

Bold values indicate correct expression recognition and others indicate incorrect recognition.

Table 4 FER Confusion Matrix Using Depth Faces with ICA-LDA

Expression	Anger	Happy	Sad	Surprise	Fear	Disgust
Anger	**85%**	0	5	0	0	10
Happy	0	**85**	10	5	0	0
Sad	0	0	**85**	15	0	0
Surprise	0	0	0	**87.50**	12.50	0
Fear	0	2.50	15	0	**87.50**	0
Disgust	0	0	15	0	0	**85**
Average			**85.83**			

Bold values indicate correct expression recognition and others indicate incorrect recognition.

Then, LBP was tried on the same database that achieved the average recognition rate of 89.20% as shown in Table 5. Furthermore, LDP was employed and achieved the better recognition rate than LBP, that is, 90.83% as shown in Table 6. Finally, LDP-PCA-LDA was applied with HMM that showed superiority over the other feature extraction methods achieving the highest recognition rate (i.e., 98.33%) as shown in Table 7. Figure 9 shows FER performances using different approaches where LDP-PCA-LDA shows its superiority.

Table 5 FER Confusion Matrix Using Depth Faces with LBP

Expression	Anger	Happy	Sad	Surprise	Fear	Disgust
Anger	**87.50%**	0	12.50	0	0	0
Happy	10	**90**	0	0	0	0
Sad	0	0	**90**	0	10	0
Surprise	7.50	0	0	**92.50**	0	0
Fear	0	5	10	0	**85**	0
Disgust	0	0	10	0	0	**90**
Average			89.17			

Bold values indicate correct expression recognition and others indicate incorrect recognition.

Table 6 FER Confusion Matrix Using Depth Faces with LDP

Expression	Anger	Happy	Sad	Surprise	Fear	Disgust
Anger	**90%**	0	10	0	0	0
Happy	10	**90**	0	0	0	0
Sad	0	0	**92.50**	0	7.50	0
Surprise	7.50	0	0	**92.50**	0	0
Fear	0	5	7.50	0	**87.50**	0
Disgust	0	0	7.50	0	0	**92.50**
Average			90.83			

Bold values indicate correct expression recognition and others indicate incorrect recognition.

Table 7 FER Confusion Matrix Using Depth Faces with LDP-PCA-LDA

Expression	Anger	Happy	Sad	Surprise	Fear	Disgust
Anger	**97.50%**	0	2.50	0	0	0
Happy	2.50	**97.50**	0	0	0	0
Sad	0	0	**97.50**	2.50	0	0
Surprise	0	0	0	**100**	0	0
Fear	0	0	2.50	0	**97.50**	0
Disgust	0	0	0	0	0	**100**
Average			98.33			

Bold values indicate correct expression recognition and others indicate incorrect recognition.

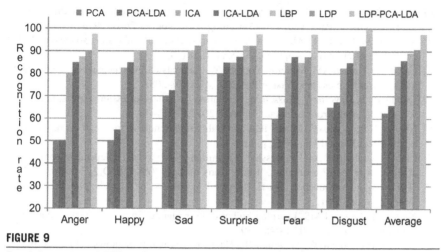

FIGURE 9

Depth image-based FER performances using different approaches.

5 CONCLUDING REMARKS

A depth video-based robust FER system has been proposed in this work using LDP-PCA-LDA features for facial expression feature extraction and HMM for recognition. The proposed method was compared with other traditional approaches and the recognition performance showed its superiority over others. However, the proposed system can be implemented in many systems such as smart home applications.

ACKNOWLEDGEMENT

This work was supported by Faculty Research Fund, Sungkyunkwan University, 2013.

REFERENCES

[1] Uddin MZ, Jehad Sarkar AM. A facial expression recognition system from depth video, In: Proc. 2014 international conference on image processing, computer vision, & pattern recognition (IPCV'14), July 21–24, Las Vegas; 2014.

[2] Kim D-S, Jeon I-J, Lee S-Y, Rhee P-K, Chung D-J. Embedded face recognition based on fast genetic algorithm for intelligent digital photography. IEEE Trans Consum Electron 2006;52(3):726–34.

[3] Padgett C, Cottrell G. Representation face images for emotion classification. Advances in neural information processing systems, vol. 9. Cambridge, MA: MIT Press; 1997.

[4] Mitra S, Acharya T. Gesture recognition: a survey. IEEE Trans Syst Man Cybern C Appl Rev 2007;37(3):311–24.

[5] Donato G, Bartlett MS, Hagar JC, Ekman P, Sejnowski TJ. Classifying facial actions. IEEE Trans Pattern Anal Mach Intell 1999;21(10):974–89.

[6] Ekman P, Priesen WV. Facial action coding system: a technique for the measurement of facial movement. Palo Alto, CA: Consulting Psychologists Press; 1978.

[7] Meulders M, Boeck PD, Mechelen IV, Gelman A. Probabilistic feature analysis of facial perception of emotions. Appl Stat 2005;54(4):781–93.

[8] Calder AJ, Burton AM, Miller P, Young AW, Akamatsu S. A principal component analysis of facial expressions. Vision Res 2001;41:1179–208.

[9] Dubuisson S, Davoine F, Masson M. A solution for facial expression representation and recognition. Sign Process Image Commun 2002;17:657–73.

[10] Buciu I, Kotropoulos C, Pitas I. ICA and Gabor representation for facial expression recognition, In: Proc. IEEE; 2003. p. 855–8.

[11] Chen F, Kotani K. Facial expression recognition by supervised independent component analysis using MAP estimation. IEICE Trans Inf Syst 2008;E91-D(2):341–50.

[12] Hyvarinen A, Karhunen J, Oja E. Independent component analysis. New York: John Wiley & Sons; 2001.

[13] Karklin Y, Lewicki MS. Learning higher-order structures in natural images. Network: Comput Neural Syst 2003;14:483–99.

[14] Bartlett MS, Donato G, Movellan JR, Hager JC, Ekman P, Sejnowski TJ. Face image analysis for expression measurement and detection of deceit, In: Proc. sixth joint symposium on neural computation; 1999. p. 8–15.

[15] Chao-Fa C, Shin FY. Recognizing facial action units using independent component analysis and support vector machine. Pattern Recognit 2006;39:1795–8.

[16] Calder AJ, Young AW, Keane J. Configural information in facial expression perception. J Exp Psychol Hum Percept Perform 2000;26(2):527–51.

[17] Lyons MJ, Akamatsu S, Kamachi M, Gyoba J. Coding facial expressions with Gabor wavelets, In: Proc. third IEEE international conference on automatic face and gesture recognition; 1998. p. 200–5.

[18] Bartlett MS, Movellan JR, Sejnowski TJ. Face recognition by independent component analysis. IEEE Trans Neural Netw 2002;13(6):1450–64.

[19] Liu C. Enhanced independent component analysis and its application to content based face image retrieval. IEEE Trans Syst Man Cybern B Cybern 2004;34(2):1117–27.

[20] Phillips PJ, Wechsler H, Huang J, Rauss P. The FERET database and evaluation procedure for face-recognition algorithms. Image Vis Comput 1998;16:295–306.

[21] Uddin MZ, Lee JJ, Kim T-S. An enhanced independent component-based human facial expression recognition from video. IEEE Trans Consum Electr 2009;55(4):2216–24.

[22] Ojala T, Pietikäinen M, Mäenpää T. Multiresolution gray scale and rotation invariant texture analysis with local binary patterns. IEEE Trans Pattern Anal Mach Intell 2002;24:971–87.

[23] Shan C, Gong S, McOwan P. Robust facial expression recognition using local binary patterns, In: Proc. IEEE international conference on image processing (ICIP); 2005. p. 370–3.

[24] Shan C, Gong S, McOwan P. Facial expression recognition based on local binary patterns: a comprehensive study. Image Vis Comput 2009;27:803–16.

[25] Jabid T, Kabir MH, Chae O. Local directional pattern (LDP): a robust image descriptor for object recognition, In: Proc. IEEE advanced video and signal based surveillance (AVSS); 2010. p. 482–7.

[26] Zhu Y, De Silva LC, Ko CC. Using moment invariants and HMM in facial expression recognition. Pattern Recognit Lett 2002;23(1-3):83–91.

[27] Cohen I, Sebe N, Garg A, Chen LS, Huang TS. Facial expression recognition from video sequences: temporal and static modeling. Comput Vis Image Underst 2003;91:160–87.

[28] Aleksic PS, Katsaggelos AK. Automatic facial expression recognition using facial animation parameters and multistream HMMs. IEEE Trans Inform Sec 2006;1:3–11.

[29] Iddan GJ, Yahav G. 3D imaging in the studio (and elsewhere...). Proc. SPIE 2001;4298:48–55.

[30] Rabiner LR. A tutorial on hidden markov modes and selected application in speech recognition. Proc. IEEE 1989;77:257–86.

Automatic classification of protein crystal images

27

Madhav Sigdel[1], Madhu S. Sigdel[1], İmren Dinç[1], Semih Dinç[1], Marc L. Pusey[2], Ramazan S. Aygün[1]

[1]*DataMedia Research Lab, Computer Science Department, University of Alabama Huntsville, Huntsville, AL, USA*
[2]*iXpressGenes Inc., Huntsville, AL, USA*

1 INTRODUCTION

Protein crystallization is the process for formation of protein crystals. Success of protein crystallization is dependent on several factors such as protein concentration, type of precipitant, crystallization methods, etc. Therefore, thousands of crystallization trials with different crystallization conditions are required for successful crystallization [1]. High throughput systems have been developed in recent years trying to identify the best conditions to crystallize proteins [1]. Imaging techniques are used to monitor the progress of crystallization. The crystallization trials are scanned periodically to determine the state change or the possibility of forming crystals. With a large number of images being captured, it is necessary to have a reliable classification system to distinguish the crystallization states each image belongs to. The main goal is to discard the unsuccessful trials, identify the successful trials, and possibly identify the trials which could be helpful. The main interest for crystallographers is the formation of large 3D crystals suitable for X-ray diffraction. Other crystal structures are also important as the crystallization conditions can be optimized to get better crystals. Therefore, it is necessary to have a reliable system that distinguishes between different types of crystals according to the shapes and sizes.

Many research studies have been done to distinguish crystallization trial images according to the presence or absence of crystals [2–6]. In our previous work [7], we presented classification of crystallization trials into three categories (non-crystals, likely-leads and crystals). Saitoh et al. [8] proposed crystallization into five categories (clear drop, creamy precipitate, granulated precipitate, amorphous state precipitate, and crystal) and Spraggon et al. [9] described classification into six categories (experimental mistake, clear drop, homogeneous precipitant, inhomogeneous precipitant, micro-crystals, and crystals). Likewise, Cumba et al. [10] classified crystallization trials into six basic categories (phase separation, precipitate, skin effect, crystal, junk, and unsure). In all these studies, the objective of the classification is

421

to identify the different phases of crystallization. In other words, classification of protein crystal images according to the shapes and sizes of crystals has not been the main focus of the previous other work.

For feature extraction, a variety of image processing techniques have been proposed. Cumba et al. [2], Saitoh et al. [11], and Zhu et al. [12] used a combination of geometric and texture features as the input to their classifier. Saitoh et al. [8] used global texture features as well as features from local parts in the image and features from differential images. Cumba et al. [10] extracted several features such as basic statistics, energy, Euler numbers, Radon-Laplacian features, Sobel-edge features, micro-crystal features, and GLCM features to obtain a large feature vector. We presented classification using region features and edge features in Ref. [13]. Increasing the number of features may not necessarily improve the accuracy. Moreover, it may slow down the classification process. Therefore, finding a minimal set of useful image features for classification is important.

This work introduces our technique for automatic classification of trial images consisting of crystals. Our focus is on classifying crystallization trial images according to the types of protein crystals present in the images. Our previous study [13] attempted to classify trial images according to the types of crystals (needle crystals, small crystals, large crystals, other crystals). This work extends our earlier work [13] on crystallization trials classification. The main objective is to improve the classification accuracy with new additional image features and using an alternate classification technique. Our feature extraction includes extracting edge related features from Canny edge image, extracting blob related features from multiple binary images, and extracting line features using Hough transform. The images are classified into four categories: needles, small crystals, large crystals, and other crystals. For the decision model, we investigate random forest classifier in addition to decision tree classifier proposed in Ref. [13].

This chapter is arranged as follows. The following section describes the image categories for the classification problem considered in this paper. Section 3 provides the system overview. Section 4 describes the image processing and feature extraction steps used in our research. Experimental results and discussion are provided in Section 5. The last section concludes the chapter with future work.

2 IMAGE CATEGORIES

The simplest classification of the crystallization trials distinguishes between the non-crystals (trial images not containing crystals) and crystals (images having crystals). In this study, we are interested in developing a system to classify different crystal types. We consider four image categories (needle crystals, small crystals, large crystals, and other crystals) for protein crystallization images consisting of crystals. Here description of each category is provided:

Needle crystals: Needle crystals have pointed edges and appear as needles. These crystals can appear alone or as a cluster in the images. The overlapping of multiple needle crystals on top of each other makes it difficult to get the correct crystal structure for these images. Figure 1 (a-c) show some sample crystal images under this category.

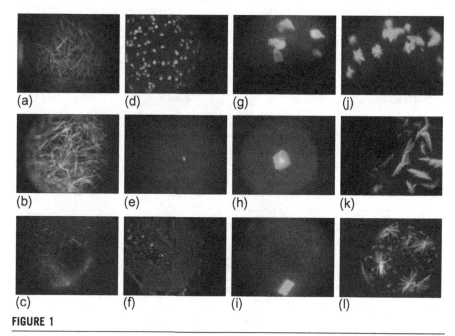

FIGURE 1

Sample protein crystallization images: (a-c) needles, (d-f) small crystals, (g-i) large crystals, and (j-l) other crystals.

Small crystals: This category contains small-sized crystals. These crystals can have two- or three-dimensional shapes. These crystals can also appear alone or as a cluster in the images. Because of their small size, it is difficult to visualize the geometric shapes expected in crystals. Besides, the crystals may be blurred because of focusing problems. Figure 1 (d-f) provide some sample images under this category.

Large crystals: This category includes images with large crystals with quadrangle (two- or three-) shapes. Depending on the orientation of protein crystals in the solution, more than one surface may be visible in some images. Figure 1 (g-i) show some sample images under this category.

Other crystals: The images in this category may be a combination of needles, plates, and other types of crystals. We can observe high intensity regions without proper geometric shapes expected in a crystal. This can be due to focusing problems. Some representative images are shown in Figure 1 (j-l).

3 SYSTEM OVERVIEW

The images of crystallization trials are collected using Crystal X2 software from iXpressGenes, Inc. The protein solutions are labeled with trace levels (<1%) of fluorescent dye. Green light is used as the flourescence excitation source while collecting the images [7]. Figure 2 shows the system diagram of the crystallization trials to classify systems. We first down-sample the images by eightfold from 2560×1920 to 320×240

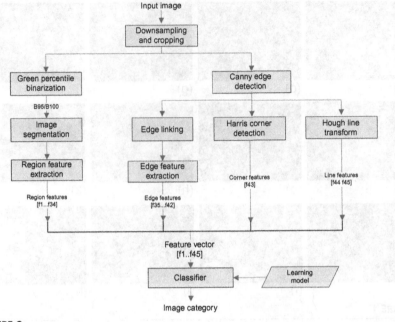

FIGURE 2

System diagram.

and crop 10 pixels at the borders from each side. This reduction enables feature extraction faster without losing necessary details for feature extraction. The downsampled image is input to the image binarization technique. Image segmentation is performed on the binary images, and region features are extracted. Likewise, Canny edge detection [14] is applied on the image. The Canny edge image is used to extract edge features, Harris corner [15] features and Hough [16] line features. Overall, we obtain a 45-dimensional feature vector for the classifier. All the image feature extraction and classifier routines are programmed in Matlab. The following section describes the image processing and feature extraction in more detail.

4 IMAGE PREPROCESSING AND FEATURE EXTRACTION

The distinguishing characteristics of protein crystals are the presence of straight lines and quadrangular shapes. Therefore, we focus on extracting geometric features of the objects (or regions) in the image. As in our previous work [13], we extract blob features from multiple binary images and edge features from Canny edge image. In addition to these features, we apply Hough line transform and extract line related features. Details of our proposed image processing and feature extraction technique is provided in the following section.

4.1 GREEN PERCENTILE IMAGE BINARIZATION

Image binarization is a technique for separating foreground and background regions in an image. When green light is used as the excitation source for fluorescence based acquisition, the intensity of the green pixel component is observed to be higher than the red and blue components in the crystal regions [7]. We utilize this feature for our green percentile image binarization. Let τ_p be the threshold for green component intensity such that the number of pixels in the image with green component below τ_p constitute $p\%$ of the pixels. For example, if $p = 90, \tau_{90}$ is the threshold of green intensity such that 90% of the green component pixels will be less than τ_{90}. Image is binarized using the value of τ_p and a minimum gray level intensity condition $\tau_{min} = 40$. All pixels with gray level intensity greater than τ_{min} and having green pixel component greater than τ_p constitute the foreground region while the remaining pixels constitute the background region. As the value of p goes higher, the foreground (object) region in the binary image usually becomes smaller.

We generate binary images using green percentile thresholds for $p=95$ and $p=99$ and extract region features. Figure 3 shows some sample thresholded images using the two methods. From the original and binary images in Figure 3, we can observe that a single technique may not yield good results for all images. For the images in rows (i) and (ii), the binary images with $p = 95$ provide better representation of the crystal objects. However, for image at row (iii), the binary image obtained using $p = 99$ provides better representation of the crystals.

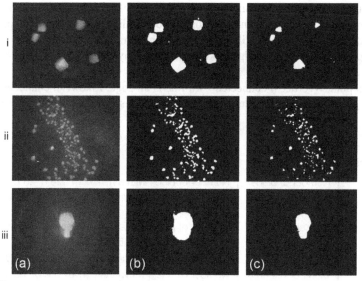

FIGURE 3

Image binarization on crystallization trial images: (a) original images, (b) Green percentile threshold ($p = 95$), and (c) Green percentile threshold ($p = 99$).

4.2 REGION FEATURES

After we generate the binary image, we apply connected component labeling to segment the regions (crystals). The binary image can be obtained from any of the thresholding methods. Let O be the set of the blobs in a binary image B, and B consists of n number of blobs. The blobs are ordered from the largest to the smallest such that area $(O_i) \geq \text{area}(O_{i+1})$. Each blob O_i is enclosed by a minimum boundary rectangle (MBR) having width (w_i) and height (h_i). It should be noted that the blobs may not necessarily represent crystals in an image. For such cases, the blob features may not be particularly useful for the classifier. Table 1 provides a list of the region features. We extract five features (area, perimeter, filled area, convex area, and eccentricity) from the three largest blobs O_1, O_2, and O_3. If the number of blobs is less than 3, value 0 is assigned. We apply green percentile image binarization with $p = 95$ and $p = 99$. From each binary image, we extract 17 region features. Thus, at the end of this step, we obtain 34 features.

4.3 EDGE FEATURES

Canny edge detection algorithm [14] is one of the most reliable algorithms for edge detection. Our results show that for most cases, the shapes of crystals are kept intact in the resulting edge image. An edge image can contain many edges which may or may not be part of the crystals. To analyze the shape and other edge related features, we link the edges to form graphs. We used the MATLAB procedure by Kovesi [17] to perform this operation. The input to this step is a binary edge image. First, isolated pixels are removed from the input edge image. Next, the information of start and end points of the edges, endings and junctions are determined. From every end point, we track points along an edge until an end point or junction is encountered, and label the image pixels. The result of edge linking for the Canny edge image in Figure 4 (b) is shown in Figure 4 (c).

Two points (vertices) connected by a line is an edge. Likewise, connected edges form a graph. Here, we use the terms edges and lines interchangeably. The number

Table 1 Region Features

Symbol	Term	Description
n	Number of blobs	Number of blobs with a minimum size of 25 pixels
ch	Convex hull area	Area of the convex hull (smallest set of pixels) that enclose all blobs
a_1,a_2,a_3	Blob area	Number of pixels in the three largest blobs O_1,O_2,O_3
p_1,p_2,p_3	Blob perimeter	Perimeter of the three largest blobs O_1,O_2,O_3
fa_1,fa_2,fa_3	Blob filled area	Number of white pixels in the three largest blobs O_1,O_2,O_3
ch_1,ch_2,ch_3	Blob convex area	Number of pixels within the convex hull of the three largest blobs O_1,O_2,O_3
e_1,e_2,e_3	Blob eccentricity	Eccentricity of the three largest blobs O_1,O_2,O_3

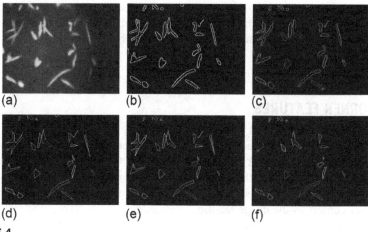

FIGURE 4

Edge detection and edge feature extraction: (a) original image, (b) Canny edge image, (c) edge linking, (d) line fitting, (e) edge cleaning, and (f) image with cyclic graphs or edges forming line normals.

of graphs, the number of edges in a graph, the length of edges, angle between the edges, etc. are good features to distinguish different types of crystals. To extract these features, we do some preprocessing on the Canny edge image. Due to the problem with focusing, many edges can be formed. To reduce the number of edges and to link the edges together, line fitting is done. In this step, edges within certain deviation from a line are connected to form a single edge [17]. The result from line fitting is shown in Figure 4 (d). Here, the margin of three pixels is used as the maximum allowable deviation. From the figures, we can observe that after line fitting, the number of edges is reduced and the shapes resemble to the shapes of the crystals. Likewise, isolated edges and edges that are shorter than a minimum length are removed. The result from removing the unnecessary edges is shown in Figure 4 (e). At the end of edge linking procedure, we extract the eight edge related features listed in Table 2. The lengths of edges

Table 2 Edge Features

Symbol	Description
η	Number of graphs (connected edges)
η_1	Number of graphs with a single edge
η_2	Number of graphs with two edges
η_c	Number of graphs whose edges form a cycle
η_p	Number of line normals
μ_l	Average length of edges in all segments
S_l	Sum of lengths of all edges
l_{max}	Maximum length of an edge

are calculated using Euclidean distance measure. Likewise, the angle between the edges is used to determine if the edges (lines) are normal to each other. We consider two lines to be normals if the angle θ between them lies between 60 and 120 (i.e., $60 \leq \theta \leq 120$).

4.4 CORNER FEATURES

Corner points are considered as one of the uniquely recognizable features in an image. A corner is the intersection of two edges where the variation between two perpendicular directions is very high. Harris corner detection [15] exploits this idea and it basically measures the change in intensity of a pixel (x,y) for a displacement of a search window in all directions. We apply Harris corner detection and count the number of corners as the image feature.

4.5 HOUGH LINE FEATURES

Hough transform is a very popular technique in computer vision for detecting certain class of shapes by a voting procedure [16, 18]. We apply Hough line transform to detect lines in an image. Once the lines are detected, we extract the following two line features—number of Hough lines and the average length of line.

5 EXPERIMENTAL RESULTS

Our experimental dataset consists of 212 expert labeled images. The images are hand-labeled by an expert into four different categories: needles, small crystals, large crystals, and other crystals. The proportion of these classes are 24%, 20%, 35% and 21% respectively. For each image, we apply green percentile binarization with $p = 95$ and $p = 99$. From each binary image, we extract 17 region features. Likewise, we extract 8 edge related features, 1 Harris corner feature, and 2 Hough line features. Therefore, we extract a total of $2 \times 17 + 8 + 1 + 2 = 45$ features per image. On a Windows 7 Intel Core i7 CPU @2.4 GHz system with 12 GB memory, it takes around 232 s to extract features for 212 images. Thus the time for feature extraction is around 1.1 s per image.

We group the feature sets into three categories—region features, edge/corner/line features, and combined features. For the classification, we test using decision tree and random forest classifier. Table 3 shows the classification accuracy using the selected classifiers and feature sets. The values are computed as the average accuracy over 10 runs of 10-fold cross validation. Region features alone does not provide good accuracies. With edge-corner-line features only, we obtain 73% accuracy with decision tree and 75% accuracy with random forest. Combining the two features improves the overall accuracy.

Table 3 Classification Correctness Comparison

	Region Features	Edge-Corner-Line Features	All Features
Decision tree	0.56	0.73	0.72
Random forest ($n = 200$)	0.63	0.75	0.78

The best accuracy is obtained with random forest classifier and combined set of features. For this combination, we obtained accuracy in the range 75-80%. Table 4 shows a sample confusion matrix using 200 trees for the random forest. The overall accuracy is 78.3%. The sensitivity for large crystals is 88%.

Among the four classes, we can observe that the system distinguishes the small crystals and needle crystals with high accuracy. Distinction between large crystals and other crystals is the most problematic. From our discussion with the expert, small and large crystals are the most important crystals in terms of their usability for the diffraction process. Therefore, it is critical not to misclassify the images in these categories into other two categories. From Table 1 , we observe that our system misses 6 small crystals (3 images grouped as other crystals and 3 images grouped as needles). Likewise, our system classifies 6 large crystals as other crystals. In overall, our system misses 12 [3+3+6] critical images. Thus, the rate of miss of critical crystals of our system is around 6% [12/212]. This is a promising achievement for crystal sub-classification of crystal categories. The average accuracy over 10 runs of 10-fold cross validation is 78%.

As the number of trees for random forest classifier is increased, the accuracy is increased up to a certain extent. Figure 5 provides the performance comparison for accuracy and computation time for training and testing versus the number of trees. The best accuracy is obtained with number of trees sampled is 200. As the number of trees parameter for random forest increases, the computation time also increases. The computation time for training and testing time increases linearly with the number of trees.

Table 4 Confusion Matrix with Random Forest Classifier (Number of Trees = 200)

Actual Class	Observed Class			
	Other Crystals	Needles	Small Crystals	Large Crystals
Other crystals	28	6	2	8
Needles	0	42	6	3
Small crystals	3	3	31	6
Large crystals	6	0	3	65

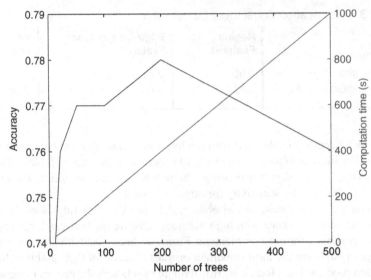

FIGURE 5

Performance comparison (accuracy and performance computation vs number of trees of random forest).

6 CONCLUSION AND FUTURE WORK

This chapter describes our method for automatic classification of protein crystals in crystallization trial images. Our method focuses on extracting geometric features related to blobs, edges, and lines from the images. Using random forest classifier, we are able to achieve classification accuracy around 78% for a 4-class problem and this is a good classification performance.

This study focused on classifying a crystallization trial image according to the types of protein crystals present in the image. We only included images consisting crystals in our experiments. In the future, we would like to perform a two-level classification. First, we plan to classify the images as non-crystals, likely-crystals, and crystals. Next, we plan to classify the sub-categories. The current work will fall under the sub-classification of crystals.

We plan to improve the accuracy of the system further. The performance of our system depends on the accuracy of image binarization. In some images, the thresholded images do not capture the shapes of crystals correctly. Therefore, the features extracted from blobs may not necessarily represent crystals. Because of this, the features extracted from those blobs are not useful. To solve this problem, we plan to investigate different thresholding techniques. Our initial study shows that using the best thresholded image for feature extraction improves the classification performance.

ACKNOWLEDGMENT

This research was supported by National Institutes of Health (GM090453) grant.

REFERENCES

[1] Pusey ML, Liu Z-J, Tempel W, Praissman J, Lin D, Wang B-C, et al. Life in the fast lane for protein crystallization and X-ray crystallography. Progr Biophys Molecul Biol 2005;88(3):359–86.

[2] Cumbaa CA, Lauricella A, Fehrman N, Veatch C, Collins R, Luft J, et al. Automatic classification of sub-microlitre protein-crystallization trials in 1536-well plates. Acta Crystallograp D Biol Crystallograp 2003;59(9):1619–27.

[3] Cumbaa C, Jurisica I. Automatic classification and pattern discovery in high-throughput protein crystallization trials. J Struct Funct Genom 2005;6(2–3):195–202.

[4] Berry IM, Dym O, Esnouf R, Harlos K, Meged R, Perrakis A, et al. Spine high-throughput crystallization, crystal imaging and recognition techniques: current state, performance analysis, new technologies and future aspects. Acta Crystallograph D Biol Crystallograp 2006;62(10):1137–49.

[5] Pan S, Shavit G, Penas-Centeno M, Xu D-H, Shapiro L, Ladner R, et al. Automated classification of protein crystallization images using support vector machines with scale-invariant texture and gabor features. Acta Crystallograph D Biol Crystallograp 2006;62(3):271–9.

[6] Po MJ, Laine AF. Leveraging genetic algorithm and neural network in automated protein crystal recognition. In: 30th Annual International Conference of the IEEE: Engineering in Medicine and Biology Society, EMBS 2008. IEEE; 2008. p. 1926–9.

[7] Sigdel M, Pusey ML, Aygun RS. Real-time protein crystallization image acquisition and classification system, Crystal Growth Design 2013;13(7):2728–36. http://dx.doi.org/10.1021/cg3016029.

[8] Saitoh K, Kawabata K, Asama H. Design of classifier to automate the evaluation of protein crystallization states. In: Proceedings 2006 IEEE International Conference on Robotics and Automation, ICRA 2006. IEEE; 2006. p. 1800–5.

[9] Spraggon G, Lesley SA, Kreusch A, Priestle JP. Computational analysis of crystallization trials. Acta Crystallograph D Biol Crystallograp 2002;58(11):1915–23.

[10] Cumbaa CA, Jurisica I. Protein crystallization analysis on the world community grid. J Struct Funct Genomics 2010;11(1):61–9.

[11] Saitoh K, Kawabata K, Kunimitsu S, Asama H, Mishima T. Evaluation of protein crystallization states based on texture information. In: 2004 IEEE/RSJ International Conference on Intelligent Robots and Systems, IROS 2004. Vol. 3. IEEE; 2004. p. 2725–30.

[12] Zhu X, Sun S, Bern M. Classification of protein crystallization imagery. In: 26th Annual International Conference of the IEEE on Engineering in Medicine and Biology Society, IEMBS'04. Vol. 1. IEEE; 2004. p. 1628–31.

[13] Sigdel M, Sigdel M, Dinc I, Dinc S, Pusey M, Aygun R. Classification of protein crystallization trial images using geometric features. In: Proceedings of the 2014 International Conference on Image Processing, Computer Vision, Pattern Recognition; 2014. p. 192–8.

[14] Canny J. A computational approach to edge detection. IEEE Trans Pattern Anal Mach Intell 1986;6:679–98.

[15] Harris C, Stephens M. A combined corner and edge detector. In: Alvey Vision Conference. Vol. 15. Manchester, UK; 1988. p. 50.

[16] Duda RO, Hart PE. Use of the Hough transformation to detect lines and curves in pictures. Commun ACM 1972;15(1):11–5.

[17] Kovesi PD. MATLAB and Octave functions for computer vision and image processing. Centre for Exploration Targeting, School of Earth and Environment, The University of Western Australia, available from: http://www.csse.uwa.edu.au/_pk/research/matlabfns

[18] Gonzalez R. Woods R. Prentice Hall: Digital image processing; 2008.

Semi-automatic teeth segmentation in 3D models of dental casts using a hybrid methodology

28

J.D. Tamayo-Quintero[1], S. Arboleda-Duque[1,2], J.B. Gómez-Mendoza[1]

[1]*Department of Electric, Electronic and Computer Engineering, Universidad Nacional de Colombia, Manizales, Caldas, Colombia*
[2]*Department of Telecommunications Engineering, Universidad Católica de Manizales, Manizales, Caldas, Colombia*

1 INTRODUCTION

The advent of new technologies has driven the development of increasingly sophisticated 3D acquisition systems [1]. 3D models originated by using those systems, also referred as point clouds, provide surface information, metrics, texture, etc. This 3D information is of great interest in different fields in the industry, such as in-process inspection, accident reconstruction, crime scene analysis, machine calibration, orthodontics, etc. [2].

Digital dental models have proven to be helpful and important for experts in odontology and orthodontics. They provide information precise enough to be used in diagnosis and prognosis [3], this has caused a number of concerns to emerge using 3D dental models is becoming a more common practice in the field.

Colombian laws in consumer protection require dental cast records of patients to be preserved during a period no less than 10 years, and according to the Association of Orthodontists [4], it is recommended that study models are retained for at least 11 years or until the patient is 26 years old. This has caused a number of concerns to emerge, like limited storage capacity, model fragility, among others.

Therefore, it is important to use the 3D digital dental models in place of physical alginate casts. Aiming to further strengthen the acceptance of such practice, 3D image processing and digital measuring tools are finding their way into orthodontics.

Surface and object segmentation is an intermediate step in artificial vision that eases object recognition and classification. A good segmentation is a key to facilitate, enhance, and achieve further interpretation of the input data.

For that reason, in this work we present an exploratory analysis of current segmentation techniques for point clouds applied to dental 3D models. This is a first step toward parameter measurement [5,6], simulation of the movement of teeth to correct malocclusions [7], planning for dental and maxillofacial surgery [8], pose estimation [9], among others.

This chapter is organized as follows: Section 2 describes briefly the process of obtaining integrated 3D point clouds from plaster dental models. Section 3 introduces the segmentation techniques applied to 3D digital dental models. Section 3.4 shows the analysis and results of applying those segmentation techniques to point clouds of dental models. Finally, Section 3.5 presents the findings and discussion of the results of this work.

2 DENTAL STUDY MODEL

Experts in dental areas use diagnostic logs, which are kept in order to document the initial condition of the patient and complement the information gathered during clinical examination. These records are commonly divided in three categories: dental models, photographs, and radiographs [10].

Dental models in dentistry are built primarily using alginate cast. They are important for diagnosis and orthodontic treatment planning, as well as to detect anomalies of pose, size, and shape of the teeth. Also, they are indispensable to assess the outcomes of treatment process [11–13].

2.1 3D MODEL ACQUISITION

The Universidad Nacional de Colombia Sede Manizales has a 3D digitizer VIVID 9i Konica (Figure 1). This scanner produces range images which constitute a valuable source of information. Since range images cover the object's geometry from a

FIGURE 1

Konica Minolta VIVID 9i 3D digitizer.

FIGURE 2

Registration.

FIGURE 3

Integration.

specific point of view, several shots are needed in order to reconstruct a whole model without occlusions.

The views acquired with the range scanner must be aligned up into a single coordinate space. This procedure is called registration (e.g., in Figure 2).

Once the views have been registered, the integration process starts. The goal of integration is to generate a well-defined mesh or data set using the information coming from all the views (partial meshes or point sets) captured during scanning (Figure 3). Furthermore, this process seeks to eliminate redundant information in regions with little variation in the surface, and to fill small holes in the surface.

In this study five dental models were used. Eight views were captured in order to construct each model, with the scanner tilted at 45°, thus achieving good detail within the object of interest. This process was conducted by the research group in Perception and Intelligent Control (PCI). For further details please refer to the Master's final technical report [14].

3 POINT CLOUD SEGMENTATION

In this section, a brief introduction on three different techniques for segmenting point clouds is given: RANdom SAmpling and Consensus (RANSAC) [15], Region Growing [16], and Maximum-Flow Minimum-Cut (Min-Cut) [17].

3.1 RANSAC

The iterative method of RANSAC was proposed by Fischer and Bolles. The technique aims to estimate the parameters of a mathematical model from a set of observed data using a method of hypothesis testing. The algorithm is used as a geometric model-based segmentation algorithm, due to its ability to automatically recognize parameterized shapes through the data.

The principle of the algorithm is as follows. If ε is the probability of choosing a sample that produces a poor estimate (outlier), then $1 - \varepsilon$ is the probability of getting a good sample (inliers). This means that the probability of catching s good samples becomes $(1 - \varepsilon)^s$. For k trials, the probability of failure becomes $(1 - (1 - \varepsilon)^s)^k$. If ρ is the desired probability of success, given for Equation (1):

$$1 - p = ((1 - \varepsilon)^s)^k \rightarrow k = \frac{\log(1 - \rho)}{\log(1 - (1 - \varepsilon)^s)} \tag{1}$$

3.2 REGION GROWING SEGMENTATION

The Region Growing algorithm is based on the idea that some features in local data do not change greatly regarding those features measured for a given sample, called seed. Therefore, regions can be "grown" if neighboring data remain homogeneous given certain constraints, commonly the spatial closeness of the data, although other features can also be included. In our work, we choose to enrich the spatial closeness with features that are based in local surface orientation and curvature, both approximated at each point in the cloud. The algorithm can be summarized as follows:

- Points are sorted according to their curvature.
- The point that has the minimum value of curvature is chosen as a seed and the region growth begins from that point (flat areas have less curvature).
- For each seed point, a list containing its closest neighbors is extracted:
  - The angle between the normal of each neighbor and the normal of the current point (seed) is compared: if the angle is less than a certain threshold, the point is added to the current region.
  - Subsequently, every neighbor is tested for the curvature value. If the neighbor's curvature is less than certain curvature threshold value then that point is turned into a new seed.
  - Current seeds are removed from the set of seeds, but remain marked as points belonging to the region. This avoids double checking points.

Regions are found once the algorithm runs out of seeds. For further details regarding Region Growing please refer to [16].

3.3 MIN-CUT

According to the results of Golovinskiy and Funkhouser [17], Min-Cut is robust to noise and is very effective for segmenting dense point clouds of outdoor urban scans. However, it requires prior knowledge of the location of the objects to be segmented, and has input parameter (namely radius and σ) that should be set in order to control the resulting segmentation, where the main cues are distances and point densities, rather than colors and textures.

The principle of the algorithm is as follows:

First of all, the structure of the point cloud as a flow graph through the K closest neighbors, which are joined together using links with different weights. Additionally, points are joined to a source and a sink, used to represent the object and the background.

The first weight is given to all edges of the point cloud and is called SmoothCost (SC), computed using Equation (2):

$$\text{SmoothCost} = e^{-\left(\frac{\text{dist}}{\sigma}\right)} \tag{2}$$

where dist is the distance between the points and σ is a free input parameter that allows modifying the smoothing effect.

The next step of the algorithm is to establish the cost of the data. In this case it is necessary to make use of the source (t) and sink (s), where the source is related to the central point of the object to segment (given manually) and sink with any point belonging to background, where the following penalty calculated by Equation (3).

$$\text{Background Penalty} = \left(\frac{\text{distocenter}}{\text{radius}}\right) \tag{3}$$

where distocenter is the expected distance to the center of the object in a horizontal plane, and is computed as in Equation (4):

$$\text{distocenter} = \sqrt{(x - \text{center} X)^2 + (y - \text{center} Y)^2} \tag{4}$$

Radius is an input parameter and can be considered as the range from the center of the object where the points belong to a region of interest by assigning a higher weight. On the other hand, z axis is not considered in Equation (4). Such constraint can be interpreted geometrically as an infinite length cylinder with radius given by radius, whose length is aligned parallel to the z axis.

Once the graph is constructed, the segmentation is given by the minimum cut where the region of interest is extracted.

3.4 FEATURE SAMPLING USING NARF

Semi-automated 3D point cloud segmentation results are highly dependent upon parameter set-up. Whenever possible, it is the user's responsibility to provide proper values for such parameter set as part of the algorithm's prior. In some algorithms, those parameters are points which are representative for the regions contained in the point set, and selecting them can be a demanding task.

In order to overcome such limitation, an automatic or semi-automatic point selection technique can be applied.

Normal-aligned radial features (NARF), presented by Steder et al. [18], aim to cope with the necessity of generating a structured subsampling of the data, taking into account elements such as spatial density (including empty areas) and robustness to noise.

According to the authors, in order to obtain NARF descriptors one must:

- calculate a normal aligned range value patch in the point, which is a small range image with the observer looking at the point along the normal,
- overlay a star pattern onto this patch, where each beam corresponds to a value in the final descriptor, that captures how much the pixels under the beam change,
- extract a unique orientation from the descriptor,
- and shift the descriptor according to this value to make it invariant to the rotation.

Resulting points are not overcrowded in high variation areas, but retain a well-defined representation of the information contained in the original cloud. Additionally, each feature vector contains the mean orientation of the local patch that it represents.

3.5 THE HYBRID TECHNIQUE

This method implemented is a contribution for semi-automatic segmentation of point cloud based in Min-Cut, NARF, and Region Growing.

Min-Cut is an efficient and powerful technique for point cloud segmentation; however, this method has a number of disadvantages as it is the prior knowledge of the center of object to be segmented and the radius value. Due to these drawbacks, we propose a method to achieve a semi-automatic segmentation without prior knowledge of the location of the objects, supplying part of that information by the means of NARF.

On the other hand, Region Growing segmentation based in local surface orientation and curvature is an efficient technique for segmenting point clouds of dental models, effectively separating the gum and teeth.

In our first work, a hybrid technique was constructed using NARF and Min-Cut, aimed to segment outdoor environments [19]. Figures 4 and 5 show some of the results obtained in that work. The streamline of the technique can be summarized as shown below:

- Two input parameters are set up prior to execution: support size and angular resolution.
- Then, we use NARF as a descriptor to obtain the target landmarks;
- The final step is to segment the cloud using each landmark as a seed in the Min-Cut algorithm.

In this work, the hybrid technique is based in NARF, Min-Cut, and Region Growing [20]. The methodology can be summarized as shown below:

- First of all, the gum is separated from teeth using the Region Growing method.
- Once gum is set apart, a set of landmarks is extracted using the NARF technique in the segmented teeth region.
- Subsequently, each landmark is used as a source in the Min-Cut method.

FIGURE 4

This is an example segmentation in outdoor environment using the first work with the hybrid technique (for easier visualization background is subsample).

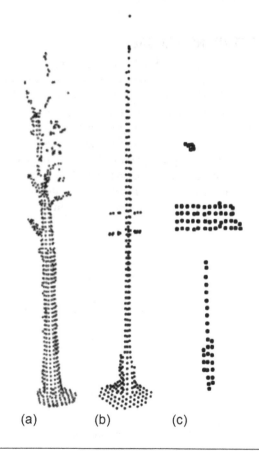

(a)   (b)   (c)

FIGURE 5

Some important objects are obtained by the hybrid technique. Tree (a), tall post (b), road sign (c).

The final segmentation is composed of the gum and a set of tooth regions. Notice that, unlike the case of outdoor scene segmentation, there is no need to preestablish angular resolution and support size. This is because overall teeth geometry does not vary greatly from one model to another.

4 RESULTS OF SEGMENTATION TECHNIQUES APPLIED TO 3D DENTAL MODELS

Exploration results obtained by applying different segmentation techniques described in Section 3 are shown in this section. Five 3D dental models were used in this analysis (Figure 10). Each cloud has approximately 50,000 points.

The tests were performed on all models; some important conclusions drawn from this analysis are mentioned. Finally, a semi-automatic segmentation methodology for 3D dental models is presented.

4.1 FIRST, A TEST USING RANSAC

As mentioned in Section 3.1, RANSAC allows automatic recognition of known forms of the data (planes, cylinders, spheres, and tori). In this case a planar model was used, with a threshold of ± 5 mm, as shown in Figure 6(a). The result obtained applying this technique is shown in Figure 6(b). The points retain colors red (dark gray in the print version) and blue (light gray in the print version) according to the region they have been assigned to. Notice that the plane in Figure 6(a) serves only as a mere illustration of the principle used by the technique, and do not correspond to the one used to obtain the classification in Figure 6(b).

This method finds the highest concentration of points in a planar model based in a planar hypothesis. In this case the highest concentration of points is found on the teeth's surface.

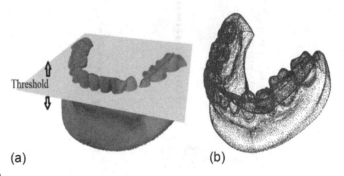

(a) (b)

FIGURE 6

(a) Planar segmentation by RANSAC with a threshold of ± 5 mm and (b) dental model segmented.

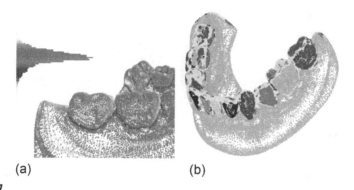

FIGURE 7

(a) Example of curvature in point clouds of dental models, (b) 3D dental model segmented using a Region Growing segmentation.

4.2 GUM EXTRACTION USING REGION GROWING

The results obtained by applying the algorithm of region growing are shown in Figure 7. The stop criteria are given comparing the points normal and then the curvature of the points. The input parameters are shown in Table 1.

In order to improve understanding and visualization, the point cloud of dental model is drawn with colors representing their curvature Figure 7(a) and the result obtained applying the Region Growing segmentation technique in a 3D dental model is illustrated in Figure 7(b).

For further information regarding neighbor search process and Kd-trees please refer to PCL, API Documentation [21] or the Flann library documentation [22].

Figure 7(b) shows some points colored in aqua blue (light gray in the print version), which are not targeted because of their high curvature or because the region generated by the region growing process do not contain enough data points to be considered as such.

Clearly this method requires some refinement that would allow merging some regions. However, this is an acceptable approximation which can be used instead of usable as start point for further refinement.

4.3 PER-TOOTH SEPARATION USING MIN-CUT

As mentioned in Section 3.3, this algorithm requires human interaction to introduce the virtual node called source (t) to segment an object of interest. We can see a clear example in Figure 8.

Table 1 Input Parameters for Region Growing Segmentation

cth	θth	N	O{.}	P
1	5	12	Tree	Point cloud

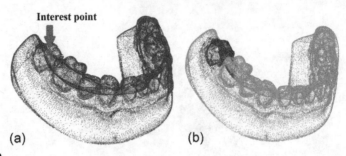

FIGURE 8

Segmentation applying the Min-Cut. (a) Selection of the interest point. (b) Segmentation of the selected tooth.

Min-Cut requires human interaction in order to set some important parameters such as the radius. For this reason, we designed a variant of the methodology used by Tamayo-Quintero and Gómez-Mendoza [19] to search the virtual nodes automatically—landmarks—i.e., a point in the centers of each object—in the ideal case—in this case each tooth, by means of NARF. The input parameters are shown in Table 2.

4.4 SEMI-AUTOMATIC SEGMENTATION (HYBRID TECHNIQUE)

The results obtained by applying the hybrid technique are shown in Figures 9 and 10. The stop criteria are mentioned in the previous techniques and the input parameter are shown in Table 3.

Table 2 Input Parameters for Min-Cut Segmentation

Interest Point (x,y,z)	σ	SmoothCost	Radius
20,0,18	0.5	0.6	15

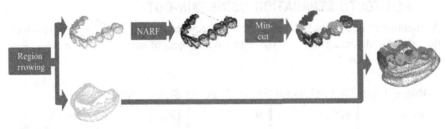

FIGURE 9

Semi-automatic segmentation proposal.

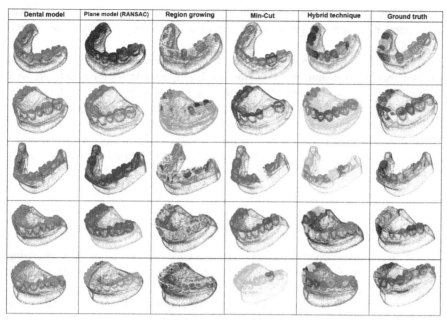

FIGURE 10

Results obtained by applying different segmentation techniques to five dental models.

Table 3 Input Parameters Used in the Proposed Methodology

cth	θth	σ	SC	Radius	ag	ss	N
1	5	0.5	0.6	15	0.02	20	12

In Figure 9, we designed a variant and this methodology is based in the hybridization of three algorithms: Region Growing, NARF, and Min-Cut. The first step is separated the gum from teeth using the region growing method then apply NARF and subsequently, each landmark is used as source in order to apply the Min-Cut. Finally, the segmentation is composed of the gum and a set of teeth. The methodology is illustrated in Figure 9, and the results obtained are shown in Figure 10.

5 COMMENTS AND DISCUSSIONS

Figure 10 shows the result of applying segmentation methods to five dental casts. The first column contains the point cloud of dental models one to five. The second column shows the segmentation using RANSAC algorithm. There is a noticeable difference in the results for model three in comparison to the other four, mainly due to teeth unevenness.

The third column presents the result of the Region Growing segmentation, where restrictions of smoothness given by the curvature and the angle between the normal are used.

The fourth column corresponds to Min-Cut-based segmentation, which separates the tooth but requiring human interaction in selecting a landmark for each tooth. As a consequence of this, the fifth column shows a methodology where landmarks are automatically selected through NARF, and then segmented using Min-Cut. Finally, the sixth column shows the Ground truth, built manually using Mesh Lab.

Results of teeth segmentation using the proposed methodology seem appropriate in appearance; however, they must be subject to analysis carried by experts in order to qualify them.

6 CONCLUSION

Dental casts contain rich information in terms of curvature and geometry, comprising semi-flat zones, highly curved zones, objects of interest with variable sizes, etc. As it happened with urban structures in our previous work [19], this data set posed an interesting segmentation problem that proved to be tackled in a more comprehensive manner through the means of a mixed methodology, composed by various well-known techniques that can be further tuned to recognize or separate a particular structure.

From this work, some achievements can be highlighted:

- Segmentation of the gum and teeth can be carried out adequately using the Region Growing algorithm based on the curvature and the angle between the normal vectors.
- The potential for Min-Cut algorithm for segmenting each tooth is evidenced.
- It is possible to apply the proposed methodology using NARF and Min-Cut, obtaining acceptable results for segmentation while reducing human interaction in setting internal parameters of the Min-Cut algorithm (landmark selection).
- Automatic radii selection for Min-Cut remains an open issue.

ACKNOWLEDGMENTS

This work was made possible thanks to the support of the Universidad Nacional de Colombia Sede Manizales, and in particular the research groups on Perception and Intelligent Control (PCI) and Soft and Hard Applied Computing (SHAC).

REFERENCES

[1] Rusu RB, Cousins S. 3D is here: point cloud library (PCL), In: 2011 IEEE International Conference on Robotics and Automation; 2011. p. 1–4, available at: http://ieeexplore. ieee.org/lpdocs/epic03/wrapper.htm?arnumber=5980567.

[2] FARO's 3D metrology solutions, Measurement Industries, available at: http://www.faro.com/measurement-solutions.

[3] Motohashi N, Kuroda T. A 3D computer-aided design system applied to diagnosis and treatment planning in orthodontics and orthognathic surgery, Eur J Orthod 1999;21:263–74. available at: http://ejo.oxfordjournals.org/content/21/3/263.full.pdf.

[4] Bell A, Ayoub AF, Siebert P. Assessment of the accuracy of a three-dimensional imaging system for archiving dental study models, J Orthod 2003;30(3):219–23. available at: http://www.ncbi.nlm.nih.gov/pubmed/14530419.

[5] Laurendeau D, Guimond L, Poussart D. A computer-vision technique for the acquisition and processing of 3-D profiles of dental imprints: an application in orthodontics, IEEE Trans Med Imaging 1991;10(3):453–61. available at: http://www.ncbi.nlm.nih.gov/pubmed/18222848.

[6] Mokhtari M, Laurendeau D. Feature detection on 3-D images. In: . p. 287–96, available at: http://ieeexplore.ieee.org/stamp/stamp.jsp?tp=&arnumber=315842.

[7] Chuah JH, Ong SH, Kondo T, Foong KWC, Yong TF. 3D space analysis of dental models, Visualization, Display, an Image-Guided Procedures, Proc SPIE 2001;4319:564–73. 2, 26, available at: http://proceedings.spiedigitallibrary.org/proceeding.aspx?articleid=905781.

[8] Heo H, Chae O-S. Segmentation of tooth in ct images for the 3D reconstruction of teeth, Image Processing: Algorithms and Systems III, Proc SPIE-IS & T Electron Imaging 2004;5298:455–66. 2, 13, available at: http://proceedings.spiedigitallibrary.org/proceeding.aspx?articleid=837263.

[9] Mok VW, Ong S, Foong KW, Kondo T. Pose estimation of teeth through crown-shape matching, Medical Imaging 2002: Image Processing, Proc SPIE 2002;4684:955–64. available at: http://proceedings.spiedigitallibrary.org/proceeding.aspx?articleid=879917.

[10] Hou H-M, Wong RW-K, Hagg U. The uses of orthodontic study models in diagnosis and treatment planning. HKDJ 2006;3(2):107–15, 3, 14.

[11] Vellini-Ferreira F. Ortodoncia: diagnóstico y planificación clínica. 1st ed. Paulo, Brazil: Editora Artes Médicas Ltda; 2002, xvii, 3, 5, 6.

[12] Acosta W, Meneses F, Morzán A, Pastor E, Tomona N. Manual de procedimientos de laboratorio en ortodoncia. 1st ed, Lima, Perú: Universidad Peruana Cayetano Heredia; 1999.

[13] Rudge SJ. A computer program for the analysis of study models. Eur J Orthod 1982;4:269–73.

[14] Morantes LJ. Caracterización de piezas dentales a partir de modelos 3D. Maestría tesis, Universidad Nacional de Colombia, Sede Manizales; 2008, available at: http://www.bdigital.unal.edu.co/3377/#sthash.4QRtCEp7.dpuf.

[15] Schnabel R, Wahl R, Klein R. Efficient RANSAC for point-cloud shape detection. Comput Graphics Forum 2007;26(2):214–26. available at: http://doi.wiley.com/10.1111/j.1467–8659.2007.01016.x.

[16] Point cloud Library (PCL), documentation, tutorial, available at: http://pointclouds.org/documentation/tutorials/region_growing_segmentation.php.

[17] Golovinskiy A, Funkhouser T. Min-cut based segmentation of point clouds, In: 2009 IEEE 12th International Conference on Computer Vision Workshops ICCV Workshops, XXXIX-B3 (September); 2009. p. 39–46. available at: http://ieeexplore.ieee.org/lpdocs/epic03/wrapper.htm?arnumber=5457721.

[18] Steder B, Rusu RB, Konolige K, Burgard W. Point feature extraction on 3D range scans taking into account object boundaries. In: 2011 IEEE International Conference on Robotics and Automation; 2011. p. 2601–8. available at: http://ieeexplore.ieee.org/lpdocs/epic03/wrapper.htm?arnumber=5980187.

[19] Tamayo-Quintero JD, Gómez-Mendoza JB. Semi-automatic 3D point cloud segmentation using a modified Min-Cut approach. In: 5th Latin American Conference on Networked and Electronic Media (LACNEM 2013); 2013. available at: http://revnoos. manizales.unal.edu.co/index.php/articulo/volumen-4-lacnem-2013.

[20] Tamayo-Quintero JD, Arboleda-Duque S, Gómez-Mendoza JB. Image segmentation techniques applied to point clouds of dental models with an improvement in semi-automatic teeth segmentation, In: IPCV'14—The 2014 International Conference on Image Processing, Computer Vision, and Pattern Recognition; 2014. p. 23–5.

[21] Point Cloud Library (PCL), API documentation, available at: http://docs.pointclouds. org/trunk/.

[22] Fast Library for Approximate Nearest Neighbors (FLANN), available at: http://www.cs. ubc.ca/research/flann/.

Effective finger vein-based authentication: Kernel principal component analysis

29

S. Damavandinejadmonfared, V. Varadharajan

Department of Computing, Advanced Cyber Security Research Centre, Macquarie University, Sydney, New South Wales, Australia

1 INTRODUCTION

The importance of reliability in verification and identification has gained lots of attention recently [1]. Finger vein is a newly proposed method of biometrics that has been able to gain many researchers' attention due to the fact that it is something internal and reliable to be used for this purpose. Furthermore, it has been proven by the medical studies that finger vein pattern is unique and stable [2]. As the data in finger vein recognition [3–5] is "image," some face recognition algorithms [6–10] have been proposed to be used in this case. Principal component analysis (PCA) [11,7,6] is one of the common and known methods of pattern recognition and face recognition [12,13] that has been used a lot in biometrics. PCA, however, is a linear method which makes it unable to properly deal with nonlinear patterns which might be in data. To overcome the mentioned drawback of PCA, kernel principal component analysis (KPCA) [14,8] was proposed, which is known to be more appropriate than PCA in many cases, such as pattern recognition and face recognition. It is because of the fact that using kernel function in the system makes it nonlinear. Kernel entropy component analysis (KECA) is also an extension on KPCA that has been introduced in finger vein area [15,16] as well as some extensions of two-dimensional PCA [17]. The mentioned reasons motivated us to conduct a comparative analysis between two known and mostly used methods called PCA and KPCA [9,18–20] in finger vein recognition. The main difference between PCA and KPCA is the fact that PCA is a linear method, whereas KPCA is the nonlinear version of PCA in which kernel transforming is used. In PCA, it is ensured that the transferred data are uncorrelated, and only preserve maximally the second-order statistics of the original data, which is why PCA is known as insensitive to the dependencies of multiple features of the pattern. In KPCA, the mentioned problem has been overcome as it is not a linear method. In KPCA, however, it is essential that

447

which kernel mapping function is chosen to be used. It could be considered very important due to the fact that each kernel mapping has particular characteristics and the data after being mapped will be in a totally different and high-dimensional space where it could be too complicated to extract the valuable features. As PCA is a well-known method of dimensionality reduction, the combination of PCA and kernel mapping will lead to a more reliable system. This work is an extension of the work of Damavandinejadmonfared and Varadharajan [21] presented in IPCV 2014 conference. There are several different types of kernel mapping which have been proven to be novel in different machine learning algorithms. In this research, we use four famous kernel mappings such as polynomial, Gaussian, exponential, and Laplacian as they have an extensive use within image processing related algorithms. Comparison in this paper is between different types of KPCA using the mentioned four kernel functions to map the data to achieve a twofold contribution; first, KPCA is appropriate enough to be used in finger vein area, and second, which kernel mapping function is the most superior one.

The remainder of this paper is organized as follows:

In Section 2, image acquisition is explained. In Section 3, PCA is explained. In Section 4, KPCA is introduced. In Section 5, experimental results on the finger vein database are given. Finally, Section 6 concludes the paper.

2 IMAGE ACQUISITION

Based on the proven scientific fact that the light rays can be absorbed by deoxygenated hemoglobin in the vein, absorption coefficient of the vein is higher than other parts of finger. In order to provide the finger vein images, four low-cost prototype devices are needed such as an infrared (IR) LED and its control circuit with wavelength 830 nm, a camera to capture the images, a microcomputer unit to control the LED array, and a computer to process the images. The webcam has an IR blocking filter; hence, it is not sensitive to the IR rays. To solve this problem, an IR blocking filter is used to prevent the infrared rays from being blocked (Figure 1).

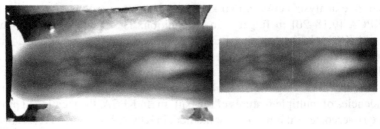

FIGURE 1

Original and cropped image.

3 PRINCIPAL COMPONENT ANALYSIS

PCA is known as a very powerful method for feature extraction. The usage of extracting eigenvectors and their corresponding eigenvalues to project the input data onto has been very common in image analysis, such as face recognition and image classification. PCA, actually, extracts the features from the data and reduces the dimension of it. When the features are extracted, a classifier can be applied to classify them and the final decision can be made. Euclidian distance is used in our algorithm which is very fast and sufficient to our purpose. In the rest of this section, PCA is explained briefly: First, the mean canter of the images is computed. m represents the mean image.

$$m = \frac{1}{M}\sum_{i=1}^{M}X_i \tag{1}$$

The mean cantered image is calculated by Equation (2)

$$w_i = X_i - m \tag{2}$$

First covariance matrix is calculated by:

$$C = WW^{\mathsf{T}} \tag{3}$$

where W is a matrix composed of the column vectors w_i placed side by side.

Assuming that λ is eigenvector and v is eigenvalue, by solving $\lambda v = Cv$ eigenvectors and eigenvalues could be obtained.

By multiplying both side by W and substitution of C, we can get the following equation.

$$WW^{\mathsf{T}}(Wv) = \lambda(Wv) \tag{4}$$

which means the first $M-1$ eigenvectors λ and eigenvalues v can be obtained by calculating WW^{T}.

When we have M eigenvectors and eigenvalues, the images could be projected onto $L \ll M$ dimensions by computing

$$\Omega = [v_1 v_2 \ldots v_L]^{\mathsf{T}} \tag{5}$$

where Ω is the projected value. Finally, to determine which face provides the best description of an input image, the Euclidean distance is calculated using Equation (6).

$$\in_k = \|\Omega - \Omega_k\| \tag{6}$$

And finally, the minimum $\in_k$ will decide the unknown data into k class.

4 KERNEL PRINCIPAL COMPONENT ANALYSIS
4.1 KPCA ALGORITHM

Unlike PCA, KPCA extracts the features of the data nonlinearly. It obtains the principal components in F which is a high-dimensional feature space that is related to the feature spaces nonlinearly. The main idea of KPCA is to map the input data to the feature space F first using a nonlinear mapping Φ when input data have nonlinearly been mapped, the PCA will be performed on the mapped data [3]. Assuming that F is centered, $\sum_{i=1}^{M}\Phi(X_i)=0$ where M is the number of input data. The covariance matrix of F can be defined as

$$C=\frac{1}{M}\sum_{i=1}^{M}\Phi(X_i).\Phi(X_i)^{\mathrm{T}} \tag{7}$$

To do this, this equation $\lambda v = Cv$ which is the eigenvalue equation should be solved for eigenvalues $\lambda \geq 0$ and eigenvactors $v \in F$.

As $Cv = (1/M)\sum_{i=1}^{M}(\Phi(X_i)\cdot v)\Phi(X_i)$, solutions for v with $\lambda \neq 0$ lie within the span of $\Phi(X_1),\ldots\Phi(X_M)$, these coefficients $\alpha_i(i=1,\ldots,M)$ are obtained such that

$$V=\sum_{i=1}^{M}\alpha_i\Phi(X_i) \tag{8}$$

The equations can be considered as follows

$$\lambda(\Phi(X_i)\cdot V) = (\Phi(X_i)\cdot Cv)\text{ for all } i=1,\ldots,M \tag{9}$$

Having $M \times M$ matrix K by $K_{ij}=k(X_i,X_j)=\Phi(X_i)\cdot\Phi(X_j)$, causes an eigenvalue problem.

The solution to this is

$$M\lambda\alpha = K\alpha \tag{10}$$

By selecting the kernels properly, various mappings can be achieved. One of these mappings can be achieved by taking the d-order correlations, which is known as ARG, between the entries, X_i, of the input vector X. The required computation is prohibitive when $d > 2$.

$$(\Phi_d(X)\cdot\Phi_d(y)) = \sum_{i_1,\ldots,i_d=1}^{N} \chi_{i_1}\ldots\chi_{i_d}\cdot y_{i_1}\ldots y_{i_d} = \left(\sum_{i=1}^{N}\chi_i\cdot y_i\right)^{d} = (x\cdot y)^d \tag{11}$$

To map the input data into the feature space F, there are four common methods such as linear (polynomial degree 1), polynomial, Gaussian, and sigmoid, which all are examined in this work in addition to PCA.

4.2 KERNEL FEATURE SPACE VERSUS PCA FEATURE SPACE

In PCA, covariance matrix of the input data is given after some processing stapes such as centring the data and calculating the mean. Then, the feature space is given by extracting the eigenvectors from this matrix. Indeed, each eigenvector has its corresponding eigenvalue whose greatness determines the value of its principal axis. Projection of the data onto a spanned subspace of the mention feature space is the actual data transformation and depending on how many principal axes to project the data onto, the dimension of the transferred data is determined. It means that the dimension of the input data can be reduced to even "one" when using just the first principal ax for projection. On the other hand, the maximum dimension data can have after transformation is equal to its original dimension when using all principal axes to project the data onto. Note that, in PCA the dimension of the feature space, where the spanned subspace is selected, is equal to the dimension of the input data. For example, let $X = [x_1, \ldots, x_N]$, where $x_t \in R^d$ meaning that we have N input data having the dimension of d. In this case, no matter how large N is, the feature space has the fixed dimension of d, which can be considered an advantage for PCA as the dimension of feature space is limited to that of input data and it does not get too high in terms of analyzing potentially large number of data.

In KPCA, however, it is different. The kernel feature space has a higher dimension than that of input data. Indeed, in KPCA, the whole input data space is mapped into kernel feature space by a specific kernel function which is nonlinear, and uses inner products. It is given by considering kernel matrix as input data space for PCA. It means that, unlike PCA, the dimension of kernel feature space is not dependent to the dimension of the input data. Indeed, it is equal to the number of input data. Let X be $[x_1, \ldots, x_N]$, for instance, and $x_t \in R^d$ meaning that we have N input data with the dimension of d. In KPCA, no matter how high the dimension of the input data d is, the kernel feature space is N dimensional as the kernel matrix (Gram matrix) is $[N \times N]$. Kernel matrix and its feature space is defined in Shawe-Taylor and Cristianini [22] as follows:

Given a set of vectors $X = [x_1, \ldots, x_N]$, the *gram matrix* is defined as the $[N \times N]$ matrix G whose entries are $G_{ij} = \langle x_i, x_j \rangle$. If we are using a kernel function k to evaluate the inner products in a feature space with feature map φ, the associated Gram matrix has entries

$$G_{ij} = \langle \varphi(x_i), \varphi(x_j) \rangle = k(x_i, x_j) \tag{12}$$

In this case, the matrix is often referred to as kernel matrix displaying as follows:

k	1	2	$\cdots$	N
1	$k(x_1, x_1)$	$k(x_1, x_2)$	$\cdots$	$k(x_1, x_N)$
2	$k(x_2, x_1)$	$k(x_2, x_2)$	$\cdots$	$k(x_2, x_N)$
$\vdots$	$\vdots$	$\vdots$	$\ddots$	$\vdots$
N	$k(x_N, x_1)$	$k(x_N, x_2)$	$\cdots$	$k(x_N, x_N)$

Mapping the data into another space nonlinearly makes this method (KPCA) nonlinear, which has been stated more superior than the linear PCA in many applications and literature. However, it can lead to the problem of complexity as the dimension of feature space is as high as the number of input data specially when analyzing a huge amount of data. It can also make it too complex to find the optimized subspace of the feature space for projection.

5 EXPERIMENTAL RESULTS

In this section, the experiments are conducted to corroborate the performance of Gaussian KPCA over other kinds of KPCA such as polynomial, exponential, and Laplacian PCA in terms of finger vein recognition. Finger vein database used in the experiments consists of 500 images from 50 individuals; 10 samples from each subject were taken. In this experiment, 4, 5, 6, and 7 images are used to train and the remaining 6, 5, 4, and 3 images are used to test, respectively. In each experiment, the accuracy is calculated using the first 100 components of the extracted features meaning that each experiment is repeated 100 times using the first 100 features to project the data onto, and also the dimension is reduced from 60% to 85% in different experiments. The results are shown in Figures 2–5. As it was expected, use of kernel

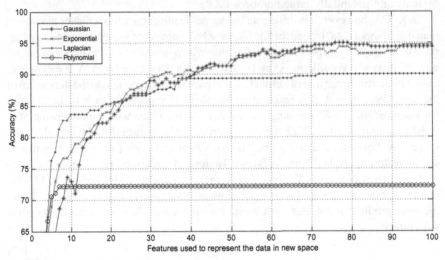

FIGURE 2

Comparison of accuracies obtained using four images to train and six to test.

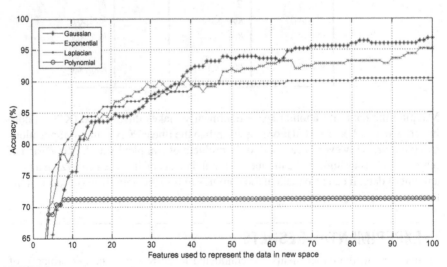

FIGURE 3

Comparison of accuracies obtained using five images to train and five to test.

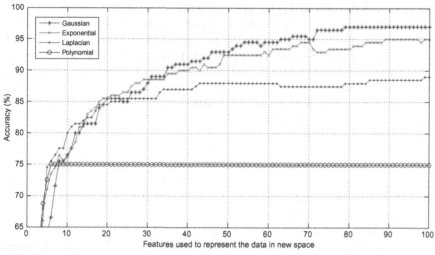

FIGURE 4

Comparison of accuracies obtained using six images to train and four to test.

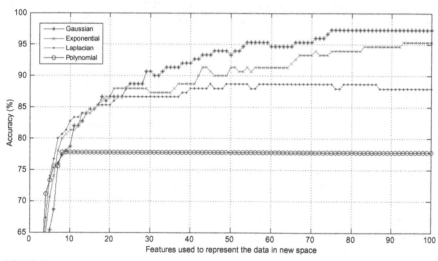

FIGURE 5

Comparison of accuracies obtained using seven images to train and three to test.

functions to map the data first and then applying PCA on the mapped data (KPCA) results in acceptable accuracies varying from over 70% up to near 100% in different experiments. Polynomial KPCA, however, seems to be the worst among all types of KPCA and there is a great discrepancy between polynomial and other kinds of kernel KPCA in terms of final outputs of the system. The results show that polynomial kernel reaches its optimized point when using even less than ten components and it remains the same no matter how many more components to be used. It could be considered an advantage as using this kernel can be faster than others as it gets to its peak in the point 10 or less than that. The accuracy in polynomial KPCA, however, is not satisfying at all and is less than the others in almost all experiments. From another point of view, when four images are used to train, the highest accuracy obtained is around 95%, while the accuracy rate almost reaches 99% when using seven images to train which means, the more the number of training images is, the higher accuracy gets.

It is observed from the results that the accuracies achieved using Laplacian KPCA are not very close to those of the exponential and Gaussian methods; it is also understood that although the accuracies of Gaussian KPCA are close to those of exponential KPCA, the exponential method in a majority of implementations results in less accuracy compared to Gaussian.

Results indicate that in the first experiment, where four images were used to train and the remaining six images to test, the difference between the accuracies obtained using Gaussian, exponential, and Laplacian were not that significant as Laplacian, exponential, and Gaussian reached 90%, 94%, and 95%, respectively. However, the more the number of training images get, the higher accuracy Gaussian KPCA obtains and its discrepancy in accuracy becomes larger to the point that leads to the conclusion that Gaussian KPCA is the most superior kernel mapping in finger vein recognition systems.

6 CONCLUSION

The performance of four different types of KPCA on finger vein recognition has been validated in this paper. The first contribution is that KPCA might not be efficient enough in image classification and recognition as it might be sometimes too time consuming and computationally expensive; however, KPCA can be very reliable and accurate as it is able to deal with nonlinear patterns in the data. Among the examined kernel mapping in this work, it is shown that not only is the Gaussian KPCA the most appropriate one in comparison with the other types of KPCA (polynomial, exponential, and Laplacian), but also this method is efficient enough to be used in finger vein recognition as for such a big data base the accuracy is very high and promising.

REFERENCES

[1] Jain AK, Ross A, Prabhakar S. An introduction to biometric recognition. IEEE Trans Circuits Syst 2004;14(1):4–20.
[2] Kumar A, Zhou Y. Human identification using finger images. IEEE T Image Process 2012;21(4):2228–44.

[3] Beng TS, Rosdi BA. Finger-vein identification using pattern map and principal component analysis, In: 2011 IEEE international conference on signal image processing and applications; 2011. p. 530–4.

[4] Song W, Kim T, Kim HC, Choi JH, Kong H-J, Lee S-R. A finger-vein verification system using mean curvature. Pattern Recogn Lett 2011;32(11):1541–7.

[5] Wu J-D, Liu C-T. Finger-vein pattern identification using principal component analysis and the neural network technique. Expert Syst Appl 2011;38(5):5423–7.

[6] Wen C, Zhang J. Palmprint recognition based on Gabor wavelets and 2-dimensional PCA&PCA, In: International conference on wavelet analysis and pattern recognition; 2007. p. 2–4.

[7] Zhao W, et al. Face recognition: a literature survey. ACM Comput Surv (CSUR) 2003;35 (4):399–458.

[8] Ebied RM. Feature extraction using PCA and kernel-PCA for face recognition. International conference on informatics and systems 2012;8:72–7.

[9] Nhat VDM, Lee S. Kernel-based 2DPCA for face recognition, In: 2007 IEEE international symposium on signal processing and information technology; 2007. p. 35–9.

[10] Yu C, Qing H, Zhang L. K2DPCA plus 2DPCA: an efficient approach for appearance based object recognition, In: 2009 3rd international conference on bioinformatics and biomedical engineering; 2009. p. 1–4.

[11] Lin S, Ph D. An introduction to face recognition technology. Pattern Recogn 1997;1995:1–7.

[12] Zuo W, Zhang D, Wang K. Bidirectional PCA with assembled matrix distance metric for image recognition. IEEE T Syst Man Cybern B Cybern 2006;36(4):863–72.

[13] Zhang D, Zhou Z-H. Two-directional two-dimensional PCA for efficient face representation and recognition. Neurocomputing 2005;69(1–3):224–31.

[14] Kim KI, Jung K, Kim HJ. Face recognition using kernel principal component analysis. Signal Process 2002;9(2):40–2.

[15] Damavandinejadmonfared S. Kernel entropy component analysis using local mean-based k-nearest centroid neighbour (LMKNCN) as a classifier for face recognition in video surveillance camera systems, In: IEEE international conference on intelligent computer communication and processing (ICCP); 2012. p. 253–6.

[16] Damavandinejadmonfared S. Finger vein recognition using linear kernel entropy component analysis, In: IEEE international conference on intelligent computer communication and processing (ICCP); 2012. p. 249–52.

[17] Damavandinejadmonfared S, Varadharajan V. Finger vein recognition in row and column directions using two dimensional kernel principal component analysis, In: The 2014 international conference on image processing, computer vision, and pattern recognition; 2014.

[18] Peng H, Yang A.-P. Indefinite kernel entropy component analysis. In: 2010 International Conference on Multimedia Technology (ICMT). 29–31 Oct. 2010. p. 1, 4.

[19] Jenssen R. Kernel entropy component analysis. IEEE T Pattern Anal Mach Intell 2010;32 (5):847–60.

[20] Shekar BH, Sharmila Kumari M, Mestetskiy LM, Dyshkant NF. Face recognition using kernel entropy component analysis. Neurocomputing 2011;74(6):1053–7.

[21] Damavandinejadmonfared S, Varadharajan V. Effective kernel mapping for one-dimensional principal component analysis in finger vein recognition, In: The 2014 international conference on image processing, computer vision, and pattern recognition; 2014.

[22] Shawe-Taylor J, Cristianini N. Kernel methods for pattern analysis. New York, NY: Cambridge University Press; 2004 p. 462.

Detecting distorted and benign blood cells using the Hough transform based on neural networks and decision trees

30

Hany A. Elsalamony

Mathematics Department, Faculty of Science, Helwan University, Cairo, Egypt

1 INTRODUCTION

Naturally, the human blood consists of a complex combination of plasma, red blood cells (RBCs), white blood cells (WBCs), and platelets. Plasma is the fluid component, which contains melted salts and proteins. RBCs make up about 40% of blood volume. WBCs are less, but greater in size than RBCs. The platelet cells are similar particles, which are smaller than WBCs and RBCs [1].

Anemia occurs when the blood has lower than the normal number of RBCs or insufficient hemoglobin. RBCs are made inside the spongy marrow of the body's larger bones. Bone marrow is always making new RBCs to replace old ones. Normal RBCs die after 120 days in the bloodstream. Their job is carrying oxygen and removing carbon dioxide (a waste product) from the body. In addition, RBCs are disk-shaped and move easily through blood vessels, and they contain an iron-rich protein called hemoglobin. This protein transmits oxygen from the lungs to the rest of the body [1]. In sickle-cell anemia, the body makes sickle-shaped RBCs. Sickle cells contain abnormal hemoglobin called sickle hemoglobin or hemoglobin S, which contributes to the cells developing a sickle, or crescent, shape. Sickle cells are very dangerous because of their rigidity and stickiness, which cause the cells to clump, blocking blood flow in the blood vessels of the limbs and organs. The blocked blood flow can cause pain, organ damage, and increased probability of infection. Moreover, the abnormal sickle cells usually die after only about 10-20 days, and the bone marrow cannot make new RBCs fast enough to replace the dying ones [1]. Figure 1 illustrates the danger of sickle-cell anemia and its various types.

Sickle-cell anemia is most common in people whose families originate from Mediterranean countries, Africa, South or Central America (especially Panama and the Caribbean islands), Saudi Arabia, and India. In the United States of America, approximately 70,000 to 100,000 people suffer from the condition, and they are

457

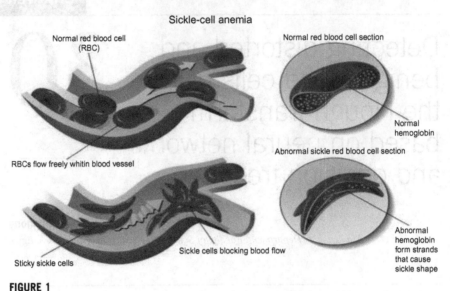

FIGURE 1

Kinds of RBCs and sickle-cell anemia.

mainly African Americans. The discovery of this disease depends on blood test analysis that can specifically detect sickle cells [1].

Recently, microscopic-image analysis has been used as an impressive diagnostic tool for detecting irregular blood cells [1]. The Hough transforms is the most important technique applied to image analysis and segmentation for the detection of blood cells. The transform depends on extracting features related through the segmentation of the microscopic image. Generally, the Hough transforms used today were invented by Richard Duda and Peter Hart in 1972, who called it a "generalized Hough transforms" after the related 1962 patent of Paul Hough [2,3]. Figure 2 shows a simple example of a pixel lying on a definite circle (solid circle), and the classical circular Hough transform (CHT) voting pattern (dashed circles) for the applicant pixel.

On the other hand, data mining techniques have gained popularity as illustrative and predictive applications of image analysis, and researchers have used the two techniques on blood cell detection data. The neural network (NN) is one of these techniques, and it has been successfully applied in the identification and control of dynamic systems. In 1986, David Rumelhart introduced concepts related to the NN when he presented a back-propagation process, which used many layers throughout the network.

Another technique of data mining is the classification and regression tree (C&R), which is the most common and powerful technique for classifying data and predicting outcomes in the decision tree (DT). It can generate understandable rules and handle both continuous and categorical variables [4]. The C&R tree algorithm had been popularized by Breiman, Friedman, Olshen, and Stone in 1984, before Ripley in 1996 [5]. The popularity of DT techniques is due to two features: (1) the procedures are relatively straightforward to understand and explain, and (2) the

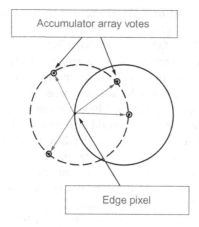

Accumulator array votes

Edge pixel

FIGURE 2

Voting in classic circular Hough transforms.

procedures address a number of data complexities, such as nonlinearly and interactions, that commonly occur in real data [4].

This chapter is divided into two parts. In the first part, I apply a proposed algorithm to detect benign and distorted blood cells (sickle-cell anemia) and to count them depending on the segmentation of their shapes using CHT, watershed, and morphological tools. In the second part, I introduce an algorithm for checking and analyzing the resulting cell data variables (e.g., area, convex area, perimeter, and eccentricity) by applying the most important techniques in data mining, NN and DT (C&R tree), to get the right decision for diagnosis [6].

To this end, the chapter is organized as follows: Section 2 focuses on the related work which is presenting a literature review on the work in this chapter, and Section 3 presents the definition and features of the Hough transform. Section 4 provides an overview of the NN. Section 5 discusses the C&R of DTs, and the proposed algorithm is presented in Section 6. In Section 7, the experimental results show the effectiveness of each model, and I offer a conclusion in Section 8.

2 RELATED WORK

In recent years, research on the blood cells' detection and diagnosis of diseases using image processing has grown rapidly. In 2010, Y M Hirimutugoda and Gamini Wijayarathna presented a method to detect thalassaemia and malarial parasites in blood sample images acquired from light microscopes and investigated the possibility of rapid and accurate automated diagnosis of red blood cell disorders. To evaluate the accuracy of the classification in the recognition of medical image patterns, they trained two back propagation Artificial Neural Network models (3 layers and 4 layers) together with image analysis techniques on morphological features of RBCs. The three layers had the best performance with an error of 2.74545e-005 and 86.54%

correct recognition rate. The trained three layer ANN acts as a final detection classifier to determine diseases [7].

In December 2012, D.K. DAS, C. CHAKRABORTY, B. MITRA, A.K. MAITI, and A.K. RAY introduced a methodology using some techniques of machine learning for characterizing RBCs in anemia based on microscopic images of peripheral blood smears. In the first, for reducing unevenness of background illumination and noise they preprocessed peripheral blood smear images based on geometric mean filter and the technique of gray world assumption. Then watershed segmentation technique applied to erythrocyte cells. The distorted RBCs, such as, sickle cells, echinocyte, tear drop, acanthocyte, elliptocyte, and benign cells have been classified as dependent on their morphological shape changes. They observed that when a small subset of features used by using information gain measures, the logistic regression classifier presented better in performance. They achieved highest prediction in terms of overall accuracy by 86.87%, sensitivity to 95.3%, and specificity was 94.13% [8].

In May 2013, Thirusittampalam, Hossain, Ghita, and Whelan developed a novel tracking algorithm that extracted cell motility indicators and determined cellular division (mitosis) events in large time-lapse phase-contrast image sequences. Their process of automatic, unsupervised cell tracking was carried out in a sequential manner, with the interframe cell's association achieved by assessing the variation in the local cellular structures in consecutive frames from the image sequence. The experimental results indicated that their algorithm achieved 86.10% overall tracking accuracy and 90.12% mitosis detection accuracy [9].

Also in May 2013, Khan and Maruf presented an algorithm for cell segmentation and counting via the detection of cell centroids in microscopic images. Their method was specifically designed for counting circular cells with a high probability of occlusion. The experimental results showed an accuracy of 92% of cell counting, even at around 60% overlap probability [10].

An algorithm presented by Mushabe, Dendere, and Douglas in July 2013 identified and counted RBCs as well as parasites in order to perform a parasitemia calculation. The authors employed morphological operations and histogram-based thresholds to detect the RBCs, and they used boundary curvature calculations and Delaunay triangulation to split overlapped cells. A Bayesian classifier with their RGB pixel values as features classified the parasites, and the results showed 98.5% sensitivity and 97.2% specificity for detecting infected RBCs [11]. In 2014, Rashmi Mukherjee presented an evaluation the morphometric features of placental villi and capillaries in preeclamptic and normal placentae. The study included light microscopic images of placental tissue sections of 40 preeclamptic and 35 normotensive pregnant women. The villi and capillaries characterized based on preprocessing and segmentation of these images. He applied principal component analysis (PCA), Fisher's linear discriminant analysis (FLDA), and hierarchical cluster analysis (HCA) to identify placental (morphometric) features, which are the most significant from microscopic images. He achieved 5 significant morphometric features (>90% overall discrimination accuracy) identified by FLDA, and PCA returned three most significant principal components cumulatively explained 98.4% of the total variance [12]. From this literature survey, it was noticed that research work has been done towards anemia-affected RBCs' characterization using computer vision approach. The proposed work methodology has described in Section 6.

3 HOUGH TRANSFORMS

The Hough transform is a popular feature extraction technique that converts an image from Cartesian to polar coordinates. Any point within the image space is represented by a sinusoidal curve in the Hough space. In addition, two points in a line segment generate two curves, which are overlaid at a location that corresponds with a line through the image space. Even though this model form is very easy, it is deeply complicated for the case of complex shapes due to noise and shape imperfection, as well as the problem of finding slopes of vertical lines. The CHT solved this problem by putting a transformation of the centroid of the shape in the x-y plane to the parameter space [13].

There are three essential steps common to all CHTs. First, a CHT contains an accumulator array computation of high gradient foreground pixels, which chosen as candidate pixels. Then they are collected "votes" in the accumulator array. Center estimation is the second step. It predicts the circles centers by detecting the peaks in the accumulator array that produced through voting on candidate pixels. The votes are accumulated in the accumulator array box according to a circle's center. Figure 3 shows an example of the candidate pixels (solid dots) falling on an actual circle (solid circle), as well as their voting patterns (dashed circles), which coincide with the center of the substantial circle. The third step in a CHT is radius estimation; if the same accumulator array has been used for more than one radius value, as is commonly done in CHT algorithms, the radii of detected circles must be estimated as a separate step [2]. The radius can be clearly estimated by using radial histograms; however, in

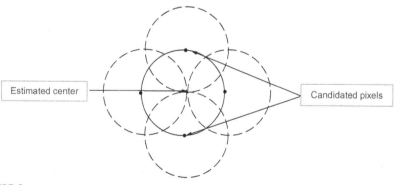

FIGURE 3

Circle center estimated.

phase-coding, the radius can be estimated by simply decoding phase information from the estimated center located within an accumulator array [2]. For this chapter, I have used a CHT to detect and count RBCs, even if they are hidden or overlapped. Watershed and morphological functions are used to enhance and separate overlapped cells during the segmentation process.

4 OVERVIEW OF NN

Now, NN with back propagation is the most popular artificial NN construction, and it is known as a powerful function approximation for prediction and classification problems. Historically, the NN has been viewed as a mutually dependent group of artificial neurons that uses a mathematical model for information processing, with a connected approach to computation introduced by Freeman in 1991 [4,14]. The NN structure is organized into layers of input, output neurons, and hidden layers, as in Figure 4.

The activation function may be a simple threshold function, a sigmoid hyperbolic tangent, or a radial basis function [15].

$$y_i = f\left(\sum w_{ij} x_i\right) \tag{1}$$

Back propagation is a common training technique for an NN. This training process requires the NN to perform a particular function by adjusting the values of the connections (weights) between elements [6,16]. Actually, three important issues related to the NN need to be addressed: selection of data samples for network training, selection of an appropriate and efficient training algorithm, and determination of network size [17,18].

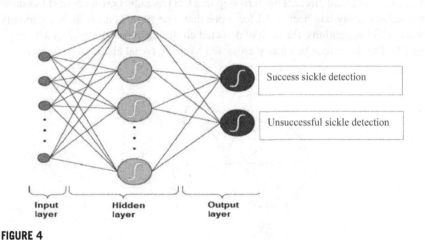

FIGURE 4

The structure of a neural network.

Moreover, an NN has many advantages, such as the good learning ability, less memory demand, suitable generalization, fast real-time operating, simple and convenient utilization, adeptness at analyzing complex patterns, and so on. On the other hand, an NN has some disadvantages, including its requirement for high-quality data, the need for careful *a priori* selection of variables, the risk of over-fitting, and the required definition of architecture [14].

5 OVERVIEW OF THE CLASSIFICATION AND REGRESSION TREE

C&R trees are the most common and popular nonparametric DT learning technique. In this chapter, I only use a regression tree for numeric data values. C&R builds a binary tree by splitting the records at each node according to a function of a single input variable. The measure used to evaluate a potential splitter is diversity. This method uses recursive partitioning to split the training records into segments with similar output variable values [4]. Moreover, the impurity used at each node can be defined in the tree by two measures: entropy, as in Equation (2), and Gini, which has been chosen for this chapter. The equation for entropy follows.

$$\text{Entropy}(t) = -\sum_j p(j \mid t) \log p(j \mid t) \tag{2}$$

The Gini index, on the other hand, generalizes the variance impurity, which is the variance of distribution related to the two classes. As in Equation (3), the Gini index can also be useful as the expected error rate if the class label is randomly chosen from the class distribution at the node. In such a case, this impurity measure would have been slightly stronger at equal probabilities (for two classes) than the entropy measure. The Gini index, which is defined by the following equation, holds some advantages for an optimization of the impurity metric at the nodes [19].

$$g(t) = 1 - \sum_j p^2(j \mid t) \tag{3}$$

When the cases in a node are evenly distributed across the categories, the Gini index takes its maximum value of $1-(1/k)$, where k is the number of categories for the target attribute. Furthermore, for all cases in the node that belong to the same category, the Gini index equals zero.

6 THE PROPOSED ALGORITHM

The goal of this chapter is to describe a process for detecting and distinguishing between benign and distorted blood cells in a colored microscopic image. This work can help doctors, physicians, chemists, and anyone else who cares about blood cell detection and analysis, and determination of diseases. The proposed algorithm is divided into two steps, as shown in Figure 5.

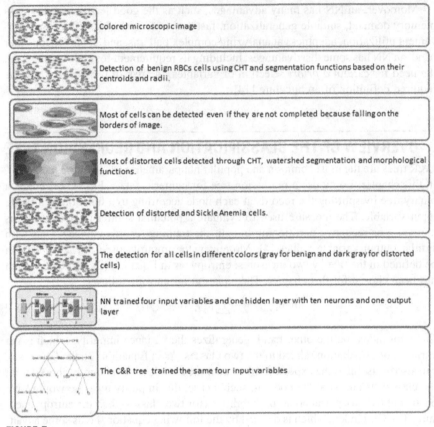

Colored microscopic image

Detection of benign RBCs cells using CHT and segmentation functions based on their centroids and radii.

Most of cells can be detected even if they are not completed because falling on the borders of image.

Most of distorted cells detected through CHT, watershed segmentation and morphological functions.

Detection of distorted and Sickle Anemia cells.

The detection for all cells in different colors (gray for benign and dark gray for distorted cells)

NN trained four input variables and one hidden layer with ten neurons and one output layer

The C&R tree trained the same four input variables

FIGURE 5

The main points of the proposed algorithm.

In the first step, I apply a CHT with morphological functions to the bright and dark intensity of cells to detect and count benign and distorted blood cells. In the second step, I use NN and a C&R tree to test and check the performance of the proposed algorithm for diagnosing a patient with sickle-cell anemia, evaluating which process is more effective than the other. Classification and prediction depend on the detected cells' data variables (e.g., area, convex area, perimeter, and eccentricity) to reduce the errors in detection operation and ensure final diagnosis of sickle-cell anemia. The first part of the CHT includes many operations:

- *Cell polarity* indicates whether the circulating blood cells are brighter or darker than the background.
- *Computation* (two-stage) calculates the accumulator array of the CHT. It is based on computing radial histograms; radii are clearly applying the estimated cell centers along with the image information [20].

- The *sensitivity factor* is the sensor of the accumulator array in the CHT. Detection includes weak and partially hidden or overlapped cells; however, higher sensitivity values increase the risk of false detection.

This stage also determines the edge gradient threshold, given that cells generally have a darker interior (nuclei) surrounded by a bright halo. The edge gradient threshold is very useful for determining edge pixels, and both unhealthy and strong blood cells can be detected based on their contrast by setting a lower value in the threshold. The system detects fewer cells with weak edges when the value of the threshold is increased [15].

The final stage is the segmentation process, which displays the input image with all the contoured benign (gray) and distorted (dark gray) RBCs. Through this operation, the area, convex area, perimeter, and eccentricities for each cell are measured. In addition, the good and distorted cells can be counted, and the patient can be diagnosed with sickle-cell anemia. These measures are used as input variables to train the NN and C&R tree; but the output (target) measured based on the solidity (S), which it is the area of cell divided by its convex area, as in Equation (4):

$$S = \frac{area_c}{(convex\,area_c)} \tag{4}$$

$$T_c = \begin{cases} 1 \text{ if } 0.95 < S_c \le 1 \\ 0 \text{ if } 0 \le S_c \le 0.95 \end{cases} \tag{5}$$

where $area_c$ is the area in each cell, and convex $area_c$ represents its convex area for all detected cells (benign and distorted). The target T_c can have two values, 1 and 0, based on the solution of Equation (4). As a result, if any solidity value S_c is >0.95 up to 1 (perfect cell), T_c takes the value 1 with the decision benign. On the other hand, if T_c takes the value 0, then the S_c value is ≤ 0.95 according to Equation (4), with the decision that the cell is distorted and may be sickled.

The back-propagation NN has been trained and tested using 4 variables as an input layer, 10 neurons in the hidden layer, and 1 neuron in the output layer. Moreover, three kinds of samples are applied: training, validation, and testing samples. The samples are presented in the network during the training process by 80% and 20% for testing process, and the network is modified according to the error. Accordingly, only 10% are used for the validation samples to measure network generalization and to pause training when generalization stops improving. The remaining 10% of all cell samples are introduced as a testing sample that has no effect on training and thus provides an independent measure of network performance during and after training. In addition, the mean square error (MSE) is applied, with the MSE defined as the average squared difference between outputs and targets. For the MSE, lower values are better, and zero means no error. Table 1 illustrates the description of the formed cells' data, which is automatically computed for all cells (benign and distorted).

Apart from the NN, the recursive binary C&R tree has been applied to the term of regression because all variables contain numeric values, as shown in Table 1. In this

Table 1 Blood cell variables

#	Variable	Type	Domain
1	Area	Ranged	163:1376
2	Convex area	Ranged	187:1781
3	Perimeter	Ranged	58.97056:218.2082
4	Eccentricity	Ranged	0:0.965444268
5	Target	Binary	(1 for benign cell, 0 for distorted cell)

table, all variables range in type, and only the output (target) variable has binary values (e.g., 1 for benign cells and 0 for distorted cells). The binary tree is divided into two branches based on the Gini index and recursively trained with a maximum tree depth of five levels, and it stops when it achieves a parent branch minimum of 2% and a child branch minimum of 1%.

Finally, the performance of each classification model is evaluated using three statistical measures: classification accuracy, sensitivity, and specificity. These measures are defined as true positive (TP), true negative (TN), false positive (FP), and false negative (FN). A TP decision occurs when the positive prediction of the classifier coincides with a positive prediction of the previous segmentation. A TN decision occurs when both the classifier and the segmentation suggest the absence of a positive prediction. An FP occurs when the system labels the benign cell (positive prediction) as a malignant or distorted one. Finally, An FN occurs when the system labels a negative (malignant) cell as positive. Moreover, the classification accuracy is defined as the ratio of the number of correctly classified cells to the total number of cells, and it is equal to the sum of TP and TN divided by the total number of RBCs (N), as shown in the following equation [9].

$$\text{Accuracy} = \frac{\text{TP} + \text{TN}}{N} \tag{6}$$

Sensitivity refers to the rate of correctly classified positives, and it is equal to TP divided by the sum of TP and FN.

$$\text{Sensitivity} = \frac{\text{TP}}{\text{TP} + \text{FN}} \tag{7}$$

Specificity refers to the rate of correctly classified negatives, and it is equal to the ratio of TN to the sum of TN and FP [9].

$$\text{Specificity} = \frac{\text{TN}}{\text{TN} + \text{FP}} \tag{8}$$

7 THE EXPERIMENTAL RESULTS

As mentioned above, the experimental results are displayed in two parts. The first part is concerned with the detection and segmentation of RBCs in order to distinguish between benign and distorted cells (caused by sickle-cell anemia), with the cells counted automatically. The second part involves checking the previous detection process exported from part one by predicting and categorizing the segmentation results using the two most famous classification models in data analysis: the NN and the C&R tree [6,21].

In part one, the detection process begins with importing and reading the microscopic colored image of RBCs. All cells (benign or distorted) are then detected using CHT, a watershed process, and morphological techniques for enhancing the detection process. In the same way, CHT is applied to the conditions of cell polarity to determine all dark and bright cells according to their intensity. A two-stage technique subsequently computes the accumulator array of the CHT. The sensitivity of this accumulator array for the proposed algorithm is 0.97 for brightness and 0.90 for darkness, and the edge gradient threshold is set at 0.2 to detect fewer cells with weak edges. Actually, these conditions help the CHT to detect most of the benign RBCs (near to the circle in shape), those positioned singularly or overlapping, and even those attached to other distorted cells. Figure 6 shows the original image of RBCs in (a), and the proposed algorithm is illustrated in detail from (b) to (f).

In Figure 6(b), a mask of balls is constructed using centroids and radii for each cell, which have been previously determined. In this case, and after the masking process, many overlapping benign cells appeared as one big region according to the shape and size of the normal cells. For that reason, the watershed process in Figure 6(c) is applied to get the optimum separation in this abnormal shape of cells. In fact, to get the optimal separation of overlapped cells, their centroids are used to put marks on them as in Figure 6(d). Now the cells within each cell blob have been separated and marked, as in Figure 6(e). Finally, by applying all the previous steps, the benign cells are contoured by gray lines, extracted to count, and distinguished from the other distorted cells, which are also shown in the second step of part one. This detection operation indicates 109 benign cells out of 180 detected cells (benign and distorted) in the image. In fact, the remaining cells (71) may be considered to be detection errors, distorted cells (sickle-cell Anemia), platelets, or even WBCs. The image in the figure does not have any WBCs, but if WBCs exist in other images, the proposed algorithm can easily detect and count them, as in Figure 7. On the other hand, platelets have been neglected because the algorithm concentrates only on RBCs and those distorted cells that occur with sickle-cell anemia [21].

Additionally, the algorithm has identified 177 cells, representing a 99.98% success ratio according to the image in Figure 6(a). Therefore, the next step is trying to discover how many of the 71 nonbenign cells are currently or potentially sickle cells. First, all 71 strange shapes (crescent, elliptic, platelets, and unknown) are discovered and displayed using the previous steps of benign cell detection. Figure 8 illustrates the last two steps of the proposed algorithm, which is applied to the distorted cells.

In Figure 8(a), a colored, segmented image shows all unknown distorted shapes with a noise similar to that produced by platelets, and so on. The current and potential sickle cells are detected without any noise in Figure 8(b). As a result, the deformed cells (current or potential sickle) appear to number 57 out of 71. The final detection

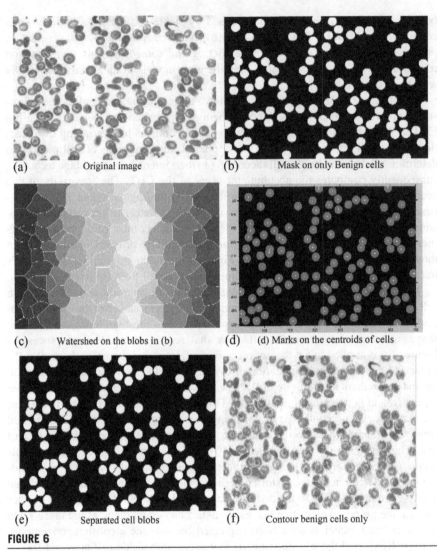

(a)   Original image   (b)   Mask on only Benign cells

(c)   Watershed on the blobs in (b)   (d)   (d) Marks on the centroids of cells

(e)   Separated cell blobs   (f)   Contour benign cells only

FIGURE 6

(a) The original image, (b) the healthy cells masked, (c) watershed for each blob region, (d) a small mark on each cell's centroid, (e) the cell blobs separated, and (f) the final detected benign cells.

of distorted cells is contoured by blue lines, as shown in Figure 8(c). In Figure 8(d), the final detection and tracking of all cells (benign by gray color and distorted with dark gray color) has been completed.

In this experiment, the NN consists of 4 input variables, 10 neurons in one hidden layer, and 1 output layer. The network succeeds after 65 of 1000 maximum iterations of the epoch, with a performance value of 0.0189, a gradient of 0.0165, and six

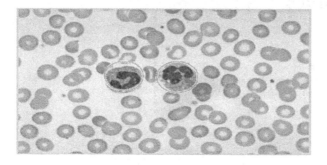

FIGURE 7

The detected WBCs.

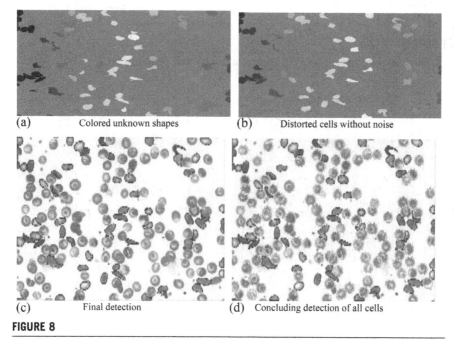

(a)   Colored unknown shapes

(b)   Distorted cells without noise

(c)   Final detection

(d)   Concluding detection of all cells

FIGURE 8

(a) All unknown shapes, (b) the distorted cells, (c) the final detection of only distorted cells, and (d) the final detection of all cells.

validation checks, as shown in Figure 9(a). In Figure 9(b), the best validation performance is shown as 0.00010338 at epoch 59, with the training in a dark gray line, validation in a gray line, and the test in a red line. In the same context, the MSE of training, validation, and testing processes are 2.059e−2, 1.03383e−2, and 1.17910e−2, respectively.

Figure 10 shows the confusion matrices for training, validation, and testing processes. In this figure, the predictions of the NN model are compared with the original

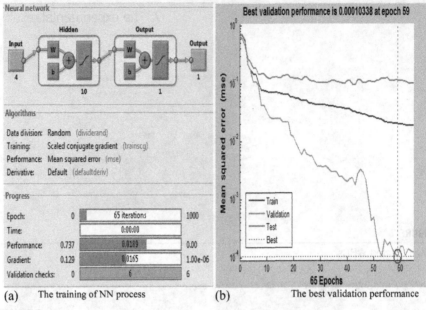

(a)   The training of NN process   (b)   The best validation performance

FIGURE 9

(a) The back-propagation NN, and (b) the best validation performance.

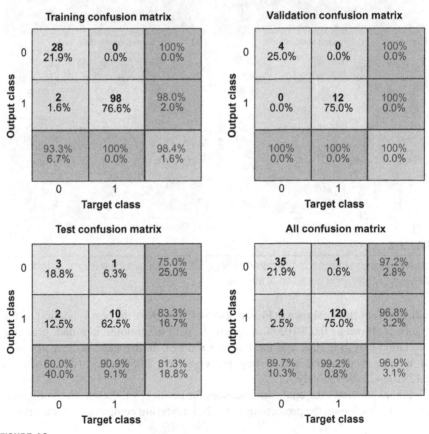

FIGURE 10

The confusion training, validation, and testing matrices.

classes of the target T_c to identify the values of TPs, TNs, FPs, and FNs. These values are computed to construct the confusion matrix, in which each cell contains the number of cases classified for the corresponding combination of desired and actual classifier outputs; it achieved 96.9%. Accordingly, accuracy, sensitivity, and specificity approximate the probability of the positive and negative labels being true and assess the usefulness the algorithm on an NN model. The accuracy, sensitivity, and specificity classifications of NN have achieved 98.4, 100, and 93.3% success with training samples, respectively.

Yet importantly, the NN agreed with the detection of cells using the proposed algorithm by about 96.9%.

Next, I apply the C&R tree to the mentioned input and target variables. The tree is carried out with a maximum depth of 5, a maximum of five surrogates, and the use of the Gini index to measure impurity. As in the previous example, the tree has trained 144 or 80% of all samples, and used 36 samples in validation and testing (i.e.. 20%). As a result, the tree achieved 95.83% agreed with the target in the training process, whereas, in the testing samples (cells), achieved 92.86% correct. Moreover, the most important and effective determined input variable is the eccentricity around 0.6786. The area variable comes in after eccentricity about 0.2576, followed by the perimeter variable around 0.0358 and the convex area variable at the end about 0.0279. Therefore, when using the C&R tree, the diagnosis may depend on the eccentricity, and, if necessary, the area variables, to distinguish the benign cells from the distorted ones.

Furthermore, the accuracy, sensitivity, and specificity in training samples have achieved 89.8%, 100%, and 82.1%, respectively. On the other hand, in the test samples, the accuracy, sensitivity, and specificity achieved approximately 81.25%, 100%, and 66.7%, respectively. Although the C&R tree is easier to apply to exported data than the NN is, it has achieved only about 92.9% success, while NN has achieved 96.9%. Clearly, the previous application of NN and C&R tree for the output data tends to show that NN is preferred and more effective than the C&R tree for making predictions from these data. In other words, the NN appears to be more effective at testing and checking the efficiency of the data resulting from the proposed algorithm in order to detect the sickle cells among all those distorted and, thus, to diagnose sickle-cell anemia. Finally, Matlab 2013a has been used to build the algorithm on Windows 7 with the processor Intel ® Core™2Duo CPU T5550@ 1.83 GHz, 2.50 GB RAM, and a 32-bit operating system. The optical Nikon microscope digitized all blood cell images.

8 CONCLUSIONS

The microscopic-image analysis of human blood cells is a valuable tool for detecting distorted blood cells. Sickle-cell anemia is one of the most important types of anemia. This chapter presents a proposed algorithm for detecting and counting the sickle cells among all healthy and distorted cells in a microscopic colored image, even if those cells are hidden or overlapped. I have used an algorithm with a CHT to detect benign and distorted blood cells. I then classified the exported variable data (e.g., area, convex area, eccentricity, and perimeter) for all detected cells (benign and distorted) as input variables, constructing a solidity measure for all cells as a target variable. In the next step, I applied the NN and regression tree to produce the right decision for diagnoses and to check the effectiveness of the proposed detection algorithm. Based on the experimental results, these procedures have demonstrated high accuracies, and these models appear successful at predicting the healthy and distorted cells present in blood from a person with sickle-cell anemia. I calculated the performance of the models, using three statistical measures: classification accuracy, sensitivity, and specificity. As a result, I have concluded that this algorithm has correctly segmented and classified about 99.98% of all input cells, which may have contributed to the improved diagnosis of sickle-cell anemia. The experimental results have shown that the effectiveness reaches to 96.9% in the case of applying an NN and 92.9% when using a C&R tree. Therefore, the proposed algorithm is very effective for detecting benign and distorted RBCs, and the NN is more efficient than a C&R tree for testing the quality of the detection algorithm.

REFERENCES

[1] U. S. Department of Health & Human Services, National Institute of Health, 2014. http://www.nhlbi.nih.gov/.

[2] Image Processing Toolbox, is available through MATLAB's help menu, or online at: http://www.mathworks.com/help/images/index.html.

[3] Stockman GC, Agrawala AK. Equivalence of Hough curve detection to template matching. Commun ACM 1977;20:820–2.

[4] Elsalamony HA, Elsayad AM. Bank direct marketing based on neural network. Int J Eng Adv Technol IJEAT 2013;2(6):392, ISSN: 2249-8958.

[5] Breiman L, Friedman JH, Olshen RA, Stone CJ. Classification and regression trees. Belmont, CA: Wadsworth; 1998.

[6] Devi BR, Rao KN, Setty SP, Rao MN. Disaster prediction system using IBM SPSS data mining tool. Int J Eng Trends Technol (IJETT) 2013;4(8):3352, ISSN Volume: 2231.

[7] Hirimutugoda YM, Wijayarathna G. Image analysis system for detection of red cell disorders using artificial neural networks. Sri Lanka J Biomed Inform 2010;1(1):35–42.

[8] Das DK, Chakraborty C, Mitra B, Maiti AK, Ray AK. Quantitative microscopy approach for shape-based erythrocytes characterization in anaemia. J Microsc 2013;249(Pt 2):136–49. Received 7 August 2012; accepted 11 November 2012.

[9] Thirusittampalam K, Hossain MJ, Ghita O, Whelan PF. A novel framework for cellular tracking and mitosis detection in dense phase contrast microscopy images. IEEE J Biomed Health Informat 2013;17(3):42–653.

[10] Khan HA, Maruf GM. Counting clustered cells using distance mapping. In: International conference on informatics, electronics & vision (ICIEV); 2013. p. 1–6.

[11] Mushabe MC, Dendere R, Douglas TS. Automated detection of malaria in Giemsa-stained thin blood smears, In: 35th annual international conference of the IEEE engineering in medicine and biology society EMBC; 2013. p. 3698–701.

[12] Mukherjee R. Morphometric evaluation of preeclamptic placenta using light microscopic images. Biomed Res Int 2014;2014:9 pages. Article ID 293690.

[13] Fleyeh H, Biswas R, Davami E. Traffic sign detection based on AdaBoost color segmentation and SVM classification, In: EUROCON conference, IEEE, 1-4 July; 2013. p. 2005–10.

[14] Freeman WJ. The physiology of perception. Sci Am 1991;264(2):78–85, University of California, Berkeley.

[15] Chaudhuri B, Bhattacharya U. Efficient training and improved performance of multilayer perceptron in pattern classification. Neurocomputing 2000;34:1–27.

[16] Wikipedia, the free encyclopedia, (Redirected from Neural network), last modified 21 Oct 2014. http://en.wikipedia.org/wiki/Neural_network#History of the neural network analogy.

[17] YuBo T, XiaoQiu Z, RenJie Z. Design of waveguide matched load based on multilayer perceptron neural network. In: Proc ISAP, Niigata, Japan; 2007.

[18] Mitchell TM. Machine learning. New York: McGraw-Hill; 1997.

[19] Brown SD, Myles AJ. Decision tree modeling in classification. In: Brown SD, Tauler R, Walczak B, editors. Comprehensive chemometrics. Oxford: Elsevier; 2009. p. 541–69.

[20] Atherton TJ, Kerbyson DJ. Size invariant circle detection. Image Viscion Comput 1999;17(11):795–803.

[21] Elsalamony HA. Sickle anemia and distorted blood cells detection using Hough transform based on neural network and decision tree. In: Proc. international conference on image processing, computer, vision, and pattern recognition. IPCV'14, Worldcomp'14, Las Vegas, Nevada, USA; 2014. p. 45–51.

Registration, matching, and pattern recognition

3

Improving performance with different length templates using both of correlation and absolute difference on similar play estimation ☆

31

Kyota Aoki, Ryo Aita

Graduate school of Engineering, Utsunomiya University, 7-1-2, Yoto,
Utsunomiya, Tochigi, Japan

1 INTRODUCTION

There are many videos about sports. There is a large need for content-based video retrievals. The amount of videos is huge, so we need an automatic indexing method [1]. We proposed the method to retrieve shots including a similar motion based on the similarity of the motion of a sample part of videos [2–5].

In former works, we used the correlation of motions and the correlation of textures [6]. We have a good performance using both the correlation of motions and the correlation of textures.

This paper proposes the method to retrieve the plays using only motion compensation vectors in MPEG videos. Using multiple features, the performance increases. Many works try to index sport videos using the motions in the videos. Many works try to understand the progress of games with tracking the players. Many of the works use the motion vectors in MPEG videos. They succeed to find camera works. They are zoom-in, zoom-out, pan, etc. However, no work retrieves a play of a single player from only motions directly. Of course, camera works have an important role in understanding videos. Sound also has some roles in understanding videos. Many works use camera works and sound for understanding sport videos. Those feature-combining methods have some successes about retrieving home runs and other plays. However, those works did not success to retrieve plays from only motions. Recently, many works focused on retrieval combining many features and their relations [7,8].

☆IPCV paper: Improving Performance using both of Correlation and Absolute Difference on Similar Play Estimation

In this paper, we try to propose a method that retrieves similar plays only from motions. With the help of texture, the performance of similar play retrieval increases. We showed that the combination both of motions and textures show better performance about similar play retrieval [9]. However, in many games, there are changes of fields and spectators. The colors of playing fields changes with the change of seasons. The motion based method can works with textures, sound, and camera works. In a previous paper, we proposed the method to estimate similar plays only from motions in motion compensation vectors in MPEG videos [10]. There are many motion estimation methods [11,12]. However, they need large computations. The method gets the motions from motion compensation vectors in MPEG videos, and makes the one-dimensional projections from the X motion and Y motion. The motion compensation vector exists at each 16×16 pixel's square. Very sparse description of motions is the motion description made from the motion compensation vector. The one-dimensional projection represents the motions between a pair of adjacent frames as a one-dimensional color strip. The method connects the strips in the temporal direction and gets an image that has one space dimension and one time dimension. The resulting image has the one-dimensional space axis and the one-dimensional time axis as the temporal slice [13–15]. Our method carries information about all pixels, but the temporal slice method does only about the cross-sections. We call this image as a space-time image. Using the images, the method retrieves parts of videos as fast as image retrievals do. We can use many features defined on images.

Our previous work uses a single template space-time image, and retrieves similar plays as the play described in the template space-time image [10]. However, using absolute difference and correlation, we can use different templates. Using different templates, they need not to be a same length. In our old works, for retrieving the pitches in baseball games, the best length of template is 20 frames. However, the experiments are restricted.

A long space-time image template is good for retrieving the same play in the template. However, in a similar play retrieval, the long template of a space-time image is not robust about the change of the duration of a play. A short space-time image template is robust about the change of the duration in a similar play retrieval. However, a short space-time image template is weak in the discrimination power.

This paper discusses the effects of the duration of templates in similar play retrieval using correlation and absolute difference in similar play retrieval on only motions. First, we show the over-all structure of the proposed method. Then, space-time image is discussed. Next, we discuss the similarity measures based on correlation and absolute difference. Then, we shows the experiments on a video of a real baseball game on a Japanese TV broad cast. And last, we conclude this work.

2 STRUCTURE OF THE PROPOSED METHOD

The proposed play retrieving method is the composition of a correlation and an absolute difference of motion space-time images [1–6]. We describe the space-time image as ST (space-time) image in the followings. In MPEG video, each

16×16 pixels' block has the motion compensation vector. Using the MPEG motion compensation vector as the motion description, the size of the description is 1/64 of the original frames. In other word, the static texture description is 64 times larger than the motion descriptions in size. The static texture description is 96 times larger than the motion description in total amount with the consideration of the vector size.

The color description fits for describing the static scenes. The motion description does for describing the dynamic scenes. A play in a sport is a composition of motions. Therefore, the motion description fits for describing plays in a sport. For retrieving the same play in a video, we can use any similarity measures. However, our goal is the retrieval of similar plays from videos. The speed of a play may change. In this case, the similarity measure must be robust about the absolute amount of motions. Our motion retrieval method uses the simple correlation as the similarity measure. The simple correlation works well in the similar play retrieval in sport videos. Using correlation as the similarity measure, there is no hint for the absolute amount of motions. As a result, there are some error retrievals. In the relative motion space, there is no difference between large motions and small motions.

The absolute difference is a major difference feature. In similar play retrieval, the absolute difference shows poor performance in our preparation experiments [10]. However, with other similarity measures the absolute difference can work some role for distinguishing the similarity measured with the correlations.

The proposed similar play retrieving method uses both of the correlation and the absolute difference between a template ST image and the ST image from videos. We can easily differentiate the large motion difference with the absolute difference. In sport videos, the absolute difference can find the camera motions. Composing the correlation based measure and the absolute difference based measure, we construct the composite similar play retrieval method.

Figure 1 shows the structure of the proposed method. We use absolute difference and correlation separately. Therefore, there is no need to use same length of templates.

3 1D DEGENERATION FROM VIDEOS

There are many degeneration methods. Some works use the temporal slices [9,16,17]. The temporal slices are easy to make and represent videos in small representation. The temporal slice is the sequence of the set of selected pixels in frames. There is no information about other pixels. These works make the temporal slices from color and textures in videos.

In this paper, we makes 1D degenerated representation using the statistical features of the set of pixels. The main statistical features are mean, mode, and median. We uses the mean for making 1D degeneration [9]. For treating sports, the motions in videos are important.

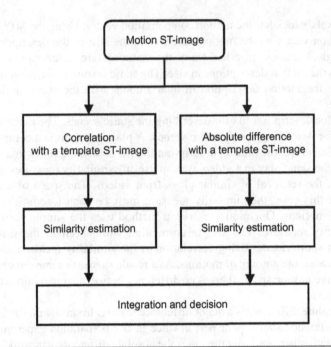

FIGURE 1

Outline of the proposed similar play estimating method.

3.1 MOTION EXTRACTION FROM MPEG VIDEOS AND CONSTRUCTION OF SPACE-TIME IMAGE

From an MPEG video, we get a two-dimensional image describing motion compensation vectors in a video. In the following, we abbreviate space-time image as ST image. The ST image has a space axis and time axis. The ST image represents the sequence of frames in one two-dimensional image. The ST image is a very compact description of a video, and it is easy to treat.

3.2 MOTION COMPENSATION VECTORS FROM MPEG VIDEOS

First, we must have the motions in an MPEG video. An MPEG video is a sequence of GOP (Group of Pictures). Each GOP is starting from I-frame, and has B-frames and P-frames. The motion compensation vector is block wise. The block size is 16×16. There is a 640×480 MPEG video. The image of motion compensation vector is only 40×30 pixels.

3.3 SPACE-TIME IMAGE

We have the motion vector (two-dimensional) on every motion compensation block. The amount of information is $2/16 \times 16 \times 3$ of the original color video. This is very small comparing with the original color frames. The baseball games can long about 2 h. This video has 200k frames. If we compare frame by frame, there needs a huge computation. There is a large difficulty to retrieve similar parts of a video.

We can retrieve similar parts of videos using classical representative frame wise video retrieve method. However, it is difficult to retrieve similar part of videos based on the player's motions, because motion leads a change of subsequent frames.

We can use many feature-based methods to retrieve similar part of videos. However, the applicability of the method depends on the features selected to use. The generality of the method may be lost using specified features.

This paper uses the one-dimensional degeneration for reducing the amount of information without lost generality. We make one-dimensional degeneration of each frame as:

$$I_{1dx}(x) = \frac{\sum_{y \in [0, Y_{max}]} I_{2d}(x, y)}{Y_{max} + 1} \tag{1}$$

$$I_{1dy}(y) = \frac{\sum_{x \in [0, X_{max}]} I_{2d}(x, y)}{X_{max} + 1} \tag{2}$$

Equation (1) makes one-dimensional degenerated description of X-direction from a two-dimensional image. Equation (2) makes one-dimensional degenerated description of Y-direction from a two-dimensional image. In Equations (1) and (2), $I_{2d}(x,y)$ stands for the intensity at the pixel (x, y). (X_{max}, Y_{max}) is the coordinate of the right-upper corner.

The resulting one-dimensional degenerated description is defined as:

$$I(j) = \frac{j \leq X_{max} \rightarrow I_{1dx}(j)}{j > X_{max} \rightarrow I_{1dy}(j - X_{max} - 1)} \tag{3}$$

There are two directions to make a one-dimensional degeneration. We use both two directions that are X-axis and Y-axis using Equations (1) and (2). In each color plane, we have a one-dimensional-degenerated description. We connect the two degenerated descriptions onto X-axis and the transposed projection onto Y-axis. We represent the X-direction motion in red, and Y-direction motion in green. There is no value in blue. Then, we have a one-dimensional degenerated color strip from the motion compensation vector. In the color strip, red represents the X-direction motion and green does the Y-direction motion. For the convenience, we set 255 in blue when both of X- and Y-direction motions are zero.

We connect the one-dimensional color strips describing motion frames on time passing direction. Connecting one-dimensional color strips, we have a color image that has one space axis and one time axis. In this paper, we describe this image as ST image. In the following experiments, we use the 320×240 pixels half-size frames. In the MPEG format, each 16×16 pixels block holds a motion compensation vector. This leads to reduce the amount of information into 1/256. The resulting motion image is 20×15 pixels. The 1D degenerated description is 7/60 of the original 20×15 pixels image. As a result, the usage of the ST image of motion compensation vector in MPEG video reduces the amount of information into 0.045%

from the original half-size video frames. In the ST image used in this paper, X-axis holds the space and Y-axis does the time. There is no reduction in information in time axis.

The similar motion retrieval estimates what kind of motions exists on a place. It is same as the cost of the retrieval on images to retrieve similar part of videos on an ST image.

There are many similar image retrieval methods. They can be applied in ST images describing videos' motions. This paper uses the correlation between two images. We normalize the resulting correlations for compensating the variance among videos. We have two independent correlations between two ST images from each color plane. The blue plane exists for only the convenience for our eyes. We use an X-direction motion and a Y-direction motion in red and green planes.

3.4 MATCHING BETWEEN TEMPLATE ST IMAGE AND RETRIEVED ST IMAGE

All ST images have same space direction size. The estimated motion image is $X \times Y$ pixels. Then, the size of the space axis of ST images is $X + Y$ pixels. For computing the correlations between the template ST image and any part of retrieved ST image, there is no freedom on space axis. There is only the freedom on time axis. If a template ST image is $S \times t$ and a retrieved ST image is $S \times T$, the computation cost of correlations is $S \times t \times T$.

In a baseball game, the length t of an interesting play of a video is short. Therefore, the computational cost of correlations is small enough to be able to apply large-scale video retrieval. Because of the shortness of the retrieved part, there is no need to compensate the length of the part. There is no very slow pitch or no very fast one. There is no very slow running or no very fast one.

4 SIMILARITY MEASURE WITH CORRELATION AND ABSOLUTE DIFFERENCE IN MOTION RETRIEVING METHOD

4.1 SIMILARITY MEASURE IN MOTION SPACE-TIME IMAGE BASED ON CORRELATIONS

We use the mutual correlation as the measure of similarity. We have two-dimensional correlation vectors. They are X-direction motion, Y-direction motion. If there is a similar motion between the template and the retrieved part of ST image, both of the two correlations are large. We use the similarity measure shown as follows:

$$S_C(I_T, I_V) = \min_{p \in \{x, y\}} \left(\text{NCol}(I_{Tp}, I_{Vp}) - \text{Th}_p \right) \tag{4}$$

$$\text{NCol}\left(I_{Tp}, I_{Vp}\right) = \frac{\text{Col}\left(I_{Tp}, I_{Vp}\right) - \frac{\sum_{I_{V'p} \in V} \text{Col}\left(I_{Tp}, I_{V'p}\right)}{|V|}}{\text{SD}_{I_{V'p} \in V}\left(\text{Col}\left(I_{Tp}, I_{V'p}\right)\right)} \tag{5}$$

In Equation (4), $S_C(I_T, I_V)$ is the similarity between an ST-image I_T and I_V. I_T is a template ST-image. I_V is a part of ST-image from a video. $\text{NCol}(I_{Tp}, I_{Vp})$ is the normalized correlation between I_{Tp} and I_{Vp} over a video V. The normalized correlation is normalized on the pair of the template ST-image and the ST-image from a video over the video. Th_p is the threshold. p is one of x and y that represent the X-direction motion and Y-direction motion. This similarity measure is scalar.

Equation (5) is the formal definition of NCol. SD is a standard derivation over the video V. Col is the correlation.

4.2 SIMILARITY MEASURE IN MOTION SPACE-TIME IMAGE BASED ON ABSOLUTE DIFFERENCES

We use the absolute difference as the measure of similarity in the motion description. In the case, we have two-dimensional absolute differences. They are the absolute differences based on both of X-direction motion and Y-direction motion. If there is a similar motion between the template and the retrieved part of the ST image, both of the two absolute differences are small. We use the similarity measure shown in the following equation:

$$S_D(I_o, I_1) = \min_{p \in \{x, y\}} \left(\text{NABD}\left(I_{0p}, I_{1p}\right) - \text{Th}_p\right) \tag{6}$$

$$\text{NABD}\left(I_{Tp}, I_{Vp}\right) = \frac{\frac{\sum_{I_{V'p} \in V} \text{ABD}\left(I_{Tp}, I_{V'p}\right)}{|V|} - \text{ABD}\left(I_{Tp}, I_{Vp}\right)}{\text{SD}_{I_{V'p} \in V}\left(\text{ABD}\left(I_{Tp}, I_{V'p}\right)\right)} \tag{7}$$

In Equation (6), $NABD(I_{0p}, I_{1p})$ is the normalized negation of absolute difference between I_{0p} and I_{1p}. I_{0p} and I_{1p} are ST images. Th_p is the threshold. p is one of x and y that represent the X-direction motion and Y-direction motion. This similarity measure is scalar.

Equation (7) is the formal definition of NABD. SD is a standard derivation over the video V. ABD is the absolute difference between two ST-images. In Equation (7), the terms in the numerator are placed reverse order from a normal position. This implements the negation.

5 EXPERIMENTS ON BASEBALL GAMES AND EVALUATIONS

5.1 BASEBALL GAME

This paper treats baseball game MPEG videos. In baseball games, players' uniforms change between half innings. The pitch is the most frequent play in a baseball game. There is a large number of pitches. This paper uses a single play of a pitch as a template. Using this template, the proposed method retrieves large number of pitches using similar motion retrieval.

Motion based similar video retrieval can find many types of plays based on the template. A few repeated plays are not pitches. This paper distinguishes a pitch and other plays.

5.2 EXPERIMENTAL OBJECTS

This paper uses a whole baseball game for experiments. The game is 79 min, 132485 frames in a video. In the game, there are right-hand pitchers and a left-hand pitcher. There are 168 pitches. 31648 frames represent the camera works that catch the pitching scenes.

5.3 EXPERIMENT PROCESS

The experimental videos are recorded from Japanese analog TV to DVD. Then, the recorded videos are reduced into 320×240 pixels and encoded MPEG1 format. Most plays of pitches are very short. Therefore, there is no reduction on time direction. There are 30 frames in 1S. There are all parts, including telops, sportscasters, and computer graphics. The first step of our experiment is the extraction of motion compensation vectors. The motion compensation vector is at each 16×16 pixel blocks. In every motion compensation block, we have a motion compensation vector. The similar play retrieval in motion frames uses a continuous sequence of frames as a template and retrieves the shots, including pitches of a video.

5.4 CORRELATION-BASED SIMILARITY MEASURE IN PITCHING RETRIEVAL

In this experiment, we use template pitches. The pitches include the pitch shows the best performance in our previous work. Around the pitch, we search the best length and the starting point of the template ST-image. In the experiments, the lengths of the template ST-images are 15, 20, 25, 30, and 40. The F-measures are 0.818, 0.846, 0.849, 0.863, and 0.781 respectively.

Table 1 shows the relations between the performances and the length of templates using correlation for calculating similarities. Using correlation for the similarity measure, the 40 frames of length is too long for retrieving pitches in baseball games. Comparing the 30 frames of length, the performance of the 40 is 10% lower than one of the 30.

Table 2 shows the relation between the performance and the starting point of 30 frames template ST-images. In a range of six frames from 120125 to 120131, the F-measures keep over 0.84.

Table 1 Performance with Correlation

Length	Recall	Precision	F-Measure
15	0.809	0.828	0.818
20	0.845	0.847	0.846
25	0.821	0.879	0.849
30	0.887	0.840	0.863
40	0.803	0.760	0.781

Table 2 Performance with Correlation by Starting Frame in 30 Frames Length Template ST Image

Starting Frame	Recall	Precision	F-Measure
120115	0.565	0.646	0.602
120120	0.750	0.693	0.720
120125	0.892	0.799	0.842
120127	0.839	0.871	0.854
120129	0.887	0.840	0.863
120131	0.815	0.887	0.849

5.5 ABSOLUTE DIFFERENCE BASED SIMILARITY MEASURE IN PITCHING RETRIEVAL

The length of durations of templates affects the performance a little. In the experiments range, the shortest one is the best one. The 15 frames length template retrieves all pitches. Moreover, it is best in F-measure (Table 3).

5.6 COMBINATION BOTH OF CORRELATIONS AND ABSOLUTE DIFFERENCES

For retrieving the precise pitches in videos, we need to use the correlation-based similarity. Combining the correlation based similarity and the absolute difference based similarity, we can improve the performance of the similar pitch retrieval.

Table 3 Performance with Absolute Difference

Length	Recall	Precision	F-Measure
15	1.000	0.190	0.319
20	0.988	0.190	0.318
25	0.976	0.189	0.316
30	0.970	0.186	0.312
40	0.976	0.180	0.303

Using the correlation based similarity or the absolute difference based similarity, we have no difficulties to find the proper set of thresholds. In the correlation based similarity or the absolute difference based similarity, two thresholds work in each X- and Y-direction motions.

We use logical conjunction to combine the correlation-based similarity and the absolute difference-based similarity. We can use logical disjunction. However, minimum is the extension of logical conjunction. We select logical conjunction in this paper. We have four thresholds in the combination. It is difficult to optimize all thresholds at once with short processing time. We divide the optimization of thresholds into two steps. They are the correlation-based similarity threshold optimization, and the absolute difference-based one.

First, we optimize the thresholds in the absolute difference based similarity. Then, we do ones in the correlation-based similarity. In the absolute difference based experiments, the recalls are high enough. This leads the decision. Of cause, there is no difference on the results between the correlation based first and the absolute difference based first.

Table 4 shows the result of the experiments. The templates are same in the previous experiments. Using the same length templates in absolute difference and correlation, the F-measure is 0.865. In number, there is 158 recalls and 39 errors. The error retrieval rate is 0.000297. This is 99.97% precision. This precision is very high. In the best mix of the templates' lengths, the absolute difference measure uses the 15 frames in the length of the template. The correlation one uses 30 frames in the length of the template. The range of the correlation's template includes the one of the absolute difference's one. Using the best mix both of absolute difference and correlation, the F-measure is 0.910. In number, there is 151 recalls and 13 errors. This error retrieval rate is 0.0000981. This is 99.99% precision. The number of error retrievals decreases 26. This is 67% decrease.

The best mix of two similarities works well. The F-measure of the best mix one increases 5% from the single correlation similarity. There is a difference in the best length of templates between the similarity based on absolute difference and the one based on correlation.

Table 4 Performance with the Combination of Correlation and Absolute Difference

Template Length (Correlation + Absolute Difference)	Recall (%)	Precision (%)	F-Measure
20+20	94.0	80.0	0.865
30+15	89.9	92.2	0.910

6 CONCLUSIONS

This paper discusses the length of templates on the retrieval of similar plays in sport MPEG videos using similar motion retrieval based on both of correlation and absolute difference. For recognizing sport videos, the motions represent important meanings. In the cases, there must be similar video retrieval methods based on the motions described in the videos. The proposed similar play retrieval method is the combination of correlation and absolute difference motion based on only motion compensation vectors in MPEG videos.

The experiments show that the similar play retrieval works well using correlation and absolute difference on ST-images made from motion compensation vectors in MPEG videos. Moreover, the best mix of the length of templates in absolute difference and correlation is better than the same template. Classical works using MPEG motion compensation vector only use global-scale motions. However, the proposed method utilizes local motions. The proposed combination of correlation-based similarity measure and absolute difference-based similarity measure works well in our experiments. Using both similarity measures, the proposed method gets some more performance than a single correlation based similarity measure based on motion based ST-images.

REFERENCES

[1] Hu W, Xie N, Li L, Zeng X, Maybank S. A survey on visual content-based video indexing and retrieval. IEEE Trans Syst Man Cybern C Appl Rev 2011;41(6):797–819.
[2] Aoki K. Video retrieval based on motions, JIEICE technical report, IE, 108, 217, pp. 45–50; 2008.
[3] Aoki K. Plays from motions forbaseball video retrieval. In: Second international conference on computer engineering and applications, 2010; 2010. p. 271–5.
[4] Aoki K. Play estimation using multiple 1D degenerated descriptions of MPEG motion compensation vectors. In: Fifth international conference on computer sciences and convergence information technology, 2010; 2010. p. 176–81.
[5] Aoki K. Play estimation using sequences of multiple 1d degenerated descriptions of mpeg motion compensation vectors, In: Proceedings of the eighth IASTED international conference on signal processing, pattern recognition, and applications; 2011. p. 268–75.
[6] Aoki K, Fukiba T. Play estimation with motions and textures in space-time Map description. In: Workshop on developer-centred computer vision in ACCV 2012. Lecture Notes in Computer Science, vol. 7728; 2012. p. 279–90.
[7] Fleischman M, Roy D. Situated models of meaning for sports video retrieval. In: Proceedings of the NAACLHLT2009, Companion Volume; 2007. p. 37–40.
[8] Sebe N, Lew MS, Zhou X, Huang TS, Bakker EM. The state of the art in image and video retrieval. Lecture Notes in Computer Science, vol. 2728; 2003, pp. 7–12.
[9] Peng S-L. Temporal slice analysis of image sequences. In: Proceedings CVPR '91. IEEE computer society conference on computer vision and pattern recognition, 1991; 1991. p. 283–8.

[10] Aoki K, Aoyagi R. Improving performance using both of correlation and absolute difference on similar Play estimation. In: 2014 6th international conference on digital image processing, proceedings; 2014. p. 289–95.

[11] Aoki K. Block-wise high-speed reliable motion estimation method applicable in large motion, JIEICE technical report. IE, 106, 536, pp. 95–100; 2007.

[12] Nobe M, Ino Y, Aoki K. Pixel-wise motion estimation based on multiple motion estimations in consideration of smooth regions, JIEICE technical report. IE, 106, 423, pp. 7–12; 2006.

[13] Ngo C-W, Pong T-C, Zhang H-J. On clustering and retrieval of video shots through temporal slices analysis. IEEE Trans Multimedia 2002;4(4):446–58.

[14] Bouthemy P, Fablet R. Motion characterization from temporal cooccurrences of local motion-based measures for video indexing, In: 14th international conference on pattern recognition, ICPR'98, Brisbane; August 1998. p. 905–8.

[15] Keogh E, Ratanamahatana CA. Exact indexing of dynamic time warping. Knowl Inf Syst 2005;7(3):358–86.

[16] Ngo CW, Pong TC, Chin RT. Detection of gradual transitions through temporal slice analysis. In: IEEE Computer Society conference on computer vision and pattern recognition, 1999, vol. 1; 1999. p. 41.

[17] Ngo C-W, Pong T-C, Chin RT. Video partitioning by temporal slice coherency. IEEE Trans Circuit Syst Video Technol 2001;11(8):941–53.

Surface registration by markers guided nonrigid iterative closest points algorithm

32

Dominik Spinczyk

Faculty of Biomedical Engineering, Silesian University of Technology, Zabrze, Poland

1 INTRODUCTION

Registration is a process to find correspondence between data sets, and generally could be divided into geometry-based or intensity-based methods [1]. Nowadays, in many multimedia applications input data set are represented as point cloud (segmented surfaces of the objects, etc.). Then in the processing pipeline data sets should be register, to find the correspondence between data sets. The most popular approach, in this case, is iterative closest point algorithm (ICP) [2]. This algorithm was proposed by a few researchers independently [3,4]. The ICP is an iterative algorithm and consists of two steps. The first step is to find a correspondence between target and source points, based on Euclidean distance between points. In the second step, the updated version of result transformation is calculated using equation:

$$f(S,T) = \frac{1}{N_s} \sum_{i=1}^{N_s} ||T_i - \text{Rot}(S_i) - \text{Trans}(S_i)||^2 \tag{1}$$

where T, S are target and source set of points, N_s is number of source points (equals number of target points), and Rot, Trans are rotation and translation components of final transformation.

The updated version of final transformation in current iteration is based on close-form solution of mean square error problem. The classical approach used only one rigid or affine transformation for whole data sets. In literature the description of disadvantages of the classical ICP approach [5] can be found:

- problem of finding global minimum of cost function depends on an initial guess of final transformation,
- the algorithm is sensitive to improper correspondences,
- long time of computation—one of the most time-consuming operation is retrieving correspondences.

Due to these disadvantages researchers proposed a lot of classical approach rectifications:

- registration only subsets of points,
- improvement of finding correspondence problem,
- quantity measure of proper correspondence,
- elimination of improper correspondence,
- modification of computing minimum of cost function.

The standard ICP approach cannot be used to track surface of objects that change their shape in time. Amberg [6] proposed nonrigid version of ICP by the following equation:

$$E(X) = E_d(X) + \alpha E_s(X) + \beta E_1(X) \tag{2}$$

where X is the unknowns organized in a $4n \times 3$ transformation matrix; $E_d(X)$ is distance measure between all target points and transformed source points, in contrast to classical ICP. X is not a single rotation or translation but a collection of affine transformation for each point; $E_s(X)$ is stiffness regularization, topology matrix is created based on points neighborhood to preserve the shape of object during iterations; we use square matrix topology (every point has four neighbors). α is stiffness vector, which influences the flexibility of cloud shape; $\beta E_1(X)$ is a factor used for guiding registration, based on known position of landmarks in source and target sets of points. β is a weighting factor, used to fade out the importance of landmarks toward the end of the registration process.

The implemented nonrigid ICP algorithm consists of two iterative loops. In the outer loop, the stiffness factor α is gradually decreased with uniform steps, starting from higher values, which enables recovery of an initial rigid global alignment, to lower values, allowing for more localized deformations. For a given value of α, the problem is solved iteratively in the inner loop. The condition of changing stiffness vector is threshold norm of transformation difference from adjoining iterations. In our implementation β is constant and equals 1. The above equation can be transformed into the system of linear equations, which is solved by computing pseudo-inverse matrix (see Amberg et al. [6] for details). This is the iterative algorithm, where each iteration consists of two main steps, namely finding correspondences between source and target points and computing affine transformations for each source point. If the second step is modified by the solution proposed by Amberg, that causes better results, corresponding problem remains critical for final results.

2 MATERIALS AND METHODS

Improvement of finding correspondences was implemented. Classically finding correspondences are done by searching Euclidean distance between closest points in source and target or in normal vector of source point direction. The general idea of presented approach was to take into account knowledge about markers' positions not only in computing transformation phase but also in finding correspondence phase in every algorithm's iteration. Decision to test a few approaches of finding correspondences was done:

- searching along normal vectors in source points, following the initial rigid registration based on Horn algorithm [7],
- along static marker vector displacement, where marker vectors are calculated only once at the preliminary stage. Marker vector is defined by positions of specific marker in source and target point cloud,
- along dynamic marker vector displacement, where marker vectors are calculated in each iteration based on constant positions of nearest marker points in matrix topology. Transformed source point in each iteration is treated as a new origin of dynamic marker vector.

Classical Euclidean distance is treated as baseline to compare the obtained results. Generally it is challenging to verify registration approach. We used global and local criteria for evaluation:

- global measurement: average distances between nearest source and target points, average distances between correspondences,
- local measurement—quality of correspondences: average correspondence assignment error of points nearest to the markers and the number of correspondences for every target points.

Data set consists of abdomen surfaces acquired by six volunteers on free breathing using time-of-flight sensor Mesa SR4000 [8]. Intensity map example of input data is presented in Figure 1. As markers 15 mm white squares attached to the abdomen were used, which corners were manually segmented by two users.

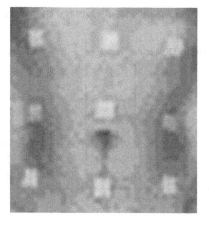

FIGURE 1

Example of input data: intensity map for ToF camera of abdomen with nine square markers.

3 RESULTS

For the different methods of finding correspondences, evaluation scores: surface distances, correspondence distances and average marker error, are presented in Tables 1 and 2.

4 DISCUSSION AND CONCLUSIONS

The implemented nonrigid ICP algorithm showed average residual distance of 0.68 mm (Euclidean distance not included). A further analysis of registration accuracy was focused on finding correspondence problem. Four methods for this

Table 1 Surface distances for four variants of ICP

ID	Surface Distance [mm]				
	Initial	E	NH	SM	DM
1	5.83	0,21	0.6	0.69	0.63
2	12.04	0.12	0.74	0.87	0.61
3	25.16	0.03	0.03	0.06	3.43
4	19.84	0.14	1.04	0.51	3.56
5	5.21	0.004	0.21	0.28	0.28
6	10.76	0.16	0.15	0.09	1.94

E, the Euclidean distance; NH, normal vectors with initial rigid registration; SM, static; DM, dynamic markers vectors.

Table 2 Correspondence distances and average marker error for four variants of ICP

ID	Correspondence Distance [mm]				Marker Error [number of unit]			
	E	NH	SM	DM	E	NH	SM	DM
1	0.26	0.18	0.25	0.58	12.42	10.81	4.45	0.76
2	0.12	0.27	0.33	0.87	7.02	6.28	2.12	1.49
3	0.04	0.03	0.03	1.7	2.57	2.9	1.86	0.44
4	0.14	0.22	0.15	0.88	4.3	4.63	3.6	0.72
5	0.04	0.07	0.1	0.1	4.05	2.61	3.11	4.69
6	0.16	0.07	0.06	0.53	2.25	1.89	0.75	0.09

E, the Euclidean distance; NH, normal vectors with initial rigid registration; SM, static; DM, dynamic markers vectors.

problem were tested: Euclidean distance treated as base line, normal shooting with initial rigid registration—marker-based Horn algorithm, static marker vectors (computing only one at the beginning of registration process), and dynamic marker vectors (computing in every iteration). For "near" cloud, where stiffness vector is constant for almost every iterations in nonrigid ICP, Euclidean distance is good enough. Unlike "near" clouds, "far" clouds, where stiffness vectors are changing for few iterations, Euclidean distance seems to be not enough. There are a lot of gaps in registered source cloud (Figure 2). To improve it, static and dynamic marker vectors were proposed. If marker is not only used in computing transformation step but also in computing correspondences step for each iteration, correspondence assignment error of points nearest to the markers decreased from 5.4 to 2.0 of confused neighbors. Normal shooting approach was also evaluated, but results were worse than other cases, while combination normal shooting and initial rigid registration significantly improved results (Figure 2). To use Horn algorithm at least three noncollinear corresponding points in source and target should be known. It helps to overcome the problem of the relative displacement of the source and target point clouds, which is not taking into account when Euclidean distance is used.

Because it is difficult to measure directly the quality of correspondences, observation was proposed in a few steps. Correspondence map (Figure 2) showed spatial distribution of the feature, number of correspondences assigned to every target point (desirable value is 1). It is easier to compare correspondence map globally with different cases using correspondence map histogram (Figure 3). Average correspondence assignment error of points nearest to the markers allows to measure the quality of correspondence points from cloud, which are nearest to the markers.

The results show improvement when markers are used not only in computing transformation phase but also in finding correspondence phase in every algorithm's iteration [9]. To make the proposed changes more universal k-nearest neighbor method and radius constraint could be used to apply the marker information to not only every point in the cloud but also the nearest points to the markers. For points that are not near a marker, the Euclidean distance was used. The score results for three selected values (i.e., 5, 10, and 15%) of the radius constraint selected as percent of the cloud width were calculated. The results are presented in Figure 4. For the most demanding criterion (5%), the results showed improvement.

The convergence of ICP algorithm is topic of research [10]. In presented approach no reliability weighting is used (weighting is always equal 1), the residual in an optimal step ICP is always decreased, because neither finding a new deformation, nor finding new closest points can increase residual. A formal proof for rigid case, which can be applied to presented approach can be found in Ref. [2]. Danilchenko and Fitzpatrick [11] proposed principal access approach to taking into account local character of anisotropic noise in rigid point

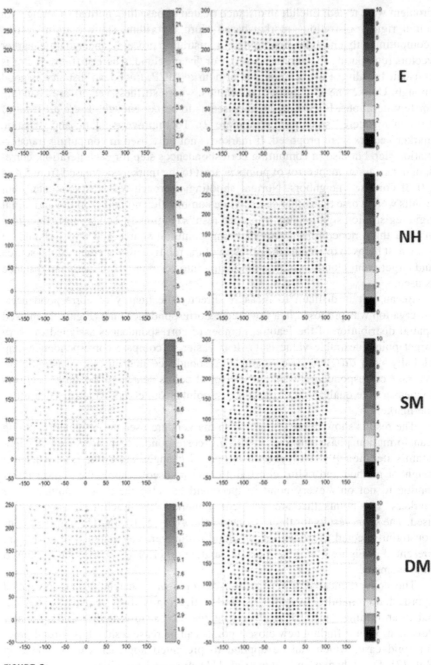

FIGURE 2

Distance map [mm] (left column) and correspondence map [number of units] (right column) for different modifications of ICP computing correspondence: Euclidean distance (E), normal shooting with initial rigid registration (NH), static marker vectors (SM), and dynamic marker vectors (DM).

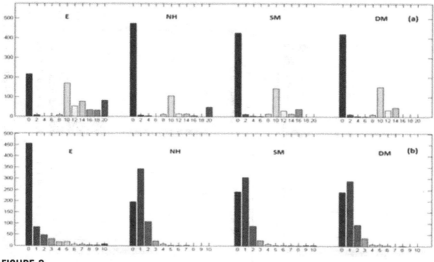

FIGURE 3

Distance map histogram [mm] (a) and correspondence map histogram [number of units], (b) in different modifications of ICP computing correspondence: Euclidean distance (E), normal shooting with initial rigid registration (NH), static marker vectors (SM), and dynamic marker vectors (DM).

registration and Maier-Hein et al. [10] used this approach to rigid anisotropic weighting ICP algorithm and ToF data. In future work this approach can be generalized to nonrigid ICP.

Presented approach may be used in different medical, entertainment, and industrial applications, where nonrigid point clouds should be registered, when initial relative position of clouds is that finding correspondences by Euclidean distance or normal shouting is not enough. The proposed changes do not introduce complex calculations. Initial calculation of rigid registration allows to solve the problem of unknown transformation matrix initialization. Comparing to classical nonrigid ICP the disadvantage of proposed approach is that initial corresponding positions of markers in source and target point clouds are needed.

ACKNOWLEDGMENT

The study was supported by National Science Center, Poland, Grant No UMO-2-12/05/B/ST7/02136.

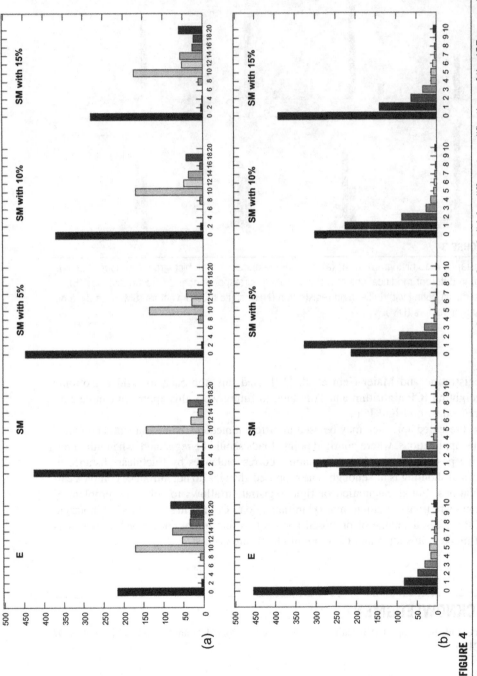

FIGURE 4

Distance map histogram [mm] (a) and correspondence map histogram [number of units], (b) for different modifications of the ICP computing correspondence algorithm: static marker vector (SM) and static marker vector with 5, 10, and 15% radius constraints for the ToF camera.

REFERENCES

[1] Wyawahare M, Patil P, Abhyankar H. Image registration techniques: an overview. Int J Signal Proc Image Process Pattern Recogn 2009;2(3):11–28.

[2] Salvia J, Mataboscha C, Fofib D, Forest J. A review of recent range image registration methods with accuracy evaluation. Image Vision Comput 2007;25:578–96.

[3] Besl P, McKay N. A method for registration of 3D shapes. Pattern Anal Mach Intell 1992;14(2):239–56.

[4] Chen Y, Medioni G. Object modeling by registration of multiple range images. Image Vision Comput 1992;10(3):145–55.

[5] Rusinkiewicz S, Levoy M. Efficient variants of the ICP algorithm, In: Proc. 3rd international conference on 3D digital imaging and modelingStanford, CA: Stanford University; 2001. p. 145–52.

[6] Amberg B, Romdhani S, Vetter T. Optimal step nonrigid ICP algorithms for surface registration, In: Proc. IEEE conference of computer vision and pattern recognition CVPR; 2007. p. 1–8.

[7] Horn B, Hilden H, Negahdaripour S. Closed form solution of absolute orientation using orthonormal matrices. J Opt Soc Am A 1988;5:1127–35.

[8] http://www.mesa-imaging.ch/swissranger4000.php – Mesa-Imaging – manufactor website: SR4000 Data Sheet.

[9] Spinczyk D (2014). Surface registration by markers guided non-rigid iterative closest points algorithm. Proc. 2014 international conference on image processing, computer vision, and pattern recognition.

[10] Meier-Hein L, Franz A, Santos T, Schmidt M, Fangerau M, Meinzer H, et al. Convergent iterative closest-point algorithm to accommodate anisotropic and inhomogenous localization error. IEEE T Pattern Anal Mach Intell 2012;34(8):1520–32.

[11] Danilchenki A, Fitzpatrick J. General approach to first-order error prediction in rigid point registration. IEEE Trans Med Imaging 2011;30(3):679–93.

An affine shape constraint for geometric active contours

33

Mohamed Amine Mezghich, Maweheb Saidani, Slim M'Hiri, Faouzi Ghorbel

GRIFT Research Group, CRISTAL Laboratory, Ecole Nationale des Sciences de l'Informatique (ENSI), Campus Universitaire de la Manouba, Manouba, Tunisia

1 INTRODUCTION

Precise object of interest detection is of high need in many applications of image processing such as medical imaging, tracking of moving object, and 3D object reconstruction. There have been several works in this field of image segmentation and object detection. Among them we can distinguish the classical active contours which are intensity-based models [1–5] and the constrained models by a prior knowledge that are driven both by global geometrical [6–9] or statistical [10–14] shape information and a local image information like gradient or curvature. There have been promising results given that the classical snake models can detect object with smooth contours whereas the level set-based models have the additional ability to detect simultaneously many objects in the image. However, several work of the prior knowledge-driven models reached good segmentation results by detecting partially occluded shapes presenting missing part in low contrast or very noisy image. To define prior knowledge, the authors use either shape alignment [7] or registration [9] between the contour of the target shape and the shape of reference or a distance between invariant shape descriptors like [8]. All these work manage the case of Euclidean transformations (translation, rotation, and scale factor). But in real situations, the object of interest can submit large transformations (affine or projective cases) and distortions. Hence the class of rigid transformations is not appropriate to model this type of movement between the shape of reference and the target one. To our knowledge, there has been only the work of Foulonneau et al. [15] that treats the case of affine transformations. Although this approach, which is based on the distance between an invariant set of Legendre descriptors of the target and reference shapes, presented good results, this method suffers from the instability of the Legendre moments and the order that has to be fixed empirically. Besides, the method requires a heavy execution time to achieve satisfactory results. In order to extend the work of shape priors presented in Refs. [16,17], we propose in this research a geometric approach to manage the class of affine transformations [26] that can occur between the shape of interest and the reference one. Prior knowledge is obtained by aligning the evolving contour and the template using an alignment method which is based on Fourier descriptors. For this purpose, we will start by introducing our approach in the case of rigid transformations. Then we generalize the idea by treating the case of affine ones that often occur in real situations. We will also propose a geometric method based on a set of complete and stable set of invariant shape descriptors to manage the case of mutireferences. Combining the proposed shape prior information with the level set-based model, the improved model can retain all the advantages of the active contour model and have the additional ability of being able to represent the global shape of an object. The remainder of this paper is organized as follows: In Section 2, a description of the outlines of the used shape alignment method in both cases (Euclidean and affine transformations) will be presented. In Section 3, we will briefly recall the principle of the used edge-based active contours, then we will move to present the proposed shape prior. Experimental results are presented and commented in Section 4. Finally, we conclude the work and highlight some possible perspectives in Section 5.

2 SHAPE ALIGNMENT USING FOURIER DESCRIPTORS

In this section, we recall the used alignment methods to define the proposed energy in both cases rigid and affine transformations.

2.1 EUCLIDEAN SHAPES ALIGNMENT

It is well known that the closed contour of a planar object can be given by its parametric representation

$$\gamma : [0, 2\pi] \to C$$
$$t \to x(t) + iy(t) \tag{1}$$

Let γ_1 and γ_2 be centered (according to the center of mass) and normalized arc length parameterizations of two closed planar curves having shapes F_1 and F_2. Suppose that γ_1 and γ_2 have a similar shape under rigid transformation.

In shape space this is equivalent to have:

$$\gamma_1(t) = \alpha e^{i\theta} \gamma_2(t + t_0) \tag{2}$$

where α is the scaling factor, θ the rotation angle, t_0 is the difference between the two starting points of γ_1 and γ_2.

Rigid motion estimation is obtained by minimizing the following quantity introduced by [18]:

$$E_{rr}(\gamma_1, \gamma_2) = \min_{(\alpha, \theta, t_0)} \left\| \gamma_1(t) - \alpha e^{i\theta} \gamma_2(t + t_0) \right\|_{L^2} \tag{3}$$

If α is equals to 1 [19], showed that Equation (3) is a metric in shape space and corresponds to the Hausdorff distance between the two shapes. In practice, this result implies the uniqueness of the motion's parameters so obtained. Using Fourier descriptors $C_k(\gamma_1)$ and $C_k(\gamma_2)$, minimizing $E_{\rm rr}$ becomes equivalent to minimize $f(\theta, t_0)$ in Fourier domain

$$f(\theta, t_0) = \sum_{k \in Z} \left| C_k(\gamma_1) - \alpha e^{i(kt_0 + \theta)} C_k(\gamma_2) \right|^2 \tag{4}$$

[18] proposed an analytical solution to compute t_0 and θ. t_0 is one of the zeros of the following function:

$$g(t) = \sum_k \rho_k \sin(\psi_k + kt) \sum_k k\rho_k \cos(\psi_k + kt)$$
$$- \sum_k k\rho_k \sin(\psi_k + kt) \sum_k \rho_k \cos(\psi_k + kt) \tag{5}$$

where $\rho_k e^{i\psi_k} = C_k^*(\gamma_1) C_k(\gamma_2)$, θ is chosen to satisfy Equation (6) and minimize $f(\theta, t_0)$ where t_0 is one of the roots of Equation (5).

$$\tan\theta = -\frac{\sum_k \rho_k \sin(\psi_k + kt_0)}{\sum_k \rho_k \cos(\psi_k + kt_0)} \tag{6}$$

Having the value of θ and t_0 that minimize $f(\theta, t_0)$, the scaling factor is given by

$$\alpha = \frac{\sum_k \rho_k \cos(\psi_k + kt_0 + \theta)}{\sum_k C_k^*(\gamma_2) C_k(\gamma_2)} \tag{7}$$

Based on Nyquist-Shannon theorem and B-spline approximation of the $g(t)$'s curve, Persoon and Fu [19] proposed the first implementation of this method of shape alignment and its application in rigid motion estimation for video compression. In Figure 1, we give an example of two aligned curves with the used method.

The estimated motion's parameters are presented in Table 1. The associated $g(t)$'s curve is presented in Figure 2. The zeros of $g(t)$ are drawn with circles.

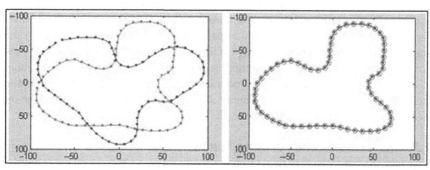

FIGURE 1

Example of two curves before (a) and after (b) shape alignment.

Table 1 The Estimated Parameters of Synthetic Rigid Motion

Rotation (°)	Scaling	Difference Between Starting Point
−45	1	0

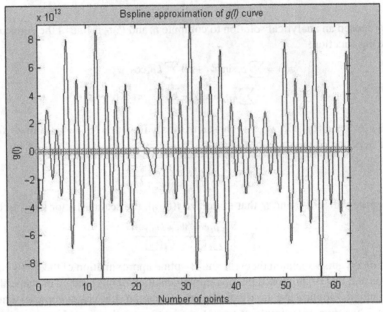

FIGURE 2

Example $g(l)$'s curve.

2.2 AFFINE SHAPE ALIGNMENT

In order to define affine invariant shape prior from a reference shape, we have to perform shape matching between the target and the template shapes F_1 and F_2. To correctly estimate the affine motion parameters, we have to deal with the same number of points which is not relevant if we consider two different points of view. For this purpose, in Ref. [20], the author proposes to use the affine reparametrization of curve which is invariant under affine transformation. We will start by presenting the affine reparametrization procedure of a given curve. Then we will describe our method of affine motion's parameters estimation.

2.2.1 Reparametrization of closed curve

If we take the same object in two different camera sides, we found a different number of contour points in each image. Consequently, we proceed by normalization of curves under affine transformation. Given the shape front, its edge pixels are extracted and traversed to yield a discrete closed curve which is a parametric equation $\gamma(t) = (u(t), v(t))$, where $t \in \{0, \ldots, N-1\}$ and $\gamma(N) = \gamma(0)$. We use the affine arc length reparametrization to normalize closed curves under affine transformations that can be expressed by:

$$s_a(t) = \frac{1}{L_a} \int \left\| \gamma'(t) \wedge \gamma''(t) \right\|^{\frac{2}{3}} dt, t \in [a, b] \tag{8}$$

$$L_a = \int_a^b \sqrt[3]{\left| \gamma'(t) \wedge \gamma''(t) \right|} dt \tag{9}$$

where L_a is the total affine arc length of the considered curve, $\wedge$ represents the cross product between two vectors and, $\|\cdot\|$ denotes the Euclidean norm.

2.2.2 Contours alignment using geometrical affine parameters estimation

We consider two closed curves O_1 and O_2 which define the same shape. O_1 and O_2 are said to be related by an affine transformation if and only if:

$$h(l) = \alpha A f(l + l_0) + B \tag{10}$$

where B is a translation vector, A is a linear transformation, l_0 is the shift value, f and h are the affine reparametrization of two contours having the same affine shape. In the Fourier space we get:

$$U_k(h) = \alpha e^{2i\pi k l_0} A U_k(f) + b\delta_k \tag{11}$$

where $U_k(h)$ and $U_k(f)$ are, respectively, the Fourier coefficients of f and h.

So estimation of affine motion can be resumed to the estimation of its three parameters: the affine matrix A, the shift value l_0, and finally the scale factor α if we consider a normalization under translation.

Estimation of the scale factor α

The scale factor can be estimated using the following formula:

$$\alpha^2 = \frac{\det\left(U_k(h), U_k^*(h)\right)}{\det\left(U_k(f), U_k^*(f)\right)} \tag{12}$$

where $(U_k(h), U_k^*(h))$ and $(U_k(f), U_k^*(f))$ are 2×2 matrix formed by Fourier coefficients on some fixed index k and U^* is the U complex conjugate.

Computation of the shift value l_0

Let's consider $M_1 = (U_{k_1}(h), U_{k_2}(h))$ and $M_2 = (U_{k_1}(f), U_{k_2}(f))$

$$l_0 = \frac{\arg\left(\det\left(M_2\right)\right) - \arg\left(\det\left(M_1\right)\right)}{(k_1 + k_2)} \tag{13}$$

where k_1 and k_2 are two fixed index and $\arg(U)$ is the complex argument of U.

Computation of the matrix A's parameters

Since scale factor α and shift value l_0 have been previously estimated (Equations 12 and 13), we are going to estimate affine matrix A parameters. Lets O_1, O_2 be two curves and U_f, U_h, respectively, their Fourier coefficients. In Fourier space we have (Equation 14)

$$U_k(h) = \alpha e^{2i\pi k l_0} A U_k(f) \tag{14}$$

Using matrix, we have the following formula:

$$\begin{pmatrix} u_2(k) \\ v_2(k) \end{pmatrix} = \alpha e^{2i\pi k l_0} \begin{pmatrix} a_1 & a_2 \\ a_3 & a_4 \end{pmatrix} \begin{pmatrix} u_1(k) \\ v_1(k) \end{pmatrix} \tag{15}$$

So we have to estimate a_1, a_2, a_3, and a_4. This system can be represented as following:

$$\begin{cases} u_2(k_1) = \alpha e^{2i\pi k_1 l_0} a_1 u_1(k_1) + e^{2i\pi k_1 l_0} a_2 v_1(k_1) \\ v_2(k_1) = \alpha e^{2i\pi k_1 l_0} a_3 u_1(k_1) + e^{2i\pi k_1 l_0} a_4 v_1(k_1) \\ \qquad \vdots \\ u_2(k_n) = \alpha e^{2i\pi k_n l_0} a_1 u_1(k_n) + e^{2i\pi k_n l_0} a_2 v_1(k_n) \\ v_2(k_n) = \alpha e^{2i\pi k_n l_0} a_3 u_1(k_n) + e^{2i\pi k_n l_0} a_4 v_1(k_n) \end{cases} \tag{16}$$

Then to estimate matrix A's parameters (Equation 14), we have to resolve a system with $2N$ equations and four unknown parameters that can be written as

$$K_{2N \times 4} A_4 = U_{2N} \tag{17}$$

The solution of the system (Equation 16) can be obtained by

$$KA - U = e \tag{18}$$

So we have to minimize the quadratic error e by using the pseudoinverse of K. We show by the following figure an example of affine motion estimation between two synthetic curves after contours resampling (Figure 3). The final result of curves alignment after affine motion estimation is presented by Figure 4. The estimated motion parameters are presented in Table 2.

2.3 DISCUSSION

Having the parameters of the affine or Euclidean transformations between the two contours, we perform the alignment of the two curves to determine the regions of variability between shapes by computing the product function of the signed distance

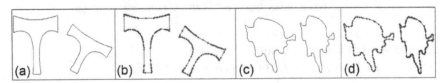

FIGURE 3

Two different shapes after affine deformations ((a) and (c)) and curve resampling ((b) and (d)).

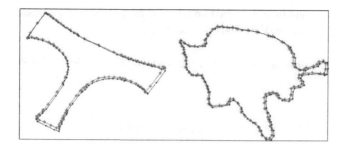

FIGURE 4

Results of affine shape alignment.

Table 2 The Estimated Affine Motion Parameters

	l_0	α	A
Shapes of (b)	0.002	1.003	$\begin{pmatrix} 0.860 & -0.47 \\ 0.52 & 0.865 \end{pmatrix}$
Shapes of (d)	0	2.004	$\begin{pmatrix} 0.962 & 0.002 \\ 0.1037 & 0.966 \end{pmatrix}$

functions associated to level set functions of, respectively, the target and the reference object after alignment given by

$$f_{\text{prod}}(x, y) = f_{\varnothing_{\text{ref}}}(x, y) \cdot f_{\varnothing}(x, y) \tag{19}$$

where $f_{\varnothing_{\text{ref}}}$ and $f_{\varnothing}$ are the two binary images associated, respectively, to $\varnothing_{\text{ref}}$ and $\varnothing$. See Ref. [16] for more details. By construction, the product function f_{prod} is negative in the areas of variability between the two binary images $f_{\varnothing_{\text{ref}}}$ and $f_{\varnothing}$ due to occlusion, clutter, or missing parts, whereas in positive regions, the objects are similar. Thus, in what follows, we propose to update the level set function $\varnothing$, only in regions of variability between shapes to make the evolving contours overpass the spurious edges and recover the desired shapes of objects. This property recalls the narrow band technique used to accelerate the evolution of the level set functions [4].

2.4 GLOBAL MATCHING USING AFFINE INVARIANTS DESCRIPTORS

In presence of many templates, we have to choose the most suitable one according to the evolving curve. Let α and β be positive real numbers, and k_0, k_1, k_2, and k_3 four positive integers.

Let C_n^x and C_n^y be the complex Fourier coefficients of the coordinates (u, v). $\triangle$ denotes the determinant.

$$\triangle_n^m = \begin{vmatrix} C_n^x & C_m^x \\ C_n^y & C_m^y \end{vmatrix} \tag{20}$$

In Ref. [20], the author introduced two sets of invariant descriptors I and J which are, respectively, given by (Equations 21 and 22).

$$\forall k - \{0, k_0, k_1, k_2\}, I_{k_1} = |\Delta_{k_1, k_0}|, I_{k_2} = |\Delta_{k_2, k_0}|, I_k = \frac{\Delta_{k, k_0}^{k_1 - k_2} \Delta_{k_1, k_0}^{k_2 - k} \Delta_{k_2, k_0}^{k - k_1}}{\left|\Delta_{k_1, k_0}^{k_2 - k - \alpha}\right| \left|\Delta_{k_2, k_0}^{k - k_1 - \beta}\right|} \tag{21}$$

$$\forall k - \{0, k_0, k_1, k_2\}, J_{k_1} = |\Delta_{k_1, k_3}|, J_{k_2} = |\Delta_{k_2, k_3}|, J_k = \frac{\Delta_{k, k_3}^{k_1 - k_2} \Delta_{k_1, k_3}^{k_2 - k} \Delta_{k_2, k_3}^{k - k_1}}{\left|\Delta_{k_1, k_3}^{k_2 - k - \alpha}\right| \left|\Delta_{k_2, k_3}^{k - k_1 - \beta}\right|} \tag{22}$$

In Refs. [21,22], the authors have shown experimentally that such descriptors are complete and stable. The completeness guarantees the uniqueness of matching. The stability gives robustness under nonlinear shape distortions and numerical errors. In Ref. [20], the author demonstrates that the shape space S can be considered as a metric space with a set of metrics. Hence, the Euclidean distance (Equation 23) between the set of the presented invariants can be used to compare the evolving curve and the available templates.

$$d_p(\mathbf{F}, \mathbf{H}) = \|\{I_n(f)\} - \{I_n(h)\}\|_{\mathbb{P}} = \left(\sum |I_n(f) - I_n(h)|^p\right)^{1/p} \tag{23}$$

For any real number p such that $p > 1$. Where f and h are two normalized affine arc length reparametrization of two objects having, respectively, the shapes F and H. The shape having the minimum distance according to the evolving active contour is used as template.

3 SHAPE PRIOR FOR GEOMETRIC ACTIVE CONTOURS

Geometric active contours are iterative segmentation methods which use the level set approach [2] to determine the evolving front at each iteration. Several models have been proposed in literature that we can classify into edge-based or region-based active contours.

In Ref. [4], the level set approach is used to model the shape of objects using an evolving front. The evolution's equation of the level set function $\varnothing$ is

$$\varnothing_t + F|\nabla_\varnothing| = 0, \tag{24}$$

F is a speed function of the form $F = F_0 + F_1(K)$ where F_0 is a constant advection term equals to (± 1) depends of the object inside or outside the initial contour. The second term is of the form $-\varepsilon K$ where K is the curvature at any point and $\varepsilon > 0$. To detect the objects in the image, the authors proposed to use the following function which stops the level set function's evolution at the object boundaries.

$$g(x, y) = \frac{1}{1 + |\nabla G_\sigma \times f(x, y)|} \tag{25}$$

where f is the image and G_σ is a Gaussian filter with a deviation equals to σ. This stopping function has values that are closer to zero in regions of high image gradient and values that are closer to unity in regions with relatively constant intensity. Hence, the discrete evolution equation is:

$$\frac{\varnothing^{n+1}(i,j) - \varnothing^n(i,j)}{\Delta t} = -g(i,j)F(i,j)|\nabla\varnothing^n(i,j)| \tag{26}$$

It's obvious that the evolution is based on the stopping function g which depends on the image gradient. That's why this model leads to unsatisfactory results in presence of occlusions, low contrast, and even noise. To make the level set function evolve in the regions of variability between the shape of reference and the target shape, we propose the new stopping function as follows:

$$g_{\text{shape}}(x,y) = \begin{cases} 0, \text{ if } \varnothing_{\text{prod}}(x,y) \geq 0, \\ \text{sign}(\varnothing_{\text{ref}}(x,y)), \text{ else} \end{cases} \tag{27}$$

where $\varnothing_{\text{prod}}(x,y) = \varnothing(x,y)\dot{c}\,\varnothing_{\text{ref}}(x,y)$, $\varnothing$ is the level set function associated to the evolving contour, while $\varnothing_{\text{ref}}$ is the level set function associated to the shape of reference after alignment. As it can be seen, the new proposed stopping function only allows for updating the level set function in the regions of variability between shapes. In these regions, g_{shape} is either 1 or -1 because in the case of partial occlusions, the function is equal to 1 in order to push the edge inward (deflate) and in case of missing parts, this function is equal to -1 to push the contour toward the outside (inflate). This property recalls the Balloon snake's model proposed by Cohen [23] in which the direction of evolution (inflate or deflate) should be precise from the beginning. In our work, the direction of evolution is handled automatically based on the sign of $\varnothing_{\text{ref}}$. The total discrete evolution's equation that we propose is as follows:

$$\frac{\varnothing^{n+1}(i,j) - \varnothing^n(i,j)}{\Delta t} = -\left(wg(i,j) + (1-w)g_{\text{shape}}(i,j)\right)F(i,j)|\nabla\phi^n(i,j)| \tag{28}$$

w is a weighting factor between the image-based force and knowledge-driven force. See Ref. [16] for our proposed shape prior for a region-based active contours.

4 EXPERIMENTAL RESULTS

4.1 ROBUSTNESS OF THE PROPOSED SHAPE PRIORS

We present in Figure 5 an example of successive evolutions between several shapes of different topologies under the proposed shape priors only ($w = 0$). By the first row, the initial shape is a simple square while the target is a tree leaf. For the second row, the final shape obtained after several iterations in the first row is used as initial contour. The template in this case consists of two contours. This experiment proves that the proposed shape constraint can act on the topology of the original curve. Finally, by the third row, we show the ability of our shape prior to detect objects with holes.

This simulation shows that the proposed shape priors can well constrain an active contour to take a given shape (known as reference) and handling nontrivial geometric shapes with holes and complex topologies.

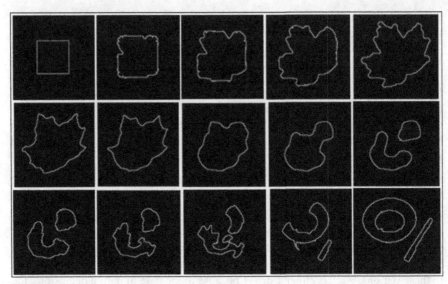

FIGURE 5

Curve evolution under the proposed shape prior only.

4.2 APPLICATION TO OBJECT DETECTION

We will devote this section to present some satisfactory results obtained by the proposed model in the case of Euclidean transformations, then the general case of the affine ones will be treated. The algorithm is as follows: We first evolve the active contour without shape prior until convergence (i.e., $w = 1$) to reduce the computational complexity and to have a good estimation of the parameters of the geometric transformation as in Refs. [8,11]. This first result provides an initialization for the model with prior knowledge. Then the model will evolve under both forces (data and prior forces) with more weight assigned to prior knowledge (generally $w \leq 0.5$) to promote convergence toward the target shape.

4.2.1 Case of Euclidean transformation

To assess the performance of the method, we have experimented the proposed method in medical imaging. The template is given by image 1 of Figure 6 which corresponds to the left ventricle of the heart. The aim is to detect the true contours of the left ventricle of the heart which are partially occluded by the valve. The second row of Figure 6 shows several iterations of curve evolution until convergence without prior knowledge. Starting with final this result, and based on the reference shape after rigid motion estimation, the evolving front continues its evolution until the curve reaches the desired contours (third row).

The aligned curves which are used to compute the prior energy are presented in Figure 7. We present by Table 3, the estimated rigid motion parameters.

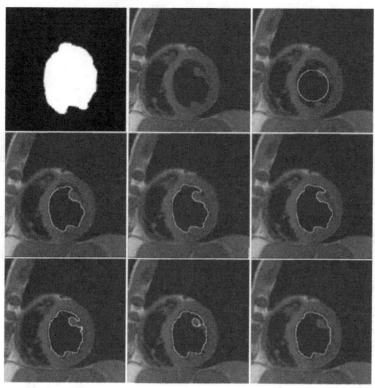

FIGURE 6

First row: The template, test image, initial curve. Second row: The active contours without shape prior. Third row: The active contours with shape prior.

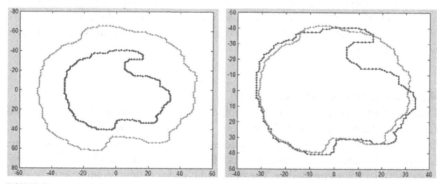

FIGURE 7

First image: Curves before alignment, Second image: Curves after alignment.

Table 3 The Estimated Motion's Parameters

Rotation (°)	Scaling	Difference Between Starting Points
−0.802	1.571	1.312

FIGURE 8

Tracking of the mouse in video sequence. First row: The active contours model without shape prior. Second row: The active contours model with shape prior.

We end this part of experiments by applying the active contour with shape prior to object tracking. In Figure 8, the goal is to track the mouse in a video sequence with cluttered background. We suppose that the movement of the mouse through frames is rigid thus the presented method of shape alignment is used. The convergent contour in frame i is used as a template in frame $i+1$.

Results seem to be satisfactory. Although, the presented rigid motion estimation method solves some situations and leads to interesting detection results. Other types of transformations such as stretching can only be solved by the class of relevant transformations. Thus the goal of the next section is to present some obtained results within this framework.

4.2.2 Case of affine transformation

Consider for this first experiment, the spider object, image (a) of Figure 9, obtained from MCD database (url: http://vision.ece.ucsb.edu/zuliani/Research/MCD/MCD. shtml). The (b) image is the object of interest which is obtained from (a) after affine transformation and partial occlusion. As a first step, we perform object (b) segmentation without prior knowledge. The obtained contour is then aligned with the contour of the (a) object to determine the regions of occlusions. We present in (c) the result of shape alignment. The estimated values are $\alpha = 2, l_0 = 0, A = [0.5, 0.2, 0, 2]$. By Figure 10, we present the obtained results without and with shape prior. We

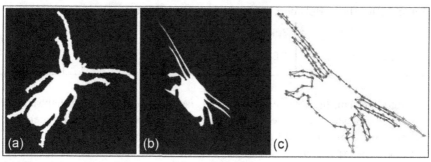

FIGURE 9

Spider's shapes alignment.

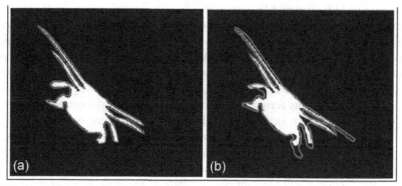

FIGURE 10

Detection without, image (a), and with, image (b), affine prior knowledge.

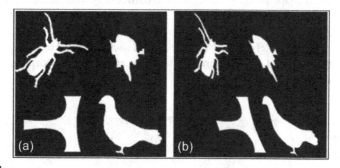

FIGURE 11

Image (a): The available templates. Image (b): The transformed object.

considered in this experiment four templates (a spider, a chopper, a device, and a bird), see Figure 11. We were based on the set of the presented invariant shape descriptors to choose the suitable reference according to the occluded spider (image (b) of Figure 11).

Table 4 Distances Between the Occluded Spider and the Used Templates

	Spider	Chopper	Bird	Device
The occluded spider	0.037	0.46	0.44	0.53

Table 4 presents the obtained Euclidean distance between the target shape and the available templates. We notice that the minimum distance can be easily identified because the suitable form in this experiment is distinguishable.

In the next experiment, a mosaic application is considered. The mosaic images that are considered are taken from the Bardo Museum of Tunisia which contains the biggest collection of mosaic images in the world. In mosaic images, objects are composed of tessellas and are often partially occluded as they are shown by images (c) and (d) (Figure 12).

So, given that in mosaic images the objects are often repeated and in order to study the robustness of our method, we try to find to true contour of an occluded object based on another one having the same shape. We have approximated the perspective projection to an affine transformation which is often used in the literature according to the acquisition conditions. Let's consider the (c) image. As it's shown, this image contains many forms. Among all forms available in these two images, (c) and (d), taken from two sides, we use the Euclidean distance between the affine invariant Fourier descriptors to localize two lions. The left one is partially occluded. We will use the right lion of the (d) image as template in order to have a better segmentation. In the last figure, images (a) and (b), we present the used curves to perform shape alignment and shape prior computation. The estimated values are $\alpha = 1$, $l_0 = -0.52$, $A = [-0.002, -0.003, 2.003, -0.35]$. We present by the (c) image the obtained curves alignment result and by the (d) image the segmentation result based on the proposed shape prior. Such results are particularly interesting since it can be used for mosaic images restoration under partial occlusions and missing parts. The underlying idea is to extract similar forms using minimal distance between descriptors in order to define prior knowledge for such occluded or cluttered objects based on the presented affine shape alignment method for the purpose of a good segmentation result (Figure 13).

FIGURE 12

Some mosaic images from the Bardo Museum of Tunisia.

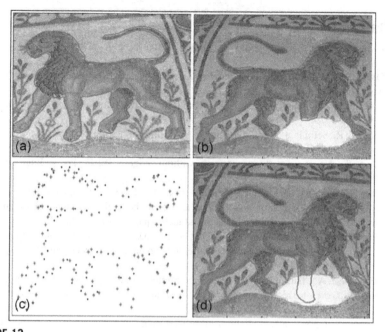

FIGURE 13

Robust object detection in mosaic image.

5 CONCLUSIONS

We presented in this paper an alternative approach to incorporate prior knowledge into a level set-based active contours in order to have robust object detection in case of large shape distortion that can be analyzed by the class of affine transformations. We presented also a geometric solution to choose the reference shape in case of many available templates, given that the statistical approach needs a training set and PCA. Then the application of a given classifier like Bayesian classifier to determine the appropriate reference shape like the work of Fang and Chan [24]. Given that the proposed approach invokes only pixels of the regions of variability between the shape of reference and the object of interest in the process of curve evolution and based on the fast Fourier transform for affine motion estimation and invariants computation, the method is faster compared to Refs. [15,25] where at each iteration shape descriptors are calculated for a given order that has to be set empirically. The obtained results are promising in the case of real and simulated data and the method can be used for the restoration of mosaic images in the archeological field. As future perspectives, we are working on integrating our model in the context of 3D object reconstruction from silhouettes sequence in order to refine the obtained 3D model.

REFERENCES

[1] Kass M, Witkin A, Terzopoulos D. Snakes: active contour models. Int J Comput Vis 1988;1:321–31.

[2] Osher S, Sethian JA. Fronts propagating with curvature-dependent speed: algorithms based on Hamilton-Jacobi formulation. J Comput Phys 1988;79:12–49.

[3] Caselles V, Kimmel R, Sapiro G. Geodesic active contours. Int J Comput Vis 1997;22:61–79.

[4] Malladi R, Sethian J, Vemuri B. Shape modeling with front propagation: a level set approach. PAMI 1995;17:158–75.

[5] Chan T, Vese L. Active contours without edges. IEEE Trans Imag Process 2001;10:266–77.

[6] Charmi MA, Mezghich MA, M'Hiri S, Derrode S, Ghorbel F. Geometric shape prior to region-based active contours using Fourier-based shape alignment. In: IEEE international conference on imaging systems and techniques; 2010. p. 478–81.

[7] Charmi MA, Derrode S, Ghorbel F. Using Fourier-based shape alignment to add geometric prior to snakes. In: International conference on acoustics, speech and signal processing; 2009. p. 1209–12.

[8] Foulonneau A, Charbonnier P, Heitz F. Contraintes géométriques de formes pour les contours actifs orientés région: une approche basée sur les moments de Legendre. Traitement du signal 2004;21:109–27.

[9] Mezghich MA, Sellami M, M'Hiri S, Ghorbel F. Shape prior for an edge-based active contours using phase correlation, In: European signal processing conference; 2013. p. 1–5.

[10] Leventon M, Grimson E, Faugeras O. Statistical shape influence in geodesic active contours. In: Proc. IEEE conference on computer vision and pattern recognition; 2000. p. 316–23.

[11] Fang W, Chan KL. Incorporating shape prior into geodesic active contours for detecting partially occluded object. Pattern Recogn 2007;40:2163–72.

[12] Chen Y, Thiruvenkadam S, Tagare HD, Huang F, Wilson D, Geiser EA. On the incorporation of shape priors into geometric active contours. In: Proc. IEEE workshop on variational and level set methods in computer vision; 2001. p. 145–52.

[13] Vandergheynst P, Bresson X, Thiran JP. A priori information in image segmentation: energy functional based on shape statistical model and image information, In: International conference on image processing; 2003. p. 425–8.

[14] Duay V, Allal A, Houhou N, Lemkaddem A, Thiran JP. Shape prior based on statistical map for active contour segmentation. In: International conference on image processing; 2008. p. 2284–7.

[15] Foulonneau A, Charbonnier P, Heitz F. Affine invariant geometric shape priors for region-based active contours. PAMI 2008;8:1352–7.

[16] Mezghich MA, M'Hiri S, Ghorbel F. Fourier based multi-references shape prior for region-based active contours. In: Mediterranean electrotechnical conference; 2012. p. 661–4.

[17] Mezghich MA, M'Hiri S, Ghorbel F. Invariant shape prior knowledge for an edge-based active contours. In: International conference on computer vision theory and applications; 2014. p. 454–61.

[18] Mokadem A, Avaro O, Ghorbel F, Daoudi M, Sanson H. Global planar rigid motion estimation, applied to object-oriented coding. In: International conference on pattern recognition; 1996. p. 641–5.

[19] Persoon E, Fu KS. Shape discrimination using Fourier descriptors. IEEE Trans Syst Man Cybern 1977;7:170–9.

[20] Ghorbel F. Towards a unitary formulation for invariant image description: application to image coding. Ann Telecommun 1998;153:145–55.

[21] Chaker F, Ghorbel F. Apparent motion estimation using planar contours and Fourier descriptors. In: International conference on computer vision theory and applications; 2010.

[22] Ghorbel F, Chaker F, Bannour MT. Contour retrieval and matching by affine invariant Fourier descriptors, In: International association for pattern recognition; 2007.

[23] Cohen L. On active contour models and balloons. Graph Model Im Proc 1991;53:211–8.

[24] Fang W, Chan KL. Using statistical shape priors in geodesic active contours for robust object detection. In: International conference on pattern recognition; 2006. p. 304–7.

[25] Derrode S, Charmi MA, Ghorbel F. Fourier-based shape prior for snakes. Pattern Recogn Lett 2008;29:897–904.

[26] Mezghich MA, Saidani M, M'Hiri S, Ghorbel F. An affine shape constraint for geometric active contours. In: International conference on image processing, computer vision, and pattern recognition; 2014.

A topological approach for detection of chessboard patterns for camera calibration

34

Gustavo Teodoro Laureano[1], Maria Stela Veludo de Paiva[2], Anderson da Silva Soares[1], Clarimar José Coelho[3]

[1]Computer Science Institute (INF), Federal University of Goiás (UFG), Goiânia, Brazil
[2]Engineering School of São Carlos (EESC), Electrical Engineering Department, University of São Paulo (USP), São Paulo, Brazil
[3]Computer Science and Computer Engineering Department (CMP), Pontifical Catholic University of Goiás (PUC-GO), Goiânia, Brazil

1 INTRODUCTION

The camera calibration aims to determine the geometric parameters of the image formation process [1]. This is a crucial step in many computer vision applications especially when metric information about the scene is required. In these applications, the camera is generally modeled with a set of intrinsic parameters (focal length, principal point, skew of axis) and its orientation is expressed by extrinsic parameters (rotation and translation). Both intrinsic and extrinsic parameters are estimated by linear or nonlinear methods using known points in the real world and their projections in the image plane [2]. These points are generally presented as a calibration pattern with known geometry, usually a flat chessboard.

Many studies have given attention to the camera calibration area, most of them are dedicated to the parameters' estimation phase and the refinement location of calibration points [3–6], however the automatic detection of calibration patterns is an issue not always addressed. Tsai [7] and Zhang [8] are examples of the most cited papers related to this area. They propose closed form solutions for the estimation of intrinsic and extrinsic parameters using 3D and 2D calibration patterns, respectively. Hemayed [9] and Salvi et al. [10] present reviews about some related works.

Camera calibration is a much discussed topic but the lack of robust algorithms for features detection difficults the construction of automatic calibration process. Calibration pattern recognition is a hard task, where lighting problems and high level of ambiguities are the principal challenges. For this reason, applications for camera

517

calibration often require user intervention for a reliable detection of the calibration points. The hand tuning of points is tedious, imprecise and require user skill [11], what is a difficult task in most cases. Others works need a complete identification of the calibration pattern. This is a severe constraint due to illumination or occlusion problems.

Currently, there is an increasing demand for systems with multiple cameras, such as augmented reality applications and 3D reconstruction, which makes the manual calibration an impracticable task or time consuming. Some tools for automatic camera calibration are available. The Bouguet MATLAB Toolbox [12] implements a semiautomatic calibration process. The application asks the user to define four extreme points that represent the area where an algorithm searches for the calibration points given the number of rows and columns of the pattern. The OpenCV library [13] is a very popular computer vision library that offers an automatic way to detect chessboard patterns in images using the *findChessboardCorners()* function. The method performs successive morphological operators until a number of black and white regions' contours be identified and, subsequently, four corners are extracted of each contours, comprising the calibration point set. The pattern is recognized only if all rectangles are identified. In an online system this restriction causes a considerable loss of image frames, since is not always possible to detect all the chessboard rectangles.

Fiala and Shu [14] use an array of fiducial markers, each one with a unique self-identifying pattern. The described methodology is robust to noise and it is not necessary to identify the entire calibration pattern. In the other hand, the markers are complex and require a special algorithm to recognize them. Escalera and Armingol [15] identify the calibration points as the intersections of lines. The methodology uses a combined analysis of two consecutive Hough transforms to filter the collinear points inside the pattern. The assumption that all points of interest are collinear makes this algorithm very sensitive to distortions, limiting its use only to cameras with low radial distortion.

The system named CAMcal [16] uses the Harris corner detection and a topological sort of squares within a geometric mesh. Furthermore, the system must to detect three circles to determine orientation of the pattern. Harris corner detection is time consuming, sensible to noise, needs an empirical threshold to select interesting points, and does not produce good results to the specific features of the chessboard image [17]. Usually, this operator finds many features that do not belong to the calibration pattern, especially for images with complex backgrounds.

This work presents extended description of work [18] which describes a system for automated detection of chessboard patterns for camera calibration. Initially, a fast and specific x-shaped corner operator is performed to retrieve initial interesting points. A geometric mesh is created from all the x-corners using Delaunay triangulation. A topological filter is proposed exploiting the regularity of the pattern. The color and the neighborhood of the triangles are analyzed and only those triangles that match with the pattern are taken as valid. Each remaining point defines a valid x-corner and a refinement location is performed locally.

The calibration process does not depend of the whole calibration pattern to be detected. The algorithm can be executed whenever a minimum number of points is defined. The algorithm is fast enough to be used in online applications and with complex backgrounds.

2 X-CORNER DETECTOR

The first stage of the algorithm is the features detection. Corners x-shaped are identified analyzing the number of high-contrast alternations in the neighborhood of each pixel. Considering $V = \{\mathbf{p}_1, \mathbf{p}_2, \ldots, \mathbf{p}_n\}$, the neighborhood of a central pixel $\mathbf{p}_c$ defined by all pixels in the Breseham's circle border [19], the number of alternations is computed by Equation (1):

$$N_{\text{alt}} = \sum_{i=1}^{n} \begin{cases} 1, & I(\mathbf{p}_i) > T_{\text{h}} \wedge I(\mathbf{p}_{i-1}) < T_{\text{l}} \\ 1, & I(\mathbf{p}_i) < T_{\text{l}} \wedge I(\mathbf{p}_{i-1}) > T_{\text{h}} \\ 0, & \text{otherwise} \end{cases} \qquad (1)$$

where $\mathbf{p}_i \in V$, $I(\mathbf{p}_i)$ represents the pixel intensity of $\mathbf{p}_i$, T_{l} and T_{h} are the inferior and superior threshold, respectively. Alternatively, both thresholds can be defined by: $T_{\text{l}} = m - g$ and $T_{\text{h}} = m + g$, with $m = \frac{1}{n} \sum_{i=1}^{n} I(\mathbf{p}_i)$.

The pixel $\mathbf{p}_c$ is classified as a x-corner if $N_{\text{alt}} = 4$ and $T_{\text{l}} < I(\mathbf{p}_c) < T_{\text{h}}$. For Equation (1), when $i = 0$, $i - 1 = n$ is assumed. Figure 1 shows the covered area by this detector.

The variable g models the operator sensibility. Considering a previously blurred image, the number of alternations imposes large part of the restriction required for a proper classification. Thus the variable g has little effect on the final result. In this work, g is empirically defined with value 10.

This detector can be seen as a specification of the detector proposed in Rosten and Drummond [20], which is considered very fast. Since only a small portion of the

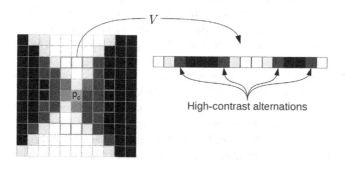

FIGURE 1

Typical neighborhood of a x-corner. Set V represents a circular border around central pixel $\mathbf{p}_c$ with four high-contrast alternations.

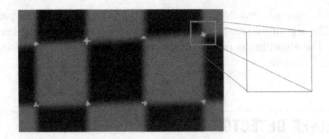

FIGURE 2

X-corner detector response. Light pixels define found corner positions in the image.

neighborhood of the pixel is analyzed, the computational cost is reduced. Other similar detectors can be found in Zhao et al. [17] and Sun et al. [21]. Figure 2 shows a typical result of this detector over a chessboard image.

Equation (1) does not guarantee that only one pixel is classified as a x-corner in its neighborhood. To deal with this problem, the cost described by Equation (2) is associated with each corner and a nonmaximum suppression is performed [22].

$$\max \left(\sum_{i \in dark} |I(\mathbf{p}_i) - m|, \sum_{i \in light} |I(\mathbf{p}_i) - m| \right) \qquad (2)$$

The classes *dark* and *light* contains the dark and light pixels, respectively. The right corner is the one with the highest associated cost.

3 TOPOLOGICAL FILTER

The identification of valid corners is an important step because not all x-corners present in the image belong to the calibration pattern. In this work, the identification of valid x-corners is made considering the regularity neighborhood of the chessboard image. This problem can be extended to the task of creating geometric meshes in computer graphics. In a mesh composed of basic components such as triangles, vertices are connected according to their neighborhood [23].

The Delaunay triangulation is a classic problem in computational geometry. Given a set of points in a plane, the only valid triangulation is one where the circumcircle of each triangle contains no other vertex [24]. This constraint ensures that the triangles are formed by the more closely vertexes. The mesh allows to define the neighborhood of each point. Figure 3 gives an example of this triangulation. Guibas et al. [25] present an algorithm for incremental triangulation that runs in time $O(n \log(n))$.

Using the geometric mesh, the vertices and triangles are submitted to a topological filter to exclude those not satisfying the regularity of the pattern. The corners

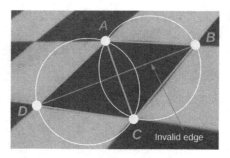

FIGURE 3

A Delaunay triangulation example. Considering *A*, *B*, *C*, and *D* four image corners, the valid triangulation if formed by the triangles $\Delta(A, B, C)$ and $\Delta(A, C, D)$.

(or vertexes) share internal triangles of different colors in a regular manner. Each square of the chessboard pattern is represented by two triangles of the same color. Each triangle has no more than two neighboring triangles that form two squares with different colors alike. The internal vertexes have in common a maximum of eight triangles. Valid triangles have its interior filled with a single color.

Even after the projected image plane, the neighborhood relationship between the corners is still maintained. This restriction allows evaluating if corners really belong to the calibration pattern. Thus, are considered valid:

1. Those triangles that do not have color transitions in its interior;
2. Only those triangles that have a neighbor with the same color;
3. Those triangles that have only two neighbors of the same color and different color triangle taken as reference.

This filter is applied to the grid until there are no more invalid triangles. In the end, the vertices that do not form any triangle are also removed.

To avoid the use of thresholds in the comparison of colors, this filter uses a binarized version of the image. This is an important step to validate the points. If the binarization process fails, noisy points can be identified and actual points can be disregarded. To minimize these effects, this work uses adaptive binarization described in the work of Bradley and Roth [26]. This algorithm handles well with large variations in illumination and runs in linear time for any window size.

The binarization phase can be influenced by problems from the acquisition of images due to lighting variations and also by the fluctuation of the intensities of the pixels. In the regions near to the edges, a range of values may be wrongly considered black or white pixels. This behavior can generate white triangles with black borders and black triangles with white edges. In practice, the verification of color transition is made in a region of an innermost triangle, ignoring the edges. Figure 4 shows intermediate results of the algorithm including detected x-corners, initial mesh over the binarized image, and after the topological filtering.

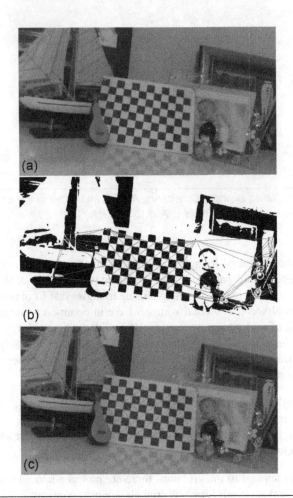

FIGURE 4

Mesh generation and topological filter results. (a) Initial x-corners, (b) triangulation over binarized image, and (c) valid triangles after topological filter.

4 POINT CORRESPONDENCES

The next step of the algorithm associates each vertex to the real coordinates of the pattern. This is done by analyzing the relative position of each corner. First two neighboring triangles of the same color are arbitrarily selected: T_1 and T_2. Three vertices make the triangle T_1, the origin of the coordinate system is defined by the vertex that has T_2 as its opposite triangle. For the remaining, vertices are assigned the directions x and y of the Cartesian plane (Figure 5).

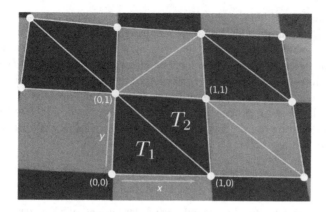

FIGURE 5

Propagation of coordinates. The triangles T_1 and T_2 define the origin and the direction of coordinates, respectively.

The propagation of coordinates consists in establishing the relative coordinates of the vertices neighbors. Given a triangle T whose vertices have already defined coordinates, where the origin is v_o, v_x and v_y are the vertices with the x and y directions, respectively. Triangle T_v is defined as a neighbor triangle of T with a different color. If triangles T_v and T are neighbors then they share an edge e and T_v has a opposite vertex to T, named v_v. The coordinates of the opposite vertex needs to be determined, thus:

1. If $v_x \in e$, then $v_v = \left[v_t^{(x)} \quad 2v_t^{(y)} - v_y^{(y)} \right]^T$;

2. If $v_y \in e$, then $v_v = \left[2v_t^{(x)} - v_y^{(x)} \quad v_t^{(y)} \right]^T$;

It is understood by $v^{(\cdot)}$ the coordinate $(\cdot)$ of vertex v. Similarly, T_{op} shares a border e_{op} with T_v, then $v_{op} = \left[v_h^{(x)} \quad v_v^{(y)} \right]^T$, where v_h is the third vertex of T_v and v_{op} is the opposite vertex to e_{op}.

For each visited triangle, the vertexes coordinates of the current and opposite triangles are propagated. The algorithm performs recursively for each neighbor triangle to the pair T_v and T_{op}. It makes the algorithm $O(n/2)$, where n is the number of triangles in the mesh.

5 LOCATION REFINEMENT

The x-corner detector, described in Section 2, identifies the position of corners with low accuracy where the only information available is the position of discrete pixels. Since the quality of the calibration is directly dependent to the precision which the position of features is found, there is a need for a refinement [1].

Traditional algorithms, such as Harris and Stephens detector [27] and Shi and Tomasi [28], run throughout the image and use thresholds to select the features of interest. The subpixel precision is achieved by maximizing functions fitted to the square of the intensity profile of the local neighborhood of each pixel. The threshold has a direct impact on the quality of response of these detectors, so corners are usually classified as the N pixels with greater response to the operator.

Chen and Zhang [4] propose a new detector specially designed to fit x-shaped corners. Considering the neighborhood of a pixel as a surface, its Hessian matrix can be expressed as:

$$\mathbf{H} = \begin{bmatrix} I_{xx} & I_{xy} \\ I_{xy} & I_{yy} \end{bmatrix} \tag{3}$$

where I_{xx}, I_{xy}, and I_{yy} are the second partial derivatives of pixel $I(x,y)$. Thus, the x-corner detector is described as:

$$S = \lambda_1 \cdot \lambda_2 = I_{xx} \cdot I_{yy} - I_{xy}^2 \tag{4}$$

where λ_1 and λ_2 are the Eigen values of $\mathbf{H}$.

In order to avoid unnecessary computation, this operator is only applied in regions defined by the valid vertices of triangle mesh. The real x-corner is the pixel with largest negative value of S and the refined coordinates $[x_0+s, y_0+t]^\mathrm{T}$ is given by:

$$s = \frac{I_y \cdot I_{xy} - I_x \cdot I_{yy}}{I_{xx} \cdot I_{yy} - I_{xy}^2}, \quad t = \frac{I_x \cdot I_{xy} - I_y \cdot I_{xx}}{I_{xx} \cdot I_{yy} - I_{xy}^2} \tag{5}$$

6 EXPERIMENTAL RESULTS

In this section, the detector response is evaluated considering an image database and by means of experimental tests with two different cameras. The image database is provided by the toolbox for MATLAB prepared by Bouguet [12]. This database consists of 20 images of a chessboard calibration pattern, accounting 156 x-corners arranged as 12×13 matrix, being presented in different orientations. This set represents a common situation to most of systems where the pattern images are first captured and calibration is performed in an off-line manner.

Figure 6 shows some examples of these images and Table 1 summarizes the results obtained for each one. The results are generated by applying the algorithm in each image and counting the number of corners identified. Analyzing Table 1, the vast majority of points is detected.

The mean accuracy of the algorithm is 85.38%; however, two images (images 5 and 18) require attention by the low percentage of detected points. They represent situations where the calibration plane is very inclined to the camera. In this

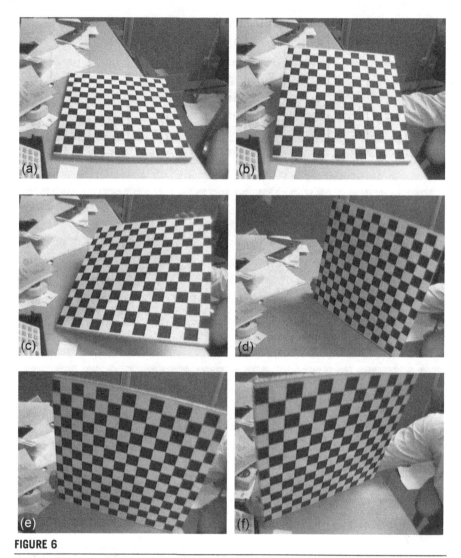

FIGURE 6

Examples of Bouguet database images. (a) Image 1, (b) image 2, (c) image 4, (d) image 9, (e) image 17, and (f) image 19.

case it is expected that the corners are uncharacterized by high perspective distortion and lack of focus in the image. Another aspect to be considered is that images in this database are of low contrast, which difficults the identification of alternations of high contrast. Figure 7 shows examples the best and worst for Bouguet images.

Table 1 Results for the Bouguet Database

Image	1	2	3	4	5	6	7	8	9	10
Corners	151	154	147	153	51	149	132	110	143	153
%	96.79	98.72	94.23	98.08	32.69	95.51	84.62	70.51	91.67	98.08
Image	11	12	13	14	15	16	17	18	19	20
Corners	152	155	156	138	121	154	155	61	111	118
%	97.44	99.36	100.00	88.46	77.56	98.72	99.36	39.10	71.15	75.64

The rows named "Corners" list the number of detected x-corners and rows named "%" list the hit rate.

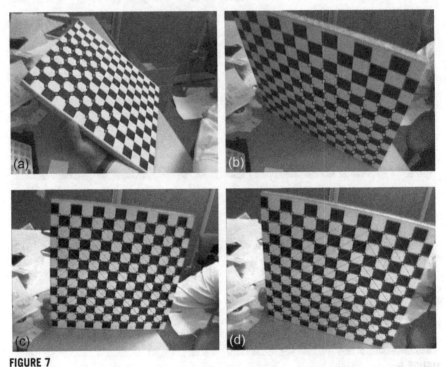

FIGURE 7

Worst (images 5 and 18) and best (images 13 and 17) result in the Bouguet database. (a,b) In images 5 and 18, few points are found due to pattern inclination. (c,d) In images 13 and 17, the pattern is fully detected.

In general, the algorithm was able to find the most calibration points. If the two worst images are discarded, the accuracy of success rises to 90.88%, which reflects the efficiency of the methodology. The absence of some points in the final result does not mean they were not detected. Both the presence of a false calibration point as the loss of a filter response influences on the neighborhood of these points. From a calibration perspective, where the presence of outliers affects substantially the camera parameters, it is more prudent to consider only those points that perfectly match with the regularity of the pattern.

For the online experiments, two different cameras were used: (1) Philips Webcam SPC990NC e and (2) Microsoft Webcam HD 5000. The calibration pattern used is formed by squares with 2.5 cm of width and forms a matrix of 11×7 x-corners. For each camera were tested 14 real images of the calibration pattern in various orientations and distances.

The algorithm runs on a sequence of captured frames. The amount of detected points presented in the second and fourth column of Table 2 corresponds to the average of the points detected in 10 frames for each position of the calibration pattern.

Figure 8 shows some of the images used in the second experiment. Once the pattern is completely visible, the algorithm has a high success rate, while the missed corners tend to arise when there is a more accentuated inclination of the plane in relation to the camera. In both experiments no false positives were identified, which confirms the robustness of the filter used. To illustrate the efficiency of the topological filter and propagation of coordinates, Figure 9 shows the result of the algorithm using complex backgrounds and partial occlusion of the pattern. The occluded corners do not interfere in the propagation of correct coordinates. Thus, it is possible to use the maximum of features identified for the estimation of camera parameters. The last column shows the reprojection plan calibration calculated from the detected points.

Table 2 Results for the Online Detection

	HD 5000		SPC900nc	
	x-Corners	**%**	**x-Corners**	**%**
Image 00	77	100	73	94.80
Image 01	77	100	77	100
Image 02	77	100	77	100
Image 03	73	94.80	76	98.70
Image 04	77	100	73	94.70
Image 05	77	100	77	100
Image 06	77	100	76	98.70
Image 07	77	100	77	100
Image 08	77	100	77	100
Image 09	77	100	76	98.70
Image 10	75	97.40	72	93.50
Image 11	70	90.90	76	98.70
Image 12	72	93.50	75	97.40
Image 13	70	90.90	77	100
Mean		97.68		98.23

FIGURE 8

Example of images used in the second test. The left column shows all x-corners and the triangulation. The right column shows the topological filter result.

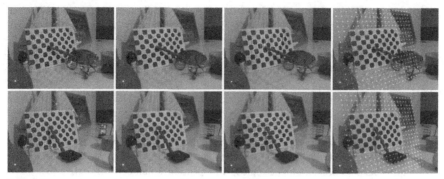

FIGURE 9

Results with complex backgrounds and partial occlusion.

7 CONCLUSIONS

This work proposes a methodology for automatic detection of chessboard calibration patterns. The algorithm runs automatically without any user intervention. It can detect the calibration points both in simple and complex background scenes where the calibration points mix with other image characteristics. The proposed methodology is robust to the presence of noise and also when the pattern cannot be fully identified. A partial identification of the pattern allows the calibration process to consider the max of detected points. In conditions where few points are available most picture frames are utilized.

REFERENCES

[1] Hartley R, Zisserman A. Multiple view geometry in computer vision. 2nd ed. New York: Cambridge University Press; 2003. ISBN: 0521540518.

[2] Trucco E, Verri A. Introductory techniques for 3-D computer vision. Upper Saddle River, NJ: Prentice Hall PTR; 1998. ISBN: 0132611082.

[3] Dutta A, Kar A, Chatterji BN. A novel window-based corner detection algorithm for gray-scale images. In: Sixth Indian conference on computer vision, graphics & image processing, ICVGIP'08. Washington, DC: IEEE Computer Society; 2008. p. 650–6. Available at: http://ieeexplore.ieee.org/lpdocs/epic03/wrapper.htm?arnumber=4756131 [accessed September 15, 2012].

[4] Chen D, Zhang G. A new sub-pixel detector for x-corners in camera calibration targets. In: 13th international conference in central Europe on computer graphics, visualization and computer vision, Winter School of Computer Graphics (WSCG-short papers)' 2005, Václav Skala - UNION Agency, University of West Bohemia. Plzen. Czech Republic: Citeseer; 2005. p. 97–100. Available at:http://citeseerx.ist.psu.edu/viewdoc/download?doi=10.1.1.87.5833&rep=rep1&type=pdf [accessed November 8, 2011].

[5] Hu X, Du P, Zhou Y. Automatic corner detection of chess board for medical endoscopy camera calibration. In: Proceedings of the 10th international conference on virtual reality continuum and its applications in industry (VRCAI '11). New York: ACM; 2011. p. 431–4. Available at: http://doi.acm.org/10.1145/2087756.2087837.

[6] Krüger L, Wöhler C. Accurate chequerboard corner localisation for camera calibration. Pattern Recogn Lett 2011;32(10):1428–35. Available at: http://linkinghub.elsevier.com/retrieve/pii/S0167865511001024 [accessed November 28, 2012].

[7] Tsai RY. An efficient and accurate camera calibration technique for 3D machine vision. In: Proceedings of IEEE conference on computer vision and pattern recognition; 1986. p. 364–74.

[8] Zhang Z. A flexible new technique for camera calibration. IEEE Trans Pattern Anal Mach Intell 2000;22(11):1330–4. Available at: http://ieeexplore.ieee.org/lpdocs/epic03/wrapper.htm?arnumber=888718 [accessed November 8, 2011].

[9] Hemayed EE. A survey of camera self-calibration. In: Proceedings of the IEEE conference on advanced video and signal based surveillance; 2003. p. 351–7. Available at: http://ieeexplore.ieee.org/lpdocs/epic03/wrapper.htm?arnumber=1217942.

[10] Salvi J, Armangué X, Batlle J. A comparative review of camera calibrating methods with accuracy evaluation. Pattern Recogn 2002;35:1617–35. Available at: http://www.sciencedirect.com/science/article/pii/S0031320301001261 [accessed December 7, 2012].

[11] Bennett S, Lasenby J. ChESS—quick and robust detection of chess-board features. In: CoRR; 2013. p. 1–13. [abs/1301.5] Available at: http://www-com-serv.eng.cam.ac.uk/~sb476/publications/ChESS.pdf [accessed May 6, 2013].

[12] Bouguet J-Y. Camera calibration toolbox for matlab (2008). http://www.vision.caltech.edu/bouguetj/calib_doc/.

[13] G. Bradski. Open computer vision library (OpenCV). In: Dr. Dobb's J Softw Tools, 2000. http://www.opencv.willowgarage.com/.

[14] Fiala M, Shu C. Self-identifying patterns for plane-based camera calibration. Mach Vision Appl 2007;19(4):209–16. Available at: http://link.springer.com/10.1007/s00138-007-0093-z [accessed May 21, 2013].

[15] De la Escalera A, Armingol JM. Automatic chessboard detection for intrinsic and extrinsic camera parameter calibration. Sensors 2010;10(3):2027–44. Available at: http://www.pubmedcentral.nih.gov/articlerender.fcgi?artid=3264465&tool=pmcentrez&rendertype=abstract [accessed November 28, 2012].

[16] Shu C, Brunton A, Fiala M. A topological approach to finding grids in calibration patterns. Machine Vision Appl 2009;21(6):949–57. Available at: http://link.springer.com/10.1007/s00138-009-0202-2 [accessed June 25, 2013].

[17] Zhao F, Wei C, Wang J, Tang J. An automated x-corner detection algorithm (axda), J Softw 2011;6(5):791–7. Available at: https://academypublisher.com/~academz3/ojs/index.php/jsw/article/view/0605791797 [accessed June 27, 2013].

[18] Laureano GT, Paiva MSV, Soares AdS. Topological detection of chessboard patterns for camera calibration. In: IPCV'13—the 2013 international conference on image processing, computer vision, and pattern recognition; 2013.

[19] Bresenham J. A linear algorithm for incremental digital display of circular arcs. Commun ACM 1977;20(2):100–6.

[20] Rosten E, Drummond T. Machine learning for high-speed corner detection. In: Proceedings of the 9th European conference on computer vision—volume part I, ECCV'06. Berlin, Heidelberg: Springer-Verlag; 2006. p. 430–43. Available at: http://link.springer.com/chapter/10.1007/11744023_34 [accessed June 23, 2013].

[21] Sun W, Yang X, Xiao S, Hu W. Robust checkerboard recognition for efficient nonplanar geometry registration in projector-camera systems. In: Proceedings of the 5th ACM/IEEE international workshop on projector camera systems (PROCAMS '08); 2008. p. 2:1–7. Available at:http://dl.acm.org/citation.cfm?id=1394625 [accessed June 25, 2013].

[22] Nixon MS, Aguado AS. Feature extraction & image processing for computer vision. 3rd ed. Oxford: Academic Press; 2012. p. 37–82. ISBN: 9780123965493. http://dx. doi.org/10.1016/B978-0-12-396549-3.00002-1.

[23] Bern M, Eppstein D. Mesh generation and optimal triangulation. Comput Euclidean Geom 1992;1(1):23–90.

[24] de Berg M, Cheong O, van Kreveld M, Overmars M. Computational geometry: algorithms and applications. 3rd ed. Santa Clara, CA: Springer-Verlag TELOS; 2008. ISBN: 978-3-540-77974-2.

[25] Guibas L, Knuth D, Sharir M. Randomized incremental construction of Delaunay and Voronoi diagrams. Algorithmica 1992;7(1-6):381–413. Available at: http://link. springer.com/article/10.1007/BF01758770 [accessed September 15, 2012].

[26] Bradley D, Roth G. Adaptive thresholding using the integral image. J Graph GPU Game Tools 2007;12(2):13–21. Available at: http://www.tandfonline.com/doi/abs/10.1080/2151237X.2007.10129236.

[27] Harris C, Stephens M. A combined corner and edge detector. In Taylor CJ, editor. Proceedings of the alvey vision conference. Alvey Vision Club; September 1988. p. 23.1–23.6. http://dx.doi.org/10.5244/C.2.23. Available at: http://www.bmva.org/bmvc/1988/avc-88-023.html [accessed May 22, 2011].

[28] Shi J, Tomasi C. Good features to track. Computer vision and pattern recognition. Proceedings CVPR '94., 1994 IEEE computer society conference on. 1994. p. 593–600. http://dx.doi.org/10.1109/CVPR.1994.323794. Available at: http://ieeexplore.ieee.org/xpls/abs_all.jsp?arnumber=323794 [accessed May 23, 2013].

Precision distortion correction technique based on FOV model for wide-angle cameras in automotive sector

35

Haijung Choi[1], Jeong Goo Seo[1], Dae Hyuck Park[1], Eui Sun Kang[2]

[1]SANE Co., Ltd, Seoul, Korea
[2]Soongsil University, Seoul, Korea

1 INTRODUCTION

A driver assistance system to reduce the traffic accident rate analyzes data collected from various sensors installed in a vehicle and provides its result to the driver. Around View Monitor (AVM) system is used to prevent collision accidents during parking and driving by composing data received from more than three cameras installed around the vehicle and providing surrounding image information to driver.

In general, a passenger car is equipped with four cameras with wide-angle lenses mounted on the front, rear, left, and right sides of a vehicle to capture the maximum field of horizontal and vertical images from the surroundings. A wide-angle lens, which can capture a picture with a wide angle greater than 120° with a short focal length, generates radial distortion by which a ray of light that enters the lens farther from its center is more curved than a ray of light that enters the lens closer to its center due to the effect of a curved lens. This phenomenon often occurs in fish-eye lenses used in AVM systems, and such distortion is more severe near the edge of the image than at the center.

In order to correct the distortion of a fish-eye lens, two methods have been used: approximation of distortion functions into polynomial forms and the field of view (FOV) model, which is a geographical model based on nonlinear distortion characteristics. In the polynomial distortion model, computational complexity increases as the order of polynomials increases and the difficulty of application increases as the view angle of the fish-eye lens becomes larger. However, the FOV model is more efficient than the polynomial distortion model because its design is based on the nonlinear distortion of fish-eye lenses, although it might have additional distortion when there is an error in the location of the distortion center.

To solve this problem, this chapter proposes a method to estimate a distortion center to accurately correct the distortion that occurs in the camera image signals from an ultra-wide viewing angle greater than 190°. In particular, this chapter proposes a method to find the center point of distortion that can minimize distortion using a lattice-patterned 2D plane and the FOV distortion model to correct distortion.

The remainder of this chapter is organized as follows. In Section 2, previous studies related to distortion correction are described, whereas the proposed distortion center estimation method using 2D planes is described in Section 3. In Section 4, the experiment environment and results are discussed, and the conclusion is presented in Section 5.

2 RELATED RESEARCH

A complex calculation is required to transform 3D camera images into 2D planar images that can be processed by computers. To reduce such computational complexity, a pinhole camera model is used. A pinhole camera, which was used to locate the center point of an image, converts 3D information into 2D planar pixel units based on the optical image received through a small hole. In order to convert 3D spatial coordinates into 2D image coordinates, external parameters such as the installation height and direction of the camera, and internal parameters such as the focal length and center point of camera are required. The focal length in the internal parameter refers to a distance between the focal point and the image sensor charge coupled device (CCD) and complementary metal oxide semiconductor (CMOS), which is represented by

$$x_{\text{screen}} = f_x \left(\frac{X}{Z} \right) + C_x, y_{\text{screen}} = f_y \left(\frac{Y}{Z} \right) + C_y \tag{1}$$

Here, x_{screen} and y_{screen} refer to the coordinates on the 2D plane, whereas f is the distance between the focal point and the image plane. In addition, Z is the distance between the object and the focal point, whereas C is the displacement of the coordinate center in the projection plane. Using Equation (1), the location where the image appears on the 2D plane can be calculated. However, because only a small amount of light passes through a pinhole camera, a long exposure time is required to create an image. In order to collect a large amount of light, a curved lens is used, thereby obtaining images by collecting the curved light. When the obtained image is projected onto a 2D plane, a problem of image distortion can occur due to the characteristics of the lens. The distortion by a lens can be divided into two types: radial distortion, which is generated more severely in an area farther from the center, and tangential distortion, which creates an elliptical distortion distribution.

The typical type of lens which is installed in the vehicle is fish-eye lens and they can create radial distortion. To resolve the radial distortion problem, three methods can be employed: the method of using the center point of distortion, distortion parameters, and internal parameters; the method of performing polynomial distortion iteratively to transform the distorted curves caused by radial distortion into straight lines; and the method of using image information only. Heikkila [1] proposed a method of finding the center of distortion and internal parameters by using chessboard-like images, in which a method to find parameters that can integrate distortion correction and a camera calibration process was introduced. However, this method has a drawback that could increase iterative calculation complexity when the distortion is excessively severe, although it can be efficient when distortion is moderately severe.

In Ref. [2], three orthogonal planar patterns were introduced to cover an entire 180° image with a specific pattern of asymmetrical distortion. This method locates a vanishing point where distorted curves converge to a single point and then defines that as the center point of distortion, thereby performing distortion restoration. This method does not depend on distortion models of parameters due to the special structure of the apparatus, and therefore, it has an advantage in that it can be applied to various lenses, although it is not appropriate for a case where radial asymmetric distortion is generated.

In Ref. [3], a center radius was defined using the center of a sphere and the position of a single distorted point. A corrected position value was then used to restore the distorted curves into straight lines. Then, new radii at all positions in the image were obtained to be applied in the FOV model. This method can be used for real-time processing because it uses low-order polynomials to change curves into straight lines, although it has a weakness in terms of accuracy compared to other existing methods.

In Ref. [4], distortion parameters based on the assumption that lines were straight prior to distortion were found using the characteristics of the pinhole camera model in order to minimize the curvature of the lines, and then, they were applied to the tangential distortion correction method.

In Ref. [5], the longest curved lines were extracted and removed from 2D images, and then the correction of the remaining curves was performed. However, this method has several drawbacks in that curve detection is performed slowly whereas the removal of the curves may not be carried out accurately owing to the use of a single fixed threshold value for curve removal. To overcome these drawbacks, a method was proposed in Ref. [6] to detect and remove the lines quickly using Hough transformation.

The FOV model, which is based on nonlinear lens distortion characteristics, corrects distortion under the assumption that the center of an image and the center of lens distortion are the same. However, in the case of cameras using lenses with special functions and a number of layers, an error of the center point might occur during the manufacturing process, thereby creating a fine center point error in the projection onto the 2D plane. Therefore, not only can distortion correction not be performed correctly, but also additional distortion of the image can occur after distortion correction. To solve this problem, a method was proposed in Ref. [7] to correct distortion after estimating a center by selecting three straight lines in the image plane to decrease computation complexity.

In addition, a method was presented in Ref. [6] to estimate the center of distortion by extracting a curve from the projected 2D image and modifying it into an undistorted straight line, thereby finding the direction in which the center of the extracted curve is changed. However, its accuracy varies depending on the number of detected lines and the existence of lines around the distortion center.

This chapter proposes an accurate distortion correction method through the estimation of the distortion center of a lens using the FOV model and 2D patterns in order to correct radial distortion.

3 DISTORTION CENTER ESTIMATION METHOD USING FOV MODEL AND 2D PATTERNS

3.1 DISTORTION CORRECTION METHOD CONSIDERING DISTORTION CENTER ESTIMATION

The process of distortion correction considering the distortion center is shown in Figure 1. In this chapter, a 2D planar image of a chessboard pattern was used first to correct distortion of an image from a fish-eye lens quickly. Using the distorted chessboard pattern, a distortion coefficient was estimated by applying the FOV model.

The center of distortion was found using the estimated distortion coefficient and distorted curve component. Based on the center of distortion (C_x, C_y), a lookup table

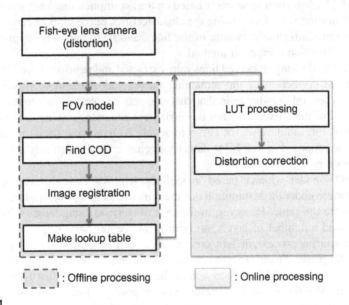

FIGURE 1

Distortion correction algorithm of 2D planar pattern.

(LUT) is produced, which represents the relationship between distorted location and 2D planar location using the FOV model. Distortion can be corrected by applying the LUT produced offline to real images.

3.2 FOV DISTORTION MODEL

The FOV model [3,4] calculates a location value in the image over the plane through the coordinate in which distortion occurs when radial distortion is detected once a video image is acquired by a fish-eye lens. Figure 2 shows the FOV model.

The distance from the center of a sphere to one point of the planar image is r_u, whereas r_d is the distance to the distorted location projected onto the sphere plane. Since the FOV model is based on the optical model, it is derived by trigonometric functions with regard to the angle ω. Once a point (A) is moved to a point (B) due to radial distortion projected onto the plane of the sphere and acquired by a fish-eye lens, it is projected onto the image sensor, thereby producing radial distortion. The FOV model can compute r_d and r_u using the distortion functions and their inverse functions.

$$r_d = \frac{1}{2\omega} \arctan\left(2r_u \tan\omega\right) \tag{2}$$

$$r_u = \frac{\tan\left(r_d \tan\omega\right)}{2\tan\omega} \tag{3}$$

The above equations are rearranged using radius R as

$$\frac{R \times r_d}{\sqrt{R^2 - r_d^2}} \tag{4}$$

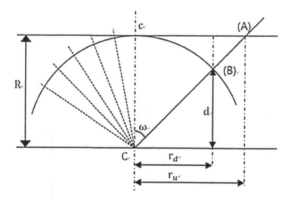

FIGURE 2

FOV model.

3.3 DISTORTION COEFFICIENT ESTIMATION OF THE FOV MODEL

According to the principle of the camera model [8], a straight line in 3D should be a straight line after being projected onto a 2D surface by a camera if there is no distortion. This means that the larger the difference between an actual straight-line component and a projected straight line, the larger the distortion is. Conversely, the less the difference is, the less the distortion is. The degree of camera distortion can be verified by the distortion coefficient ω of the FOV model. In the FOV model, $q_{\omega i}$ is a point of restoration of distorted point p_i by the distortion coefficient ω. The distortion parameter estimation from Ref. [9] expresses a relationship of $D^{-1}(\omega, p_i)$ with regard to the distortion coefficient, which can solve the linear equation of the least squares distance when the estimation is applied to the algorithms from p_1 to p_n.

By solving the equation of the i and j functions where the error function $E_{ij}(\omega)$ is minimized with regard to the distortion coefficient ω, the distortion coefficient ω can be estimated. Using this method, distortion correction can be performed by using the distortion correction coefficient with regard to the camera distortion center.

$$q_{\omega i} = [x_{\omega i}\, y_{\omega i}]^{\mathrm{T}} = D^{-1}(\omega, p_i) \tag{5}$$

$$E(\omega) = \sum_{i=1}^{n} \|y_{\omega i} - L(x_{\omega i})\|^2 \tag{6}$$

$$arg \min_{\omega} \sum_{i=1}^{n}\sum_{j=1}^{m} E_{ij}(\omega) \tag{7}$$

Using the distortion coefficient estimation method, once a chessboard pattern is captured, distortion correction can be executed quickly using only the distortion coefficient. Nonetheless, a fine error in the components of the row and column of the chessboard was discovered through experiment. In the case of an ultra-wide-angle camera, the calibration error becomes larger near the edge of the image than at the center owing to the characteristics of the lens. Thus, distortion correction using the FOV model is appropriate (Table 1).

Table 1 Measurement of Distortion Center Estimation Result in the AVM Camera

	Cod$_x$	Cod$_y$
CAM #1	10	−9
CAM #2	10	0
CAM #3	4	3
CAM #4	−4	7

3.4 DISTORTION CENTER ESTIMATION METHOD USING 2D PATTERNS

The distortion center estimation method using 2D patterns is proposed to overcome the limitation of the distortion correction method using the distortion coefficient ω of the FOV model. In this chapter, a chessboard pattern was shot to estimate the center of distortion followed by projecting it onto an actual straight line in the image data of corrected distortion, thereby estimating the center of distortion using the value of the distance difference between the straight lines.

In order to estimate the center of distortion, first the distortion in the 2D patterns was corrected using the distortion coefficient of the FOV model. Then, a certain range surrounding the center of distortion, which was determined while applying the FOV model, was set to the detection window of the center of distortion.

Next, straight lines are generated by following the detected points using the method described in Ref. [10] in the detection window of the center of distortion. Figure 3 shows the straight lines used to compute the distortion error and detection window in which the distortion center is expected. In the chessboard pattern, where a number of crossing points of straight lines can be found; crossing points of $M \times N$ representing every corner point are found, and then vertical M straight lines and horizontal N straight lines using the main outer points are generated based on the outermost points, thereby determining whether crossing points are present in the center within the straight lines. The smaller the vertical and horizontal distortions are, the closer the point is to the center of distortion, which also means it is closer to a straight line. Thus, a center of distortion can be estimated by computing the error between the straight line and the distortion. To estimate the center of distortion, distances in the row and column directions are added, and an equation for the straight line that is closest to the center of distortion and C_x, C_y is solved. Therefore, the distances to the

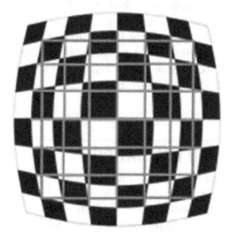

FIGURE 3

Example of the detection window of the distortion center and straight-line components.

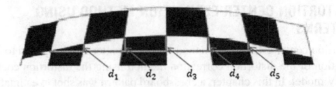

FIGURE 4

Distortion error.

distortion points $\left(p_{ij,c_x,c_y}\right)$, where there are error points with the straight line $\left(L_{i,c_x,c_y}\right)$ are computed.

Figure 4 shows an example of errors between the distortion and a straight line, which represents distances d_n between the blue-colored straight line and the distortion in the 2D chessboard pattern. The points detected in the figure are used to determine the degree of distortion. That is, the distances between the crossing points and the straight line are computed in the vertical and horizontal directions, thereby summing the distances of the inner points $(d_1 + \cdots + d_n)$ to calculate the distortion error.

$$E_{ij}\left(c_x, c_y\right) = \left\| L_{i,c_x,\,c_y} - p_{ij,\,c_x,\,c_y} \right\|^2$$
$$E_{ji}\left(c_x, c_y\right) = \left\| L_{j,c_x,\,c_y} - p_{ji,\,c_x,\,c_y} \right\|^2 \tag{8}$$

$$arg \min_{c_x c_y}\left(\sum_{i=1}^{n}\sum_{j=1}^{m} E_{ij}\left(c_x, c_y\right) + \sum_{j=1}^{m}\sum_{i=1}^{n} E_{ji}\left(c_x, c_y\right) \right) \tag{9}$$

In other words, it finds the minimum sum-of-squares difference between the actual straight-line component and the projected line component. By using this function for distance computation, the minimum distance to the straight-line component of row (m) and column (n) is calculated to estimate the distortion center (c_x, c_y).

The distortion center estimation method using 2D patterns performs precise distortion correction by finding the minimum distortion distance. Precise distortion correction can be achieved by applying the least distortion distance estimation method to the FOV distortion correction model using 2D patterns. An LUT is produced with regard to the distortion locations on the 2D plane using the estimated distortion center, thereby being applied to the actual image.

4 EXPERIMENT AND EVALUATION

In order to verify the result of the distortion correction algorithm, the following distortion correction experiment device was developed. The experiment environment was configured using notebook computers, USB cameras, wide-angle lenses, and chessboard patterns as the hardware configuration. The target image was a 2D black and white chessboard pattern with 6 horizontal rows and 11 vertical columns. One square of the chessboard was $163_{\text{pixel}} \times 163_{\text{pixel}}$ while the actual size was 45 mm^2.

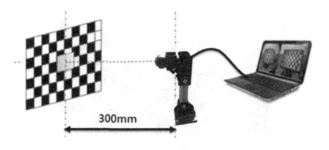

FIGURE 5

Experiment environment for distortion correction using wide-angle lens camera.

FIGURE 6

Distortion correction using the FOV model.

As shown in Figure 5, the experimental environment was prepared to perform real-time processing for the proposed algorithm, in which a 2D chessboard was positioned at the center and a real-time camera image taken with a wide-angle lens was sent to the personal computer for distortion correction.

Once the accurate distortion center (C) is set in the FOV model and the distortion is corrected, all straight lines can be restored almost completely as shown in Figure 6. This result is obtained because the distortion center was set repeatedly in the distortion correction process.

However, additional distortion was generated as shown in Figure 7 when distortion correction was performed again assuming that the distortion center was the center point of the image where there was an error from the lens distortion center. The analysis result of the distortion center showed that when a fine error of -30 pixels in the X direction and $+30$ pixels in the Y direction was applied to the same image, a phenomenon representing a fine curve with a specific directivity was found. This means that more severe distortion was found in proportion to the distortion center. The reason for this fine center error while projecting it onto the 2D plane is due to a mismatch of the center point with regard to the optical axis occurred during the camera manufacturing process in the case of cameras with a number of layered lenses. Therefore, while applying the FOV model, which does not estimate the center of distortion separately, there is a problem of deterioration of distortion correction

FIGURE 7

Result of the distortion center error (X axis: −30 pixels, Y axis: +30 pixels).

accuracy as the error of the distortion center of the lens and the center point of the image becomes larger.

The experiment to determine the error of the measurement angle using the Zhang algorithm [11], which is regarded as a representative method of distortion correction, produced four measurement results as shown in Table 2. In addition, it was verified that deflection of the lens center was discovered in the X direction, to the right of the Y axis, and in upper portion of the image.

Accordingly, this chapter solved the problems that straight lines were expressed as curves due to no estimation of the distortion center in the FOV model and deflected representation by means of precise correction of the distortion center. Figures 8 and 9 show the correction result after the distortion center in the FOV model was estimated in the horizontal and vertical directions.

In the case of incorrect distortion correction due to the displaced distortion center, the image was corrected only in either the vertical or horizontal direction as shown in Figure 8(a) and (b), respectively. This phenomenon occurred because of the incorrect designation of the distortion center axis for the distortion correction. To minimize this error, the precise center axis can be found using the distortion center estimation method by means of 2D patterns such as a chessboard pattern. This resulted in minimizing the distortion correction error that might occur owing to instrument error while configuring the experiment or camera mounting (Table 3).

Table 2 Estimation Result of Distortion Center Using the Zhang Algorithm

	Cod_x	Cod_y
First measurement	12.1	−1.13
Second measurement	12.03	−1.01
Third measurement	6.96	−1.87
Fourth measurement	10.43	−0.78

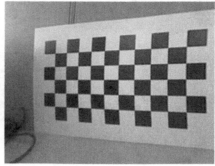

FIGURE 8

Estimation of the distortion center in the (a) vertical and (b) horizontal directions using the FOV model.

FIGURE 9

Correction result using the distortion center estimation method.

Table 3 Result of the Proposed Distortion Estimation Method

	Cod_x	Cod_y
First measurement	10	−11

Figure 10 shows the distortion correction results as image data were received in real time from the 190° wide-angle camera. As shown in Figure 11(a), distorted correction can be found in the distorted monitor image in the horizontal and vertical directions. Figure 11(b) shows the distorted result image when the original image was corrected while (c) and (d) show the full unwrapped images of (b). If images collected from a wide-angle lens are corrected in a distorted manner, they are transformed into images of infinite size so that cropping at an appropriate scale should be used to produce images for monitoring and composition.

FIGURE 10

Result of the distortion center correction using 2D planar patterns.

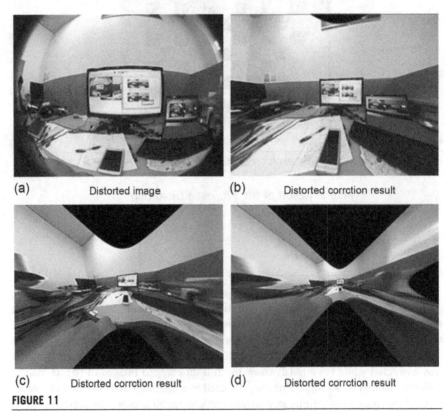

(a)   Distorted image   (b)   Distorted corrction result

(c)   Distorted corrction result   (d)   Distorted corrction result

FIGURE 11

Experiment result using actual image. (a) Distorted image, (b) distorted correction result, (c) distorted correction result, (d) distorted correction result.

As shown in Figure 12, there was a significant difference in the image interface matching before and after the distortion center estimation application. The distortion center estimation can be more influential on the composition of a number of camera inputs than on a single camera input.

5 APPLICATION OF ALGORITHM TO PRODUCTS IMPROVING VEHICLE CONVENIENCE

We study on products which provide us with safety and convenience of vehicle. This algorithm can be applied in a way that wide-angle camera can be used to recognize danger information at the place where clear view is not secured for the driver. It can be applied to the rear view camera and SVM system.

(a) Image composition prior to application
of the distortion center estimation value

(b) Image composition after application
of the distortion center estimation value

FIGURE 12

Comparison between image compositions before and after distortion center estimation.
(a) Image composition prior to application of the distortion center estimation value,
(b) image composition after application of the distortion center estimation value.

5.1 REAR VIEW CAMERA

The algorithm is used for rear view camera to correct the distortion in one channel image. It is very important algorithm for rear view camera whose angle is linked to the steering angle as giving driving direction in accordance with steering angle.

In the screen having wide angle of 190°, the information on steering angle is received using the CAN signal and driving direction is expressed in a way that it is laid over the corrected image. If distortion correction is not done precisely, there happens error in driving direction of vehicle. In addition, inconsistent errors can be occurred in accordance with steering angle. To solve these problems, this algorithm is very important. Figure 13 shows resulting image where FOV distortion correction algorithm and steering angle overlay are applied.

5.2 SURROUND VIEW MONITORING (SVM) SYSTEM

This algorithm is indispensable for SVM system of vehicle. This study was started to develop own SVM system and this algorithm made the SVM technology to complete.

This is a device for safer and more convenient driving as receiving four wide-angle images from front, rear, left, and right sides of vehicle to check surrounding images in the vehicle during driving or parking. SVM system is configured as Figure 14 and Freescale's i.mx6 Processor was used in this system.

SVM system gets the wide-angle camera images from four channels in analog signal and four channel images are digitalized by TW6865 and converted into data for image processing. Then, using the algorithm suggested in this chapter, the

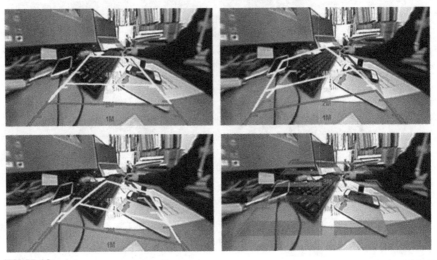

FIGURE 13

Screen of overlay in which the steering angle control is applied to the wide-angle compensation algorithm.

FIGURE 14

Configuration of SVM system.

FIGURE 15

3D SVM image screen.

distortion correction is conducted based on the estimated center of the image. And 3D SVM is configured by texture mapping four channel images on 3D SVM model (Figure 15).

6 CONCLUSION

In recent years, vehicles have used image processing technologies increasingly while black-box systems for vehicles and AVM systems have been widely used as embedded systems for information recording, parking assistance, safe driving, and the prevention of traffic accidents. Such systems record all details of the surrounding areas using an ultra-wide-angle lens (190°) with high resolution. In order to use such images, distortion correction is necessary to enable users to monitor these images.

This chapter proposed a distortion correction method for a camera model in which the distortion center correction method was optimized using the FOV model, and distortion center was found using 2D patterns. Through the proposed method, complete distortion correction can be achieved in the vertical and horizontal directions so that images without size and pattern distortion can be used for image processing, image recognition, and monitoring by users. In general, cameras for AVM systems use high-precision center point estimation. Our algorithm can produce high quality and minimum error of AVM top views from images acquired from inexpensive cameras.

ACKNOWLEDGMENTS

This work was supported by the Technology Innovation Program (or Technology Innovation Program, "0043358, Information Composition and Recognition System for surrounding images possible for top view and panorama view of resolving power less than 10 cm) funded By the Ministry of Trade, Industry & Energy (MI, Korea)" and "R&D Infrastructure for Green Electric Vehicle (RE-EV) through the Ministry of Trade Industry & Energy (MOTIE) and Korea Institute for Advancement of Technology (KIAT)."

REFERENCES

[1] Heikkila J. Geometirc camera calibration using circular control points. IEEE Trans Pattern Anal Mach Intell 2000;22(19):1066–77.
[2] Kim W, Baik YK, Lee KM. A parameter-free radial distortion correction of wide angle lenses using distorted vanishing points, In: 14th Japan-Korea Joint Workshop on Frontiers of Computer Vision (FCV); 2008. p. 53–58(1).
[3] Jo YK. Barrel distortion compensation of fisheye lens for automotive omnidirectional camera module system. Master's thesis of Dongguk University; 2010.
[4] Devernay F, Faugeras O. Straight lines have to be straight-automatic calibration and removal of distortion from scenes of structured environments. Mach Vision Appl 2001;13(1):14–24.
[5] Thorsten T, Hellward B. Automatic line-based estimation of radial lens distortion. Integr Comput Aided Eng 2005;12(2):177–90.
[6] Kim BK, Chung SW, Song MK, Song WJ. Correcting radial lens distortion with advanced outlier elimination, In: IEEE International Conference on Audio, Language and Image Processing (ICALIP); 2010. p. 1693–9.
[7] Wang A, Qiu T, Shao L. A simple method of radial distortion correction with centre of distortion estimation. J Math Imaging Vision 2009;35(3):165–72.
[8] Shah S, Aggarwal J. Intrinsic parameter calibration procedure for a (higher distortion) fisheye lens camera with distortion model and accuracy estimation. Pattern Recogn 1996;29(11):1775–88.

[9] Chao T-w. Wide-scoped top-view monitoring and image-based parking guiding, Master's Thesis; 2009.

[10] Harris C, Stephens MJ. A combined corner and edge detector, In: Alvey Vision Conference; 1988. p. 147–52.

[11] Zhang Z. A flexible new technique for camera calibration. IEEE Trans Pattern Anal Mach Intell 2000;22(11):1330–4.

Distances and kernels based on cumulative distribution functions

36

Hongjun Su, Hong Zhang

Department of Computer Science and Information Technology, Armstrong State University,
Savannah, GA, USA

1 INTRODUCTION

A kernel is a similarity measure that is the key component of support vector machine ([1]) and other machine learning techniques. More generally, a distance (a metric) is a function that represents the dissimilarity between objects.

In many pattern classification and clustering applications, it is useful to measure the similarity between probability distributions. Even if the data in an application is not in the form of a probability distribution, they can often be reformulated into a distribution through a simple normalization.

A large number of divergence and affinity measures on distributions have already been defined in traditional statistics. These measures are typically based on the probability density functions and are not effective in detecting global changes.

In this paper, we propose a family of distances and kernels that are defined on the cumulative distribution functions, instead of densities. This work is an extension of our previous paper in IPCV'14 ([2]).

This paper is organized as follows. Section 2 introduces traditional kernels and distances defined on probability distributions. In Section 3, a new family of distance and kernel functions based on cumulative distribution functions is proposed. Experimental results on Gaussian mixture distributions are presented in Section 4. In Section 5, we discuss the generalization of the method to higher dimensional spaces. Section 6 provides conclusions and proposals for improvements.

2 DISTANCE AND SIMILARITY MEASURES BETWEEN DISTRIBUTIONS

Given two probability distributions, there are well-known measures for the differences or similarities between the two distributions.

551

The Bhattacharyya affinity ([3]) is a measure of similarity between two distributions:

$$B(p,q) = \int \sqrt{p(x)q(x)}\,dx$$

In [4], the probability product kernel is defined as a generalization of Bhattacharyya affinity:

$$k^{\text{prob}}(p,q) = \int p(x)^\rho q(x)^\rho\,dx$$

The Bhattacharyya distance is a dissimilarity measure related to the Bhattacharyya affinity:

$$D_{\mathrm{B}}(p,q) = -\ln\left(\int \sqrt{p(x)q(x)}\,dx\right)$$

The Hellinger distance ([5]) is another metric on distributions:

$$D_{\mathrm{H}}(p,q) = \sqrt{\frac{1}{2}\int \left(\sqrt{p(x)} - \sqrt{q(x)}\right)^2 dx}$$

The Kullback-Leibler divergence ([6]) is defined as:

$$D_{\mathrm{KL}}(p,q) = \int \left(\ln\frac{p(x)}{q(x)}\right)p(x)\,dx$$

All these similarity/dissimilarity measures are based on the point-wise comparisons of the probability density functions. As a result, they are inherently local comparison measures of the density functions. They perform well on smooth, Gaussian-like distributions. However, on discrete and multimodal distributions, they may not reflect the similarities and can be sensitive to noises and small perturbations in data.

Example 1. Let p be the simple discrete distribution with a single point mass at the origin and q the perturbed version with the mass shifted by a (Figure 1).

$$p(x) = \delta(x)$$
$$q(x) = \delta(x-a)$$

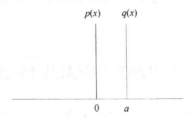

FIGURE 1

Two distributions.

The Bhattacharyya affinity and divergence values are easy to calculate:

$$B(p,q) = \int \sqrt{p(x)q(x)}dx = 0$$

$$D_B(p,q) = -\ln\left(\int \sqrt{p(x)q(x)}dx\right) = \infty$$

$$D_H(p,q) = \sqrt{\frac{1}{2}\int \left(\sqrt{p(x)} - \sqrt{q(x)}\right)^2 dx} = \infty$$

$$D_{KL}(p,q) = \int \left(\ln\frac{p(x)}{q(x)}\right)p(x)dx = \infty$$

All these values are independent of a. They indicate minimal similarity and maximal dissimilarity.

The earth mover's distance (EMD), also known as the Wasserstein metric ([7]), is defined as

$$W_p(\mu,v) = \left(\inf_{\gamma \in \Gamma(\mu,v)} \int d(x,y)^p d\gamma\right)^{1/p}$$

where $\Gamma(\mu,v)$ denotes the set of all couplings of μ and v. EMD does measure the global movements between the distributions. However, the computation of EMD involves solving optimization problems and is much more complex than the density-based divergence measures.

Related to the distance measures are the statistical tests to determine whether two samples are drawn from different distributions. Examples of such tests include the Kolmogorov-Smirnov statistic ([8]) and the kernel based tests ([9]).

3 DISTANCES ON CUMULATIVE DISTRIBUTION FUNCTIONS

A cumulative distribution function (CDF) of a random variable X is defined as

$$F(x) = P(X < x)$$

Let F and G be CDFs for the random variables with bounded ranges (i.e., their density functions have bounded supports). For $p \geq 1$, we define the distance between the CDFs as

$$d_p(F,G) = \left(\int |F(x) - G(x)|^p dx\right)^{1/p}$$

It is easy to verify that $d_p(F,G)$ is a metric. It is symmetric and satisfies the triangle inequality. Because CDFs are left-continuous, $d_p(F,G) = 0$ implies that $F = G$.

When $p = 2$, a kernel can be derived from the distance $d_2(F,G)$:

$$k(F,G) = e^{-\alpha d_2(F,G)^2}$$

To show that k is indeed a kernel, consider a kernel matrix $M=[k(F_i, F_j)]$, $1 \le i$, $j \le n$. Let $[a,b]$ be a finite interval that covers the support of all density functions $p_i(x)$, $1 \le i \le n$.

$$d_2(F_i, F_j) = \left(\int_a^b |F_i(x) - F_j(x)|^2 dx \right)^{1/2}$$

This metric is induced from the norm of the Hilbert space $L^2([a,b])$. Consequently, the kernel matrix M is positive semidefinite, since it is the kernel matrix of the Gaussian kernel for $L^2([a,b])$. Therefore, k is a kernel.

The formula for $d_p(F,G)$ resembles the metric induced by the norm in $L^p(R)$. However, a CDF F cannot be an element of $L^p(R)$ because $\lim_{x \to \infty} F(x) = 1$. The condition of bounded support will guarantee the convergence of the integral. In practical applications, this will not likely be a limitation. Theoretically, the integral could be divergent without this constraint. For example, let F be the step function at 0 and $G(x) = x/(x+1)$, $x \ge 0$. Then

$$d_1(F, G) = \int_0^\infty \frac{1}{x+1} dx = \infty$$

Given a data sample, $(X_1, X_2, \ldots, X_n)$, an empirical CDF can be constructed as:

$$F_n(x) = \frac{1}{n} \sum_{k=1}^n I_{X_i < x}$$

which can be used to approximate the distance $d_p(F,G)$.

When $p = \infty$, we have

$$d_\infty(F, G) = \max_x |F(x) - G(x)|$$

The distance d_∞ is similar to the Kolmogorov-Smirnov statistic ([8]).

The distance measures defined above satisfy certain desirable properties of invariance.

Proposition 1 $d_p(F,G)$ is invariant under a translation. Let $F_{+a}(x) = F(x-a)$ be the CDF of $X+a$, a translation of the original random variable. Then

$$d_p(F_{+a}, G_{+a}) = d_p(F, G)$$

Proof The CDF of $X+a$ is $F_{+a}(x) = F(x-a)$

$$d_p(F_{+a}, G_{+a}) = \left(\int |F(x-a) - G(x-a)|^p dx \right)^{1/p}$$
$$= \left(\int |F(u) - G(u)|^p du \right)^{1/p} = d_p(F, G)$$

Proposition 2 $d_p(F,G)$ is invariant under a reflection. Let $F_{-1}(x)$ be the CDF of $-X$, a reflection of the original random variable. Then

$$d_p(F_{-1}, G_{-1}) = d_p(F, G)$$

Proof For a continuous random variable, $F_{-1}(x) = P(-X < x) = 1 - F(-x)$

$$d_p(F_{-1}, G_{-1}) = \left(\int |(1 - F(-x)) - (1 - G(-x))|^p dx \right)^{1/p}$$

$$= \left(\int |F(-x) - G(-x)|^p dx \right)^{1/p}$$

$$= \left(\int |F(u) - G(u)|^p du \right)^{1/p} = d_p(F, G)$$

Proposition 3 Let $F_c(x)$ be the CDF of $cX, c > 0$, a scaling of the original random variable. Then

$$d_p(F_c, G_c) = c^{1/p} d_p(F, G)$$

Proof

$$F_c(x) = P(cX < x) = F(x/c)$$

$$d_p(F_c, G_c) = \left(\int |F(x/c) - G(x/c)|^p \, dx \right)^{1/p}$$

$$= \left(\int |F(u) - G(u)|^p c \, du \right)^{1/p}$$

$$= c^{1/p} \left(\int |F(u) - G(u)|^p \, du \right)^{1/p}$$

$$= c^{1/p} d_p(F, G)$$

Example 2. Consider the same example as in the previous section. The CDFs of the distributions are illustrated in Figure 2.

The proposed distance function has the value:

$$d_p(F, G) = \left(\int_0^a 1 \, dx \right)^{1/p} = a^{1/p}$$

For $p < \infty$, the distance value is dependent on a. The kernel value is:

$$k(F, G) = e^{-\alpha d_2(F, G)^2} = e^{-\alpha \sqrt{a}}$$

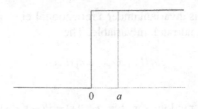

0   a

FIGURE 2

CDFs.

The computation of the distance $d_p(F, G)$ is straightforward. For a discrete dataset of size n, the complexity for computing the distance is $O(n)$. On the other hand, the computation of earth mover's distance requires the Hungarian algorithm ([10]) with a complexity of $O(n^3)$.

4 EXPERIMENTAL RESULTS AND DISCUSSIONS

The CDF-based kernels and distances can be effective on continuous distributions as well.

A Gaussian mixture distribution ([11]) and its variations, shown in Figure 3, are used to test the kernel functions. The first chart shows the original Gaussian mixture. The other two distributions are obtained by moving the middle mode. Clearly the second distribution is much closer to the original distribution than the third one.

Indexed in the same order as in Figure 3, the Bhattacharyya kernel matrix for the three distributions is:

$$\begin{pmatrix} 1 & 0.775 & 0.715 \\ 0.775 & 1 & 0.715 \\ 0.715 & 0.715 & 1 \end{pmatrix}$$

The Bhattacharyya kernel did not clearly distinguish the second and the third distributions when comparing to the original. There is no significant difference between the kernel values k_{12} and k_{13}, which measure the similarities between the original distribution and the other two perturbed distributions.

The kernel matrix of our proposed kernel is:

$$\begin{pmatrix} 1 & 0.123 & 1.67 \times 10^{-6} \\ 0.123 & 1 & 4.68 \times 10^{-5} \\ 1.67 \times 10^{-6} & 4.68 \times 10^{-5} & 1 \end{pmatrix}$$

The CDF-based kernel showed much greater performance in this example. The kernel values k_{12} and k_{13} clearly reflect the larger deviation (less similarity) of the third distribution from the original.

This is due to the fact that the density-based Bhattacharyya kernel does not capture the global variations. The CDF-based kernel is much more effective in detecting global changes in the distributions.

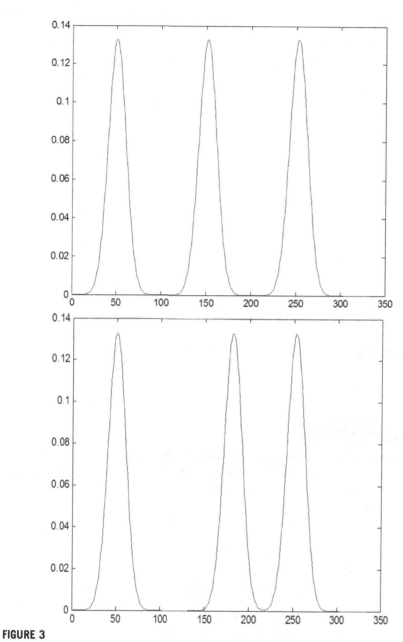

FIGURE 3

A Gaussian mixture and variations.

(Continued)

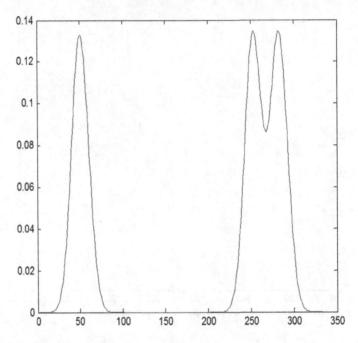

FIGURE 3, CONT'D

5 GENERALIZATION

This method can be extended to high-dimensional distributions. Let F and G be n-dimensional CDFs for the random variables with bounded ranges. Then we can define the distance measures similar to the 1D case.

$$d_p(F, G) = \left(\int |F(x) - G(x)|^p dx \right)^{1/p}$$

When $p = 2$, a kernel can also be defined from the distance $d_2(F, G)$.

The advantages of CDF can be maintained in the high-dimensional cases. For example, the translation invariance and the scaling property can be established in a similar fashion. The 2D extension is especially interesting because it is directly associated with image processing. However, there exist challenges commonly associated with extensions to high-dimensional spaces. For example, there will be significant cost in directly computing high-dimensional CDFs. If m points are used to represent a 1D CDF, an n-dimensional CDF would need m^n points.

6 CONCLUSIONS AND FUTURE WORK

In this paper, we presented a new family of distance and kernel functions on probability distributions based on the cumulative distribution functions. The distance function was shown to be a metric and the kernel function was shown be a positive definite kernel. Compared to the traditional density-based divergence functions, our proposed distance measures are more effective in detecting global discrepancy in distributions. Invariance properties of the distance functions related to translation, reflection, and scaling are derived. Experimental results on generated distributions were discussed.

Our distance measures can be extended to high-dimensional spaces. However, the calculation of distance using CDFs may incur heavy computational cost. For future work, we propose to develop an algorithm that computes the distance measure directly from the data, bypassing the explicit construction of CDFs.

REFERENCES

[1] Boser BE, Guyon IM, Vapnik VN. A training algorithm for optimal margin classifiers. In: Proc. fifth annual workshop on computational learning theory - COLT '92; 1992. p. 144.

[2] Su H, Zhang H. Distances and kernels based on cumulative distribution functions. In: Proc. 2014 international conference on image processing, computer vision, & pattern recognition; 2014. p. 357–61.

[3] Bhattacharyya A. On a measure of divergence between two statistical populations defined by their probability distributions. Bull Calcutta Math Soc 1943;35:99–109.

[4] Jebara T, Kondor R, Howard A. Probability product kernels. J Mach Learn Res 2004;5:819–44.

[5] Hellinger E. Neue Begründung der Theorie quadratischer Formen von unendlichvielen Veränderlichen. J Reine Angew Math (in German) 1909;136:210–71.

[6] Kullback S, Leibler RA. On information and sufficiency. Ann Math Stat 1951;22(1): 79–86.

[7] Bogachev VI, Kolesnikov AV. The Monge-Kantorovich problem: achievements, connections, and perspectives. Russ Math Surv 2012;67:785–890.

[8] Smirnov NV. Approximate distribution laws for random variables, constructed from empirical data. Uspekhi Mat Nauk 1944;10:179–206 (In Russian).

[9] Gretton A, Borgwardt KM, Rasch MJ, Scholkopf B, Smola A. A kernel two-sample test. J Mach Learn Res 2012;13:723–73.

[10] Munkres J. Algorithms for the assignment and transportation problems. J Soc Ind Appl Math 1957;5(1):32–8.

[11] Bishop C. Pattern recognition and *machine learning*. New York: Springer; 2006.

Practical issues for binary code pattern unwrapping in fringe projection method

37

M. Saadatseresht[1], R. Talebi[2], J. Johnson[2], A. Abdel-Dayem[2]

[1]*Department of Geomatics Engineering, College of Engineering, University of Tehran, Tehran, Iran*
[2]*Department of Mathematics and Computer Science, Laurentian University, Sudbury, Ontario, Canada*

1 INTRODUCTION

Due to the growing need to produce three-dimensional (3D) data in various fields such as archeology modeling, reverse engineering, quality control, industrial components, computer vision and virtual reality, and many other applications, the lack of a stable, economic, accurate, and flexible 3D reconstruction system that is based on a factual academic investigation is recommended. As an answer to that demand, fringe projection has emerged as a promising 3D reconstruction direction that combines low computational cost with both high precision and high resolution. Research studies have shown [1] that the system based on digital fringe projection has acceptable performance, and moreover, it is insensitive to ambient light.

The major stages of fringe projection method are:

- A sinusoidal pattern is projected over the surface of the object by using a projector, as illustrated in Figure 1.
- A digital camera is used to capture the pattern that has been phase modulated by the topography of the object surface.
- The captured pattern is analyzed to extract topographical information.
- A phase-unwrapping algorithm is executed to resolve discontinuities on the extracted phase.
- A phase to height conversion method is used to materialize the third dimension in every pixel.

Practical considerations regarding the fringe projection system in general and the binary code unwrapping method in particular are the focus of this paper. Section 2 highlights the previous research into fringe analysis. In Section 3, practical issues for fringe pattern generation are described. Section 4 describes the details of binary code generation for phase ambiguity resolution and evaluation of this unwrapping method.

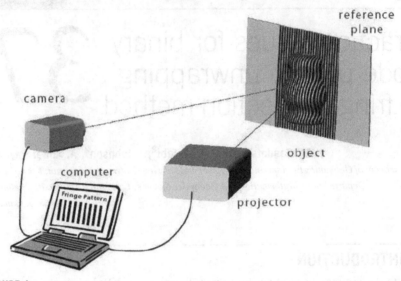

FIGURE 1

Fringe projection arrangement from [2].

In Section 5, practical issues for fringe pattern photography are described. Section 6 offers concluding remarks and suggestions for future work.

2 PRIOR AND RELATED WORK

There have been many advances regarding structured light systems for 3D shape measurement such as multiple level coding, binary coding, triangular coding, and trapezoidal coding. Fringe projection 3D shape measurement improves upon the usual structured light systems because high-resolution (as high as camera resolution and projector) results in a correspondingly high speed. Furthermore, phase of each pixel, which includes modulated depth information, is calculated through gray-level intensities. The captured phase can be transformed to height (depth) for each pixel after discontinuities in the phase have been resolved by phase unwrapping.

Phase detection approaches have been based on a variety of approaches such as Fourier transform [3–6,14], interpolated Fourier transform [7], continuous wavelet transform [8–10,15], 2D continuous wavelet transform, discrete consign transform, neural network [11], phase locked loop, spatial phase detection, and phase transition.

3 PRACTICAL ISSUES FOR FRINGE PATTERN GENERATION

Fringe pattern generation is the process of projecting a sinusoidal pattern over the surface of an object and capturing the pattern by taking a picture of it with a digital camera. The object used for illustration is a chalky white sculpture of a woman without any sudden change in depth in its topography as shown in Figure 2.

FIGURE 2

Object used for experimentation.

In our previous work [1], an experimental study and implementation of a simple fringe projection system have been reported that was based on a multi-wavelength unwrapping approach. In that work, a classification of 3D reconstruction systems was also presented. In later work [12], a new method of phase unwrapping was implemented that is based on time analyses approaches. The fringe projection system provided an experimental environment in which the two unwrapping methods could be compared. Experimental results have shown that the digital code pattern unwrapping method is a stable and reliable method that results in a higher level of precision in the reconstructed 3D model at the cost of using more pictures. Using the same object to evaluate each unwrapping technique, it was found that binary code pattern unwrapping resulted in a more accurate point cloud.

Matlab high-level functions were used to produce the processing software to analyze the images and create the 3D models. Although there are other available choices of programming languages for image processing, Matlab has unique advantages for working in this field. In fact, we have created a magnificently powerful yet simple tool by taking advantage of Matlab's image processing capabilities. Processing functions will be described by showing fragments of Matlab code.

In the fringe pattern generation algorithm, creating the fringe patterns for one row will repeat for all the similar rows. Therefore, only one row of the algorithm will be explained. Assume that the projector has 100 width pixels. Assume that one fringe pattern is to be created with wavelength of 20 ($T = 20$), wave frequency of ω, three fringe shifts ($N = 3$), fringe shifting of 120°, and shifted phase value of p_0. Accordingly, the phase $P = \omega t + p_0$ is a function of the pixel position ($t = 1{:}n$). The wave frequency is $\omega = 2\pi/T$. Therefore, $a_0 + (b_0 - a_0)*(1 + \cos(P))/2$ expresses a sinusoidal function with values between a_0 and b_0.

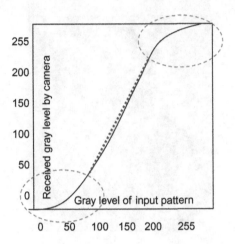

FIGURE 3

Photometric calibration of the projector-camera system. Red area: should not be considered in input gray level of pattern; dotted green line: middle area after gamma correction to make linear photometric projection function for the projector-camera system.

The brightness level of the fringe patterns in image pictures converts nonlinearly with the level of brightness in the projected patterns due to the radiometric behavior of the projector-camera system (Figure 3).

This nonlinear behavior will cause acute problems in producing the phase map. In order to avoid this problem, the range of black-and-white areas in the fringe patterns was changed from 0-255 to 50-200. Hence a_0 and b_0 were defined as $a_0 = 50$ and $b_0 = 200$. However, when working with shiny or very bright objects, defining the b_0 value to 150 will help significantly reduce calculation errors and leads to better results in practice.

Phase $P = \omega t + p_0$ as a function of t is illustrated in Figure 4. The next step toward making the middle part of the function a linear photometric function is to do gamma correction. It is done by applying a calibrated exponential function on input gray levels or directly using a look-up-table between input-output gray levels. So we have:

$I = a_0 + (b_0 - a_0) * [(1 + \cos(P))/2]^{\wedge}\gamma$ which γ is the gamma parameter.

Considering the fact that by growing the t value the phase P will be increased, in immense values of P, Matlab will calculate the cos(P) with some volumes of errors, due to approximation of the Taylor expansion (truncation error).

Therefore, in calculating the phase P, it is better to calculate the value of function cos(P) after omitting the $2*k*\pi(2k\pi)$ coefficients where k is an integer number used to count the number of coefficients of 2π. For calculating the reduced phase, the following code was used:

$P = P\text{-floor}(P/(2*pi))*2*pi$.

The fringe patterns should result in an 8-bit integer picture. Accordingly, the following command was used to convert the real I values to integer values:

$I = \text{uint8}(\text{round}(I))$.

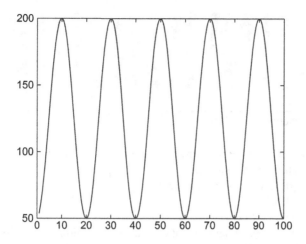

FIGURE 4

Calculated fringe patterns assuming values $a_0 = 50$ and $b_0 = 150$.

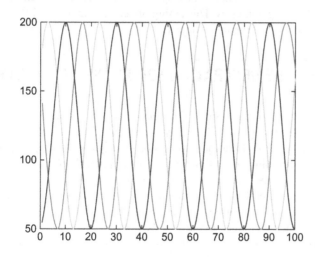

FIGURE 5

Shifted fringe patterns (120°) profiles in color.

Figures 4, 5, and 6 show the calculated fringe patterns function, shifted fridge patterns profiles (120°), and shifted fringe patterns for 0, 120, and −120°.

As it is clear, changing p_0 in relation $P = \omega t + p_0$ causes to shift the fringe pattern in x-axis. If it supposes $\gamma = 0$ then for each pixel, after projecting three patterns, there are three intensities:

I1 = a+b*cos (φ-2π/3)
I2 = a+b*cos (φ)
I3 = a+b*cos (φ+2π/3)

FIGURE 6

Shifted fringe patterns a: 0 b: 120 c: −120.

Solving this equation set with three unknowns a, b, and φ (fi) gives us the output phase φ for each pixel individually:

fi = atan (sqrt(3)*(I1-I3)/(2*I2-I1-I3));

a = (I1+I2+I3)/3;

b = sqrt(3*(I1-I3)^2+(2*I2-I1-I3)^2)/3;

a is the computed texture and b is data modulation. If b limits to infinity, then fi will be unstable and highly effected from noise so is not validate. It means the quality of the extracted fi depends on how far are the value of (I1-I3) and (2*I2-I1-I3) from zero.

After computation of wrapped phase φ, the final phase $\Phi = \varphi + 2k\pi$ in which k is unknown ambiguity parameters. This ambiguity can be solved by different methods that will be described in the next subject.

4 BINARY CODE GENERATION FOR PHASE AMBIGUITY RESOLUTION

Since phase modulation analysis uses the arctan function, it yields values in the range $[-\pi, +\pi]$. However, true phase values may extend over 2π range, resulting in discontinuities in the recovered phase and imprecision in the phase-unwrapping results. The procedure of determining discontinuities on the wrapped phase, resolving them, and achieving the unwrapped phase is called phase unwrapping.

Considering the fact that in each row, the fringe patterns will be repeated every 20 pixels, as a result, the phase ambiguity of each pixel will be increased with the amount $2*\pi i$ in each 20 pixels. In view of the above remark, if the phase ambiguity of each pixel is equal to $k*2*\pi$ ($2k\pi$), therefore k values will be distributed in k = 0-1-2-3-4. Generally, k goes from 0 to ceil (n/T − 1) giving k coefficients for phase ambiguity.

Assuming width of the projector equal to 1280 pixels (n = 1280) and 1280 pixels/ 20 pixels/area = $64 = 2^6$ areas to be coded. Consequently, six binary pictures (code patterns) will be needed to code 64 areas.

The code value will be a number between 0 and 63 which actually is the 2π coefficients in phase ambiguity and can be used to unwrap the phase. It is mandatory to create one black and one white binary pattern in order to convert the gray-level pictures to binary. Hence, a threshold value should be defined based on the gray value norm and for each code if norm value is greater than the threshold, then it is going to change to one, otherwise it is going to change to zero. Therefore, the number of binary code patterns will be raised to eight as can be seen in Figure 7.

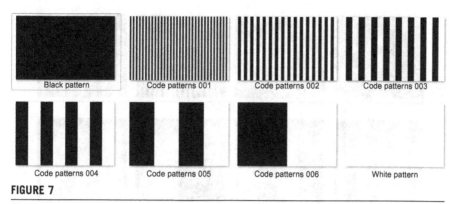

FIGURE 7

Binary fringe patterns: black pattern, code patterns 001-006, white pattern.

5 PRACTICAL ISSUES FOR PROJECTED FRINGE PATTERN PHOTOGRAPHY

Three crucial points should be considered regarding the optical arrangement and calibration in the projected fringe pattern photography:

- The position of the projector and camera should not be moved at all during the process of taking pictures. The camera should not be touched at all, and the pictures should be taken using a remote controller. These modest facts are significantly crucial in view of a very simple optical fact that if the camera lens moves one-hundredth of a millimeter, the picture pixels will move in scale of 10 or 20 (pixels) according to the distance between the camera and the reference plane.
- The projector and the camera should be focused on the object. Regarding the camera, it comes with better practical results if the camera setting be set on auto focus. Additionally, the projector should warp enough by choosing a precise focusing value that the pixels of the projected patterns on the objects should not be distinguishable from a near distance.
- The projector brightness level has to be chosen very precisely to avoid any distribution of the white lights fraction on the black part of the projected patterns on the object. The level of brightness can be set using the projector settings or by choosing smaller values (150 or even 100 instead of 255 as the gray values) for patterns on the brighter areas. These variables are mostly differing from one to other practical attempts. They are highly related to the level of brightness of the sculpture, how much light it will reflect, and how much dark or bright is the room or the wall behind the object.

Three fringe patterns and eight code patterns were created and projected on the object and reference plane separately. Figures 8 and 9 present the binary code patterns and projected fringe patterns on the object and reference plane, respectively.

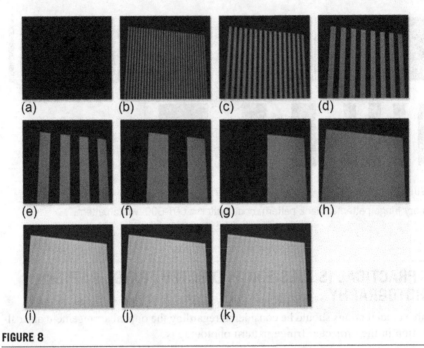

FIGURE 8

(a)-(h) Binary patterns projected on the reference plane. (i)-(k) Fringe patterns projected on reference plane.

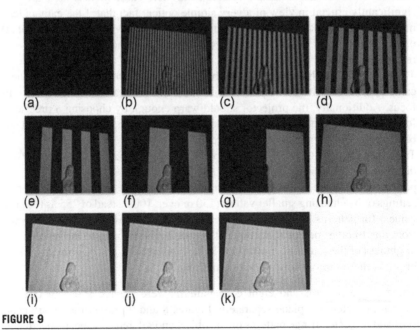

FIGURE 9

(a)-(h) Binary patterns projected on the object. (i)-(k) Fringe patterns projected on the object.

6 THREE-DIMENSIONAL RECONSTRUCTION

It is possible to specify shadow areas using the fringe patterns. The threshold value for the mentioned operation is 20 using a 3 by 3 mask.

A=(I1+I2+I3)/3;

MSK=abs(I1-A)<TH & abs(I2-A)<TH & abs(I3-A)<TH

Figure 10 demonstrates the output resulting from applying the shadow recognition mask.

6.1 HOW TO COMPUTE THE INITIAL (WRAPPED) PHASE

The wrapped phase can be calculated using the following command:

Wrapped Phase=atan2(sqrt(3)*(I1-I3),2*I2-I1-I3).*MSK;

Figures 10 and 11 illustrate ambiguity code of the scene before and after object placement (Figures 12–15).

6.2 HOW TO COMPUTE THE UNWRAPPED PHASE VIA TWO PREVIOUS OUTCOMES

Unwrapped phase=wrapped phase+code*2*pi

As can be seen in Figure 16, due to some minor errors in retrieving the code patterns in areas of varying white to black patterns, some artifacts have been created in the phase map.

FIGURE 10

Shadow recognition output.

FIGURE 11

Reference plane wrapped phase.

FIGURE 12

Object wrapped phase obtained by the phase-shifting fringe analyses method.

FIGURE 13

Retrieved reference plane code patterns.

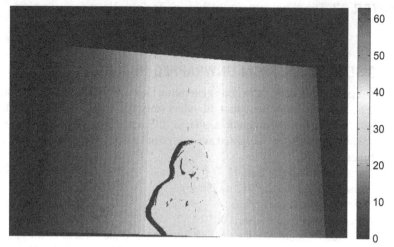

FIGURE 14

Retrieved object code patterns (0-63).

FIGURE 15

Reference plane unwrapped phase.

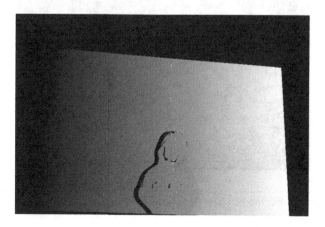

FIGURE 16

Unwrapped object phase with some artifacts.

6.3 NOISE REMOVAL FROM UNWRAPPED PHASE

Because of problem in ambiguity code generation especially in boundaries of black-white areas, there are unwanted phase blunders (mistakes). We use median filter to detect these noises. If filter outcome has large difference with respect to the initial phase, we substitute it by the weighted average of neighbors. We can apply this filter several times.

```
ctdot;a=medfilt2(uwPhase,[1 7]);
c=filter2([1 2 3 0 3 2 1]/12,uwPhase);
b=abs(a-uwPhase)>(1.5*pi);
uwPhase=uwPhase.*~b+c.*b;
```

As can be seen (Figure 17), the median filter reduced the level of artifacts in significant scale. Compare Figure 16 before filtering with Figure 17 after filtering.

6.4 COMPUTE DIFFERENTIAL PHASE

Now object phase is subtracted from background phase using the following code to yield differential phase map of Figure 18. The depth can be computed after calibration of the differential phase image.

```
[p1,msk1,rgb1]=phaseproc(dir1,TH,FILTER);
[p2,msk2]=phaseproc(dir2,TH,FILTER);
dp=p1-p2;
msk=msk1.*msk2;
dp=dp.*msk;
```

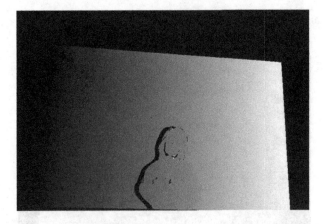

FIGURE 17

Unwrapped phase after median filtering to reduce artifacts.

FIGURE 18

Phase map with some artifacts.

6.5 NOISE REMOVAL FROM DIFFERENTIAL PHASE

As can be seen, the phase map (Figure 18) has very low contrast and object topography is not clear. This is because of phase mistakes with very large or very small values. Hence, we improved the previous phase map using the following filter:

dp(abs(dp)>15 | dp>-4)=0;

dpf=abs(dp);

After erasing these mistakes, we can see the much improved object topography in the phase map of Figure 19.

There are yet some phase errors especially at the edges. We can correct these errors using a filter previously used in phase computation. Like with phase

FIGURE 19

Phase map after filtering.

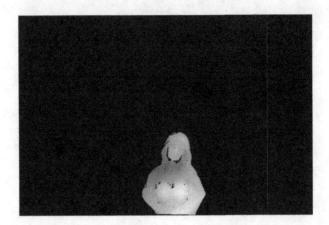

FIGURE 20

Final phase map with modulated height information.

computation, we can apply this filter several times by which we obtain the further improved phase map of Figure 20.

   ···a=medfilt2(dpf,[1 7]);
   ···c=filter2([1 2 3 0 3 2 1]/12,dpf);
   ···b=abs(a-dpf)>.5;
   ···dpf=dpf.*~b+c.*b;

6.6 HOW TO MAKE RGB TEXTURE IMAGE FROM PROJECTED FRINGE PATTERN IMAGES

RGB=(projected fringe pattern1+projected fringe pattern2+projected fringe pattern3)/3

As can be seen from the texture image of Figure 21, there are some unwanted periodic patterns and these could be removed by using phase filtering techniques

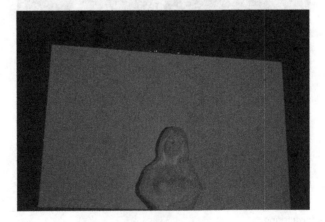

FIGURE 21

Object texture resulting from averaging operation.

in the frequency domain. However, a better method is possible as a result of binary code pattern unwrapping being used for ambiguity resolution. The idea is to use projected white code to obtain RGB texture image.

6.7 OBJECT CROPPING

To diminish the size of point cloud data, we crop texture and phase images to object area (Figures 22 and 23) using the following code.

```
xmin=1000;xmax=1600;ymin=900;ymax=1600;
dpf=dpf(ymin:ymax,xmin:xmax);
rgb1=rgb1(ymin:ymax,xmin:xmax,:);
```

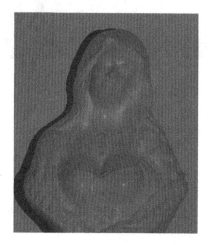

FIGURE 22

Cropped texture image.

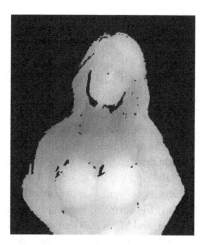

FIGURE 23

Cropped phase map.

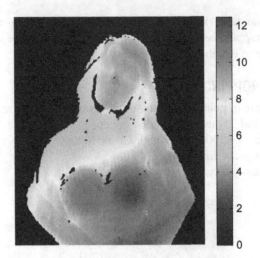

FIGURE 24

Colored depth map.

To show colored depth map (Figure 24):
imshow(dpf,[])
colormap(jet(256));
colorbar

6.8 CONVERT DIFFERENTIAL PHASE TO DEPTH AND 3D VISUALIZATION

SC is scale factor to convert pixel value (phase) to depth (pixel unit).
[x,y]=meshgrid(xmin:xmax,ymax:-1:ymin);
x=x(dpf~=0);
y=y(dpf~=0);
z=dpf(dpf~=0)*SC;

6.9 ACCURACY EVALUATION OF 3D POINT CLOUD

Previously [1,12,13], the level of preciseness in the cloud point was revealed by direct observation of 3D visualizations. Here, cloud points are converted to inputs suitable for a 3D printer and precision is judged by comparison of the object printed with the original object that was to be reconstructed.

A variety of 3D mesh reconstructed models of the woman were created based on point clouds created by Matlab (e.g., Figure 25). Models were created by scientific/academic/trial version of "Geomagic" software. Many other programs are also capable of reading 3D (point cloud) file formats, for example, Microstation Point Cloud tools, Arc GIS Cloud Extension, and Mesh Lab to name a few. These applications are capable of providing the function to convert point clouds to many kinds of 3D models (e.g., wired mesh, 3D mesh) that can be used in applications with varying demands.

FIGURE 25

Woman sculpture point cloud created by Matlab.

Geomagic was used to create a 3D file in .stl format, a format that is supported by most of the mentioned point cloud analyzing applications and that can be read by a 3D printer. The workspace of the 3D printer (the cavity into which objects to be printed are placed) is limited and it could not house the original sculpture of the woman if we wanted to print it directly. A picture of the object printed from the .stl file is presented in Figure 26. The print size was arbitrarily specified to the 3D printer software to be one quarter the size of the original sculpture.

Left, right, and back views are given in Figures 27–29.

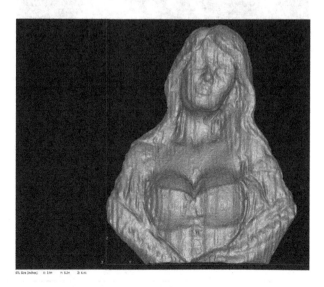

FIGURE 26

3D printing of point cloud of Figure 25 with STL size (inches) $X=3.94$, $Y=5.24$, $Z=6.41$.

FIGURE 27

3D printing of point cloud left side view with STL size (inches) $X=3.94$, $Y=5.24$, $Z=6.41$.

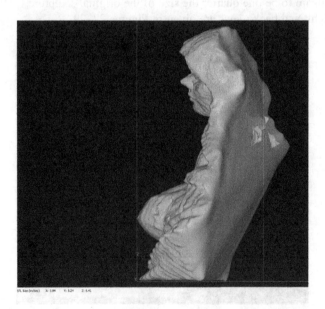

FIGURE 28

3D printing of point cloud right side view with STL size (inches) $X=3.94$, $Y=5.24$, $Z=6.41$.

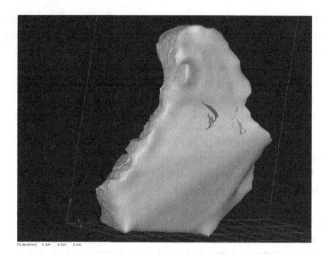

FIGURE 29

3D printing of point cloud back side view with STL size (inches) $X=3.94$, $Y=5.24$, $Z=6.41$.

Imperfections are apparent in all of the 3D printings. There are holes in the neck area because there is so little information in that area being given to the printer. The thickness of the material used for printing, some kind of plastic inserted as cartridges in the 3D printer is greater than the depth information given by the point cloud in this region. The nose height is greater than the original object yielding a shape that is more pointed and not as round. That could have been introduced by the software for point cloud to 3D model conversion because this does not show up in previous renderings of the object.

7 SUMMARY AND CONCLUSIONS

A new phase-unwrapping method, called binary code pattern unwrapping, was introduced and illustrated within a reconstruction system based on digital fringe projection. Along the way, practical issues had to be overcome and these and their solutions were enumerated. The fringe projection method, of which phase unwrapping is one step, was illustrated by showing the results obtained at the end of each stage of the process. The unwrapping method impacts results of later steps and binary code pattern unwrapping was found to produce a more accurate point cloud of the object in both depth and width directions compared with the previously studied multiwavelength unwrapping, but with tradeoffs.

In binary code pattern unwrapping, at least three shifted fringe patterns should be projected on the object. The projected fringe patterns should also have 120° phase difference. According to our practical results, the camera and projector should be close to each other, and the camera and projector optic axes should be parallel to the reference plane axis. Considering the mentioned optical calibration and system setting, three pictures should be taken from the object while the fringe patterns are projected on it. Next, the phase of the assorted patterns should be calculated. This process will be repeated with and without the presence of the object. In fact, it has been shown that the depth properties of the object can actually be calculated using the subtraction results of the object phase and the reference plane phase.

The main contributions reported here to ongoing research are as follows:

- Implementation and creation of practical parameterized experimental tools based on theories in the fringe projection method
- The development of a new phase-shifting process that reduces the number of pictures in fringe projection method
- Illustration that, by reducing the size of the fringe patterns, the level of preciseness of both height and details of the 3D model will increase
- Investigation of the optical arrangement of the fringe projection method and illustration by example of how failure in optical arrangement may cause failure in the whole method.
- Investigation of the reasons that may cause those errors concluding that in order to achieve the maximum level of preciseness, a controlled environment and precise metric equipment are mandatory.

Further research is expected, particularly with regard to the first contribution listed above with a view to creating a cellular device mobile scanner and a real-time scanning 3D measurement system. The richness of the Fourier transform method and the wavelength transition method that provide for modeling 3D phenomena has not been fully tapped by our approach. The mentioned methods have their own advantages in reducing the number of pictures and this may be beneficial in creating a real-time 3D modeling system. We have provided a general tool that applies to the phase-shifting fringe analyses method. A challenging problem for the near future is to provide more accurate, more stable, and more economic methods to create 3D models of any desirable elements of human life.

REFERENCES

[1] Talebi R, Abdel-Dayem A, Johnson J. 3-D reconstruction of objects using digital fringe projection: survey and experimental study. In: Proc. ICCESSE 2013: international conference on computer, electrical, and systems sciences, and engineering. World academy of science, engineering and technology, 78; 2013. p. 714–23.
[2] Gorthi SS, Rastogi P. Fringe projection techniques: whither we are? Opt Laser Eng 2010;48(2):133–40.
[3] Su X, Chen W. Fourier transform profilometry: a review. Opt Laser Eng 2001;35(5): 263–84.
[4] Tavares PJ, Vaz MA. Orthogonal projection technique for resolution enhancement of the Fourier transform fringe analysis method. Opt Commun 2006;266(2):465–8.

[5] Li S, Su X, Chen W, Xiang L. Eliminating the zero spectrum in Fourier transform profilometry using empirical mode decomposition. J Opt Soc Am 2009;A 26(5):1195–201.

[6] Dai M, Wang Y. Fringe extrapolation technique based on Fourier transform for interferogram analysis with the definition. Opt Lett 2009;34(7):956–8.

[7] Vanlanduit S, Vanherzeele J, Guillaume P, Cauberghe B, Verboven P. Fourier fringe processing by use of an interpolated Fourier-transform technique. Appl Opt 2004;43(27): 5206–13.

[8] Dursun A, Ozder S, Ecevit FN. Continuous wavelet transform analysis of projected fringe patterns. Meas Sci Technol 2004;15(9):1768–72.

[9] Zhong J, Weng J. Spatial carrier-fringe pattern analysis by means of wavelet transform: wavelet transform profilometry. Appl Opt 2004;43(26):4993–8.

[10] Gdeisat MA, Burton DR, Lalor MJ. Spatial carrier fringe pattern demodulation by use of a two-dimensional continuous wavelet transform. Appl Opt 2006;45(34):8722–32.

[11] Tangy Y, Chen W, Su X, Xiang L. Neural network applied to reconstruction of complex objects based on fringe projection. Opt Commun 2007;278(2):274–8.

[12] Talebi R, Johnson J, Abdel-Dayem A. Binary code pattern unwrapping technique in fringe projection method. In: Arabnia HR, Deligiannidis L, Lu J, Tinetti FG, You J, editors. Proc. 17th international conference on image processing, computer vision, & pattern recognition (IPCV'13); 2013. p. 499–505vol. I/II.

[13] Talebi R, Johnson J, Abdel-Dayem A, Saadatseresht M. Multi wavelength vs binary code pattern unwrapping in fringe projection method. J Commun Comput 2014;11:291–304.

[14] Berryman F, Pynsent P, Cubillo J. The effect of windowing in Fourier transform profilometry applied to noisy images. Opt Laser Eng 2001;41(6):815–25.

[15] Gdeisat MA, Burton DR, Lalor MJ. Eliminating the zero spectrum in Fourier transform profilometry using a two-dimensional continuous wavelet transform. Opt Commun 2006;266(2):482–9.

Detection and matching of object using proposed signature

38

Hany A. Elsalamony

Mathematics Department, Faculty of Science, Helwan University, Cairo, Egypt

1 INTRODUCTION

The object detection plays an important role in the area of computer vision research. Nowadays, many of its applications require the locations of objects in images. In fact, there are two closely related definitions, object presence detection, and object localization. The determinations of one or more of an object class are presented (at any location or scale) in an image, which means of an object's presence detection or image classification, and can be suitable for image retrieval based on an object [1]. While the object localization means finding the object location and scale an image.

Many of the object detection algorithms are following the model of detection by parts, which was introduced by Fischler and Elschlager [2]. They used the object structural modeling and reliable part detectors' methods. The basic idea behind this model is to identify that the individual parts of an object detector are easier to build than that for the full object [3,4]. Actually, these methods of object detection are depending on sliding a window or template mask through the image to classify each object falls in the local windows of background or target [5,6]. In fact, this approach has successfully used to detect rigid objects such as cars and faces, and has even applied to articulated objects such as pedestrians [7–9].

Later, a frequency model is proposed, which is dependent on a moving background containing repetitive structures. The authors considered special temporal neighborhoods of the pixels, which they have applied local Fourier transforms in the scene [10]. The feature vectors are generated to build a background model. However, they are applied their model for moving object and backgrounds, on both synthetic and real image sequences [11].

On the other hand, another popular approach is depending on extracting the local interest points through the image and then classifies the regions, which contained these points, instead of looking at all possible sub-windows, as in the previous [12]. The greatest common divisor of the above approaches is that they can fail when the regional image information is insufficient (target is very small or unclear), and this is considered as a weakness of them [13].

In this way, the image matching based on features is depending on analyzing the extracted features and find the corresponding relationship between them [12]. The image matching is not accurate enough because the images are often noisy, in different illuminations and scales. Recently, extracted features are widely applied in the field of object matching. In 1999, the scale invariant feature transforms (SIFT) presented by Lowe, when a robust descriptor and difference-of-Gaussians detector was used [14,15]. It is interesting to note that the advantages of SIFT; that it is applied on invariant rotation or image scale, is about its computation, which is very hard to calculate and take a time because it needs to extract 128 dimensional descriptors to work [16]. This problem was solved in 2008 by Bay, who proposed speeded up to robust features (SURF); 64 dimensions modeled it. The experiments of SURF have assumed the integrated images to compute a rough approximation of the Hessian matrix, and this is tended faster than SIFT [17,18]. In 2009, Lue and Oubong compared SIFT and SURF; they have pointed out that SURF is better in performance but is not efficient in rotational changes [19]. In fact, the effective power of SURF has been reduced because the ignoring of features in geometric relationships [19,20].

This chapter presents proposed algorithm depending on the object geometrical shape, and relationship between outer points of the objects' contours. It is divided into two parts; one is constructing an own signature for any object in an image and the other is matching operation among all object shapes' signatures to get exactly which they are described. In addition, four steps have to process through these parts. Firstly, constructing signatures for all objects in an image and saving them as data in the system. Secondly, constructing signatures for all test input objects. The comparisons between inputs and saved signatures, which they have determined before, have operated using statistical methods in the third step. Finally, these signatures have used to detect and define the objects in the image.

In fact, the proposed approach introduces an idea to detect an object dependent on its outer shape by constructing an own signature, which let the object to be free from constraints such as rotation, size, and its position in the image. This proposed idea will may use in many fields like identifying the kinds of plants, fruits, and any other objects based on their shapes. The succeeding section is discussing SURF method because it is the most important one in the object detection and matching ways.

The rest of this chapter is organized as follows. Section 2 introduces an overview on SURF. A brief overview on image segmentation is discussed in Section 3. In Section 4, the proposed algorithm of detection and matching has been illustrated. The algorithm's experimental results are detailed in Section 5 and the conclusion in Section 6.

2 OVERVIEW ON SURF METHOD

The initial mention of SURF was by Bay in 2006. It has four major stages: Hessian matrix, localization of these points, orientation assignment, and descriptor, which is depended on Haar wavelet response's sum [18]. In the first, Hessian matrix is based on detection in scale space of interested points. Additionally, the determinant of Hessian matrix has used as a preference to look for local maximum value, and the detection of SURF interested point is based on theory of scale space. Equation (1) illustrates in details the components of Hessian matrix. In this equation, there is a point $X = (x, y)$ in an image I, the Hessian matrix $H(X, \sigma)$ in X at scale σ has defined as follows:

$$H(X, \sigma) = \begin{pmatrix} L_{xx}(X, \sigma) L_{xy}(X, \sigma) \\ L_{xy}(X, \sigma) L_{yy}(X, \sigma) \end{pmatrix} \tag{1}$$

where $L_{xx}(X, \sigma)$ represents the convolution of the Gaussian second-order partial derivative. $\delta^2 g(\sigma)/\delta x^2$ with the image I in a point X, and similarly for $L_{xy}(X, \sigma)$ with $\delta^2 g(\sigma)/\delta x \delta y$ and $L_{yy}(X, \sigma)$ by $\delta^2 g(\sigma)/\delta y^2$.

To speed up the convolution, 9×9 box filter is utilized to approximate integral image and the second-order Gaussian partial derivatives with $\sigma = 1.2$ [18]. The symbols D_{xx}, D_{xy}, and D_{yy}, are denoting the convolution results' approximations. The determinant of Hessian matrix is

$$|H_{approx}| = D_{xx} D_{yy} - \left(w D_{xy} \right)^2 \tag{2}$$

where w is recommended as 0.9, that is the relative weight of the filter responses [17,18]. The step after is dividing the image into many regions, each one contains different scale image templates.

The second stage is the interested point localization. First step in this stage is setting a threshold to the detected Hessian matrix of extreme points. Second step, to obtain these points a nonmaximum suppression in a $3 \times 3 \times 3$ neighborhoods have applied. The bases of selecting a feature point are that only the point with value bigger than the neighboring 26 points' value has chosen as a feature point [18].

The third stage is the orientation assignment, that is starting by calculating the Haar wavelet (Haar side: $4s$, where s is the scale at which the interest point was detected) responses in the x and y direction within a circular neighborhood of radius $6s$ around the interest point. The responses have centered at the interested point and weighted with Gaussian ($2s$). At that moment, the sum has calculated for all responses within sliding orientation window of size $\pi/3$ to estimate the leading orientation, then determining the sum of horizontal and vertical responses within the window. A local orientation vector has produced with the two collected responses, such that the longest vector over all windows defines the orientation of the interest point.

Last stage in SURF is the descriptor based on sum of Haar wavelet responses. For the extraction of the descriptor, the first step consists of constructing a square template region (the size is $20s$) oriented along the selected orientation and centered on the interested point. The region splits up regularly into smaller 4×4 square subregions. For each subregion, Haar wavelet responses have computed at 5×5 regularly spaced sample points. Simply, the Haar wavelet response in horizontal direction is denoted by d_x, also the Haar wavelet response in vertical direction by d_y. The responses d_x and d_y are first weighted with a Gaussian ($\sigma = 3.3s$) centered at the interested point. Moreover, the responses $|d_x|$ and $|d_y|$ are extracted to bring in information about the polarity of changes in the intensity. Hence, the structure of each subregion has four-dimensional descriptor vector V_{sub}:

$$V_{sub} = \left(\sum d_x, \sum d_y, \sum |d_x|, \sum |d_y|\right) \tag{3}$$

From the previous, by multiplying all 4×4 subregions results in a descriptor vector of length are $4 \times (4 \times 4) = 64$ [17,18]. Additionally, to judge whether the two feature points of images are matched or not, the distance of the characteristic vector between two feature points is calculated. Finally, it is interesting to note that SURF ignores the geometric relationship between the features, which is very important characteristic of many objects in the image. For that reason, this chapter presents proposed algorithm to detect and matching objects based on own constructed signatures.

3 OVERVIEW ON IMAGE SEGMENTATION

The segmentation idea is splitting an image into many various regions containing every pixel with similar characteristics such that; texture information, motion, color, whereas the detection stage has to choose relevant regions and assign objects for further processing [3,21]. In addition, these regions should strongly related to the detected objects or features of interest to be meaningful and useful for image analysis and interpretation. Actually, the transformation from gray scale or color image in a low-level image into one or more other images a high-level image, which is depending on features, objects, and scenes, represents the first step in significant segmentation. Generally, the accurate partitioning of an image is the main challenging problem in image analysis, and the success of it depends on consistency of segmentation [12].

On the other hand, segmentation techniques are divided into either contextual or noncontextual. The noncontextual techniques do not care about account of special relations between features in an image and group pixels together based on some global attribute, for example, gray level or color. However, contextual techniques mainly are exploiting these relations, for example, pixels with similar gray levels, and close spatial locations grouped with each other [1,3]. Actually, the proposed algorithm is trying to exploit the segmentation contextual techniques in object detection and classification. Succeeding section illustrates in details the idea for the suggested algorithm.

4 THE PROPOSED ALGORITHM

The proposed object detection and matching framework are divided into three parts. They are consisting of segmentation, construction of objects' signatures in image, and matching them to classify the object based on its signature [13]. The segmentation process represents the main stone in this algorithm, which is giving initial hypotheses of object positions, scales and supporting based on matching. These hypotheses are then refined through the object signature classifier, to obtain final detection and signatures matching results. Figure 1 describes all steps of the proposed algorithm [22].

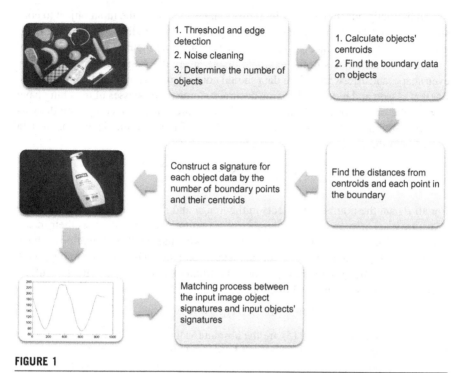

FIGURE 1

The proposed algorithm steps.

This figure starts by an example of original RGB image with all different objects, many morphological functions and filters (edge detection, erosion, dilation, determination the number of objects, watershed segmentation, etc.) are applied to enhance the work of this image. The areas, centroids, orientations, eccentricities, convex areas for every object can easily be determined. Moreover, the boundary points (x_{ij}, y_{ij}) for each object are calculated individually, where i represents the number of objects and j is the number of boundary points related to an object. These boundary points and the objects' previous information are saved to start construction of own proposed signature for every object based on all these information. The relation among all these information and Euclidian distance from objects' centroids (x_{tc}, y_{tc}) is plotted and saved as an individual signature for each object, that is shown in Figure 1 by one object. These signatures for all objects are saved and waiting for matching with any input object's signature, as in Section 5. Moreover, the contour is drawn around all objects and tracing the exterior boundaries of them.

The third part of this proposed algorithm after segmentation and constructing signatures is the matching process between input and saved objects' signatures as in the above. Two different ways in matching process have used to make a comparison between them in accuracy and activity; one is using statistical measures related to the signatures and the second is using SURF [22].

Additionally, all shown steps in Figure 1 have applied on the input object to construct its signature. Actually, the matching process is depending on statistical measures on both types of objects' signatures (saved ones and input). Firstly, as shown in Figure 1, not all objects in the example image are in the same size, orientation, or even shape, and afterwards, their data should not be equal in length or characteristics. For that reason and more in checking accuracy, some preprocesses of matching have carried out; one is sorting all the data of all signatures, and then computing the variability in the dataset by calculating the average of the absolute deviations of data points from their mean. The equation for average deviation is

$$\text{AVD} = \frac{1}{n} \sum_{j=1}^{n_i} \left| x_{ij} - \overline{x_i} \right| \tag{4}$$

For all i's are the number of objects in the image and j's are the number of object's signature data, x_{ij} represents the number of signature's data points, $\overline{x_i}$ is their mean, and n_i is the number of signature data rows. Secondly, the results of Equation (4) have applied on all input and saved objects to make a comparison between them for get the exact matching by least error. Equation (5) introduces a method for calculate differences between the results of Equation (4):

$$\text{DIF} = \text{ABS}\left(\text{ADV}_{\text{Saved}} - \text{ADV}_{\text{Input}}\right) \tag{5}$$

The components of Equation (5) are the absolute value of the difference between the two results of Equation (4) related to saved and input object signatures. The decision of matching based on the least value of DIF, which is given the exact matched object.

5 EXPERIMENTAL RESULTS

The experimental results are divided into two parts; one is representing the objects and their signatures in images and the second is showing the results of matching and comparing a proposed algorithm with SURF methods.

Figure 2 presents a sample of experimentally clear and unclear images, which contain some standard geometrical shapes in (a), some kinds of objects varying in shapes, and luminance intensity in (b)–(f). Sequentially, the signatures have been constructed for the most distinct mentioned objects.

In Figure 3, all objects are individually be defined, detected, and matched by its signatures in the proposed algorithm.

It is interesting to note that the similarity is cleared in signatures for the stand ellipse (its major axis parallel to the y-axis) and horizontal one (its major axis parallel to the x-axis) because it is the same shape but different position. Evidently, the square shape has four identical peaks in its signature because the equality of its sides; furthermore, the circle's signature is one-line parallel to the x-axis and far away its radius length. On the same way, many objects' signatures are nearest to each others, for example, the object (1, 2) (i.e., in the row 1 and column 2 in Figure 3) is closer in signatures with objects in cells (9, 2), (9, 4). In the same context, signatures of objects (1, 3) and (5, 4) are seemed to correspond to some. These last cases are happened

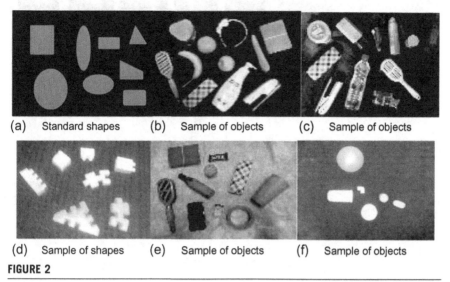

(a)   Standard shapes   (b)   Sample of objects   (c)   Sample of objects

(d)   Sample of shapes   (e)   Sample of objects   (f)   Sample of objects

FIGURE 2

Images of famous regular shapes in (a) and from (b) to (f) other types of different objects.

because the shape's nature of the original objects not because mistakes or big errors in the proposed algorithm.

Actually, the proposed algorithm has applied on about 120 different shapes, positions, orientations, and intensity luminance of objects in RGB images. Furthermore, signature's determination for all objects has achieved 100% without any errors (in data, or wrong signature construction) for all objects.

Second part of the proposed algorithm is matching of input and saved signatures. Table 1 presents the matching process that is depending on Equations (4) and (5); the decision in this process is based on the least value in Equation (5). Obviously, Table 1 shows all input objects images in first row. Regularly, the first column represents all positions (1-11) of objects in their main image if are scanned from left to right. Sequentially, Table 1 consists of x rows and y columns, which contain a set of values, represent the smallest value of errors calculated by Equation (5). For example, in the cell (1, 1), the proposed algorithm is selected a least value (0.1097) in a row (1), which indicates to the first object in the image. Clearly, this value indicates to the exact object position selected in the main image of Figure 2(b). In this case, the input object has been completely different in its position and orientation; however, the proposed matching algorithm is overcome that and succeeded. In fact, all other objects have been matched by the same way and have achieved 100% for that image.

Table 2 presents error values for another image in the matching process based on objects' signatures, which are applied on unclear image in Figure 2(d). As in Table 1, all cell's values represent the DIF of Equation (5), and the least value indicates to exact match of objects in an image and the input one. Clearly, as seen one mismatching is found in second row column two; however, this mismatching is acceptable because the objects in second and third columns are so close to each other in shape.

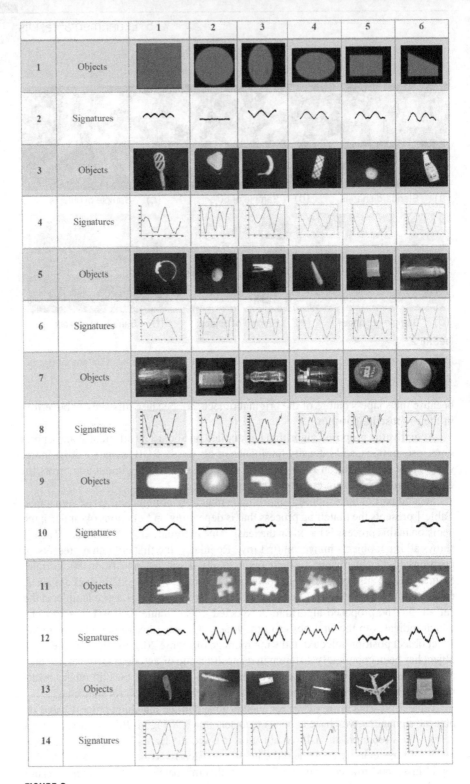

		1	2	3	4	5	6
1	Objects						
2	Signatures						
3	Objects						
4	Signatures						
5	Objects						
6	Signatures						
7	Objects						
8	Signatures						
9	Objects						
10	Signatures						
11	Objects						
12	Signatures						
13	Objects						
14	Signatures						

FIGURE 3

Different objects and their signatures.

Table 1 The Matching Process of Objects' Signatures

1	0.1097	23.32694	5.452305	3.462439	27.57506	14.90506	12.47566	25.51032	1.590916	5.577318	20.90324
2	23.23969	0.022453	17.89709	19.88695	4.22567	38.25444	10.87373	2.160928	24.94031	28.92671	2.446154
3	5.145352	18.07189	0.197253	1.792613	22.32001	20.16010	7.220604	20.25527	6.845967	10.83237	15.64818
4	2.327028	20.89021	3.015577	1.025711	25.13833	17.34177	10.03893	23.07359	4.027643	8.014045	18.46651
5	27.72588	4.508644	22.38328	24.37314	0.260521	42.74063	15.35993	2.325263	29.4265	33.4129	6.932345
6	15.20056	38.4178	20.54316	18.5533	42.66592	0.185809	27.56651	40.60118	13.49994	9.513541	35.99409
7	12.41719	10.80005	7.07458	9.064446	15.04818	27.43193	0.051229	12.98343	14.1178	18.1042	8.376351
8	26.05026	2.833021	20.70765	22.69752	1.415102	41.06501	13.6843	0.64964	27.75087	31.73728	5.256722
9	1.948574	25.16581	7.291179	5.301313	29.41393	13.06617	14.31453	27.34919	0.247959	3.738443	22.74211
10	5.332486	28.54972	10.67509	8.685225	32.79785	9.682263	17.69844	30.7331	3.631871	0.354532	26.12602
11	17.84909	5.368144	12.50649	14.49635	9.616267	32.86384	5.483138	7.551525	19.54971	23.53611	2.944443

Table 2 The Matching Process of Objects' Signatures

1	0.056373	9.911202	6.924778	17.52564	4.48623	4.075137	9.227283
2	7.716881	2.250695	0.735729	9.86513	12.14674	11.73564	1.566775
3	6.836034	3.131541	0.145117	10.74598	11.26589	10.8548	2.447622
4	16.82239	6.854813	14.87723	0.759622	21.25225	20.84115	7.538732
5	4.465828	14.4334	11.44698	22.04784	0.035971	0.447064	13.74948
6	3.9633	13.93088	10.94445	21.54531	0.466557	0.055463	13.24696
7	9.283804	0.683772	2.302652	8.298207	13.71366	13.30257	0.000148

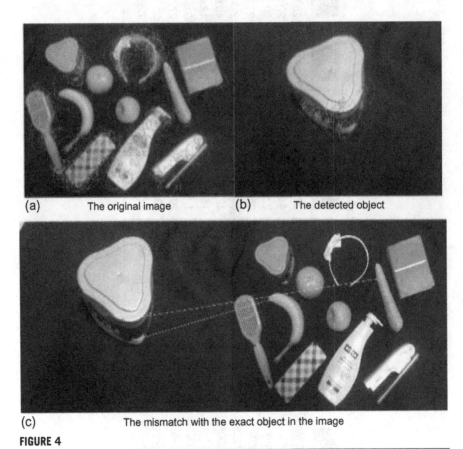

(a)   The original image   (b)   The detected object

(c)   The mismatch with the exact object in the image

FIGURE 4

The SURF example with the mismatch an object. (a) The original image; (b) the detected object; (c) the mismatch with the exact object in the image.

As the same way in Tables 1 and 2, all other objects have been selected based on their signatures and have achieved 96% in the matching process. On the other hand, by applying SURF on the same image with different input objects, some mismatching is found if the input object has changed in his position or orientation; even so, this mismatching has not happened with the proposed algorithm under the same constraints. Figure 4 illustrates SURF Work in an example for this mismatching with the second object in second column of Table 1 by 100 strongest feature points.

In this figure, the input object in the left is mismatched with its corresponding object in the original image. Additionally, this mismatch repeats many times with the test objects using SURF. From the previous results, although SURF method and proposed algorithm have presented to detect and matching objects in an image; however, the presented algorithm is more effective and accurate in objects matching process than SURF and simply in use by some humble statistical equations without any constraints as in the other methods. Next section shows the conclusion of this work.

In Figure 5, another example for mismatching of objects using SURF method whereas exact matching has illustrated in Figure 6.

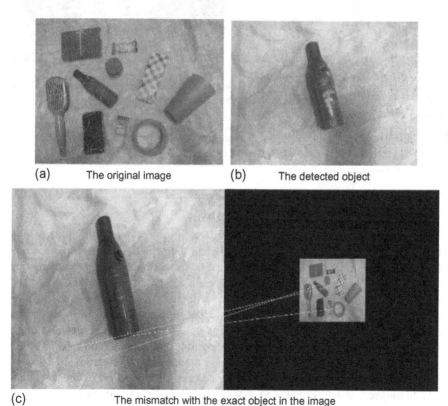

(a)   The original image   (b)   The detected object

(c)   The mismatch with the exact object in the image

FIGURE 5

The SURF example with the mismatch an object. (a) The original image; (b) the detected object; (c) the exact matching with the exact object in the image.

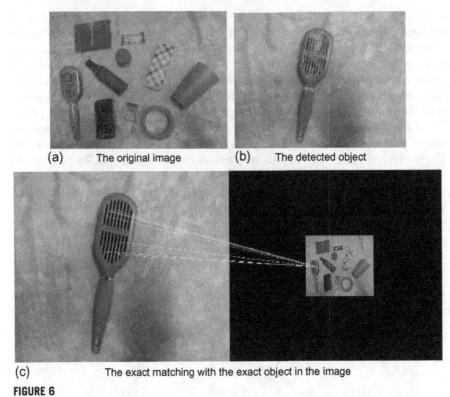

(a)   The original image   (b)   The detected object

(c)   The exact matching with the exact object in the image

FIGURE 6

The SURF example with the exact match an object. (a) The original image; (b) the detected object; (c) the exact matching with the exact object in the image.

6 CONCLUSIONS

This chapter has presented proposed algorithm for object detection and matching based on its own signature using morphological segmentation tools. The algorithm has divided into three parts; first is segmentation process, second is the construction of object signatures, and the last part is the matching based on them to classify and define the object. Actually, this signature has a singularity, simply in use, saving it on a small memory, and working in a variety of light levels. Moreover, the proposed algorithm matched the objects neither among object's blobs nor regions of interest; but among the constructed signatures. On the other hand, SURF method has been presented for comparison with the proposed method on the experimental results. Many difficulties are appeared in matching process, such as object in unusual intensity luminance, shape, orientation, position, different sizes, or unclear image of objects; but the proposed algorithm has overcome on them, while SURF has not done. The performance has been tested 120 from a wide variety of different objects;

it has been achieved 100% in the case of constructing object signatures, also it has achieved 96% of exact matching whereas SURF has achieved 85% for all experimental objects.

REFERENCES

[1] Elsalamony HA. Automatic video stream indexing and retrieving based on face detection using wavelet transformation. In: Second international conference on signal processing systems (ICSPS) 5-7 July, 2010; 2010. p. 153–7.

[2] Fischler M, Elschlager R. The representation and matching of pictorial structures. IEEE Trans Comput 1973;C-22(1):67–92.

[3] Bouchard G, Triggs B. A hierarchical part-based model for visual object categorization. In: IEEE computer society conference on computer vision and pattern recognition; 2005.

[4] He L, Wang H, Zhang H. Object detection by parts using appearance, structural and shape features. In: International conference on mechatronics and automation (ICMA); 2011. p. 489–94.

[5] Huttenlocher D, Lilien R, Olson C. View-based recognition using an eigenspace approximation to the Hausdorff measure. IEEE Trans Pattern Anal Mach Intell 1999;21(9):951–5.

[6] Lai K, Bo L, Ren X, Fox D. Detection-based object labeling in 3D scenes. In: International conference on robotics and automation, 2012; 2012.

[7] Gavrila D, Philomin V. Real-time object detection for smart vehicles. In: Proceedings. 7th international conference on computer vision; 1999. p. 87–93.

[8] Rowley HA, Baluja S, Kanade T. Human face detection in visual scenes. Adv Neur Inf 1995;8.

[9] Viola P, Jones M, Snow D. Detecting pedestrians using patterns of motion and appearance. In: IEEE conference on computer vision and pattern recognition; 2003.

[10] Zahn C, Roskies R. Fourier descriptors for plane closed curves. IEEE Trans Comput 1972;21(3):269–81.

[11] Ali I, Mille J, Tougne L. Space–time spectral model for object detection in dynamic textured background. Pattern Recogn Lett 2012;33(13):1710–6, ISSN 0167–8655.

[12] Veltkamp RC, Hagedoorn M. State of the art in shape matching. Technical Report UU-CS-1999-27, Utrecht; 1999.

[13] Elsalamony HA. Automatic object detection and matching based on proposed signature. In: International conference on audio, language and image processing (ICALIP), 16-18 July, 2012, vol. 1; 2012. p. 68–73.

[14] Lowe DG. Distinctive image features from scale-invariant key points. Int J Comput Vis 2004;60:91–110.

[15] Lowe DG. Object recognition from local scale-invariant features. In: Proceedings of the international conference on computer vision, Greece, 1999; 1999.

[16] Ke Y, Sukthankar R. PCA-SIFT: a more distinctive representation for local image descriptors. In: Proceedings of the IEEE conference on computer vision and pattern recognition, USA, 2004; 2004.

[17] Bay H, Ess A, Tuytelaars T, VanGool L. Surf: speeded up robust features. Int J Comput Vis Image Und 2008;110:404–17.

[18] Bay H, Tuytelaars T, VanGool L. Surf: speeded up robust features. In: Proceedings of the European conference on computer vision, Austria, 2006; 2006.

[19] Juan L, Gwun O. A comparison of SIFT, PCA-SIFT and SURF. Int J Image Process 2009;3:143–52.

[20] Amit Y, Geman D, Wilder K. Joint induction of shape features and tree classifiers. IEEE Trans Pattern Anal Mach Intell 1997;19(11):1300–5.

[21] Darwish AA, Ali HF, El-Salamony HAM. 3D human body motion detection and tracking in video. In: The 14th IASTED international conference on applied simulation and modeling, Spain, June 15-17, 2005; 2005.

[22] Elsalamony HA. Object detection and matching using proposed signature and surf. In: Eightenth international conference. Image processing, computer vision, and pattern recognition. IPVC'14, Worldcomp'14 proceeding, Las Vigas, Nevada, USA, July 21-24, 2014; 2014. p. 377–83.

Index

Note: Page numbers followed by *f* indicate figures and *t* indicate tables.

Printed in the United States
By Bookmasters